Warfare in the Ancient Near East to 1600 BC

'Hamblin's book is a goldmine of information – both textual and archaeological – on ancient Near Eastern warfare before the Late Bronze Age.'

Professor Robert Drews, Vanderbilt University

For many historians, military history began in Classical Greece. Chronologically, however, half of recorded military history occurred before the Greeks rose to military predominance. In this groundbreaking and fascinating study, William J. Hamblin synthesises current knowledge of early ancient Near Eastern military history in an accessible way, from the Neolitihic era until the Middle Bronze Age.

Drawing on an extensive range of textual, artistic, and archaeological data, *Warfare in the Ancient Near East to 1600 BC* offers a detailed analysis of the military technology, ideology, and practices of Near Eastern warfare, focusing on key topics including: recruitment and training of the soldiers; the logistics and weaponry of warfare, with emphasis on the shift from stone to metal weapons; the role played by magic; narratives of combat and artistic representations of battle; the origins and development of the chariot as a mode of military transportation; fortifications and siegecraft; and developments in naval warfare. Hamblin pays particular attention to the earliest-known examples of holy war ideology in Mesopotamia and Egypt, and argues that this era laid the foundation for later Near Eastern concepts of holy war, and that such understandings remain of vital significance in the world today.

Illustrated throughout, including maps of the region, this book is essential for experts and non-specialists alike.

William J. Hamblin is Associate Professor of History at Brigham Young University, specializing in Near Eastern and military history. He is co-author of *World History to 1648* (1993).

Warfare and History
General Editor
Jeremy Black
Professor of History, University of Exeter

Warfare in the Ancient Near East
to 1600 BC

Holy Warriors at the Dawn of History

William J. Hamblin

LONDON AND NEW YORK

First published 2006
by Routledge
2 Park Square, Milton Park, Abingdon, Oxon, OX14 4RN

Simultaneously published in the USA and Canada
by Routledge
270 Madison Avenue, New York, NY 10016

Routledge is an imprint of the Taylor & Francis Group, an informa business

Typeset in Bembo by Taylor & Francis Books
Printed and bound in Great Britain by The Cromwell Press, Trowbridge, Wiltshire

British Library Cataloguing in Publication Data
A catalogue record for this book is available from the British Library

Library of Congress Cataloging-in-Publication Data
Warfare in the ancient Near East to c. 1600 BC / [edited by] William J. Hamblin.
     p. cm. – (Warfare and history)
   Includes bibliographical references and index.
     1. Military art and science–Middle East–History. 2. Middle East–History,
Military–To 1500. I. Hamblin, William James. II. Series.

U31.W37 2005
355'.00939'409013--dc22

                              2005006029

ISBN10: 0-415-25589-9 (pbk)
ISBN10: 0-415-25588-0 (hbk)

ISBN13: 978-0-415-25589-9 (pbk)
ISBN13: 978-0-415-25588-2 (hbk)

For Loree, Ken, Karen and Alex

– of course

For Scott Nelson: the Better Man

And for Blake Donnek,
who dared to dream of a world without war

"Mightiest of the mighty, hero in battle, let me sing his song!"

Gilgamesh and the Bull of Heaven, Sumer, c. 2000 BCE (EOG 169)

Contents

CONTENTS

Illustrations

Preface

While working on this book over the past few years, my motto, along with Shakespeare's Prospero, has necessarily been: "Me, poor man, my library was dukedom large enough" (*Tempest*, I, ii, 126). As anyone who has written a book can attest, it is both an exhilarating and an exasperating experience. It is also, paradoxically, a most lonely endeavor that can only be accomplished with the assistance of many friends and colleagues.

It is my pleasure to thank numerous people and institutions for their generous assistance in writing this book. The History Department and the College of Family Home and Social Sciences at Brigham Young University (BYU) provided a much-needed sabbatical and research funds to complete this book. The Institute for the Preservation of Ancient and Religious Texts at BYU provided resources for released time from teaching and for hiring a research assistant. Likewise BYU's General Education and Honors Program, Middle East Studies Program, and Kennedy Center for International Studies, were all liberal with resources for travel and research. Jake Olmstead provided helpful research assistance. John Gee, William "Bill" Gay Associate Research Professor of Egyptology at The Institute for the Preservation of Ancient and Religious Texts, BYU, was very accommodating with his advice on matters Egyptological. Michael Lyon, artist and scholar, produced the illustrations. Prof. Dr. Eric Gubel, Senior Keeper of Antiquities in Royal Museums of Art & History in Brussels, kindly provided a digital photograph of one of the cylinder seals from that collection.

On a more personal level, I would like to thank my wife's family for admirable restraint in limiting the number and frequency of questions to my wife concerning why her errant husband was not attending certain mandatory family functions. My father gave a fine rendition of Pope Julius to my less than adequate Michelangelo; it is a matter of no little irritation that, while undergoing chemotherapy no less, he finished two books in the time it took me to finish this one. I am more than thrilled that his personal "al-Qaeda cells" have been defeated. Finally, I must thank my wife and children for their unending patience and support. To them I can only say: I have at last emerged from the dungeon.

William J. Hamblin
Provo, Utah, 2005

Abbreviations

A1 Albert Kirk Grayson, *Assyrian Rulers of the Third and Second Millennia BC (to 1115 BC)*, The Royal Inscriptions of Mesopotamia, Assyrian periods, v. 1 (Toronto: University of Toronto Press, 1987)

AAA Edwin Yamauchi (ed.), *Africa and Africans in Antiquity* (East Lansing: Michigan State University, 2001)

AAE John Baines and Jaromir Malek, *Atlas of Ancient Egypt* (New York: Facts on File, 1980)

AAK Walter Wreszinski, *Atlas zur altaegyptischen Kulturgeschichte* (Leipzig: Hinrichs, 1923–1936), cited by volume, part, and plate (*tafel*) number

AAM Anton Moortgat, *The Art of Ancient Mesopotamia* (New York: Phaidon, 1969), cited by page or figure number (§)

AANE Pierre Amiet, *Art of the Ancient Near East* (New York: Harry N. Abrams, 1980), cited by page or plate number (§)

AE Walter B. Emory, *Archaic Egypt* (Harmondsworth: Penguin, 1961)

AEA Dieter Arnold, *The Encyclopedia of Ancient Egyptian Architecture* (Princeton: Princeton University Press, 2003)

AEAB Miriam Lichtheim, *Ancient Egyptian Autobiographies Chiefly of the Middle Kingdom: A Study and an Anthology*, Orbis Biblicus et Orientalis 84 (Freiburg: Universitätsverlag, 1988)

AEF A. Lawrence, "Ancient Egyptian Fortifications", *JEA*, 51 (1965): 69–94

AEL Mariam Lichtheim, *Ancient Egyptian Literature*, 3 vols (Berkeley: University of California Press, 1975–1980)

AEMK Stephen Quirke, *The Administration of Egypt in the Late Middle Kingdom: The Hieratic Documents* (Whitstable, UK: SIA Publishing, 1990)

AEN Karola Zibelius-Chen, *Die ägyptische Expansion nach Nubien: Eine Darlegung der Grundfaktoren* (Wiesbaden: Dr. Ludwig Reichert Verlag, 1988)

AF Hans Goedicke, "Ankhtyfy's Fight", *Chronique d'Egypte* 73 (1998): 29–41

AFC Joan Aruz (ed.), *The Art of the First Cities: The Third Millennium BC from the Mediterranean to the Indus* (New York: Metropolitan Museum of Art, 2003)

AH   Ekrem Akurgal, *The Art of the Hittites* (New York: Abrams, 1962), cited
            by page or plate number (§)

AI   Georges Roux, *Ancient Iraq*, 3rd edn (London: Penguin, 1992)

AIB   Lawrence Michael Berman, "Amenemhet I", PhD dissertation, Yale
            University, 1985

ALB   Amihai Mazar, *Archaeology and the Land of the Bible: 10,000–586 BC*
            (New York: Doubleday, 1990)

AM   Eva Strommenger, *5000 Years of the Art of Mesopotamia* (New York:
            Harry N. Abrams, 1964), cited by page or plate number (§)

AMT   Linda Ellis (ed.), *Archaeological Method and Theory: An Encyclopedia* (New
            York: Garland, 2000)

AN   Torgny Säve-Söderbergh, *Ägypten und Nubien* (Lund: Haken Ohlssons
            boktryckeri, 1941)

ANE   Amelie Kuhrt, *The Ancient Near East c. 3000–300 BC*, 2 vols (London:
            Routledge, 1995)

ANEP   James B. Ptrichard (ed.), *The Ancient Near East in Pictures, Relating to the
            Old Testament*, 2nd edn (Princeton: Princeton University Press, 1969)

ANET   James B. Ptrichard (ed.), *Ancient Near Eastern Texts, Relating to the Old
            Testament*, 3rd edn (Princeton: Princeton University Press, 1969)

AR   Kirk Albert Grayson, *Assyrian Royal Inscriptions*, 2 vols (Wiesbaden:
            Harrassowitz, 1972)

ARE   James Henry Breasted, *Ancient Records of Egypt*, 5 vols (Chicago: Uni-
            versity of Illinois Press, 1906; reprint, 2001)

ARM   *Archives Royale de Mari* (Paris: Imprimerie Nationale, 1950 ff.), cited by
            volume number and text number (e.g. 1.10 = volume 1, text 10)

AS   Peter Akkermans and Glenn Schwartz, *The Archaeology of Syria: From
            Complex Hunter-Gatherers to Early Urban Societies, (ca. 16,000–300 BC)*
            (Cambridge: Cambridge University Press, 2003)

ASD   Rivkah Harris, *Ancient Sippar: A Demographic Study of an Old-Babylonian
            City (1894–1595 BC)*, Uitgaven Van Het Nederlands Historisch-Archae-
            ologisch Instituut Te Istanbul, 36 (Istanbul: Nederlands Historisch-
            Archaeologisch Instituut, 1975)

AT   D. Wiseman, *The Alalakh Tablets* (London: British Institute of Archae-
            ology at Ankara, 1953); cited by page or tablet number (§)

AUP   Giorgio Buccellati, *The Amorites of the Ur III Period*, Publicazioni del
            Seminario di Semitistica, Richerche 1 (Naples: Intituto Orientale di
            Napoli, 1966)

AW   Yigael Yadin, *Art of Warfare in Biblical Lands in the Light of Archaeological
            Study*, 2 vols (Jerusalem: International Publishing Company, 1963)

BAE   Ian Shaw, "Battle in Ancient Egypt: The Triumph of Horus or the
            Cutting Edge of the Temple Economy?", in Alan B. Lloyd (ed.), *Battle
            in Antiquity* (Swansea: Duckworth, 1996), pp. 239–69

BAH   Walther Wolf, *Die Bewaffnung des Altägyptischen Heeres* (Leipzig:
            Hinrichs'sche Buchhandlung, 1926)

BH	Percy E. Newberry, *Beni Hasan*, 4 vols (London: Kegan Paul, Trench, Trubner, 1893–1900); cited by volume and page (e.g. 2:31), or volume and plate number (§), and a small letter indicating (a) right (b) center, or (c) left portion of a mural (e.g. 2 §5b = volume 2 plate 5, middle section)
BI	H. S. Smith, *The Fortress of Buhen: The Inscriptions* (London: Egyptian Exploration Society, 1976)
BSMK	Alan R. Schulman, "Battle Scenes from the Middle Kingdom", *Journal for the Society for the Study of Egyptian Antiquities*, 12/4 (1982): 165–83
C	Century: e.g. {21C} = twenty-first century BCE
C1/2	I. E. S. Edwards *et al.* (eds), *Cambridge Ancient History, vol. 1, part 2: Early History of the Middle East* (Cambridge: Cambridge University Press, 1971)
C2/1	I. E. S. Edwards *et al.* (eds), *Cambridge Ancient History, vol. 2, part 1: History of the Middle East and the Aegean Region, c. 1800–1380* (Cambridge: Cambridge University Press, 1973)
CAM	Michael Roaf, *Cultural Atlas of Mesopotamia and the Ancient Near East* (New York: Facts on File, 1990)
CANE	Jack M. Sasson (ed.), *Civilizations of the Ancient Near East*, 4 vols (New York: Macmillan, 1995)
CB	Steven A. LeBlanc, *Constant Battle: the Myth of the Peaceful, Noble Savage* (New York: St. Martin's, 2003)
CG	Robert Drews, *The Coming of the Greeks: Indo-European Conquests in the Aegean and the Near East* (Princeton: Princeton University Press, 1988)
CH	James Mellaart, *Catal Huyuk: A Neolithic Town in Anatolia* (New York: McGraw-Hill, 1967), cited by page, figure number (f.) or plate number (§)
COT	P. Bar-Adon, *The Cave of Treasure: The Finds from the Caves in Nahal Mishmar* (Jerusalem, 1980)
CS	William W. Hallo and K. Lawson Younger (eds), *Context of Scripture*, 3 vols (Leiden: Brill, 1997–2002)
CT	R. O. Faulkner, *The Ancient Egyptian Coffin Texts*, 3 vols (Warminster: Aris & Phillips, 1973–1978; reprint 1994), cited by spell number (§) rather than page
DAE	Ian Shaw and Paul Nicholson (eds), *Dictionary of Ancient Egypt* (New York: Abrams, 1995)
DANE	Piotr Bienkowski and Alan Millard, *Dictionary of the Ancient Near East* (Philadelphia: University of Pennsylvania Press, 2000)
Diod.	Diodorus, *Diodorus on Egypt: Book I of Diodorus Siculus' Historical Library*, trans. Edwin Murphy (Jefferson, NC: McFarland, 1985)
DZ	T. Maeda, "The Defense Zone during the Rule of the Ur III Dynasty", *Acta Sumerologica*, 14 (1992): 135–72
EA	Eric Meyers (ed.) *The Oxford Encyclopedia of Archaeology in the Near East* (Oxford: Oxford University Press, 1997)

EAA	R. Miller, E. McEwen and C. Bergman, "Experimental Approaches to Ancient Near Eastern Archery", *World Archaeology*, 18/2 (1986): 178–95
EAE	Donald B. Redford (ed.), *Oxford Encyclopedia of Ancient Egypt*, 3 vols (Oxford: Oxford University Press, 2001)
EBD	E. McEwen, R. Miller and C. Bergman, "Early Bow Design and Construction", *Scientific American*, 264/6 (June 1991): 76–82
EBP	Michael Hoffman, *Egypt before the Pharaohs*, 2nd edn (Austin, TX: University of Texas Press, 1991)
EBS	Steve Vinson, *Egyptian Boats and Ships* (Princes Risborough: Shire Publications, 1994)
ECI	Donald B. Redford, *Egypt, Canaan and Israel in Ancient Times* (Princeton: Princeton University Press, 1992)
ED	"Early Dynastic": the Mesopotamian Early Bronze Age {2900–2300}. Divided into several sub-phases: ED I {2900–2650}; ED II {2650–2550}; ED IIIA {2550–2400}; ED IIIB {2400–2300}. (AFC xx–xxi; slightly different dates given in AI 502–3)
EDE	Toby A. H. Wilkinson, *Early Dynastic Egypt* (London: Routledge, 1999)
EDS	Harvey Weiss (ed.), *Ebla to Damascus: Art and Archaeology of Ancient Syria* (Washington DC: Smithsonian Institute, 1985)
EE	A. Spencer, *Early Egypt: The Rise of Civilization in the Nile Valley* (London: British Museum, 1993)
EEH	Joan Oates, "A Note on the Early Evidence for Horse and the Riding of Equids in Western Asia", in M. Levine, C. Renfrew and K. Boyle (eds), *Prehistoric Steppe Adaptation and the Horse* (Cambridge: McDonald Institute, 2003): 115–25
EER	Paolo Matthiae, *Ebla: An Empire Rediscovered* (New York: Doubleday, 1981)
EG	Alan Gardiner, *Egyptian Grammar*, 3rd edn (London: Oxford University Press, 1957)
EHA	Hans Nissen, *The Early History of the Ancient Near East, 9000–2000 BC* (Chicago: University of Chicago, 1988)
ELH	P. Moorey, "The Emergence of the Light, Horse-drawn Chariot in the Near East c. 2000–1500 B.C.", *World Archaeology*, 18/2 (1986): 196–215
EM	J. Postgate, *Early Mesopotamia: Society and Economy at the Dawn of History* (London and New York: Routledge, 1992)
EMO	R. Faulkner, "Egyptian Military Organization", *Journal of Egyptian Archaeology*, 39 (December, 1953): 32–47
EOG	Andrew George, *The Epic of Gilgamesh* (London: Penguin, 1999)
EOK	Gae Callender, *Egypt in the Old Kingdom: An Introduction* (London: Longman, 1998)
EP	Alan Gardiner, *Egypt of the Pharaohs* (Oxford: Oxford University Press, 1961)

ET   Martha Joukowsky, *Early Turkey: Anatolian Archaeology form Prehistory through the Lydian Period* (Dubuque, Iowa: Kendall/Hunt Publishing, 1996)

EWA   Donald B. Redford, "Egypt and Western Asia in the Old Kingdom", *Journal of the American Research Center in Egypt*, 23 (1986): 125–43, cited by item number (§) rather than page

EWP   Rebine Schulz and Matthias Seidel (eds), *Egypt: World of the Pharaohs* (Cologne: Könemann, 1998)

EWT   Stuart Piggott, *The Earliest Wheeled Transport: From the Atlantic Coast to the Caspian Sea* (Ithaca, NY: Cornell University Press, 1983)

EWW   Ian Shaw, *Egyptian Warfare and Weapons* (Princes Risborough: Shire Publications, 1991)

FA   Doyne Dawson, *The First Armies* (London: Cassell, 2001)

FB   Walter Emery *et al.*, *The Fortress at Buhen: The Archaeological Report* (London: Egypt Exploration Society, 1979)

FI   Dominique Collon, *First Impressions: Cylinder Seals in the Ancient Near East* (London: British Museum, 1987), cited by figure number (§) rather than page

FP   Robert B. Partridge, *Fighting Pharaohs: Weapons and Warfare in Ancient Egypt* (Manchester: Peartree Publishing, 2002)

FSW   Douglas R. Frayne, "A Struggle for Water: A Case Study from the Historical Records of the Cities of Isin and Larsa (1900–1800 BC)", *Canadian Society for Mesopotamian Studies Bulletin*, 17 (May 1989): 17–28

GDS   Jeremy Black and Anthony Green, *Gods, Demons and Symbols of Ancient Mesopotamia: An Illustrated Dictionary* (London: British Museum, 1992)

GG   Othmar Keel and Christoph Uehlinger, *Gods, Goddess and Images of God in Ancient Israel* (Minneapolis: Fortress Press, 1998), cited by figure number (§) rather than page

GH   O. Gurney, *The Hittites*, 4th edn (London: Penguin, 1990)

GJ   Brigitte Jaroš-Deckert, *Das Grab des Jnj-jtj.f, die Wandmalereien der XI. Dynastie* (Mainz am Rhein: Verlag Philipp von Zabern, 1984)

GP   Toby Wilkinson, *Genesis of the Pharaohs* (London: Thames and Hudson, 2003)

GT   T. Jacobsen, "Historical Data", in H. Frankfort (ed.), *The Gimilsin Temple and the Palace of the Rulers of Tell Asmar* (Chicago, University of Chicago Press, 1940), 116–200

HAAE   Bill Manley, *The Penguin Historical Atlas of Ancient Egypt* (London: Penguin, 1996)

HAE   Nicolas Grimal, *A History of Ancient Egypt* (Oxford: Blackwell, 1992)

HE1   Michael Astour, "An Outline of the History of Ebla (Part I)", in Cyrus Gordon, ed., *Eblaitica*, vol. 3 (Winona Lake, IN: Eisenbrauns, 1992), pp. 3–82

HE2   Michael Astour, "A Reconstruction of the History of Ebla (Part 2)", in Cyrus Gordan, ed., *Eblaitica,* vol. 4 (Winona Lake, IN: Eisenbrauns, 2002), pp. 57–195

HEA   Alexander Badawy, *A History of Egyptian Architecture*, 3 vols (Berkeley and Los Angeles, 1954–68)

Her.   Herodotus, *The History*, trans. David Greene (Chicago: University of Chicago Press, 1987), cited by book and paragraph

HTO   T. Jacobsen, *Harps that Once: Sumerian Poetry in Translation* (New Haven: Yale University Press, 1987)

HW1   Philo H. J. Houwink ten Cate, "The History of Warfare According to Hittite Sources: the Annals of Hattusilis I (Part I)", *Anatolica*, 10 (1983): 91–109

HW2   Philo H. J. Houwink ten Cate, "The History of Warfare According to Hittite Sources: the Annals of Hattusilis I (Part II)", *Anatolica*, 11 (1984): 47–83

ICN   Henry G. Fischer, *Inscriptions from the Coptite Nome, Dynasties VI–XI*, Analecta Orientalia 40 (Rome, 1964)

IS   A. H. Gardiner, T. E. Peet and J. Cerny, *The Inscriptions of Sinai*, 2nd edn, 2 vols (London: Egypt Exploration Society, 1952–1955)

ISP   Jaromir Malek, *In the Shadow of the Pyramids: Egypt during the Old Kingdom* (Norman, OK: University of Oklahoma Press, 1986)

ITM   Edward Brovarski and William J. Murnane, "Inscriptions from the Time of Nebhepetre Mentuhotep II at Abisko", *Serapis* 1/1 (1969): 11–33

IYN   Marcel Sigrist, *Isin Year Names*, Institute of Archaeology Publications, Assyriological Series, vol. 2 (Berrien Springs, MI: Andrews University Press, 1988)

JCS   *Journal of Cuneiform Studies*

JEA   *Journal of Egyptian Archaeology*

JNES   *Journal of Near Eastern Studies*

JRAS   *Journal of the Royal Asiatic Society*

KH   Trevor Bryce, *The Kingdom of the Hittites* (Oxford: Clarendon Press, 1998)

KS   Samuel Noah Kramer, *The Sumerians: Their History, Culture, and Character* (Chicago: University of Chicago Press, 1963)

L   Wolfgang Heimpel, *Letters to the King of Mari: A New Translation, with Historical Introduction, Notes, and Commentary* (Winona Lake, IN: Eisenbrauns, 2003)

LA   Wolfgang Helck and Eberhard Otto, *Lexicon der Äegyptologie*, 7 vols (Wiesbaden: Otto Harrassowitz, 1975–1992)

LB   Yohanan Aharoni, *The Land of the Bible: A Historical Geography*, 2nd edn (Philadelphia: Westminster, 1979)

LC   M. Roth, *Law Collections from Mesopotamia and Asia Minor* (Atlanta: Scholars Press, 1995)

LD   Piotr Michalowski, *The Lamentation Over the Destruction of Sumer and Ur* (Winona Lake: Eisenbrauns, 1989)

LHAEE   Alessandro Roccati, *La Litterature Historique Sous l'Ancien Empire Egyptien* (Paris: Les Editions du Cerf, 1982)

LKA   J. Goodnick Westenholz, *Legends of the Kings of Akkade* (Winona Lake, IN: Eisenbrauns, 1997)

LMB   Patty Gerstenblith, *The Levant at the Beginning of the Middle Bronze Age* (Winona Lake, IN: Eisenbrauns, 1983)

LYN   Marcel Sigrist, *Larsa Year Names*, Institute of Archaeology Publications, Assyriological Series, vol. 3 (Berrien Springs, MI: Andrews University Press, 1990)

M   The following reference provides a map

MAEM   R. Ritner, *The Mechanics of Ancient Egyptian Magical Practice* (Chicago: The Oriental Institute, 1993)

Man.   Manetho, *Manetho*, trans. W. G. Waddell, Loeb Classical Library 155 (Cambridge MA: Harvard University Press, 1940), cited by fragment number (§) rather than page

MAS   B. Foster, "Management and Administration in the Sargonic Period", in M. Liverani (ed.), *Akkad: The First World Empire: Structure, Ideology, Traditions* (Winona Lake, IN: Eisenbrauns, 1993), 25–39

MB   Whitney Davis, *Masking the Blow: The Scene of Representation in Late Prehistoric Egyptian Art* (Berkeley: University of California Press, 1992)

MBA   Yohanan Aharoni and Michael Avi-Yonah, *Macmillan Bible Atlas*, 2nd edn (New York: Macmillan, 1977), cited by map number (§) rather than page

MC   Piotr Michalowski, "The Royal Correspondence of Ur", PhD Dissertation, Yale University, 1978

ME   Timothy Potts, *Mesopotamia and the East: An Archaeological and Historical Study of Foreign Relations, c. 3400–2000 BC* (Oxford: Oxford University Committee for Archaeology, 1994)

MFM   Stephanie Dalley, *Myths from Mesopotamia: Creation, the Flood, Gilgamesh, and Others*, 2nd edn (Oxford: Oxford University Press, 2000)

MHT   Trevor R. Bryce, *The Major Historical Texts of Early Hittite History* (Brisbane: University of Queensland, 1983)

MK   S. Dalley, *Mari and Karana: Two Old Babylonian Cities* (London and New York: Longman, 1984)

MKT   H. E. Winlock, *The Rise and Fall of the Middle Kingdom in Thebes* (New York: Macmillan, 1947)

MM   Jack Sasson, *The Military Establishments at Mari* (Rome: Pontifical Biblical Institute, 1969)

MW   Graham Philip, *Metal Weapons of the Early and Middle Bronze Ages in Syria-Palestine*, 2 vols (Oxford: BAR International Series, 1989)

NEA   G. Gaballa, *Narrative in Egyptian Art* (Mainz Am Rhein: Verlag Philipp Von Zabern, 1976)

OAC   Mogens Trolle Larsen, *The Old Assyrian City-State and its Colonies* (Copenhagen: Akademisk Forlag, 1976)

OBLTA   Robert M. Whiting, Jr., *Old Babylonian Letters from Tell Asmar*, Assyriological Studies, No. 22 (Chicago: Oriental Institute of Chicago, 1987)

OBTR   Stephanie Dalley, *The Old Babylonian Tablets from Tell Al Rimah* (London: British School of Archaeology in Iraq, 1976), cited by text number (§) rather than page

OHAE   Ian Shaw (ed.), *The Oxford History of Ancient Egypt* (Oxford: Oxford University Press, 2000)

OW   Arthur Ferrill, *The Origins of War: from the Stone Age to Alexander the Great* (London: Thames and Hudson, 1985)

PA   Jak Yakar, *Prehistoric Anatolia: The Neolithic Transformation and the Early Chalcolithic Period* (Tel Aviv: Tel Aviv University, 1991)

PAE   D. Potts, *The Archaeology of Elam* (Cambridge: Cambridge University Press, 1999)

PE   I. E. S. Edwards, *The Pyramids of Egypt*, 5th edn (Harmondsworth: Penguin, 1993)

PH   Yuhong, Wu, *A Political History of Eshnunna, Mari and Assyria during the Early Old Babylonian Period (From the end of Ur III to the death of Shamshi-Adad)* (Changchun: Institute of History of Ancient Civilizations, Northeast Normal University, 1994)

PI   Jerrold S. Cooper, *Presargonic Inscriptions* (New Haven: The American Oriental Society, 1986)

PS   Toby A. H. Wilkinson (editor and translator), *Royal Annals of Ancient Egypt: the Palermo Stone and its Associated Fragments* (London: Kegan Paul International, 2000)

PSE   Emma Swan Hall, *Pharaoh Smites his Enemies* (Munich: Deutscher Kunstverlag, 1986)

PT   R. O. Faulkner, *The Ancient Egyptian Pyramid Texts* (Oxford: Clarendon Press, 1969), cited by "utterance" rather than page

R1   Douglas Frayne, *Royal Inscriptions of Mesopotamia, Early Periods, Vol. 1: Pre-Sargonic Period (to 2334 B.C.)* (Toronto: University of Toronto Press, 2004)

R2   Douglas Frayne, *Royal Inscriptions of Mesopotamia, Early Periods, Vol. 2: Sargonic and Guitian Period (2334–2113 B.C.)* (Toronto: University of Toronto Press, 1993)

R3/1   Dietz Otto Edzard, *Royal Inscriptions of Mesopotamia, Early Periods, Vol. 3/1: Gudea and His Dynasty* (Toronto: University of Toronto Press, 1997)

R3/2   Douglas Frayne, *Royal Inscriptions of Mesopotamia, Early Periods, Vol. 3/2: Ur III Period (2112–2004 B.C.)* (Toronto: University of Toronto Press, 1997)

R4   Douglas Frayne, *Royal Inscriptions of Mesopotamia, Early Periods, Vol. 4: Old Babylonian Period (2003–1595 B.C.)* 2 vols, *Royal Inscriptions of Mesopotamia, Babylonian Period* (Toronto: University of Toronto Press, 1990)

RA1   A. Kirk Grayson, *Royal Inscriptions of Mesopotamia, Assyrian Periods, Vol. 1: Assyrian Rulers of the Third and Second Millennia BC (to 1115 BC)* (Toronto: University of Toronto Press, 1987)

RA3   Ronald J. Leprohon, "The Reign of Amenemhet III", PhD dissertation (University of Toronto, 1980)

RGTC   *Répertoire Géographique des Textes Cunéiformes,* in *Beihefte zum Tübinger Atlas des Vorderen Orients. Reihe B, Geisteswissenschaften,* 7 (Wiesbaden: Dr. Ludwig Reichert, 1977 ff.)

RH   Jerrold S. Cooper, *Reconstructing History from Ancient Inscriptions: the Lagash-Umma Border Conflict* (Malibu, CA: Undena Publications, 1983)

RLA   Erich Ebeling (ed.), *Reallexikon der Assyriologie* (Berlin: W. de Gruyter, 1932–2000)

RTU   Richard L. Zettler and Lee Horne (eds), *Treasures from the Royal Tombs of Ur* (Philadelphia: University of Pennsylvania Museum, 1998), cited by page, or by item number (§)

SAF   Helga Seeden, *The Standing Armed Figurines in the Levant* (Munich: Beck'sche Verlagsbuchhandlung, 1980), cited by page, plate number (§), or figure number (#)

SD   P. Smither, "The Semna Dispatches", *Journal of Egyptian Archaeology,* 31 (1945) pp. 3–10; cited by dispatch number (§) rather than page

SDA   Andre Parrot, *Sumer: the Dawn of Art* (New York: Golden Press, 1961)

SGAE   Wolfgang Decker, *Sports and Games of Ancient Egypt* (New Haven: Yale University Press, 1987)

SHP   Horst Klengel, *Syria, 3000–300 BC: A Handbook of Political History* (Berlin: Akademie Verlag, 1992)

SI   Claude Obsomer, *Sesostris Ier: Etude chronologique et historique de règne* (Brussells: Connaissance de l'Egypte Ancienne, 1995)

SIP   K. Ryholt, *The Political Situation in Egypt during the Second Intermediate Period, c. 1800–1550 BC* (Copenhagen: Carsten Niebuhr Institute of Near Eastern Studies, 1997)

SP   Bjorn Landstrom, *Ships of the Pharaohs: 4000 Years of Egyptian Ship-building* (Garden City, NY: Doubleday, 1970)

SSN   H. E. Winlock, *The Slain Soldiers of Neb-hepet-Re Mentu-hotpe* (New York: Metropolitan Museum of Art Egyptian Expedition, 1945)

SW   Alan R. Schulman, "Siege Warfare in Pharaonic Egypt", *Natural History: The Journal of the American Museum of Natural History,* 73/3 (March 1964): 13–21

TEM   Francesco Tiradriti (ed.), *The Treasures of the Egyptian Museum* (Cairo: American University in Cairo Press, 1999)

THL   *Treasures of the Holy Land: Ancient Art from the Israel Museum* (New York: The Metropolitan Museum of Art, 1986)

TS   R. B. Parkinson (translator), *The Tale of Sinuhe and Other Ancient Egyptian Poems, 1940–1640* (Oxford: Oxford University Press, 1997)

TSH   Jacob Klein, *Three Shulgi Hymns: Sumerian Royal Hymns Glorifying King Shulgi of Ur* (Ramat-Gan, Israel: Bar Ilan University Press, 1981)

USP   Benjamin R. Foster, *Umma in the Sargonic Period*, Memoirs of the Connecticut Academy of Arts and Sciences, vol. 20, April 1982 (Hamden, CN: Archon Books, 1982)

VAE   R. B. Parkinson, *Voices from Ancient Egypt: an Anthology of Middle Kingdom Writings* (Norman, OK: University of Oklahoma Press, 1991)

WAM   Erkki Salonen, *Die Waffen der Alten Mesopotamier* (Helsinki: Studia Orientalia, 1965)

WBC   Lawrence H. Keeley, *War Before Civilization: The Myth of the Peaceful Savage* (Oxford: Oxford University Press, 1996)

WH   Gernot Wilhelm, *The Hurrians* (Warminster, Wilts.: Aris & Phillips, 1989)

WM   Albert Glock, *Warfare in Mari and Early Israel* (PhD Dissertation, University of Michigan, 1968)

WV   M. Littauer and J. Crouwel, *Wheeled Vehicles and Ridden Animals in the Ancient Near East* (Leiden: Brill, 1979), cited by page, and by figure number (§)

Y   "Year of king"

Introduction

For many historians, military history begins with the classical Greeks. *Warfare in World History*, for example, starts with the battle of Thermopylae {480 BCE}.[1] The very useful *Reader's Guide to Military History* has one entry on ancient Egypt and another on the ancient Near East, but eight on the classical Greeks and another eleven on the Romans.[2] The *Art of War in World History* devotes eleven of its 1069 pages to warfare before the Greeks.[3] Likewise, the *World History of Warfare* devotes only twenty-nine pages to the pre-Greek and Persian Near East.[4] This common misconception of military history beginning at Greece is off by a mere 2500 years. In purely chronological terms, half of all recorded military history occurred before the battle of Marathon {490 BCE}.

On the other hand, there is certainly some justification for the Hellenocentric approach to early military history, largely because the surviving source material for Greek military history alone probably exceeds the entire corpus of surviving militarily significant sources from the ancient Near East from 3000–500 BCE. Furthermore, the sources for ancient Near Eastern military history are written in a number of obscure and difficult languages which are seldom studied by military historians. All these languages still present numerous philological difficulties and uncertainties. Compounding these problems, we find that many of the sources are laconic, tendentious, fragmentary, and contextually obscure. Furthermore, many modern scholarly studies on ancient Near Eastern military matters are published in specialist journals of limited accessibility, often burdened by nearly impenetrable technical jargon and abbreviations and a bewildering array of unpronounceable transcriptions of ancient words. Despite these problems, however, there is a vast vista of ancient Near Eastern military history which remains essentially *terra incognita* to many military historians. The goal of this study is to synthesize our current knowledge of early ancient Near Eastern military history in a form that is accessible to the broader range of military historians who do not specialize in ancient Near Eastern studies.

Those general surveys of military history which deal with the ancient Near East to some degree frequently do so by giving a brief passing nod to Thutmose III {1504–1452 BCE} at Megiddo, Ramesses II {1304–1237 BCE} and the Hittites at Kadesh, the Assyrian Empire {930–612 BCE}, and perhaps the Bible, before turning to the Greeks.[5] Important as these events and periods are, they are but a small portion of the vast array of ancient Near Eastern military history, and the repeated emphasis on these same events necessarily distorts the overall under-standing of warfare in the ancient Near East. Indeed, this present study concludes at the end of the Middle Bronze Age {c. 1600 BCE}, before the battles of Megiddo {1482 BCE} or Kadesh {1274 BCE} took place. Even within this lim-ited timeframe I found myself hard-pressed to selectively synthesize the available source materials into the 544 pages of this book.

Geographically this study encompasses the modern countries of Turkey (Ana-tolia), Syria, Lebanon, Israel, Palestine, Jordan, Egypt, Iraq (Mesopotamia), wes-tern Iran, and the modern states of the Arabian Peninsula. However, due to the nature of the surviving sources, most of the emphasis will be on Mesopotamia and Egypt. Chronologically, this study ranges from the origins of warfare to the end of the Middle Bronze Age around 1600 BCE; again because of the nature of the surviving sources, the focus will be on the period from roughly 3000 to 1600 BCE. The selection of the year 1600 for ending this study is based on three con-siderations. First, major social and political transformations occurred around this time, as reflected in material culture; scholars use these transformations as the cri-teria for the transition from the Middle to the Late Bronze Ages. Second, this period of transformation is marked politically by the fall of Babylon to the Hittites {1595 BCE} and the beginning of the rise of New Kingdom Egypt in Thebes {1569 BCE}. Finally, the sixteenth century BCE witnessed the final emergence of fully developed chariot warfare, creating the "chariot age", which would dom-inate Near Eastern military history for the next half millennium or more (which I hope to examine in a future study). I will present both a narrative of military his-tory and an examination of military systems and ideologies of different kingdoms and cultures in the ancient Near East during this period

Chronological issues

Chronological notation conventions

Unless other wise noted, all dates are BCE (Before the Current Era = BC) or, in other words, before the traditional year of the birth of Christ. I have adopted the convention of placing dates within pointed brackets { }, with parentheses ( ) used to identify sources, and square brackets [ ] marking editorial insertions into quotations of sources, to help contextualize and clarify the intent of the source. A number followed by a "C" refers to a century: hence {25C} means the twenty-fifth cen-tury BCE. A number preceded by a "Y" refers to a regnal year: thus {Y 15} refers to the fifteenth year of the reign of the king under discussion. Regnal years are generally also translated into the equivalent years of our current calendar when known.

Sources for chronology[6]

While scholars of modern military history can sometimes temporally define mili-tary events down to the hour and even minute, historians of the ancient Near East often debate about which century a ruler lived in. The systems of scholarly periodization of the ancient Near East present the non-specialist with a bewildering variety of names and periods which I have attempted to simplify and systematize. There are a number of different methods by which scholars attempt to discover chronological information for the ancient Near East. Each of these methods has its advantages and limitations; the most secure dates are based on a complementary combination of as many chronological methods as available.[7]

The overall goal of these methods is an attempt to establish absolute chronology, in which ancient events are correlated to precise years in our modern calendar. For much of the ancient period, in most of the regions of the ancient Near East, dates for an absolute chronology are unfortunately not available with certainty; historians must therefore rely on other forms of periodization based on estimates derived from a combination of other dating techniques. These include:

- Synchronism, which searches for the correlation of chronologically significant events in one text with another, or with astronomically datable events.
- Dendrochronology, the study of the patterns of tree rings for certain species of trees which vary according to differing climatic conditions for each year, allowing the year a tree was chopped down to be determined.
- Radiometric dating, which provides approximate dates derived from measuring the decay of radiological elements (such as Carbon 14) found in all organic matter.
- Relative or stratigraphic dating, based on analysing the relative position of an artifact in relation to other artifacts found at a given site (EA 5:82–8).
- Typological dating, comparing form, pattern, color, material, and construction techniques of the remains of material culture (EA 450–3). This type of dating is generally associated with pottery typologies, but weapon typologies are also very important for military history.

By painstakingly fitting together thousands of minute technical chronological data from these and other forms of dating, archaeologists have been able to identify the broad chronological patterns of ancient Near Eastern history, and establish an absolute chronology for much of the history of Mesopotamia and Egypt. Unfortunately, a number of ambiguities and uncertainties in the data permit several different overall ways of interpreting the chronological information, and hence different chronologies.

For the most part this study will not deal with technical questions of chronology. Instead, I will accept the "Middle Chronology", as used in the standard reference works such as *The Oxford Encyclopedia of Ancient Egypt* (EAE), *The Oxford Encyclopedia of Archaeology in the Near East* (EA), and *Civilizations of the Ancient Near East* (CANE).[8] Specific chronological charts for regional periodization will be provided for each chapter. I should emphasize, however, that there is ultimate uncertainty in much of the chronological information from the early ancient Near East. Generally speaking, the older the date the more uncertain the chronology.

While all dates given here are more or less problematic, I will use the abbreviation "c." (for the Latin *circa*, or "approximately") when giving chronological information that is especially dubious. Even though the dates given are often mere guesses, I have chosen to use dubious dates rather than no dates at all, in order to help the reader keep at least a relative sense of chronological periodization and development through time. We must remember, however, that these dates are sometimes little more than chronological pegs on which mentally to hang our information, rather than temporal absolutes.

Periodization

There are a number of additional different ways scholars categorize ancient chronological information besides trying to give a date in our modern calendar. The first is the appearance of writing, which alone allows us to give precise dates and specific names to people, places and events. Periods before writing are *prehistoric*, while societies with surviving written source materials are *historic*. The transition point between prehistoric and historic is different for each region of the world. Some regions of the world—Australia for example—remained prehistoric until the eighteenth century CE. In Egypt, on the other hand, the first evidence of writing is about 3000 BCE; thus, before 3000 is *prehistoric*, while after 3000 is *historic*. However, it is generally the case that the first evidence of writing is often so sparse and laconic that it provides the historian with very minimal information—sometimes nothing more than the name of a king. We thus often speak of a *protohistoric* period, where the number of written texts is so limited that it provides us with only fragmentary historical knowledge.

A second method of periodization is based on archaeological study of the primary material used for tool making: stone, copper, bronze, or iron. Broadly speaking, archaeologists speak of three great "ages" in the ancient Near East: Stone Age, Bronze Age, and Iron Age (EA 4:267–73). The Stone Age itself is divided into subperiods: Paleolithic (Old Stone Age), Epipaleolithic (Late Old Stone Age)[9] and Neolithic (New Stone Age). In addition, there is a transitional period from the use of stone to the use of metal, in which the first signs of working copper appear; this period is known as the Chacolithic ("Copper–Stone" Age), which generally corresponds with late Neolithic in most regions of the ancient Near East.

This system of periodization by tool manufacturing has its own particular set of problems. First, based on the tools alone, no absolute chronology can be determined; assigning specific years in the modern calendar to each "age" results from synchronisms (discoveries of chronological matches or overlaps) with historical texts, radiometric dating, and archaeological stratigraphy. Second, each of these archaeological ages begins at a different absolute date in different regions of the Near East. Thus, the Bronze Age in Egypt begins later than the Bronze Age in Mesopotamia. Some isolated regions of the world, such as parts of New Guinea or the Amazon, for example, were still in some ways in the "Stone Age" until the early twentieth century. Third, the dividing line for these periods generally represents centuries of transition. Stone or bronze tools often remained in widespread simultaneous use for centuries after their "ages", according to the archaeologists' periodization, technically ended. From the military history perspective, this system is somewhat unsatisfactory. In Egypt, for example, flint arrow heads were still in widespread use during the Middle Kingdom, even though Egypt was technically in the Middle Bronze Age by that time. It must be remembered that the transition between tool ages is based on when the technology *first* appears, not on when it is universally adopted. For the ancient Near East, the following is a very rough periodization by tools (based on EA 4:269–70), with the caveat that each region has its own specific chronology with different periods of transitions. Egypt, in particular, generally entered these phases several centuries later than the rest of the Near East. Table A shows a chronology of the Ancient Near East, based on the materials used for tool making.

Table A Chronology of the Ancient Near East, based on tool making

Epipaleolithic	Epipaleolithic (Mesolithic)	c. 18,000–8500
Neolithic	Pre–Pottery Neolithic	c. 8500–6000
	Pottery Neolithic	c. 6000–4500
Chalcolithic	Chalcolithic	c. 4500–3300
Bronze	Early Bronze	c. 3300–2000
	Middle Bronze	c. 2000–1600
	Late Bronze	c. 1600–1200
Iron	Iron Age I	c. 1200–925

Archaeologists also classify chronological periods based on a matrix of material culture discovered at, and named after, specific archaeological sites where a particular combination of material culture was first discovered. Thus we find in Egypt a discussion of the Faiyum culture, the Moerian period, as well as the Maadi, Badarian, Naqada or Gerzean; all of these, however, are simply specific regional subphases of the Neolithic period in Egypt. These periods of material culture are often subdivided into phases, which are generally given Roman numerals. In order to minimize confusion and complexity, throughout this study I will mainly use the dynastic and tool-based methods of periodization since these are the most relevant to military history. I will generally convert pottery-based subphases of material culture into their dynastic or tool-typology equivalents. At the beginning of each chapter I will provide a chart which attempts to correlate all these different forms of periodization for the region under consideration.

Historical geography and ethnography

The historical geography and ethnography of the ancient Near East is also a complicated subject. One problem is that the modern location for most place names mentioned in ancient texts is not known for certain. Even capitals of major empires, like Akkad of the Akkadians and Washukanni of Mitanni, have not been identified with certainty. The same place might be called different names in different languages; place-names can also change with time. The kingdom of Mitanni, for example, was anciently called Mitanni, Maitta, Hurri, Khanigalbat, Khabigalbat, Naharina and Nahrima (DANE 200). Furthermore, different scholars often translate a single ancient term differently; likewise the English, German, French, or Italian usages are sometimes quite distinct. All of this is further complicated by the fact that many ancient sites are called by their modern Arabic names, even after the ancient name has been discovered. Thus, the ancient Ebla is also frequently called by its modern Arabic name Tell Mardikh. For the non-specialist, this can create immense confusion. As a general rule I will select one standardized modern spelling for ancient place names, and consistently use it throughout this study. Alternate place-names will generally be given in parentheses or in notes; all alternate spellings in quotations and translations will be standardized. Thus, for example, I will consistently use the modern standard English spelling for the city of Aleppo, rather than Yamkhad (ancient Near Eastern name), Beroea (Hellenistic name) or Halab (Arabic name).

Different ancient peoples at different times also defined themselves and others differently, and such ethnonyms (names of peoples) could change through time. Many different ethnic groups inhabited the same region simultaneously, with some groups disappearing and others appearing in different periods. Migration was common in the ancient Near East, causing frequent changes in ethnography. Furthermore, what groups called themselves was often different from what foreigners called them. For clarity for the non-specialist, I have decided to use a simplified, standardized, and consistent—though necessarily somewhat arbitrary—system for describing ancient ethnography. Broadly speaking, I will use the following terms for peoples living in the following modern regions:

Anatolian	Ancient people of modern Turkey
Phoenician	Ancient maritime people of the Levant coast of modern Syria, Lebanon, and northern Israel
Syrian	Land-based peoples of modern Syria and Lebanon
Canaanite	Peoples of modern Israel, Palestine, and Jordan
Egyptian	Peoples of the Nile Valley below Aswan (First Cataract)
Libyan	Peoples of the deserts to the west of the Nile
Nubian	Peoples south of Aswan in northern modern Sudan
Mesopotamians	All ancient peoples living in the Tigris and Euphrates river valleys in modern Iraq and southeast Syria. Mesopotamians included a number of different ethnic and linguistic groups such as Sumerians, Akkadians, Assyrians, and Babylonians, who will be introduced in the appropriate chapters.
Elamite	Peoples of south-western Iran
Highlander	Mountain pastoral herders in the Zagros Mountains of Western Iran and south-eastern Turkey

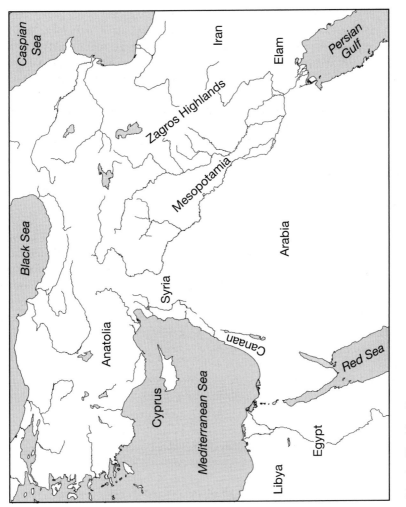

Map 1 The Near East

Nomad	Desert and steppe pastoral herders. It should be emphasized that Early Bronze nomads were generally not horse and camel riders. They usually migrated and fought on foot. By the Middle Bronze Age some nomads were beginning to ride equids and camels, but there is no evidence of large bodies of cavalry or camelry used by ancient nomads in battle.

Using this method is unsatisfactory in many ways. It is rather like calling ancient Gauls or Franks by the modern term French; or, more drastically, like referring to the Iroquois as New Yorkers. While recognizing the problems with this approach, my goal is to make ancient ethnography and geography more accessible to modern readers. When introducing new ethnonyms I will always try to place them in their proper geographical and chronological setting and give variant spellings. Thus, when, introducing the Hittites and Luwians, I will say they are "Anatolian" peoples, even though the land the Hittites and Luwians inhabited was not called Anatolia until nearly a thousand years after the age of the Hittite Empire.

Sources

Before roughly 1820 CE, all of our knowledge of the ancient Near East was found in the Bible and in classical Greek and Latin sources. During the nineteenth century the decipherment of ancient Egyptian {1822–1843 CE} and the cuneiform writing systems {1802–1852 CE}, along with the rapid development of the discipline of professional archaeology, transformed our knowledge of the ancient Near East. Indeed, the rediscovery of the lost history of the ancient Near East through archaeology and the philological decipherment of dead languages is one of the great intellectual sagas of mankind.[10] Nearly all of the sources for ancient Near East history used in this book have been discovered through archaeology in the past two centuries. From these two centuries of archaeological effort we have four types of source materials available for the study of warfare in the ancient Near East:

1   texts, in a wide range of genres including royal inscriptions, year names, autobiographies, hymns, letters, administrative texts, myths, epics, and other literature;
2   martial artwork: artistic representations of arms and combat, generally patronized by kings for royal propaganda and aggrandizement, or as religious veneration and thanksgiving to the gods;
3   fortifications;
4   weapons and other military-related artifacts.

Each of these categories of evidence is complementary, offering different perspectives on ancient warfare, but each also has special methodological problems relating to their interpretation. Some of the technical issues relating to specific artifacts, art, or texts will be introduced throughout this study. Here some general methodological considerations will be discussed.

Textual sources

The textual sources of ancient Near Eastern military history before 1600 are largely in three primary languages: Sumerian, Akkadian (including Old Assyrian and Old Babylonian dialects), and Egyptian. Hittite texts become crucial for Anatolia and Syria in the eighteenth and seventeenth centuries. A large archive of administrative and economic texts also exists in Eblaite, which are of indirect interest to the military historian.[11] There are a number of other ancient Near Eastern languages which are poorly attested or poorly understood, or for which we only have a body of names mentioned in texts written in other languages. These include Elamite, Hurrian, Amorite, Byblos Syllabic, and Old Canaanite; these languages have few significant texts for military history.[12] The linguistic Babel of the ancient Near East is further compounded by the fact that many crucial secondary studies are in German, French, and Italian.

Another problem in dealing with ancient Near Eastern sources is that there are a number of different ways to transliterate ancient words and names and to translate technical military terms. Some of the translations I have cited use different transliteration systems. I have opted to follow the spelling and transliteration systems found in the *Oxford Encyclopedia of Ancient Egypt* (EAE), the *Oxford Encyclopedia of Archaeology in the Near East* (EA) and the *Dictionary of the Ancient Near East* (DANE). In order to make understanding easier for the non-specialist, I have standardized alternative spellings in sources which use different spelling and transliteration systems. Thus, I use the spelling "Montuhotep" for the famous Middle Kingdom Egyptian rulers. If sources I quote use the alternative spellings Mentuhotep or Mentuhotpe, I have simply changed their spelling to conform to the EAE system without comment.

Likewise, certain technical military terms can be translated in different ways by different translators. I have chosen to standardize many of these as well. For example, the Egyptian term *imy-r* can be translated in different ways according to context. In texts relating to work crews it is perhaps best rendered as "overseer". In a military context the translation of "commander" is probably more appropriate. The problem is that different English words are sometimes used by different translators to translate this single Egyptian word. Thus, many of the translations I am quoting have been slightly modified by me for consistency of translation of technical military terminology. I generally give a transliteration of the original term I am translating when the concept is first introduced. I also make extensive use of square brackets [ ] to indicate my insertion of explanatory terms into a translation to provide background for the non-specialist reader. For example, when a text states "I am the lord of the land" (L 249), I might modify it to read "I [the god Shamash] am the lord of the land [of Mari]" to clarify the context.

I have made a consistent effort to give as many sources in translation as possible. Throughout this study I have given preference to citing English translations in accessible editions, though this has not always been possible. I have generally not given full bibliographic references to the standard editions for these sources in the original languages. Instead, I have included references to translations or commentaries which include full bibliography on original language editions and studies. Those who wish to consult the original languages can find that information in the secondary literature and commentary on the translations I have cited. Such primary studies are thus at most one bibliographic step away in my notes and references. I have also adopted a fairly extensive system of abbreviations to keep the size of the notes and parenthetical references to a minimum. These abbreviations can be found on pages xv–xxiv.

Art and weapons

Martial art and surviving weapons are a crucial source for the military history of the ancient Near East. Throughout my study I have made extensive use of such sources. Unfortunately, due to publication costs, it has been impossible to include illustrations of all the items I discuss in the text. Whenever I make reference to a particular work of martial art or weapon I attempt to give references to recent and accessible publications which have reproduced that art, preferably in color. I will frequently give multiple references to reproductions of the same piece of art to help those attempting to track them down. I also try to get a full verbal description for those who cannot get access to the images, though such descriptions are invariably inadequate.

The interpretation of martial art has its own set of methodological problems which I will discuss on occasion throughout the text. Three major problems are idealization, contextualization and anachronism. Idealization is where the martial scene is presented in an idealized or ritualized context—how things should have been, rather than how they really were. This is a nearly ubiquitous problem with ancient Near Eastern martial art, since nearly all of it was patronized by kings or nobles in order to glorify their martial achievements. The second problem, contextualization, is more subtle. It is attempting to determine what precisely the art is intended to depict. For example, the famous "Standard of Ur" includes scenes of Sumerian war-carts trampling defeated prostrate enemies (AFC 98–9; FA 84; AW 1:132–3). The question is: does the art mean to depict war-carts in the midst of battle as they knock down enemies in combat, or does it show an after-battle triumph where the war-carts are paraded among the corpses of the dead who have already been killed by infantry? Such questions plague the interpretation of a great deal of ancient martial art. Finally, there is the question of anachronism; this is especially a problem in the context of ritual or mythological martial art. Here the essential problem is: do the weapons of the kings and gods represent the actual weapons used in battle at the time the art was made, or are they idealized mythical weapons which are no longer actually used in combat? Here the example of

10

Christian religious art depicting the archangel Michael with a sword is analogous. Such art in medieval churches may depict actual contemporary weapons, while a depiction of Michael in a twentieth-century church—still with his sword rather than a machine gun—is clearly anachronistic. Likewise the British Royal Horse and Foot Guard continue to parade with archaic weapons and uniforms that are no longer used in actual combat. Four thousand years from now an archaeologist might be puzzled by what seems to be the continued use of sword-armed cavalry in the age of machine-guns, tanks and airplanes.

What is war?[13]

For anyone who has been in one, it seems silly to ask the question "what is war?". Only those who have experienced it can really know, and for them there can be little doubt as to what it really is. I have been fortunate to never have experienced war at first hand. I missed the Vietnam War by only a few months, with a draft number of 53. In one sense this should disqualify me from even discussing the topic. By what arrogance do I—who have never killed anyone or had anyone try to kill me—talk about warfare? But in reality, that is not my purpose here. My function is to collect, synthesize and present what the peoples of the ancient Near East had to say about warfare. My function is that of interlocutor, to serve as an intermediary for voices of ancient warriors—now dead for thousands of years—and let them tell their stories. I am, of course, not so naïve as to believe that I can tell their stories without necessarily distorting their past through the prism of my own ideas, beliefs, ignorance, and limitations. But, as much as possible, my goal is to present and elucidate the ancient texts, art, and artifacts related to war.

For the purpose of this study, I am not overly concerned with formulating a precise definition of warfare; I am actually rather dubious that such a thing could be done, or if it could that it would be very useful. Different definitions of warfare are often related to the fact that anthropologists, archaeologists, historians, and other scholars, although all dealing with the same phenomenon, each approach the issue by asking different types of questions and attempting to answer those questions with different types of evidence and methodologies. Our concern, then, should not be defining "what is war?", but rather, "what type of model or definition for warfare is most helpful in understanding the issues and questions related to the strengths and limitations of a given discipline, methodology or body of evidence?" A universally useful definition of war is not only unattainable, but undesirable. Rather, such definitions should be viewed as more or less useful models for answering a specific range of questions with certain types of methodology. The overall issue of warfare should be explored with as many different perspectives and methodologies as possible. My goal here, however, is not to formulate an idealized model describing what "tribal warfare", "chiefdom warfare", or "state warfare" was supposedly like (FA 48–73). Rather, I will pay close attention to the evidence we have describing what was actually done by specific individuals at specific times and places. My particular approach here is thus historical, though I will gratefully incorporate the insights provided by anthropology, archaeology, and other disciplines as frequently as possible.

It is odd that, in attempting to define warfare, so little attention is often paid to the indigenous concepts of warfare of the peoples being studied. Rather than trying to decide what *we* think warfare is, we should begin by asking ourselves what do *they*—the objects of our study—think warfare is. This is the important anthropological distinction between insider and outsider perspectives and forms of discourse. It is more interesting to the historian to discover what the ancient peoples thought *they* were doing when they fought wars, than how modern scholars choose to describe or model what *we* think ancient peoples were doing. From the perspective of ancient Near Eastern peoples, war was conceived of as something altogether different from the activity often described as war by anthropologists, archaeologists, and historians. Feeding and equipping armies certainly occurred in the ancient Near East. Ancient soldiers marched and fought, and killed and died, just like modern soldiers. But for ancient Near Easterners that was not what was really important about war. For the ancients, *war was the means by which the gods restored cosmic order through organized violence undertaken in their name by their divinely ordained kings*. Or, to put it in Clauswitzian terms, "war is the continuation of *divine* policy by other means". Whatever other modern models we might wish to apply to our study of ancient Near Eastern warfare to help illuminate certain questions, this definition must never be far from our mind. Throughout this study I will try to pay careful attention to the ideologies of warfare as conceived by ancient Near Easterners.

To the modern mind this definition of war is almost incomprehensible, particularly since in the wake of 9/11—the destruction by terrorists of New York's World Trade Center in September 2001—we tend to view warfare in the name of God as something abhorrent. In reality, however, throughout most of history and in most regions and cultures, there has been an intimate connection between religion and warfare, so much so that one could argue that ancient Near Eastern warfare was, in many ways, a form of religious worship and mass sacrifice.

To the modern advocating the superiority of the veneration of a god of love and peace, the ancient would simply reply: "Why would I possibly want to worship a god who cannot bring victory in battle?" To the outsider, four thousand years removed from this world-view, there is something unsatisfying and even disturbing in this perception of war. But only when we understand this key concept—that ancient Near Eastern war isn't really about maces and javelins and fortresses, but is a theomachy, a "war of the gods"—can we begin to understand ancient Near Eastern warfare. From their perspective it is not that humans cynically invoke the gods to justify fighting their human wars. It is that the gods use the humans to fight their divine wars. The cosmic war between good and evil, order and chaos, is ongoing; the gods simply recruit mortals to fight in that war. To understand the ancient Near Eastern view of war is to read of the acts of the gods in Homer's *Iliad* not as literary metaphor but as an absolutely authentic description of the actual presence of real, cosmicly powerful beings using humans as their pawns.

But, to return to the world-view of the twenty-first century: rather than attempting a narrow definition of warfare and ignoring all war-like human behavior that does not fit this definition, I will, instead, adopt a loose and broad definition of war and war-like activities. In its most universal form, warfare is simply organized violence between rival human groups. Under this broad definition, "gang wars" over drug territory in a ghetto would be a form of warfare. Thus, in some sections of this book I will take this perspective, considering fighting between small forager tribal groups as just as "authentic" a form of warfare as World War Two. But most of the attention of this book will be focused on state-sanctioned organized violence, directed at either destroying rival political entities, or forcing them into submission. Much of ancient Near Eastern warfare also had an important economic component, either to enrich the gods, king and warriors directly, through the acquisition of slaves, plunder, or tribute, or indirectly, by controlling access to important rare resources such as tin, lapis lazuli, or cedarwood for building timber. All of these factors—religion, politics, and economics—had an overlapping and integrated impact on war-making in the ancient Near East; although we view them as causally separate, they would generally not be clearly distinguished in the minds of ancient kings and warriors.

CHAPTER ONE

The Neolithic Age and the origin of warfare {to c. 3000}

The origin of war

The question of how, why, when, and where warfare began is a complicated one that is frequently burdened by many uncorroborated assumptions; proposed answers are sometimes blissfully unhindered by evidence. Even asking the very question begins to limit the possible range of answers, since asking "when did war begin" implies that there was a time when there was no war. In theory we must allow for the possibility that warfare has always been known among humans. Attempts to answer this question are also intimately connected to assumptions about human nature – are humans (or more specifically male humans) inherently violent? – which are beyond the purview of historians.[1] Asking these questions also implies that we know what war "really" is, and that we have sufficient evidence from the past to allow us to clearly identify its presence or absence. Both of these assumptions are dubious. As discussed in the introduction, I doubt an objective and universally applicable definition of war can be formulated. Rather, the nature of war has varied from culture to culture throughout history, with war meaning different things to different people at different times and places.

What war meant to a Paleolithic forager, an Egyptian pharaoh, or a modern politician, may be quite different things, but that is not to say that those phenomena should not all be seen as warfare. The mother whose son died in a cattle raid in Neolithic Anatolia undoubtedly grieved just as much as the mother of an Iraqi or American soldier killed in the Gulf War; the fact that some modern scholars might be unwilling to say that "primitive" Neolithic raids are "real" war hardly changes the poignancy of the mother's grief (WBC 3–24). But the debate over what "real" war is misses the real point that should be the focus of our attention. Although, using historical methods, we may not be able to answer questions concerning when, where, why, and how war began, we can contribute to the discussion by instead asking: "by what types of evidence can we know that war occurred in the past?" In reality all that we are actually able to discuss is our first *evidence* for war, not the actual origin of war. The Near Eastern evidence discussed below indicates

14

that war probably existed millennia before the first surviving written texts that describe war. War was already commonplace by the time the first writing appears. Some of our earliest writing describes a mythic or legendary past in which warfare was present, which may thus serve as possible evidence for prehistoric warfare.

We are therefore left with four types of archaeological evidence which may point to the existence of prehistoric war: martial art, weapons, human skeletons with weapon trauma, and fortifications (WBC 36–9). Two of these forms of evidence are not, in fact, helpful in trying to identify the origins of war. Weapons are a dubious indicator, since almost all Neolithic weapons – axe, dagger, spear, javelin, bow, and sling – were also used in hunting and other non-military activities. Thus the presence of a bow may indicate hunting rather than war. (The mace, as discussed below, may be a uniquely militant tool.) A skeleton with weapon trauma is also not conclusive evidence for warfare, since the person may be a victim of murder rather than war. However, the presence of a large number of skeletons with weapon trauma in mass or simultaneous burials is probably conclusive evidence that they died in warfare, though even here it could point to mass execution or ritual human sacrifice. Practically speaking, this leaves us three types of archaeological evidence that can point to the existence of war: art depicting conflict, mass burial of skeletons with weapons trauma, and fortifications. Near Eastern examples of each of these types of evidence will be discussed below. It must be emphasized that, while the presence of these types of evidence should be sufficient to demonstrate that war occurred, their absence does not necessarily demonstrate that war did not occur. Absence of evidence is not evidence of absence. Many, if not most, wars in ancient Near Eastern history have left no archaeologically discernable evidence that they were fought. Artistic evidence for archaic warfare found in early cave paintings from Late Epipaleolithic or early Neolithic Spain {10,000–6000} show organized humans fighting and killing each other with bows (FA 52–5; OW 20–3). Likewise some Epipaleolithic or early Neolithic mass burials with skeletons with weapon trauma have been found in Germany and at Jebel Sahaba in the northern Sudan (FA 52–3; OW 23–4). Overall, however, such archaeological evidence is quite sparse for periods before the late Neolithic. Warfare clearly existed, but there is no evidence to show it was endemic.

Most arguments for warfare in the Epipaleolithic and early Neolithic periods are in fact based on anthropological analogy. The assumption here, and it is only an assumption, is that human societies go through a sort of evolutionary progress from "bands" of foragers to "tribes", then "chiefdoms" and finally "states".[2] This is essentially an anthropological model for the evolution of human social and political organization in which it is assumed that human social groups that modern anthropologists classify in certain categories will behave in similar patterns, even though they may be separated by thousands of years or tens of thousands of miles, and have completely different languages, cultures, and religions. Thus, if one finds evidence for warfare in a thirteenth-century CE chiefdom in North America (WBC 68–9), it is seen as evidence that warfare would have similarly occurred in "chiefdoms" in the Near East in 6000 BCE or Africa in 500 CE. Likewise the fact that some twentieth-century CE tribal groups in the Amazon or New Guinea fight wars (FA 56–60), is viewed as evidence that ancient human groups classified by anthropologists as tribes should also have fought wars.[3] The problem with this approach is that, while some tribal groups clearly engage in warfare, others do not. Some human groups resolve conflict through arbitration and mediation, others through violence. And the same group might negotiate in one circumstance and fight a war in another. Thus, while anthropology can tell us a great deal about the range of possible human social behavior, it cannot tell us that a specific tribe or town in Anatolia in 5000 BCE did or did not engage in warfare.

My suspicion – and it is only a suspicion – is that war began at least in the Paleolithic times when different foraging clans first began to interact (CB 55–127). Much of this interaction was undoubtedly peaceful and friendly, such as the exchange of goods or intermarriage. If anthropological analogy is any guide, however, it seems likely that conflicts would also have occurred, be it competition for food or other resources, kidnapping women, or personal offense taken for a petty insult. In such circumstances conflict could turn to fighting, and as groups rallied to support and defend their clansmen, fighting could turn into tribal war. A death or injury needed revenge; stolen property or kidnapped women needed to be recovered. This is not to say that wars always occurred between different foraging clans, only that competition and conflict between rival clans created the social circumstances in which tribal wars could occur.

The "military threshold"

Rather than attempting to answer the question of when and why war began through anthropological models, I will take an historical approach and ask two questions: what is our earliest archaeological evidence of warfare (artistic, skeletal, or fortification); and, when do the various regions of the Near East cross what I will call the "military threshold"? By military threshold, I mean the point at which warfare has essentially become endemic in a region, and at which all peoples in a region are forced to militarize their societies to one degree or another. In the Near East this seems to have first occurred as early as the sixth millennium in Anatolia, and is closely related to the culmination of a process we call the Neolithic Revolution.

The Neolithic Revolution[4]

Epipaleolithic {c. 18,000–8500} human hunting bands had low population density and were scattered in small clans of a few dozen people living in temporary camps and wandering in seasonal migration patterns; as time progressed some of these seasonal camps in ideal ecological zones with plentiful food had the capacity to develop permanent villages with populations in the low hundreds. Anthropological analogy would suggest that Epipaleolithic hunting clans were territorial and could have had periods of competition and conflict with other clans, possibly creating flashes of tribal warfare (AS 39–40; CB; WBC). However, there is little evidence for Epipaleolithic warfare in the Near East.

The Neolithic period in the ancient Near East {c. 8500–4500} witnessed a number of fundamental technological, social, and economic developments which laid the foundation for the eventual crossing of the military threshold. These include the development of the domestication of plants and animals, metallurgy, boats, social stratification, the development of large cities with the capacity for monumental building, the worship of militant gods, and the foundation of warlike royal dynasties. Evidence for the crossing of the military threshold as early as the sixth millennium can be found in weapons, art, and fortification, as well as mythic recollections written down in later periods. Each of these developments was a slow process, taking centuries if not millennia. Some developments occurred earlier or more rapidly in one area than another, but the increasing network of international trade and cultural contacts – developed largely in pursuit of rare and valuable resources such as metal, precious stones, and building wood – meant that developments in one region of the Near East were eventually copied in all others. The cumulative effect was the formation of new human social structures based on the city-state, and the crossing of the military threshold.

Domestication of plants and animals

A fundamental development of the Neolithic period is the domestication of plants and animals. The move from hunting and foraging to domestication seems to have emerged from both ecological and demographic factors. Ecologically there seems to have been an increasing desiccation in the Near East during the Neolithic period, forcing more people to live in progressively smaller regions with the best water and food resources. At the same time we see a rise in population, bringing increasing competition for decreasing resources.

Domestication of plants and animals emerged as strategies to bring greater control and security to food resources, and to intensify the amount of food that could be produced from a given tract of land. Domestication of plants, including wheat, flax, barley, beans and peas, allowed increasing sedentarization in the Near East, with villages becoming permanent sites of habitation and slowly growing in size. Domestication of animals such as cattle, sheep, goats, pigs, and dogs increasingly supplanted hunting and fishing as a major source of food. Initially these developments occurred in upper Mesopotamia, Syria, and Anatolia, where these plants and animals were indigenous in the wild. Eventually these domestication practices moved into the river valleys, where irrigation techniques were first practiced. In the long run, irrigated agriculture in the great river valleys of the Near East would prove far more productive, giving those regions significant agricultural surpluses and laying the foundation for the rise of the large city-states of the late fourth millennium.

A related important development during the early Neolithic that was to have crucial impact on military history was the formation of two symbiotic systems of food production, agricultural and pastoral, which in turn would create two differing social systems: farmers and nomads (AS 68–79, 126–31). Although today nomads as a significant military force in world history have essentially disappeared – largely due to the development of the airplane, motorized transportation, and food and water preservation and storage technologies – the complex interrelationship of cycles of cooperation and conflict between nomad and city formed a constant theme in the military history of the Near East and the world until as late as the early twentieth century CE, when Arab nomads participated in the liberation of Damascus and the fall of the Ottoman Empire in World War One.[5]

Domestication had a number of significant indirect effects on the military potential of human societies. First, increasing competition for dwindling resources could lead to conflict and, potentially, to militarism. Second, domestication of plants required the new farmers to remain in a single location. Their survival depended on retaining control of their farms. If a forager or nomad band was threatened it could migrate. When a sedentary band was threatened, it could not flee; it had to submit or fight. This basic fact laid the foundation for the eventual development of fortifications and siegecraft. From the military perspective the domestication of the donkey, for which we have evidence by at least the early fourth millennium (EA 2:255), also came to play a significant role in military logistics. As a pack animal the donkey would prove invaluable for collecting and moving surplus resources, trade goods, and for campaign logistics. The full military impact of the domestication of animals will be discussed in Chapter Five.

Agricultural surpluses

Whereas nomads were restricted as to the maximum size of their herds (and hence food surplus) by the carrying capacity of their grazing land, agriculturalists could create large food surpluses simply by planting and harvesting more food than they needed for their families. The ability to produce food surpluses created the possibility for both increasing population and, more importantly, for some of the population to specialize in non-food-producing activities, including warfare. The major problems for agricultural food surpluses were storage and spoilage. These problems were resolved by the development of pottery {seventh millennium}, which, when properly sealed and stored, could preserve grains and other food products for years. The development of pottery permitted storage and transportation of surplus food supplies. Militarily the combination of agricultural surpluses and pottery storage systems laid the foundation for the rise of a specialized warrior class who could control and gather much of a region's food surplus. This, in combination with using donkeys, boats, and eventually carts for transport, created military logistics, with the potential for the extension of military operations in time and space.

Boats

Our earliest evidence for boats comes from Syria in the Upper Euphrates around 5000, where small model boats were discovered at Tell Mashnaqa. These earliest boats were reed canoes covered with pitch and propelled by paddling or punting. Similar models have been discovered at a number of other sites from Iraq in the fifth millennium (AS 167–8; EA 5:30–4). River craft developed on the Nile at roughly the same time. From the military perspective boats facilitated transportation and communication in the two great river valleys, the Nile and Mesopotamia. The ability to move men, supplies, and equipment more easily and cheaply along these great river systems meant that it was easier to exercise military power within the river valleys than outside them. As we shall see, river transportation facilitated the formation of larger, more powerful, and longer lasting military states in the river valleys than outside them. The eventual development of sea-going vessels will be discussed later.

Increasing population

Agricultural surpluses allowed for an increase in both the number and the size of settlements in the Near East throughout the Neolithic period. Rising populations brought increased contact between various Neolithic clans and villages. Contact could be peaceful, involving trade, intermarriage and cultural exchange. On the other hand, competition for resources could create rising tensions, possibly leading to war. Rising population naturally created the possibility for increased army size, and thus larger and more complex campaigns.

Monumental building and fortifications

The development of monumental building in the Neolithic had three components: the ability to mobilize enough manpower to erect monumental buildings; the development of the engineering skills necessary to do so; and a cultural impetus creating the desire to build large communal structures. The earliest form of monumental building in the Near East was the temple, but militarily the building of fortifications is most important. The earliest evidence we have for fortifications will be introduced later, but, generally speaking, fortification building is our clearest indicator that a society has crossed the military threshold. The fact that a people are willing to spend the time and resources necessary to build fortifications implies that they perceive a serious and long-standing military threat, transcending low-level feuding, raiding, or brigandage.

Weapons and the origin of metallurgy {9000–2000}[6]

There are several important military implications of the development of weapons during the Neolithic period. First, all ancient Near Eastern weapons – with the probable exception of the mace – originated as Neolithic tools. During the Neolithic, weapons and tools were generally made of flint, chert, or obsidian. Basic hunting weapons of the Neolithic – axe, javelin, sling, bow and arrow, dagger, and spear – are found in numerous Neolithic camps and burials. However, each of these tools had both peaceful and military uses: axes for chopping and shaping wood, projectile points for hunting, and knives for domestic cutting of food or other materials. The mere presence of these tools alone is thus not necessarily a clear archaeological indicator of warfare.

All metal weapons were based on stone prototypes. Metal weapons developed different forms during the Bronze Age, but the basic prototypes for Bronze Age metal weapons can be found in Neolithic hunting weapons. The origin of metal-working was one of the most momentous developments in military history, leading ultimately to metal weapons. Although this process originated in Neolithic times, developments continued for several millennia. The earliest evidence for the use of metal dates to the early ninth millennium at Cayonu in Anatolia, in the form of drilled and polished malachite (copper) as ornamental beads. Copper was the early metal of choice because it exists abundantly as a metal in its natural geological context, is easy to polish and drill, and can be hammered into different shapes. For the next three millennia {9000–6000} the only known copper objects continue to be native copper beads and pins; a small four-centimeter awl is the largest known metal object from this period. This type of small ornamental metal-working is sometimes called "trinket metallurgy". By the sixth millennium this type of trinket copper-working had spread into northern Mesopotamia, Iran and Baluchistan (south-west Pakistan). Additionally, the technique of annealing – heating native copper at low temperatures to facilitate hammering and prevent cracking – also developed during this period, laying the foundation for the eventual smelting of metal. From the perspective of military history, metal-working was irrelevant during the early Neolithic, since all weapons in that period continued to be made of flint, chert, or obsidian (CAM 34). This was to change in the city of Can Hasan in southern Anatolia, however, where a copper shaft-hole mace-head was discovered dating to the sixth millennium, the earliest known metal weapon, and the earliest large metal object in the world (EA 4:5b; CANE 3:1503b; ET 125). It was probably made in imitation of a stone mace. Furthermore, it was found with the skeleton of a man in a house in a level of the city that was destroyed by fire, presumably in war. The mace wielding warrior apparently died in battle defending his doomed home (CAM 46).

The fact that the earliest discovered large metal object was a mace is significant, for the only purpose of a mace is to kill. The mace may be a Neolithic weapon uniquely developed for warfare. The antecedents to the mace are both the club and the axe. The club, in its simplest form of a heavy stick, is probably the earliest human weapon. The Paleolithic axe was formed from binding a sharpened rock to the club. A Neolithic mace is distinguished from the axe in that there is generally no cutting edge on a mace; it is simply a rounded heavy weight fastened to a wooden shaft. In theory a mace could be used for hunting – for dispatching a wounded prey, for example. In practice, however, a knife or an axe would do just as well, for if a hunted prey is already disabled by archery, then any weapon could be used to kill it. Uninjured animals, on the other hand, are generally too fast to be caught and injured by a man with a mace. There is no real reason to design a mace to complement the axe in the Neolithic hunting arsenal. Even if it eventually came to be used by Neolithic hunters, the question is: why make a mace in the first place? Whereas an axe can have a non-military use – chopping wood – the only purpose of a mace is to kill. The mace is specifically designed for smashing things, specifically skulls and bones.

The next phase in Near Eastern metallurgy {5000–3000} was the development of smelting and casting (EA 4:6; CANE 3:1503–6). Copper smelting is first in evidence at Catal Hoyuk in Anatolia in the early sixth millennium, and later at Tall-i-Iblis {c. 5000} and Tepe Ghabristan in Iran {c. 4500}, where a smelting workshop was discovered including crucibles, molds, a furnace and twenty kilograms of copper ore. The oldest known metal spearhead was found in Mesopotamia dating to the early fifth millennium (EA 4:3b). During this period the main metal used for weapon-making was copper or arsenic-copper. Burials at Susa in south-western Iran from the late fifth millennium included 55 copper axes. By the fourth millennium copper smelting and casting was known in Syria, Canaan (Nahal Mishmar), and Mesopotamia as well, where weapons included largely axes, maces, and spearheads. In other words, logically enough, copper smelting and casting began in Anatolia and Iran, where copper was abundant and where earlier copper trinket metalworking had existed for several millennia. Although some early copper objects could have been traded into Mesopotamia and Egypt, copper metallurgy was transmitted as an already fully developed technology into metal-poor Mesopotamia and Egypt, whose new metal industries were completely dependent on imports for their raw materials.

The development of metal weapons is another sign of a probable movement towards the military threshold. For ordinary hunting and household activities, stone tools probably served nearly as well as metal tools. Given the relative expense of the earliest metal objects the average householder would probably not be able to afford a metal axe for chopping household firewood, or a metal tipped javelin for hunting antelope. Eventually, of course, metal tools became common and inexpensive enough that they could be owned by ordinary householders. But initially, metal weapons were rare and expensive, and affordable only by the elites. While an aristocrat might have used a metal javelin for hunting, there seems to be little need for a metal axe, since aristocrats did not cut their own wood. Although it cannot be known for certain, the earliest metal axes, spearheads, and daggers were probably used only by the elites specifically for warfare; the appearance of metal weapons is thus most likely a sign of militarism.

The need for access to metal mines and markets by the emerging metal industries of Egypt and Mesopotamia was one of the driving factors behind Chalcolithic and Bronze Age imperialism (CAM 35). Once a society became dependent on copper, it found itself increasingly drawn to securing access to the needed ores. In Anatolia where there is ample copper ore, this did not create a serious problem. But in Mesopotamia and Egypt, with limited copper resources, the search for metal became an impetus to imperialism, leading emerging city-states to explore and trade to obtain copper and, later, tin. When these peaceful methods proved insufficient or unstable, they would move to raiding, controlling, or conquering metal resources. The search for metal became a spur to imperialism, and the possession of metal-armed armies likewise maximized the possibility for military success in that imperialism.

The third phase in Near Eastern weapon metallurgy is the development of bronze {3000–2000} (EA 4:8–11; CANE 3:1506–7). Copper is a relatively soft metal which doesn't hold an edge well. While useful for making large heavy objects such as maceheads and heavy axes, it is less effective with thinner spearheads, knife blades or projectile points. Alloying roughly 10 percent tin with 90 percent copper created bronze, a much harder alloy that holds a sharpened edge nicely and thus was more useful for bladed weapons and projectile points. The actual tin content of the earliest Near Eastern bronze varied from 2–15 percent. The earliest known bronze objects date to about 3000 in Syria – hence the beginning of the Bronze Age. Bronze was used in Mesopotamia by the twenty-eighth century and in Egypt by 2700. However, throughout the period we call the Early Bronze age {3000–2000}, most metal weapons continued to be made from arsenic-copper rather than tin-bronze (MW 1:182–3). Copper ores with trace elements of arsenic create a melted copper that is less viscous, and hence easier to cast with superior results. Although there are some rare examples of the tin-copper alloy we call bronze, most of the weapons in the Near East during the Chalcolithic and Early Bronze age are in fact arsenic-copper weapons (CANE 3:1505–6). For example, a hoard of metal objects found in Susa dating to roughly 2500 contained forty-eight copper objects, of which six (12 percent) had 2 percent tin, and four (8 percent) had 7 percent tin; none had the 10 percent tin content traditionally associated by modern scholars with true tin-bronze. In other words, four-fifths of the copper objects found in this hoard contained no tin at all, and those with tin were weak bronze alloys.

Another important thing to note is that, throughout the Chalcolithic and Early Bronze ages, stone weapons continued to be used alongside metal weapons. At first metal weapons were undoubtedly rare and precious, used only by the elites – they were weapons for gods and kings. As time progressed, however, the proportion of metal to stone weapons steadily increased, culminating in the Middle Bronze age when we begin to see the overwhelming predominance of metal weapons. Since Near Eastern martial art is nearly entirely the product of the royalty and nobility, depictions of weapons probably tend to show elite rather than common armament. Another characteristic of the Bronze Age weapons industry that may distort our data is the fact that metal was quite valuable and invariably taken as plunder and recycled when damaged. Our finds of metal weapons are not statistically random, but are significantly skewed by the fact that most of them are intentionally buried, either in tombs (generally of the elites), in votive offerings to temples, or in hoards buried for hiding and eventual recovery (EA 4:1–5). The fundamental problem with early bronze-making was that there were no good tin sources in the Near East that were accessible to ancient mining technologies (DANE 292). One source may have been available in the Taurus Mountains, but if it was exploited it produced only a small quantity of tin that was insufficient for the burgeoning demands of the Near East bronze industries. The main source for tin throughout the Early and Middle Bronze ages was Afghanistan (known to the Sumerians as Aratta or Tukrish), which also supplied all of the Near East's lapis lazuli, a highly valued semi-precious stone (EA 4:8–9; CANE 3:1507–9). From the Near Eastern perspective, tin, lapis lazuli and gold were all of roughly equal value. One of the reasons metal armor was not used extensively in the Early and Middle Bronze periods was that it was inordinately expensive. But whereas lapis lazuli and gold were used purely for ornamental purposes, tin had a crucial military purpose as well, being the key ingredient in making superior bronze weapons. The "Tin Road" trade route from Afghanistan to Elam and Sumer thus became a key strategic artery, and by the middle of the third millennium had been firmly established with regular trade. From Mesopotamia tin was shipped, with at least a 100 percent markup in value, to Anatolia, Syria, and ultimately Egypt. The best-documented example of this tin trade is the Assyrian Middle Bronze merchant colony at Kanesh (Nesha) in Anatolia {2000–1750}, where a surviving merchant archive describes shipping 80 tons of tin over a fifty-year period to the city-states of Anatolia from Assyria and originally from Afghanistan (see Chapter Eleven). Throughout the Bronze Age Near East, tin was the strategic resource that was as vital to ancient military systems as oil is to modern armies.

Because of the relative scarcity of tin supplies it was not until the Middle Bronze age {2000–1600} that true tin-bronze became the predominant metal alloy for weapon making. Thus, in a sense, true Bronze Age warfare begins only in the Middle Bronze age. This increase in the overall bronze supply also allowed, for the first time, armies to be equipped entirely with bronze weapons – although the use of non-metal arrowheads seems to have continued, probably because shooting an arrow often meant losing the arrow and bronze arrowheads were still too expensive to lose. By the end of the Middle Bronze period bronze body armor was beginning to appear, but only for the elite chariot warriors. The specific details of the impact of metal weapons on different regions of the Near East will be discussed in subsequent chapters.

Militant gods

The precise nature of the gods worshipped in the Neolithic period is uncertain because of lack of any textual evidence. What is clear, however, is that when writing first appears in the Near East, war-gods were already well established and widely worshipped, as discussed in the following chapters. Given the conservative though syncretistic nature of ancient Near Eastern religions, it is quite likely that the worship of war-gods antedates their first appearance in iconography and texts by at least several centuries. This would place the worship of war-gods in the Near East no later than the mid-fourth millennium in both Egypt and Mesopotamia, and probably much earlier. It is unclear if the worship of militant gods increased militarism among the worshippers, or if a warlike people naturally gravitated towards worshipping warlike gods. Most likely the relationship was symbiotic. However that may be, it is probable that those groups worshipping warlike gods developed militant social institutions and engaged in a higher frequency and greater intensity of warfare. However the worship of militant gods may have first originated, their worship is another sign that a people have probably crossed the military threshold.

Warlike royal dynasties

The creation of a military aristocracy centered around a warlord-king – a ruler with the economic, ideological, and coercive power to mobilize the entire society for war – was a crucial step in the movement to cross the military threshold. Rulers for whom warfare was a means of ideological legitimization, personal aggrandizement, and increasing wealth were rulers who would be more likely to bring cities into war. The alliance of warlord-kings with priests was a key ingredient in the crossing of the military threshold. Priests, speaking in the name of the gods, could legitimize or even command the military endeavors of kings, while plunder from victory in battle would be shared with the gods by donations to the priest-controlled temple institutions.

All of these developments – social, economic, political, technological, and religious – had their origins in the prehistoric Neolithic and Chalcolithic period. By the time writing first appears in Egypt and Mesopotamia, both of those societies had already crossed the military threshold. As Arther Ferrill aptly put it: "as soon as man learned how to write, he had wars to write about" (OW 31). The following sections in this chapter will examine the specific evidence for warfare and militarism in the major regions of the Neolithic Near East.

Neolithic Anatolia {to 11,000–5500}

The early Neolithic in Anatolia {11,000–6500} broadly parallels similar developments throughout the Near East: shift from hunting to village-farming economies, domestication of plants and animals, and development of pottery by around 6500. Most of the Early Neolithic settlements of Anatolia are similar to other contemporary villages in the Near East: small sites with a mixed food-collecting and hunting economy, and no fortifications. Some, like Cayonu {8250–5000} (EA 1:444–7) and Nevali Cori {8300–5000} (EA 4:131–4) in south-eastern Turkey, had monumental communal and religious buildings, indicating that they had sufficient population and social organization to have built fortifications if they had been needed. Their absence implies the lack of a serious and sustained threat. At the early Neolithic site of Hallan Cemi Tepesi a triangular stone mace head was discovered, possibly a war weapon (ET 87).

Fortifications

The famous wall and tower at Jericho {c. 7000} are often considered the oldest fortifications in the world (see p. 29). Jericho, however, was essentially an isolated example of fortress-building designed to respond to a serious but isolated military threat. In Anatolia, on the other hand, we find a cluster of fortified or quasi-fortified sites – Catal Hoyuk (Çatal Höyük), Asikli Hoyuk (Aşikli Höyük), Kurucay Hoyuk (Kurucay Höyük), and Hacilar – all with fortifications dating to the mid-to-late Neolithic period. The site of Asikli Hoyuk {seventh millennium} in central Anatolia has closely packed houses and a defensive wall of mud brick (EA 1:123–4; PA 187–9). Kurucay Hoyuk {6000–5500} has a late Neolithic fortified stone wall with projecting semi-circular towers (PA 166–72).

Catal Hoyuk (Catal Huyuk) {6500–5500}[7]

The site of Catal Hoyuk is one of the best preserved in the Neolithic Near East. For the military historian it is notable for both its walls and its wall paintings. The walls at Catal Hoyuk are rather peculiar, and could perhaps be described as proto-fortifications. Most of the houses are built adjoining one another, sharing walls with other houses, but with no doors between dwellings. The outer walls of the outermost houses of the village thus formed a solid wall surrounding the entire complex (CH 68–9). Individual houses were entered by ladders through holes in the roof, while entry into the village as a whole was made by ladders which were leaned against the outside walls, or through a fortified gate (CH 70). What this effectively created was a walled city which could be defended from the rooftops on the outer perimeter. The outer walls, while certainly a barrier to occasional raiders and brigands, were not much thicker than the interior walls, and would not have offered a serious obstacle to a determined enemy. None the less, an enemy breaking through an outer wall would have access only to a single dwelling. To get to the next dwelling he would have to break through another wall, or climb a ladder up through the roof-door. Catal Hoyuk probably represents a transitional phase in fortification; a first effort to protect a city with minimal additional expenditure of resources and labor. Weapons found at Catal Hoyuk include stone daggers, spearheads, arrowheads, and maces (ET 101; CH 209, 213, §113–15, xiv); although copper trinket metallurgy was known at Catal Hoyuk, all weapons in the late Neolithic were from flint or obsidian.

The earliest substantial Neolithic art of Anatolia – the wall paintings at Catal Hoyuk – do not show explicitly military themes. We do have scenes of men hunting with bows and perhaps slings, weapons which would eventually be turned to warfare.[8] Another scene shows a deer hunt with bows and lassos (CH §62). Most of the hunters wear a flowing leopard-skin kilt and are armed with a bow or a club/mace. Between the two hunting scenes is a third scene, which has been interpreted as a hunting dance (CH 174, §61), which is certainly an excellent possibility. It may also, however, represent a war dance or victory celebration, or even a battle. Twelve men are shown in running postures but are facing in different directions. Seven are armed with bow and/or club/mace, five are unarmed. No animals are present, but none of the men seem to be directly confronting each other. What points to a possible military context is that three of the men are headless, and one of the headless men is armed with a bow. One unarmed man stands in the middle, tied to two of the headless men. If the painting represents a hunting dance, as Mellaart believes, why are there headless men, and why are some men tied together? An alternative interpretation is that the scene shows an after-battle victory celebration in which bound prisoners are brought forward and decapitated.

From the military perspective another intriguing wall painting of Catal Hoyuk comes from Room 7, which shows carrion birds hovering over headless bodies (CA 169, §45–9). This has been interpreted as representing the exposure and excarnation of bodies before burial (CH 167–8). The decapitation of the bodies may also relate to the preservation and veneration of ancestral skulls (CH 65–6, 84) such as are found at the "skull house" at Nevali Cori (Nevali Çori) (EA 4:133). On the other hand, the painting in Room 7 may depict the decapitated bodies of enemies killed in battle and left to be devoured by vultures, a military practice memorialized in very early martial art in both Mesopotamia (Stele of Vultures, AFC 190–1, cf. FI §887), and Egypt (Battlefield Palette and Narmer Palette, EWP 29). A different vulture scene shows a man with a bow or sling in one hand and a mace or club in the other standing over a headless body flanked by two vultures (CH §46). Mellaart believes the standing man is "ward[ing] off the two vultures from the small headless corpse" (CH 166), although this runs counter to his overall interpretation of people intentionally exposing the dead to be eaten by vultures (CH 167–8) – why chase the vultures away if you intentionally expose the corpses? A very fragmentary scene shows a man who seems to be carrying a human head, perhaps a war trophy (CH §51). If this military interpretation is correct, the 8000-year-old murals of Catal Hoyuk would be the oldest military victory memorial in the world.

Unfortunately, all of the evidence at Catal Huyuk which I have interpreted from a military perspective is ambiguous. The overlapping exterior walls may be intended for protection, but might also simply be a quirky way to save building materials and time. The mace may be a war weapon, or might be used to dispatch a deer wounded by arrows on a hunt. The headless corpses amid the vultures may be war dead, or may be a form of exposure of the dead known anciently in the Near East, most closely associated with Zoroastrianism and Tibet.[9] Dancing armed men may be preparing for the hunt or celebrating victory in battle. These ambiguities make certainty of interpretation impossible.

Hacilar {5700–4800}[10]

The military interpretation of Catal Hoyuk, given above, is strengthened by the fortifications and destruction levels of the late contemporary site of Hacilar. The originally unwalled village was destroyed around 5500, and rebuilt with a defensive wall 1.5–3 meters thick. It was destroyed again in 5250, and rebuilt with stronger "fortresslike characteristics" (EA 2:449b). It was destroyed again and abandoned around 4800. Can Hasan was also destroyed by fire at roughly the same time

(ET 125), leading some to postulate a period of significant military upheaval in the late sixth millennium. In other words, expanding from the proto-fortifications of Catal Hoyuk, true fortified cities appear in Anatolia by the mid-sixth millennium, suffering destruction in war and rebuilding in an even more strongly fortified condition. This is strong evidence that Anatolia had crossed the military threshold at this time.

Warfare in Neolithic Syria {10,000–4000}

The Early Neolithic Period {10,000–6800}[11]

As elsewhere in the Near East, the Neolithic period in Syria was one of transition from foraging to farming and nomadism through the domestication of plants and animals, presumably in response to ecological change at the end of the Pleistocene period. There are a few surviving signs of militarism in the Syrian Neolithic. Neolithic weapons – flint arrowheads, javelins, knives, and stone axes (AS 19–20, 26–7, 79–80; ED 67, 71, 74) – all had hunting or other domestic functions and are not sure indicators of war. None the less, the discovery of a number of skeletons with embedded projectile points, as well as a burned house with a number of skeletons inside, indicate that violence, and probably warfare, was present in the Neolithic (AS 76–7). An international "arms trade" also makes its first appearance in the early Neolithic, with the development of obsidian trade over hundreds of miles from the volcanic regions in eastern Anatolia into Syria (AS 82). Obsidian creates a finer and sharper edge for tools, and was highly prized by Neolithic peoples. Although most Neolithic obsidian projectile points or blades were not primarily intended for military purposes in the Neolithic, the search for such scarce resources created international trade and contact between scattered groups; competition for these resources was one of the key factors contributing to inter-clan tension, potentially leading to tribal warfare.

As time progressed the number and size of Neolithic villages expanded, increasingly engaging in food production (farming and herding) rather than food gathering. The size of early Neolithic villages in Syria ranged from 1 to 12 hectares, with a population of the largest of these Neolithic villages, such as Abu Hureyra (12 hectares) perhaps reaching 1000 people; the population of most settlements, however, numbered in the hundreds (AS 59). Neolithic villages had enough manpower and social organization to begin to undertake monumental building, such as rough stone walls several meters high and terraced platforms for ritual purposes at Halula and Tell Sabi Abyad {c. 7000} (AS 63–5), roughly contemporary with Catal Hoyuk in Anatolia and Jericho in Palestine. Despite possessing the logistical and organizational capability to build such large stone walls, however, none of these early Neolithic sites seem to have been fortified, pointing to a lack of serious and sustained military threat in the early Neolithic; by 6000 Syria had not yet crossed the military threshold.

Late Neolithic Syria {6800–4000} (AS 99–180)

By around the sixth millennium spreading Neolithic Syrian farming villages began to be integrated into a the broader regional Mesopotamian cultural and agricultural system of the Late Neolithic, subdivided into the Halaf Period {5900–5200} and the Ubaid Period {5200–4000}.[12] This phase is characterized by the development of pottery, increasing similarities of material culture throughout different regions (indicating ongoing interregional contacts), numerous scattered small villages, as well as the development of a few large villages of over 1000 people. Some sites, like Bouqras, show signs of organized uniform village planning, perhaps pointing to the beginnings of social hierarchy and emerging elites. Overall, however, the Late Neolithic is characterized by egalitarian, self-sufficient, and autonomous communities.

Like the early Neolithic, the late Neolithic archaeological data presents little evidence of extensive militarism. As its name indicates, the "Burnt Village" level at Tell Sabi Abyad was destroyed by fire around 6000, possibly indicating destruction in military conflict. However, the fire has also been interpreted as a ritual act of destruction; bodies found inside the burned homes had died before the conflagration (AS 112–14, 148). Unfortunately, a burn level at an archaeological site is not certain evidence of warfare, since fires may be started accidentally or even intentionally in non-military contexts. A burial pit at Tepe Gawra contained 24 bodies which seem to have been "thrown into the pit without any attendant ritual" (AS 148); they may have been victims of warfare.

There is evidence of some changes in the nature of archery in the Syrian late Neolithic. It has been suggested that the expanding use of smaller projectile points may represent some type of change in bow technology. The decline in frequency of projectile point finds during the Late Neolithic is probably due to the spread of agriculture leading to the decreasing importance of hunting as a source of food, and therefore a decrease in the practice of archery (AS 128, 132–3). Two Late Neolithic Syrian pots have paintings of archers with quivers in a hunting context (AS 133). We also have the first evidence of the sling in the form of thousands of clay sling bullets (AS 128,132). In the seventh millennium we also find the first evidence of the use of copper in Syria, harbinger of the later development of metal weapons; however, at this period metal objects are only small ornamental objects such as beads (AS 133).

The last phase of the Late Neolithic is known as the Ubaid period {5200–4000} (AS 154–80; M = CAM 53), known for increasing uniformity of pottery styles, housing structure and other aspects of material culture between Mesopotamia and Syria. It has been speculated in the past that this uniformity may be related to migration or even conquest (AS 154), but it must be emphasized that uniformity of material culture does not demonstrate shared ethnicity nor the existence of a single political entity – the existence of Japanese cars in the United States, for example, is not evidence that Japan conquered the United States. It does indicate, however, that the Ubaid was a period of increasing long-distance social and economic contacts. At Ubaid-period Tell Mashnaqa two small clay miniatures of boats were found, the first evidence of riverine sailing on the Upper Euphrates. The actual boats were apparently bundled reed canoes coated with bitumen, similar to those used until recently by the Marsh Arabs of southern Iraq (AS 167–8). The ability to move men and supplies up and down the Tigris and Euphrates rivers would become important factors in later Mesopotamian warfare. The first signs of the use of copper for tools rather than ornamentation also appear; a copper axehead was made in the late Ubaid period, transitional with the following Chalcolithic period (AS 169). Signs of warfare during the Ubaid period in Syria are still relatively rare. None the less, by about 4000 a number of key technologies and practices are in place that will allow the eventual transition across the military threshold.

Neolithic Canaan {8500–4300}[13]

Before 8500 Syria and Canaan were inhabited by Epipaleolithic hunting and foraging bands known by archaeologists as the Natufian culture. The ecology of the region was wetter then, allowing human occupation of areas which are now deserts. The region was sparsely populated, with humans organized into small kinship-based bands not much larger than a hundred people. There is no evidence of warfare before the Neolithic period, although small-scale tribal conflicts undoubtedly occurred. Hunting technologies developed during the Epipaleolithic {10,500–8500}, which would lay the foundation for warfare in the following millennia. These included the bow and arrow and javelin, with flint or bone projectile points (THL 42). Likewise flint axes and daggers were in use for hunting and domestic purposes, which could also double as weapons if needed.

The beginning of the pre-pottery Neolithic period {8500–6000} is characterized by the transition from food gathering to food production, the rise of permanent dwellings, and new burial practices. It is during this early Neolithic period that the first signs of fortification in the Near East, and indeed the world, appear at the site of Jericho (Tell el-Sultan) in modern Palestine.[14] Human settlement at Jericho was based on the perennial springs of the region. Initially foragers were attracted to the rich plant and animal life at the springs, where they built a small shrine and dwelling huts in the Epipaleolithic. By the eighth millennium, however, the development of agriculture had transformed this foraging settlement into a city with a population between 1000 and 3500 (depending on presumed density), which was continuously occupied for nearly 2000 years. During this period the people of Jericho built a massive defensive wall of large unhewn stones, almost three meters wide and four meters high. A deep dry moat eight meters wide was cut in the rock, and a round tower was constructed, measuring 8.5 meters in diameter and 7.7 meters high (FA 76; AW 1:115; THL 45).

The appearance of such massive fortifications a thousand years before fortification in other regions has led some to question their purpose, claiming the walls were designed to protect the community from flash floods out of the wadis to the west. However, it seems dubious that protection from flash floods would require such a massive four-meter-high wall – indeed the ditch alone should have proved sufficient for flood control. The stronger interpretation is that the wall and tower had a military purpose. It is possible that these defensive walls were designed to protect Jericho against rival proto-towns in the region – nearly two dozen proto-towns are known in Canaan and Jordan during this period. But it seems more likely that the walls were designed to defend the community from local raiders who were attracted to the rich springs at Jericho and the food surpluses collected there from their early Neolithic agriculture. Such walls would have been an insuperable barrier to hunting or nomadic clans bent on a quick plundering raid at the oasis. It is likely that the Neolithic fortress of Jericho was built in response to a very specific, local, but ongoing threat, rather than reflecting a rise in regional militarism.

Tools with a possible military function – such as flint axes, knives, and projectile points – are found throughout the region (ALB 46, 50, 52), but no other certain signs of militarism are known in the Neolithic period {8500–4300}. The archaic walls of Jericho remained in use throughout this period, however, and were rebuilt twice; a similar, though less massive wall was found at Beidha (ALB 45). We have no evidence of other fortification building at other Neolithic sites.

Based upon anthropological analogy we can perhaps assume that conflicts arose between rival proto-towns, and between sedentarists and hunting nomads, but such claims remain nothing but assumptions. There was increasing desiccation of the region throughout the Neolithic period. Many sites in the Sinai, Negev (southern Israel), and Jordan, which had flourished in the early Neolithic period, show either significant occupational gaps or complete abandonment during parts of the later Neolithic (ALB 48–9). Whatever the ultimate cause of such declines in settlement – probably a combination of ecological degradation due to both desiccation and overuse of resources – such stress would create the conditions for increasing conflict over decreasing resources, and warfare may have been a catalyst in the abandonment of some of these Neolithic sites.

Neolithic Elam and Iran {7000–3400}[15]

Only 10 percent of Iran is arable, the rest being mountain, steppe, or desert. Throughout the Neolithic outside of Elam there were only sparse settlements leaving limited archaeological remains. Ancient Elam was roughly coterminous with the modern province of Khuzistan in south-western Iran, a region of flat terrain watered by tributaries of the Tigris with good agricultural potential. The modern province of Fars was also the center of another zone of city building which would give rise to the ancient city-state of Anshan. The mountains of the Zagros, running from north-west to south-east, were home to highland pastoral tribes who would on occasion play an important role in the military history of Mesopotamia. As with the rest of the Near East, evidence for militarism in early Neolithic Iran is slight. It is not until the late fifth millennium that we begin to see sure signs of warfare.

Susa {4300–3400}

The major site showing military activity in Elam was Susa. The region of Susa had been occupied by small Neolithic villages since the eighth millennium. In the late fifth millennium, some of the surrounding Neolithic villages, such as Chogha Mish, were abandoned, perhaps due to warfare. The population seems to have migrated towards larger centers, perhaps for protection, with Susa being adopted as a new regional ceremonial center around 4300.[16] The "Apadana" section of Susa I {4300–3800} included a 2.1-meter-thick mud brick wall – four times as thick as the usual walls of the period; this may have served as a citadel for the ruling elite (PAE 46–7). The city had a population of only a few thousand people, serving as a ceremonial center for at least forty surrounding villages. At some point it was destroyed by fire, presumably in warfare, and partially abandoned. Arsenic-copper was smelted during this period, with metallurgical technology stimulated from the Fars highlands (PAE 50). Burials at Susa from the late fifth millennium included 55 copper axes, possibly for elite warriors. On the other hand, military images are notably absent from the seals of Tal-i Bakan during this period (PAE 53).

During the Susa II period {3800–3100}, Susa shows strong cultural relations with Sumer and the city-state of Uruk in Mesopotamia. Political power in Elam was no longer centralized in Susa, but diffused among smaller towns such as Chogha Mish and Abu Fanduweh, each with a population of several thousand. The exact nature of the relationship between Sumer and Elam during this period is a subject of strong debate (PAE 52–67). In the absence of historical documents, the military implications of this relationship cannot be determined, but it is certainly possible that Sumerian military power was exerted in some form in Elam during this period (see pp. 37–9). The abrupt appearance of Uruk-style pottery and proto-writing system at Susa, and more broadly in Elam as a whole, strongly suggests the migration of people from Sumer to Elam – whether as merchants, the courtiers of a married princess, peaceful colonists, or military conquerors is not clear. The question of the overall significance of the "Uruk expansion" will be discussed in Chapter Two.

Anshan (Tel Malyan)[17]

Anshan, near modern Shiraz in Fars province, had been occupied since 6000 BCE, but the region was sparsely populated before the late fourth millennium. It became a major center of military power during the Proto-Elamite period {3400–2800}, when the city served as the administrative center of the region with a large copper smelting installation, and a probable population of several thousand. Militarily, it is most notable for its massive city walls. Built on a stone foundation and protected by a mud-plaster glacis, the main wall is some five kilometers long, made from brick on a stone foundation. There are two parallel inner walls, indicating an emerging understanding of concentric fortifications. The innermost wall is made of brick and is five meters thick. The walls enclosed an area of 200 hectares, although only a portion of this was occupied. These fortifications made the city the most powerful military bastion east of Mesopotamia. It is unclear if the enemies of Anshan were local nomads and highlanders from within Fars, or outside invaders, but it seems that such massive and sophisticated fortifications would be excessive to deal with occasional bedouin raids.

Neolithic Egypt {to 3500}[18]

Our understanding of the origins of warfare in Egypt must take into account the ecological transformation of the Sahara from savannah to desert which had occurred by the fourth millennium BC. In the past few decades the emergence of the science of climatology and the history of climates has allowed scholars to more fully understand how past environments differed, often dramatically, from current ecological conditions. Temperature, rainfall and other ecological conditions have fluctuated during the past 20,000 years. During this period the Sahara region has oscillated between dry and wet phases. During the wet phases the Sahara received sufficient rainfall to create a savannah ecology, with a wide range of animals flourishing there (EAE 1:385–9; GP 60–1). Between 7000 and 3500 (late Epipaleolithic and Neolithic) the regions surrounding the Nile Valley that are currently desert were much like the current Sub-Saharan savannah, home to large herds of antelope, ibex, elephant, giraffe, ostrich, and cattle, and to lions (GP 83–112). During this period Egypt and the Sahara were also home to semi-nomadic foragers congregating in seasonal camps following the migration of animals and the natural cycles of the maturation of plants used as food; these foragers also availed themselves of food and other resources from the Nile valley.

Thus, for several thousand years, hunting and herding bands lived seasonally in the savannah surrounding the Nile Valley, and within the Nile Valley itself. Humans in Egypt lived in small hunting and fishing camps, mixed with some proto-agriculture – as witnessed by grinding stones and the microlithic sickles used for harvesting grains. Human settlements in this period were generally temporary seasonal camps. Population was small and societies were probably organized into kinship-based clans.

Although few details are known, it seems probable that these seasonal foragers engaged in tribal warfare. The oldest discovered cemetery in the Nile Valley at Gebel Sahaba in Nubia (northern Sudan) – broadly dated to roughly 12,000–9000 – provides the earliest evidence of tribal warfare, for roughly half of the 59 skeletons at site 117 had flint projectile points among the bones, probably indicating death in battle; some had evidence of multiple healed wounds, perhaps indicating repeated fighting.[19] An extended period of drought beginning in the sixth millennium led to the desiccation of the Sahara savannah, stimulating increased migration into the Nile Valley as well as a transformation from food gathering to food production through the domestication of plants and animals {6000–4000}. The hunters and herders who had formerly roamed the once fertile savannah were forced by this desiccation to slowly congregate in the Nile valley, causing mounting competition for increasingly scarce resources. A number of new ideas, technologies, and domesticated plants and animals developed during this period, laying the foundation for Egyptian civilization and its military system.

Rock art from herders in the Eastern Desert also provides evidence of warfare in Egypt by at least the fourth millennium, and probably earlier. A recently discovered vase from Abydos Tomb U–239 {early fourth millennium} depicts four mace-armed warriors with ostrich feathers and animal-tail loincloths executing a band of prisoners (GP 79). A similar mace-armed warrior in a boat is depicted in rock art from near contemporary Wadi Abu Wasil (GP 79). These figures are dressed and armed quite similarly to the figures on the famous "Hunter's Palette", dating from a few centuries later (GP 96), indicating a widespread use of a common set of tribal military equipment: loincloth, feathered headdress, tails of bulls or other animals as belts, with weapons including spears, bows, maces, and axes, and a tribal banner or totem. All of this evidence implies that low-level tribal warfare was at least occasionally a part of the life of Egyptian hunting clans, an interpretation bolstered by anthropological analogy.

Neolithic Mesopotamia {9000–3500}[20]

As with the rest of the Near East, there is little evidence for warfare in Neolithic Mesopotamia. The Epipaleolithic period {16,000–9000} is characterized by small foraging bands scattered unevenly throughout the region. The standard tool kit included obsidian blades acquired from eastern Anatolia, indicating some long-distance contacts and exchanges, even if indirect. Most of the excavated sites from this period are in the uplands or highlands. In part this may be because the earliest agriculture developed around the regions where wild wheat and barley grew naturally with normal rainfall. On the other hand, the earliest sites and settlements in the river valleys are buried in three meters or more of silt accumulated over the past eight thousand years, are now beneath the water table (CAM 51–2), and are thus largely inaccessible to archaeologists.

The development of incipient agriculture and domestication in the Early Aceramic Neolithic {9000–7000} began in northern Mesopotamia, Syria, and Anatolia, where wild wheat, barley, goats, and sheep facilitated the transition. Small Neolithic agricultural villages of the period, such as Jarmo (EA 3:208–9), had only a few hundred people, practicing a mixture of herding (sheep and goats), farming (wheat, barley, lentils), and hunting with both flint and imported obsidian weapons.

A number of developments occurred during the Pottery Neolithic phase {7000–5000}. As discussed on p. 18, pottery allowed storage of food surpluses, allowing people more easily to remain at a single site all year, along with increasing the population. Agriculture was becoming more prominent as a source of food, but hunting was still widely practiced. A number of important sites such as Tell Halaf (EA 2:460), Tepe Gawra (EA 5:183–5), and Samarra {6000–5000} (EA 4:472–3) have been excavated from this period, revealing small villages of a few hundred people. In the sixth millennium we see the beginnings of monumental building, mainly small temples. During this period we also see the development of several zones with distinctive pottery styles (CAM 49, 53). The military implications of this fact are unclear, since pottery styles cannot be translated with confidence into either ethnic or political boundaries. None the less, it is clear that during this period there are ongoing contacts throughout Mesopotamia and Syria.

It is during this late Neolithic period that we begin to see the first evidence of warfare in Mesopotamia. Most prominent is the fortification of the site of Tell al-Sawwan near modern Samarra, where around 6000 a thick brick wall and a three-meter-wide moat were constructed to defend the settlement (EA 4:473). Clay sling bullets were discovered at Hassuna, but these could have been used for hunting rather than war. Trinket metallurgy begins to be seen in Mesopotamia in this period.

Ubaid {5000–4000} and early Uruk {4000–3500} periods

The final phase of the Neolithic era in Mesopotamia is called the Ubaid period, after a shared style of pottery and material culture that spreads throughout much of Mesopotamia and Syria. Ubaid-style pottery was also discovered on the north-east coast of Arabia, and in Qatar and Bahrain, indicating that ocean-going vessels existed during the period, initiating the Persian Gulf trade which would culminate in the military expeditions discussed in Chapters Two and Three. This period shows clear evidence of increasing settlement size, social stratification, inter-regional contacts, and monumental building. The impressive temple complex at Eridu in Sumer shows that communities had the capacity for monumental building during this period (EA 2:258–9; CAM 52), as do the large buildings at Arpachiyeh with stone walls 1.5 meters thick.

None the less, there is still sparse evidence for either fortification or war during this period. Despite its magnificent temple complex, Eridu seems to have been unfortified in the fifth millennium. Eridu may have been a sacrosanct ceremonial center during this period, supported by many surround villages and towns, rather than a politically oriented city-state. Some have suggested that some of the legendary prediluvian kings of the Sumerian Kinglist may have been associated with Eridu in this period (C1/2:107). There is some evidence of war: at the end of the Ubaid period the "Round House" at Tepe Gawra, which seems to have served as a citadel, was destroyed by fire, possibly in war (EA 5:184b). By around 4000 we also see the shift to the Chalcolithic period, where tools and other large objects begin to be made from arsenic-copper. A copper spearhead, the oldest yet discovered, was found in Mesopotamia dating to the early fifth millennium (EA 4:3b). A painting on a bowl from Tepe Jowi shows a man with a bow in one hand and possibly a mace in the other; he wears a loincloth and a feather in his hair (AANE §186). Thus in the Early Uruk period there were a number of behind-the-scenes developments which laid the foundation for the crossing of the military threshold in Mesopotamia that occurred in the Late Uruk period {3500–3000}, discussed in Chapter Two.

CHAPTER TWO

Early Dynastic Mesopotamia {3500–2334}

Early Mesopotamia and Egypt were the heartlands of the great river valley economic, social and political systems that produced the earliest advanced civilizations in world history. From the military perspective, these two river valleys both witnessed the development of intimately intertwined militant religion and kingship, manifesting their warlike ideologies by the creation of martial art and inscriptions. Though warfare in the Near East had been going on for centuries, it is with the first written and artistic records of Egypt and Mesopotamia that true military history begins. This chapter will examine the rise of the military states in Mesopotamia. These developments should be compared with comparable contemporary events in Early Dynastic and Old Kingdom Egypt (see Chapters Twelve and Thirteen).

The following chart (Table 2.1) shows the major periods of Early Mesopotamian history. The exact dates for the division between the different phases and subphases of the Early Dynastic period are interpreted differently by different scholars (compare with AI 502–3 and C1/2:998–1001).

Table 2.1: The major periods of Early Mesopotamian history

Late Uruk	3500–3000
Jamdat Nasr	3000–2900
Early Dynastic I	2900–2650
Early Dynastic II	2650–2550
Early Dynastic IIIA	2550–2400
Early Dynastic IIIB	2400–2300

The Late Uruk (Pre-Dynastic) period {3500–3100}[1]

A number of developments in the Late Uruk period collectively formed the catalyst which caused Mesopotamian civilization to definitively cross the military threshold. These included the urban revolution, an increase in the size and amount of monumental building leading to fortifications, the development of ideological art, much of it with military themes, and the rise of social stratification with domination by martial kings and elites. The formulation of a complex administrative organization, capable of collecting and dispersing surpluses and running a city-state, laid the foundation for kings capable of mobilizing armies in the thousands of men and keeping them in the field for months. The invention of protowriting (from mnemonic accounting devices), which occurred in Uruk around 3400, was a key component of the new bureaucratic state (PAE 58–67; EA 5:352–8). In addition to allowing an expanded and more efficient bureaucracy, writing would eventually permit the state ideology, both religious and military, to be recorded and preserved, thus creating military history.

The city-states of the Late Uruk and subsequent periods were both quantitatively and qualitatively different from the towns of the Neolithic period. The shift of agriculture from the rain-fed lands around Mesopotamia into the river valleys had a significant impact on population growth. As irrigation developed in the river valleys agricultural productivity and surpluses expanded, in part because of higher productivity per acre and in part because of multiple crops per year in the hot climates of Mesopotamia. At the same time the rivers allowed the easy collection and transportation of these surpluses into one central location. The combination of irrigation and river transport meant that cities were no longer dependent solely on the land immediately surrounding the city, but could collect surpluses from tracts of land all up and down the river system. The overall impact was to allow the possibility of having cities many times larger than had been possible during the Neolithic period, creating the first city-states.

An examination of city size during the urban revolution gives a sense of the overall growth of population. In the late Ubaid period {4500–4000} there were very few settlements as large as ten hectares, which could have held a maximum population of around 2000. By the Early Uruk period {4000–3500}, Uruk (Warka, Erech, Unu)[2] encompassed 70 hectares, two other cities were 50 hectares, and a final two 30 hectares each (M = CAM 58–9). The population in these cities might have ranged from 7000 to 20,000. By the Late Uruk period {3500–4000} Uruk had reached more than 200 hectares in area, and was the greatest city of the age, with a population as high as 40,000 to 50,000 – twenty times greater than the largest towns of the Neolithic period. Cities of this size could probably field armies of several thousand men, and perhaps up to 5000 with maximum effort, compared to the dozens or hundreds of men who composed earlier Neolithic tribal armies. We must also note that the great cities that were developing in the Late Uruk had a number of villages and small towns as satellites, which were politically integrated into the city-state and which supplied some of their surplus resources to the central city. However, as the great cities continued to grow in size, the number of smaller villages began to decrease rapidly; presumably their populations migrated into the large centers. Part of the reason for this might have been the greater security inside the great cities, pointing to increasing warfare in the region.

These new cities were ruled by a hierarchy of priests and kings with the majority of wealth and power in their hands, though they were always dependent on town councils for making major decisions. They organized a central hier-archical government overseeing a stratified society. A large percentage of the peo-ple of the new Mesopotamian city-states were no longer directly engaged in agriculture designed to produced the food to be consumed by their own families. Rather, they increasingly entered non-food-producing occupations such as priests, scribes, craftsmen and merchants. The development of economic specialization gave rise to military specialists, who would develop into military professionals, elites, and ultimately martial aristocracies. Monarchical rule was not absolute, requiring advice and consent by the city council of elders. None the less, the new kings of Mesopotamia had far more military resources at hand than any earlier rulers. One of the primary functions of these new kings (*lugal*: "big man") was that of warlord, to protect and expand the power of the city-state.[3]

The centralization of power in the hands of allied royal and priestly classes was associated with the emergence of a divinely mandated martial ideology. Using their new wealth and surplus resources, the kings and priests embarked on a flamboyant program of monumental building of immense temples, palaces and city fortifications. The most lavish building projects were temples, such as the great Eanna ("House of Heaven") temple complex at Uruk (CAM 61–3). None the less, massive monumental fortifications were also built, such as the great mud-brick wall of Uruk, built around 3000, which had a circumference of six miles; its ruins can still be seen 5000 years later. By the Early Dynastic period all Mesopo-tamian cities were fortified with such huge mud-brick walls.

During this period a royal ideology of divine kingship developed in which the king was chosen by the gods as his representative on earth; this could sometimes encompass the idea of the king as son of god, or as a god incarnate (EM 260–74). When the king acted as warlord, he was acting under the express command of the gods as revealed through divination and oracles. The gods themselves were the ultimate arbiters of war. It is probably not unimportant that the patron goddess of Uruk – where we first see evidence of this new ideology – was Inanna ("Lady of Heaven", the Akkadian Ishtar), patroness of love and war. In the absence of early written texts – all proto-writing of the Late Uruk period is administrative – the development of an ideology of martial kingship can only be seen in the new styles of martial art.

The "Priest-King"[4]

The earliest Mesopotamian art was largely ornamental and often abstract. This type of art continued throughout the Late Uruk period, during which we also find the first ideologically-rich martial art, from both sculpture and cylinder seals. The use of cylinder seals in Mesopotamia dates back to the fourth millennium. They were made from small two-to-five centimeter long cylinders of stone, similar to large oblong beads, which were rolled on wet clay as a type of seal to show own-ership, rather like a medieval signet ring. The art on cylinder seals is often called glyptic art, which provides us with a number of important martial scenes as sources for military history. Originally designed simply as a stamp to indicate identity and ownership, they rapidly developed into an extraordinarily sophisticated and elegant art form, like gem-cutting and cameos in medieval and Renaissance Europe.[5]

A problem with interpreting glyptic art for the military historian is that much of it focuses on mythological and religious themes, creating a methodological question concerning the reliability of the weapons depicted: are the weapons and combat techniques authentic to the contemporary age, or are they stylized representations of archaic weapons in contemporary retellings of ancient myths. An analogous problem might be if an archaeologist were to insist that twenty-first-century warriors used swords in combat because he found depictions in twenty-first-century Christian churches and religious art of the archangel Michael wielding a sword. Thus, if a Middle Bronze cylinder seal shows a god wielding a mace in a mythological scene, we cannot be certain that the mace was actually used in real combat during the Middle Bronze Age, since the scene may be a stylized anachronistic representation which originated centuries earlier, with the god becoming iconographically standardized as wielding a mace in subsequent art. Another problem with glyptic art is that many of the cylinder seals are quite small, measuring only one or two inches. Although many of the scenes depicted are of extraordinary detail and quality, many others are quite abstract, and it is often difficult to interpret the details of weapons.

Most art of early Mesopotamia was religious in nature, and presumably Late Uruk martial art was also fundamentally religious in purpose. None the less, the glorification of the martial deeds of the gods, legendary heroes, or kings clearly points to a fundamental martial ideology as a significant indicator that Mesopotamia had crossed the military threshold by the mid-fourth millennium. This new martial art is exemplified by the emergence of the "Priest-king", an iconographically stylized figure of a tall bearded man wearing a kilt or long robe, a flat round cap, with his shoulder-length hair in a bun. The image of the Priest-king appears in Uruk, as well as Susa II iconography in Elam. There are a number of different scenes:

- Hunting: armed with a bow, hunting either lions (AFC 22) or bulls (AFC 23);
- Armed with a bow and a long, mace-like weapon resting on his shoulder (PAE 68/3);
- Two siege scenes: both show the Priest-king armed with a bow, shooting enemies while besieging a city. The first shows prisoners with arrows protruding from their legs fleeing from the Priest-king. The city is represented by a wall and a large palace or temple behind it. The building has three curved horn-like lines coming from its side which have been interpreted as either actual architectural features or a divine aura around a temple; they could also, on the other hand, represent flames coming from the burning of the besieged citadel, palace, or temple. This scene could represent an attack on an enemy city, or perhaps the ritual slaughter of captured prisoners before the temple of the gods (AFC 24; PAE 68/1, 70; FI §743). The second shows a number of

bound prisoners around the city, with one man on the ramparts and another falling from the ramparts; this is clearly a siege scene, but the building lacks the horns/flames (PAE 68/2). These represent the earliest depictions of sieges in history;

- Boat scene: the Priest-king sits in a large boat holding a mace in one hand and rope in the other to which are tied two kneeling bound prisoners. This points to the military use of boats by at least the late fourth millennium;

- Execution of prisoners: two different scenes show the king armed with a six-foot-long broad-headed thrusting spear, held point downward, overseeing the torture or execution of bound prisoners (#1 = AFC 23; AAM §L–3; #2 = PAE 68/5);

- Ritual activities (AFC 25, §8; AAM §L–1–2): making offerings at a temple (AFC §9).

The Priest-king, armed variously with spear, mace, and bow, is thus shown in a whole sequence of martial activities, including hunting, fighting enemies, assaulting fortified cities, transporting captives by boat, and torturing or executing bound prisoners.

The problem of interpreting the Priest-king is one of context: is he intended to represent a god or a mythical figure? Does each image represent the same great conqueror king? Or is it a stylized figure representing a number of different kings, each of whom is depicted in the same way? The kings of Egypt were always shown in stylistically similar images, and it is generally impossible to tell which king is represented without an inscription. Does each scene represent a separate discrete historical event, or are they idealized depictions? Does the distribution of the Priest-king iconography represent the zone of political domination of a single state, or is it merely that the Priest-king iconographic style was copied in several different politically independent regions? Unfortunately, in the absence of historical texts from this period, it is impossible to answer these questions with certainty.

A military maximalist interpretation of the Priest-king would argue that the art depicts the real military activities of one or more actual kings who extended Uruk's military power into southern Mesopotamia. The appearance of the Priest-king iconography in Elam represents the extension of Uruk military power into that region as well. All of this may be part of what is called the "Uruk expansion" (see pp. 40–42). Minimally, the Priest-king iconography demonstrates that martial kingship was ideologically highly developed in Uruk by the late fourth millennium; Mesopotamia had clearly crossed the military threshold.

Other Late Uruk martial art {3500–3000}

Not all martial art of the Late Uruk period was specifically associated with the figure of the Priest-king, although the themes were precisely parallel. Hunting was a major martial theme in Late Uruk art. The most famous is the Uruk lion hunt, showing the Priest-king with a bow and another man with a spear battling four lions.[6] A similar scene shows the king with a bow followed by a servant with quiver and arrows; the king is hunting bulls and an onager (AFC 23; AAM §A–4; FI §683). Another cylinder seal shows a man with a bow hunting an antelope (AAM §A–2). Hunting scenes do not necessarily point to warfare, but they do show a desire to emphasize royal prowess with weapons; the theme of the martial hunter-king endures in the Near East through the Sassanid period[7] and into Islamic times.

The importance of the bow in Late Uruk Mesopotamia is emphasized in two other cylinder seals. One shows the king at target practice with a bow, shooting a boar target mounted on a pole (FI §682). Another shows an early arms factory making bows and bronze daggers, and perhaps javelins as well (FI §742). Individual combat is depicted showing a man grappling with another and stabbing him with a short javelin or dagger (AFC §22). A siege scene shows defenders on the city ramparts throwing stones at attackers who appear to be torturing or executing a prisoner (FI §748). Other scenes also show the beating or execution of bound prisoners (FI §746); another shows kneeling bound prisoners attacked by vultures or perhaps mythic winged creatures (FI §887). The marshaling of troops or vassal clans in preparation for battle or in victory celebrations may be depicted in a scene showing men with banners with large balls on top, seated before an enthroned figure (FI §15).

The "Uruk Expansion" {3500–3000}[8]

The Late Uruk period also witnessed a phenomenon known as the Uruk Expansion, which is characterized archaeologically by the spread of a similar style of material culture of pottery, bowls, clay tablets, and cylinder seals from Sumer (southern Mesopotamia) to far beyond its original core zone; during this period Uruk-style material culture spreads to northern Mesopotamia, Syria and western Iran. The cause of this expansion seems to have been largely economic. Mesopotamia has few natural resources besides clay, reeds, and grain. The massive population growth and high demand for prestige and luxury products by the new emerging Sumerian elites created an extensive search outside the Mesopotamian valley for metal (initially copper, then tin, lead, silver, and gold; ME 143–76), stone (for building, and semi-precious stones like lapis lazuli for ornamentation; ME 177–216), and building timber. The Uruk expansion occurred during most of the Late Uruk period, but rapidly declined by the thirty-first century. Some Sumerian centers, like Habuba Kabira in Syria, were simply abandoned. In others, like Susa, Sumerian cultural influence also declined rapidly.

The Uruk expansion took three forms. First, and most intense, new colonies were founded and occupied, largely by Sumerians. Second, Sumerian merchants and craftsmen, and perhaps other colonists as well, took up residence in already existing indigenous towns in northern Mesopotamia, Syria and Elam, bringing with them Sumerian technology, culture, and other social practices. Third, many cities on the highland fringes were regularly visited by Sumerians or were indirectly influenced by secondary exchanges. The spread of Sumerian influence and colonies seems to have developed along major trade routes to high-demand resource areas. The demand for natural resources in exchange for luxury and prestige items from Sumer created a shared interest between Sumerian merchants and peoples in the resource rich zones. The major Uruk Expansion trade routes included (HE1 14–18; M = CAM 64–5):

1   Elam, with Susa as a major colonial center;
2   NW Iran, with Godin Tepe as center on the Lapis Lazuli (and later Tin) Road to Afghanistan;
3   The Tigris route via Nineveh and Tepe Gawra;
4   North to Tell Brak in the Khabur triangle for copper, gold, and silver from Anatolia;
5   The Euphrates route to Tell Habuba in Syria for cedars, other timber, and metals;
6   The Euphrates route, with extensions southwest to Egypt via Canaan or the Mediterranean Sea; Sumerian-style motifs have been found on some Pre-dynastic Egyptian artifacts, though the precise implications of these connections are disputed;
7   Persian Gulf route to Bahrain and Oman.

The intensity of trade and Sumerian influence varied in each of these areas, with the greatest evidence for direct Sumerian colonization being around Habuba Kabira in Syria and in Susa in Elam.

From the perspective of military history the important question is what role, if any, did military conquest play in the Uruk expansion. The essential question is whether the expansion of Sumerian cultural influences and material culture can be explained in purely social and economic terms, or do we need to posit a military component? The evidence is insufficient for a certain answer. It seems that a military component is not absolutely *necessary*, but the evidence fits more nicely together if we assume that Sumerian armies were involved to some degree in the Uruk expansion. It seems likely that warfare was a component in the expansion, but that the phenomenon was not primarily military in nature. This is reflected most clearly in the fact that some of the Sumerian colonies were strongly fortified; Habuba Kabira in Syria is the most striking example, with three-meter-thick mud-brick walls with numerous projecting square towers and strongly fortified gates (AS 190–7). Sumerian military occupation of Susa and other parts of Elam is also a possibility, but there are also arguments against this (PAE 52–69). Some have argued that the Sumerian military system was not yet logistically advanced enough to conquer Susa. But the distance from Uruk to Susa is only about 160 miles, requiring a campaign of only 10–14 days. Susa could also have been approached by the Karkheh river. Contemporary Egyptian armies found operations of this sort completely feasible (see Chapter Twelve). The artistic sources mentioned above demonstrate that militarism was a fundamental part of Sumerian kingship at this time, making it likely that international relations between Sumerian kings and outside peoples would have had a strong military edge to them; this was certainly the case a few centuries later.

Unfortunately, in the absence of written texts, all of this remains speculative. The problem of interpreting both the military significance of the Priest-king iconography and the military significance of the Uruk expansion are examples of the difficulty of doing military history in the absence of texts.

Legends of the Uruk period

We have no historical texts for the Uruk period. On the other hand, later Sumerian legendary recollections may reflect some of the historical situation in the Uruk age. The most important historical tradition is the Sumerian King-list.[9] The precise significance and meaning of the King-list for fourth-millennium history is uncertain. It was clearly composed in its final form in the Isin-Larsa period (see Chapter Six) as a propaganda tool for the legitimization of the kings of Isin. The text can be divided into three phases: the antediluvian kings who ruled before the "great flood" (KS 328; C1/2: 107–8), a group of protohistoric kings (KS 328–329), a few of whom can be confirmed by other inscriptions, and the historic kings, whose names are also known from other sources (KS 329–40). The antediluvian kings have reigns of tens of thousands of years; after the flood the protohistoric rulers reign for hundreds of years, while the historic rulers have ordinary human reigns seemingly based on actual chronological information.

From the military perspective, a number of things are important to note. First, kingship "descends from heaven" (KS 328); it is a divinely ordained institution. Second, kingship is bestowed by the gods on a certain city, and can be taken away from that city as well. Thus "kingship", or perhaps what we would call the hegemony of Sumer, is transferred from city to city by the gods. The mechanism by which kingship is transferred is warfare. The King-list repeatedly uses standardized formulae to describe shifts in the balance of power in Sumer: "city-X was defeated [in war]" or "city-X was abandoned [by the gods]" or "city-X was smitten with weapons" after which "its kingship was carried off to city-Y". Thus, when the gods granted victory in battle, they were revealing whom they had chosen to be the new hegemon of Sumer.

The Sumerian King-list mentions a great flood, but when this was thought to have occurred relative to our modern chronological system cannot be determined. But two things are clear about kingship in antediluvian times. First, kingship passed between five different cities before the flood; each city in succession lost its hegemony when it was "abandoned" by the gods, and the "kingship was carried off" to another city. In military terms I take this to imply that Sumerian myths and legends remember that warfare and power struggles among Sumerian city-states occurred in the mythic antediluvian times, which historically are probably recollections of the fourth millennium. Second, after the great flood, kingship was re-established by the gods and given to the rulers of the city of Kish, at which time we move from legend into the very beginning of the proto-historical period.

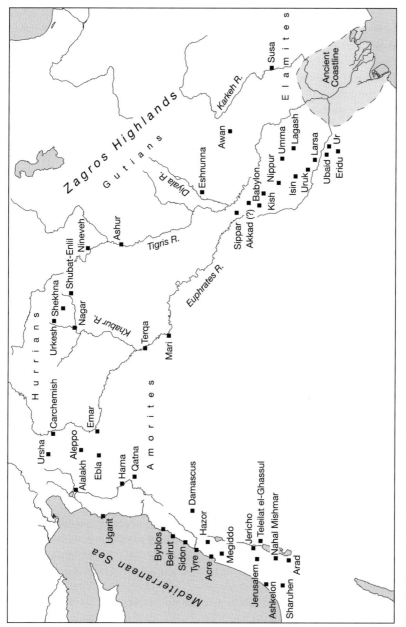

Map 2 Bronze Age Mesopotamia and Syria

Early Dynastic I {2900–2650}[10]

The end of the Uruk expansion occurred in the protohistoric period. The precise causes are uncertain, but a shift in the balance of power in Sumer itself, and increasing military conflict between rival Sumerian city-states, may have been contributing factors, perhaps related to the legendary establishment of hegemonic kingship at the city-state of Kish (EM 28–32; KS 328).

A number of characteristics of Early Dynastic Mesopotamia must be emphasized. One problem with Early Dynastic military history is that we do not have firm regnal years for most of the kings. We can generally tell the relative order of kings for a number of cities, and we can often determine synchronisms – that a certain king of one city was a contemporary of the king of another. But we do not know the length of reigns for almost any kings other than some of those mentioned in the Sumerian King-list, which is extremely unreliable for the Early Dynastic period. This means we can place the kings in order and determine if they were early or late in a given century, but, for the most part, we cannot give precise regnal years. In the following discussion I will give dates for most kings, but it should be emphasized that these are quite speculative and should be used only as broad chronological indicators.

Politically Sumer in the Early Dynastic period was divided into a number of separate and feuding independent city-states engaged in complex patterns of cooperation, alliance, conflict, and war.[11] During much of the Early Dynastic period there was endemic warfare between these city-states, rather like classical Greece. The scale of this warfare was in many ways rather limited. Umma and Lagash, whose ongoing feud is the best documented (RH), are only about twenty-five miles apart. The entire area encompassed by the vast majority of Early Dynastic military sources is only 300 miles across. The greatest distance of a known military campaign in the Early Dynastic period, a conflict between Kish and Elam (PI 35), amounted to a distance of no more than 160 miles. Most military operations occurred within a few days' march of the home city.

There was a great deal of cultural, linguistic, and religious unity among the Sumerians, despite their political disunity. We are provided with only a highly stylized legendary account of the history of this period in the King-list, which seems to suggest a succession of city-states. In fact, synchronisms from other contemporary records indicate that many of the dynasties mentioned in the King-list clearly overlap rather than being sequential. It appears that, whatever else was occurring in power politics in Mesopotamia, only one king was able to claim the title of "king of Kish" at a time. This did not mean he ruled all of Mesopotamia, but that he was the first among equals; I will describe this ruler as the hegemon, and his rule as hegemony. This hegemony also seems to have ben associated with religious responsibilities of maintaining the Tummal temple of the god Ninlil at Nippur (KS 46–9). An inscription describing which kings undertook repairs of that shrine broadly matches the patterns of Sumerian hegemonic kingship as described in the King-list.

To properly contextualize the Sumerian martial inscriptions of the Early Dynastic period, it must be remembered that the fundamental purpose of Sumerian inscriptions was to commemorate dedications and gifts to the gods. Most of the inscriptions are almost always associated with giving gifts of land, precious things, or temple buildings to the gods. The inscriptional evidence does not permit us to write a complete military history of Early Dynastic Sumer; rather we are given numerous snapshots of individual conflicts and military incidents. None the less, we have enough data to give us a good sense of warfare in the Early Dynastic Age.

Kish {c. 3100–2700?} (EA 3:298–300; DANE 171)

According to Sumerian legend, the period scholars now call Early Dynastic I was dominated by the hegemony of the kings of Kish (KS 328). Throughout the Sumerian period the title "king of Kish" (lugal Kish) meant hegemon of Sumer, and every warlord claiming universal domination of Mesopotamia adopted "king of Kish" as one of his titles (PI 37, 40, 102). We cannot know for certain the precise period of the hegemony of Kish. The King-list itself gives each of the rulers reigns of hundreds of years, and the dynasty as a whole a duration of 24,510 years. The last two rulers on the Kish king-list, Enmebaragesi and his son Agga (EM 28–32; KS 238; PI 18) are known from other records to have been contemporaries of Gilgamesh, king of Uruk, who dates to around 2700 (DANE 128–9). If we assume that each of the twenty-three kings of Kish were historical figures, however mythically remembered, who ruled for an average of around twenty years each, the entire period of Kish hegemony in Sumer would have lasted somewhat over 400 years. Since the dynasty's hegemony ended around 2700 under the last king, Agga, this would place the beginning of the Kish dynasty around 3100. Of course, such numbers are very rough and can only give us the broadest sense of chronology.

Militarily, little is known of the period of Kish, which has left scant inscriptions or martial art – only a fragment of two warriors and an image of a bound prisoner of war (AFC 89–92). Excavations of royal tombs from Kish show the use of metal weapons and the burial of several early war-carts (EA 3:298; see pp. 132–41). From the persistence of the title "king of Kish" as the rough equivalent of "emperor" in later Mesopotamia, we can assume their hegemony was substantial for at least part of the period. A few of their rulers have left us brief military hints. Etana, the eleventh from the end of the dynasty {c. 2900}, was said to have "made firm all the lands" (KS 328), which may refer to some type of political hegemony but could equally be a ritual or religious phenomenon – he is also said to have "ascend[ed] into heaven" (KS 328; C1/2:109–10), reflecting the connection of Sumerian kingship with the gods. The later legend of Etana gives a more detailed account of this (MFM 189–202). The legend records the founding of the city by the gods, and their primordial preparation for its defense:

> The Sebitti [seven warrior gods] barred the gates [of Kish] against armies.
> [The Anunnaki gods] barred them against [other] settled peoples.
> The Igigi [gods] would patrol the city. (MFM 190)

Enmebaragesi {c. 2700} (PI 18; C1/2:110) is said to have "plundered the weapons of the land of Elam" (KS 328; PAE 87) some 160 miles to the east. This is the first textual reference to war between Sumer and the neighboring Elam, indicating the logistical reach of Sumerian armies of the period. Enmebaragesi was succeeded by his son Agga, under whom "Kish was defeated [in battle by Gilgamesh of Uruk], and its kingship was carried off to [the temple] Eanna [in the city of Uruk]" (KS 328).

Gilgamesh and the rise of Uruk {c. 2780–2560}

The shift of hegemony in Sumer from Kish to Uruk illustrates a problem in Sumerian legendary historiography. Later Sumerian tradition is unequivocal in attributing Uruk's rise to hegemony to Gilgamesh (EOG 143–8), but the King–list gives five kings ruling before Gilgamesh (KS 328–9); presumably Gilgamesh's predecessors before the rise of Uruk to hegemony. The dynasty begins four generations before Gilgamesh with "Meskiaggasher, son of [the god] Utu" {c. 2780–2760} who "entered the sea and ascended the mountains" (KS 328–9). If this deed is historical rather than mythical, it may imply that Meskiaggasher was perhaps the first known Sumerian king to take to the sea in war, and raided into the Zagros mountains for timber, metal, or stone.

Three of the early legendary kings of Uruk became epic heroes, perhaps because of early development of a heroic court poetry centered on martial deeds in Uruk. However that may be, Enmerkar {c. 2760–2740} and his son Lugalbanda {2740–2720} were attributed in Sumerian legend with an invasion and siege of Aratta, a mythical and wealthy land to the north-east of Mesopotamia, the source of tin and lapis lazuli.[12] It is generally thought that Aratta was in central or eastern Iran, or perhaps Afghanistan (ME 12–4). We need not suppose that Enmerkar and Lugalbanda actually campaigned to Afghanistan, but rather than Meskiaggasher's "ascent to the mountains" and Enmerkar's siege of Aratta probably reflect legendary recollections of Early Dynastic campaigns into the Zagros highlands in western Iran to secure the immediate source of lapis lazuli and tin, rather than their original source in Afghanistan.

The greatest warrior-king of early Uruk, however, was Gilgamesh {c. 2700–2680}, who was destined to become the premier epic hero of the Near East, and whose tales were told and retold for the next two-and-a-half millennia (EOG). The military aspects of the Gilgamesh epic are discussed elsewhere, since they probably reflect warfare in the age of their actual composition rather than in the time of the historic Gilgamesh (see pp. 126–8). It is quite certain that Gilgamesh was a historical ruler, but it is difficult to disentangle the epic-hero from the historic king. He is attributed with building the massive ten-kilometer circuit of walls around Uruk (CAM 60; EA 5:294–8; C 1/2:110–12). Like his predecessors, Gilgamesh the epic hero is also a wanderer in search of cedarwood from Lebanon (EOG).

The most historical part of the epic tradition of Gilgamesh may be the tale of the defeat of Agga (Akka), the last of the hegemonic kings of Kish.[13] Agga sent envoys to Uruk demanding that Gilgamesh submit to Kish and pay tribute. Gilgamesh convened the "assembly of his city's elders" for a consultation. Gilgamesh proposed, "let us not submit to the house of Kish, let us wage war!" But the elders demurred and refused to give their consent. Ignoring the will of the city council, Gilgamesh instead "placed his trust in the [war] goddess Inanna, took no notice of what his city's elders said", going directly to the "assembly of the city's young men" of military age, who supported the call for war:

> You are their king and their warrior!
> O crusher of heads [with a mace in battle],
> Prince beloved of [the god] An
> When he [Agga king of Kish] arrives why be afraid?
> The army [of Kish] is small
> And a rabble [of untrained troops] at the rear,
> Its men will not withstand us! (EOG 145–6)

With the young warriors of the city aroused, Gilgamesh prepared for war:

> Now make ready the equipment and arms of battle,
> Let weapons of war return to your grasp!
> Let them create terror and a dread aura,
> So when he [Agga of Kish] arrives fear of me overwhelms him,
> So his good sense is confounded and his judgment undone! (EOG 146)

Agga is quick to respond to this challenge to the Hegemony of Kish. "It was not five days, it was not ten days, [when] Enmebaragesi's son Agga [king of Kish] laid siege to Uruk" (EOG 146). Gilgamesh sends one of his "royal bodyguard" to negotiate, but he is captured and beaten by Agga, whereupon:

> Gilgamesh climbed up on the wall [of Uruk]
> His dread aura overwhelmed those [too] old and [too] young [to fight]
> But put weapons of war in the hands of Uruk's young men.
> At the door of the city gate they stood [marshaled] in the roadway,
> Enkidu [Gilgamesh's companion] went forth from the city gate
> [leading the army of Uruk into battle against Agga].
> Gilgamesh raised his head on the rampart....
> A myriad [of the enemy] did fall [to defeat]
> A myriad [of Uruk] did rise [to victory]
> A myriad did thereby roll [dead] in the dust,
> He [Gilgamesh] cut down the horns of the [royal] boat [of Agga]
> In the midst of his army he took prisoner Agga, king of Kish. (EOG 147–8)

With Agga as prisoner, Gilgamesh proceeded to negotiate from a position of power. Agga finally agreed that "Uruk, the smithy of the gods, its great rampart, a cloudbank resting on the earth, is given into your charge" (EOG 149); in other words Uruk became independent of Kishite vassalage. In return Gilgamesh set Agga free. This account is interesting in reflecting the fact that the king did not have absolute power, but had to consult the city councils before making war. The old men of the council of elders cautioned against war, while the council of the young warriors carried the day for war.

The predominance of Uruk in Sumer was said to have continued for perhaps a century {c. 2680–2560}, but no military details are known for the subsequent rulers. The period of Uruk hegemony corresponds roughly with what archaeologists call the Early Dynastic II period {2650–2550}. By the end of the first dynasty of Uruk, their hegemony was rapidly passing to the city of Ur.

The First Dynasty of Ur, and the royal tombs {c. 2560–2450}[14]

According to the King-list, the city of Ur came to hegemony in Sumer after the first Dynasty of Uruk. Royal inscriptions of this period provide little information of military matters beyond mere mentions of the names of kings, which none the less have the merit of confirming the basic historicity of the Sumerian King-list, at least for this period (PI 97–101; KS 329).

From the perspective of the military historian, the spectacular treasures from the royal tombs of Ur include a number of artifacts of the greatest importance. The cemetery of Ur contained hundreds of tombs, of which sixteen are called "Royal Tombs" because of the richness of their content and because of human sacrifices buried with the kings and queens, presumably to accompany them into the afterlife. The absence of inscriptions makes it impossible to know for certain who was buried in the tombs, but a tentative list has been reconstructed (AFC 96). The tombs thus cannot be precisely dated, but are generally placed in late Early Dynastic II through early Early Dynastic IIIA, around 2550–2450.

A number of weapons and other military artifacts have been preserved in the royal tombs of Ur, which generally reflect precisely the weapons depicted on contemporary martial art. The weapons include: copper daggers (RTU §147–8); a stunning ceremonial dagger in gold (AFC §54; RTU §146; AM §xv; AW 1:140–1); spike-like javelins (RTU 162, §140; AW 1:134); broad-headed spears (RTU 162, §141–2); and socketed axeheads (AW 1:136–7; RTU §149–51); no archery equipment was found in the tombs. There were also weapons found in ordinary tombs in the Ur cemeteries: a preliminary count included 58 spears, 171 daggers and 309 axes.[15] If these numbers are proportional to the actual use of weapons it may give an impression of the troop-types of Sumerian armies.

Body army was likewise absent, but the oldest known copper helmets were found still on the skulls of sacrificed bodyguards sent to accompany their kings in the afterlife (AFC §56; AW 1:49). The beautiful golden helmet-crown of Meka-lamdug {c. 2510} (AM §xvi; AANE §45; FA 83) could have been worn by the king in battle, but it would have afforded little protection; it is somewhat similar to the helmet worn by Eanatum (AM 66), but I suspect the battle version was in bronze. There were apparently no metal helmets found in the non-royal graves, which probably indicates that most helmets were leather. Only elite soldiers and royal guards had metal helmets. Some art from the royal tombs also display martial themes, such as symbolic lions, representing the triumphant king, trampling prostrate enemies (AFC §57; RTU §13). A bodyguard in a sheepskin robe with an axe attends the king at a banquet (RTU §17). Bronze daggers are also common weapons in the art (AFC §58; RTU 74, §21).

The "Standard of Ur"[16]

The most important artistic source for military history from the royal tombs is the famous Standard of Ur, a box inlaid with shell and lapis lazuli depicting a scene of victorious warfare of the king of Ur. It was discovered in tomb PG 779, which is associated with Ur–Pabilsag, who died around 2550 (AFC 96–7). The martial side of the box is divided into three panels, depicting different phases of combat. I believe it should be read from the bottom to the top. In the bottom panel four Sumerian war-carts charge across a battlefield strewn with enemy corpses. These war-carts are described in detail later (see Chapter Five). Each war-cart is pulled by four equids, and has a driver and a warrior, who wields either a javelin or an axe. The middle panel shows a line of eight infantrymen on the left side, and another half a dozen collecting enemy prisoners on the right. The eight are all dressed the same and carry the same weapons. The men wear sheepskin kilts, and have long capes running from their shoulders to their ankles. The capes are fastened at the neck and open at the front, leaving the arms free for combat. The capes are polka-dotted, which some have interpreted as leopard skins, but are more likely simply colorful designs. Each wears a leather cap or metal helmet fastened under the chin, perhaps similar to the helmets found in the royal tombs (AFC §56). Each of the men is armed with a medium-size thrusting spear, held underhand. The right half of the middle panel shows the soldiers of Ur rounding up prisoners. All of them have been wounded and have several gashes with flowing blood. Some of the Ur soldiers have collected booty in their arms and are brandishing knives or clubs as they herd the prisoners.

On the top panel the prisoners are brought before the king on the right side, naked and bleeding from their wounds. King Ur-Pabilsag stands in the center of the panel, reviewing the prisoners. Behind the king are three soldiers, each armed with spears and axes. In the rear is the royal chariot, held by the axe-armed driver. The elite warriors and charioteers all seem to be dressed in sheepskin or fringed leather kilts and wear sheepskin cloaks over one shoulder. The common soldiers wear the polka-dotted capes; both classes have the same caps or helmets.

As I interpret it the Standard of Ur depicts the aftermath of a victorious battle rather than the actual combat. The chariots race across the field, pursuing the fleeing foe and trampling the dead. The middle panel shows the infantry following the chariots collecting the booty and wounded enemy as prisoners. The final panel shows the triumph celebration where the booty and prisoners are brought before the king. The Standard shows two classes of Sumerian warriors, charioteers and infantry; there is no sign of archers and none of the corpses or wounded have any missiles protruding from them. The four weapons depicted are javelins (only thrown by charioteers), medium-size thrusting spears, and axes or daggers for close combat. We are not shown, however, how the enemy was defeated. Was there a phase of missile exchange? Was there an infantry melee? Did the chariots charge, drive by throwing javelins, or only pursue an enemy already broken by the infantry? Despite these unanswered questions, the Standard of Ur is a striking piece of martial art, both for its depiction of war-carts, arms and armor, and for its evocation of the martial spirit of the Sumerian kings.

A lesser known, but equally important Ur war-scene comes from a cylinder seal, which I believe depicts a Sumerian army on the march, with infantry, war-carts, dogs, pack animals, and boats.[17] The scene shows two parallel panels, one on the river and one on land, which I interpret to show an army on campaign with part marching on the bank of the river, accompanied by other troops and supplies on boats in the river. The upper panel shows a boat with a seated royal figure being paddled by another man. On shore is a soldier with a long lance who accompanies a donkey bearing a load of supplies. The bottom panel shows the army on land accompanying the fleet on the river, with a two-wheeled war-cart ridden by a man with an axe (?) pulled by long-eared equids. The chariot is followed by a dog and three soldiers, one with an axe and two with long spears.

Although we know little of the actual military history of the First Dynasty of Ur, the royal tombs provide crucial examples of weapons and martial art, giving us invaluable insights into the Sumerian military system.

Early Dynastic IIIA {2550–2400} and IIIB {2400–2250}

With the beginning of Early Dynastic III, we enter our best-documented period for military history before the rise of the Akkadian empire of Sargon. We are especially fortunate to have a series of martial inscriptions from the kings of Lagash. Around 2500 we have vague records of a Mesilim who claimed the title "king of Kish" and who is remembered in later inscriptions as arbitrating a boundary dispute between Lagash and Umma (PI 40), an apparent reflection of his position of overlord. However, little is known of his military activities (KS 53).[18]

The warrior-kings of Lagash {2495–2345}[19]

Early Dynastic IIIA could be called the age of the warlords of Lagash, who provide us with our richest sources of both military narratives and martial art of the Early Dynastic Age. Interestingly, Lagash is nowhere mentioned in the Sumerian King-list, an oversight which is generally thought to reflect a propaganda statement by the kings of early Middle Bronze Isin about the illegitimacy of the kings of Lagash. The rise to hegemony of Lagash in Mesopotamia begins with the victories of Urnanshe.

Urnanshe of Lagash {c. 2495–2475}

The first Mesopotamian king for whom we have a detailed contemporary account of warfare is Urnanshe of Lagash, who fought against both Umma and Ur. The background to this war relates to an ongoing struggle between Umma and Lagash over control of agricultural land, diversion of irrigation water through building canals and dams, and failure to share the agricultural produce from certain shared tracts of land (RH 22–3; PI 54–5).

> [Urnanshe, king] of Lagash, went to war against the leader of Ur and the leader of Umma: [Urnanshe] the leader of Lagash defeated the leader of Ur. He captured Mu[...] the admiral, captured Amabaragesi and Kishibgal the officers, captured Papursag, son of U'u, captured [...] the officer, he made a burial mound [for the war dead]. He [then] defeated the leader of Umma. He captured Lupad and Bilala the officers, captured Pabilgaltuk ruler of Umma, captured Urtulsag the officer, captured Hursagshemah the quartermaster-general, and he made a burial mound [for the war dead]. (PI 25)

Urnanshe's inscription contains the first textual reference we have to the Mesopotamian custom of building burial mounds for the war dead at the site of a victory. We also have an iconographic representation of this in the famous Stele of Vultures, where the dead are shown placed in a pile by the victors while people carried baskets of earth to bury the corpses (AAM §121; see p. 55). When a Mesopotamian king claimed to have "raised a mound" after a battle it indicated that he was victorious, because his troops were in possession of the battlefield and therefore buried the war dead. Urnanshe emphasized his capture of important enemy officers, including the king of Umma, Pabilgaltuk. We do not know the fate of these captives; in later texts they are often tortured or executed, but are also often returned to their thrones as vassals of the victorious king. In addition to his military victories, Urnanshe also "built the walls of Lagash" (PI 25, 28–9), a defensive action emphasizing the military threat of his age.

Some of the inscriptions of Lagash mention overseas voyages through the Persian Gulf to Dilmun (modern Bahrain; DANE 45; EA 1:266–8) for timber and stone for temple building (PI 23, 24, 28–30). Although not explicitly military ventures, these voyages indicate that seagoing vessels were capable of sailing the Persian Gulf during this period, and this maritime technology would lay the foundation for the eventual naval conquests of the Akkadians in the Persian Gulf (see pp. 80–1, 84).

Urnanshe was succeeded by his son Akurgal {c. 2475–2455}, about whom we have no military information (PI 33), and then by his grandson Eanatum, the greatest warlord of Early Dynastic Mesopotamia.

Eanatum I (Eannatum) {c. 2455–2425}[20]

According to Sumerian martial ideology, kings did not win victory in battle by their own strength and wisdom, but by the gift of the gods. Eanatum is no exception.

> Eanatum, king of Lagash, granted strength by [the high god] Enlil, nourished with special milk by [the mother goddess] Ninhursag, given a fine name by [the war goddess] Inana, granted wisdom by [the god of wisdom] Enki, chosen in her heart by [the divination goddess] Nanshe the powerful mistress, who subjugates foreign lands for [the war god] Ningirsu [patron god of Lagash] . . . beloved spouse of [the war goddess] Inana. (PI 37)

Not only was Eanatum granted these special gifts by the gods, he was in fact the son of god on earth. According to one of Eanatum's inscriptions, the war god Ningirsu, "warrior [and son] of [the high god] Enlil", "implanted [his] semen for Eanatum in the womb" of Eanatum's mother. Thus, the hero-king was not a mere man, but a demi-god, son of the war god, destined to fulfill the gods' commands and restore the proper divine order in Sumer through victorious battle. When Eanatum finally matured, "Ningirsu, with great joy, gave him the kingship of Lagash" (PI 34).

Lagash had been engaged in an ongoing struggle with Umma over disputed agricultural land between the two cities for a generation or two. Attempted arbitration ultimately failed, leading to renewed hostilities (RH 22–4). Eanatum's first campaign was against his nearest rival, the city-state of Umma under their king Enakale.[21] The great war between Lagash and Umma is recorded in the longest and most detailed battle narrative of the Early Dynastic period. According to Eanatum, the king of Umma "acted haughtily" and broke the divinely established order by usurping the "Gu'edena", an agricultural region between Umma and Lagash. Eanatum observed the city of Umma making military preparations to seize and retain control of this disputed agricultural land.

> Eanatum, who has strength [in war] . . . declared: "Now then, O Enemy [king of Umma]!" [He] proclaimed for evermore: "The ruler of Umma – where is he recruiting [soldiers for the war]? With [other] men [foreign mercenaries?] . . . he is able to exploit the [agricultural region] Gu'edena, the beloved field of Ningirsu. May he [the war god Ningirsu] strike him down!" (PI 34; cf. PI 55)

This warlike provocation of seizing land from Lagash would have justified military action by Eanatum, but the king was further compelled to battle by an oracular dream.

> Eanatum who lies sleeping – [his] be[loved] master [the war god Ningirsu] approaches his head [in an oracular dream, and says:] "Kish itself [the sacred

city of divine kingship] must abandon Umma.... The sun-[god] will shine at your right [in battle], and a [crown?] will be affixed to your forehead. O Eanatum, you will slay [the enemy from Umma] there. [The burial mound with] their myriad corpses will reach the base of heaven. In Umma [...] the people of his [king Enakale's] own city will rise up against him and he will be killed within Umma itself [during the rebellion of his own people].' (PI 34)

Enakale, king of Umma, was not merely the enemy of Lagash, but the enemy of the gods, who prophesied his defeat in battle. Eanatum does not go to war for plunder or personal glory, but at the express command of the gods.

The description of most of the beginning of the battle is unfortunately broken, but the narrative picks up again in mid-combat. "He [king Eanatum] fought with him [king Enakale]. A person shot an arrow at Eanatum. He was shot through by the arrow and had difficulty moving. He cried out in the face of it" (PI 34). This text shows both the use of archery in Sumerian warfare – which is unclear in the art of the period – and the fact that the kings fought in personal combat.

The next part of the text is again broken, but it is obvious that, despite his serious wound, Eanatum leads the army of Lagash to victory. After the victory, a treaty is made, in which Enakale of Umma is forced to cede land to Lagash

Eanatum, the man of just commands, measured off the boundary with the leader of Umma, left [some land] under Umma's control, and erected a monument on that spot [of the victory].... He defeated Umma and made twenty burial mounds for [the battle dead, indicating very high casualties in the war, or perhaps a number of different encounters].... Eanatum restored to [the god] Ningirsu's control his beloved field, the Gu'edena. ... Eanatum erected a [victory] monument in the grand temple of Ningirsu. (PI 34–5)

The defeated Enakale of Umma is thereafter forced to swear a peace oath.

Eanatum gave the great battle net of [the supreme god] Enlil to [Enakale] the leader of Umma and made him swear to him by it. The leader of Umma swore to Eanatum: "By the life of Enlil, king of heaven and Earth! I may exploit the field of Ningirsu as a[n interest-bearing] loan.... Forever and evermore, I shall not transgress the territory of [Lagash, the city of the god] Ningirsu! I shall not shift the [course of] its irrigation channels and canals! I shall not smash its [boundary] monuments! Whenever I do transgress, may the great battle net of Enlil, king of heaven and earth, by which I have sworn, descend upon Umma!" Eanatum was very clever indeed! He made up the eyes of two doves with kohl, and anointed their heads with cedar [resin]. He released them to [the high god] Enlil, king of heaven and earth [as an offering]. (PI 35)

53

Doubting the sincerity of this oath taken under extreme duress, Eanatum forced Enakale to repeat the exact same oath by five additional gods (PI 35–7). As we shall see, Eanatum's distrust was justified. Some time after the initial victory, the oath was broken just as Eanatum had feared: "the leader of Umma smashed the [boundary and victory] monument" that Eanatum had set up after his victory, and occupied the disputed lands. The war god Ningirsu again "gave the order to Eanatum [to go to war], and he destroyed [the city of] Umma" (PI 39–40).

With its rival Umma subjugated, Lagash was now one of the most powerful states in Sumer, but was yet by no means predominant. In subsequent years he launched a whole series of campaigns throughout Mesopotamia. In his first campaigns he "defeated Elam and Subartu [northern Mesopotamia], mountainous lands of timber and treasure . . . he defeated Susa [the capital of Elam]" (PI 37), and "defeated the ruler of Urua, who stood with the standard [of the god of the city] in the vanguard [of the battle line]" (PI 43), another indication of Sumerian kings fighting in the front ranks. Thereafter he turned to subdue the rival city-states of Sumer.

> He defeated Uruk, he defeated Ur, he defeated Kiutu. He sacked Uruaz and killed its ruler. He sacked Mishime and destroyed Arua. All the foreign [non-Sumerian] lands trembled before Eanatum, the nominee of Ningirsu. Because the king of Akshak [a city near Baghdad] attacked, Eanatum . . . beat back Zuzu, king of Akshak . . . and destroyed [Akshak]. (PI 41–2, 43)

His initial victories over these city-states established his pre-eminence in Sumer, so that "to Eanatum, ruler of Lagash, Inana [the war goddess], because she loved him so, gave him the kingship of Kish", meaning official status as hegemon over Sumer (PI 41). Thereafter,

> Elam trembled before Eanatum, he drove the Elamite back to his own land. Kish trembled before Eanatum; he drove the king of Akshak back to his own land. (PI 42)

Eanatum's new status as hegemon, however, was not entirely secure. Realizing they could not defeat him individually, his defeated rivals began to form coalitions against him:

> He defeated [a coalition of the kings of] Elam, Subartu and Urua at the [battle of the] Asuhur [canal]. He defeated [a coalition of the kings of] Kish, Akshak and Mari at the Antasura of Ningirsu. (PI 42)

By the time of his death Eanatum was supreme in southern Mesopotamia, and hegemon of Sumer, but his defeated enemies chafed under the domination of Lagash, and grasped the first opportunity to rebel under Eanatum's successor and brother, Enanatum I (see pp. 60–1).

The Stele of the Vultures[22]

Eanatum's great victory over Umma, which left twenty burial mounds of enemy dead and launched Eanatum on his career towards domination of Sumer, was celebrated in the famous "Stele of the Vultures", which could perhaps be better entitled "The Victory of Ningirsu through Eanatum". This stele is perhaps the greatest surviving piece of Early or Middle Bronze martial art from ancient Mesopotamia, and merits detailed attention.

The stele is unfortunately broken and fragmentary, but the overall sense is clear. The entire stele shows the victories of Eanatum, but each side shows a different sphere, the celestial and the terrestrial. The divine side, probably the more significant from the Sumerian perspective, is divided into two panels. The upper panel shows the bearded and powerful war god Ningirsu, father of Eanatum and

Figure 1 The "Stele of the Vultures", king Eanatum of Lagash, Sumer {c. 2440}

Source: Louvre AO 50; drawing by Michael Lyon.

divine patron of the city of Lagash. Ningirsu holds his mace in his right hand, and holds the "great battle net" of Enlil in his left hand – surmounted by an emblem of the mythical Sumerian lion-headed eagle Anzu (also called Imdugud, GDS 107–8; AAM §117; AM §70a) – by which the defeated king of Umma was forced to swear an oath that, if he broke the treaty, "the great battle net of Enlil ... [will] descend upon Umma" (AM §67; PI 35), precisely as depicted in the stele. The soldiers of Umma are caught in the net, and the head of one – presumably the king of Umma who is trying to escape – is being crushed by the mace of Ningirsu (AM §67, 69). Behind Ningirsu, and about half the size of the god, stands a figure in a feathered crown holding a battle standard crested with Anzu (AAM §118). This is probably Ninhursag, mother and councilor to Ningirsu. The standard, possibly an actual bronze standard of Lagash (PI 43), is Anzu, precisely the same emblematic creature on Ningirsu's battle net. When the standard is carried into battle it thus represents the presence of Ningirsu going into battle beside the king – a motif mentioned in numerous Mesopotamian inscriptions.

The lower register is quite fragmentary, but clearly shows the edge of a chariot on the left, and the top of the head of Ninhursag facing the chariot on the right (AAM §118). This type of chariot of the gods was led in processions at the temple of Ningirsu at Lagash, where the king Eanatum greets the god and shares the booty of the victory with him. It is possible that the chariot and Anzu standard were actually brought into battle as a sign of the divine presence of Ningirsu, rather like the biblical Ark of the Covenant (Judges 5.20; Joshua 6; 1 Samuel 4–6); hence the emphasis given by Eanatum on his later capture of the standard of the enemy king of the city of Urua (PI 41, 43). The overall meaning of the celestial side of the stele is that Ningirsu grants victory in battle to his son and earthly representative, Eanatum, king of Lagash.

The other terrestrial side of the stele shows the earthly results of Ningirsu's divine intervention on behalf of Eanatum (AFC 190). This side is divided into four panels, which are probably intended to be read chronologically from top to bottom. It must be emphasized that the panel does not show the army of Lagash in actual combat, but at the moment of victory. In the top panel the sky is filled with vultures – from which the stele gets its name – who fly off with the severed arms and heads of the dead soldiers of the defeated army of Umma (AM §120). Beneath the hovering vultures, on the right side of the panel, the victorious army of Eanatum marches gloriously over the corpses of their fallen enemy (AM §66). King Eanatum leads the army wearing a thick sheepskin kilt and long sheepskin robe on his left shoulder and a helmet similar to the golden helmet of Meka-lamdug from the Royal Tombs of Ur (see p. 48). He is armed with what is sometimes called a sickle-sword, but what may be a scepter or club (see pp. 66–71). Behind him his troops are marshaled in a very interesting formation, which is sometimes described as a phalanx (AM §68). The soldiers are beardless, with long hair flowing down to their shoulders. They all wear helmets, which might be of copper similar to those found in the royal tombs of Ur (AFC §56; AW 1:49). One text mentions the delivery of a copper/bronze helmet and spearhead, implying that the two go together as a warrior's equipment (PI 71). However, it may be that only the elite bodyguards, like those buried in the royal tombs, had metal helmets, the rest making due with leather caps.

The front of the formation is protected by four large body-length shields – only the heads and feet of the soldiers are visible. The shields are rectangular – about one and a half meters tall and a meter wide; each has six round, evenly spaced disks. It is impossible to tell what the shields are made from, but a contemporary body shield from Mari (AFC §99) is made of long reeds bound together with leather straps and a large handle two-thirds of the way up. By analogy it is likely that the Lagash shield were made of reeds and covered with leather. It appears that every soldier did not have his own shield. Rather, only the front rank of the formation carried the shield in both hands, forming a solid shield wall. This is apparent from two characteristics. First, between each shield we see six spears thrust forward, and each spear is held by two hands, which means the men in the rear ranks cannot hold a shield. A second feature which points to most soldiers being shieldless is that in the second panel, discussed below, none of the soldiers have shields, nor do those in the Standard of Ur (AFC 98–9). Thus, the overall formation is seven men deep. The front man carries a shield, probably with both hands for ease of maneuverability and bearing the weight. The rest of the men in the following six ranks thrust their spears between the shields.

The right half of the first panel is generally ignored, but is important for understanding the scene. The army of Lagash is trampling the dead on the left portion of the top panel, while on the right the diminutive and chaotic soldiers of Umma – some fallen, some tumbling, some standing – flee in terror (AFC 190).

Only the upper left portion of the second panel has survived (AAM §119; AM §66). On the right Eanatum, in precisely the same dress as on panel one, rides his war-cart into battle. In his right hand he holds a sickle-sword (or club or mace) and in his left hand he holds a long lance which he is thrusting out against the enemy over the heads of his donkeys (see p. 55). Most of the war-cart and the equids pulling it is missing, but from its size it is clearly a four-wheeled vehicle, and essentially the same in structure as the war-carts found in the Standard of Ur, though rendered in more detail (see pp. 49–50); the javelin quiver contains eight javelins and an axe. Behind Eanatum stands his driver, who is mostly effaced by damage to the stele; his arm by Eanatum's hip is holding an axe (or a javelin?). Behind Eanatum marches the infantry of Lagash. They are dressed in sheepskin kilts, with some type of sash (leather or colored cloth?) over their left shoulders. They wear precisely the same helmets as the soldiers in the first panel, and are armed with spears and narrow-bladed socketed axes, some of which have been found by archaeologists (RTU §151; AW 1:136–7). They seem to be marching in fairly ordered ranks.

Several questions of interpretation arise here. First, are the infantry in panel two the same as those in panel one, but in a different phase of the battle? Or are they an entirely different tactical unit, performing a different function? One interpretation suggests that they represent the same troops in different phases of the battle. In defensive positions, or when advancing slowly, the Sumerian infantry remained behind the large body-shields. When attacking, however, they abandoned the shields, which were too bulky to use at a run, and charged forward without them. The other interpretation maintains that some of the infantry fought without the shields, and were assigned to tactically support the war-carts at a run. According to this interpretation, the heavy infantry fought from behind their shield wall throughout the entire battle, while different units of light, shieldless infantry supported the war-carts. Another question derives from the placing of Eanatum relative to the infantry. In both the first and second panels, Eanatum precedes his army into battle. Does this represent actual tactical practice, or is it a symbolic representation of the king as leader of the army? Most importantly, did the war-carts generally precede the infantry into battle? In other words, did war-carts charge against enemy formations supported by infantry, or did the infantry defeat other infantry while the war-carts supported with javelins, or pursued fleeing enemies. Unfortunately, the evidence from Early Dynastic Sumer is insufficient to answer these questions with certainty.

Of the third panel, only a triangular fragment of the center-left survives, showing the aftermath of the battle (AAM §121). The left shows a burial mound: the dead of Umma – and perhaps the casualties of Lagash as well – are stacked in a mound, while workers bring baskets full of dirt to bury them. This is the burial mound whose "myriad corpses will reach to the base of heaven" (PI 34) as prophesied in Eanatum's dream. The right side of this fragment shows the rich bounty from the reconquest of the field of Gu'edena, the result of Eanatum's victory. In the far right corner we see the feet of Eanatum, supervising the scene. At his feet a cow lies bound to a stake, which is probably either to be sacrificed to the gods, or will be eaten by the troops. The message of this panel is also clear. The result of war is death to the enemies of the god Ningirsu and his beloved city of Lagash, and prosperity and bounty for the people of Lagash.

Only the barest sliver of the fourth panel remains, but it provides enough information to reconstruct some of the scene. In the far left of the panel we see a hand grasping the end of a long lance in precisely the same way that Eanatum grasps the end of his lance from his chariot in the second panel. I suggest that the fourth panel showed another chariot scene parallel to that in the second panel, or perhaps the king standing and using his lance. The precise length of the lance is difficult to tell, but by comparing its proportional length to the size of Eanatum in the surviving figures, the lance would seem to be three to three-and-a-half meters long. All of this implies that, in addition to using javelins from the war-carts, the Sumerians also used long lances, which the chariot warrior would thrust over the backs of the equids against the enemy. On the far right of the fourth panel we see the tops of four heads, three facing to the right. Only the tops of their heads are visible, and they are set very close together. They seem to be wearing helmets similar to those worn by the soldiers of Lagash in the first and second panels. It may be that they are part of the advancing army of Lagash, but no weapons are visible above their heads (as they should be by analogy to panel two). Furthermore,

Eanatum is always shown on the stele preceding his army, never following it. I suggest they are probably enemy soldiers who have turned to flee from the irresistible onslaught of Eanatum's chariot.

The fourth figure, who is taller and slightly larger than the others, faces left, about to be stabbed in the face by Eanatum's lance. He seems to be raising his hand to ward off the blow. This figure probably represents the enemy leader, at the moment of his defeat by Eanatum. A fragment of the inscription by this head reads "king of Kish" (PI 37). This may simply be a phrase from a longer part of the now lost inscription, but some have speculated that this refers to the name of the man who is being attacked by Eanatum – Eanatum himself is likewise identified in a superscription on the stele (PI 37). In other words, the fourth panel may show Eanatum's victory over the king of Kish. This makes some sense in the context of the inscriptions, since, as Eanatum's oracular dream prophesies, "Kish itself must abandon Umma, and, being angry, cannot support it [Umma]" (PI 34), implying that Kish was an ally of Umma in the war. This scene would thus represent the aftermath of the original victory over Umma in which the "king of Kish" is likewise overthrown, paving the way for Eanatum to take that title of hegemony in Sumer, as he ultimately does (PI 42).

Ironically the Stele of the Vultures may not be a representation of the actual battle, but rather of the oracular dream in which Ningirsu ordered Eanatum to go to war with Umma and promised him victory.

Most of the elements of Eanatum's dream are depicted in the stele. On the celestial side we see the appearance of the God Ningirsu holding his enemies trapped in the great battle net. On the other side we see the defeat of the army of Umma and the huge burial mound reaching to the height of heaven. In the small upper fragment of the lowest panel we see a figure about to be skewered by Eanatum's lance, who is possibly identified in the inscription as the "king of Kish" (PI 37), whom the oracular dream promises "must abandon Umma" and "cannot support Umma". The stele thus nicely illustrates how oracular dreams, divine intervention, and actual combat were all inextricably intertwined in Sumerian warfare.

Other artistic sources

Additional Early Dynastic martial art supplements the more famous Standard of Ur and Stele of the Vultures. Most of the martial art of the Early Dynastic period often does not have sufficient chronological context to be attributed to a specific ruler or dynasty. All of the art exhibits similar styles and themes. These sources are important to help us avoid interpreting Sumerian martial art based only on the artistically most famous and most frequently reproduced items – in other words, generalizing from limited examples. Some very fragmentary figures from Kish (AFC §48–9) show close parallels with similar scenes from contemporary Mari and Ebla (see pp. 241–8), which allows us to fill in some conceptual gaps.

In scenes of close-grappling melee combat, either with humans, animals, or mythic monsters, the preferred melee weapons include the mace (FI §79), short thrusting spear (or javelin) held overhand (FI §61, §78, §942), the axe, and the dagger, held either overhand (FI §83, §758; AAM §46) or underhand (FI §837). In one scene a warrior has grabbed his enemy by the hair and is thrusting his dagger into his neck (FI §837). Wrestling and boxing are also depicted as sports (AM §46; AANE §437; AAM §48). The bow is occasionally shown (FI §758, §933; ME 110; AFC §99), indicating its use in this period even though absent from the Standard of Ur and the Stele of the Vultures. Several scenes also show javelins used from boats for hunting (FI §695–7; FI §934); presumably they would have been used in river warfare as well (AMM §44).

A number of Early Dynastic maceheads were dedicated as temple offerings, indicating the continued use of that weapon.[23] One example has four carved lion-heads projecting out of the sides of the mace (AAM §38), which may be related to lion-headed maces which kings said they dedicated to the gods.[24] The mace was possibly considered the premier royal weapon of the Sumerians. From Gudea's dynasty at Lagash alone we have twenty-nine surviving votive maceheads (E3/1:225–6 for catalog list). Based on archaeological evidence alone, we would con-clude that the stone mace was the major weapon of the Sumerians. However, these maces may reflect the continuation of traditional ritual use of the mace – rather like a royal scepter (AM §65) – rather than its use it combat. The priority of the mace in ritual did not necessarily translate into its priority in combat, where it seems to have largely been replaced by the axe, as found in the artistic and textual sources. In the Stele of the Vultures the god Ningirsu still wields a mace, while all humans on the terrestrial battlefield use axes (AM §66–7; cf. SDA 169). This emphasizes that caution needs to be used when trying to reconstruct combat weapon-use from archaeological evidence alone. What gets preserved in the archaeological evidence is often based not on what weapons were used in combat, but on what weapons were used in rituals, in temple dedications, or in tombs.

Enanatum I {c. 2425–2405}[25]

Upon the death of Eanatum he was succeeded by his brother Enanatum I. Urluma, king of Umma, the son of Enakale who had been humiliated in the wars with Lagash, took the opportunity afforded by the succession to attempt to regain the disputed land:

> Urluma, ruler of Umma, recruited foreigners [as mercenaries][26] and trans-gressed the boundary channel of [the god] Ningirsu, [saying]: "Antasura is mine! I shall exploit its produce!" [The god Ningirsu] spoke angrily [through a prophetic oracle]: "Urluma . . . has marched on my very own field. He must not do violence against Enanatum, my mighty male!' Enanatum beat back Urluma. (PI 47–8)

Urluma's rebellion against the hegemony of Lagash was apparently not the only one, for a later inscription informs us that the gods "granted kingship of Lagash to

Enanatum, put all foreign lands [Elam, northern Mesopotamia] in his control, and set the rebellious lands [of Sumer] at his feet" (PI 51). Thus, though the details are not known, it appears that Enanatum faced a serious rebellion upon his succession; he claims to have retained control over Sumer, but if so, it was quite tenuous.

Enmetena {c. 2405–2385} (PI 54–68)

Some of Enanatum's claims may have been propagandistic hyperbole (RH 30–1), for the war between Umma and Lagash continued. The conflict erupted over the failure of Umma to pay the grain tribute that had been established by earlier treaties:

> When, because of [Umma's failure to deliver] that barley, he [Enanatum I] sent envoys to him [Urluma], having them say to him, "You must deliver my barley!" Urluma spoke haughtily with him: "[The] Antasura [agricultural zone] is mine, it is my territory!" he said. He levied the Ummaites and foreign [mercenaries] were dispatched there. At the [battle of the] Ugiga-field, the beloved field of [the god] Ningirsu, Ningirsu destroyed the Ummaite army. (PI 77)

More details are provided in the inscription of Enmetena, son and successor to Enanatum I:

> Enanatum, [father of Enmetena and] ruler of Lagash, fought with him [Urluma of Umma] in the Ugiga-field, the field of Ningirsu. Enmetena, beloved son of Enanatum, [commanding the army of Lagash], defeated him [Urluma]. He [Urluma] had abandoned sixty teams of asses on the bank of the Lumagirnunta-canal, and left the bones of their personnel strewn over the plain. He [Enmetena] made burial mounds in five places there for them. (PI 55, 77)

This inscription has a number of interesting features. It states that Enanatum fought with Urluma, but does not mention a victory. Rather, his son Enmetena is said to have defeated Urluma. This can be understood in one of two ways. Either Enanatum fought Urluma and was defeated, after which Enmetena took revenge, or that Enanatum declared the war but was too old to fight, and the actual battle was fought by his son Enmetena (RH 29–30). Whatever the actual events, this incident reminds us of an important characteristic of ancient Near Eastern inscriptions. A king never writes an inscription or raises a monument in which he admits defeat.[27] Since, due to the vagaries of archaeological preservation and discovery, we lack inscriptions from Umma's side of this war, the conflict appears at first glance to be nothing more than an endless succession of brilliant victories by Lagash orchestrated by the god Ningirsu. The reality was obviously quite different, hinted at by the fact that Enanatum is said to have fought Urluma, but not to have defeated him. The other interesting item in this inscription is the mention of the capture of "sixty teams of asses", meaning, presumably, sixty teams for war-carts. The implications of this for Sumerian war-cart warfare are discussed in Chapter Five.

In the aftermath of the battle, Urluma escaped. The army of Lagash followed the fleeing king to the walls of Umma, where Enmetena "sent [envoys to Umma, saying]: 'Be it known that [Umma] will be completely destroyed! Surrender!' " (PI 85). Urluma apparently refused to surrender and was overthrown and killed in a coup. He was replaced by Il, a priest of the temple at Zabala, who usurped the throne. Umma apparently made peace thereafter, but the underlying conflict over the disputed agricultural and water rights continued, with Enmetena prevailing (PI 55). Most of Enmetena's other inscriptions deal with temple building or other ritual activities. He does mention that he "built a fortress along the Sala-[canal] in the Gu'edena [agricultural zone], and named it 'Building-that-Surveys-the-Plain' for him. He built a wall for the Girsu ferry terminal" (PI 67). These were watch-towers and provincial fortifications designed to observe and protect against troops or raiders from Umma.

Enmetena's control over other parts of Sumer was likewise weakened. A building report mentions that

> He [Enmetena] cancelled [labor and tribute?] obligations for the citizens of Uruk, Larsa and Patibira. He restored [the first] to [the goddess] Inana's control at Uruk, he restored [the second] to [the god] Utu's control at Larsa, and he restored [the third] to [the god] Lugalemush's control at the Emush [temple in Patibira]. (RH 31)

The obvious import of this inscription is that there were certain obligations of labor or resources that these city-states had been required to make, but that Enmetena "restored" them to the city-states. The implication here is that his hegemony over these city-states was lost, at least to some degree. This is confirmed by another text which states that "Enmetena ruler of Lagash and Lugalkiginedudu, ruler of Uruk, established brotherhood" (RH 31). "Brotherhood" here implies peaceful relations, but more specifically, independent equal kings called themselves "brothers". Whereas his uncle Eanatum had "defeated Uruk" (PI 41–2) and established hegemony over the city, Uruk is now regarded as a fully independent equal of Lagash, whose obligations of labor and tribute were "restored". This may hint at the initial military victory by Uruk which laid the foundation for the rise of that city to predominance under subsequent rulers (see pp. 63–6). Thus, under Enmetena, the hegemony of Lagash which had been established by Eanatum was beginning to be undermined.

En-entarzi {c. 2367–2350}

Unfortunately we know almost nothing of the military history of Lagash during the next forty years {c. 2385–2343}.[28] The vague indications we have point to the decreasing military might of Lagash. There is a brief account that during the reign of En-entarzi {c. 2373–2360} 600 Elamites raided the land of Lagash, but they were intercepted and captured by local troops.

> Luenna, the *sanga* [temple administrator], fought with 600 Elamites who were carrying off booty from Lagash to Elam. He defeated the Elamites and [took] 560 Elamites [prisoner].... They are in Eninmar. He [Luenna] recovered five vessels of pure silver, twenty [...] five royal garments, and fifteen hides. (KS 331)

Such raids and counter-raids were probably not uncommon in Early Dynastic Sumer, but records of such events have rarely survived. The fact that this raid was dealt with by the local commander probably points to a military system in Lagash that was still relatively strong. On the other hand, the fact that the raid occurred at all, and that there is no record of a retaliatory attack by Lagash against Elam, probably points to the declining prestige and overall military strength of Lagash during these decades.

Uru'inimgina (Urukagina) {c. 2343–2335}[29]

The growing weakness of Lagash is emphasized by the fact that its last king of this period, Uru'inimgina, was a usurper: "Ningirsu ... granted the kingship of Lagash to Uru'inimgina, selecting him from among the myriad people; [Uru'inimgina] replaced the customs of former times" (PI 71); this implies that there was a period of social anarchy at the time (PI 74–5). The disorders and weakness of Lagash increased the threat of outside intervention, causing Uru'inimgina to "[re]build the wall of [the city of] Girsu" (PI 70). But this was a case of too little too late. The year names[30] on several tablets mention sieges of Lagash by "the leader of Uruk" in the fourth {2340} and sixth years {2338} of Uru'inimgina (RH 34), for a new great warlord had arisen who in one terrible day would erase the century-and-a-half of domination of Lagash over Umma.

The Second and Third Dynasties of Uruk {2410–2316}

The power vacuum created by the declining military strength of Lagash in the twenty-fourth century was filled by Uruk, ruled by the epic hero Gilgamesh three hundred years earlier. Lugalkiginedudu (Lugalkinishedudu) {c. 2410–2390} seems to have initiated the revival of fortunes for Uruk by becoming king of both Uruk and nearby Ur. It is not clear if he took Ur by force, but the impression from the text points to some type of diplomatic union of the states (PI 101–3): "[The god] An, king of all lands, and [goddess] Inana, queen of [the temple] Eana, Lugalkiginedudu, king of Kish – when Inana combined lordship with kingship for Lugalkiginedudu, he exercised lordship in Uruk and kingship in Ur" (PI 102). In this text he also claims the title "king of Kish", which the kings of Lagash had ceased using. If not pure hyperbole, this probably implies some type of hegemony in Sumer for Uruk.

We have no military records for the next two kings of Uruk, Lugalkisalsi {c. 2390–2375} (PI 103–4) and Urzage {c. 2375–2360} (PI 104). However, they retained the dual monarchy of Uruk and Ur (PI 103), and Urzage, at least, continued his claim to be "king of Kish" (PI 104), pointing to ongoing predominance of Uruk during the early twenty-fourth century. The fourth king of Uruk, Enshakushana {c. 2360–2340} (PI 104–6) spread Uruk hegemony into northern Sumer with a campaign against Kish and Anshak.

> For [the god] Enlil, [divine] king of all lands, Enshakushana, lord of Sumer and king of the nation [of the Sumerians] – when the gods commanded him, he sacked Kish and captured Enbi'ishtar, king of Kish. [He defeated] the leader of Akshak and the leader of Kish, having sacked their cities [...] [He] dedicated the statues [of the gods of Akshak and Kish], their precious metals and lapis lazuli, their timber and treasure to [the god] Enlil at Nippur. (PI 105)

According to this inscription, Enshakushana conquered Kish and Akshak (near Baghdad) in northern Sumer; his offerings at the temple of Nippur implied some type of alliance or suzerainty over that city as well. Taken as a whole, control of Ur, Uruk, Nippur, Kish, and Akshak gave Enshakushana power over western, central and northern Sumer. This left only Lagash in the south-east still outside of the domination of Uruk. Lagash became the target of the last and greatest of the warlords of Uruk, Lugalzagesi.

Lugalzagesi (Lugalzaggissi) {2340–2316}[31]

Lugalzagesi was the son of king U'u of Umma, and great-grandson of Il, who had usurped the throne from Urluma after his disastrous defeat at the battle of the Ugiga-field (see p. 62). Before becoming king of Umma, Lugalzagesi had been an important priest of Nisaba, patron goddess of Umma (PI 94). His relationship to the city of Uruk is somewhat mysterious; he claims he was "brought up by Ningirim the mistress of Uruk" (PI 94), perhaps implying an intimate relationship with the city from his youth. It is probable that he became king of Uruk through marriage or some type of peaceful acquisition, rather than by war (RH 34). In his major royal inscription he lists "king of Uruk" (PI 94) as his first title, and he is called king of Uruk, not Umma, in the Sumerian King-list (KS 330). This would imply that the sieges by the "king of Uruk" against Lagash and Girsu mentioned in several year names were undertaken by Lugalzagesi himself, and are the same events as the sieges described in the Uru'inimgina inscription. By combining the city-state of Ur with the kingdom of Uruk, which had conquered most of Sumer under the previous kings, Lugalzagesi was master of all Sumer except the old dual city-state of Lagash-Girsu, to which he turned his attention.

The initial attacks by Lugalzagesi against Lagash were unsuccessful. A fragmentary inscription describes these initial campaigns. "He [Lugalzagesi] besieged
Girsu [the second major city of the kingdom of Lagash]. Uru'inimgina battled him
and [drove him off] at [Girsu's] wall. [. . .] He [Lugalzagesi] returned to his city
[Umma], but came a second time [to attack Girsu]" (PI 78). The year names also
mention at least three failed sieges against Lagash by the "king of Uruk", presumably Lugalzagesi (RH 34).

Although the details are not known, around 2335 Lugalzagesi inflicted a
crushing defeat against Lagash, in which he sacked and destroyed the city. We have
a poetic lament by a priest of Lagash who witnessed the final destruction of
his city.

> [Lugalzagesi] the leader of Umma set fire to the Ekibira [temple]. He set fire
> to the Antasura [temple] and bundled off its precious metals and lapis-lazuli.
> He plundered the palace of Tirash, he plundered the Abzubanda [temple], he
> plundered the chapels of [the gods] Enlil and Utu. He plundered the Ahush
> [temple] and carried off its precious metals and lapis-lazuli. (PI 78–9)

The account goes on in this vein, describing the desecration and plundering of
another dozen shrines. The priest-scribe making this account was in a sense
creating a judicial record of the crimes and sacrilege of Lugalzagesi, and ends his
account with a prayer and curse:

> The leader of Umma [Lugalzagesi], having sacked Lagash, has committed a sin
> against Ningirsu. The hand which he [Lugalzagesi] has raised against him
> [Ningirsu] will be cut off! It is not [because of] a sin of Uru'inimgina, king of
> Girsu [that Lagash was sacked]! May Nisaba, the god of Lugalzagesi, ruler of
> Umma, make him [Lugalzagesi] bear the sin [for plundering the temples of
> the gods]! [PI 79]

In a sense this bitter prayer was answered, for Lugalzagesi would eventually himself
be defeated and overthrown by Sargon of Akkad; if the scribe who wrote this
curse lived to see that day he undoubtedly rejoiced and praised his gods.

But the day of retribution was not to come for another twenty years, which
were filled with triumph upon triumph for Lugalzagesi. Using the plunder and
slaves from the sack of Lagash, Lugalzagesi was able to muster an even stronger
army for a series of campaigns over the next two decades. If he was not already
king of Uruk in 2335, he became such within the next few years and seems to
have moved his capital there, using "king of Uruk" as his principle title.

Having thus conquered the last independent city-state of Sumer, Lugalzagesi
claimed the title of high king of Kish.

> When [the high god] Enlil, [divine] king of all the lands, gave to Lugalzagesi
> the kingship of the nation [of Sumer], [Enlil] directed all the eyes [of the other

rulers of the] land [of Sumer] toward him [Lugalzagesi, in obedience], put all
the lands at his feet [in submission], from east to west made them subject to
him. (PI 94)

Here we see that, in typical Sumerian fashion, it is the gods who decided to grant
Lugalzagesi supreme kingship in Sumer. Later in the inscription Lugalzagesi lists
the Sumerian cities that "rejoice" under his kingship. It presumably lists his conquests or vassal states, and includes Uruk, Ur, Larsa, Umma, Zabala, Kidingir, and
Nippur (PI 94). Lagash and Girsu, though conquered by Lugalzagesi, are notably
absent from the list – perhaps there was little rejoicing in those devastated cities.

With Sumer fully secure, Lugalzagesi turned his attention to the Semitic-
speaking lands to the north, campaigning along both the Tigris and Euphrates
rivers:

> Then, from the Lower Sea [Persian Gulf], along the Tigris and Euphrates to
> the Upper [Mediterranean] Sea, he [the god Enlil] put their routes in good
> order for [Lugalzagesi's armies to march, and for communication and trade].
> From east to west Enlil permitted him no rival; under him the lands rested
> contentedly, the people made merry, and the suzerains of [the various vassal
> city-states of] Sumer, and the rulers of other lands [along the Tigris and
> Euphrates] conceded sovereignty to him [Lugalzagesi] at Uruk. (PI 94)

Some scholars doubt the historicity of Lugalzagesi's conquests outside of Sumer,
attributing the inscription to royal hyperbole. It is true that there is little confirming evidence for his conquests, although the city of Mari was sacked twice
during this period, which could be attributed to campaigns by Lugalzagesi and
later by Sargon (CAH 1/2:331). On the other hand, there is nothing inherently
improbable about Lugalzagesi being able to campaign up the Tigris and Euphrates.
After all, Sargon and his successors would do the same a few decades later. Mesopotamian armies of this time had the capacity to campaign over distances of several
hundred miles. The lack of confirming evidence is probably due to the fact that
Lugalzagesi was overthrown by Sargon shortly after his Tigris and Euphrates
campaigns, leaving him no time to consolidate these fresh conquests. In a sense
Lugalzagesi's campaigns of the unification of Sumer paved the way for the rise of
Sargon. By undermining the independent military strength of each individual
Sumerian city-state, Lugalzagesi made it possible for Sargon to take all of Sumer by
one great military victory – the defeat of Lugalzagesi himself, as will be chronicled
in the next chapter.

The sickle-sword[32]

Yadin, followed by many subsequent scholars, believed that the so-called "sickle-
sword" originated in Mesopotamia in the twenty-fourth century. I see several
phases of development of this weapon, with the classic sickle-sword emerging only

in the Middle Bronze Age. The earliest evidence we have of a possible sickle-sword-style weapon comes from Early Dynastic Mesopotamia {2900–2300} (MW 1:143). An Early Dynastic fragment of sculpture from Telloh shows a man with a sickle-like weapon on his shoulder (AM §44a; AW 1:136; see Figure 2a). This weapon was also known in Early Dynastic Syria, where a cylinder seal depicts a man slaying a lion and a bull with a javelin wielded overhand in his right hand and a sickle-shaped weapon in his left hand (FI §78). There are two questions about these weapons: are they made from copper/bronze or wood? Do they have a cutting edge or were they used as clubs? There is insufficient evidence give us a certain answer. As discussed below, I suspect that these Early Dynastic weapons represent fighting clubs, essentially the same as the similar weapons found in Egypt (AW 1:158–9, 166–7; see p. 426).

The next example of a possible Early Dynastic sickle-sword comes from the famous "Stele of Vultures" of king Eanatum of Lagash {c. 2440 (see Figure 1)}.[33] Here, however, the ambiguities are only increased. King Eanatum is shown in two different scenes holding the same curved sickle-like object. In the top scene the upper portion of the object is missing, while in the bottom scene the upper portion is partially defaced. The main oddity of this weapon is that it is clearly shown as being composed of (at least) three separate parallel pieces. A first glance this feature might seem to be ribbing on the metal, as is found in some depictions of daggers. But the object seems to be bound together in at least two places with thin ropes. Since copper/bronze objects were invariably cast as a single piece, it seems unlikely that the artist was trying to depict a metal sickle-sword, or at least not of the classical type found in the Middle Bronze period. None of the other soldiers in this scene are carrying this type of object. While it is possible that this object was a sickle-sword, there is clearly ambiguity here. It may, in fact, be a scepter rather than a weapon; an image of an enthroned deity from the Early Dynastic period shows the god holding both a mace and a curved club-like object in his left hand, which broadly resemble the proposed early sickle swords (AM §65; cf. FI 821). Another possibility is that Eanatum's weapon is actually a whip used to goad the equids in the chariot, such as is clearly depicted in several chariot scenes;[34] the most clear comparison is to an Old Babylonian scene (WV §31).

The case against Eanatum's weapon being a sickle-sword is bolstered by the fact that the type of object held by Eanatum disappears during the subsequent Akkadian and Ur III periods {2300–2000}. If this object is the ancestor of the classic Middle Bronze sickle-sword, why does it disappear during the Akkadian period? Instead, the Akkadian sickle-sword-like weapon is clearly a type of axe. The haft and the blade of the Akkadian weapon would be about 60–75 cm long, judging by its proportion to the body – when the tip is resting on the ground the edge of the handle reaches to about the lower hip (FI §540, §781; see Figure 2c–e). The haft is completely straight until the last foot or so, which has a slight curve to it. A broad rectangular axe blade is fastened to the upper curved part of the haft; the wooden haft sometimes extends beyond the upper edge of the axe blade (FI §567, §781). The rectangular axe-blade seems to be epsilon-shaped (FI §781; see Figure 2b–c).

(a) (b) (c)

(d) (e) (f)

Figure 2 Early and Middle Bronze Age weapons (drawings by Michael Lyon)

(a) Warrior with throwing or fighting stick, similar in form to later "sickle swords" {c. 3000} (Relief from Telloh; Louvre AO 2350); see AM §44a.

(b) Akkadian stele of warrior carrying a sheathed dagger on a belt in his right hand; an Akkadian war-axe showing the shape of the head and rivets is sheathed in his belt, partially obscured by a sash {23C}; (Iraq Museum 59205) see AM §119.

(c) Uruk: Neo-Sumerian god with war-axe in age of Shulgi {21C} (British Museum, 116719); see FI §781.

(d) Mari: The goddess Ishtar holding a curved axe in her left hand; colored mural from the Palace of Zimri-Lim, "The Investiture of the king by Ishtar" {18C} (Louvre); see SDA §346.

(e) Cylinder seal from Mari showing a god carrying a classic "sickle-sword" standing on a prostrate enemy {18C} (Louvre AO 21988); see FI §191.

(f) Classic "sickle-sword" from Abydos, Egypt {19C} (Museum of the Oriental Institute, Chicago); see AW 1:172b.

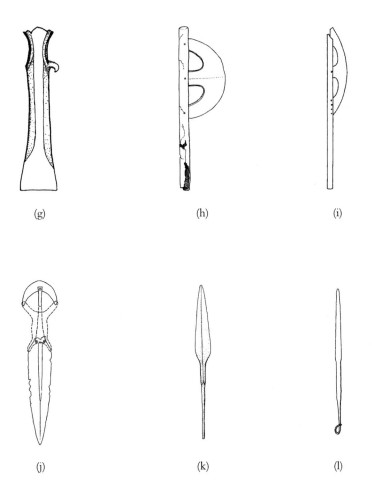

(g) Narrow-bladed "chisel" axe from Ras Shamra, Syria (Louvre); see MW 2:276, §418.

(h) Middle Kingdom Egyptian semi-circular axe; see EWW §23c.

(i) Middle Kingdom Egyptian broad-bladed axe (British Musuem); see AW 1:154.

(j) Middle Bronze Age broad-bladed dagger from Tel Rehov, Israel; see MW 2:434, §628.

(k) Broad spearhead from Serrin, Syria (Oxford, Ashmolean Museum); see MW 2:315, §47.

(l) Spiked javelin head from Khirbet el-Krimil, Israel (Jerusalem, Hebrew Union College); see MW 2:336, §156.

In a badly damaged relief of Sargon in a victory procession, he is followed by several attendants carrying what seem to be this type of "sickle-axe".[35] The clearest example of this weapon comes from a fragment of an Akkadian relief from Nasriyeh showing courtiers bringing tribute. In the upper-right-hand portion of this relief a soldier escorting prisoners is carrying a clearly depicted version of this axe (ME 108). In the lower-left section another man holds a sheathed bronze dagger in one hand, and a vase in the other. Inside his belt is a rectangular sickle-axe, about 75 cm long in proportion to his body (AAM 137; see Figure 2b). The sickle-axe is partially obscured by a sash, but enough of the top remains to show that the upper portion of the haft is partially curved and the haft extends beyond the top of the blade, just as in the other examples. Another clear example can be found in the twentieth-century relief of Anubanini in Iran (ME 20; PAE 319). The axehead is riveted to the metal bands which encircle the haft. I will call this weapon the "rectangular sickle-axe". I believe what occurred is that during the Akkadian period a rectangular axe blade was bolted to the curved scepter-club of the Early Dynastic period, representing the first step in the evolution towards the classic sickle-sword.

At around 2000 the form of the Akkadian-style rectangular sickle-axe splits into two different forms of the weapon: the Babylonian curved sickle-axe, and the classic sickle-sword. The Babylonian version probably originated as a shift in the form of the axe blade from the original Akkadian rectangular blade to a semi-circular curved version of the sickle-axe found on Neo-Sumerian and early Old Babylonian cylinder seals (AW 1:150; AAM §138; FI §167, §772). The difference is subtle, but noticeable, and is transitional to the Babylonian curved sickle-axe. The Babylonian-style "curved sickle-axe" is held in precisely the same way in precisely the same ritual contexts as the Akkadian "rectangular sickle-axe". In some of the depictions it is possible to see that the blade of the curved sickle-axe is quite clearly a separate object from the wooden haft – they are not a single piece of cast bronze (SDA §383, 384; FI §538). The best examples of this come from the remarkable murals at the palace of Zimri-Lim in Mari {c. 1765 (Figure 2d)}. Here the war-goddess Ishtar holds a sickle-axe in her hand; the painting shows the curved wooden haft in one color, to which is attached a different colored crescent-shaped axe blade, on the top of the haft (SDA 279; AW 1:172). Overall the weapon has the distinctive curve of the Old Babylonian sickle-axe. Another mural from the palace shows the war-goddess with three hafted weapons in a quiver on her back – a mace, an axe, and a curved sickle-axe, again with distinctive colors for the haft and blade (SDA 282–3).[36]

The other line of development from the Akkadian rectangular sickle-axe leads to the classic Middle Bronze sickle-sword, found in both art and archaeology.[37] A very clear cylinder seal from Mari {1765} shows the new-style sickle-sword with precisely the features of the surviving archaeological examples of the classic sickle-sword, but depicted in the same ritual context of the earlier Akkadian sickle-axe (FI §191; Figure 2e). Ritually speaking, in depictions of royal and divine iconography, the weapon was the same, even though the actual form of the weapon had gone through several transformations. In the classic sickle-sword the blade is actually rectangular (like the Akkadian sickle-axe). Essentially someone seems to have taken the Akkadian rectangular sickle-axe, and cast the entire thing in bronze, haft and blade, while retaining the original axe-like form. As with the Akkadian rectangular sickle-axe and the Babylonian curved sickle-axe, the sharp blade of the weapon occupies only the upper third, betraying its origin from the axehead.

From surviving archaeological examples we can see that the classic sickle-sword kept the distinctive quasi-rectangular form of the blade which was modeled after the Akkadian rectangular sickle-axe. Thus the Akkadian sickle-axe diverged into two different forms in the Middle Bronze Age: the curved sickle-axe, and the classic sickle-sword. The curved sickle-axe continued the original curvature of the haft, but kept the wooden haft and metal blade of the original. It seems likely that the sickle-"sword" is actually a version of the axe, where the original wooden haft and metal blade are combined together and cast in a single piece. This would have served to decrease breakage both of the haft and of the joint between haft and blade. The weapon also invariably appears only in royal and ritual contexts in both artistic and archaeological evidence. It is quite probably an elite or royal weapon (MW 1:170–1).

During the Middle Bronze Age the new sickle-sword spread rapidly through-out the Near East, appearing in Elam, Syria, Canaan, and eventually Egypt.[38] Egypt seems to have been the last region to acquire the weapon. It doesn't appear in Middle Kingdom Egyptian art, making it likely that the weapon was initially acquired by Egyptians through trade or plunder from Canaan. There is mention of thirty-three "scimitars" – literally "reaping implements" (ECI 79 n49) – taken as plunder in Syria during the reign of Amenemhet II {1929–1895}. Presumably these are versions of the sickle-swords found in the royal tombs of Byblos in Syria and Shechem in Canaan during this period. The weapon does not seem to have been manufactured in Egypt until the New Kingdom, when it frequently appears in a modified form as the Egypt *khopesh* (*ḫpš*), or scimitar, where the haft of the weapon is reduced to about one third and the blade extended to two thirds (AW 1:206–7; FP 51).

Warfare in Early Dynastic Elam {2900–2334}[39]

Although ethnically distinct and speaking their own language, the Elamites had in many ways been integrated economically and culturally with Sumer during the Uruk expansion of the late fourth millennium. These bonds remained strong throughout the Early Dynastic period, during which we also have our first records of warfare between Elam and Sumer. In the Susa III phase of Elamite history {3100–2700}, the early cultural predominance of Uruk expansion-style material culture is replaced by pottery and art styles derived from the eastern highlands of Fars and Luristan. Some speculate that this might be associated with the movement of nomadic highlanders into Elam, perhaps associated with "Awan", a name in Sumerian records for northern Elam (PAE 88–9, 97–8).

An Elamite kingdom, with its capital at Susa and encompassing south-western Iran, flourished during the Early Dynastic or Proto-Elamite period (PAE 71–84;

EA 5:106–10). The precise boundaries and nature of this state are uncertain. Cultural influence from Elam, including pottery styles and proto-Elamite tablets, are found throughout much of south-western and central Iran, indicating widespread cultural influence and merchant activity. In some ways, the Elamites became the suppliers for overland trade to Sumer for lapis lazuli, tin, and other Iranian products. How much political or military influence Elam might have exerted in other parts of Iran is unknown.

Militarily, all we know of Elam during the Early Dynastic period derives from incidental references in Sumerian texts. The Sumerian King-list states that "Ur was defeated in battle and its kingship carried off to Awan" (KS 329) – either a city-state in Elam or an alternate Sumerian name for the region as a whole. Its location in the King-list would place the event in late Early Dynastic II, perhaps around 2550. Assuming there is some historicity to this claim, it would imply a major Elamite invasion of Sumer – perhaps Awan highlanders – which may have resulted in the vassalage of one or more Sumerian city-states to the Elamites (PAE 88). Shortly thereafter, perhaps 2525, Enna'il, King of Kish, claims to have "vanquished Elam", probably ending this vassalage (PI 21).

The major recorded wars of earliest Elamite history are with Eanatum of Lagash, who mentions campaigns in Elam a number of times in his inscriptions (PI 37, 41–44; PAE 89). Lagash, on the south-east edge of the Mesopotamian floodplain, was the closest Sumerian city-state to Elam, and had the most frequent economic relations with it (PAE 91). Eanatum claims to have defeated Elam, "the mountainous land of timber and treasure" (PI 37), and "made burial mounds" in it (PI 41). The details are elusive, but economic texts from Lagash in subsequent decades show extensive trade in grain, spices, wood, and silver (PAE 91). It is possible that Lagash exercised some type of suzerainty over Elam during the late twenty-fifth century. Arrowheads, daggers, and a four-wheeled chariot were discovered in excavations at Susa dating to roughly this time (PAE 95), indicating the movement of Sumerian war-cart technology into the region by the twenty-fifth century. With the decline of Lagash military power beginning around 2400, the Elamites became independent again, and took to raiding their former suzerains. A text from about 2360 describes a raid by 600 Elamites into Lagash (KS 331). It was undoubtedly only one of many. Thereafter we have no military information on Elam until the invasion of Sargon of Akkad and his successors in the late twenty-fourth century.

CHAPTER THREE

The Akkadian empire {2334–2190}

With the rise of the Akkadian empire we see a number of new characteristics appearing in Mesopotamian military history.[1] First, there is a fundamental shift in military power away from the ethnic Sumerians to Semitic-speaking peoples of central and northern Mesopotamia. Second, although a few kings of the Early Dynastic period campaigned outside of the confines of Sumer itself, for the most part the military history of the Early Dynastic period focused on struggles among rival Sumerian city-states. With the rise of Akkad, Mesopotamia, Syria, and Elam are all integrated into one diplomatic and political system. Third, the Akkadian warlords introduced new policies of destroying the walls of conquered cities to eliminate their capacity to rebel, and of installing Akkadian governors in conquered cities rather than keeping the indigenous kings as vassals (R2:11–12), who presumably were supported by Akkadian garrisons. Thus, rather than trying to establish himself as hegemon over rival vassal kings who had been defeated, Sargon deposed those kings and took direct rule over an empire administered by appointed governors.

The origins of the Akkadian empire are obscured by lack of sources, and by many late legendary accounts. The site of Sargon's capital at Akkad is unknown, although there is a general consensus that it was probably located in the region of modern Baghdad at the confluence of the Tigris and Euphrates (EA 1:41–4). The eventual discovery of this site may produce additional information about the Akkadian Empire from tablets and monuments. Before the rise of Sargon, Akkad had never played an important political or military role in Mesopotamia.

Sargon (Sharrukin) {2334–2279}[2]

Interpreting the military career of Sargon is complicated both because most of his inscriptions lack chronological data, and because of the large number of legends which grew up about him, making it sometimes difficult to distinguish between history and legend. In this section I will mainly use contemporary sources written during the lifetime of Sargon or his immediate successors.

If the later legends are to be believed, Sargon was a usurper of the throne. He began his career as the dependent ruler of Akkad under the hegemony of his overlord Ur-Zababa, king of Kish, whom legend claims he served as cup-bearer

(KS 330). He may have been installed as governor of Akkad by Ur-Zababa. In his early reign[3] he rebelled against Ur-Zababa, perhaps after the latter had been weakened and his authority undermined in wars with Lugalzagesi of Uruk. Sargon successfully secured his independence, defeating several subsequent rulers of Kish during his early reign, and finally conquering the city of Kish itself. This early phase of his career, centering on the struggle with Kish for independence and predominance in central Mesopotamia, apparently lasted from 2334 to around 2320.

With his position in Akkad and central Mesopotamia finally secure, Sargon faced an even greater challenge. While Sargon was struggling with Kish, Lugalzagesi of Uruk had risen to prominence in Sumer and even campaigned up the Euphrates and Tigris (see pp. 64–6). It seems likely that, during some part of Sargon's early reign, he was in some sense a vassal of Lugalzagesi – though the royal inscriptions of Sargon would of course never admit such a thing. Sargon's conquest of Kish was probably viewed by Lugalzagesi as an upstart vassal taking too much power. War broke out (R2:9–22, 31), and at the battle of Uruk {c. 2316}, Sargon defeated the army of Uruk, including "fifty governors" or vassal rulers of Lugalzagesi; one suspects that some of Lugalzagesi's vassals may have deserted him at a key moment in the battle, hoping his defeat would allow them independence, not realizing, of course, that Sargon was ultimately a greater threat to their independence than Lugalzagesi. Sargon claims to have personally captured the aging king Lugalzagesi (R2:16, 21), and to have led him captive in triumph to the Gate of Enlil at Akkad.

> Sargon, king of Akkad, steward of the goddess Ishtar, king of the world, anointed priest of the god Anum, lord of the land, governor [on earth] for the god Enlil, was victorious over Uruk in battle, conquered fifty governors [of Lugalzagesi] with the [divine] mace of the god Ilaba, as well as the city of Uruk, and destroyed [Uruk's] walls. Further, he captured Lugalzagesi, king of Uruk, in battle [and] led him off to the gate of the god Enlil in a neck stock. (R2:13)[4]

Sargon forced his royal captive to watch the erection of a victory stele (R2:15); Lugalzagesi's ultimate fate is uncertain, but presumably he was executed, as was the Akkadian custom with captured kings: Naram-Sin "captured three kings and brought [them] before the god Enlil", after which they were apparently executed. Other captured kings were marched through cities in triumph, after which they were executed "before the gods" in their temples (R2:112, 138, 222).

Following his victory over Uruk, Sargon faced a new challenge. The Sumerian vassal rulers had asserted their independence after the fall of their overlord Lugalzagesi to Sargon, requiring him to undertake at least four additional campaigns in Sumer to secure Lugalzagesi's entire former domain (R2:10–15).

> Sargon, king of Akkad, was victorious over Ur in battle, conquered the city and destroyed its walls. He conquered Eninmar, destroyed its walls, and

conquered its districts and Lagash as far as the sea [Persian Gulf]. He washed his weapons in the sea. He was victorious over Umma in battle, conquered the city, and destroyed its walls. (R2:14)

The important after-battle ritual washing of weapons was designed to cleanse them of blood and purify them (HTO 243). When inscriptions describe Sargon's weapons being washed "in the Upper and Lower Seas" (the Mediterranean and Persian Gulf) (R2:11, 32, 97), it was meant to indicate that Sargon had reached the end of the world, and could therefore ritually cleanse his weapons, since there was nothing left to conquer (R2:11, 14, 17).

The destruction of the walls of conquered cities, while not unknown before, became a standard policy under Sargon. Presumably the city walls were not entirely destroyed, but were left with major breaches or without gates, rendering them indefensible and thereby making rebellion a very dubious proposition. The fact that so many cities in the Akkadian empire repeatedly rebelled despite their ruined city walls is an indicator of the great hatred the conquered people had for their Akkadian overlords. A related policy undertaken by Sargon was to install loyal Akkadians as governors of conquered cities rather than allowing conquered kings to remain as vassal rulers: "from the Lower Sea to the Upper Sea citizens of Akkad held the governorship [of conquered cities]" (R2:14). Sargon is also sometime credited with creating the world's first standing army, based on one of his inscriptions where he claims "5400 men daily eat in the presence of Sargon" (R2:29). This passage probably has reference to Sargon's palace establishment rather than an actual standing army, and references to ration distribution to ministers, scribes, priests, courtiers, and perhaps even servants at the palace of Akkad. It is quite likely that a portion of those 5400 men were in fact the Royal Bodyguard who formed a permanent standing army.

The exact chronological order of his subsequent conquests is uncertain, though we can identify four regions where Sargon campaigned: Elam, Subartu (northern Tigris), Syria, and perhaps south-central Anatolia. With Sumer secure, Sargon turned towards a traditional enemy of Mesopotamia, Elam, in south-western Iran.[5] His inscriptions describe thirteen cities or regions which he defeated and plundered, along with capturing a number of governors and generals, including both "Khishibrasini, king of Elam" and his son Lukh'ish'an. A victory stele erected at Susa shows Sargon, with thick beard and long hair tied in a braided bun at his neck, leading prisoners and booty in triumph after his capture of the city.[6] Elam was apparently not permanently subdued, however, for Sargon's son Rimish was compelled to campaign there again (see pp. 78–80).

Sargon also campaigned into northern Mesopotamia (C1/2:430–2). A vague tradition records his victories in Subartu (northern Tigris), where he "defeated them, cast [their dead bodies] in heaps [of burial mounds], and overthrew their widespread host" (C1/2:430). Nineveh and Ashur, the homeland of the Assyrians, were clearly ruled by Sargon's successors, and presumably were conquered at this time. The practice of piling the corpses of dead enemies and burying them on the battlefield is noted in the inscriptions, which seems to have served both as a religious ritual, and as a victory monument reminding would-be rebels of the price of defeat (R2:53, 56, 129, 144). For example, "when [Shulgi] destroyed the land of Kimash and Hurtum, he dug a ditch and heaped up a pile of corpses" (R3/2:141; E4:387).

Sargon's campaigns up the Euphrates are more clearly documented in his own inscriptions (R2:12, 15, 28–31). Sargon began his campaign by seeking authorization from the gods for his proposed conquest of Syria. At the city of Tuttul in the middle Euphrates ...

> Sargon, the king, bowed down to the god Dagan in [his temple in the city of] Tuttul [seeking oracular confirmation for his plan to conquer Syria]. He [the god Dagan, through an oracular pronouncement] gave to him [Sargon] the Upper Land [Syria], [including the cities of] Mari, Yarmuti, and Elba as far as the Cedar Forest [of Lebanon] and the Silver [Taurus] Mountains. (R2:28–9)

Archaeological evidence shows destructions of Mari and Ebla at this period, probably by the invasion of either Sargon or his grandson Naram-Sin (AS 277–9).

There are also later legendary sources which claim that Sargon invaded south-central Anatolia and attacked Purushkhanda, in defense of Mesopotamian merchants who were being abused by local rulers. There is no confirmation of this campaign in contemporary Akkadian sources, but it is not inherently implausible, since Anatolia was an important source of silver for Mesopotamia, and would therefore have been an attractive source of plunder for Sargon (C1/2:426–9).

Overall, Sargon was clearly the greatest Mesopotamian conqueror before the Assyrian period some 1500 years later. In military terms his achievements are remarkable:

> Sargon, king of the world, was victorious in thirty-four battles. He destroyed the [city] walls [of his enemies] as far as the shore of [both] the seas. He moored the ships of Meluhha [Indus Valley], Magan [Oman], and Dilmun [Bahrain] at the quay of Akkad.... 5,400 men daily eat in the presence of Sargon. (R2:28–29) ... He [the god Enlil] gave to Sargon [all the land from] the Upper Sea [to] the Lower [Sea]. Sargon [became] king of the [entire] world. (R2:32)

He created the largest empire the world had yet known, stretching from the Persian Gulf to the Mediterranean, and encompassing most of modern Iraq and Syria, and over twice the size in population and land of contemporary Egypt.[7] From another perspective, however, Sargon's empire was what we would call today a humanitarian disaster, for "the god Enlil instructed [Sargon to conquer the world] and he showed mercy to no one" (R2:32). This merciless feature of Sargon's conquests, imitated by all his successors, fomented widespread hatred for Akkadian rulers, creating a constant underlying threat of rebellion. When the great warlord finally died, his entire empire rose in revolt, only to be further suppressed by mass devastation by his son Rimush (see pp. 78–80).

Sargon as the ideal warrior-king (LKA 57–139)

The reality of Sargon the Warlord as unifier of Mesopotamia was amplified by subsequent generations. For later Mesopotamians Sargon served as the exemplar of the conquering warlord, a mythic role similar to Alexander's or Caesar's in Europe – two subsequent kings of Assyria took his name. In the past few decades scholars have been able to reconstruct the legendary account of the life of Sargon. Although the historical value of these texts for understanding Sargon's historic reign is limited – rather like the *Alexander Romance* in relation to the historic Alexander – the legends are useful to illuminate the warrior mentality of the age. Although these literary texts cannot necessarily be viewed as reliable history, they do provide narrative detail of a typical military campaign that is often lacking in the terse and propagandistic royal inscriptions.

Sargon is described as ever eager for war: "Sargon girds his loins with his terrible weapons. In the palace, Sargon opens his mouth. Speaking to his warriors he declares: 'My warriors! With [the land of] Kanish I desire war!' " (LKA 109–11). Sargon recognizes the logistical and intelligence problems facing his army in campaigning far from Akkad. When his advisors warn him, "The road, O my Lord, that you wish to travel – it is month-long, it is dangerous" (LKA 111–13), Sargon summons merchants "who spy out the regions" to provide him with intelligence to properly plan for the march (LKA 115–21).

On the eve of battle, Sargon is depicted as giving a speech to his assembled warriors, admiring their "courage, strength, vigor [and] heroism" (LKA 63). His warriors are compared to "strong bulls" (LKA 67). His champion responds, "Tomorrow, Akkad will commence battle. A festival of warriors will be celebrated" (LKA 63). The army is encouraged to act bravely "so the king [Sargon] will proclaim you 'My Warrior' and erect your statue in front of his own statue" (LKA 66–7). "My Warrior" may have been a technical term for personal guards. The reference here to making monuments commemorating the bravest warriors on campaign may mean that some soldiers depicted along with the king on Akkadian monuments may represent actual individuals. The soldiers are described as wearing fine robes adorned with gold (LKA 67–9), perhaps like those depicted on the Alabaster Victory Stele (AM §119; AFC §131). These may be robes of honor given as another type of reward for heroic soldiers.

Sacrifices, prayers, and divination preceded and followed battle.[8] Armies are divided into center lines and two flanks (LKA 87, 181), and the troops are divided into battalions (*kisri*) (LKA 65), armed with "maces and copper battleaxes" (LKA 137). Sargon naturally fights in the front ranks (HTO 244–5), and is compared to a lion in battle: "Was it not because of his frightening radiance and his bellowing roar that no one dared to approach him? I, Sargon, am your raging lion . . . When there is combat, invoke my name!" (LKA 99–101). This may be an allusion to shouting the king's name as a battle-cry. On another occasion the men shout "Charge, man against man!" (HTO 37) to launch an attack.

Even after the battle is won, the enemy's capital must be besieged to win the final victory. Some narrative details of siegecraft are provided:

> Sargon undermined [the walls of] the city, broadened the Gate of the Princes, [he made a breach] two *iku* [c. 120 meters] wide. He cast it down; in the highest part of its wall he made a breach; he smote all of his wine-intoxicated men. Sargon placed his throne before the gate. Sargon opens his mouth, speaking to his warriors. He declares, "Come on! Nur-Daggal [the enemy king] ... Let him stir himself! Let him humble himself! Let me behold [him surrender]." (LKA 123–5)

With his city walls undermined, Nur-Daggal panics and surrenders, negating the need for an assault into the breach. In victory the Akkadian army strips the countryside of both humans and animals, leaving the conquered city a heap of ruins depopulated for miles around (LKA 71–3, 91).

Rimush {2278–2270}[9]

Even during Sargon's lifetime, there were hints of rebellion among the conquered peoples of Mesopotamia (R2:30; C1/2:433). It is clear there was substantial dissatisfaction with Akkadian rule, and upon Sargon's death most of the empire rose in revolt. Sargon's son and successor Rimush probably spent most of his short reign trying to keep his empire in one piece. It is difficult to obtain an accurate picture of the extent and success of these rebellions, since they are only mentioned in the Akkadian annals after they have been suppressed; successful rebellions are never discussed.

Rimush recorded a lengthy inscription in which he details his suppression of these rebellions. His inscription, however, is highly formulaic, repeating over and over that a city revolted, Rimush defeated it, killed and captured a certain number of men, captured the rebel leaders, and destroyed the walls of the rebellious city. Here is an example:

> Rimush, king of the world, was victorious over Adab and Zabala in battle and struck down 15,718 men. He took 14,576 captives. Further, he captured Meskigala, governor at Adab, and Lugalgalzu, governor of Zabala. He conquered their two cities and destroyed the walls of both of them. Further, he expelled many men from their two cities and annihilated them. (R2:41)

After six campaigns, Rimush had apparently suppressed the rebellion, concluding that, like his father, he "[was] king of the [entire] world – the god Enlil did indeed grant kingship to him. ... He took away their tribute [from defeated enemies from] as far as the Lower Sea [Persian Gulf]" (R2:46).

The inscriptions of Rimush introduce a new element into Akkadian military practice: mass slaughter, enslavement, and deportation of defeated enemies, and the total annihilation of their cities (R2:42, 44, 46, 48). The policy was that, if a city rebelled against the king of Akkad, that city should be utterly destroyed as a warning to others contemplating revolt. Rebellion against the king was tantamount to rebellion against the gods. Table 3.1 summarizes the casualty reports from Rimush's inscriptions, emphasizing the widespread human suffering caused by Akkadian imperialism.

The names of a number of important captured aristocrats are also given, including Kaku, king of Ur (R2:46–7). Since Ur had been previously captured by Sargon, this would indicate either that he had left Kaku as vassal prince of Ur, or that Kaku restored kingship in Ur as part of the rebellion. Other cities in Sumer are described as being ruled by rebellious "governors" (*ensi*). To the extent that the figures given by Rimush are not pure fabrications – he repeatedly insists "by the gods Shamash and Ilaba I swear that [these] are not falsehoods, [but] are indeed true", perhaps protesting too much (R2:49, 54, 57–8) – these numbers undoubtedly represent casualties among the entire civilian population of the defeated cities, rather than just numbers of soldiers.[10] If so, they represent the first evidence for a new policy of mass destruction as punishment for rebellion, one which will endure for several thousand years in the Near East, bearing terrible fruit under the Assyrians and Babylonians, and which continues to be practiced by some modern Middle Eastern tyrants who, like the ancient Akkadians, rule with blood and horror upon the earth.

Having solidified his rule, Rimush launched a campaign against Parahshum in Elam, winning a great victory at the battle of the Middle River {c. 2273}, for which we have a detailed description (PAE 103–6; ME 100–2).

> Rimush, king of the world, was victorious in battle over Abalgamash, king of Parahshum. Zahara, Elam, [Gupin, and Meluhha,][11] had assembled in Parahshum for battle, but he [Rimush] was victorious [over them] and struck down 16,212 men [and] took 4,216 captives. Further, he captured Emahsini, king of Elam, and all the [nobles?] of Elam. Further, he captured Sidga'u, general of Parahshum, and Sargapi, general of Zahara, in between [the cities of] Awan and Susa, by the "Middle River". Further, he heaped up over them a

Table 3.1 Summary of enemy casualties from Rimush's campaigns

City	Killed	Captured	Expelled	Source
Adab and Zabala	15,718	14,576	–	R2:41
Umma and KI.AN	8900	3540	3600	R2:43–4
Ur and Lagash	8049	5460	5985	R2:45–6
Three battles in Sumer	11,322	–	14,100	R2:47–8
Kazallu	12,052	5862	–	R2:48, 51
Parakhshum (Elam)	16,212	4216	–	R2:52

burial mound in the area of the city. Further, he conquered the cities of Elam, destroyed their walls, and tore out the foundations of Parahshum from the land of Elam. [Thereby] Rimush, king of the world, ruled Elam. The god Enlil showed him [the way to victory] ... When he conquered Elam and Parahshum, he took away 30 minas [roughly a pound each] of gold, 3,600 minas of copper and 300 male and female slaves and dedicated [them] to the god Enlil. (R2:52–5)

An interesting element of this inscription is the reference to troops from Meluhha – the Indus Valley civilization – serving in the anti-Akkadian coalition at the battle of the Middle River.[12] Rimush saw this victory as definitive for his reign, describing himself in later inscriptions as "Rimush, king of the [entire] world: the god Enlil gave to him all the land. He holds the Upper Sea and the Lower Sea and all the mountain [lands] for the god Enlil" (R2:59). Overall Rimush managed to keep much of the Akkadian empire together after significant rebellions, and solidified Akkadian power in Elam.

Manishtusu {2269–2255}[13]

According to later legend, Manishtusu usurped the throne after the murder of his brother in a palace coup; certainly Rimush's reign was rather short. As was usual at Akkadian succession, his reign began with a general uprising of most conquered provinces, which was probably an extension of the revolts against his predecessor Rimush: "all the lands ... which my father Sargon left had in enmity revolted against me [Manishtusu] and not one stood fast" (C1/2:437–8). There is no account of his suppression of this revolt, but he apparently maintained control over most of the empire. An inscription from Ashur indicates that the local ruler Azuzu recognized Manishtusu as his overlord (A1:8).

The military affairs of Manishtusu's reign are poorly documented. His single martial inscription alludes to two great campaigns:

Manishtusu, king of the world: when he conquered Anshan and Shirihum [in south-west Iran], had ... ships cross the Lower Sea [Persian Gulf]. The cities across the Sea, thirty-two [in number], assembled for battle, but he was victorious [over them]. Further, he conquered their cities, struck down their rulers, and after he roused them [his troops] plundered as far as the Silver Mines. He quarried the black stone of the mountains across the Lower Sea, loaded [it] on ships, and moored [the ships] at the quay of Akkad. He fashioned a statue of himself [and] dedicated [it] to the god Enlil (R2:75–6).

Here we see a first campaign into eastern Elam, solidifying and even expanding the conquests of his brother in that region. (Anshan is Tal-i Malyan near modern Shiraz, while Shirihum is the area west of modern Bandar Abbas.) Thereafter, he launched a major maritime campaign "across the Lower Sea", or the Persian Gulf.

The specific target of this offensive is not named, but there are three lands generally reached via the Persian Gulf during this period: Dilmun (Bahrain), Magan (Oman) and Meluhha (Indus delta). Most scholars assume it to be Oman, since it is a source of the "black stone" which is probably diorite (R2:117). None of the three regions can be excluded, however. Given the mention of a Melluhan contingent allied with the Elamites at the earlier battle of the Middle River against Rimush, it is possible that Manishtusu's expedition included a punitive raid on the Indus delta as well. The ability of the Akkadians to launch a successful maritime expedition in the Persian Gulf in the twenty-third century BC indicates a fairly sophisticated level of administration and logistics, as well as ocean-going naval technology. Manishtusu's ocean campaign (c. 2260) comes almost a century after Weni's maritime campaign against Canaan (c. 2340) (see pp. 336–40); together these events represent the beginning of recorded naval warfare.

Naram-Sin {2255–2218}[14]

After his grandfather Sargon, Naram-Sin was the greatest of the Akkadian warlords. The widespread use of terror and massacre by his uncle Rimush to suppress revolts had done little to endear the people of Mesopotamia to their Akkadian rulers, and Naram-Sin's rule was likewise inaugurated with a massive revolt.[15]

> When the four quarters [i.e. the entire world] together revolted against him, [which] no king whosoever had [ever] seen [before]: when Naram-Sin, the mighty, [was] on a mission for the goddess Ishtar, all the four quarters together revolted against him and confronted [him] (R2:96).... Through the love which the goddess Ishtar showed him, he was victorious in nine battles in one year, and the [three] kings whom [the rebels] had raised [against him], he captured. (R2:113)

Of course the suppression of the rebellion was not nearly as straightforward as Naram-Sin wanted to make it seem. The exact order of the different phases of the rebellion and its suppression cannot be established, since the inscriptions lack a chronology. None the less, it is clear that the rebellions nearly toppled the empire.

As the rebellion began, the newly independent city-states elevated anti-Akkadian rulers as new kings, and organized large coalitions to oppose Naram-Sin. Akkad's old rival Kish rebelled under Iphur-Kish, rallying half-a-dozen cities to his cause, enlisting the aid of Amorite bedouins (shadu) (R2:104, 109), serving as an ominous precursor to the Amorite invasion and migration into Mesopotamia in subsequent decades (see pp. 157–9). As leader of the rebel coalition, Iphur-Kish mustered his force and marched toward Akkad, where "he drew up battle lines [before the city] and awaited battle" at the "Field of the God Sin" (R2:104).

With a rebel army at the gates of Akkad, Naram-Sin was seriously threatened: "Naram-Sin, the mighty, [mobilized] his young men there [in Akkad], and he held

Akkad. He closed [the city gates]" against Iphur-Kish (R2:104–5; LKA 255–7). Rather than face a lengthy siege, which would only give other cities the opportunity and motive to join the rebellion, Naram-Sin mustered his army and immediately attacked Iphur-Kish. "In the field of the god Sin the two of them engaged in battle and grappled with each other. By the verdict of the goddess Ishtar-Annunitum, Naram-Sin, the mighty, was victorious over the Kishite [Iphur-Kish] in battle at Tiwa", capturing "300 officers and 4932 captives" (R2:105–6). Thereafter Naram-Sin pursued the routed rebels:

> Further, he [Naram-Sin] pursued him [Iphur-Kish] to Kish, and right beside Kish, at the gate of the goddess Ninkarrak, the two of them engaged in battle for a second time, and grappled with each other. By the verdict of the goddess Annuntium and the god Anum, Naram-Sin, the mighty, was [again] victorious over the Kishite in battle at Kish. (R2:106)

Another 3015 men were captured in battle, and the city and its walls were destroyed.[16]

The immediate threat to Akkad was thus averted, but unfortunately for Naram-Sin, rebellion spread rapidly throughout Sumer. Ur and Uruk had joined Iphur-Kish's coalition (R2:109), but, because of Naram-Sin's swift response and victory, they were apparently unable to arrive with their armies in time to face Naram-Sin in the initial battles. After the fall of Kish, rebellion continued in southern Sumer under the leadership of Amar-Girid of Uruk, who formed an alliance with nearly all the Sumerian city-states including Ur, Lagash, Umma, Adab, Shuruppak, Isin, and Nippur (R2:107). Amar-Girid "drew up battle lines" near Ashnak (R2:108). Wasting no time, Naram-Sin "hastened" to successfully attack Amar-Girid (R2:108), thereby apparently crushing the rebellion in Sumer. In all, Naram-Sin was victorious in nine battles in a single year {2255}, capturing three of the rebel kings (R2:113, 115–17; LKA 260–1). By any military standard it was a remarkable victory.

In grateful recognition for the divine intervention that preserved Naram-Sin's rule and saved city of Akkad, the people of Akkad spontaneously prayed that the gods might accept Naram-Sin as one of their own – at least if you believe Naram-Sin's account:

> In view of the fact that [Naram-Sin] protected the foundations of his city [Akkad] from danger, [the citizens of] his city requested from [the following gods] – Ishtar in [the temple of] Eanna, Enlil in Nippur, Dagan in Tuttul, Ninhursag in Kes, Ea in Eridu, Sin in Ur, Shamash in Sippar, (and) Nergal in Kutha – that [Naram-Sin] be [made] the god of their city, and they built within Akkad a temple [dedicated] to him [as a god]. (R2:114)

Thereafter Naram-Sin took the title "king of the four quarters", meaning the entire world, and was frequently called the "god of Akkad" (C1/2:440). As with

Alexander the Great, it is impossible to determine whether this self-deification was megalomania, shrewd propaganda, or a sincere religious belief – or, most likely, a combination of all three.

The rebellion against Akkadian rule was not limited to Sumer, however; city-states in northern Mesopotamia (Subartum) revolted as well. Naram-Sin apparently undertook two campaigns in this region.[17] The first, up the Tigris river valley, is poorly documented (R2:125–30). He claims to have "smashed the weapon of all of [the land of] Subartum" and to have conquered "fourteen fortresses" (R2:141–3); Naram-Sin boasts of having "reached the source of the Tigris River and the source of the Euphrates River" during his campaigns (R2:140).

With the Tigris Valley subdued, Naram-Sin turned his attention to the Euphrates, where the revolt was galvanized under the leadership of the lord of Apishal, swearing to fight Naram-Sin "whether I die or keep myself alive" (R2:91, 141).[18] One inscription gives us a feel for the nature of Naram-Sin's campaign and an itinerary of his march against this northern rebellion (cf. R2:125). The rebels mustered their troops and marched to the battle of Mt. Bashar (Jebel Bishri on the west bank of the Euphrates in Syria):

> Naram-Sin, went from Ashimananum to Shishil. At Shishil he crossed the Tigris River and [went] from Shishil to the [east] bank of the Euphrates River. He crossed the Euphrates River and [went] to [Mount] Bashar, the Amorite mountain.... He [Naram-Sin] marched to Habshat. Naram-Sin, [going] from the Euphates River, reached Bashar, the Amorite mountain. He personally decided to fight: [the two armies] made battle and fought one another. By the verdict of the goddess Ishtar, Naram-Sin, the mighty, was victorious in battle over Apishal at [Mount] Bashar, the Amorite mountain.... He struck down in the campaign a total of 9 chiefs and 4,325 men. Naram-Sin, the mighty captured [?] captives and the king of Apishal.... [He captured] leaders and chiefs, as well as 5,580 captives. [Enemy casualty list for this campaign]: Total: 6 generals. Total: 17 governors. Total: 78 chiefs. Total: [?] captains.... [Grand] total: [?] kings. [Grand] total: 13 generals. [Grand] total: 23 governors. Grand total: 2,212 chiefs. Grand total: 137,400 men [including civilian casualties?]. The god Enlil showed [him the way and] Naram-Sin, the mighty, struck down as many as there were in the campaign, and captured [them]. (R2:91–4)

Despite the probable hyperbole in the total of 137,400 casualties he claims to have inflicted on his enemies, this inscription makes clear the magnitude of the opposition to Naram-Sin, with over two dozen city-states allied against him, together with the Amorite tribesmen from the Syrian Desert (R2:93).

His subjugation of the rebellion in the northern Euphrates left him in a position to undertake further campaigns into Syria (R2:163, 167). Naram-Sin's inscription describing his conquest of Armanum (Aleppo?) and Ebla contains the most important description of fortifications and siegecraft for this period.[19]

Whereas, for all time since the creation of mankind, no king whosoever had destroyed Armanum [Aleppo?] and Ebla, the god Nergal, by the means of [his divine] weapons opened the way for Naram-Sin, the mighty, and gave him Armanum and Ebla [through conquest]. Further, he gave to him [by conquest] the Amanus [Mountains], the Cedar Mountain, and the Upper Sea. By means of the [divine] weapons of the god Dagan, who magnifies his kingship, Naram-Sin, the mighty, conquered Armanum and Ebla. Further, from the [west] side of the Euphrates River as far as [the city of] Ulishum, he smote the people whom the god Dagan had given to him for the first time, so that they perform service for the god Ilaba, his god. Further, he totally [conquered] the Amanus, the Cedar Mountain (RS2:163, 167).

The regions described here are all in western Syria. The Amanus Mountains are the range north-west of modern Antioch, while the Cedar Mountain is in modern coastal Syria or Lebanon. From central Syria Naram-Sin marched to the Mediterranean Sea and to "Talkhatum", apparently in south-central Anatolia (C1/2:442–3). At least large portions of Syria were incorporated into the Akkadian empire, with Nagar (Tell Brak) in northern Mesopotamia becoming the main Akkadian administrative center, flourishing during this period (AS 279–80).

With Syria subdued and his conquests extended to the "Upper Sea" or the Mediterranean, Naram-Sin turned his attention to the Akkadian overseas domain in the Persian Gulf, which had been established by his father Manishtusu. His army "crossed the [Lower] Sea and conquered Magan [Oman], in the midst of the sea", capturing its ruler Manium (R2:97, 117, 138, 140, 163). Naram-Sin also attacked Elam and Parahshum in south-western Iran, but these campaigns are poorly documented (R2:130, 167; PAE 106–8; ME 105–16). There is archaeological evidence of direct Akkadian rule in Elam in the form of victory monuments and other Akkadian artifacts.

Ominously, the inscriptions of Naram-Sin include a vague reference to "smiting the people and all the [Zagros] Mountain Lands for the god Enlil" (R2:138, 140). Mountain Peoples, or highlanders (*shadu*) is a somewhat vague term, but is generally understood to refer to fierce mountain tribes of the Zagros Mountains. Evidence of direct Akkadian rule in part of the central Zagros is found in copper and stone votive maceheads which were discovered in the area (ME 112). Most importantly, the famous Victory Stele of Naram-Sin describes a punitive campaign against the highlander tribal confederation of the Lullubu in the central Zagros (AANE §49; Figure 3): "Satuni, the king of the the highlanders of Lullubum assembled together ... [for] battle. ... [Naram-Sin] heaped up a burial mound over them ... [and] dedicated [this object, the stele] to the god [who granted victory]" (R2:144). The Lullubu highlanders who "assembled together" to attack Akkad were an ominous precursor to the invasion of Akkadian empire by Gutian highlanders within a few years after Naram-Sin's death (see pp. 102–4).

Akkadian martial art

Given the warlike nature of the Akkadian kings, the fact that we have only nine surviving pieces of Akkadian monumental martial art – all but two of them fragmentary – clearly emphasizes the point that we are at the mercy of random chance for both survival and discovery of our evidence for ancient Near East military history. I will examine each of these pieces here for the insights they can give us into Akkadian military history.

1a Victory Stele of Sargon (Susa).[20] King Sargon, identified by an inscription, is shown in procession with soldiers and prisoners (AM §115). This badly damaged stele, which is a small fragment of a much larger original relief that probably included item 1b below, consists of only half of two panels. The upper panel shows a row of naked prisoners with their arms bound behind them at the wrist. The lower, more important panel shows Sargon leading a victory procession. Sargon is dressed in a robe, with his long hair and beard precisely matching the famous bronze bust of an Akkadian ruler (9, below). He may have a dagger in his belt. Two characteristics of the stele make it slightly possible that Sargon is riding in a war-cart. First, there is a triangle of damaged rough stone in front of Sargon, about waist high. It is in high relief, and if Sargon were walking one would expect this portion of the panel to be in low relief, as is the rest of the background on the stele. This piece of the stele is in the rough shape of the upper front of a two-wheeled war-cart from the period (see WV §8, §13, §17, §18, §31), but is too damaged to see any confirming details. Something is there, which has the vague shape of a war-cart; if it is not a war-cart, what is it? Second, Sargon is taller than the rest of his soldiers; this may be because of the widespread tradition in Near Eastern martial art of representing the king as larger than ordinary mortals, but may also be because he is standing on a war-cart. The bottom and front part of image that would have shown the wheels and equids are both missing. Sargon is followed by a courtier carrying either a standard, a banner, or perhaps a parasol. Behind march five soldiers with long pleated robes on their left shoulders and carrying large Akkadian battle-axes.[21]

1b The Prisoner Stele of Sargon (Susa). This shows prisoners led by an Akkadian soldier with an axe (AFC §127).[22] This is likely, but not certainly, a different piece of stele 1a. It shows an Akkadian soldier in a kilt with a broad-headed battle-axe escorting naked prisoners with their arms bound behind their backs at the wrist.

2 The War-net stele of Sargon (Susa) (AAM §126–7; AFC 193). This highly fragmentary relief shows a war-net scene based on iconography quite similar to Ningirsu's war-net on the Stele of the Vultures (see pp. 55–9). Here Sargon holds a net in which a dozen enemy prisoners are ensnared. As with Ningirsu's net, one prisoner is trying to escape and is being bashed on the head by Sargon's mace. Sargon is presenting the net to the war goddess Ishtar

(Sumerian Inana) who is seated on her throne. All we see is her skirt, and a mace over her shoulder (presumably in a quiver on her back), which iconographically point to Ishtar.

3   Stele of Rimush (two sides) (from Telloh) (AFC §129a–b; Figure 5e, p. 219).[23] All that survives of this stele is one triangular fragment with reliefs on both sides. Parts of three panels of war-scenes are shown on either side. On side one, the upper panel depicts two archers with their tasseled quivers on their backs, and vague outlines of bows; they are very similar to an archer from an Akkadian cylinder seal (AFC §139). The second panel of side one shows an archer with a drawn bow. In front of him, a soldier with an axe dispatches a naked enemy. The third panel shows a man wielding his pike with two hands, stabbing a fallen enemy who is missing from the fragment. The second side, panel one, shows a soldier carrying a large axe. On the second panel, a soldier dispatches a kneeling man pleading for his life. Behind him, a soldier with a long 2.5-meter pike escorts a prisoner. This man's marching stance with his pike is very similar to that in the Victory Stele of Naram-sin (4). On the feet just below the pikeman is the head of an archer with the top of his bow visible. Taken together we see four archers, three axemen and two pikemen.

4   Victory Stele of Naram-Sin (AANE §49; Figure 3). The the most famous Akkadian martial monument,[24] this stele shows the king and his army ascending into the Zagros Mountains and defeating the Lullubu highlanders. This scene is the first in the history of Mesopotamian martial art to attempt to depict the natural terrain of the battlefield in a single scene rather than in stylized panels. The terrain shows a number of ridges covered with trees and a high mountain peak in the background. The inscription reads in part, "Satuni, the king of the highlanders of Lullubum assembled together . . . [for] battle.... [Naram-Sin defeated them and] heaped up a burial mound over them . . . [and] dedicated [this object, the stele] to the god [who granted victory]" (R2:144). The Lullubu soldiers, with their distinctive long braided ponytails, are shown in an utter rout. Several lie dead; one has an arrow or javelin protruding from his neck. Another falls from the mountain. Two more run away, one with a broken pike. The Lullubi king Satuni stands before Naram-Sin, begging for his life. The Akkadian army, on the other hand, marches boldly forward in good order. All six of the Akkadian soldiers wear kilts and helmets, broadly similar to those shown in the earlier Sumerian Standard of Ur and Stele of the Vultures (Figure 2). They all also have narrow-bladed axes for melees. Two carry war banners, two hold 2.5-meter pikes at the butt, resting the shaft on the shoulder like a rifle on the parade-ground. The fifth Akkadian has a bow, while the sixth seems to have an axe. The heroic Naram-Sin leads his army into battle on the crest of the mountain, standing twice as tall as anyone else, and stepping on the bodies of fallen enemies. He has a similar kilt, but has a thick beard and long hair, and wears a horned crown symbolic of his divinity. In his hand he carries an axe, a bow, and an arrow. His bow is often said to be the earliest representation of a composite bow, an issue that will be discussed below (pp. 89–95).

Figure 3 The "Victory Stele" of Naram-Sin, Akkadian {c. 2230}
Source: Louvre, Sb 4; drawing by Michael Lyon.

5   Darband-i-Gawr rock cut relief of Naram-sin (AAM §157; Figure 5d, p. 218).
    This gives a different version of the events depicted on Naram-Sin's victory
    stele (4). The king is shown in precisely the same martial pose, striding for-
    ward to victory carrying a bow and a mace or axe. Beneath him are the fallen
    bodies of the dead Lullubu highlanders, again with long braided ponytails.

6   Royal Stele of Naram-Sin (from Pir-Hussein), (AFC §130).[25] This stele shows
    the king in courtly robes in a ritual pose. In each hand he holds the haft of a
    weapon, probably an axe or a mace; unfortunately, the heads of both weapons
    are missing.

7   Alabaster Victory Stele (from Nasiriyya). The three fragments show a triumph
    scene of yoked prisoners and booty with an armed Akkadian escort.[26] Frag-
    ment A (left, AM §119), shows two Akkadian soldiers bearing booty, includ-
    ing two nicely rendered bronze daggers in leather sheaths and belts. The
    Akkadian solider wears a long kilt with a sash-like fringed robe over his
    shoulder, and a helmet/cap with stripes, either striations on metal, or colored
    bands. The solider has a broad-headed axe thrust in his belt. A comparison
    with the dress of soldiers in combat leads me to suspect that this is the court
    dress of the bodyguard, rather than combat dress. Fragment B (center, AM
    §136), shows a line of naked prisoners with their arms bound behind them at

the elbows, yoked together at the neck with long poles. The middle soldier has a beard and a long braided ponytail similar to the Lullabi soldiers on the Naram-Sin Victory Stele (4; see also 8). Fragment C (right, AFC §131) shows an Akkadian guardsman wearing the same robes and helmet as the soldier in Fragment A. He holds a broad-headed battle-axe which is nicely rendered, showing the details of the blade and how it was riveted to the haft. Above him are the feet of another guardsman with what appears to be the spiked-shape head of a spear pointing downward.

8　Vase. This shows a bound highlander captive, with long beard and braided hair similar to that of the Lullubu (SDA 190–1; AANE §367), and the prisoners in 4 and 7.

9　Cast bronze bust of Sargon or Naram-Sin. Technically not a piece of martial art, this is however the most striking example of royal iconography, and shows details of how the hair of the king, and possibly other warriors, was braided and bound for combat.[27]

Other sources of martial art

Akkadian period weapons included the mace, dagger, bow, javelin, narrow-headed axe, broad axe, spear, and pike, all of which are depicted on contemporary cylinder seals; several have surviving archaeological examples. Contest scenes depicting grappling with animals or mythical creatures may show ancient wrestling stances (FI §95–101 §703), and presumably Akkadian warriors were trained to fight without weapons. In other hand-to-hand combat the dagger is frequently used (FI §566, §876). A finely rendered and well preserved glyptic scene shows four armed men, one with bow, arrow, and quiver, one with javelin, and two with small narrow-headed axes (AFC §139, §150; FI §641). The two-handed long spear or pike makes a frequent appearance in Akkadian art. In one scene two gods attack a seven-headed monster with longs spear held overhand with both hands (FI §840).

The mace is actually the most frequently represented weapon in Akkadian cylinder seals, but it appears mainly in mythical scenes of combat between heroes, monsters, and gods, where the mace is a primary weapon (FI §445, 516, §779, §849; AFC §143–4, §156–7; AM §113b). Sometimes maces appear in ritual poses, but other times they are used in combat (FI §126), where a broken mace shaft is a symbol of defeat (AFC §156; AM §113b). Some scenes show maces with handles roughly a meter long which would best be wielded with two hands (FI §103–5, §126, §896). One god holds two large maces, one in each hand (FI §896). The widespread presence of the mace in Akkadian glyptic art may be because of iconographic conservatism resulting in representing archaic weapons in mythical scenes, since the mace is rarely seen in actual combat scenes between humans. Thus, these mythic scenes may not tell us about real Akkadian weaponry, but they certainly show the importance of the mace in earlier times.

Mesopotamian archery and the Akkadian composite bow[28]

In 1963 Yigael Yadin, in his magisterial study *The Art of Warfare in Biblical Lands*,[29] argued that two Akkadian stelae depict "the very first representation of the composite bow in the history of ancient weapons". He maintained that the Akkadian composite bow "explains ... [how] the Akkadians were able to conquer and gain dominion over Mesopotamia.... It is indeed no exaggeration to suggest that the invention of the composite bow with its comparatively long range was as revolutionary, in its day, and brought comparable results, as the discovery of gunpowder thousands of years later" (AW 1:47–8). Yadin later included a then newly discovered archery scene from Mari as a third example of what he believed to be the composite bow in Akkadian times (Figure 5c, p. 218).[30] Since Yadin, many scholars have accepted this interpretation.[31] The standard interpretation holds that, during the Akkadian period, the combination of the greater range and power of the composite bow, with the added penetrating power of bronze arrowheads, gave a decisive tactical advantage to Akkadian archers. Thus, the Akkadian conquests were due at least in part to the new technological innovation of the composite bow with bronze-tipped arrows.

In order properly to evaluate Yadin's argument, we need to re-examine the evidence for the development of Mesopotamian archery, some of which has been published since Yadin's book, and some of which Yadin did not consider. The crux of Yadin's argument for the development of the composite bow in the twenty-fourth century is based on an interpretation of three artistic depictions of the bow. As far as I can tell, no one has presented any archaeological or textual evidence for the composite bow before the Middle Bronze period. Yadin's argument, then, rests entirely on the iconographic interpretation of these three pieces of martial art. To properly interpret their significance, these depictions need to be placed in the broader context of Mesopotamian artistic representations of bows and archery.

The bow was known in the Neolithic Near East by at least 6000, and undoubtedly much earlier (EBD). Many figures depicted at Catal Hoyuk {c. 6000} use the bow (CH 171, §54, 61–4; xiii). Likewise Syrian pottery {sixth millennium}[32] and Mesopotamian pottery {c. 4200} have examples of hunter/warriors with bows (AANE §186); these weapons seem to be simple wooden self bows. The bow is also well represented in Pre-Dynastic {3500–3000} Mesopotamian martial art. The Priest-king figure (see pp. 37–39) is shown using the bow for hunting and in a siege. The most famous archery scene is the Uruk lion-hunt,[33] in which the nocks of the bow are clearly recurved. However, this scene is not the most informative. Less well-know are cylinder seals showing the Priest-king hunting bulls using the same type of bow (Figure 5a, p. 218; AFC 23; FI §683), and in target practice (FI §682). In two siege scenes the Priest-king again uses the same bow (AFC 24; FI §743; PAE 68/2), which is also found in a mythological Early Dynastic hunting scene (FI §993). Burials at Susa in Elam from the early third millennium included copper arrowheads (PAE 95). All of these depictions seem to show the same type of bow. It is fairly large proportionally (c. 100 cm), going from above the head to the waist when drawn. It is also clearly recurved at the nocks or tips of the bow. The most pronounced recurvature is found on the Uruk lion-hunt stele, but every example shows some degree of recurvature at the nocks. My suspicion is that the Uruk stele artist was simply exaggerating the size of the nocks because of the difficulty of working in a basalt medium with only copper or stone carving tools.

While some have interpreted this Pre-Dynastic bow as composite (PAE 67), the most decisive argument against a Pre-Dynastic composite bow comes from a Pre-Dynastic cylinder seal showing an arms factory (Figure 5b, p. 218; FI §742). In this scene, five unstrung bows are shown. They are all essentially straight when unstrung, although they show a clear difference in thickness – thicker in the limbs and thinner in the handle and nocks. But each shows a pronounced hook-like recurvature at the nock, very similar to the nocks on the drawn bow of the Uruk lion-hunt stele. The fact that the overall shape of the bow is not recurved in the slightest when unstrung implies that the weapon is probably a self bow with some type of highly recurved nocks for the bow string. Another crucial piece of evidence comes from Uruk, where a stele shows the Priest-king carrying a bow which is not drawn and may be unstrung (PAE 68/3). This bow may exhibit some recurvature of the limbs and also has the curved nocks.

In overall structure, this Pre-Dynastic bow appears quite similar to the late Early Dynastic bow from Mari, which Yadin believes is a composite bow (Figure 5a, p. 218).[34] In the Mari scene the archer seems to be depicted as he begins to draw the bow, which certainly appears to be recurved. This creates a problem: if the Mari bow is definitely composite, as Yadin argues, one would have to argue that the Pre-Dynastic Mesopotamian bow, which seems to have the same basic shape and type of recurvature, should also be composite. This would place the origin of the composite bow in Mesopotamia at around 3400, a thousand years earlier than Yadin suggests. It also ignores the fact that in the bowyer scene mentioned above, the bow has no recurvature when unstrung (FI §742). If the bow in Pre-Dynastic art is not composite, there is no reason to believe the Mari bow is either.

Archery does not appear frequently in either the art or texts of the Early Dynastic period. This has led Yadin to conclude that "the bow ... was not used by the Sumerian army" (AW 1:47). There are, however, several examples of its use. Two cylinder seal from Early Dynastic Susa show the use of a bow (FI §758, §933; ME 110), but these are from Elam. The Early Dynastic archery scene from Mari also shows archery, but this is from Syria. None the less, although there were significant cultural differences between Mari and Sumer, there were also many parallels in military equipment; a martial scene from Mari shows the use of the bow (AFC §99). In textual evidence, an inscription of king Eanatum of Lagash {2455–2425} claims that "a person shot an arrow at Eanatum. He was shot through by the arrow and had difficulty moving" (PI 34), indicating the use of archery on the battlefield among the Sumerians. The infantry on the Stele of the Vultures are protected by large body-length rectangular shields (FA 82; AM §66–9), which makes sense as a defense against missiles (see p. 55). There is thus limited evidence for the use of the bow among the Early Dynastic Sumerians.

Furthermore, although there is no artistic evidence of the bow among the Sumerians in the Neo-Sumerian period {c. 2200–2000}, there is extensive textual evidence for their use of the bow at that time. In a twenty-second-century myth the god Ninurta uses the bow (HTO 244). Gudea of Lagash {2141–2122} had a bow for a chariot he built (R3/1:96–7). A twenty-first-century text mentions the use of a bow in battle (LD 61), while king Shulgi of Ur {2094–2047} mentions conscripting archers for his army (R3/2:101). Hymns of Shulgi also mention the king shooting a bow in battle (TSH 79), while a quiver is among objects dedicated to the god Ningirsu (R3/1:34). The importance of archery is further emphasized in the seal of "Kalbaba, bowmaker (^{GIS}.ban-dim), servant of [king] Ishbi-Erra [of Isin, {2017–1985}]" (R4:12). The possession of seals was generally associated with the elite of Mesopotamian society; Kalbaba was thus an important man, perhaps the king's personal bowyer. What we actually have in the sources is evidence for the extensive use of the bow in Pre-Dynastic art, limited evidence for the bow in Early Dynastic sources, and extensive evidence again Akkadian and Neo-Sumerian sources. It is impossible to tell if this reflects a change in the importance and practice of archery, or a change in the nature and survival of our sources.

In the 2048 the king of Ebla sent Shulgi of Ur tribute (*gun*) consisting of "500 *tilpānu*-weapons of *sudiānum*-wood and 500 containers (^{GIS}.kab-kul) of the same wood."[35] This text leads us to the complicated problem of the philology of ancient weapon names, an issue with many ambiguities leading to possible confusion. Eichler has argued that the *tilpānu* is a javelin,[36] while Groneberg has made a strong argument that it should be a bow.[37] I believe that the fact that the 500 *tilpānu*-weapons are sent along with 500 "containers" strongly points to the *tilpānu* being a bow, in which case the 500 "containers" would obviously be quivers. Otherwise, of what use are the 500 "containers" for javelins? At any rate, if the *tilpānu* here is in fact a bow, as seems probable, it is said to have been made out of the same *sudiānum*-wood which is used to make the quivers. The most straightforward reading of this evidence is that the *tilpānu*-bow of the twenty-first century is an ordinary self bow made from wood, not a composite bow. It is, of course, possible that the *sudiānum*-wood is used only for the wooden part of a composite bow, or that these bows were self bows, while other weapons were composite bows. Once again, the evidence is inconclusive.

The Akkadian artistic sources provide Yadin with two pieces of evidence that are crucial to his argument: one shows Naram-Sin holding an undrawn strung bow, the other shows an Akkadian warrior drawing a bow. Yadin argues that Naram-Sin's bow "bears the two characteristic features of the composite weapon; it is small – about 90 centimeters from end to end (an estimate based on its relationship to the size of the figure holding it); and its arms tend to recurve near the ends and then become straight" (AW 1:47). In actuality there are a number of other artistic representations of the use of the bow by Akkadians, which serve to muddy the interpretative waters. The two sources discussed by Yadin need to be compared with six others showing an undrawn Akkadian bow, and two others with drawn bows.

We have a number of examples of gods or kings posing in Naram-Sin's "archer stance" from his Victory Stele, showing the Akkadian bow strung but not drawn.[38]

- Naram-Sin's famous victory stele (4 in the list on p. 86; Figure 3, p. 87) shows the conqueror holding a 95-cm bow which recurves and becomes quite straight toward the end. Indeed, about a third of each limb appears straight in this example.[39]
- Often neglected in the study of the Akkadian composite bow is the parallel, but less famous, war monument of Naram-Sin, the rock-cut relief at Darband-i Gawr (5 on p. 87; Figure 5d, p. 218).[40] This source is important because it shows Naram-Sin in precisely the same dramatic stance, holding a bow in the same way. However, at Darband-i Gawr, Naram-Sin's bow does not appear to be a composite bow. Whereas the tips of Naram-Sin's bow are straight and parallel with the string for about one third of the limb on the Victory Stele, at Darband-i Gawr the bow is shorter (70 cm to the stele's 95 cm) and immediately curves away from the string; it is actually more triangular in shape. Now it is, of course, possible that Naram-Sin is depicted using two different types of bows, but it is equally possible that the differences between the bows of the two monuments are based on artistic style rather than technological substance. Assuming Naram-Sin had a powerful and expensive composite bow, why would he use an ordinary self bow in battle, or order a monumental propaganda depiction of himself with the inferior weapon?
- Another soldier on the Naram-Sin victory stele also holds a bow (c. 90 cm). The bottom part of the image of the bow is damaged, but the top part shows that the bow is smaller than Naram-Sin's, and has less recurvature towards the tip; in style it seems midway between Naram-sin's bow on the stele and that on the Darband-i Gawr relief.
- A god holds a somewhat longer bow (102 cm) and arrow; the bow shows very little recurvature towards the tips (FI §761; AM §113a; SDA §237; AFC §139).
- A god holds a rather small, undrawn bow (67 cm) which displays moderate recurvature towards the tips (FI §849).
- A cylinder seal shows an Akkadian archer with an undrawn bow (94 cm) and a quiver with tassel.[41] Here the fine work of the artist shows a moderate recurving of the limbs toward the nocks, but it is less pronounced than in the Naram-Sin stele.
- In the lower right corner of the right fragment of the Victory Stele of Rimush (p. 86) we see the head and top of the bow of an archer (AFC §129; AAM §135). This bow, on the same stele as the drawn bow that Yadin saw as composite, shows no recurvature and no straightening at the end. The slight outline of the bottom of a bow on the other side of this stele in the upper left panel also appears to have no recurvature and no straightening at the nock.

Also, the ends of two other bows on the Rimush stele show no straightening at the nocks.

In summary, these examples show a range in both size and recurvature: 95 cm, strong recurvature (Naram-Sin stele); 90 cm, moderate recurvature; 67 cm, moderate recurvature; 94 cm, moderate recurvature; 102 cm, little recurvature. From this evidence we note that Naram-Sin's weapon on his victory stele is of average length, but is by far the most recurved of all these weapons. Yadin's deduction that the Akkadians used the composite bow is thus a generalization from an atypical example.

We also have three depictions from the Akkadian period of a drawn bow.

- Yadin's example comes from Akkadian monumental martial art (Figure 5e, p. 219).[42] Yadin believes that the bow's "arms still curve outward slightly" at full extension (AW 1:47; AFC §129), but if so, it is quite slight. In my view, the shape of this flexed bow is much closer to that of a self bow than the classic composite bow (EBD 78–9); it is certainly less recurved than the next example.
- A god draws a bow which remains quite recurved in form (FI §876).
- An archer shooting a bow; the image is unclear, but there is not much apparent recurvature (FI §685).

Of these latter three examples, I would classify one drawn bow as recurved, and two as not recurved. This leaves the evidence for the Akkadian recurved (and hence composite) bow ambiguous. It either means that the Akkadians used both the composite bow and the regular self bow, or that the Akkadian artists were not overly concerned with accurately representing the weapons they saw. None the less, when recurvature on Akkadian bows is seen, it is a distinctive enough feature that it seems unlikely that it would have appeared as an arbitrary artistic aberration. If the composite bow was known to the Akkadians, it was certainly not universally used by Akkadian archers; some, probably most, would have continued to use self bows.

Thus I would suggest that, while the existence of the composite bow among the Akkadians is possible, it is still uncertain. More to the point, however, the military impact of the Akkadian composite bow, if it existed, is also unclear. The mere technological capacity to make composite bows would not necessarily translate into a tactical revolution on the battlefield. What percentage of all Akkadian troops used the bow? What proportion of these had composite bows (if any) instead of self bows? How many bronze (as opposed to copper or flint) arrowheads were available? One Neo-Sumerian text mentions that the king himself shot "flint-tipped arrows" (HTO 330). If the king is still using flint arrowheads, how widespread could bronze arrowheads be? How many arrows could each archer realistically shoot in a battle or siege? There is no hard evidence to answer any of these questions. If the composite bow existed in Akkadian times I would suggest that it was a rare and expensive weapon used by kings and other elites. As discussed elsewhere (p. 255), the expense of making bronze (as opposed to copper or flint) arrowheads would probably limit the overall tactical impact of the Akkadian composite bow. A few dozen archers in an army of several thousand would not be tactically decisive.

Old Babylonian martial art also has a few representations of the bow, but the surviving textual and artistic evidence does not give a great importance to the weapon. One scene shows a god holding a bow in the Naram-Sin archer stance; it is a short weapon with little or no recurvature (FI §160, §686). A scene from Ebla shows an archer hunting with a quiver and what appears to be a short self bow (AANE §451; SDA 292). During the Middle Bronze period, the god Ashur gives the king of Assyria a bow at his investiture, indicating its continued importance as a royal ceremonial weapon (A1:21). King Anubanini of Lullubi (modern Luristan) is also depicted in the Naram-Sin pose, trampling a fallen enemy. In one hand he holds an axe, and in the other a bow and arrow; the bow itself is not recurved, but has slightly recurved tips where the string is attached (PAE 319; ME 20). In the Old Babylonian version of the *Epic of Gilgamesh*, the hero arms himself with dagger, axe, and "his quiver with the bow from Anshan" in south-west Iran (EG 113). In the Beni Hasan murals in Egypt, Canaanite warriors have bows similar to those of the Egyptians – though this may be the artistic convention of an Egyptian artist who is told to draw a Canaanite with a bow, and draws the Canaanite with an Egyptian bow, the only weapon the artist knows (AW 1:166–7). The textual evidence for the bow from Mari, again indicating its relative unimportance, is discussed on pages 254–5.

If, as Yadin argues, the composite bow existed in Mesopotamia in the twenty-fourth century with revolutionary military impact, the following questions become difficult to answer. Why does the bow seem to decline in importance in later evidence from Mesopotamia and Syria? Assuming the composite bow made archery more effective, one would expect its use to increase, not decline, relative to the Akkadian period. Why did the composite bow not spread to Canaan and Egypt by the Middle Bronze Age, if it had already existed in Mesopotamia for several centuries? Most other Syrian military technologies – fortifications, axes, chariots – spread quite rapidly to Canaan. Assuming the Beni Hasan murals are accurate in showing the Canaanites using Egyptian-style bows, why are the Canaanites not using the superior composite bow if the technology had been known to their Syrian neighbors for centuries? Why are arrowheads so sparsely attested in martial tombs with other weapons burials? Why does archery appear to play a relatively minor role in warfare in the Mari archives? Why are charioteers not shown using a bow in martial art before the eighteenth century (see Chapter Five)? Why do we not see the rapid spread of body armor and shields from the late third millennium for protection from the new, more powerful composite bow?

I would argue that the most probable interpretation of the evidence is that the composite bow – or at least an efficient version that could be produced in reasonable quantities – developed only in the nineteenth or eighteenth century. The dramatic military impact one would expect from the development of a new weapon like the composite bow, with twice the range and penetrating power of the self bow (EBD), only begins to be seen in the eighteenth century. We also find textual evidence for the increasing weight of bronze arrowheads which could have been shot from the more powerful bows (ARM 18.5; MK 63; see pp. 254–5). During the seventeenth century we see marked evidence of the use of the bow from chariots, and the weapon is introduced into Egypt probably in the seventeenth century by the Hyksos (see Chapter Eighteen). Increased use of body armor and shields is found in the seventeenth century and throughout the Late Bronze Age, but is not found in the Akkadian and Old Babylonian periods. If the Akkadians did have the composite bow, it was either a less efficient version of the weapon, or it was so difficult and expensive to make that only the elites could afford it, and therefore its tactical importance before the late Middle Bronze Age was limited.

Akkadian and Neo-Sumerian military systems[43]

Only a partial understanding of the Akkadian and Neo-Sumerian military systems can be obtained from fragmentary bits and pieces of information. Sumerian city-states apparently organized their population into "clans", each with a different name and emblem, who were called up in labor corvees for construction of canals, dikes, and temples (R3/1:78). Presumably, a similar organization existed for recruiting levees for warfare, which were treated administratively as a type of labor duty to the state. Each band of warriors served within a kinship or socially related group. Each Sumerian family owed military service to the state. Shulgi named one of his years "the year the citizens of Ur were conscripted as spearmen". He also describes his "conscription with the bow and arrow; nobody evaded it – the levy being one man per family" (R3/2:101). These levees were recruited on an ad hoc basis for a specific war, with soldiers returning to their homes after the campaign (MAS 27). As a special privilege, the military and labor conscription required of a city could be cancelled. For example, Ishme-Dagan of Isin {1953–1935} "relieved the citizens of Nippur from military service … and made the nation content" (R4:32–4, 89).

Sargon is sometimes credited with having created the first-known standing army in the world. His claim that "5400 men daily eat in the presence of Sargon" (R2:29, 31), however, refers not just to soldiers, but to priests, scribes or other court functionaries see (see p. 75). None the less, a substantial number of the 5400 were probably soldiers. On the other hand, it is very likely that earlier rulers also had professional guards. Texts of Amarsin mention the elite *gardu*, translated as "royal body guard" (R3/2:239), who were probably professional troops. A seal from the reign of Sumu-El of Lagash mentions an "Iemsium, lieutenant of the elite soldiers (*ugula aga.us.sag.ga*)" (R4:136), perhaps another professional regiment. There is a group know as the *aga-ush* – "followers of the crown" – who seem to be professional full-time soldiers as opposed to levees (MAS 27). Soldiers are sometimes described as receiving land in return for military service.[44]

The Akkadians and Neo-Sumerians had a sophisticated bureaucracy over all aspects of the state, including the military (EM). City governors (*ensi*) seemed to have had responsibility for military recruitment and supplies in their jurisdiction (MAS 26–7). Within the homeland, cities were expected to provide supplies and accommodation for armies passing through their province. Numerous Sumerian and Akkadian economic texts describe the requisitioning of food and equipment for government use, although it is not clear if this is for labor gangs or soldiers (MAS 26). From the Mesopotamian perspective, there was probably no distinction.

Surviving archives describing the disbursement of supplies and equipment to soldiers demonstrate that, at least by the Akkadian period, Mesopotamians had developed a well organized commissary system which kept detailed records of the collection and distribution of supplies.[45] The archive recorded "the number of workers [or soldiers] and how long they worked on the one hand, and the number of times they had been fed on the other" (USP 25). They dealt with the collection, storage and distribution of grain, foodstuffs, personnel, livestock (including donkeys), textiles, and equipment, including weapons (USP 38). A typical record reads:

> 580 shu-loaves [of bread,] 29 jars of 30/30 beer did the chief of the work troops receive. 20 loaves, 1 pot of 30/30 beer to the soldier of Adda. The bread and beer are a disbursement. Year 5, month 5, day 27.

This extensive and complex bureaucracy facilitated the creation of the Akkadian army and the management of the lands conquered by the armies.

The capture of booty was a major purpose of war. Several "booty tablets" (*namrak*) have survived from the Neo-Sumerian period, giving lists of booty taken on a campaign and its disbursement (R3/2:236). A portion of the booty was generally donated to the temples of the gods, for practical use by the priests. One text mentions, for example, the "booty dedicated to the god Shara [taken as plunder] from the city of Sharithum" (R3/2:238). Since the gods were the most important allies of the king, and granted him victory, they deserved their share of the plunder just as any other allied king would, even though this portion of the plunder was not of immediate practical military use. Part of the booty was directly distributed to soldiers, both for food while on campaign, and as rewards after battle (R3/2:108, 110). Great victory feasts were held for the "heroes" of the campaign, in which captured animals were roasted (R3/2:109, 239). Finally, a portion of the booty went to the king, some of which would eventually be recycled to fund the army. The logistical and economic costs of maintaining this standing army may have caused Sargon to create the world's first predatory army – a force which is too large to be maintained by the economic resources of the kingdom, and must perforce campaign every year to provide plunder for its own upkeep (war must feed war). A number of the texts focus on the plunder and captives taken from conquered regions, indicating these important economic aspects of Akkadian warfare (R2:23–4, 31, 60–7).

The commander-in-chief of the Akkadian and Sumerian army was the king, who regularly campaigned in person. However, the king was served by a number of different types of military officers, although the specifics about their differences and functions are sometimes obscure. The Sumerian epic *Gilgamesh and Agga* has a section where Gilgamesh lists five military offices in order of ascending rank (EOG 148):

ugula	lieutenant (overseer)
nubanda	captain
ensi	governor (or perhaps colonel in a military sense)
shagina	general
shagina erin	"general of the army", or perhaps field marshal

Shagina (Sumerian GIR.NITA, roughly "general") was probably the highest military office, and occurs repeatedly in inscriptions (R3/2:349, 353). Successful generals were honored in royal inscriptions (R2:32). Generals also appear as military governors of conquered cities; for Mari we have a list of seven generals who governed the city for the Akkadians (R2:231–7; R3/2:143), with several others governing Elam (R2:302–8). Under Naram-Sin a warrior named Lugal-uru-si was "general of the land of Sumer and Akkad" (R2:103), the supreme army commander under the king, and perhaps the same as the *shagina erin*. As in many ancient societies, generals often held many additional government and religious offices – Caesar, for example, served as a priest as Pontifex Maximus. Under king Shusin, Irnanna served simultaneously as governor, a *sanga* priest of the god Enki, and the GIR.NITA of several different provinces (R3/2:323–4). In addition to his military duties, general Babati served as royal steward, accountant, canal inspector, and *sanga* priest (R3/2:341–2). Likewise, city governors (*ensi*) are often described as participating in campaigns, and seem to have ranked immediately under the general.

The second most frequently mentioned military office is *nubanda*, roughly equivalent to captain (R2:93; R3/2:239). They were clearly of lower rank and more numerous than the generals. We can get a sense of the relative status, rank, and numbers of Akkadian period officers by some of Naram-Sin's prisoner lists. He claims during one of his extended campaigns to have captured six *shagina* (generals), seventeen *ensi* (city governors), 78 *rabi'anu* (nomad "chiefs"), and 2000 *nubanda* (captains) (R2:92–3). At the battle of Tiwa, Naram-Sin captured the GIR.NITA (general) of Kish, along with four of his *nubanda* (captains) (R2:105–6). *Nubandas* were often assigned specific types of duties; under Shusin we hear of "Lugalmagure, captain of the watch" (*nubanda ennuga*) serving as governor of Ur (R3/2:326, 418).

The Akkadian army was also organized into military units, though these seem to have been rather flexible in size. The basic term for a military unit was *kiseri*, or regiment; Sargon is said to have mustered nine *kiseri* against Uruk (R2:16). Several records describe companies of roughly 200 men commanded by a *nubanda* (MAS 26 n11). The professional nature of the Akkadian army allowed it to campaign at rapid speeds; a Naram-Sin inscription describes a forced march in which the

Akkadian army moved at over twice the normal rate of march for several days running (R2:125). Soldiers on campaign are described as eating "bread [baked] on coals" and "drinking water from skins" (LKA 179). Some type of camp fortifications on campaign seem to be implied when Naram-Sin "made firm the foundations of the army camps" (R2:141).

Manishtushu (R2:75–6), Naram-Sin (R2:97, 117) and Shar-kalli-shari (R2:192) all claim to have undertaken maritime expeditions in the Persian Gulf. Conquest of the coast of the Persian Gulf allowed Akkadians to control much of the maritime trade of the region, with merchants arriving in Akkad from Meluhha (the Indus valley), Magan (Oman), and Dilmun (Bahrain) (R2:28–30). The captain of a boat is also called a *nubanda* (R3/1:41), like his land-based counterparts. The "chief sea-captain", or admiral, is called *nam-garash* (R3/247–8); this inscription has specific reference to trading activities, but presumably this officer would be involved in any naval military affairs as well.

Weapons in the Akkadian and Sumerian arsenals included lance, spear, javelin, narrow-headed axe, broad battle-axe (or scimitar-axe), mace, dagger, and bow. Weapons were kept in a special arsenal, sometimes inside a temple complex, which were protected by images of divine beings. King Gudea {2141–2122} gave a description of one of these arsenals: "in the inner [arsenal] where the weapons hang, [at] its Battle Gate, [Gudea] posted the warriors 'deer-of-six-heads' and 'Mount Sinjar' " (R3/1:85) – the latter apparently being images of mythical warrior demons slain by Ningirsu.[46]

A ritual blessing given by Imdugud, a mythical dragon-like creature, to the epic hero Lugalbanda, describes the arms of a Sumerian king:

> May your flint-tipped arrow hit its man . . .
> May it be sharp like the point of an axe . . .
> May [the god] Ninurta, Enlil's son,
> Cover your crown with the helmet, "Lion of Battle" . . .
> When you have wielded the net in the mountain,
> May the net not let loose [your enemies]. (HTO 330–1)

The throwing net mentioned here was used to entangle enemies (HTO 236), perhaps as depicted on the Stele of the Vultures (AM §66–9, see Figure 1, p. 55).

A description of a ritual inspection tour by Gudea of Lagash included a catalog of some of the weapons at the temple arsenal at Lagash:

> Gudea brings to [the god] Ningirsu . . . [the officer] Shul-shaga . . . holding the seven-spiked mace, and opening the *Ankar*, the Battle-Gate [to the arsenal], that the
>
> > dagger blades [*eme-gir*]
> > the *mitu* ["dead-man"] mace,
> > the "floodstorm" weapon

> the "bitter one" [*khurratum*]
> and all the weapons of war;

> might all exactly hit their targets, that he might flood all the lands of [the god] Enlil's enemies. Gudea brings along with himself [for the inspection] to [the temple of] Ningirsu the mighty weapon "Slaughterer of a Myriad", which subdues all lands in battle, [and] the officer of [the temple] Eninnu, hawk of the rebel land, [and] his general Lugalkurdub.[47]

This text apparently refers to a special blessing for weapons before battle. Weapons were often viewed as magical objects, as gifts from the gods imbued with divine power which was the real source of victory (R2:133). Many of these special ceremonial weapons were made of very precious and rare materials and given evocative names such as "Mace-unbearable-for-the-regions", "Three-headed-lion-mace", and "slaughterer-of-a-myriad" (R3/1:34). Sargon claimed that "the god Ilaba, mighty one of the gods – the god Enlil gave to [me] his weapons". Sargon ascribes his victory over Uruk to the power of the "mace of the god Ilaba"; perhaps something similar to a mace he dedicated to the gods as a victory trophy (R2:13, 17–18). Bur-Sin of Isin donated a "three-headed gold mace with heads of lapis-lazuli as a great emblem for Ninurta" (IYN 30). Sargon's grandson Naram-Sin wielded this same mace (or another of the same name) in battle (R2:94). At his coronation Naram-Sin was given "a weapon of heaven from the temple of the god Enlil" (R2:85), as well as divine weapons of the gods Dagan and Nergal (R2:133), and Ishtar (LKA 195, 199); Shu-sin received the *a'ankara* weapon from Ninlil (E3/2:302, 307; cf. R4:391). The *shibirru* weapon – sometimes called a "scimitar" – was apparently a special weapon of kingship (LKA 199–200). What distinguished a divine weapon from an ordinary one is unclear. They may have been ancestral weapons preserved in the temples, or weapons that were manufactured with a special ritual and consecration by the priests. Meteoric iron was worked by the Akkadians (R2:68); such a mace could perhaps have been described as coming "from heaven". These weapons of the gods are said to have the power to make the enemy panic in battle (R3/1:93).

Akkadian martial ideology

The god Enlil, whose major temple was E-kur ("mountain house") at Nippur, was the particular focus of Akkadian martial devotion. Sargon became ruler by the "verdict" of Enlil, and ruled as his "governor" (R2:10, 13, 19, 34, 133). Enlil called Manishtusu "by name", granting him the "scepter of kingship" (R2:77). Enlil granted Sargon "surpassing intelligence", thereby insuring that Sargon had "no rival" in the world (R2:34, 11, 14, 20, 29, 31, 45).

The kings ruled as they were "instructed" by the gods, presumably through oracles and divination. Divination often preceded battle. Enlil's instructions included the command to "show mercy to no one", which the Akkadian rulers followed religiously (R2:32, 34, 56, 192–3): "Naram-Sin, the mighty, by the authority of the god Enlil, showed mercy to no one in those battles" (R2:138). The gods also "go before" or "open the way" for the king in battle, granting victory (R2:50, 133; LKA 181).

The link between Akkadian kings and the gods was strengthened and emphasized under Naram-sin, who was no longer merely the representative of the gods, but the "spouse of the goddess Ishtar-Annumitum" (R2:88). When he defeated a rebellion of "the four quarters" (i.e. the entire world), thereby saving the city of Akkad from destruction, Naram-Sin was proclaimed a god, and a temple was dedicated to him (R2:113–14). Thereafter, his name was always written with a divine determinative – a linguistic marker indicating the name of a god. His son Shar-kalli-shari also claimed divinity in one of his inscriptions (R2:206).

Shar-kalli-shari {2217–2192}, and the decline of the Akkadians[48]

Naram-Sin's son and successor, Shar-kalli-shari ("king of all kings") was the last of the great Akkadian rulers, but was unable to retain power over the vast empire his father had controlled by brutal repression. As with all Akkadian kings, the exact chronology of his reign is uncertain. He is noted as a great temple builder, who undertook resource gathering expeditions to Syria and Lebanon (R2:185–91, 193); he may have been more interested in religious and cultural pursuits than in warfare. Be that as it may, at some point during his reign a major rebellion broke out, which is described in terms similar to those used by Naram-Sin:

> When the four quarters together revolted against him [Shar-kalli-shari], from beyond the Lower Sea as far as the Upper Sea, he smote the people and all the Mountain Lands for the god Enlil and brought their kings in fetters before the god Enlil. Shar-kalli-shari, the mighty, by the authority of the god Enlil, showed mercy to no one in those battles. (R2:192–3)

Although he claims to have suppressed this rebellion, it is clear that his victory was tenuous. Whereas his ancestors consistently called themselves "king of the four quarters [of the world]", Shar-kalli-shari is satisfied with "King of Agade", as were his feeble successors.

Shar-kalli-shari's inscriptions are far fewer and less instructive than those of Sargon and Naram-Sin, but a basic picture begins to emerge of an empire in crisis. In his "year names" he mentions three campaigns, claiming victories in all. The Amorites were defeated in their mountain stronghold at Bashar (R2:183), where Naram-Sin had fought them earlier. Shar-kalli-shari claims to have defeated the Elamites at the battle of Akshak, near modern Baghdad (R2:183; PAE 108). Significantly, rather than campaigning into the heart of Elam, Shar-kalli-shari fought the Elamites as they were invading the Tigris valley. Finally, the Gutian highlanders from the Zagros mountains under their ruler Sharlak were defeated (R2:183), but not destroyed. In a few years Sharlak reappears as Sharlagab (KS 330), a Gutian warlord ruling in Mesopotamia (see pp. 102–4).

Thus Shar-kalli-shari's inscriptions reveal the empire surrounded by powerful and militant enemies: the Amorites to the north-west; the Gutians to the east, and the Elamites to the south-east. These problems were further complicated by the internal revolt of recalcitrant city-states. Although royal defeats are never mentioned in the Akkadian annals, they were obviously occurring with increasing frequency, and would culminate with the collapse of the Akkadian state shortly after Shar-kalli-shari's death. The Gutian invasion and collapse of Akkad will be discussed in the next chapter.

CHAPTER FOUR

The Neo-Sumerian period {2190–2004}

The Neo-Sumerian period is characterized by the cultural and political revival of Sumerian peoples after a century-and-a-half of domination by Semitic Akkadians. The collapse of the Akkadian empire was in part caused by, and at the same time facilitated, the migration of highlander warlords known as Gutians into Mesopotamia. For over half a century these foreign warlords dominated local peoples, but were never accepted by them as legitimate leaders. Sumerian kings first achieved local independence, and then ousted the foreign warlords, creating the culturally dynamic Third Dynasty of Ur. The Neo-Sumerian age lasted less than a century-and-a-half, however, ending with a second wave of outsiders invading Mesopotamia. This time, Semitic Amorite warlords from Syria were successful in integrating themselves into Mesopotamian civilization, creating a new political and military order that transitioned into the Middle Bronze Age.[1]

Gutian warlords {c. 2190–2115}[2]

At the death of Shar-kalli-shari the military crisis of Akkad was exacerbated by an apparent civil war in which four kings ruled in only three years {2192–2190}. There are vague allusions in the inscriptions to inter-city warfare during this period (R2:209–18), which the Sumerian King-list succinctly summarizes: "Who was king? Who was not king? Igigi, the king; Nanum, the king; Imi, the king; Elulu, the king – the four of them were kings but reigned only three years." (KS 330). Although Dudu {2189–2169} finally emerged as ruler of Akkad, by that time his domain had been reduced to one city-state among many in central Mesopotamia.

During this period of chaotic anarchy, Gutian highlanders emerge as a major military power in Mesopotamia. Earlier vague allusions to Gutians appear in Akkadian texts, where they are described as highlanders of the Zagros Mountains to the east of Akkad (ME 24–7), but their first major reference is to the defeat of the Gutian king Sharlak by Shar-kalli-shari, mentioned on pp. 100–1 (R2:183). Thereafter, Gutian warbands appear in Mesopotamia, first as devastating raiders,[3] and eventually as conquerors. The specific pattern of Gutian conquest is unclear. From the military perspective, the fall of Akkad was characterized by both internal revolts and outside invasion. The city-states of Sumer, Elam, and northern Mesopotamia all became independent, while outsiders simultaneously invaded Mesopotamia. Mountain highlanders from many surrounding regions seem to have participated in his migration, including the Hurrians (from the northern mountains), Lullubi (neighbors of the Gutians in the Zagros mountains), Elamites from the south of Zagros, Amorites from the Jebel Bishri region of Syria, and perhaps the obscure Umman-Manda.[4] Archaeological data confirms the devastation of a number of cities in northern Mesopotamia during this period (RA3:710). Later epic literature describes, with considerable hyperbole, the panic and devastation of these invasions.[5] The Akkadian armies are defeated, the land devastated, cities are destroyed, and the rites of the gods blasphemed (LKA 271–7); all of Mesopotamia is overrun (LKA 315).

The most important invaders were the Gutians, described as fierce and lawless barbarians from the mountains. Some of the Gutian warlords managed to establish themselves as kings over some of the city-states of Mesopotamia. The Sumerian King-list mentions twenty-one Gutian rulers reigning for a period of about 90 years, with each king ruling for only a few years (KS 330); an alternative possibility is that many of these Gutian kings were contemporaries. They should not be seen, however, as forming a coherent dynasty ruling all of Mesopotamia. It is more likely they were loosely allied warlords who ruled as a foreign military aristocracy over a number of city-states. Perhaps it is best to view them as broadly similar to the Germanic kingdoms following the fall of Rome.

The Sumerians viewed this period as one of chaos and devastation:

> The Gutians [are] the fanged serpent of the mountain, who acted with violence against the gods, who carried off the kingship of the land of Sumer to the mountain land, who filled the land of Sumer with wickedness, who took away the wife from the one who had a wife, who took away the child from the one who had a child, who put wickedness and evil in the land of Sumer. (R2:284)

Military sources for this period range from vague to non-existent. Only the campaigns of the Gutian king Erridu-pizir have substantial documentation. An inscription describing the revolt of one of his rebellious vassals, the king of Madga, is perhaps reflective of the anarchy of the age:

> Erridu-pizir, the mighty, king of Gutium and the four quarters, hastened [to confront] him [the rebellious king of Madga]. [Since the Gutian ruler of Madga] feared [Erridu-pizar] he retreated [into his own original] mountain [homeland], and [Erridu-pizir] hunted him down, captured him, led him away [captive, and executed] him. Erridu-pizir, the mighty, king of Gutium and the four quarters took [him] away by force through the gate of the god of Gutium, struck him, and killed him, the king [of Madga]. (R2:221–2)

Here we see a Gutian warlord ruling a city in Mesopotamia as the vassal of another Gutian. When a conflict arises between the two, the vassal flees back to his original mountain homeland, hoping vainly to escape the wrath of his lord.

Erridu-pizir's greatest victory was a campaign against the rival highlander Lullubi tribe in the Zagros. Erridu-pizir provides an itinerary for his campaign into the mountains, forcing mountain passes and capturing the enemy commanders and mountain strongholds:

> KA-Nisba, king of Simurrum, instigated the people of Simurrum and Lullubi [highlanders] to revolt. Amnili, general of [the enemy Lullubi] ... made the land [rebel] ... Erridu-pizir, the mighty, king of Gutium and of the four quarters hastened [to confront] him. He proceeded [through] the peaks of Mount Nisba. In six days he conquered the pass at Mount Hamemepir ... entered its pass. Erridu-pizir, the mighty, pursued him [Amnili] and conquered the pass at Mount Nuhpir. Further, he struck down Amnili, the [Lullubi] ... on its summit ... In a single day he ... conquered the pass of Urbillum at Mount Mumum. Further, he captured Nirishuha. (R2:226–7)

Gutian domination in Mesopotamian was not universal. Many Sumerian cities, like Ur, Uruk, Umma, Lagash, and Mari, achieved some degree of independence during this period. Their few inscriptions, however, provide little concrete military information. From these independent Sumerian city-states arose a nationalistic anti-Gutian movement aimed at ousting the hated invaders. The most successful leader of this movement was Utuhegal of Uruk {2117–2111}, who is credited with driving out the Gutians and inaugurating the Neo-Sumerian period (see pp. 105–7).

Gudea, Second Dynasty of Lagash {2155–2122}[6]

While the Gutians dominated much of Sumer, the city of Lagash remained independent under the kings of its Second Dynasty. Although this period is renowned as a cultural golden age under king Gudea {2141–2122}, the Second Dynasty of Lagash has not produced many military inscriptions, leaving our understanding of warfare during this period rather vague. The corpus of inscriptions from Lagash focuses instead on temple building and other ritual activities. When compared to his lovingly detailed description of temple building, Gudea's most important campaign is laconically described: "Gudea defeated the cities of Anshan and Elam and brought the booty there from to Ningirsu in his Eninnu [temple]" (R3/1:35). Indeed, the allusion to the campaign only occurs in the context of describing the materials gathered to build his beloved temples.

From the inscriptions of Lagash, it would seem that there was relative peace during the reign of Gudea. Gudea praises the god Ningirsu, who "opened for him all the roads leading from the Upper to the Lower Sea" (R3/1:33), which presumably meant for trade rather than for warfare. His inscriptions describe bringing building materials, precious metals and jewels from Lebanon, Elam, the Persian Gulf, Magan (Oman), and the Meluhha (Indus valley) (R3/1:33–4, 78). None of Gudea's numerous splendid statues depicts the king in any martial context (SDA

202–17). This is generally true of the next several centuries of Mesopotamian art; for whatever reason, martial themes are seldom depicted (SDA 196–251);[7] martial art essentially disappears during the Neo-Sumerian period.

Unlike the first dynasty, described in Chapter Two, the second dynasty of Lagash was not an expansionist state, but apparently had a sufficiently strong military to insure its own survival. Several of the year-names are associated with the construction of ritual divine weapons for dedications at temples. These include "the year the wooden [shaft] of the [divine weapon of Ningirsu] 'Mow-down-a-myriad' was made"; "[the war-god] Ningirsu's mace with fifty heads was fashioned" (R3/1:27, 33, 75). But even these are, strictly speaking, ritual rather than military activities. It remained for the warlike king Utuhegal of Uruk finally to drive the hated Gutians from Sumer.

Puzur-Inshushinak (Kutik-Inshushinak) and the Elamites {c. 2120–1990}[8]

The collapse of Akkadian power allowed local nobles in Elam to gain independence for the first time in a century, recreating their Elamite kingdom based at Susa. Puzur-Inshushinak, who began as an Akkadian vassal viceroy in Elam, eventually asserted his independence, taking the title "mighty king of Awan [Elam]" by the end of his reign. His main martial inscription describes his rise to power in Elam, capturing two rival kings "Kimash and Hurtum" and "crushing under his feet in one day 81 towns and regions". The king of Shimashki, a land east of Elam, "grabbed his feet", begging for mercy, and was allowed to live as a vassal of Puzur-Inshushinak (PAE 123). Claiming imperial titles from the crumbling Akkadians, Puzur-Inshushinak proclaimed that "[the god] Inshushinak looked graciously upon him and gave him the four quarters of the earth" (C1/2:653).

Predominant in Elam, Puzur-Inshushinak turned his attention to Mesopotamia. A text from Ur from the reign of Urnammu lists several regions of central Mesopotamia as being under the rule of Puzur-Inshushinak, including Eshnunna and Akkad itself. This brought Puzur-Inshushinak into conflict with the rising power of Urnammu of Ur (see pp. 108–9). Urnammu claims he "liberated Akshak, Marad, Girkal, Kazallu, and their settlements, and for Usarum, whatever [territories] were under the subjugation of [Puzur-Inshushinak] of Anshan" (CS 2:409a; PAE 124–5). Elamite incursions into Mesopotamia were thus temporarily forestalled, but a century later they would return to sack Ur itself (see p. 120).

Utuhegal of Uruk {2117–2111}[9]

The overthrow of the Gutian warlords occurred in the reign of Utuhegal, king of Uruk. Seizing the opportunity afforded by the uncertainty surrounding the ascension of a new Gutian monarch named Tirigan, Utuhegal rebelled against his

Gutian overlord. He left a vivid inscription of his victory over the Gutians which contains one of the most detailed military narratives of the third millennium, illustrating one of the fundamental principles of ancient Near Eastern warfare: that the decisions of the gods, even if inscrutable, control the course of history.

> The god Enlil, lord of the foreign lands, commissioned Utuhegal, the mighty man, king of Uruk, king of the four quarters, the king whose utterance cannot be countermanded, to destroy [the Gutian] name. Thereupon Utuhegal went to the [war] goddess Inanna, his lady, and prayed to her, saying: "My lady, lioness of battle, who butts the foreign lands, the god Enlil has commissioned me to bring back the kingship of the land of Sumer. May you be my ally."
>
> The enemy [Gutian] hordes had trampled everything. Tirigan, the king of Gutium, had [seized kingship in Sumer] ... but no [Sumerian lord] set out against him [in battle]. He had seized both banks of the Tigris River. In the south, in Sumer, he had blocked water from the fields. In the north, he had closed off the roads and caused tall grass to grow up along the roads of the land.

The foundation of Utuhegal's success was that the god Enlil chose him to "destroy [the Gutian] name". What this meant in practical terms is uncertain, but it likely has reference to oracles presented by the prophets of Uruk calling upon Utuhegal to overthrow the Gutians. Utuhegal, however, does not act alone.

> Utuhegal, the mighty man, went forth from Uruk and set up [a war banner?] ... in the temple of the god Ishkur [in Uruk]. He called out to the citizens of his city [Uruk], saying: "The god Enlil has given Gutium to me. My lady, the goddess Inanna, is my ally" ... Utuhegal made the citizens of Uruk and Kullab [a suburb of Uruk] happy. His city followed him [in the decision to go to war] as if they were just one person.

Having received oracles of victory from the gods Enlil and Inanna, Utuhegal summons a city council at the plaza before the temple of Ishkur. He announces the oracles and he rallies the citizens of Uruk to support his rebellion against the Gutians. This incident emphasizes that Sumerian kings had to rely on the support of their citizens for war, and that oracles could sway public opinion in these matters one way or another. With the support of the city, Utuhegal launches his campaign.

> Utuhegal arranged in correct array his select elite troops. After Utuhegal departed from the temple of the god Ishkur [in Uruk], on the fourth day he set up [camp] in the city of Nagsu on the Iturungal canal. On the fifth day he set up [camp] in the shrine Ilitappe. He captured Ur-Ninazu and Nabi-Enlil, generals whom [Tirigan, king of the Gutians] had sent as envoys to the land of

Sumer, and put handcuffs on them. After he departed from the shrine Ili-tappe, on the sixth day he set up [camp] at Karkar. He proceeded to the god Ishkur and prayed to him, saying: "O god Ishkur! The god Enlil has given me his weapon. May you be my ally."

The reference to "select elite troops" is important, demonstrating a ranking of the quality and value of soldiers. Utuhegal's itinerary is our most detailed description of a Sumerian army on the march. He emphasizes his daily piety, repeatedly calling on the gods for assistance, attempting to act in accordance with the will of the gods in battle. A rough estimate of a day's march for a Sumerian army can be determined from Utuhegal's itinerary. The next passage notes that battle took place "upstream from Adab" some fifty miles north of Uruk, which was reached after a six-day march, thus averaging about eight to nine miles a day. Utuhegal then describes the day of battle.

> In the middle of that night [Utuhegal] got up, and at daybreak proceeded to a point upstream from Adab. . . . In that place, against the Gutians, he laid a trap and led his troops against them. Utuhegal, the mighty man, defeated their generals. Then Tirigan, king of Gutium, fled alone on foot to Dabrum. . . . Since the citizens of Dabrum realized that Utuhegal was the king to whom the god Enlil had granted power, they did not let Tirigan go. The envoys of Utuhegal captured Tirigan along with his wife and children at Dabrum. They put handcuffs and a blindfold on him. Utuhegal made him lie at the feet of the god Utu and placed his foot on his neck. [Thus Utuhegal] removed [the Gutians and] . . . brought back the kingship of the land of Sumer. (R2:284–7)

Utuhegal's use of a stratagem to trick the Gutian should remind us that, although relying on the will of the gods for victory, the Sumerians none the less also fought wars in the real world of weapons, supplies, and tactics. Even if Enlil had promised victory, Utuhegal still used a stratagem. This auspicious victory over Tirigan was remembered in later years in books of divination (C1/2:462). The mention that Tirigan "fled [the battle] alone on foot" undoubtedly has reference to the standard use of war-carts in battle at this time.

Utuhegal's victory, although decisive, was apparently not complete. Most of southern Mesopotamia rallied to his support, but the full extent of his domain is not certain. He did not, however, found a stable dynasty. After a reign of only seven years he died, according to legend, by accidental drowning while inspecting a dike. Real political power in Sumer passed into the hands of Urnammu, the onetime governor of Ur, founder of the glorious Third Dynasty of Ur.

The Third Dynasty of Ur {2112–2004}[10]

The Third Dynasty of Ur (or Ur III) witnessed the last flowering of Sumerian cultural achievement; indeed, most of the literature, art, and architecture generally associated with Sumer was produced during Ur III. Militarily, this was also a period of Sumerian ascendancy in Mesopotamia, in which the kings of Ur were the dominant military force in the region.

Urnammu {2112–2095}[11]

Although best known for his cultural achievements in law, literature, and art, and for the building of the magnificent ziggurat of Ur, Urnammu also played an important military role as well. Unfortunately, his surviving inscriptions focus on his building projects, leaving us with fragmentary information about his military activities. Furthermore, as is often the case in early Mesopotamian military history, a precise chronology of Urnammu's campaigns cannot be established from the fragmentary evidence.

Under Utuhegal of Uruk, Urnammu had served as governor of Ur; some scholars suspect that he was the son-in-law of Utuhegal (R3/2:9). While governor of Ur for Utuhegal, Urnammu engaged in a border dispute with Lagash, defeating them and annexing a portion of their land with the acquiescence of Utuhegal (R3/2:10). Upon the death of his suzerain Utuhegal, Urnammu declared himself an independent king {2112}, initially ruling only the city-state of Ur and its surrounding land; the fortifications of Ur were significantly strengthened early in his reign (R3/2:11, 19, 25–6). Later the fortifications of Nippur were also refurbished (R3/2:76).

The anarchy of the Gutian period left brigands and pirates infesting both Mesopotamia and the Persian Gulf. Part of Urnammu's achievement was to "put the road in order from the south to the north" (R3/2:14) and to resume trade with Magan (Oman) in the Persian Gulf (R3/2:41, 47). This restoration of order and trade in Mesopotamia laid the foundation for the economic and cultural renaissance of the Neo-Sumerian period. One of Urnammu's claims was to have cleared out the brigands and to have made river and land travel secure (CS 2:409). As part of this process he mentions the "sea-captains" who "had control of the foreign maritime trade" in the Persian Gulf; Urnammu "established freedom" for the Sumerian maritime traders (CS 2:409a). These "sea-captains" can be interpreted in one of two ways. It could simply refer to non-Sumerian merchants who had taken control of ocean trade during the Gutian anarchy. On the other hand, they may be Persian Gulf pirates who were pillaging Sumerian merchants, in which case Urnammu is describing the first anti-pirate naval campaign in history. He also mentions the return of a "Magan-boat" at Ur, probably a reference to a boat capable of sailing the Persian Gulf to Magan-Oman (CS 2:409a).

Urnammu undertook a number of campaigns which resulted in the hegemony of Ur in Sumeria. His armies conquered Lagash in battle, absorbing the city into his domain, although leaving it to be governed by local aristocrats (R3/2:47). He also defeated his former masters at Uruk (R3/2:16). Eventually he "banished malediction, violence and strife" – which is to say he defeated his rivals and subdued brigands. Ur's predominance in Mesopotamia was ritually recognized in a coronation festival at Nippur, culminating in his declaration as "king of the lands of Sumer and Akkad" who "restored the ancient state of affairs", which is to say, he restored Sumerian rule in a unified Mesopotamia.[12]

Although Urnammu's direct military power was limited to central and southern Mesopotamia, he formulated an alliance with Mari to the north-west in Syria to oppose the growing power of the Amorite nomads in the Syrian steppe, who increasingly threatened Mesopotamia throughout Ur III.[13] This alliance was sealed by the marriage of Urnammu's son with Taram-Uram, the daughter Apil-Kin, king of Mari (R3/2:86).

At some point in his reign Urnammu began to campaign to the east outside of Mesopotamia. As noted above, the Elamite kingdom under Puzur-Inshushinak had taken advantage of the power vacuum in Mesopotamia following the collapse of Gutian power in Mesopotamia to sieze several Sumerian city-states (R3/2:48). Urnammu campaigned into "highland Elam", defeated the coalition of the Elamite king, and liberated the Sumerian city-states (R3/2:19–20, 65–6; PAE 124–5).

There are fragmentary inscriptions describing campaigns by Urnammu against the Gutians as well. Although driven from dominance in Mesopotamia by the campaigns of Utuhegal, the Gutians had not been decisively crushed, and still represented a serious potential threat to Mesopotamia. Gutarla, king of the Gutians, still had garrisons in parts of Mesopotamia, from which he conducted raids (R3/2:67). Urnammu campaigned victoriously against the Gutians "in their mountain", binding "the bloody hands of the Gutian" prisoners (R3/2:11, 21). Even this victory did not fully break the Gutians, however, for, according to Urnammu's funerary lament, he died in battle against them in 2095, when his army broke and fled, leaving him stranded on the battlefield: "in the place of slaughter they [the army of Ur] abandoned [their king] Urnammu [in battle] like a broken pitcher".[14] This is one of the rare examples of Mesopotamian royal inscriptions describing the defeat and death of a king in battle.

Shulgi {2094–2047}[15]

Shortly after the death of his father Urnammu in battle, Shulgi carried out a punitive campaign against the Gutians to avenge his death (R3/2:20). Thereafter, for the most part, the early years of Shulgi's reign are generally associated in his year-names with peaceful religious and building activities. There were, however, some military undertakings; in his seventh year {2088}, the highlander "Su people, and the lands of Zabshali [northwest Iran], from the border of Anshan to the Upper Sea, rose like locusts" and invaded Mesopotamia. Shulgi undertook a punitive expedition against them (DZ 138–9).

In the second half of his reign {2076–2047}, however, war becomes increasingly common, with about half the year-names associated with campaigning. In the last part of his reign Shulgi undertook a generally expansionist policy, leading to conquests throughout Sumer and hegemony abroad, which was continued by his son Amarsin, creating a Sumerian empire.

Shulgi's campaign against Der {2076} contains some interesting tactical details. On the eve of battle Shulgi apparently destroyed some irrigation dikes, flooding the enemy's positions: "The banks of the River Diyala and the River Taban he smashed, and in a swamp he annihilated the enemy. [In] the land which he inundated he smashed his enemy's weapon" (R3/2:142–3). Thereafter, Shulgi undermined the walls of Der and destroyed the city: "I [Shulgi] arrived at the rebellious land [of Der]; [my army] ripped out the brickwork [of its walls] by its foundation. May the city I have smitten not be restored! The houses which I destroyed were ruined heaps" (R3/2:103). After the destruction of Der, Shulgi built two fortresses – Shulgi-Nanna and Ishim-Shulgi – to maintain Sumerian control of the region (R3/2:103), assigning Ur-Suena as military governor of the area (R3/2:190).

Thereafter Shulgi was at war on a regular basis. One of his major efforts was in the north against the Hurrian invaders, who had migrated into much of northern Mesopotamia during the Gutian period. Shulgi launched three multi-year wars against them in the upper Tigris region. Although he was generally successful in these campaigns, the Hurrians remained an important and growing military power.[16] Most of Shulgi's campaigns are only vaguely described, with standardized formula such as "the year X was destroyed". Some of these sites cannot be securely identified. Shulgi claimed victory over Karahar {2071}, Harshi {2068}, Shasru {2053}, and Simashki (R3/2:104, 108; 451). At some point in the latter part of his reign, Shulgi added to his original title "mighty man, king of Ur", the title "king of the Lands of Sumer and Akkad" and "king of the four quarters [of the world]" (R3/2:149), indicating his claim to military pre-eminence in Mesopotamia (R3/2:111–16).

We are given more detail on a few of his campaigns. Over the course of twenty years Shulgi campaigned against the recalcitrant Hurrian stronghold of Simurrum five times {2069, 2068, 2062, 2050, 2049}, eventually capturing the city and its king Tappan-Darah. This was considered a great victory, as it is referenced several times in later oracular literature (R3/2:104–5). Attempting to improve relations with Elam, Shulgi married his daughter to the "governor of Anshan" in 2065. The alliance was unstable, however, and he invaded and defeated Anshan in 2061 (R3/2:104–5).

There are signs in the later part of Shulgi's reign of increasing military stress. In 2059 he built the "Wall of the Land", also known as the "Wall Facing the Highland". The location of Shulgi's wall is not certain, but it was probably aimed at preventing incursions by the Tidnumite nomad tribe of the Amorites (R3/2:106). The "highlands" possibly refers to Mount Bishri (Bashar) to the west of the Upper Euphrates, which had been a haunt of Amorite nomads since the days of Naram-Sin two centuries earlier. If so, the wall was the first attempt to limit or control the access of the Amorites into central Mesopotamia. The building of the wall was left in the care of his general Puzur-Shulgi; part of the letter in which Shulgi orders the building of the wall has survived:

The wall is to be finished in the period of one month! There are to be no further inquiries pertaining to these building activities! For now the Tidnum [tribe of the Amorite nomads] have come down from the mountain. (R3/ 2:106)

This letter seems to indicate that the building of the wall was taking longer than expected and presumably going over budget, and that part of the reason for this was that the Tidnum nomads were harassing the builders, having already "come down from the mountain".

This wall seems to be the first phase of the more famous "wall that repels Amorites" which was built by Shusin against incursions by Amorite nomads, representing the beginning of a shift from an offensive posture against highlanders to defensive walls to limit their raids. This represents a significant psychological shift in the martial mentality of the age: the Amorites, Hurrians, and Gutians cannot be decisively defeated – the best we can do is hold them at bay. This "great wall" mentality, more famous in its monumental Chinese manifestation, became fundamental to the Ur III martial policy in the twenty-first century. The wall was accompanied by the development of military garrison colonies and cities along a defensive zone facing the Zagros Mountains to attempt to prevent incursions from highlanders (DZ 153–6). The wall and defensive zone may have been initially successful, for we hear of no further Tidnum incursions for over twenty years. On the other hand, as noted below, the policy was ultimately to fail.

In the last five years of Shulgi's reign {2051–2047} Ur was involved in repeated campaigns against coalitions of partially subdued Hurrian city-states in northern Mesopotamia. The problems began with a coalition between the city of Simurrum – which Shulgi had already defeated three times – and the highlanders of Lullubu. Shulgi claims to have defeated them in 2051. If so, it was not a decisive victory, for in 2050 they were back in alliance with Urbillum (modern Arbil) and Karahar. The campaigns of 2049–2047 were directed against another rebel coalition of Kimash, Hurti, and Harshi (R3/2:107–9; 455), whose defeated dead he "heaped up [in] a pile of corpses" (R3/2:141). The need for repeated campaigns against Hurrian and Lullubi coalitions again points to declining military strength, perhaps associated with the fact that Shulgi was by now probably in his sixties or seventies, and may have been too old to effectively rule or lead his armies. Despite such mixed success in warfare, Ur was none the less the predominant military power of Mesopotamia at the death of Shulgi.

Military themes in the Shulgi hymns (TSH)

The court of king Shulgi of Ur {2094–2047} – who proclaimed himself a divinity – prepared a number of panegyric hymns praising the king's divine qualities, including his military prowess. It goes without saying that the king is handsome, strong, courageous and brave (TSH 73–5). By all accounts Shulgi was a superb athlete; he boasts of having run from Nippur to Ur (over 100 miles) some 1500 years before Phidippides' more famous effort in Greece (R3/2:97, 157; Her. 6.106), in which he was later emulated by Ishme-Dagan of Isin (R4:37).

The Shulgi hymns provide us with some detailed literary narratives of actual combat in Neo-Sumerian times. One of Shulgi's hymns gives an epic description of a battle against the Gutians. Despite its hyperbole, poetic language and ritual setting, the hymn provides a useful window into the characteristics of Sumerian battle. The battle begins with an exchange of missile fire:

> I will raise my spear against [the enemy]
> I will set up my banner against the border of the foreign land
> I will fill my quiver,
> My bow will distend, ready to shoot, like a raging serpent,
> The barbed arrows will flash before me like lightening
> The *barbar*-arrows, like swiftly flying bats
> Will fly into the "mouth of its battle".
> Slingstones will pour down on its people;
> Heavy clay lumps, like the "hand stones",
> Will be striking on their back.
> The crushed people of the rebellious land,
> I will cut down with my bow and sling like locusts. (TSH 79)

Following the missile exchange, the battle transforms into a bloody melee with maces and axes:

> My [mace?] will sharpen its teeth at the "head of the land"
> My *mitum*-weapon will shed the blood of the people like water.
> My weapon, the double-edged axe,
> Will [spill?] their blood, which will cover the [land]
> Having been spilled on the highland, the contents of a broken wine-jug ...
> In its wadis the blood will flow like water. (TSH 79)

In many periods of history, being taken captive after a battle or siege was often only marginally more satisfactory than dying. But in the ancient Near East the plight of the prisoner was particularly miserable. Royal prisoners were often marched naked and in stocks back to the capital of the victorious king, where they were paraded in triumph, brought before the gods, and ritually debased by having the victorious king stand on their heads or bodies in the courtyards before the temples of the gods. The great hero Shulgi boasts that he will "set my foot on his [the defeated king's] head ... I will make him die amid dripping blood" (TSH 77); the enemy was ritually executed by being disemboweled (TSH 77) in what probably amounted to a form of human sacrifice.

In the aftermath of the battle the adults were often killed, children were enslaved, and the fields and city destroyed.

The children of the foreign land, he made them embark on his ships
The adults he killed in revenge.. . .
The hero avenged his city,
Whatever has been destroyed in Sumer, he destroyed in the foreign [Gutian]
land . . . In its cultivated fields of shining barley, he caused weeds to grow,
He destroyed its wide and large trees with the axe.. . .
The king, after he destroyed the city, ruined the city walls . . .
He dispersed the seed of the Gutians like seed-grain. (TSH 85)

Many other prisoners were kept as slaves and sent to work on agriculture, canal
digging, mining, and quarrying or building projects (USP 47–50).

After the victory, great plunder is brought back to Sumer in a triumphal
procession:

The pure lapis-lazuli of the foreign land he loaded into leather-bags
He heaped up all its treasures
Amassed all the wealth of the foreign land,
Its fattened oxen and fattened sheep.
He invokes the name of [the god] Enlil,
He invokes the name of [the god] Ninlil
The hero [Shulgi], having carried out a noble revenge in the foreign land
[The king rode in] his shining royal *magur*-boat . . .
Shulgi, the righteous shepherd of Sumer,
Placed his feet upon [his enemy's neck]
Upon a throne he took seat.
The *sim* and *ala*-drums resounded for him,
The *tigi*-drums played for him music:
"My king has destroyed the foreign land, you have plundered its cities
Like a wild bull in the mountain",
Sang the singers a song for him. (TSH 85–7)

Shulgi then enters the temple of Enlil, dedicating the plunder to the gods, and
receiving in return a divine decree of long, prosperous, and victorious rule (TSH
87–9). In another context it is clear that the soldiers also received their fair share of
plunder. After defeating the Elamites, the king "brought the booty to the god
Enlil, my lord, in Nippur, and marked it for him. The remainder I presented as a
gift to my troops" (R3/2:66).

Amarsin (Amar-Suena) {2046–2038}[17]

Overall the reign of Amarsin is rather poorly documented for military affairs.
Amarsin succeeded his father Shulgi in the midst of an ongoing war with Urbillum, against which he dispatched his general Niridagal in 2045 (R3/2:236), Niridagal seems to have decisively defeated that city, which is later listed as having an

Ur-appointed military governor (R3/2:324). Thereafter Amarsin turned his attention to the north, launching two expeditions under general Haship-atal against Shashrum and Shuruthum in 2043 and 2041. According to the reconstruction of events by Frayne (R3/2:238–9), the campaign went northwest from the Diyala river, also conquering the cities of Rashap and Arrapha. In 2040 Amarsin invaded Huhnuri in Elam (R3/2:239). At some point in his reign he built a "watchtower" in Ur, but its precise military function, if any, is obscure (R3/2:259).

Some idea of the size of the empire of Ur can be discerned by the seal inscriptions of Ur-appointed city governors. Eventually the rulers of Ur are known to have had dependent governors in at least sixteen Mesopotamian cities, including Umma, Push, Kish, Lagash, Kazallu, Nippur, Sharrakum, Adab, Ishkun-Sin, Shuruppak, Marad, Simudar, Kutha, Uruk, and Eresh (R3/2:xli–xliv, 3, 271–7). There were undoubtedly other governors as well, for whom we lack records, along with additional vassal states. There were other cities with known Sumerian governors outside of Sumer itself, including Ashur, Babylon, Eshnunna, Simurrum, and Susa in Elam (R3/2:271–7); Ashur was governed by a general (GIR.NITA) named Zarriqum (R3/2:278, A1:9).

At the height of its power the empire of Ur III was divided into three zones, each with a different relationship to the city of Ur.[18] In the central heartland of Sumer and Akkad (southern and central Mesopotamia), the cities were ruled by governors directly appointed by the king of Ur, directly paying taxes (*bala*) of goods and services. The second zone, along the central Tigris valley and parts of Elam, were conquered lands which had garrisons of soldiers (*erin*) with military commanders (*shagina*) appointed from Ur. These provinces paid the "tribute of the provinces" (*gun mada*) in livestock and other products. In one year alone this tribute amounted to 28,000 cattle and 350,000 sheep (CAM 102). The third zone consisted of allied and vassal states, who had their own independent rulers but who were dependent in some way on Ur. This region is rather amorphous and informal, with changeable relations with specific cities, but included at different times parts of western Iran, the upper Tigris, the middle Euphrates and parts of Syria. These regions sent ambassadors to Ur, intermarried with the royal family, and sent various forms of tribute or diplomatic gifts (HE2:85–101). The middle Euphrates, including Mari and Ebla, seemed to have some type of tributary status to Ur (HE 2:125–33), while ambassadors were received from as far away as Byblos on the Mediterranean coast (EH2:122). In 2048 Shulgi received tribute (*gun*) from Ebla consisting of "500 *tilpānu*-weapons of *sudiānum*-wood and 500 containers (ᵍⁱˢ.*kab-kul*) of the same wood" (HE2:128–9), which I interpret to be 500 bows and quivers (see p. 91). This substantial tribute in weapons points to some type of vassalage on the part of Ebla to Ur, and further emphasizes the importance of archery in Neo-Sumerian armies.

Amarsin's overall predominance in Mesopotamia is reflected in his continuing claim to the title "king of the four quarters [of the world]". Later legends remember that, during Amarsin's reign, "the homeland revolted" (R3/2:236), but this cannot be confirmed by any contemporary documents. It seems succession occurred without incident.

Shusin {2037–2029} and the Amorite Wars

Militarily speaking, Shusin's reign is one of the better documented of the Ur III dynasty (R3/2:285–359). As noted above, most of Shusin's predecessors had focused their attention on the conquest of the Tigris valley in north-eastern Iraq. With this flank stabilized, Shusin turned his attention to the west and the middle Euphrates basin. Early in his reign he entered into a military alliance with the north Euphrates city-state of Simanum (north-east Syria) through the marriage of his daughter Kunshi-matum to Arib-atal, son of king Pusham.[19] Although the details are unknown, in 2036 a coup occurred in which Pusham and his family were ousted from power. The perpetrators of the coup are not named, but they may have been Hurrians, and they received assistance from the Amorite nomads. With the help of the gods Enlil and Inanna, Shusin – who "makes the foreign country tremble" – launched a campaign against the rebels in Simanum in 2035, which quickly turned into a much larger extended war with the Amorites.

From his base at Ashur, Shusin led the army of Ur northward up the Tigris, capturing Nineveh, Talmush, and Habura. At this time Nineveh seems to have been in the domain of the Hurrian king Tish-atal of Urkish (modern Mozan), who appears to have dominated the upper Tigris during the early Ur III period, and who may have been Shusin's uncle.[20] Shusin continued his march up the Tigris, eventually reaching Simanum, where Shusin "smote the heads of Simanum, Habura, and the surrounding districts". With the rebels defeated, Pusham and his family were restored to the throne.

We are provided with some details of the fate of prisoners from this campaign, who were deported and settled in a new town on the frontier of Nippur, perhaps to work on Shusin's defensive wall described below. Shusin boasts: "Since the [mythical] days of decreeing the fates [at the foundation of the world], no king has established a town for the god Enlil and the goddess Ninlil on the frontier of Nippur, with people he had captured." This type of mass deportation of citizens from defeated cities would become a standard practice throughout Mesopotamian history. Conquered people became in many ways a form of war plunder, to be collected and transported just like silver or lapis lazuli or building timber. Warfare created a mobile market of displaced migrant workers whom the kings could move to support new agricultural or building projects.

Despite this victory, Shusin was forced to deal with an ongoing threat from the Amorite nomads, which his grandfather Shulgi had temporarily suppressed twenty years earlier, in around 2059. The Amorite nomads of the Tidnum tribe had apparently been raiding, or migrating into, the agricultural land along the middle Euphrates, since Shusin's continuing campaign in 2034 is said to have been undertaken in order to "remove any cause for complaint from the [people who work the] furrows of the [agricultural] land [by] vengeance [against the] Tidnum [nomadic raids]" (R3/2:290). Perhaps using the newly conquered Simanum as a base, in 2035 Shusin launched an attack against the Tidnum Amorite nomads, possibly advancing as far as Aleppo (Yamhad) (R3/2:290, 299, 301). He claimed that "the big mountains [where the Amorites live] were subdued ... the towns, the populations, and their settlements, were turned into ruins".

Despite these claims, the campaign was far from decisive, for in the following year, 2034, Shusin decided to build "the Amorite wall called 'It keeps [the] Tidnum [nomads] at a distance' " (R3/2:290, 328). A letter from the building commissioner to king Shusin provides an informative description of the wall:

> To Shusin, my king ... thus says Sharrum-bani, the high commissioner, your servant. You have sent me as an envoy in order to build the great wall "It keeps Amorites at a distance". I am presenting to you how matters stand. The Amorites are descending upon the land. You have instructed me to build the wall, to cut off their path so that they may not overwhelm the fields by a breach between the Tigris and Euphrates.... As a result of my building activities the wall is now 26 *danna* long. When I sent for word to the area between the two mountains it was brought to my attention that the [Amorites] were encamped in the mountains. [The Hurrians at] Simurrum had come to their aid. Therefore I proceeded to the area "between" the mountain ranges of Ebih in order to do battle.[21]

The text is somewhat vague, but it seems the Amorites had already crossed the Euphrates, probably in the north, and were raiding southward between the Euphrates and the Tigris. The wall was being built from the banks of the Tigris to the Euphrates to forestall further penetration southward into central and southern Mesopotamia. Ruins of this earth and clay wall – estimated to have been about 170 miles (280 km) long – can still be seen north of Baghdad.[22] The wall would thus be similar to Nebuchadnezzar's later "Wall of Media". The "mountain ranges of Ebih" have not been identified with certainty, but might perhaps have reference to the twin mountains Abd al-Aziz and Sinjar in northern Mesopotamia. The building of this wall shows the concern over the growing military threat from the Amorites, who would eventually participate in the destruction of the empire of Ur. None the less, Shusin's campaigns were successful in temporarily holding the Amorite threat at bay.

The Zagros highlanders posed a simultaneous threat which was opposed with a vigorous campaign in 2031 against Indasu, king of Zabshali (R3/2:301–6). Shusin describes their depredations as being "like a swarm of locusts from the border of Anshan (in south-east Iran] to the Upper [Mediterranean] Sea", listing over a dozen subsidiary tribes or city-states who formed a confederation against Ur. Details of the battle are lacking; attention is paid to killing, scattering, and decapitating the enemy, finally piling their corpses into a heap. The captured leaders were bound and brought as captives before the god Enlil. Others scattered, attempting to ...

save their lives by fleeing to their cities, [but Shusin marched] against their cities, screeching like an Anzu [dragon]. He turned their cities into ruined heaps; he destroyed their walls. He blinded the men of those cities ... and established them as slaves in the orchards of the gods ... [the women] he offered as a present to the weaving mills of the god Enlil and the goddess Ninlil. (R3/2:309–12)

Other captives were enslaved and forced to work in the silver and gold mine at Bulma, one of the conquered cities. In addition to slaves, Shusin lists livestock and "leather sacks filled with gold and silver" and bronze as his booty. In triumph, Shusin created a monument depicting himself trampling the captive king Indasu, along with the names of ten other captured leaders of the coalition.

A fragmentary inscription describes a naval campaign of Shusin to "Magan [Oman], along with its provinces ... [and] the other side of the sea ..." (R3/2:201), which could have been an extension of Shusin's Elamite campaign. The combination of his campaigns on the Upper Euphrates, against Elam, and in the Persian Gulf allowed Shusin to claim the ancient Akkadian title of ruler from the "Lower to the Upper Sea" (R3/2:302, 317), maintaining the Third Dynasty of Ur as the dominant power in Mesopotamia.

Ibbisin (Ibbi-Suen) {2028–2004} and the fall of Ur[23]

Ibbisin's reign marked the decline and collapse of the Ur III dynasty, unleashing an ensuing period of invasion and chaos. Ibbisin's year names and inscriptions show far more concern with religious ritual than with the collapsing military and political situation of Ur. None the less, a number of campaigns are mentioned. For the most part these were defensive in nature, against provinces or cities which had earlier submitted to Ur, but had now gained independence.

In 2023 {Y6} Ibbisin undertook repairs and expansion on the walls of Nippur and Ur, perhaps reflecting a perception of an increasing threat to the heartland (R3/2:363). In a propagandistic inscription describing the building of the walls, Ibbisin wrote: "in order to make the land secure and to make the highlands and lowlands bow down before him, he surrounded his city with a great wall, whose loop-holes cannot be reached, and which is like a yellow mountain" (R3/2:369). How a defensive wall on a city in Sumer would make the highlanders "bow down" before the king of Ur is not explained. The defensive attitude, perhaps an extension of the great wall mentality, could not mask an increasingly desperate military situation.

The fall of the empire of Ur is rather well documented by the standards of the Early Bronze Age. Psychologically for Mesopotamians it was rather like the fall of Rome in the West, and from the military perspective it marks the end of the Early Bronze Age and the beginning of the Middle Bronze. A number of factors contributed to the fall of Ur. Internal political instability is reflected in the defection and independence of a number of city-states in both the heartland and the periphery of the empire, which had been brought into submission by the campaigns of Shulgi, Amarsin, and Shusin. "The lands that had been in obedience to Ur were split into factions" (LD 43). By 2027 {Y2} Eshnunna and the province of Simurrum had cast off allegiance, leading Ibbisin to send an army against them the next year (R3/2:366, 362). The campaign was apparently a failure, because the defections increased rapidly: Susa and Elam in 2026 {Y3}, Lagash in 2024 {Y5}, Umma in 2023 {Y6}, and Nippur in 2022 {Y7}. Girsu became independent under kings Ur-Ningirsu and Ur-Nanshe (R3/2:427–31).

Although we lack full documentation, other cities undoubtedly followed suit, while "brigands roamed the roads" (LD 42). More ominously, the Elamites were not only independent, but becoming increasingly hostile towards Ur, which would culminate in their destruction of the city. In an effort to stabilize the situation in Elam, Ibbisin "marched [eastward] with heavy forces against Huhnuri [near modern Behbehan] the 'open mouth' of the land of Anshan" in 2020 {Y9} (R3/2:363). This operation was indecisive, however, for he was back in 2015 {Y14}: Ibbisin "roared like a storm against Susa, Adamdun and the land of Awan [in Elam]; he made them submit in a single day and took their lords as bound captives", dedicating part of the plunder to the gods. The booty from this war appears to have caused a temporary economic boom in Ur, but was insufficient to save the state (R3/2:364, 371–2). Overall, prices of foodstuffs increased manifold during this period.[24]

At the same time the situation was also rapidly degenerating on the north-west frontier, where the Amorites were becoming an increasing military threat. A series of letters exchanged between Ibbisin and his governors in the north-west shed an interesting light on the unfolding crisis. Despite the defection of south-eastern Mesopotamia, Isin remained temporarily loyal under its governor Ishbi-Irra. From 2020 to 2010 {Y9–19}, the degenerating situation began to threaten the grain supply to Ur. Ishbi-Irra, governor of Isin, wrote to Ibbisin explaining the situation:

> Thus says Ishbi-Irra, your servant: You have instructed me to proceed on an expedition to Isin and Kazallu in order to purchase grain. The market price of grain has reached one gur [of grain] per shekel [of silver].... Word having reached me that the hostile Amorites had entered into the midst of your land I brought all of the 72,000 gur of grain into Isin. And now all of the Amorites have entered into the land. One by one they have seized all the fortifications. Because of the Amorites I have been unable to thresh the grain. They are too strong for me, I am trapped [in the city of Isin].[25]

Here we see a countryside overrun by Amorite nomads to the extent that the Sumerians are simply hiding in their cities, unable to harvest their fields as the price of grain skyrockets. At some point Ishbi-Irra, exasperated with the weakness of Ibbisin, declared his independence, leading to war with his former overlord (see pp. 159–62).

In 2013 {Y17} Ibbisin made the enigmatic claim that "this year the Amorites of the southern border, who from ancient times have known no cities, submitted to Ibbisin, king of Ur" (R3/2:364; AUP 94). Importantly, the text does not a claim military victory over the Amorites, but only that they "submitted", perhaps in return for a payment of tribute. This "submission", however, apparently represented the formation of some type of coalition between Ibbisin and the Amorites against Ishbi-Irra, the erstwhile governor of Isin; it may be alluded to in mythic terms in the following inscription: "[the god] Enlil, my helper, has summoned the Amorites from their mountain, Elam will come to my side and catch Ishbi-Irra [rebel governor of Isin]" (AUP 95). Thus, as has happened on occasion in history, when two rivals are locked in a civil war for the control of an empire, one may turn to outside barbarians for assistance, buying short-term victory at the cost of long-term security. What exactly this submission or coalition entailed is unclear; while it may have represented a temporary set-back for Ishbi-Irra, it was a major victory for the Amorite invaders, whose spread throughout Mesopotamia was thereby facilitated.

Instead of providing military assistance to his beleaguered governor, Ibbisin berated Ishbi-Irra for dereliction of duty and malfeasance:

> Thus says your king Ibbi-Sin: . . . You received twenty talents of silver to buy grain and you proceed to buy two gur of grain for each shekel, but to me you send one gur for each shekel. How is it that you permitted the Amorites, the enemy, to enter my land against Puzur-Numushda, the commandant of Badigihursagga? I sent you weapons with which to strike; how is it that you sent the "men without heads" [fools? decapitated soldiers?] who are in the land against the Amorites from the north? (R3/2:367)

The degenerating relations between Ibbisin and his governor eventually led to civil war. By 2010 {Y19} Ishbi-Irra of Isin had declared independence from the ineffectual Ibbisin, and had begun carving out his own state in central Mesopotamia. The situation was described by Puzur-Shugli, governor of Kazallu, apparently the last governor in the region loyal to Ibbisin:

> [Ishbi-Irra] has built the wall of Isin. . . . He has taken Nippur, set his men as the garrison, and captured Nigugani, the highest priest of Nippur. He has made [his general] Idi enter Malgium and plundered Hamasi. He has put Zinnum, governor of Subartu, in prison. He has returned Nur-Ahum, governor of Eshnunna, Shu-Enlil, governor of Kish, and Puzur-Tut, governor of Borsippa, to their [former] positions [from which Ibbisin had removed them for disloyalty?]. . . . Ishbi-Irra proceeds at the head of his army. . . . He captured the banks of the Tigris, Euphrates, [and] the Abgal and Me-Enlila canals. He brought in Idin-Malgium [as an ally.] He quarreled with Girbubu, the governor of Girkal . . . and took him prisoner. His battle cry lies heavy upon me. Now he has set his eye upon me. I have no ally, no one to go [to battle] with! Although his hand has not yet reached me, should he descend upon me, I shall have to flee.[26]

By this time, however, Ibbisin was in no position to help his last loyal governor in central Mesopotamia. "Ur's king sat immobilized in the palace, all alone. Ibbi-Sin was sitting in anguish in the palace, all alone. In the Enamtila, the palace of his delight, he was crying bitterly" (LD 43).

By 2007 {Y22} the chaos had reached the capital of Ur. Amorite nomads from the north, along with Gutian highlanders and Elamites, overran all of Mesopotamia. Ibbisin records an obscure inscription: "Ibbisin, king of Ur, held firm the city of Ur . . . which had been devastated by the 'flood' which had been commanded by the gods and which shook the whole world" (R3/2:365). Many scholars view this statement as a euphemistic metaphor: the "flood" is a flood of enemies who overran much of the kingdom, but were unable as yet to capture Ur itself. Indeed, this same flood metaphor is used to describe the attack of Gutians and Elamites against Ur (LD 41).[27] The next year, 2006 {Y23} Ibbisin also describes the coming of a "stupid monkey" to Ur, which some scholars see as a euphemism for an attack by an enemy king (R3/2:365). In 2005 {Y24}, the final year of Ibbisin's reign, a fragmentary inscription describes the Elamites as "smiting Ur", ending the dynasty (R3/2:366); Ibbisin was dragged in chains to Elam (LD 39; PH 7).

The Lament for Ur

An important document describing the fall of Ur is *The Lamentation over the Destruction of Sumer and Ur* (LD) – a kind of Sumerian *City of God*. Although clearly a literary text filled with hyperbole, it none the less contains a vivid description of how the Sumerians viewed the fall of their civilization, with numerous details on military matters. As with all affairs in human life, the destruction of Ur is, from the Sumerian perspective, the result of the inscrutable decrees of the gods: "the gods An, Enlil, Enki, and Nimah decided its fate. Its fate, which cannot be changed, who can overturn it – who can oppose the commands of An and Enlil?" (LD 39, 37). For although "Ur was indeed given kingship [by the gods] . . . it was not given an eternal reign" (LD 59). The war goddess "Inanna handed over victory in strife and battle to a rebellious land . . . revolt descended upon the land [of Sumer], something that no one had ever known, something unseen [until now]" (LD 41).

To accomplish this decreed destruction, the gods unleashed the foreign barbarians, the Amorites, Gutians, and Elamites. The god "Enlil then sent down Gutium from the mountains. Their advance was as the flood of Enlil that cannot be withstood, . . . the teeming plain [of Sumer] was destroyed [by the Gutian invaders], no one moved about there" (LD 41). The Gutians settled in the land like a nest of vipers: "the snake of the mountain [the Gutians] made his lair there, it became a rebellious land; the Gutians bred there, issued their seed" (LD 45). The Elamites, who would actually destroy Ur, were also unleashed by the gods. "Enlil brought down the Elamites, the enemy, from the highlands . . . Fire approached [the god] Ninmar in the shrine Guabba, large boats were carrying off its precious metals and stones [as plunder]" (LD 47). Likewise the nomadic

Amorites from the west joined in the slaughter: "To the south, the Elamites stepped in, slaughtering ... To the north, the [Amorite] vandals, the enemy ... The [Amorite] Tidnumites daily strapped the mace to their loins [for battle]" (LD 51–3).

The culmination of these invasions was the siege of Ur by the Elamites. The lament of the poet, who may have been an eyewitness, provides our most vivid account of a siege from ancient Mesopotamia:

> Laments sounded all along its city wall,
> Daily there was a slaughter before it.
> Large axes were sharpened in front of Ur,
> The spears, the arms of battle, were being launched,
> The large bows, javelin, and siege-shield gather together to strike,
> The barbed arrows covered its outside [wall] like a raining cloud,
> Large stones [from slings], one after another, fell with great thuds....
> Ur, which had been confident in its own strength, stood ready for slaughter,
> Its people, oppressed by the enemy, could not withstand their weapons.
> Those in the city who had not been felled by weapons died of hunger,
> Hunger filled the city like water, it would not cease....
> Its people dropped their weapons, their weapons hit the ground....
> Ur – inside it there is [only] death, outside it there is [only] death,
> Inside it we are being finished off by famine,
> Outside it we are being finished off by the Elamite weapons....
> Elam, like a swelling flood wave, left only the spirits of the dead....
> [Ur's] refugees were unable to flee, they were trapped inside the walls. (LD 61–3)

Surrounded and starving, the citizens of Ur finally give way to despair, dissension, and treachery:

> In Ur no one went to fetch food, no one went to fetch drink,
> Its people rush around like water churning in a well,
> Their strength has ebbed away; they cannot even go on their way,
> [The god] Enlil afflicted the city with an inimical famine,
> He afflicted the city with something that destroys cities, that destroys temples,
> He afflicted the city with something that cannot be withstood with weapons,
> He afflicted the city with dissatisfaction and treachery. (LD 55)

In the end, the Elamites breached the walls and sacked the city, and "Ur, like a city that has been wrought by the hoe, became a ruined mound" (LD 59). "The soldiers of Shimashki and Elam, the enemy, dwell in their [the Sumerians'] place, [Sumer's] shepherd [king] is captured by the enemy, all alone; Ibbisin is taken to the land of Elam in fetters" (LD 39).

Much of the rest of the *Lamentation* consists of poetic descriptions of the desolate scene after the fall of Ur, with temples deserted, cities destroyed, unplanted weed-infested fields, and livestock captured. People were massacred, leaving "corpses floating in the Euphrates" (LD 42), while others were enslaved (LD 53). The few survivors are "refugees, like stampeding goats, chased by dogs" (LD 47) who were "scattered as far as Anshan" (R4:17). The text lists many major Sumerian cities destroyed by invading Gutium and Elamites, repeating the refrain, "Alas, the destroyed city, my destroyed temple." With these invasions the old Sumerian order and the Early Bronze Age ended. The new political and military order of Mesopotamia was to be forged by Amorite warlords (see Chapter Six).

Ideal warfare in the Epic of Ninurta

Though describing a mythical tale of the gods, the Epic of Ninurta (HTO 233–72) provides our most detailed literary account of the Neo-Sumerian army at war.[28] Written in the twenty-second century, shortly after the overthrow of the Gutian highlanders from Mesopotamia, the myth centers around the great struggle between the god Ninurta and Azag, a demonic ruler of the Zagros Mountains to the north-east of Sumeria and personification of the Sumerian view of the highland warriors such as the Gutians. Azag is plotting to "take away the kingship and sacred offices" of Ninurta in Sumeria, just as the Gutians had done (HTO 239). Azag is a "fearless warrior", a "killer out of the highland", a "towering man" and "true fighter" whose highland "warriors constantly come raiding the cities" of Sumeria (HTO 237–8).

Ninurta is roused to anger by these incursions, and raises an army to destroy Azag. The advance of his army to battle is compared with the terror and destructiveness of a rising storm and flood:

> Rising, the lord [Ninurta] abutted heaven
> Ninurta marching to battle kept abreast of the hours
> A very storm he went to war,
> Rode on seven gales against the rebel country.
> Javelins he held cradled in the arm,
> The *mittu*-mace opened its mouth against the mountains,
> The weapons raged at the hostile horde.
> The evil wind and the south storm were tethered to him,
> The flood storm strode at their flanks,
> And before the warrior went a huge irresistible tempest,
> It was tearing up the dust, depositing it again
> Evening out hill and dale, filling in the hollows;
> Live coals [lightening] it rained down [from heaven]
> Fire burned, flames scorched. (HTO 240–1)

Mesopotamia was a land criss-crossed by rivers and canals, and boats were used to transport troops and supplies in almost all campaigns. This is reflected in the epic, as Ninurta "hastened toward battle" in "the boat Makarnuntaea – 'boat sailing from the royal quay' " (HTO 241). As Ninurta approached the land of Azag, he sent spies and agents "slipping into the rebel country" to "cut off communication between its cities" (HTO 241). His agents "brought an enemy captive back" to interrogate, while bringing additional information about the enemy's movements and preparations (HTO 242).

When combat finally came, Ninurta's "heart was brightening for him from pleasure in this lion-headed mace". The pre-battle arming of Ninurta is described like "the embrace of the beloved". In pre-battle preparations, a small portable shrine for the gods was established for prayer, sacrifice, and divination (HTO 243). The marshaling of troops for battle is described as preparations for a religious ritual, "the festival of manhood, [the war-goddess] Inanna's dance" (HTO 243). This may refer either to a pre-battle war-dance undertaken in honor of Inanna, or a description of actual combat as being a ritual dance honoring Inanna. This relationship of dancing with war may point to the rote-learning of combat actions and marching in unison in the form of a ritual war-dance. In some ways these war-dances are probably the origin of martial arts – the teaching of stylized patterns of combat through dance.

Throughout the myth, Ninurta's mace, named Sharur, is described as a sentient being who spies for Ninurta and gives him council (HTO 236–8). This may simply be the personification of a divine weapon, but may alternatively reflect a practice of giving weapon-titles to great champions of the king, just as Ninurta himself is called the sky-god "An's mace" (HTO 242). Elsewhere in the epic, Ninurta's soldiers armed with long spears are simply called his "long spears" (HTO 244). Ninurta holds a war council, and his councilors advise caution, fearing the power of Azag in his mountain retreats: "we will prove no match for Azag; we ought not to enter the highland!" (HTO 244).

Naturally, Ninurta is not dissuaded by their fears, but marshals his troops for combat.

> The lord [Ninurta] stretched the thigh
> [The chariot pulled by a] donkey steed was mounted
> He girded himself with warbelt
> Cast over the highland his long august shadow . . .
> Unto Azag's stronghold [in the highland] he attained
> And stood in the front line of battle. . . .
> He gave his [regiment of] long spears instructions . . .
> The lord called upon his weapons, set out most completely arrayed.

The battle itself is described as overwhelming natural chaos, with the sky darkening under the rising dust cloud caused by the combatants.

> Into the fray the warrior [Ninurta] rushed . . .
> Bow and battle-sling he wielded well,
> Shattered was the [army of the] highland, it dissolved
> Before Ninurta's battle array
> As the warrior [Ninurta] ordered his weapons "gird yourself" [for battle].

The sun marched no longer [through the sky], it had turned into a moon;
In the highland the [mountain] peaks were wiped from [view]
The day was made black like pitch [from the dust] (HTO 244).

The enemy king Azag, however, described as a gigantic dragon which struck fear into the hearts of the gods, was not yet defeated: "Azag rose to attack in the front line of battle" (HTO 245–6). At least in mythic texts, kings challenge each other to single combat (HTO 297), or use champions (HTO 309–10); one such champion is described as wearing a lion skin (HTO 316). Such a single combat occurs between Ninurta and Azag, described metaphorically as a struggle between the natural forces of desert and water (HTO 245–7). The enemy "sent arrows flying at [Ninurta] . . . and threw elite troops against him like bolts of lightening" (HTO 258). The combat culminated in Ninurta's final charge:

Howling like a storm, [carrying] his long spear,
Ninurta . . . rammed his battalion like a prod into the highland. . . .
The *mittu*-mace smote [enemy] heads with its bitter teeth,
The *shita*-weapon, which plucks out hearts, gnashed its teeth,
The long spear was stuck [through the enemy] into the ground
While blood flowed from the hole it made. (HTO 248)

Ninurta is described as a "warrior, striding into battle, trampling down all before him, putting a fighter's hand to the *mittu*-mace, reaping like grain the necks of the [enemies]" (HTO 235). At last Azag's army begins to collapse:

The warrior [Ninurta] set up a howl loudly in the highland . . .
He battered the heads of the enemy horde,
The highland was brought to tears,
The lord [Ninurta] bound up [captured] soldier teams like looted goods . . .
Ninurta passed through the [dead] enemies
Laid them out as if they were fatted calves. (HTO 249–50)

Azag is killed by Ninurta, who celebrates his victory by ritually dismembering Azag's corpse, perhaps in imitation of the god Marduk's dismemberment of the monster Tiamat at creation (MFM 254–5). Abuse of enemy corpses in Mesopotamia should probably be understood in this mythic context.

The victory was followed a cleansing ritual in which the arms and body were cleaned from the gore of battle.

The lord [Ninurta] rinsed belt and weapon in water,
Rinsed the *mittu*-mace in water,
The warrior wiped his brow –
And sounded the victory cry over the corpse [of Azag];
He carved up Azag, who he had killed like a fatted calf (HTO 250).

This ritual is probably alluded to in several royal inscriptions in which the kings wash their weapons in the waters of the ocean (R2:11, 14, 17, 32, 97).

With Azag and the highland army defeated, Ninurta brings civilization, irrigation and agriculture to the area (HTO 250–4), including fortifications to protect Sumeria: "He made a bank of stones against the highland . . . and placed it as a bar before the country [of Mesopotamia] like a great wall" (HTO 252). He then is able to exploit the "gold and silver . . . copper and tin" of the region (HTO 255), as well as numerous types of stones and gems (HTO 256–68). Returning to his boat Makarnuntaea, which had been left in the river valley, Ninurta sails home in triumph, where he is met with hymns praising his great victory (HTO 268–71).

What we have in the epic of Ninurta is a complete description of the ideal Neo-Sumerian campaign, from its inception to the triumphal return of the king to his capital. Although this ideal model could not always be fully followed in reality, it is likely that Sumerian kings made conscious efforts to have their real campaigns conform as closely as possible to this ideal.

Triumphal procession

After victory the warriors celebrated a triumphal procession, to honor both the heroes and the gods. The "Hymn to Inanna", the goddess of war, describes such a triumph, which concludes with the ritual sacrifice of prisoners of war.

> Drums, silver inwrought, they are beating for her –
> Before holy Inanna, before her eyes, they are parading –
> The great Queen of Heaven, Inanna, I will hail!
> Holy tambourines and holy kettledrums they are beating for her . . .[29]
> The guardsmen [sag-ursag] have combed their hair for her . . .
> They have made colorful for her the back hair with colored ribbons . . .
> On their bodies are sheep skin robes, the dress of divinities . . .
> They are girt with implements of battle . . .
> Spears, the arms of battle, are in their hands . . .
> Playfully, with painted buttocks, they engage in single combat . . .
> Captive [enemy] lads in neck stocks bewail to her their fate . . .
> Daggers and maces rage before her . . .
> The kurgaru [warriors] mounted on chariots swing the maces . . .
> Gore is covering the daggers, blood sprinkles . . .
> In the courtyard of the place of assembly
> The temple administrator-priests are shedding blood
> As loudly resounds there the music of tigi-harps, tambourines and lyres.
> (HTO 115–17)

It is likely that celebrations like this were organized for most victorious armies, and probably represent the archaic origins of the later Roman triumphs.

Warfare in the Epic of Gilgamesh

The *Epic of Gilgamesh* is a Mesopotamian literary epic which tells of the adventures of Gilgamesh, king of Uruk. The historical Gilgamesh reigned as king in the early twenty-seventh century (see pp. 46–8), and is noted for constructing the walls of Uruk (EOG 1). He was worshipped as a deified king by the twenty-fourth century, by which time it is assumed oral tales were told of the famous ruler. The oldest extant parts of the Gilgamesh epic cycle date from the twenty-first century in Sumerian. By the eighteenth and seventeenth centuries, nearly a thousand years after the death of the historical Gilgamesh, the epic had reached its classical form in Old Babylonian (EOG lx). Thus, from a military perspective, the epic probably best reflects military practices of the late third or early second millennium.

The *Epic of Gilgamesh* provides a number of interesting descriptions of military activities associated with the battle against the monster Humbaba (EOG 22–47). Gilgamesh represents the ideal Mesopotamian martial king, who "has no equal when his weapons are brandished" (EOG 4). The first part of the epic focuses on Gilgamesh's battle with Humbaba on Mount Lebanon (EOG 19); although mythic, it none the less represents the military ideal, if not necessarily the reality.

The description of Gilgamesh's preparations and march to Lebanon probably reflect actual practices on military campaigns. When Gilgamesh conceives of the plan to attack Humbaba, his first act is to cast new bronze weapons: axes and daggers with "gold mountings" (EOG 20). He then summons the town assembly, composed of the elders and the "young men of Uruk who understand combat" (EOG 20–1). In other words, the assembly is composed of the military-age males who debate issues of war and peace, broadly paralleling similar institutions in early Greece. This body debates Gilgamesh's military proposal; the elders advise the king of the perils of his proposed undertaking, objecting that "you are young, Gilgamesh, borne along by emotion; all that you talk of you don't understand" (EOG 22). Gilgamesh laughs at their fears, and in the end the assembly gives him advice and prays to the gods to bless him (EOG 28–9). They advise Gilgamesh "not to rely on your own strength alone", but to take Enkidu as counselor and war-companion (EOG 28). They also give advice in the form of a military proverb: "who goes in front will save his comrade, who knows the road shall guard his friend" (EOG 28), apparently meaning that proper scouting and intelligence will protect an army.

Gilgamesh's companion on the campaign against Humbaba, then, is Enkidu, a "savage man from the midst of the wild" (EOG 7); he probably represents the Mesopotamian view of highland hunters and nomads who are said to have never tasted bread and beer (EOG 14). Enkidu is explicitly said to have been "born in the uplands" where the monster Humbaba dwells (EOG 13, 18), which are associated with "the mountain of cedar" in Lebanon (EOG 34, 39). In strength and military prowess he is described as being the "equal" of Gilgamesh (EOG 11, 13) – although Gilgamesh defeats him in a wrestling match (EOG 16). He is repeatedly said to be as "mighty as a rock from the sky" (EOG 5, 10), possibly a reference to meteoritic iron, the hardest substance known to the Mesopotamians.

Having prepared his weapons, met with the council of the military assembly, and selected his companion-at-arms, there remains the crucial issue of consulting the will of the gods and gaining their support. For this Gilgamesh consults his mother, the goddess-priestess Ninsun. In historical terms the "goddess" Ninsun was probably represented by her mortal high priestess, who led divination rituals and presented oracular responses from the gods, broadly paralleling the Pythia at Delphi or the Sybil at Cumae. Ninsun performs various purification rituals, climbs to the top of a ziggurat, and invokes the blessings of Shamash the sun-god on Gilgamesh and Enkidu, concluding with a ritual in which she adopts Enkidu as her son, and thus as Gilgamesh's brother (EOG 24–7). In a badly damaged portion of the tablet, Gilgamesh and Enkidu also perform various rituals to insure their safety and victory in battle (EOG 27). Such divination and the reception of favorable oracles were crucial for any military undertaking; no one in Bronze Age Mesopotamia expected victory in battle if their plans were not approved by the gods (see pp. 186–92).

The *Epic of Gilgamesh* thus presents us with three phases of military preparation which were probably normative for most Bronze Age armies: 1, preparation of weapons, equipment, and supplies; 2, consultation with the assembly of military-age men to determine the battle plan and selection of those to participate in the expeditionary force; and 3, divination and invocation of the gods to insure divine authorization and blessing. Elements of these three phases of military preparation can be seen in many other historical and literary sources.

The march from Uruk to the Cedar Mountain is described, with regular stops for food and encampment. The emphasis in this section of the epic is on preparing a special evening ritual which allows Gilgamesh to receive five oracular dreams; each was a nightmare, filled with distressing images causing Gilgamesh to fear that his mission will fail. Enkidu, however, cleverly interprets each dream as reflecting a positive outcome for Gilgamesh (EOG 30–7). This doubtless reflects actual practices on campaigns. Oracular dreams were widely regarded as authentic communications from the gods throughout the Ancient Near East. As such, the dreams of the commander of an expedition were particularly important. Such dreams always needed professional dream interpreters to explain their meaning, and a clever interpreter like Enkidu could make almost any omen or dream seem to favor his ruler's plans.[30]

On the campaign, and in battle, Gilgamesh and Enkidu encourage each other. "Let your shout resound like a kettle drum, let the stiffness leave your arms, the tremors your knees," Gilgamesh proclaims, encouraging his friend on to battle. "We shall go on together, let your thoughts dwell on combat; let him who goes first be on guard for himself, and bring his comrade to safety" (EOG 38–9). When Gilgamesh's courage fails him at the sight of the terrifying monster Humbaba, Enkidu berates him: "why, my friend, do you speak like a weakling? With your spineless words you make me despondent.... Don't draw back, don't make a retreat! Make your blow mighty!" (EOG 41).

As in heroic Greece, one of the principle goals of the warrior is to garner fame from battle. Gilgamesh decides to fight Humbaba in order to "establish for ever a fame that endures, how Gilgamesh slew ferocious Humbaba!" (EOG 43). Details of the battle itself are sparse. Gilgamesh and Enkidu fight hand to hand with dagger and axe; no missile weapons are mentioned (EOG 39, 44–5, 70). As with a Homeric duel, the battle begins with challenges and taunts; Humbaba boasts, "I will slit the throat and gullet of Gilgamesh, I will feed his flesh to the locust bird, ravening eagle and vulture" (EOG 41). Again paralleling Homeric literature, humans can also challenge and threaten the gods. Later in the epic, Enkidu threatens the goddess Ishtar that he will "drape your arms in your guts" (EOG 52). When, with the help of great winds sent by the god Shamash, they finally subdue Humbaba, the monster pleads for his life (EOG 43). When Gilgamesh refuses to relent, Humbaba curses them: "May the pair of them not grow old, besides Gilgamesh his friend, none shall bury Enkidu", after which Gilgamesh slits his throat while Enkidu cuts out his lungs (EOG 44). Thereafter they plunder the cedar forest – Humbaba's kingdom – and take the timber back to be made into a monumental door for the temple of Enlil, while Gilgamesh carries the head of Humbaba home in triumph (EOG 47), where he purifies himself and washes his weapons (EOG 48).

CHAPTER FIVE

War-carts and chariots

Among the many military innovations in the Bronze Age Near East, two would have an impact on warfare for thousands of years: the enlistment of animals into military service, and the creation of machines to facilitate war-making. The crucial role played by animals in warfare has declined only in the twentieth century CE. Machines, on the other hand, are playing an increasingly dramatic role in warfare; some would argue that we may be on the verge of seeing machines become more important than men in determining the outcome of war. All of this began in Sumeria with the donkey and the wheel.

Animals and warfare (MK 156–65)

One of the most important and long-lasting Neolithic military innovations was the use of animals in warfare (CAM 36–7). There were five ways in which animals eventually became employed in the ancient Near East to supplement human war efforts: for guarding humans, and supplementing their sense of smell and hearing (dogs); as a mobile source of food (goats, sheep, cattle); transporting food and equipment as pack animals (donkeys, mules, horses, camels); pulling wheeled vehicles (donkeys, onager-donkey hybrids, mules, horses, oxen), and for riding (donkeys, mules, horses, camels).

The oldest military animal partner of humans was the dog, which has been domesticated in the Near East since at least the tenth millennium. Dogs were originally used for hunting and protection, a function they continued in the military context. Watchdogs appeared with paramilitary functions protecting cities, fortresses and camps (EA 2:166–7; EAE 1:229–31; AEMK 82–4). They occasionally accompanied soldiers into combat: "the frenzied dogs were wagging tails before the enemy, [as if asking] 'have you killed a victim?' and were drooling slaver on their forepaws" (HTO 245; FI §723; AM §64). Although there are some examples of tamed lions or cheetahs, these were probably rare, and were used more for court spectacle than for day-to-day protection (EAE 1:513–16).

The next use of animals in warfare was as a source of food. With the beginnings of the domestication of animals in the Neolithic period, humans were able to shift from hunting to herding, creating a more reliable and controllable food source.

Animals had a significant advantage over other possible military food sources such as grain or fruit, in that animals could move themselves along with the army, rather than requiring a man, pack animal or vehicle to carry them. On the other hand, in arid regions animals competed with humans for water, required supervision and protection, and, depending on the gait and speed of an animal, could slow an army down. In the ancient Near East goats, sheep, and cattle were the main mobile food sources which accompanied armies on campaign; on the other hand, donkeys, mules, horses, and camels, though primarily draft and pack animals, were also eaten when necessary.

The most significant military use of animals in the Chalcolithic and Early Bronze Age was the pack animal. The donkey, in particular, was domesticated and used to carry burdens in all aspects of Near Eastern life: domestic, agricultural, mercantile, and military. Throughout the Early and Middle Bronze ages, the donkey (or donkey-onager hybrid) was the primary means of land transportation (EA 2:255–6; EAE 1:478–9; AW 1:166–7). The military use of the donkey permitted armies to stay in the field longer, to campaign over greater distances, and to have extended marches in desert terrain (AEL 1:25–6). On the other hand, although we know donkeys were ridden, there is no evidence of donkeys being extensively ridden in combat situations.

The fourth possible use of animals in ancient Near Eastern warfare was as draft animals to pull wheeled vehicles. In the late fourth millennium {c. 3300–2800} kings in Mesopotamia were conveyed in palanquins (FI §711) or on thrones dragged on wheel-less sledges by bovines (FI §10; WV §2); while the sledge was the ceremonial precursor to the chariot, it obviously had little military potential. The wheel seems to have developed from modifications made to log rollers for sledges. It is possible that wheeled vehicles appear in Mesopotamia as early as the thirty-second century, though the ambiguous depiction in our evidence may show a sledge on rollers rather than true wheels (WV 13, §1). In addition to carrying loads, the earliest archaic vehicles were used for the ritual transport of images of the gods. Indeed, in Mesopotamian mythology the gods are frequently described as riding in wheeled vehicles.[1] Kings were also conveyed on vehicles in ceremonial processions. There is evidence that wheeled vehicles were extensively used for the transportation of goods, supplementing pack animals and boats (EA 1:433–4); Hammurabi's law code {c. 1760} includes laws concerning renting wagons, drivers, and oxen (ANET 177). During the Bronze Age the use of equids to pull wheeled vehicles in battle was their most important military role.

By about 2700, wheeled vehicles begin to be used in warfare in the form of war-carts which will be discussed in detail below.[2] Militarily, wheeled vehicles were probably used to carry supplies on campaign, and, along with boats and pack animals, remained the primary means of transporting supplies and military equipment throughout the Near East. Despite the fact that the Egyptians had ample trade relations with Syria, where war-carts and wheeled vehicles were known during the Early Bronze Age, there is no evidence of the extensive use of wheeled vehicles in Egypt before the New Kingdom {after 1570}, well over a thousand years after the first appearance of the wheel in Mesopotamia.[3] Presumably the fact that nearly all of inhabited Egypt is within a few miles of the Nile rendered the use of wheeled vehicles irrelevant for any type of long-distance travel, which could be accomplished more efficiently and quickly by boat. Furthermore, the existence of numerous irrigation canals and ditches in the fertile river valleys of Egypt and Mesopotamia complicated travel by wheeled vehicles. In this context it must be emphasized that early wheeled vehicles were not necessarily superior in either speed or carrying capacity to simple pack animals or boats, and the mere knowledge of the existence of wheeled vehicles did not necessarily constitute a compelling reason for their widespread use or adaptation for transportation.[4] The Egyptians adopted the widespread use of wheeled vehicles only at the very end of the Middle Bronze Age in the seventeenth century, probably in response to the introduction of the war-chariot by the Hyksos.[5]

The final military use of animals was combat riding. The precise date and place for the origin of equid[6] riding is still somewhat controversial, due to the limitations of evidence and ambiguities of interpretation. It seems to have first occurred on the Eurasian steppe in the third millennium, although some scholars argue that it may have begun as early as the early fourth millennium.[7] Given human nature, it seems likely that informal riding was spontaneous and simultaneous with the first domestication of equids; but this is something quite different from developing an entire culture of horse-riding. Furthermore, it must be emphasized that domestication of equids does not necessarily imply riding, nor does riding necessarily imply military equestrianism. Nor does military equestrianism necessarily imply fighting from horseback, since horses can be ridden by mounted infantry, scouts, and messengers, and riders can dismount to fight.

In the Near East, the donkey was probably domesticated no later than the late fourth millennium, and is widely used as a pack and draft animal until the present day. Onagers were probably not domesticated, as they tend to be intractable (EEH 117a). Onager-donkey hybrids, however, were widely used and highly prized in the late Early Bronze Age; the *kunga* onager-donkey hybrid could cost forty times as much as an ordinary donkey (EEH 117a). The first evidence for the domesticated horse appears in Mesopotamia by the late third millennium (EEH 117b). Equid riding is first documented from the royal tombs of Ur {2550–2400}, where a cylinder seal shows a man riding an animal, possibly with a weapon in his hand (RTU 65). More clear evidence comes from the twenty-third (FI §685) and twenty-first centuries.[8]

For our purpose, however, the crucial question is not the appearance of equid riding, but of equid riding in combat. There is some evidence of early horse riding in combat. An Akkadian seal {23C} shows a man riding an equid holding what could be a javelin (EEH 118). Another scene shows an equid rider in a combat context trampling a fallen man (EEH 118). A Canaanite ruler is shown riding an equid while holding an axe during the reign of Amenemhet III {1843–1797} (IS pl. 39). However, these scenes may depict riding an animal *to* battle rather than *in* battle. The tightest interpretations of the evidence point to the beginning of the *widespread* use of mounted warriors in the Near East probably occurring in the early Iron Age, perhaps around the tenth or ninth centuries.[9] Although horses or donkeys may have been ridden on campaign, or used by scouts or messengers, we have no evidence for widespread combat equestrianism in the Early or Middle Bronze ages in the Near East. Either as draft animals for vehicles, or mounts, the intimate union of man and equids in war has been one of the most momentous in military history, continuing for at least 4500 years, and fading only within living memory.[10]

Two other animals with potential use in military contexts were also known in the ancient Near East, the camel and the elephant. Dromedary (one-humped) camels were indigenous to Arabia, while the Bactrian (two-humped) camel inhabited Iran and Central Asia; camels were introduced into Egypt and North Africa only during Classical times. Camels were probably domesticated by the late third millennium; an eighteenth-century Syrian cylinder seal depicts men riding a Bactrian camel (FI §738). However, the camel did not have an appreciable military impact until the Late Bronze Age.[11] Elephants were also widespread in North Africa and Syria, where they were famously hunted by Thutmose III {1504–1452}, who is said to have hunted 120 elephants in the Orontes valley in Syria (ANET 241a); there is no evidence of the use of elephants in combat in the Near East, however, until Classical times (EAE 1:467).

Sumerian war-carts {2700–2000}[12]

The evidence for the use of the Sumerian war-cart, though striking, is rather sparse. We have three types of evidence: archaeological, artistic, and textual. The remains of war-carts were discovered from burials at Kish, Ur, and Susa (WV 16; RTU 21–5, 32–8); these were found in a highly decayed state, but enough was preserved both to confirm and to elucidate the war-cart depicted in artistic sources.[13]

Early Dynastic four-wheeled war-carts {2700–2300}

The military use of wheeled vehicles first occurred in southern Mesopotamia in the twenty-seventh century, or perhaps somewhat earlier. Although there was undoubtedly a period of experimentation and development of both wheeled vehicles and their military potential, in our surviving sources the war-cart appears fully developed by no later than the middle of the Early Bronze Age in Sumer. I will here only review the artistic sources, leaving a discussion of the military use of the war-cart for later. The following are the major artistic sources for Early Dynastic four-wheeled war-carts.[14]

1   Cylinder seal on a pot from Uruk, Sumer {ED, 2900–2300} (FI 24i, p. 159, FI §499). A four-wheeled war-cart led by one man, carrying a seated man with axe; the cart's wheels are grooved for better traction.

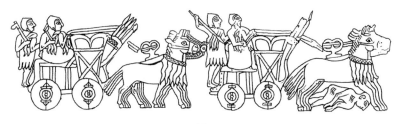

(a)

(b)

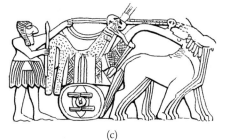

(c)

(d)   (e)

Figure 4   Early and Middle Bronze Age war-carts and chariots (drawings by Michael Lyon)

(a) Sumerian four-wheeled war-carts from the "Standard of Ur", tomb of king Ur-Pabilsag {c. 2550} (British Museum 121201); see AFC 98–9.

(b) Akkadian war-cart trampling enemies; cylinder seal from Nagar (Tell Brak, Syria) {c 2250}; see EEH 116 §2.

(c) Neo-Sumerian two-wheeled war-cart, relief from Ur {26C} (University of Pennsylvania Museum of Archaeology and Anthropology, 17086); see AFC 72 §31.

(d) Warrior in two-wheeled chariot trampling enemy; cylinder seal from Babylon {1779} (British Musuem 16815a); see WV §31.

(e) Warrior (in scale armor?) shooting a bow from a two-wheeled chariot; cylinder seal from Syria {18–17C}; see WV §36.

2 Vase painting from Khafajah {ED II, 2650–2550} (AW 1:128). A four-wheeled war-cart with studded wheel rims, carrying two men and perhaps four javelins in a side quiver-box.

3 "Standard of Ur" {ED IIIA, 2550–2400} (cover art; Figure 4a, p. 133; pp. 49–50; AFC 98–9; FA 84; AW 1:132–3; SDA 146–7; WV §3; AM §72, §x–xi). Along with the Stele of Vultures, the Standard of Ur is our most important war-cart scene. Five war-carts are depicted being drawn by long-eared equids (donkeys or donkey-onager hybrids) with barding for the animals. All the war-carts have javelin quiver-boxes; half the men hold axes in their hands, half are throwing or thrusting javelins. Judging from the gait of the equids, the war-cart on the top panel is being walked in a procession, as is one war-cart on the bottom panel; the other three, with long strides for the animals, seem to be running, while trampling the dead bodies of enemies.

4 "Stele of Vultures" of Eannatum of Lagash (from Telloh) {ED IIIA, c. 2440} (FA 82; AFC 190–1; AW 1:135; SDA 134–7; AM §66–9). The wheels are missing; this could be a four or two-wheeled vehicle. Most of the war-cart is missing, but the remaining fragment shows a war-cart with a large javelin-quiver and the king holding a javelin (or thrusting spear?) and what appears to be a proto-sickle-sword. This image is discussed in detail on pp. 55–9, Figure 1, p. 55.

5 Inlaid shell panel from Mari {ED III, 2550–2300} (AFC 159). A standard Sumerian four-wheeled war-cart with javelins in a front quiver-box, accompanied by a spear-armed foot soldier; the war-cart is trampling a corpse. Overall, the composition is similar to the that depicted on the Standard of Ur.

6 Inlaid shell panel from Mari {ED III, 2550–2300} (AW 1:139). Fragmentary; probably four-wheeled, but possible only two-wheeled war-cart.

7 Cylinder seal from Syria (Mari?) {ED III?, 2550–2300} (FI §722). A standard Sumerian four-wheeled vehicle with one rider, drawn by four equids and followed by a soldier with a javelin.

8 Cylinder seal from Kish {ED III, 2500–2350} (FI §724; ELH pl. 1). Seated figure on four-wheeled war-cart being led by another man; the war-cart has javelins in a front quiver-box and is trampling a fallen enemy.

Early Dynastic {2700–2300} two-wheeled war-carts[15]

As far as we can tell, four-wheeled and two-wheeled war-carts appear roughly simultaneously in Sumer. Both utilize essentially the same technology, and are both shown in similar military situations. The four-wheeled war-cart, discussed above, appears more frequently and in more intense military contexts than are shown in any of the representations of the two-wheeled version. The relative military merits of both will be discussed on pp. 137–41. The major artistic sources for Sumerian two-wheeled war-carts include:

9 Cylinder seal from Sumer {ED, 2900–2300} (FI §723; AM §64). Royal figure armed with axe entering a two-wheeled war-cart, accompanied by a dog and three men, two armed with axes and one with a spear.

10 Copper model from Tell Agrab {ED II, 2650–2550} (AW 1:39, 129; SDA 152–3; WV §7; AM §49). Drawn by four horses, studded block wheels; there is no apparent military context.

11 Votive plaque from Ur {ED II; 2650–2550} (Figure 4c, p. 133; AFC 72; AW 1:130; AAM §43; WV §8). The driver is standing on the ground behind the war-cart, holding the reins, and carrying a javelin; there are other javelins in the box-quiver on the war-cart. The war-cart seems to be draped with a leopard skin. It is pulled by two (possibly four) equids which are not protected by barding. It is probably part of a ceremonial scene similar to that depicted in the votive plaque from Khafajah described below.

12 Votive plaque from Khafajah {ED II?, 2650–2550} (AAM §42; AM §45; SDA 132). The overall layout of this scene closely parallels the votive plaque from Ur described above; indeed each complements the gaps in the other. A festival is in process in which the third and lowest panel shows a war-cart drawn by four equids, preceded by a man with a javelin or short thrusting spear. Although the parallel scenes depicted in the Ur and Khafajah plaques are ceremonial rather than military, these two-wheeled war-carts clearly have a martial purpose, with a javelin quiver-box, and both the driver and accompanying foot soldier armed with javelins.

The Sumerian war-cart[16]

From the archaeological and artistic evidence outlined above, we can obtain a basic understanding of the Sumerian war-cart. The classic Sumerian war-cart [^{GIŠ}.gigir] {2600–2300} was essentially a wagon adapted for military use. The four-wheeled version seems to have preceded the two-wheeled version, but by the time of its widespread military use both the two- and four-wheeled versions were used in battle. The major limitation of the four-wheeler was weight; the Sumerian war-cart had a heavy wooden frame with four solid disk wheels. The cart itself was long and narrow, allowing only one person abreast, the driver generally in front and the warrior behind. The cart was surrounded by a high front and lower side panels for protection and for the driver and rider to hold to stabilize themselves. A second major limitation on the four-wheeler was that the front wheels could not pivot independent of the vehicle as a whole, giving it a very wide turning radius. Although the royal-cart was originally pulled by oxen, which continued in use for agricultural and commercial carts, in military settings the war-cart was always pulled by equids – since bovines could move at only a few miles an hour, a war-cart pulled by oxen would be slower than a man on foot (CG 77).

Since our sources are generally vague in both naming and depicting equids, it is often not possible to determine with certainty what specific species of equid was used (WV 22–8, 41–3). Donkeys were the most common equid in Mesopotamia. Onagers (wild asses) were probably not used because they are difficult to domesticate and control; the donkey-onager hybrid was common with war-carts, being larger and stronger than the donkey, but more docile and manageable than the onager. The horse was introduced into Mesopotamia in the late third millennium; the horse or mule (horse–donkey hybrid) was probably adopted for pulling war-carts by the late Early Bronze Age (ELH 197–8). It must be emphasized that, although the Bronze Age horse was larger, stronger and faster than the donkey, it was still substantially smaller than modern horses; based on evidence from bones we can estimate that ancient horses ranged from 12–14 hands high at the shoulder (130–150 cm; one hand = eleven centimeters), while the modern Western riding horse is 15–17 hands (160–185 cm). Due to the weight of the war-cart and the limited size and strength of the draft animals, the speed of the Sumerian war-cart was rather slow. Experimentation with modern reconstructions have demonstrated that its speed ranged from 10 to 12 miles per hour, or five to six minutes per mile (WV 33), slower than the top speed of an unarmed fast man, but probably somewhat faster than the average man in a combat situation.

Development of the Sumerian war-cart

The evidence, though inadequate, allows the following hypothetical reconstruction of the development of the Sumerian war-cart. The first war-carts seem to have developed directly from ritual vehicles used for conveying divine images or kings in ceremonial processions, initially drawn by oxen rather than equids. At some point, probably in the twenty-seventh century, kings began to ride their ceremonial war-carts to the battlefield rather than simply in ceremonial processions for civic and religious purposes. Carts were also made to carry statues of the gods in ritual processions, and were dedicated to the temples (PI 100). Initially the king probably had the only war-cart on the battlefield. Presumably he rode his war-cart to the battlefield, dismounted and fought, and then rode again after the battle. For example, in the Stele of Vultures {c. 2440}, Eannatum of Lagash {c. 2455–2425} is shown in the lower panel in the only war-cart depicted in the entire battle scene (although others might have existed in the large damaged portion of the stele). In the upper register, on the other hand, Eanatum is shown fighting on foot (item 4, pp. 131–3). Military leaders were undoubtedly quickly able to recognize the military potential in the royal war-cart. The king could move among his own troops more quickly, giving orders and receiving reports. A fleeing enemy could also be pursued more quickly by war-cart. At some point the king began to ride the war-cart during the battle, and fight from it. In due course, the number of war-carts on a battlefield increased, either because members of the royal family and other nobles wanted to share in the high status of riding war-carts, or because military leaders recognized that, by increasing the number of war-carts, an army could potentially gain a tactical advantage over an enemy. Some specific changes in the design of the cart may have had military impetus. Increasing the height of the side and front panel would afford greater protection and stability to the rider. Sheep skins, strips of leather, or other types of barding, were hung on the chests of the equids for their protection (item 3, p. 134; MM 32), while a javelin quiver-box and probably other weapon containers were added to increase the ammunition supply and make it more readily accessible (item 3 above). The period roughly from 2600 to 2300 was the classic age of the Sumerian war-cart, as spectacularly represented in the military art of the Standard of Ur (item 3) and the Stele of Vultures (item 4), described above. By at least the twenty-fifth century this technology had spread up the Euphrates to Mari and south-eastern Syria (items 5 to 7).

The Sumerian war-cart in battle

The archaeological and artistic evidence can be supplemented by a few texts giving us a basic understanding of the military use of the Sumerian war-cart. The weapons of the warrior of the Sumerian war-cart were the javelin and the axe – the standard weapons of the ordinary Sumerian warrior. Javelin quiver-boxes are almost always found on the war-carts; warriors are shown wielding both javelins and axes from within the war-cart (item 1). There is no indication that the bow was used. The war-carts are almost always accompanied by foot soldiers, undoubtedly to protect the war-cart from attacks by enemy infantry. The equids are sometimes shown being led by a man (item 1), generally in a procession. The war-carts are often preceded by an armed man (items 3, 8, 11–12), or followed by a man (items 1 and 7) or a group of men (items 4 and 9) armed with javelins and/ or axes.

An important question posed by the artistic evidence is, why did the Sumerians use both four-wheeled and two-wheeled war-carts? The four-wheeler has advantages in stability and having room for a driver allowing the warrior to give his full attention to combat. Psychologically, the larger war-cart was probably more terrifying to the enemy. The two-wheeler, on the other hand, would have the advantage of speed, since it was lighter, and maneuverability, since the four-wheeler war-cart lacked a pivoting front axle and therefore had a wide turning radius. Since the Sumerians used the javelin rather than the bow – which requires two hands to shoot – as the major missile weapon from war-carts, a single warrior could drive a two-wheeler holding the reins in his left hand and a javelin or axe in his right hand, as several drivers are depicted. Overall, it seems that the two-wheeled war-cart proved to be the most effective in battle, for, as we will see on p. 145, the four-wheeled war-cart disappeared entirely from the battlefield by the early Middle Bronze Age.

Most of the war-cart scenes in Sumerian martial art are rather static. There are only two depictions of the Sumerian war-cart in which we get a sense of the actual use in battle: the Standard of Ur (item 3; cover art, Figure 5a, p. 133) and Stele of the Vultures (item 4), both dating to the twenty-fifth century. The Standard of Ur shows five war-carts. Structurally they are all almost exactly the same: four disk-wheels, a front panel between chest and neck height, and side panels about knee or thigh height. In a sense, the war-cart can be seen as a mobile shield whose high front panels provided protection to the driver and warrior from enemy missiles. All are pulled by four long-eared, long-tailed equids which have strips of sheep-skin or leather barding covering their necks and chests to protect them from enemy missiles. The war-carts are shown in two panels. The first shows a victory procession, with a single war-cart to the rear. It does not have a visible javelin-quiver, but the upper part of the top register is partly missing, so this may simply be lost. The driver, axe in hand, stands on the ground holding the reins; the equids are depicted with walking gait (all four legs visible at angles). The king – the presumed rider of the war-cart – stands at the head of three soldiers armed with spear and axe, and receives prisoners of war from other soldiers in an after-battle triumph ritual. The other four war-carts are shown in the bottom register in the midst of battle, all with javelin quivers. The equids on three of the war-carts are shown in full gallop gait, trampling the corpses of fallen enemies. The fourth war-cart, at the rear, is shown with equids walking and not trampling enemies. Each war-cart has two riders, a driver in the front and a warrior standing on the very edge at the rear. They all have sheep-skin kilts and sheep-skins flung over their left shoulders for protection to their upper torso; they also have either leather or metal helmets with a strap under the chin. Of the drivers, one holds an axe on his right shoulder (though the head of the axe is missing), holding the reins in his left hand, just like the driver in the upper panel; the image of one of the drivers is damaged and it can't be seen for certain what he is doing with his right hand. The other two drivers hold something in their right hands, it but it is uncertain what – possibly axes or a javelins.

Several things seem clear from the Standard of Ur. Both driver and warrior were expected to fight, since the drivers are also shown armed with axes. The javelins were thrown, since the javelin quiver-box attached to the war-cart contains multiple weapons. Axes were considered useful weapons for war-carts, whether to fight off infantry that might attack the war-cart, or to use when dismounted. Sumerians recognized that the greatest vulnerability of the war-cart was the equids. Since the easiest way to stop a war-cart was to kill or disable a single equid, they were given some type of protection on their chests. War-carts could move across the battlefield at a gallop and pursue fleeing enemies.

Unfortunately, there are number of ambiguities in the Standard of Ur which make a complete interpretation impossible. First, is the scene meant to depict four war-carts simultaneously, or one cart at different moments in a cartoon-like sequence? It probably shows four different war-carts, since each warrior has a different weapon. Second, does it represent a line of war-carts following one another, or a group of war-carts side-by-side? Third, are they charging formed-up enemy ranks, or chasing and overwhelming already defeated and fleeing enemies? In other words, were the war-carts used to break formed-up enemy ranks, or simply to chase down a fleeing enemy whose ranks were already broken? The Standard of Ur seems to indicate the latter, since all the enemies have their backs to the advancing war-carts; no one is making any serious resistance. Are they trampling the enemies, or riding around and beside them? In later depictions of war-carts, riding over a prostrate enemy becomes a stylized depiction of victory in battle. Unfortunately, the evidence is insufficient to answer most of these questions for certain, but it must be remembered that, whatever the artist of the Standard of Ur was trying to depict in this particular instance, it does not demonstrate that this was therefore the *only* way the war-cart could have been used by the Sumerians. It is quite possible that the Sumerians both fought from the war-cart and dismounted to fight. The war-carts could have been marshaled in line or rank depending on the tactical circumstances. They may have on some occasions attacked formed-up ranks of enemy, and on other occasions chased down fleeing enemies. There is no reason to assume the Sumerians were incapable of tactical flexibility in their use of war-carts. It is also important to emphasize that Sumerian art almost invariably depicts not actual battle, but victory *after* battle. The Standard of Ur may thus not be trying to tell us how war-carts were used to win a battle, but how they were used after the battle was already won.

The Stele of Vultures {c. 2440} (item 4; Figure 1, p. 55) shows king Eanatum of Lagash charging into battle on his war-cart, followed by a large body of infantry armed with spears and axes. The depiction may be intended as symbolic rather than tactical – the king is always said to *lead* his army into battle even if, in reality, he stands at the rear of the army. But it may also represent a real tactic of the war-carts preceding the infantry into battle. The king stands at the front of the war-cart, holding a long spear overhead in his left hand and what appears to be a proto-sickle-sword (or perhaps a club or a scepter, see pp. 66–71) in his right hand. The war-cart is also equipped with a quiver-box with half a dozen javelins, as well as a spare axe. The depiction of a spear in Eanatum's hand is unique in Sumerian warfare – all other war-cart warriors hold javelins. The spear is held overhand in the left hand, so far to the rear of the shaft that it would seem to be unbalanced. Although the head of the weapon is lost and we cannot tell the length of the spear, it is clearly not a javelin. A fragment of a parallel scene from the same stele shows the top of the largely lost fourth panel of the Stele of the Vultures.[17] There, the barest fragment at the far left of the fourth panel shows the hand of a man grasping the end of the long lance in the very same unbalanced way Eanatum holds the lance in the second panel. In the fourth panel the length of the entire lance is show, with the lance head about to be thrust into the face of the enemy king. This scene thus shows the use of a long thrusting lance from the war-cart rather than the javelin. In the upper register of the stele, Eanatum stands on the ground in front of his army, indicating that Sumerian chariot warriors could dismount and fight on the ground with axe and spear, along with the infantry. Each of the soldiers following Eanatum is similarly double-armed, with thrusting spear in one hand and an axe in the other.

Another odd characteristic of Eanatum's war-cart is that the driver appears to be standing *behind* Eanatum. The torso and head of the second figure is missing in a damaged portion of the stele, and his legs are largely hidden behind the side panel of the war-cart. The only indication of a second occupant of the war-cart is the forearm and right hand which extends to the side of Eanatum's hip, and appears to be holding an axe. The reins of the cart rest on the top of the front panel, but then disappear; Eanatum clearly is not holding them, since he has a weapon in each hand. Unless this scene is composed with unrealistic artistic license, I suspect that the reins go behind Eanatum to his left side (and hence are invisible in the scene) and are held in the left hand of the nearly obscured man to the rear of Eanatum. The Standard of Ur shows the king standing in front of the war-cart while his driver stands on the ground holding the reins in his left hand and an axe in his right, just like the largely defaced driver of Eanatum's war-cart seems to be doing. I suspect that if each man stood on opposite sides of the war-cart it would not be impossible for the man at the rear to drive, though it does seem quite awkward. On the other hand, since the equids and everything to the front of Eanatum are missing because of damage to the stele, it may be that there was originally a man leading the war-cart in front of the equids.

Another important characteristic of Sumerian war-carts depicted in art is the development of the theme of the war-cart trampling the enemy as a symbol of victory in battle. It appears most strikingly in the Standard of Ur (item 3). A precisely analogous scene, though fragmentary, occurs at Mari (item 5), and in a cylinder seal from Kish (item 8). It may also possibly have been shown in the Stele of Vultures prior to damage; the area under the war-cart is now missing, but the infantry in the register above the war-cart are trampling enemy corpses under their feet (item 4). This issue will be discussed more fully on p. 150.

These artistic representations of war-cart battle can be supplemented by occasional references to war-carts in Sumerian royal inscriptions. The most important comes from an inscription describing a battle in the agricultural Ugiga-field between king Enmetena of Lagash {c. 2400} and Urluma of Umma, in which Enmetena "confronted the retreating Urluma, ruler of Umma, at the base of the Lumagirnunta-canal, and [Urluma] abandoned his sixty teams of asses there, and left the bones of their personnel [of the war-carts] strewn over the plain" (PI 55, 77). This text describes a battle occurring on a flat open agricultural field, ideal for war-carts; unfortunately, the details of the actual battle were not recorded. The result, however, is clear: Enmetena defeated the army of Umma, which fled before him until they reached a canal which their war-carts could not cross. The warriors abandoned their war-carts and tried to flee on foot, but many were run down, either by pursuing war-carts or by infantry. The text also provides another important detail – that king Urluma had "sixty teams of asses", or, in other words, 60 war-carts. We cannot be sure that some of the war-carts did not escape, so 60 should be considered the minimum number in Urluma's army. None the less, it shows that an average Sumerian city-state could probably muster 50–80 war-carts for battle. At this point they were no longer merely ceremonial vehicles or royal conveyances, but were an important combat component in the Sumerian army. When Enmetena wished to emphasize the magnitude of his victory, he underlined the capture of 60 war-carts, rather than the total number of enemy dead or captured.

Enmetena of Lagash {c. 2400} also built a war-cart named "Ningrsu's chariot that heaps up [burial mounds of dead enemies in] defeated foreign lands" (PI 58, cf. 100); it is obviously a divine war-cart for temple ritual, but its name shows its parallel military function. The war-cart brings victory in battle, resulting in "heaping up" burial mounds of the corpses of the defeated enemies – a standard Sumerian metaphor for military victory depicted in the Stele of Vultures (item 4; Figure 1, p. 55).[18] Although to the modern mind the ceremonial aspects of the war-cart is sometimes seen to imply a lack of serious application to real combat, to the ancient mind the quasi-sacred qualities of a war-cart enhanced rather then detracted from its military value. The fact that a war-cart was dedicated to a god, carried a statue or image of a god in religious rituals, was kept in a temple treasury, and was made in imitation of the celestial vehicles used by the gods, gave the war-cart a numinous quality, making it more effective by psychologically increasing the fear of those who faced it in battle. To the mind of the Sumerian warrior, the war-cart was not the slow-moving wooden box on heavy wheels pulled by asses as often described by modern scholars; rather, it was a chariot of the gods, representing and conveying divine power to the battlefield. It was perhaps viewed by the Sumerians more like the biblical Ark of the Covenant. Indeed, against an ancient enemy, the psychological impact of the Sumerian war-cart – its size, weight, speed, heroic warrior, and divine aura – was probably as significant as its actual military impact.

The ceremonial aspect of the war-cart and chariot as the proper vehicle for royal dignity is emphasized in one of the much later Mari texts {1760s}. Here Zimri-Lim is advised about proper riding decorum:

> My lord should preserve his royal dignity. Even though you are the king of the [nomad] Haneans, you are also the king of the Akkadians. Thus my lord should not ride horses, but a chariot with mules (*kudanu*), and maintain the prestige of his sovereignty. (ARM 6.76; EEH 120b; MK 165)

The chariot as a symbol of kingship was as significant as its practical military applications in war.

The war-carts and their equid teams seem to have been housed in special stables. Uru'inimgina of Lagash describes building "a chariot-house for [the war-god] Ningirsu, a building whose awesome splendor overwhelms all the lands" (PI 80, 79). Ur-Bau, ruler of Lagash, built the "house of the donkey-stallions" (E3/1:20). These were probably building complexes for constructing, repairing, and storing war-carts and their equipment, and for the care and breeding of their equid teams.

War-carts in the Akkadian and Neo-Sumerian periods {2300–2000}

Until recently it has generally been thought that the Akkadians essentially abandoned the use of the four-wheeled war-cart in battle. Crouwel and Littauer summarized this position: the "evidence for [the] use [of war-carts] in warfare, for which they were clearly unsuitable, fades rapidly after the middle of the [third] millennium" (EA 5:344; WV 44–5). Recently published cylinder seals from ancient Nagar (Tell Brak; Figure 4b, p. 133; EA 1:355–6) in the Khabur Triangle in north-eastern Syria, however, provide some new, fairly conclusive evidence that the use of the war-cart continued unabated during the Akkadian period. Naram-Sin {2254–2218} built a large palace at Nagar, which became the major Akkadian administrative center in northern Mesopotamia. The discovery of three military scenes of four-wheeled war-carts on Akkadian-period cylinder seals from Nagar indicates the ongoing Akkadian use of the four-wheeled war-cart in battle (EEH 116, §1–4). On the other hand, none of the better-known monumental Akkadian martial art depicts the use of the war-cart. For the Akkadian four-wheeled war-cart in battle we have:

13 Akkadian cylinder seal {c. 2250} (EEH 116 §1). A four-wheeled war-cart drawn by equids with protective barding on their chests. One seated man drives the cart, with a man stepping into the war-cart behind, and another standing on the ground. The war-cart is trampling a corpse, while another wounded man on the ground is being dispatched by a warrior armed with a dagger or axe, while a vulture eagerly hovers nearby.

14 Akkadian cylinder seal {c. 2250} (EEH 116 §2; Figure 4b, p. 133). A four-wheeled war-cart drawn by equids. The seated driver is followed by one man stepping into the war-cart from the rear and another standing brandishing a dagger over his head. The war-cart is trampling a fallen corpse. Underneath this scene may be four prisoners sitting on the ground with their arms pinioned behind their backs.

15 Akkadian cylinder seal {c. 2250} (EEH 116 §4). A four-wheeled war-cart tramples an enemy and is followed by a foot soldier.

Additionally, there are two non-military Akkadian scenes with similar four-wheeled carts:

16 Cylinder seal {Akkadian, 2220–2159} (AFC §143; WV §13; SDA 189; FI §725). This mythological scene depicts a god riding in a standard four-wheeled war-cart being drawn by a griffin. The god holds a whip, but no weapons are apparent, though there may be a javelin in a quiver-box.

17 Cylinder seal {Akkadian, 2220–2159} (AM §113). God riding in a four-wheeled war-cart drawn by a griffin, similar to item 16 above.

For two-wheeled Akkadian war-carts we have:

18 Akkadian cylinder seal {2334–2193} (WV §17; FI §726). God riding in a two-wheeled celestial war-cart drawn by a griffin, similar to items 16 and 17 above.

During the Ur III period (2112–2004} there is additional evidence for two-wheeled war-carts:

19 Fragmentary scene from Ur III (AAM §192–3; WV §18). Man riding a two-wheeled war-cart with grooved disk-wheels; the upper portion is missing, so there is no indication of military use.

20 Fragments from the stele of Urnammu {2112–2095} (AFC 445). These are too damaged to determine if any military accoutrements are present.

21 Depiction of two-wheeled war-cart from Tepe Hisar, northern Iran, southeast of Caspian Sea {2350–2000} (WV §21; ELH 199). This is a badly composed scene of a man riding a two wheeled war-cart; there is no clear military context. Some have argued that the partially damaged wheel is spoked; others argue that it is a cross-bar wheel (WV 40). This may represent the spread of war-cart technology into Iran, or perhaps reflects a transitional form between the steppe war-carts of Central Asia and those of the Near East.

Thus, for the period from 2300–2000, there is an apparent shift in the *depiction* of war-cart warfare, with fewer and less dramatic military scenes. None the less, it is clear that carts continued to be used during this period (items 13–15 above). Does this apparent change in our source material reflect a change in actual combat practices, a change in the way warfare was depicted, or merely the random chance of what martial art happens to survive and to have been discovered and published? Until the recent publication of Akkadian-period cylinder seals from Nagar (EEH 116) there was no clear example of the depiction of a war-cart in a military context during that period (WV 44–5). Now there are three examples, which should serve as a reminder that, in ancient archaeology and history, absence of evidence is not evidence of absence. Much of what we claim to know about ancient history is often based on the rather random preservation and discovery of a fragmentary, obscure, and limited range of sources. None the less, despite their fixation on war, no Akkadian king is shown riding in a war-cart in battle in surviving monumental Akkadian art.

There is additional literary evidence that is generally overlooked in the discussion of war-carts in the Neo-Sumerian period. We are fortunate to have detailed textual descriptions of the Sumerian war-cart from Gudea of Lagash {2141–2122}, from precisely the period in which it is sometimes claimed that the war-cart went out of military use.[19] Gudea built a ceremonial war-cart for the god Ningirsu, taking special care in the selection and preparation of the materials:

The good shepherd Gudea [king of Lagash] … broke the seal on his storehouse [in the city of Girsu], pulled aside the wooden [bolt of the door]. Gudea checked the wood [for the war-cart] piece by piece, taking great care of it. The *mes* wood he smoothed and he split the *khalub* wood, and fitted them together to make his blue chariot…. He decorated the chariot with silver and lapis lazuli, with arrows protruding from the quiver like the [shafts] of daylight [from the sun]; he was especially careful with the *ankar* [mace], the "warrior's arm".… He harnessed to it [donkey] stallions, the "lions-summoned-for-running". Gudea fashioned for Ningirsu his beloved standard and wrote his [Ningirsu's] own name on it.[20]

The use of a mace from a war-cart is also mentioned in the epic of Ninurta (HTO 117).

A description of the completed war-cart and weapons donated by Gudea to the temple of Ningirsu provides a poetical description of the Sumerian war-cart in battle:

> The chariot named "It subdued the mountain" [lands],
> Bearing terror and dread [to the enemy],
> Drawn by the donkey "Merrily-Neighing-Wind"
> Harnessed with the other donkeys.
> The seven-spiked mace, fierce battle mace,
> Weapon unbearable from the North to the South . . .
> The *mittu*-mace, a lion-headed weapon of *hulalu* stone,
> Which does not flee from enemy lands . . .
> Nine banners
> The "warrior's arm" [mace]
> A bow [*ᴳᴵˢ-ban*] that roars like a forest of *mes*-trees,
> Its terrible arrows [*ti*] flashing like lightening in battle
> On its quiver [*mar*] a leopard and lion [were depicted]
> With a serpent flicking its tongue
> The weapons of battle
> The power of kingship . . .
> Gudea, ruler of Lagash, presented to the Temple.[21]

There is one ambiguity in interpreting the meaning of this text; Gudea is clearly describing the building of a ceremonial war-cart for use in rituals in the temple of the god Ningirsu. Does this mean that this war-cart was *purely* ceremonial, or was it taken into battle as well? However that may be, this is clearly a ceremonial *war*-cart, and represents our best contemporary description of the building, purpose, and conceptualization of the role of war-cart of this period. The war-cart was the "power of kingship", which brought "terror and dread" upon the enemy. If the military function of the war-cart had all but disappeared during the two centuries previous to Gudea, as is sometimes claimed, it is unlikely he would have so dramatically emphasized precisely those obsolete military functions in his dedicatory inscription. We should also avoid imposing modern preconceptions on ancient peoples: if a vehicle is "ceremonial" for a procession to a temple, it cannot simultaneously have a "practical" function in battle. In actuality, to some extent, all ancient battle was ceremonial; indeed, in some ways, the world of ritual was more "real" for ancient peoples than what we consider today as the world of real events.

The other striking feature of Gudea's war-cart is the emphasis on the use of the bow and arrow in war-carts, our earliest example of the bow and chariot combination which would become standard in the Late Bronze Age. The use of the bow from the chariot in Neo-Sumerian times is also implied in the Epic of Ninurta's victory over Azag. There Ninurta is said to have mounted a chariot to fight, and to have shot his bow in battle (HTO 244); although not explicit, this may imply the use of a bow from the chariot. This represents a major transition from the Early Dynastic javelin to Neo-Sumerian bow as the war-cart missile weapon, and is a key transformation in the development of the "true" war-chariot which occurs in the later Middle Bronze Age, as will be discussed on pp. 145–7.[22]

In summary, by the end of the Early Bronze Age the Sumerian war-cart was a weapon in transition. That the Sumerians retained the two-wheeled war-cart, and even experimented with using the bow from it, demonstrates that the war-cart was still considered useful in battle, even if it was not decisive. In the right terrain against the right enemy and used at the proper moment in battle, the war-cart could create a military advantage and perhaps win a battle. Thus experimentation continued in the coming centuries to discover the ideal formula for the building and use of the war-cart, leading to the innovation of the true war-chariot, and the great chariot revolution of the seventeenth century.

Middle Bronze Age and the origins of the war-chariot {2000–1600}[23]

The Middle Bronze Age saw the rise of what is often called the true war-chariot, as opposed to the early Sumerian war-cart. The transformation from war-cart to chariot required a transformation of biological, technological, social, and military factors to create the ideal vehicle for Late Bronze Age warfare. Once that proper combination of factors had developed, the war-chariot spread rapidly throughout much of the Old World, encompassing Central Asia, the Near East, Europe, India, China, and North Africa.

Scholars tend to define the "true" chariot, which would revolutionize warfare in the Late Bronze Age, by the following characteristics (CG 74–120; ELH; WV 50–5, §24–36). The chariot was drawn by horses rather than by other equids, allowing faster speed. Lighter construction techniques, two wheels instead of four, and spoked wheels rather than disk wheels, also contributed to decreasing the weight and increasing the speed of the chariot. The change from four to two wheels allowed greater maneuverability. A shift from the nose ring for controlling the horse to bit and reins, along with improved yoke and harness, created a more efficient means both for controlling the horse and for the horse to pull the chariot, again boosting maneuverability and speed. The overall impact of new lightweight construction, improved harness and horse-power, resulted by the seventeenth century in vehicles which could attain a maximum speed of thirty miles per hour for short distances, two-and-a-half times the speed of the Early Bronze Sumerian four-wheeled war-cart (CG 84). To the improved speed of the chariot was added the use of the composite bow, allowing rapid fire at a distance. The greater penetrating power of the composite bow with bronze arrowheads made the chariot a rapidly moving platform shooting the most powerful missile in the ancient arsenal.[24] It also led to the adoption of bronze scale armor for chariot warriors, and often for their horses. The fact that the bow required two hands to be shot meant that chariots were most efficient when they had a battle-team of driver and archer. This complex and expensive combination of chariot craftsmanship, composite bow-making, horse grooming and training, and metal-working for armor, created the need for large and expensive royal workshops and stables to maintain the chariots. It probably required half a dozen men – carpenter, bowyer, groom, metal-worker, and a servant or two – to maintain a single chariot in combat readiness. The building and repairing of chariot wheels is mentioned (L 377), along with reference to a courtier named Yashub-Ashar who seems to have been in charge of chariot production at Mari (MM 31).

Chariots were obviously valuable and somewhat rare, since they were given as gifts to vassals and nobles (ARM 5.66, 5.58, 10.113). The relative scarcity of both chariots and the skilled craftsmen necessary to build and repair them is emphasized in one of the Mari texts, where a nobleman, Ila-salim, requests a new chariot from the king Zimri-Lim:

> The king gave me a chariot, but when I went away between the country and the mountains, that chariot broke in the middle, and now as I travel to and fro there is not chariot for me to ride. If it please my lord, may my lord give me another chariot, so that I can organize the country until my lord comes. I am my lord's servant; may my lord not refuse me another chariot. (ARM 5.66; MK 164)

This text is interesting at a number of levels. The fact that the chariot broke in the mountains shows the problem of the use of the chariot in the rough terrain outside the flat plains. It also appears that this nobleman had the only chariot in his city; he had no other vehicle, and didn't seem to be able to borrow one. Furthermore, he had no craftsmen in his employ able to repair the chariot or build him a new one. He had to ask for one from the king. The chariot is also not used in a military context, but as a vehicle to assist the nobleman in administering his province.

Texts mention "harnessed teams" of chariot horses, grooms, and trainers (MK 161–2; ARM 18.55), indicating an organized stable system for chariot horses. For every pair of horses pulling a chariot, another half a dozen horses would be needed in reserve for breeding, training, and replacement for horses that were injured, captured or killed. All of this required a state that was wealthy and powerful enough to maintain armies with hundreds of chariots. More importantly, it required the creation of a new military mind-set focused on the tactical advantages and limitations of the chariot. As the experiences of soldiers with new technologies in the nineteenth and twentieth centuries CE amply demonstrate, it probably required several generations to fully develop such tactical expertise, and several more generations for soldiers and other elites to fully accept all the social and military changes required by the new chariot warfare. It was not until the seventeenth century that all of these complex elements were finally in place in the proper balance to maximize the military potential of chariot warfare. From the military perspective, the transition from the Middle Bronze Age to the Late Bronze Age – usually dated to around 1600 BCE – can be defined as the transition from non-chariot-centered warfare to the new chariot warfare.

Artistic evidence on the development of the chariot[25]

There are a few examples of the continued use of the four-wheeled chariot in the early Middle Bronze Age {2000–1600} in Anatolia, but depictions of four-wheeled war-carts in a military context have disappeared by the nineteenth century.[26] Throughout the rest of the Middle Bronze Age the majority of the depictions of war vehicles – nearly all from cylinder seals – are two-wheeled vehicles drawn by two horses (ELH). A rough outline of the development and use of the war-chariot can be culled from these examples. The data can be broadly divided into roughly two periods, the early Middle Bronze {2000–1800} and the late Middle Bronze {1800–1600}. It must be emphasized that our evidence is quite limited and we are essentially reduced to generalizing from inadequate data. The following is a list of our major evidence with a military context.

Early Middle Bronze evidence {2000–1800}

22 Cylinder seal, Kultepe (Karum), Anatolia {2000–1850} (WV §29; ELH §4). A single rider, a royal figure with an axe, in a chariot with two four-spoked wheels, drawn by two horses with nose rings rather than reins (cf. WV §28).
23 Cylinder seal, Uruk, Iraq {20–19C} (WV §30, p. 69). Single rider in chariot with two spoked wheels.
24 Clay tablet with cylinder seal impression, Babylon {1779} (Figure 4d, p. 133; FI §730; WV §31). The single rider is a king on a chariot with two four-spoked wheels, trampling a prostrate enemy, and followed by four soldiers in a procession before the gods.
25 Cylinder seal, Syria {19–17C} (FI §728). A single rider in a chariot with two four-spoked wheels, trampling a prostrate enemy.

Based on this – admittedly limited – evidence, we find the following characteristics of chariot warfare in the early Middle Bronze period {2000–1800}. Only the two-wheeled chariot was used for military purposes, a practice which had probably begun in the Neo-Sumerian period {2200–2000} as discussed on pp. 141–5. The Early Bronze technique of having a single rider on the two-wheeled Sumerian war-cart continued throughout the early Middle Bronze Age; all of the depictions from this period show a single rider. This obviously had its limitations, especially when facing archery to which the charioteer could not respond at a distance. The earlier Sumerian trampling-the-prostate-enemy motif, whether symbolic or tactical, continued throughout the Middle Bronze Age (items 24 and 25 above). Chariots are sometimes accompanied by infantry, who generally follow the chariot (item 24). This characteristic is also found in Neo-Sumerian chariot warfare. From hints in the depiction of equids, we find the increasing and eventually exclusive use of horses (characterized by short ears and manes) to pull chariots. Horses are first attested pulling war-carts in the Neo-Sumerian period, becoming universal during the early Middle Bronze period. The axe continued to be used by chariot warriors (item 22), but there are no early Middle Bronze artistic examples of the use of the javelin or the bow from the chariot, although the use of the bow is attested in the Neo-Sumerian texts discussed on pp. 143–5. Finally, we see a shift from disk wheels to spoked wheels (items 22–25). In other words, other than the adoption of the spoked wheel, which is the major innovation of the early Middle Bronze Age, all of the characteristics of early Middle Bronze chariot warfare were also found in the early Neo-Sumerian period. What happened during the early Middle Bronze Age seems to have been the universal adoption throughout the Near East of late Neo-Sumerian practices.

Late Middle Bronze evidence {1800–1600}

In contrast, during the later Middle Bronze period we find a number of innovations in chariot warfare depicted in our artistic sources.

26 Cylinder seal, Syria {19–17C} (FI §729). Chariot with two six-spoked wheels; single rider has quiver on his back and is followed by four soldiers on foot.

27 Cylinder seal, Syria {1850–1650} (WV §33; ELH §5). Chariot with two four-spoked wheels drawn by two horses with two riders, trampling a prostrate enemy who raises his arms to protect his face.

28 Cylinder seal, Syria {1850–1650} (WV §4; ELH §6). Chariot with two four-spoked wheels drawn by two horses; driver has a quiver on his back, while a man behind him with an axe and a dagger is either attacking him, or, more likely, stepping into the chariot to ride with him.

29 Cylinder seal, Syria {1750–1600} (ELH pl. 2). Chariot with two four-spoked wheels drawn by two horses trampling a prostrate enemy who raises an arm to protect himself; the single rider is followed by three infantrymen

30 Cylinder seal, Syria {1750–1600} (ELH pl. 3; MK 160; WV §35). Chariot with two four-spoked wheels (with metal rims?) drawn by two horses; single driver with bow and quiver on his shoulder is followed by three men on foot wearing helmets. A partially damaged lower portion seems to show a man being trampled.

31 Cylinder seal, Syria {1750–1600} (ELH pl. 4; MK 160). A single rider in a chariot with two four-spoked wheels, drawn by two horses; a prostrate body and severed head indicates a military context.

32 Cylinder seal, Syria {1750–1600} (ELH pl. 5). A single rider in a chariot with two seven-spoked wheels, drawn by two horses; the rider has a quiver on his back and is followed by four soldiers on foot. The driver seems to have a

helmet, and the hatched markings on his long skirt may indicate bronze scale armor.

33 Cylinder seal, Syria {1750–1600?} (Figure 4e, p. 133; WV 63, §36). A single rider in chariot with two eight-spoked wheels, drawn by two horses; the rider has a quiver on his back and is shooting a bow while driving. He apparently has the reins wrapped around his waist (or tied to the front panel of the chariot?); this is the first representation of this practice (WV 63), which is widely depicted in later New Kingdom Egyptian chariot warfare (e.g. EWP 198, 240). The hatched markings on his long robe may indicate bronze scale armor.

34 Cylinder seal, Anatolia {17C} (FI 57, §841). A hunting scene depicts four two-wheeled chariots each drawn by two horses on the hunt; three carry one man, one has two men. The scene is small and the details somewhat obscure, but one man seems to have a quiver on his back. Another, in a chariot with a driver, is shooting a bow; several animals seem to have arrows in them.

35 Cylinder seal, Syria {1800–1600?} (MK 162). A single rider in a two-wheeled chariot pull by two horses, followed by one man with a spear and another with a dagger.

This evidence from the late Middle Bronze period {1800–1600} attests to a number of fundamental innovations in chariot warfare. The shift from the use of the nose ring to bit and reins, allowing for more efficient driving, is first attested in Babylon in the early eighteenth century (items 24, 26–28). Although the use of a single rider remains the norm, we begin to see the driver and warrior combination that becomes predominant in Late Bronze chariot warfare (items 27, 28 and 34). The use of a lighter frame and spoked wheels decreased the weight of the chariot sufficiently to allow the cart eventually to be widened enough to allow two riders, yet remain light enough to be faster than an enemy on foot.

Evidence of a close association of archery with chariotry appears with increasing frequency, generally as a quiver and/or bow on the back of the chariot warrior (items 26, 28, 30, 32, and 34). This raises an important issue. The association of archery equipment with a charioteer does not necessarily mean the bow was shot from a moving chariot during warfare. It may simply be that the chariot warrior carried the full panoply of Middle Bronze weapons with him in his chariot, including the bow. He may have dismounted to fight and shoot his bow. Thus, in addition to the mere presence of a bow, it is important to note the appearance, for the first time, of scenes of actually shooting the bow from chariot, both by a driver alone, and by a warrior accompanied by a driver (items 33 and 34).

Chariots continue to be accompanied by infantry, as they were in the Sumerian and early Middle Bronze periods (items 26, 29, 30, and 32). This emphasizes the important potential vulnerability of the chariot to light infantry. The chariot was most effective when used with combined-arms tactics in conjunction with infantry. Thus chariot warriors continue to be armed with axe and dagger as melee weapons for dismounted combat (item 28). Finally, although the interpretation of the artistic evidence is uncertain, two charioteers have hatch-marked clothing that may be intended to represent bronze scale armor (items 32 and 33). In summary, the late Middle Bronze period {1800–1600} was one of significant innovation in chariot warfare, including the bit and rein, driver-warrior teams, archery from chariots, and the introduction of bronze armor. Thus, all of the elements of the revolutionary chariot warfare of the Late Bronze were in place by the seventeenth century.

The symbolic or tactical trampling-the-prostrate-enemy motif retains its importance in the late Middle Bronze period (items 27, 29, and 31). As noted above, the war-cart trampling scene became a standard symbol of victory in Early Bronze Sumer, appearing frequently in Middle Bronze depictions of chariots, indicating a continuity of symbolic ideology from Early Bronze war-cart to Middle Bronze chariot, as well as the probable tactical continuity in the actual use of the chariot in battle. Although the precise means of ideological and artistic transmission are unclear, by the eighteenth century the trampling scene is found in Anatolia (item 27), Syria (items 29–31) and Babylon (item 24); in other words, it has become a universal war motif throughout the Near East outside of Egypt.

In this regard, an important question for the military historian is whether the trampling scene was intended to represent an actual military tactic, or was merely a striking means to symbolize victory in battle. However this may be, it is certainly possible that war-carts could have trampled corpses, wounded or fleeing enemies, and, under the right circumstances, could in theory have broken standing enemy infantry formations as well. Two of the later Middle Bronze trampling scenes show that the victims on the ground are animate and clearly alive, raising their arms to protect themselves from the oncoming chariot (items 27 and 29; ELH §5–6).

Chariot warfare in Middle Bronze texts[27]

Compared with artistic representations of chariots, the Middle Bronze texts about chariot warfare are rather elusive. None the less, enough evidence survives to give us a broad picture of the chariot in battle. Ishme-Dagan, king of Isin {1953–1935} has left us a detailed literary description of a chariot from the early Middle Bronze, which complements Gudea's description given on pp. 143–4.[28] The hymn praises both the god Enlil, for whom the chariot was made, and Išme-Dagan, the king who ordered its construction. It provides both a detailed description of the parts of the chariot, a mythic account of the cosmic meaning of the chariot, and some hints as to its military significance (see also ARM 7.161). The chariot was built – and possibly specific elements of its design were specified – by order of Enlil in an oracle given in his temple.

> O lofty chariot; Enlil, the lord of intelligence, the father of the gods,
> Spoke about your construction, in the Ekur [temple], his sublime shrine.…

A number of specific parts of the chariot are mentioned, with a complex technical terminology for the various parts of the chariot: pole, yoke, ropes, axle, pole pin, front guard, platform, beams, side boards, and foot board. These types of items are also mentioned in several of the texts from the Mari archive, though the technical terminology is somewhat opaque (MK 162–3; ARM 18.45, 7.161). It is adorned with "silver, gold and precious stones". Since the chariot was to carry the statue of the god in ceremonial processions, it was apparently a portable temple, and is described as a microcosm of the universe.

Although the text is fundamentally mythic in function, some military details of the chariot are also mentioned. A bow may be mentioned in an uncertain passage (line 12), supplementing the mention of a bow in Gudea's chariot. Both driver and warrior are described as fighting: "[On] your [the chariot's platform], warriors [are] fighting together" side-by-side. The poem describes the god Enlil entering the chariot to go off to war, undoubtedly paralleling the practice of earthly kings.

> [Enlil] completed his great harnessing, he stepped in [the chariot]
> He embraced Ninlil, the Mother [goddess], his wife.
> [The wargod] Ninurta [son of Enlil], the hero, [went in front (as driver?)]
> The Anunnas [a class of gods] . . . [marched] after him
> The chariot shines like lightning, its bellowing [noise] a pleasure.
> [. . .] the donkeys harnessed to the yoke.
> Enlil [is in] his mighty chariot, his shining [glory] is bright.

This appears to be a textual reference to Ninurta, the war-god and son of Enlil, either driving the chariot for his father, or perhaps preceding the chariot on foot. Enlil is accompanied by the Anunnas, a class of gods, who follow or surround the chariot on foot, just as infantrymen are frequently shown accompanying chariots in the artistic sources.

The use of chariots (narkabtum) in battle is not mentioned extensively in the Mari archive (WM 144). It appears that, by 1750, the chariot had not yet become a major element of Mesopotamian warfare. There are, however, a number of hints that might point to the limited use of chariots in combat. One problem in interpreting the use of combat chariots is that the distinction between the terms for freight wagon and for chariot is unclear; both are probably best translated as cart.[29] For example, one passage mentions the itinerary of an army on the march, describing the "elite troops, chariots and gear"; it is not clear from the text if the "chariots" were war-chariots or carts carrying the gear (L 222). There are numerous references to carts for transportation purposes (L 184, 223). Chariots were clearly used for messengers and for transportation of small valuable goods. One text mentions the delivery by chariot of silver cups (MK 161). Chariots were also used in religious ceremonies (MK 161); the "golden chariot" mentioned in the Mari archive was probably intended to carry statues of the gods, or perhaps for the king in ceremonial processions (L 324; MM 32).

An additional problem in interpreting the textual evidence for chariots is the use of the term rākib ANŠE.HI.A, "rider of equids" (L 593 index). A double ambiguity exists in this phrase: is the "rider" riding the equid itself, or riding a chariot drawn by equids? Second, what specific species of equid is intended? I agree with Heimpel's interpretation that this phrase is a technical term for charioteer (L 593). Several lines of evidence point in this direction. First, the artistic evidence discussed above clearly points to the prominence of the chariot, and the rarity of actually riding equids. Second, the texts strongly imply that these "riders" are persons of importance; culturally speaking, this would associate them with chariots, the vehicles of kings and gods, as indicated by concepts of proper royal riding decorum discussed on p. 141 (ARM 6.76; EEH 120b). Third, even when discussing a single "rider", the texts use the plural for the equids (L 296, 402) – thus a single rider rides multiple animals, an impossibility if the man was riding the back of an animal, but the norm if the equids are pulling chariots.

The texts mention "riders" as royal messengers, or perhaps better ambassadors, men not just carrying a clay tablet but on special missions from the king, accompanying "high ranking servants" (L 322, 385, 402, 517). In a sense "rider of equids" almost seems like an aristocratic title in the texts rather than a description of a means of transportation. It is perhaps closer to the idea of an English "knight" in the Hundred Years War period, who did not necessarily actually fight from horseback, just as the Roman *equites* was a member of an aristocratic order and not necessarily a combat cavalryman.

There are two texts which give some indication of the actual combat use of chariots. One text implies that chariots were vehicles used by officers in battle. One army is described as having "four thousand good troops; the generals Hammu-Rabi and Dada and the diviner Kakka-Ruqqum, riders of equids, are those in the lead of those troops" (L 225). Clearly the chariot is mentioned here as a vehicle for a high official to ride to or during battle. But three chariots among 4000 men would not be sufficient to have a significant tactical effect on the outcome of a battle. On the other hand, the text does not explicitly state that there were not other combat charioteers as well, only that the three highest officers in the army were "riders of equids". The limited scale of the employment of chariots on Middle Bronze battlefields was probably related to the enormous cost of horses. One horse could cost five minas (300 shekels: MM 13), fifteen times the combat wages of a captain (see pp. 196–7). At such a cost a king would be hard pressed to field a large number of chariots, and would be wary of risking such valuable horses in combat.

There is another text, however, which points to substantial numbers of combat charioteers in battle. A general defeated an army of 500 men operating on the plains area of the middle Khabur River, and claimed to have captured "twelve riders of equids" (L 417). These were apparently important men, because they were being held for prisoner exchange for two officers. Assuming each of these is a charioteer, we have a ratio of at least one charioteer per forty infantrymen; the actual ratio was probably lower since presumably some of the charioteers escaped or were killed rather than captured. This compares nicely with the one charioteer per thirty-five infantrymen in contemporary Anatolia (MHT 27; see p. 303), and may imply there was a substantial chariot component in some northern Syrian armies in the mid-eighteenth century. It may be significant that this is a northern Syrian army, rather than an army from the Mesopotamian river valley, perhaps again pointing to northern Syria and Anatolia as the zone of greatest use of chariots in warfare.

Conclusion

In the Near East the final synthesis of all of these factors relating to chariot warfare seems to have occurred in Syria and central Anatolia in the seventeenth century among the Hittites, Hurrians, and Syrians. King Hammurabi of Babylon made an interesting observation about the relative importance of wagon vs. boat transportation in Syria and Mesopotamia: "The means [of transportation] of your [king Zimri-Lim's] land [the city of Mari in Syria] is donkeys and carts; the means [of transportation] of this land [Babylon] is boats" (L 379). Although the chariot was certainly known in Babylon, the rivers and numerous canals and irrigation ditches provided ideal avenues for transport by boat, which was faster and easier than cart transport. Furthermore, the same canals that facilitated boat transport hindered chariot transport. The situation was much the same in the Nile Valley. Thus the crucial transformation from war-cart to the true chariot occurred in the Syrian and Anatolian highlands, where carts, rather than rivers and irrigation systems, were the standard means of transport. By the end of the Late Bronze Age we begin to find texts describing the actual use of chariots in battle, especially from the Hittite archive (WV 63–5). Given the explosive and unprecedented victories of the Hittites in Anatolia, Syria, and Mesopotamia around 1600 (see Chapter Eleven), one is tempted to suspect that the Hittite Old Kingdom was the first state that fully and successfully synthesized all of these elements of chariot warfare into a single system, which would bring about the beginning of the new "chariot age" of warfare for the next half-millennium.

CHAPTER SIX

Middle Bronze Mesopotamia
{c. 2000–1600}

There are three main military characteristics of the Middle Bronze Age in Mesopotamia. First, we see the increasing importance of non-Mesopotamian peoples
who migrate into, and in various ways come to militarily dominate, Mesopotamia.
These include Elamites from south-western Iran, Hurrians from eastern Anatolia,
and most importantly Amorites from the steppe fringes of Syria. In the early
Middle Bronze period Amorite warlords managed to usurp control over most of
the city-states of Mesopotamia, establishing a series of Amorite dynasties. While
most of the population of Mesopotamia remained Akkadian or Sumerian speakers,
the military elites tended to be Amorites. The domination of Mesopotamia by
non-Mesopotamian military aristocracies was to remain a regular, though not
constant, feature of Mesopotamian military history for the next four thousand
years.[1]

   The second major military development was the disappearance of political
unity for the first two-and-a-half centuries of the Middle Bronze Age, and the
reintegration of Mesopotamia into a single state under Hammurabi of Babylon
{1792–1750}, himself a descendant of Amorite warlords. The period of disunity is
often called the Isin-Larsa period {2017–1792}, after the two dominant city-states
of Mesopotamia. The second phase is known as the Old Babylonian period
{1792–1595}, during which Babylon arises as the predominant power and
reunites Mesopotamia. The period ends in 1595 with the destruction of Babylon
by an invading Hittite army under Mursilis I (see pp. 183–4, 301–2).

Isin-Larsa period {2017–1792}

For the two centuries after the fall of Ur, southern Mesopotamia was embroiled in
a complicated see-saw struggle between numerous city-states for domination of
the region. Although the broad outline of events can be established, the precise
details are often elusive, due to numerous lacunae and ambiguities in the evidence.
The internecine and often chaotic warfare characterizing the Isin-Larsa period
culminates in the early eighteenth century as two new centers of military power
begin to emerge in Mesopotamia: Assyria in the north under Shamshi-Adad, and
Babylon in the center under Hammurabi. The Isin-Larsa period begins with the

migration of the Amorites into Mesopotamia and the fall of Ur, as described in Chapter Four.

The Amorites (MAR.TU, Amurru) {2200–2000}[2]

In some ways the predominance of the Amorites marks the commencement of the Middle Bronze Age. Beginning around 2200 from their original homeland in the Syrian steppe country to the west of Mesopotamia, they migrated throughout Syria, Mesopotamia, and Canaan during the following centuries. Amorite is a linguistic term defining an ethnic group speaking a North-west Semitic language. The name derives from the Sumerian MAR.TU (Akkadian, *Amurru*), meaning "West" or "Westerner" – a reference to the land and people in the deserts and semi-arid regions to the west of the Euphrates River. The Amorites were a nomadic people who "from ancient times have known no cities" (R3/2:364); their nomadic background is clearly reflected in Sumerian administrative texts, where Amorites are frequently associated with livestock and animal products which they exchange for manufactured goods from the cities (AUP 16–45, 282–302). From the Sumerian perspective they are described as:

> Tent dwellers buffeted by wind and rain, who dig up mushrooms at the foot of the mountain; he does not know how to bend the knee [to Sumerian royal authority]. He does not cultivate grain, but eats uncooked meat. In his life-time he does not have a house, and on the day of his death he will not be buried. The Amorite does not know house or city; [he is] an awkward man living in the mountains.[3]

From a military perspective, the Amorites were described as fierce warriors, "as powerful as the southern wind" (AUP 94), who frequently created fear among the Sumerians (AUP 336–7). "The hostile Amorites" are "a ravaging people, with the instincts of a beast, like wolves" (R3/2:299; AUP 332). Centuries later their fierceness and military prowess remained legendary; the Israelite prophet Amos describes "the Amorite, whose stature equaled the cedar, and whose strength equaled the oak" (Amos 2:9).

Nomadic herders predominated in many of the ecological zones of the Near East, both mountain pastures and steppe, during much of the Bronze Age.[4] Care must be taken to distinguish between the pastoralism of the Bronze Age and that of later periods. The full domestication and integration of the camel and horse into nomadic economies and military systems significantly changed the nature and military impact of nomadic groups in the Near East, especially after the development of horse-archery in the tenth and ninth centuries. The Arabian camel was probably domesticated by the late third millennium, but military camelry did not have extensive impact before the early Iron Age.[5]

There were, however, several military advantages for Bronze Age nomads. Their way of life created hardened warriors, with instinctive survival skills often not found in sedentary populations. As non-agricultural tribal groups, a greater percentage of their male population were available for military service, since they were not bound to agricultural work on the land for lengthy periods of time. A tribe of a few thousand could produced as many effective warriors as a city-state with many times their numbers, since most of the male population of the cities knew little of warfare and were required to spend much of their time caring for their farms. Furthermore, their lack of a central city and fields meant that they were difficult to defeat permanently, since they could simply flee into the wilderness with their herds where sedentary armies found it logistically difficult to operate for any period of time.

The agriculturalists admired the martial skills of the nomad, while despising their perceived barbarism. Uncontained nomads represented a serious military threat to sedentary kingdoms, either from raids on fields, villages, and caravans, or from widespread invasion and plunder. One standard sedentary response was to use various means to hire the nomads to provide protection and military service.

The highlander pastoralists were viewed much the same as the steppe nomads, and are described as being "warriors constantly coming to raid the cities" (HTO 238). The archetypal leader of the highlanders is the mythic demon Azag, a "fearless warrior" whose "attack no hand can stay, it is very heavy" (HTO 237, 239). Demonic warriors in mythic texts are described in terms probably reflecting the Mesopotamian view of nomad mercenaries:

> The men who went after him for the king were a motley crew
> They knew not [civilized] food, knew not drink,
> Ate not flour strewn [before the altars as offerings]
> Drank not water [poured to the gods] as a libation ...
> They set not tooth into the pungent garlic;
> They were men who ate not fish, men who ate not onions....
> [They] stunk of camelthorn and urine of the corner ...
> Around their necks hung fly-shaped beads [stolen] from anointed priests ...
> Weapons and severed heads [were] tied to their hips (HTO 35–7, cf. 222).

In the Bronze Age, nomads generally fought on foot, or occasionally in war-carts, as did all other armies. Whereas horse and camel riding were spreading during the Middle Bronze Age, actual combat on horseback was rare or unknown during this period.

The earliest recorded Amorite homeland was in the area around Mount Bashar (or Basalla, modern Jebel Bishri in Syria), the "mountain of the Amorites" (AUP 236–41; HE2 116–21). Although originally nomads and semi-nomads on the western fringes of Mesopotamia, Amorites began to migrate into Sumer in the early third millennium, drawn to the fertility and wealth of the cities in the river valley. They are mentioned in documents as living in Sumer as early as the twenty-sixth century; eventually Sumerian administrators developed a specific officer in charge of Amorite affairs, the "Inspector of the Amorites".[6] The earliest Amorites lacked political unity, being divided into several different and often feuding tribes, ruled over by tribal chiefs known as the *abum* or "father" (R3/2:297; AUP 332–6). These chiefs could hold high status in Mesopotamian society; some apparently married into royal Sumerian families (AUP 338–9). Among the most important early Amorite tribes are the Yahmadu, Tidnum (Didnum), and Yahmutum (AUP 242–5). Despite these tribal divisions, feuding Amorite clans were known to have joined together on occasion into larger confederations to fight the Sumerians (AUP 334). Another important fact to remember is that, although the Amorites were originally nomadic, by the year 2000 many can be found already settled in cities and farming villages. While generally retaining their old tribal bonds and loyalties, many Amorites had become city-dwellers or farmers. Others became semi-nomads, farming part of the year in semi-permanent houses, but wandering part of the year to care for their herds. Still others remained pure nomads, continuing to herd their animals in their original mountain and desert wilderness.

It is impossible to tell for certain if the crisis at the end of the Bronze Age was caused by the Amorites, or was created by conditions – ecological stress in pasturelands, combined with political and military weakness in sedentary lands – which facilitated the migration and conquests of the Amorites. Most likely a complex combination of factors contributed to the Early Bronze crisis, in which the Amorites were both a cause and an effect: climatic, ecological, social, and political difficulties created conditions which facilitated Amorite migration and conquest, while the Amorite migration exacerbated the already existing political crisis in Mesopotamia. It must also be emphasized that, while from an archaeological perspective this transition seems rather rapid, it in fact transpired over two hundred years, roughly equivalent to the time from Napoleon to the present day. If only one major city-state was conquered by the Amorites every five years, the cumulative effect over the course of two centuries would be the transition of power in forty city-states – in other words, most of the major cities in the Near East.

The migration of Amorites from their original homeland around Mount Bashar in Syria clearly began before 2200, and spread in all directions. However, the crisis at the end of the Early Bronze Age created a military climate of anarchy which facilitated more extensive Amorite migrations, as well as their ability to usurp power in the city-states and regions into which they migrated. From around 2200 to 1900 Amorite tribes and warlords migrated and conquered much of the Near East, seizing power in a number of important city-states in Canaan, Syria, and Mesopotamia. During this same period the Hurrians spread south and east from their core zone in the Khabur triangle (see pp. 303–7). The specific impact of Amorite conquests will be discussed in the chapters devoted to each of these regions.

The rise of the Amorites in Mesopotamia {2100–1900}

The first military appearance of the Amorites in the historical consciousness of the Sumerians occurs in the Akkadian period, when Naram-Sin {2255–2218} claims to have defeated the Amorites who formed part of a rebellious coalition against him. His son Shar-kalli-shari {2217–2192} undertook an expedition against their mountain stronghold at Mount Bashar in Syria.[7] Thereafter the Amorites appear with increasing frequency in Mesopotamian texts.

Amorite migration into Mesopotamia occurred by both peaceful and military means. Many Amorite tribes traded with Sumerian cities, and sent envoys on diplomatic missions (AUP 337–8), thereby becoming accustomed to urban ways and products (AUP 323–62); people with Amorite names were found in many cities in Sumer during the late Ur III period, but most prominently in Drehem (near Nippur), Isin, and Lagash (AUP 253–73). Some became fully integrated into Sumerian society, taking service with Sumerian lords, as indicated by references to Amorites on government ration distribution lists (AUP 34–64). Others became agriculturalists or engaged in other sedentary occupations (AUP 46–7). Still others were allowed to graze their herds in marginal pastures surrounding the rich irrigated agricultural land of Mesopotamia. Amorites passing through Sumerian land are once described as having a Sumerian military escort, presumably to prevent pillaging or other trouble (AUP 343). Increasing interaction between Sumerians and Amorites also led to some transfer of military technology; wagons or carts (*gigir*) are described as being given to the Amorites (AUP 24), though it is not certain if these vehicles were for transportation or war. The process of partial integration combined with continued nomadism in the hinterlands was to have important military consequences in the following centuries.

Most importantly from the military perspective, some Amorites who settled in Mesopotamia eventually became mercenaries or government officials (AUP 340–1, 357). As the Ur III political order disintegrated during the reign of Ibbisin {2028–2004}, high officials or military commanders of a number of city-states became functionally independent. These included the Amorite Nablanum {2025–2005}, who became king of Larsa after the fall of Ur III, as discussed on pp. 117–20. His successor, Zabaia of Larsa {1941–1933}, and others of the early dynasty continued to use the title "chief of the Amorites" (*rabian Amurrim*) as part of their royal nomenclature (R4:112, 122). At the same time, Amorite warbands invaded and conquered much of Mesopotamia, eventually taking control of a number of cities where their chiefs were established as kings. By the nineteenth century Amorite dynasties were in control of most of the major Sumerian city-states, including Larsa, Kish, Babylon, Sippar, Marad, and Urah, becoming the most powerful military force in Mesopotamia.

The rise to power of Amorite warlords in Mesopotamia is illuminated to some degree by our fragmentary knowledge of the Amorite chieftain (*rabian Amurrim*) Abda-El and his son Ushashum. They appeared around 2000 in north-central Mesopotamia, where they astutely played the game of power politics in the anarchy following the fall of Ur. Abda-El made an important alliance by marrying Ushashum to the daughter of Nur-Ahum, ruler of Eshnunna. In return for this alliance, Eshnunna was protected from Amorite raids, and could call on the clansmen for military service as allies. At the same time, other Amorites are also found serving as mercenary-allies for Ishbi-Irra of Isin in his wars against the Elamites. After a victory, Ishbi-Irra instructed his officials to divide the booty from the Elamite campaign with the Amorites, giving "890 sheep and goat skins for wrapping silver as gifts for the Amorites when Elam was defeated" (PH 10). On the other hand, Amorite soldiers also campaigned on their own accord. One text describes how "the [Amorite] tribe of Hadam has defeated 1500 troops of [Zabazuna, son of] Iddin-Sin" (PH 11), indicating that the Amorites were militarily capable of raising enough men to defeat an army of 1500 from a Mesopotamian city-state. This defeat was considered serious enough for the garrison commander of Eshnunna to be warned to "guard your city!" (PH 11).

Taken together, this evidence indicates that a judicious combination of royal marriage, mercenary service, increased wealth from plunder, and independent campaigns allowed Abda-El and other Amorite chiefs to become significant military powers in the region. In a sense the Amorites could become arbiters of the political balance of power. Those rulers who could draw the Amorites to their side gained a significant military advantage. In the end, the funeral of Abda-El was an event of international importance in Mesopotamia. A letter from Eshnunna describes how "the ambassadors of the whole land are coming for the funeral of Abda-El and all the Amorites are gathering. Whatever you intend to send [as a gift for the Amorites] for the funeral of Abda-El, your father, send separately" (OBLTA 49; PH 15–16). Presumably this process broadly paralleled the migration, integration, and conquests by Germanic peoples in the later Roman period, or Turkic peoples in the medieval Near East. The ultimate result is that, by the end of the twentieth century, most Mesopotamian city-states had come under the domination of Amorite royal dynasties, either through usurpation by Amorite warlords or conquests by outside tribes. Most of these royal dynasties of Amorite ancestry became integrated into the Mesopotamian political, cultural, and religious order, ruling in the style of traditional Sumerian or Akkadian kings. The following sections will examine the fortunes of the most important of these Amorite warlords and dynasties, culminating with the most successful of them all, Hammurabi of Babylon.

The Kingdom of Isin {2017–1794}[8]

Ishbi-Irra (Ishbi-Erra) of Isin {2017–1985}[9]

As the military situation in Mesopotamia worsened under the ineffectual leadership of Ibbisin of Ur, regional Sumerian governors and commanders were increasingly left to their own devices for defending their territory against the mounting Amorite and highlander threats. The most important of these was Ishbi-Irra of Isin {2017–1985}, the most successful Sumerian warlord of the age of the Amorite invasions. Ishbi-Irra began his career as governor of Isin for the faltering Ibbisin. Their deteriorating relations, leading to Ishbi-Irra's decision to declare independence, have been discussed earlier, on pp. 117–20.

In a remarkable letter to one of his rivals, Puzur-Shulgi of Kazallu, Ishbi-Irra outlined his justifications for usurping the kingship of Mesopotamia, and the mechanisms by which he planned to assume control:

> [The god] Enlil, my king, by his command, has given me [Ishbi-Irra] the kingship of Sumer. Enlil commanded me to bring the cities, gods and people from the bank of the Tigris to the bank of the Euphrates, from the bank of the Abnunme [canal] to the bank of the Me-Enlila [canal], and from the land of Hamasi to the sea of Magan [Persian Gulf], to the presence of Nin-Isina, to set up Isin as the chief cult place of Enlil, to make it have a reputation, to carry off spoils, and to conquer cities. Why do you [Puzur-Shulgi] resist me? I swore by [the god] Dagan, my lord: "Let my hand overwhelm Kazallu!" For each city of the land which Enlil entrusted to me, [I] will build thrones [for their gods] in Isin, and will celebrate their [divine] monthly festivals. I will settle my statues, my emblems, my *en* priests and my gods in their *giparu* chapels. Let their citizens utter their prayers before Enlil in [the temple] Ekur and before Nanna in [the temple] Ekishnugal!... [Ishbi-Irra] has taken Nippur, set his men as the garrison, and captured Nigugani, the highest priest of Nippur. (PH 9)

Here Ishbi-Irra clearly outlined the standard ideological and programmatic plan for conquest in ancient Mesopotamia. First, you must act only at the command of the gods. Second, the purpose of the conquests is always to insure proper order and worship and fame of the gods; plunder from the cities is given by the gods. Third, Ishbi-Irra offered his rival Puzur-Shulgi the chance to submit peaceably to the will of the gods: "Why do you [Puzur-Shulgi] resist me?" Fourth, the statutes of gods of captured cities and lands were apparently provided thrones in Isin, and given proper divine honors. Fifth, the priests of the gods were systematically replaced by priests appointed by Ishbi-Irra, while royal statues and emblems were set up in the temple precincts, with a garrison to insure compliance. Finally, the conquered people were required to perform some type of ritual act of allegiance to Ishbi-Irra's new order as part of their temple rituals. Although not all elements of this program are always manifest in the surviving sources, these basic elements continue across most of the Near East throughout antiquity.

His early years as independent king were spent securing his position in central Mesopotamia against both Amorite invaders and Sumerian rivals. In 2014 {Y4} he conquered the city of Girtab (IYN 13), probably from an Amorite. An unnamed city in Amorite hands was defeated in 2010 {Y8} (IYN 13; AUP 93). By this time Ishbi-Irra was well on his way to military predominance in central Mesopotamia. An agent of the king of Ur wrote the following report of Ishbi-Irra's advances to his lord Ibbisin:

> [Ishbi-Irra] has built the wall of Isin.... He has taken Nippur, set his men as the garrison, and captured Nigugani, the highest priest of Nippur. He has

made [his general] Idi enter Malgium and plundered Hamasi. He has put
Zinnum, governor of Subartu, in prison. He has returned Nur-Ahum, governor of Eshnunna, Shu-Enlil, governor of Kish, and Puzur-Tut, governor of
Borsippa to their [former] positions [from which Ibbisin had removed them
for disloyalty?].... Ishbi-Irra proceeds at the head of his army.... He captured
the banks of the Tigris, Euphrates, [and] the Abgal and Me-Enlila canals. He
brought in Idin-Malgium [as an ally]. He quarreled with Girbubu, the governor of Girkal ... and took him prisoner. His battle cry lies heavy upon me.
Now he has set his eye upon me. I have no ally, no one to go [to battle] with!
Although his hand has not yet reached me, should he descend upon me, I
shall have to flee. (PH 9; MC 253–68)

In the following years Ishbi-Irra focused attention on fortifying his domain,
building a "great wall" to protect his capital Isin, as well as several other fortifications (IYN 14–17; OBLTA 25–6). Thereafter he felt secure enough to go on the
offensive. In the meantime the city-states of Mesopotamia were coalescing into
two major confederations. The first was under the leadership of Zinnum of Shu-
bartu, and included the cities of Nippur, Girkal, Kazallu, and the Elamites. The
second was headed by Ishbi-Irra, including Eshnunna, Kish, and Borsippa. Initially
Zinnum's confederation seems to have been victorious, capturing Eshnunna, Kish,
and Bad-Ziabba and driving their kings into temporary exile. In year 12 {2006},
Ishbi-Irra campaigned northward, decisively defeating the combined army of
Zinnum of Subartu and Kindattu of Elam, thereby establishing himself as the
leading military power in central Mesopotamia (R3/2:434; PH 6–7). In the volatile situation of the collapsing kingdom of Ur, thrones could be quickly won and
lost based on a single battle, while alliances shifted in favor of the current winner.
The successful Ishbi-Irra thus quickly became the champion of Sumerians against
Elamites, Hurrians, and Amorites.

Following this victory, Ishbi-Irra was able to restore his former allies to their
thrones as vassals, thereby establishing hegemony the region.

> Ishbi-Irra took captive Zinnum, lord (*ensi*) of Subartu, plundered Khamazi
> and returned Nur-akhum, lord of Eshnunna, Shu-Enlil, lord of Kish, and
> Puzur-Tutu, lord of Bad-Ziabba each to his own place (OBLTA 23).

Presumably "returning" each of these rulers to their thrones was not an act of
selfless generosity, but a ritual of vassalization (PH 6).

The Elamites, although part of the coalition defeated by Ishbi-Irra, were by no
means decisively crushed. The following year {2005} they besieged and conquered Ur, bringing to an end any semblance of the old order. This propelled
Ishbi-Irra, now the *de facto* protector of Sumerian civilization, into a lengthy war
with the Elamites. In 2002 {Y16}, in alliance with Nur-Ahum of Eshnunna,
Ishbi-Irra launched an attack against king Kindattu of the Elamites (IYN 16; PH 7).
The war against the Elamites was probably ongoing for several years, culminating

in 1992 {Y26}, when "Ishbi-Irra the king brought down by his mighty weapon the Elamite who was dwelling in Ur" (IYN 20). His victories over the Elamites are celebrated in the poem, "Ishbi-Irra and Kindattu" (PH 6).[10] For this campaign Ishbi-Irra also allied himself with Abda-El, the Chief of the Amorites of central Mesopotamia; a document describing the dividing of Elamite booty survives, in which "890 sheep and goat skins for wrapping silver [were given] as gifts for the Amorites when Elam was defeated" (PH 10). In the next several years the struggle against the Elamites continued in southern Mesopotamia, until finally "Ur was made safe in its dwelling place" in 1987 {Y31} (IYN 21). Thus, by the end of his reign Ishbi-Erra had caused Isin to replace the devastated Ur as the dominant military power in south-central Mesopotamia and the new champion of Sumerian civilization. He had forestalled the Amorite advance, driven out the Elamites from Sumer and avenged the sack of Ur. Ishbi-Irra's victory, however, was not absolute. Both Elamites and Amorites were still powerful, and much of Sumer was still independent of Isin (M = CAM 109a).

Successors to Ishbi-Irra {1985–1787}[11]

Throughout much of the subsequent Isin-Larsa period our major source of information about military affairs is year names. It was the practice in Mesopotamia to name each year after a major event. Frequently these are religious – a great festival or the dedication of statue. Year names are also often linked with building programs of temples, canals, or fortresses. Military victories are another major category of events for year names. Furthermore, vassal cities would frequently use the year names of their overlord; thus, by seeing what city is naming its years by which king's year name, we can begin to see patterns of dominance and vassalage. It must be emphasized, however, that year names do not record all major events or military campaigns. Each year has only one name, and if a great military victory was won and a great temple built, the year may be named after the temple, and the military victory, however significant, could go completely unrecorded. By carefully collating the data from year names and royal inscriptions, Douglas Frayne has analysed the details of the shifting fortunes of the city-states and kingdoms of south-central Mesopotamia during the next two centuries.[12]

The successors to Ishbi-Irra did not record inscriptions of continued military offensives; most of their year names focus on ritual activities. This is characteristic of most of Mesopotamia during this period. Although warfare continued unabated, military affairs cease to be a significant part of ritual activities that were the focus of royal art and inscriptions. A few elements of Isin's later military history can be gleaned from the sparse sources. Shu-ilishu {1984–1975} was content to improve the fortifications of Isin (IYN 23), which continued to be maintained by subsequent kings (IYN 29–30, 32, 41). We are aware of one major campaign in the 1950s, when the city of Nippur was attacked and sacked by an unknown enemy. Iddin-Dagan {1974–1954} regained control of the city, going to great expense to rebuild the temples of this important ritual center. By 1910 Isin's predominance in Sumer was declining (CAM 109b); the northern cities were conquered by another Amorite dynasty known as Marad-Kazallu after their twin capitals, while at the same time another Amorite dynasty at Larsa was expanding northward (see pp. 163–6). For the most part the kings of Isin were content merely to retain control of their slowly dwindling kingdom by building fortifications (IYN 23, 29, 30, 32, 41). Only Erra-imitti of Isin recorded some type of counterattack: around year 1865, when he "destroyed the fortifications of Kazallu" which at that time was in the hands of Babylon (IYN 32). By 1800 Isin was a minor power in Mesopotamia, flanked by the mighty Babylon to the north and Larsa to the south; in 1794 it was conquered by its great rival Rim-Sin of Larsa; by 1787 Hammurabi absorbed Isin into his expanding empire (see pp. 172–7).

The Kingdom of Larsa {c. 2000–1762}[13]

Larsa seems to have become independent under the Amorite warlord Naplanum {c. 2025–2005} during the period of the decline of Ur. We have little information on Larsa for the next 70 years, during part of which it may have been a vassal of Isin. Larsa's ascent to military eminence began under Gungunum {1932–1906}, who spent his early military career securing his south-eastern flank by campaigns against the Elamite provinces of Bashimi {1930, Y3} and Anshan {1928, Y5} (LYN 7). He thereafter turned his attention to the kingdom of Isin, conquering the city of Ur from Isin by 1923 {Y10}, and taking the title "king of Ur" (R4:115). In subsequent years he campaigned up the Kishkattum canal; in 1914 {Y19} "by the order of [the gods] An, Enlil and Nanna, the army of Malgium was destroyed by the weapons [of Larsa]" (LYN 9). His ultimate triumph was his conquest of the supreme cultic center Nippur from Isin by 1911 {Y22} (R4:114, LYN 10; FSW 21–2), an ideological victory, allowing him to use the title "king of Sumer and Akkad" (R4:115, 118), thereby proclaiming his nominal supremacy in Mesopotamia. Many of his successors continued to use this title. Gungunum was also active in fortifying his domain, constructing the "great gate of Ur", and walls at Larsa and Ka-Geshtinanna (LYN 9–10).

At the same time that Larsa was expanding in the south, an Amorite warlord, Ibni-Shadum, founded the kingdom of Kazallu (Kazallu-Marad) northwest of Isin on the Kazallu-Arahtum canal. Although almost no details of this kingdom are known, it appears that the five Amorite kings of this dynasty conquered all the cities on the central Euphrates from Kazallu to Marad, which became the twin capitals of the state (FSW 23). In roughly this same period a third Amorite warlord named Manana founded a small kingdom north-east of Isin based on the city-states of Ilip and Akusum, to which Kish was added by king Halium (R4:660–7). Through these victories of Larsa, Kazallu, and Manana, the balance of power in Mesopotamia shifted dramatically; the previously predominant Isin was reduced to a small kingdom.

The military chaos of the period is evocatively described in an inscription of Ipiq-Ishtar, king of Malgium: "At that time all the land in its entirety came down, made a great clamor, and performed an evil deed" (R4:670). The plight of the petty ruler of a small city-state during this period is movingly expressed in an inscription by Ashduni-Yarim of Kish.

> When the four quarters [of the whole world] became hostile against me, I made battle for eight years. In the eighth year my adversary was turned to clay [= died?]. My army was reduced to three hundred men. When the god Zababa, my lord, made a favorable judgment for me and the goddess Ishtar, my lady, came to my help, I took some food to eat and went on an expedition of only a day. But for forty days I made the enemy land bow down to me. I built anew the wall [of Kish called] Inuh-Ilum. (R4:654–5)

Many kings of small threatened city-states must have had similar experiences during these internecine wars.

The death of the expansionist king Gungunum of Larsa {1906} allowed Isin to launch a temporary counter-offensive under Ur-ninurta {1923–1896}, who recaptured Nippur and several other cities on the Kishkattum canal. Ur-ninurta's offensive was finally stopped around the city of Adab by Abisare of Larsa {1905–1894}, who "defeated the army of Isin with his weapons" in 1896 {Y9} (LYN 13). Thereafter Larsa again took to the offensive against Isin under Sumu-El {1893–1865}. Expansion against the well fortified heartland of Isin proved difficult. He claimed victory over the army of Kazallu {1890} and Kish {1883} (LYN 16, 18, 19), but strategically decided to attempt to bypass and surround Isin. His most innovative strategy was economic. By conquering the small town of Eduru-Nanna-isa on the canal north of Isin, Sumu-El gained control of Isin's water supply. However, his construction of a dam in an attempt to cut off the irrigation water proved unsuccessful (FSW 23–5).

During the reign of Sumu-El two new players emerged on the political scene in southern Mesopotamia: Uruk and Babylon. It is not certain if Uruk had been a vassal of Larsa during the late 1900s, but by 1889 it is clearly an independent city-state, which Sumu-El of Larsa claims to have defeated (LYN 14, 16). It may have become independent some years earlier under its first two Amorite warlords, Alila-hadum and Sumu-kanasa (R4:439). An exact chronology for the dynasty cannot be established, but at the height of its power in the 1870s it ruled over Kisurra and Darum (R4:460), and briefly controlled Nippur. The rise of Babylon had much greater long-term implications for the future of Mesopotamia, and will be discussed below. Thus, by the mid-nineteenth century, military power in Mesopotamia was fragmented between half a dozen different Amorite-controlled city-states.

The military history of Larsa during the coming decades is only fragmentarily recorded in the year names. These were decades of low-level internecine warfare in which the kings of Larsa claimed several victories, but no major shifts in the balance of power seem to have occurred. Sin-iddinam {1848–1842} claimed to have defeated Babylon in 1845 (LYN 24), and Elam in 1843 (LYN 24). Sin-iqisham {1839–1836} seemed to feel under military pressure, for he refortified Larsa in

1837 (LYN 28), after which he claimed to have defeated "Uruk, Kazallu, the army of the land of Elam and Zambia king of Isin" (LYN 29). Overall, however, Larsa seemed generally in decline and on the defensive until the usurpation of Kudur-Mabuk.

Kudur-Mabuk {c. 1850–1834} and Warad-Sin {1834–1824}

Kudur-mabuk was an Amorite warlord operating in southern Mesopotamia in the mid-nineteenth century, probably as an ally or vassal of Larsa. Late in the reign of Sili-Adad of Larsa, the king of Kazallu invaded and defeated Larsa. Sili-Adad seems to have not been able to offer effective resistance, at which point Kudur-Mabuk usurped the throne to defeat the invaders and save the city. He "gathered the scattered [Amorite] people and put in order their disorganized troops, [he] made the land peaceful, [he] smote the head of its foes . . . [and] smashed all the enemies [of the Amorite tribes and Larsa]" (R4:220). He not only drove the king of Kazallu from Larsa but captured and sacked his capital:

> Kudur-Mabuk, father of the Amorite land . . . [with Warad-sin, his son] smote the army of Kazallu and Muti-abal in Larsa and Emutbala, [and] by the decree of the gods Nanna and Utu seized Kazallu, tore down its wall, and made it submit. (R4:206–10; LYN 31)

Thereafter he continued his victories in central Mesopotamia:

> King Kudur-Mabuk . . . by the supreme decree of the gods Enlil, Ninurta, Nanna, and Utu, having conquered Silli-Eshtar [king of Mashkan-shapir] . . . [brought him] captive in a hand-stock, in the main courtyard of the Gagis-shua, the temple of the goddess Ninlil, striding with his foot placed on Silli-Eshtar's head. (R4:266–7)

Kudur-Mabuk thus not only saved Larsa from conquest, but launched Larsa into a second period of several decades of expansion and military predominance. He was apparently quite old when he became king of Larsa, and he left much of the actual governing in the hands of his son Warad-Sin {1834–1824}, who served as co-ruler. When Warad-Sin ascended the throne in his own right it was as king of all southern Mesopotamia, including "Ur, Larsa, Lagash, and the land of Kutalla" (R4:202–6). In 1830 Warad-Sin added Zabalam (LYN 32) and in 1829 Nippur to his domain. In his tenth year Warad-Sin renovated the monumental walls of Ur (R4:236–43) and other cities (R4:253). He was succeeded as king of Larsa by his brother Rim-Sin.

Rim-Sin {1822–1763}[14]

Rim-Sin's sixty-year reign is the longest in Mesopotamian history (though it is dwarfed by Pepy II of Egypt's incredible ninety-four years {2300–2206}). Militarily he led Larsa to predominance in southern Mesopotamia, and lived to see the loss of his entire kingdom to Hammurabi of Babylon (see p. 176). We have little military information for his early reign, but the supremacy of Larsa was challenged in 1808 {Y14} by a coalition of most of the major kings of Mesopotamia (LYN 44), which Rim-Sin claims to have defeated. He . . .

> smote with weapons the army of Uruk, Isin, Babylon, Rapiqum and Sutium, seized Irnene, king of Uruk [in that battle,] and put his foot on his [Irnene's] head as if he were a snake. [He captured] the various cities of the land of Uruk. . . . The booty, as much as there was, of the various cities of the land of Uruk which I smote, I brought to Larsa. (R4:285)

The defeat of this coalition and the fall of Uruk left him pre-eminent in the south. In subsequent years he captured a number of small cities, expanding his power northward: "by the decree of the 'great mountain' [Enlil] he conquered the city . . . the city Bit-Shu-Sin, the city Imgur-Gibil, Durum, Kisurra and Uruk – their kings and their lands he overthrew, and tore down their walls" (R4:291; LYN 44–9). In year 20 {1802} he took the important cult center of Nippur, giving him great religious prestige (R4:270).

There followed a confusing five-year struggle with Babylon for control of Isin {1797–1792) in which the city seems to have changed hands several times. In 1792 {Y30}, "the true shepherd Rim-Sin with the help of the mighty weapon of An, Enlil and Enki, had Isin, the royal place, and its inhabitants – whose life he spared – taken, and he made great his fame" (LYN 60). The city was held only until 1786, when "Uruk and Isin were conquered" by Hammurabi (ANET 270). At this point Rim-Sin was probably in his eighties and no longer seems to have been an active campaigner; we have little evidence from the records of Larsa of major military campaigns, though Larsa appears as a participant in the wars described in the Mari archive. In the coming decades Larsa took part in the great six-way struggle for ascendancy in Mesopotamia (see pp. 173–7), not so much as a serious contender but as a major ally who could shift the balance of power in favor of one coalition or the other. In 1763 Hammurabi attacked his former ally, captured Larsa after a siege of four or five months (L 150–7), and incorporated the country into his kingdom (see p. 176).

The Old Assyrian Kingdom {2300–1741}[15]

The city-state of Ashur before Shamshi-Adad {2300–1814}[16]

The city of Ashur – from which the name Assyria derives – lay in northern Mesopotamia in the land known to the Sumerians in the third millennium as Subartu. Little is known of the military history of Assyria before the rise of Shamshi-Adad. The city-state had been founded by at least 2400 (OAC 28). Later traditions, as recorded in the Assyrian King-lists,[17] remember "seventeen kings who lived in tents", referring to the traditional Amorite nomadic ancestors of Shamshi-Adad (AR 1:1). The names of the first twelve of these kings bear remarkable parallels to the names of the ancestors of Hammurabi, indicating that the Amorite warlords who took control of both Assyria and Babylon were probably from related branches of one Amorite tribe (AR 1:1; OAC 36–7). These nomads are followed by another list of "ten kings whose fathers are known", but whose names are not confirmed by any inscriptional evidence (AR 1:4); these rulers also seem to be the ancestors of Shamshi-Adad, but not early rulers of Assyria (see p. 168).

This archaic section of the Assyrian King-list has no contemporary confirmation. Instead, two inscriptions indicate that, in the late third millennium, Ashur was controlled by Akkad under Manishtushu {2269–2255} (A1:8), and later by Ur III under Amar-Sin {2046–2038} (A1:9), and presumably by other southern rulers who did not leave inscriptions. On the other hand, archaic Ashur was not always dominated by foreign kings. During this period one apparently independent ruler, Ititi, dedicated booty from his victory over Gasur (Nuzi) to the goddess Ishtar (A1:7; OAC, 31–2).

Beginning about 2015 a dozen kings – numbers 26 to 38 on the Assyrian King-list – are also confirmed from sparse inscriptional evidence (AR 1:5–18, A1:11–46). The Assyrian kings began marking their independence from Ur III at this time by proclaiming in their stylized inscriptions, "[the god] Ashur is king, [the mortal ruler] is XXX, vice-regent of [the god] Ashur" (A1:13, 21); the title "vice-regent (*iššiʾak*) of Ashur" is used by all Assyrian kings of this period for whom inscriptions survive. Despite their great fame and military power in later times, the original Assyrian kingdom was merely one city-state among many in Mesopotamia, with no particular military importance.

The rise of Assyria to significance began under Puzzur-Ashur {c. 1970–1950},[18] who founded a dynasty lasting over a century-and-a-half {c. 1970–1809} until the usurpation by Shamshi-Adad (ANE 1:82). As is typical of this age, the vast majority of the inscriptions of this dynasty deal with religious affairs and temple building, giving us little military information. The major exception to this rule is an inscription by Ilu-shumma {c. 1920–1906}, who claims:

> I established the freedom of the Akkadians and their children. I purified their copper. I established their freedom from the border of the marshes and Ur and Nippur, Awal, and Kismar, Der of the god Ishtaran, as far as the city Ashur. (A1:18)

This text has been interpreted by some to imply a major military expedition or some type of political hegemony over southern Mesopotamia. However, Larsen has interpreted the "freedom" (*addurarum*) as referring to economic freedom from tariffs on the textiles and tin trade in an attempt to establish a monopoly on that trade from Mesopotamia to Anatolia (see pp. 290–1).[19]

Ilu-shumma's successor was his son Erishum I {1906–1867}, for whom a number of inscriptions survive, again with unfortunately only incidental military references which provide no information on campaigns. A blessing in a temple inscription asks that the god Ashur "give [the king] sword, bow and shield", (A1:21), perhaps indicating the major weapons of an Assyrian warrior of the period. Erishum also improved the walls of Ashur "from the Sheep Gate to the People's Gate; I made a wall higher than the wall my father had constructed" (A1:22; AR 1:11; OAC 60–3), indicating ongoing maintenance of fortifications. The military strength of the terrain of the city of Ashur was praised in a metaphorical description of the god Ashur: "Ashur is like reed swamps that cannot be traversed, terrain that cannot be trodden upon, canals that cannot be crossed" (A1:21). During this period the Assyrians were noted as great merchants on the Tin-Road to Kanesh in Anatolia, where they founded a number of merchant colonies. The military implications of this are discussed in Chapter Eleven.

Assyrian kings in the nineteenth century {1906–1814}

Assyrian military history in the nineteenth century is only fragmentarily known. The Assyrian King-list and royal inscriptions (AR 1:16–18; A1:39–46) provides the names of five kings: Ikunum, Sargon I, Puzur-Ashur II, Naram-Sin, and Erishum II. The precise dates of these rulers are not known because that portion of the document is damaged, and the royal inscriptions provide no information on military campaigns.

The rise of Shamshi-Adad {1832/1809–1776}[20]

The two centuries of fragmentation and anarchy in Mesopotamia following the fall of Ur culminated in the rise of two great Amorite warlords, both of whom were nearly successful in reuniting Mesopotamia. These were Shamshi-Adad of Assyria and Hammurabi of Babylon. These two rulers would lay the foundations for the fluctuating military and cultural predominance of Assyria or Babylon over Mesopotamia for the next 1300 years. Shamshi-Adad was not ethnically Assyrian, and did not begin his reign as ruler of Assyria. Although later Assyrian kings declared Shamshi-Adad their predecessor (CS 1:464), he was, in fact, an Amorite usurper. The Assyrian King-list begins with "seventeen kings who lived in tents" – the Amorite nomadic ancestors of Shamshi-Adad – followed by "ten kings whose fathers are known", who appear to be Amorites who had infiltrated into Mesopotamia perhaps beginning around the time of the fall of Ur III {2005}. This portion of the King-list ends with the brother and father of Shamshi-Adad (CS 1:463–4). His grandfather, Yaskur-El (or Yadkur-El) {c. 1850} may have been the Amorite ruler of the city-state of Zaralulu (Tel al-Dhibai) – one of dozens of such petty Amorite warlords during this period (PH 62–3).

Shamshi-Adad's father, Ila-kabkabu {c. 1850–1832}, was the Amorite ruler of the city-state of Terqa[21] on the middle Euphrates, and engaged in ongoing war with Mari. Their armies fought at least one major battle in which "many soldiers of [Ila-kabkabu] fell and so did those of [king] Yahdun-Lim [of Mari]", probably indicating that the battle was a draw (PH 70). Ila-kabkabu, however, was victorious in another battle, conquering the city-state of Suprum, only a day's march from Mari (PH 66–69). It is in this situation that Shamshi-Adad appears on the scene in 1832.

The Assyrian King-list provides a laconic description of the rise of Shamshi-Adad:

> Shamshi-Adad [I], son of Ilu-kabkabi: In the time of Naram-Sin [king of Assyria] he went to Kar-Duniash [i.e. Babylon]. In the eponymy of Ibni-Adad, Shamshi-Adad marched out from Kar-Duniash [in Babylonia]. He seized the town of Ekallatum [near Ashur]. He stayed in Ekallatum for three years. In the eponymy of Atamar-Ishtar, he marched out from Ekallatum. He removed [the Assyrian king] Erishum [II], son of Naram-Sin, from the throne [of Ashur]. He seized the throne [of Ashur]. He ruled as king [of Ashur] for thirty-three years [1809–1776]. (ANE 1:86)

Beyond this, the background to Shamshi-Adad's early life is quite obscure. A number of different interpretations have been offered.

A crucial problem related to the rise of Shamshi-Adad is the question of whether there are two separate rulers named Naram-Sin, or only one. The basic problem is that a king named Naram-Sin was ruling in both Eshnunna and Ashur at the same time. Is this a single person, or two people with the same name? If it is a single person, did Naram-Sin of Eshnunna conquer Ashur,[22] or did Naram-Sin of Ashur conquer Eshnunna?[23] A third scenario posits two contemporary kings, both named Naram-Sin, one the ruler of Eshnunna and one of Ashur (PH 80–7). Obviously the data is both insufficient and ambiguous, and does not allow a certain reconstruction; I will follow the interpretation that there were two distinct rulers named Naram-Sin.

Shamshi-Adad's personal reign did not begin auspiciously. His initial years, roughly 1832–1814, were spent as a minor prince at Terqa, where he was engaged in internecine wars with other petty princes. The documentation for this period is fragmentary, but Shamshi-Adad is mentioned being involved with fighting his neighbors on several occasions (PH 80), not always successfully. In 1831 he was defeated by nomadic brigands known as the Lullum, who were considered "criminals" (PH 65) and who had been marauding for some time throughout the countryside (PH 80), indicative of the anarchy of the age.

Initially a tense peace treaty was formulated between Shamshi-Adad and his most powerful neighbor, Yahdun-Lim of Mari {1820–1796}, who had earlier been at war with Shamshi-Adad's father Ila-kabkabu.

> Shamshi-Adad ... and Yahdun-Lim [king of Mari] ... took a grave oath between them by the god [Nergal], and Shamshi-Adad never committed a sin against Yahdun-Lim [i.e. he followed the treaty]. It is Yahdun-Lim who committed a sin against Shamshi-Adad [by breaking the treaty].... [The god

Nergal] went at the side of Shamshi-Adad and punished [Yahdun-Lim] so that [Shamshi-Adad's] servants killed [Yahdun-Lim in battle]. [Nergal] decided to ... turn over the city of Mari and all the banks of the Euphrates to the hand [of Shamshi-Adad, who] assigned his son [Yasmah-Addu in 1796] to the lordship of Mari; thereafter, [Yasmah-Addu] built for [Nergal] an everlasting temple [at Mari]. (PH 68)

Apparently Yahdun-Lim's "sin against Shamshi-Adad" had been to renew the war against Shamshi-Adad in alliance with Naram-Sin of Eshnunna. In this war Shamshi-Adad was defeated and ousted from the throne of Terqa around 1814, and his former domain was divided between his two enemies (PH 84). Thereafter Shamshi-Adad fled to his distant Amorite relative Apil-Sin of Babylon, the grandfather of Hammurabi.

Presumably Shamshi-Adad arrived in Babylon around 1814 with a band of Amorite warriors who had served with him at Terqa. Always on the lookout for trained mercenaries, Apil-Sin enlisted this warband, giving them land in the Kar-Dunaish area of northern Babylonia. Around 1812 some type of crisis left Ekallatum vulnerable, and Shamshi-Adad grasped the opportunity, taking his warband – either under instructions from his overlord Apil-Sin of Babylon, or perhaps entirely on his own initiative – and conquered Ekallatum, where he established himself as an independent ruler. After three years securing his base of power there, he captured Ashur around 1809.

Shamshi-Adad the Assyrian {1809–1776}[24]

With the conquest of Ashur, Shamshi-Adad was in a position to become a serious military force in Mesopotamia. By this time military power in Mesopotamia was divided into eight major kingdoms, involved in rapidly shifting alliances and balances of power politics: Ashur, Babylon, Eshnuna, Larsa, Elam, Mari, and Aleppo and Qatna in Syria. During the next twenty-five years Shamshi-Adad dominated the military scene in Mesopotamia like a colossus.

Shamshi-Adad's first order of business was to deal with Yahdun-Lim of Mari, who had been at war with Shamshi-Adad's father, and who had broken a treaty with Shamshi-Adad himself (PH 68). Yahdun-Lim's kingdom of Mari controlled the Middle Euphrates and dominated the great nomadic Amorite tribes, giving him a good source of warlike mercenaries (PH 93–9). Shamshi-Adad began by encroaching on the territory of Abi-Samar, a vassal of Yahdun-Lim, who pleaded with his overlord to make peace or come to his assistance (PH 106–7). With twelve vassal kings by his side, Yahdun-Lim fought a great battle with Shamshi-Adad, but was disastrously defeated (PH 107); Assyria thereafter overran much of the domain of Mari. In the midst of the crisis Yahdun-Lim was deposed by his son Sumu-Yama, who busied himself fortifying his land against further incursions by Shamshi-Adad. Sumu-Yama himself was assassinated by one of his own ministers, possibly at Shamshi-Adad's instigation (PH 109–10); Mari quickly surrendered to Shamshi-Adad {1796}.

With the fall of Mari, Shamshi-Adad now ruled northern Mesopotamia from the Tigris to the Euphrates, and established three provinces. In the center he reigned personally from his new capital at Shubat-Enlil (Tell Leilan, EA 3:341–7) in the Khabur Triangle of north-eastern Syria. His eldest son Ishme-Dagan ruled from the original capital at Ekallatum in Assyria, and was in charge of the frontier with the Turukkiean highlanders (who had replaced the Gutians in the Zagros mountains in western Iran), and the rival city-state of Eshnunna. His younger and inexperienced son Yasmah-Adad {1796–1776} ruled from Mari as viceroy, in charge of Syrian and Amorite nomadic military affairs. Shamshi-Adad, of course, was in ultimate command of the empire, and sent numerous letters to his sons training them and instructing them in imperial strategy; many of these letters survive in the Mari Archive, reflecting the character of the great warlord, and his imperial policies (ARM 1–6).

In Syria Shamshi-Adad claims to have marched to the sea and erected a victory monument in imitation of Sargon (C2/1:3), but if so it was a short-lived raid. His main strategic problem was Aleppo, where Zimri-Lim, the heir to the throne of Mari, had fled for protection. Shamshi-Adad and his son, the viceroy Yasmah-Adad, maneuvered to isolate and destroy Aleppo by a political and marriage alliance with Qatna, the dominant power in southern Syria. As described on pp. 257–60, Shamshi-Adad managed to gather a coalition of Qatna, Carchemish, and Ursha against an isolated Aleppo, but, for unknown reasons, they failed to take the city. It may in part be that the Syrian kings realized that Shamshi-Adad was more of a real threat to them than Aleppo, and only unwillingly participated in the anti-Aleppo campaigns. Sumu-Epuh of Aleppo {1810–1780} played the diplomatic game masterfully, forming a coalition with Shamshi-Adad's enemies in the south and east, including Sutean and Turukkean nomads, to attack him from those directions (C2/1:3; PH 114–47). The final disruption of Shamshi-Adad's hopes in the west, however, may have come from a plague which ravaged Mari at this time (PH 147–52).

On the eastern frontier Shamshi-Adad's son and viceroy Ishme-Dagan faced a series of four enemies: Turukkean highlanders to the north-east, Eshnunna to the east, Elam to the south-east, and Babylon and Larsa to the south. Babylon, with the longest border with Shamshi-Adad, seemed most intimidated by Assyrian power. Alliances in the east were unstable and opportunistic, with kingdoms attacking Assyria at one time and allying with it at another. Overall, Shamshi-Adad captured Qabra and Arrapha in the north-east (PH 181–5), but was forced to campaign regularly in the Zagros against both recalcitrant city-states and Turukkean highlanders; although he was generally victorious, the Turukkeans proved intractable in their mountain highlands, and desultory warfare continued on that front throughout most of his reign (PH 186–235). At his death, Shamshi-Adad was hegemon of Mesopotamia, but surrounded by marginally subdued enemies.

Ishme-Dagan of Assyria {1780–1741}

The death of Shamshi-Adad engendered an immediate military crisis, as recalcitrant vassals and barely subdued enemies rose up almost simultaneously to achieve independence and revenge. Although Ishme-Dagan was a competent ruler, he lacked the skill and aura of invincibility of his father, and was unable to retain control of the empire. The most disastrous event was the restoration of Zimri-Lim to the throne of Mari with the assistance of the king of Aleppo {1776}, resulting in the loss of the western portion of the empire (see pp. 261–3). Thereafter, all the surrounding kings made common cause against Ishme-Dagan, and his empire was whittled away during the coming years by Eshnunna, Mari, and Hammurabi of Babylon, until he was left with only the enclave around Ashur on the upper Tigris. The Old Assyrian kingdom had lasted less than two generations.

The Old Babylonian Empire {1894–1595}

The Foundation of the Old Babylonian Empire {1894–1793}[25]

In the third millennium, Babylon was a minor city, never playing a major political role. Its rise to importance occurred in the years of anarchy following the collapse of Ur III. As with most other cities in Mesopotamia, power in Babylon fell into the hands of an Amorite clan under the leadership of Sumu-abum {1894–1881}. Sumu-abum apparently exercised some type of suzerainty over nearby Sippar,[26] as well as being chief of several surrounding Amorite clans (PH 28–31). His son Sumu-la Il {1880–1845} permanently annexed Sippar and rebuilt its walls, which may have been damaged in his conquest. The next three successors[27] slowly added other nearby city-states by diplomacy or conquest until, in 1792, at the ascension of Hammurabi, Babylon controlled most of central Mesopotamia, including Dilbat, Sippar, Kish, and Borsippa (M = CAM 109d). Their most important victory during this period was the defeat of the rival Amorite kingdom of Marad/Kazallus, which controlled the central Euphrates basin.

Hammurabi {1792–1750}[28]

As one of the great conquerors and cultural figures of ancient Mesopotamia, Hammurabi of Babylon was the first ruler to reunite Mesopotamia in the almost 250 years since the fall of Ur III in 2005. The military aspects of his reign can be divided into three periods: early {1792–1776}, middle {1776–1764}, and late {1763–1750}.

In the first decade of Hammurabi's forty-three-year rule {1792–1781}, Babylon remained a relatively minor player in Mesopotamian international affairs, and was quite likely a vassal, at least nominally, of Shamshi-Adad of Assyria. There are three major recorded campaigns of Hammurabi before 1764 {Y29}. The most important was in 1786 {Y7} when "Uruk and Isin were conquered" at the expense of Larsa (ANET 270), providing his kingdom with new agricultural lands to exploit to improve the economic base of his state. His second campaign {1783, Y10} focused on the Tigris south of Babylon, where "the army and inhabitants of Malgia were crushed" (ANET 270). In Hammurabi's eleventh year {1782} he records that "he conquered Rapiqum and Shalibi" on the Euphrates north-west of Babylon. More details on this campaign are found in a letter from the Mari archive, in which Hammurabi claims "Shamshi-Adad forced Rapiqum out of the king of Eshnunna's control and gave it to me. Since then my garrison stayed there . . . as Shamshi-Adad's garrison stayed there" (CANE 2:910). It seems, then, that Shamshi-Adad and Hammurabi allied together and took Rapiqum from the rival city-state of Eshnunna, which Shamshi-Adad obviously saw as a greater threat than Babylon in 1782. Eshnunna's power was thereby curtailed, and Assyria and Babylon shared joint control over the city.

The middle period of Hammurabi's reign {1776–1764} begins after the death of Shamshi-Adad in 1776, at which point Assyria was ruled by his son Ishe-Dagan who was much less militarily daunting that his father. The military predominance of Assyria was quickly diluted as Hammurabi and other kings were able to undertake increasingly independent foreign policies during the rule of the ineffectual Ishe-Dagan. With the death of Shamshi-Adad a new tenuous balance of power developed in Mesopotamia between six rivals: Ibalpiel of Eshnunna {c. 1780–1760}, Ishme-Dagan of Assyria {1780–1741}, Zimri-Lim of Mari {1776–1761}, Siwe-palar-huppak of Elam {c. 1770–1750}, Rim-Sin of Larsa {1822–1764}, and Hammurabi of Babylon {1792–1750}. In addition the city-states of Aleppo and Qatna in Syria often played a role in Mesopotamian power politics, especially in relation to the affairs of Mari. This military balance of power of this period is described in a famous letter by Itur-Asdu to the king of Mari:

> There is no king who is strong by himself: 10 or 15 kings follow Hammurabi of Babylon, as many follow Rim-Sin of Larsa, Ibalpiel of Eshnunna and Amutpiel of Qatna, while 20 kings follow Yarim-Lim of Aleppo. (ANE 1:99)

During this early period Hammurabi's main military activities focused on building fortifications to protect his domain; the walls of Sippar were particularly well fortified {1768, Y25}, and the army was used for part of the labor needs: "By the supreme might which the god Shamash gave to me, with the levy of the army of my land, I raised the top of the foundation of the wall of Sippar with earth until it was like a great mountain. I built that high wall . . . for the god Shamash" (R4:335). His year names also record rebuilding the walls of Malgia {1789, Y4} and Basu {1772, Y21}, as well as constructing two fortresses, one named for the goddess Laz {1787, Y6} and the other called Igi-kharsagga {1774, Y19}. Most of his other early year names are associated with digging canals to improve economic productivity or religious rituals (ANET 270).

The Great War {1765–1763}[29]

A fascinating window on the military and diplomatic world of the eighteenth century is provided by letters from the palace archive of Mari. Most of these date to the period roughly from 1780 to 1761, when Mari was conquered by

Hammurabi.[30] This period was marked by remarkably volatile and unstable alliances as each of the six rival kings jockeyed for position, aiding, betraying, and attacking each other in dizzying turnabouts of diplomacy (CAH 2/1:178–9). Heimpel has done a masterful job of correlating and integrating the letters into a coherent picture of Mesopotamian warfare from 1765–1763. These letters give us our most complete understanding of warfare from any period of the ancient Near East; the military implications of these letters are discussed in detail in Chapters Eight and Nine. Here I will simply outline the major military events leading to the hegemony of Hammurabi.

As noted above, with the death of Shamshi-Adad the hegemony of Assyria in Mesopotamia collapsed and political order reverted to an eight-way struggle for power between Elam, Eshnunna, Assyria, Larsa, Babylon, Mari, Aleppo, and Qatna. In addition to these eight major powers there were nomadic and highlander tribes on the fringes of Mesopotamia, including the Hurrians in Anatolia to the north, Turukkeans in the Zagros mountains to the east, and Amorite tribes in the Syrian steppe to the west of the Euphrates. Each of these tribal groups took turns raiding various kingdoms, at times independently and at times as allies of one or more of the sedentary states. Each of the eight sedentary kingdoms played a machiavellian game of power-politics, formulating and breaking alliances with reckless abandon. The chaotic picture of fractious, anarchic warfare reflected in the Mari letters was probably the norm for military affairs throughout much of Mesopotamian military history, and gives quite a different picture than the pious and formulaic royal inscriptions, where the gods decree victory for a king, and it is so. Reality was always much more messy.

The final phase of Hammurabi's military history {1765–1750} begins with a crisis engendered by the growth of opposing coalitions from among the rival warlords. The unstable multi-kingdom balance of power of the middle period of Hammurabi's reign created a time of political uncertainty as alliances were formed and collapsed based on which king was perceived to be the closest to achieving hegemony. As soon as one king appeared to be nearing hegemony, everyone allied against him. In 1769 Mari, Babylon, and Elam allied against the powerful kingdom of Eshnunna, conquering that state and massacring the family of its king Ibal-pi-El II (PAE 171). King Siwe-palar-huppak of Elam rightly viewed himself as the senior partner in this enterprise. Whereas most of the allied kings called themselves "brother" – indicating an alliance among equals – they referred to themselves as the "sons" of Siwe-palar-huppak, the coalition leader. Elam thus obtained the lion's share of the spoils, including the city of Eshnunna itself (PAE 168–9; L 56–9).

This victory gave the Elamite king[31] the hope of establishing complete hegemony in Mesopotamia. Hammurabi was thus faced with a crucial decision: should he submit to de facto vassalization to Siwe-palar-huppak, or risk a major war to avert the growing power of Elam. Hammurabi recognized that he was unable to risk war with Elam on his own and turned to his long-standing ally Zimri-Lim of Mari, seeking to form an anti-Elamite coalition. Zimri-Lim realized that

Hammurabi was in a desperate position, whereas Mari, quite distant from Elam, was much more secure. As Zimri-Lim's ambassador's informed him: "Does my lord not know how badly Hammurabi king of Babylon wants to make an alliance with my lord?" He therefore drove a hard bargain in the negotiations. Neither side really trusted the other; as Zimri-Lim's ambassadors told him, "My lord will surely come to realize how exaggerated is [Hammurabi's] information and how full of lies are his words!" (CANE 2:909). But, on the other hand, neither king could hope to survive without allies in those perilous times. Hammurabi desperately needed this alliance, and in the end he got it. Allied armies from Mari, Babylon, and Aleppo together marched against the Elamite coalition in 1764 {Y30} (CAH 2/1:183; L 60–3). In the meantime, Siwe-palar-huppak was not idle. He marshaled his vassals to meet Hammurabi's advancing coalition. These included contingents from Marhashi (Iran), Subartu (Assyria), Gutium, the newly vassalized Eshnunna, and Malgi (ANET 270).

When Hammurabi occupied the smaller towns of Mankisum and Upi in the former domain of Eshnunna {1764}, the outraged king of Elam ordered Hammurabi to surrender the two cities and terminate his alliance with Zimri-Lim of Mari, or face immediate invasion by Elam. The crisis was compounded when Elamite soldiers temporarily conquered Ekallatum, Ishme-Dagan's capital, rendering him a vassal. Clearly Siwe-palar-huppak was intent on creating hegemony in Mesopotamia.[32] Hammurabi, mustering as many troops and allies as he could, met in an indecisive battle with the Elamites at Upi, while the Elamites tried to woo Hammurabi's old adversary Rim-Sin of Larsa to their side. The Elamites focused their attention on the siege of Razama in the upper Tigris basin. The siege went on for several months until it was finally relieved by the intervention of Zimri-Lim as ally of Babylon (L 65–78). This probably represents the height of Elamite power, for, after their failure at Razama, several other cities join the anti-Elamite coalition with Babylon and Mari.

In 1764 the Elamite army was active against southern Mesopotamia, but was strongly countered by a Babylonian–Mariote army on the opposite bank of the Tigris at Mankisum in the Diyala region. The Elamites attempted a siege of the strategic city of Hiritum near Sippar, but Ishme-Dagan of Assyria joined the Mari–Babylon alliance and the coalition's forces broke the Elamite siege (L 95–100). The failure and withdrawal of the Elamites led to a revolt in Eshnunna, which threw off the Elamite vassaldom and installed a new independent king (L 108–9). With their imperial plans in shambles, peace was made with between Elam and the coalition (L 110–11).

This proved to be the decisive campaign for domination of Mesopotamia. Hammurabi described it, praising the gods for their assistance but conveniently failing to mention the aid of armies from Mari and Aleppo:

> The leader [Hammurabi], after having defeated the army which Elam – from the frontier of Marhashi, also Subartu, Gutium, Eshnunna, and Malgi – had raised in masses, through the mighty power of the great gods, re-established the foundations of [the empire of] Sumer and Akkad. (ANET 270)

Thus, according to Hammurabi's official propaganda, after his victory over Elam he re-established the traditional empire of Sumer and Akkad, formally declaring himself ruler of Mesopotamia.

With the threat removed, the anti-Elamite coalition that once had united most of the Mesopotamian kingdoms began to break up, with each king pursuing an independent foreign policy (L 117–50). This renewed regional feuding presented Hammurabi with an opportunity. Hammurabi first turned on his old rival Rim-Sin of Larsa, with the continued assistance of the trusting Zimri-Lim of Mari. In 1763 {Y31} "the great gods called Hammurabi by name [through an oracle]; with his fetters he tied up the enemy [Rim-Sin], his weapon smote the army that was hostile to him, in combat he slew the evil land [of Larsa]" (R4:338–9). His year name adds additional details:

> Encouraged by an oracle given by Anu and Enlil who are advancing in front of his army, and through the mighty power which the great gods had given to [Hammurabi], he was a match for the army of Emutbal [= Larsa] and its king Rim-Sin ... thereby forcing [all] Sumer and Akkad to obey his orders. (ANET 270)

Hammurabi's great victory over Larsa made him clearly the pre-eminent military power in Mesopotamia (L 150–7). However, the victory was not without its cost; it was followed by the rapid creation of an anti-Babylonian coalition, as the remaining rulers began to see Hammurabi as the greatest threat to their independence. Hammurabi's earlier victory over the Elamites in 1763 had not resulted in the full annexation or destruction of that defeated kingdom. While Hammurabi was distracted by his Larsa campaign in 1762, king Silli-Sin of Eshnunna, the Subartu (Assyria), and the Guti highlanders marshaled an army for revenge – Elam was notably absent from this coalition. In 1761 {Y32} Hammurabi met and defeated the coalition, defeating Eshnunna and conquering the land of Mankizum (R4:339–40).

> The hero [Hammurabi] who proclaims the triumphs of [the god Marduk], overthrew in battle with his powerful weapon the army of Eshnunna, Subartu (Assyria) and Gutium and was a match for the country of Mankizum and the country along the bank of the Tigris as far as the frontier of the country Subartu. (ANET 270)

During this period of intensive conquest Hammurabi was also active both in strengthening the agricultural foundation of his state through irrigation works (R4:341), and improving its defenses by fortifications. The walls of Sippar were reconstructed (R4:335), and the fortress of Dur-Sin-muballit was built on his north-western border; he "raised high a tall fortress with great heaps of earth, whose tops were like a mountain.... I named that fortress 'Dur-Sin-muballit-abim-walidiia' [Fort Sin-muballit, father who engendered me]" (R4:342–3).

Although we are largely dependent on Zimri-Lim's archive from Mari to understand the history of the complex diplomatic relations between Mari and Babylon, it is clear from the overall results that Hammurabi played the machiavellian power-politics game of the age better than any of his rivals. With southern Mesopotamia conquered, the east subdued, and his domain secured by additional fortifications, Hammurabi turned his attention to the central Euphrates basin, where his major rival was the kingdom of Mari. It is not clear why Hammurabi went to war with his long-standing ally Zimri-Lim. Perhaps Zimri-Lim, fearing the rising power of Hammurabi, had broken the alliance. Or perhaps it was simply the next inevitable step in Hammurabi's move towards full hegemony in Mesopotamia. At any rate, in 1761 {Y33} Hammurabi "overthrew Mari and Malgi in battle ... also made several other cities of Subartu, by a friendly agreement, obey his orders" by becoming his vassals (ANET 270). Zimri-Lim apparently remained on his throne of Mari as a vassal of Hammurabi, but he remained recalcitrant and rebelled two years later. Hammurabi suppressed the rebellion of his former ally with ruthlessness, and in 1759 {Y35}, "upon the command of the gods Anu and Enlil", he "destroyed Mari's wall, and turned the land into rubble heaps and ruins" (ANET 270; R4:346).

The final years of Hammurabi's reign were focused on campaigns in northern Mesopotamia and the upper Tigris valley, where the anti-Babylonian coalition was still strong. "By the great power of the god Marduk Hammurabi overthrew the army of Sutium, Turukku, Kakmu and the country of Subartu" in 1757 {Y37} (ANET 270). Babylon's old rival Eshnunna was definitively destroyed in 1756 {Y38}, after a flood had destroyed part of the city walls, perhaps intentionally created by Hammurabi by diverting water from the canal system (ANET 270). In his last recorded campaign {1755, Y39} he again "defeated all his enemies as far as the country of Subartu" (ANET 270).

The military achievement of Hammurabi was one of the greatest of the Middle Bronze Age. Hammurabi made Babylon the center of culture of Mesopotamia, a status which it would retain for over 1500 years. His achievement, however, was also ephemeral. Since his major conquests occurred only late in his reign, he was unable to focus much attention on stabilizing his new domain. Within a decade after his death his empire began to break up during the rule of his son Samsu-iluna (see pp. 181–3).

Hammurabi and the ideal of martial kingship

Although Hammurabi's famous law code has naturally been studied mainly for its social ramifications, its introduction also provides important insights into the martial ideology of Babylonian kings.[33] Hammurabi rules because of the destiny determined by the gods; his scepter and crown are bestowed upon him "by the wise goddess Mama" (LC 78–9). Anu and Enlil "named the city of Babylon", and established "within it eternal kingship whose foundations are as fixed as heaven and earth" (LC 78; R4:334, 341); his dynasty was promised an "eternal seed of royalty" (LC 80). "Hammurabi, the pious prince, who venerates the gods ... [was chosen] to abolish the wicked and evil", which would naturally include conquering impious rival kings (LC 76). He is thus able to "stride through the four quarters of the world" conquering enemies until he "makes the four quarters obedient" to Babylon and the gods (LC 77, 80). Although he is a "warrior", wherever he conquers he is also a restorer and builder. He "restores the [conquered] city of Eridu", "shows mercy to the [conquered] city of Larsa", "revitalizes the [conquered] city of Uruk", "gathers together the scattered peoples of the [conquered] city of Isin", and "gives life to [the conquered] city of Adab" (LC 77–8). He not only conquers cities, but protects them; he "shelters the people of the city of Malgium in the face of annihilation" (LC 79); he "sustains his people in crisis, [and] secures their foundations in peace in the midst of the city of Babylon" (LC 80). Thus, Hammurabi only conquers at the command of the gods (R4:345, 351–3, 389), and does so only to restore prosperity and order, to "spread his light over the lands of Sumer and Akkad" (LC 80). Obviously, much of this is sheer propaganda; this is especially clear in his claim that he "showed mercy to the [conquered] people of the city of Mari" (LC 80). In reality he sacked the city in 1759 and mercilessly destroyed it.

Of course, Hammurabi never undertook any of his conquests on his own initiative. He is in all things the servant of the gods. Hammurabi is always "obedient to the god Shamash", who is thus his "ally" in all his conquests (LC 77); he acts only "upon the command" of the gods (ANET 270; R4:332–3). He is the "leader of the kings [of Mesopotamia], who subdues the settlements along the Euphrates River [including Mari] by the oracular command of the god Dagan, his creator" (LC 80).

With peace and prosperity restored to Mesopotamia, Hammurabi becomes a great temple builder "heaping up bountiful produce" and "supplying abundance" for the gods through donations to their temples from the plunder he has taken from war (LC 78). The epilogue to his law code summarizes the royal propaganda of the time:

> With the mighty weapons which the gods Zababa and Ishtar bestowed upon me, with the wisdom which the god Ea allotted to me, with the ability which the god Marduk gave me, I annihilated enemies everywhere, I [thereby] put an end to [the] wars [that had afflicted Mesopotamia for decades], I enhanced the well-being of the land, I made the people of all settlements lie in safe pastures, I did not tolerate anyone intimidating them [through brigandage or threat of invasion]. The great gods having chosen me, I am indeed the shepherd who brings peace, whose scepter is just. My benevolent shade is spread over my city [Babylon], I held the people of the lands of Sumer and Akkad safely in my lap. They prospered under my protective spirit, I maintained them in peace, with my skillful wisdom I sheltered them (LC 133).... Hammurabi, the lord, who is like a father and begetter to his people, submitted himself to the command of the god Marduk, his lord [to conquer the world], and achieved victory for the god Marduk everywhere. He gladdened the heart

of the god Marduk, his lord, and he secured the eternal wellbeing of the people and provided just ways for the land. (LC 134–5)

The stylized imprecations at the end of the law code include a number of curses against anyone impudent enough to challenge Hammurabi by defacing or modifying his inscriptions, illuminating some of the subliminal fears of military rulers of the age. Hammurabi curses his enemies with the things that all Mesopotamian kings feared. The god Enlil is summoned to bring to Hammurabi's enemies "disorder that cannot be quelled and a rebellion that will result in obliteration" and "the supplanting of his dynasty and the blotting out of his name and his memory in the land" (LC 136–7). The gods likewise pass judgment on the enemies, "pronouncing the destruction of his land, the obliteration of his people, and the spilling of his life force [blood] like water" (LC 137). Ea, the god of wisdom, is summoned to deprive Hammurabi's enemies "of all understanding and wisdom" and to "lead them into confusion" (LC 136). Hammurabi summons the sun-god Shamash to "confuse [his enemy's] path and undermine the morale of his army; when divination is performed for him, may he provide an inauspicious omen portending the uprooting of the foundation of his kinship" (LC 137–8). The war-gods Zababa, Ishtar, and Nergal are particularly summoned to bring military disaster on Hammurabi's enemies:

> May the god Zababa, the great warrior ... who travels on [Hammurabi's] right side [in battle], smash the weapon [of Hammuarbi's enemy] upon the field of battle; may [Zababa] turn day into night for him,[34] and make his enemy triumph over him. May the goddess Ishtar, mistress of battle and warfare, who bares [Hammurabi's] weapons [in battle][35] ... curse the kingship [of Hammurabi's enemy] with her angry heart and great fury; may she turn his auspicious [pre-battle] omens into calamities; may she smash his weapon on the field of war and battle, plunge him into confusion and rebellion, strike down his warriors, drench the earth with their blood, make a heap of the corpses of his soldiers upon the plain [of battle], and may she show his soldiers no mercy; as for [Hammurabi's enemy], may she deliver him into the hand of his enemies, and may she lead him bound captive into the land of his enemy. May the god Nergal, the mighty one among the gods, the irresistible onslaught [in battle], who enables me [Hammurabi] to achieve my triumphs, burn his [Hammurabi's enemy's] people with his [Nergal's] great overpowering weapon like a raging fire in a reed thicket; may he [Nergal] have him [the enemy] beaten with [Nergal's] mighty weapon, and shatter his limbs like those of a clay figure. (LC 138–9)

This remarkable curse is essentially an outline of the course of warfare in the Old Babylonian period: it begins with pre-battle divination and omens, the fight on the battlefield, the mound of corpses, the merciless treatment of defeated enemies, their captivity, and the final triumph of the king.

Middle Bronze Mesopotamian martial art

One of the remarkable features of the Middle Bronze Age in Mesopotamia is the near disappearance of monumental martial art. The reason for this is not clear. It may be because of changes in the cultic and ritual context in which martial art was generally produced. Alternatively, it is possible that martial art of this period was generally done in the form of fresco paintings such as those at the palace of Zimri-Lim at Mari (SDA 275–83). If so it is likely that little of this art has survived. On the other hand, when we remember that only nine fragments of martial art survive from the militant Akkadian period, the relative lack of Middle Bronze Mesopotamian martial art may simply be a matter of the failure as yet to discover any surviving remains.

This is not to say that monumental martial art is unknown from this period.[36] The most striking example is a fragment of a stele sometimes attributed, on rather flimsy grounds, to Shamshi-Adad (AAM §204–5; SDA 252). One side shows a warrior in a long ornate robe with a spear in his left hand and an axe in his right. He has one foot on the stomach of a fallen enemy; he is thrusting a spear into the man's chest while simultaneously striking him in the forehead with an axe. The opposite side of the stele fragment shows a triumph scene with a royal prisoner with his hands tied behind his back (AAM §205). An interesting feature of this stele is the simultaneous use of two different weapons in two-handed combat.

The second major martial scene shows a king with an axe in one hand and a badly worn weapon – which appears to be a sickle-sword – in the other, striding over the walls of a conquered fortress and a diminutive prostrate enemy (SDA 291c). He is followed by a soldier with a banner. One very important feature of this scene is that it is the only artistic depiction of a Middle Bronze fortress. It shows a city wall with crenellation and a large city gate flanked by two projecting towers. The gate has a clearly depicted brick arch, quite similar to the Middle Bronze gate discovered intact at Tell Dan in Israel, which can still be seen at the site (ALB 208; Figure 7, p. 278).

A third mythic scene shows a god with a long flowing robe and a triangular-shaped bow and quiver on his back, grasping a monster by the neck and stabbing him with a large bronze dagger (AAM §211; SDA 291a). Another mythic scene shows Gilgamesh and Enkidu trampling the prostrate Humbaba while slaying him with dagger and mace (AFC 482). Both of these may depict typical weapons and their use during the Middle Bronze period.

Historical and mythic scenes from cylinder seals add to our repertoire of martial art from the Middle Bronze Age. These scenes can be categorized into a number of stylized scenes. The most common shows a god, goddess or king in a victory stance with either a curved or rectangular sickle-sword in one hand.[37] Sometimes the figure is trampling a prostrate enemy.[38] The smiting scene shows a king standing with raised axe, mace or sickle-sword about to smite a cowering enemy (FI §160, 541, 763). One scene shows the god or king with sickle-sword in one hand and mace in the other (AM §157b), confirming the two-handed use of weapons shown in the "Shamshi-Adad" stele discussed above. A more distinctive scene comes from Anatolia, showing a king in battle (FI §4). The king has a cross-shaped shield, rather similar to contemporary shields in Canaan and Syria. The hand holding the shield also holds the spear, with the head facing down. He has a battle-axe in the other hand, and is standing on a dead enemy; a nearby warrior uses an underhand thrust of a dagger.

If one were to guess at patterns of Middle Bronze weapons use, based on the glyptic art, it would appear that the sickle-sword was the most common weapon, but, based on archaeology, the sickle-sword is a relatively rare find compared to spears, axes, and daggers, and appears largely in royal contexts (MW 1:142–3, 170–1; see pp. 66–71). This again points to the problem of generalizing about the norms of warfare based on mythically and ritually oriented martial art.

Samsu-iluna {1749–1712}[39]

For the first eight years of his reign Samsu-iluna was at peace; his year names focus on economic and religious activities. The new Pax Babylonica brought at least temporary prosperity, and Samsu-iluna celebrated his coronation by declaring "freedom from taxation for Sumer and Akkad" (ANET 271). Samsu-iluna's ninth year {1741} is called "the year of the Kassite army" (ANET 271). The Kassites (*Kaššu*) were tribal highlanders from the Zagros region, successors to the earlier Gutians. Kassites were eventually to succeed the Babylonians after the sack of Babylon by the Hittites in 1595. They would eventually found a dynasty that would dominate Mesopotamia from 1595–1155.[40] At this time, however, they were still highlanders from the Zagros, migrating in small groups, serving as mercenaries, or seeking opportunities for plunder in the rich cities of the Babylonian empire. No details of this first Kassite raid are known, but Samsu-iluna was apparently unable to defeat them decisively. This sign of imperial weakness provided a catalyst for widespread rebellion against Babylonian rule.

The instigator of this rebellion was Rim-Sin II of Larsa {1740–1738}, who quickly overran most of southern Mesopotamia. Samsu-iluna, however, reacted vigorously, suppressing the revolt and killing Rim-Sin II in 1738 {Y12} (R4:317, 379).

> At that time I [Samsu-iluna] defeated with weapons, eight times in the course of one year, the totality of the land of Sumer and Akkad which had become hostile against me. I turned the cities into rubble heaps and ruins. I tore out the roots of the enemies and evil one from the land. I made the entirety of the nation dwell according to my decree. (R4:376–7)

This campaign is recounted in greater detail, beginning with the mythical background in the world of the gods.

> The god Enlil, great lord, whose utterance cannot be changed – the destiny that he determines cannot be altered – looked with his joyful face at the

[warrior] god Zababa, his mighty oldest son, the one who achieves his victory, and at the [war] goddess Ishtar, his beloved daughter, the lady whose divinity is not rivaled, and spoke with them happy words: "Samsu-iluna is my mighty untiring envoy [as king on earth] who knows how to carry out the desire of my heart. May you be his shining light. May your good omen occur for him. Kill his enemies and deliver into his hands his foes that he might build the wall of Kish, make it greater than it had been previously and make you dwell in a happy abode."

The god Zababa and goddess Ishtar ... raised their faces of life brightly towards Samsu-iluna, the mighty king [of Babylon], the valiant shepherd, the creation of their hands, and joyfully spoke with him: "O Samsu-iluna, eternal seed of the gods, one befitting kingship – Enlil has made your destiny very great. He has laid a commission on us to act as your guardians for your well-being. We will go at your right side [in battle], kill your enemies, and deliver your foes into your hands. As for Kish, our fear-inspiring cult city, build its wall, make it greater than it was previously." (R4:385–6)

This type of language presumably represents oracular pronouncements and omens from court priests and prophets. Having received a divine mandate from the gods, Samsu-iluna marched to defeat the rebels in southern Mesopotamia and restore the sacred city of Kish to Babylonian rule:

Samsu-iluna, the capable king, the one who listens to the [oracles of the] great gods, was greatly encouraged by the words which the god Zababa and the goddess Ishtar spoke to him [through an oracle]. He made ready his weapons in order to kill his enemies and set out on an expedition to slaughter his foes. The year was not half over when he killed [the rebel king] Rim-Sin [II of Larsa], who had caused [southern Mesopotamia] to rebel, and who had been elevated to the kingship of Larsa. In the land of Kish [Samsu-iluna] heaped up a burial mound over him. Twenty-six rebel kings, his foes, he killed; he destroyed all of them. He defeated Iluni, the king of Eshnunna, one who had not heeded his decrees, led him off in a neck-stock, and had his throat cut. He made the totality of the land of Sumer and Akkad at peace, made the four quarters abide by his decree. At that time, Samsu-iluna, the mighty, by means of the force of his army built the city of Kish [in 1726 {Y24}]. He dug its canal, surrounded it with a moat, and with a great deal of earth made its foundations firm as a mountain. He formed its bricks and built its wall. In the course of one year he made its head rise up more than it had been before. (R4:387–8)

Thus, Samsu-iluna portrays his acts as enforcing the decree of the gods by restoring order to Mesopotamia and rebuilding the gods' sacred city of Kish. Although ultimately defeated, the revolt revealed the serious potential weakness of the Babylonian empire.

The suppression of the rebellion in the south was followed by a threat from the northeast. Eshnunna and the highlander Kassites constantly chaffed under Babylonian domination, and in 1730 {Y20} Samsu-iluna ...

> subjugated the land of Idamaraz from the border of Gutium to the border of Elam with his mighty weapon; he conquered the numerous people of the land of Idamaraz and demolished all the various fortresses of the land of Warum who had resisted him; he achieved his victory and made his strength apparent. After two months had passed, having set free and given life to the people of the land of Idamaraz who he had taken captive, and the troops of Eshnunna, as many prisoners as he had taken, he rebuilt the various fortresses of the land of Warum which he had destroyed and regathered and resettled its scattered people. (R4:389–90)

Samsu-iluna's triumph, however, was short-lived. Within a few years his control over southern Mesopotamia was again threatened. In 1721 {Y29} he lost control over Nippur (R4:425), and by 1712 {Y38} the south was permanently lost to the rising power of Iluma-Ilum {c. 1735–1710}, king of the "Sealand" (or coastal) dynasty from the coastal marshes of southern Mesopotamia. Iluma-Ilum managed to fend off three offensives from Babylon during his reign (C2/1:222); in the end the kings of Babylon were forced to acquiesce to his independence. Little is known of the Sealand dynasty; it ruled much of the Mesopotamian coastland under eleven known kings for two-and-a-half centuries {c. 1735–1460}, but few inscriptions or records survive, and almost nothing is known of its military history (AI 243; C2/1:222, 442–3).

Late Old Babylonian Kingdom {1712–1595}

Although the dynasty founded by Hammurabi would endure for another century, for all practical purposes the Babylonian empire had been reduced to central Mesopotamia by the death of Samsu-iluna. Following the death of Samsu-iluna, the deeds of later Old Babylonian kings are only sparsely recorded in inscriptions. It is clear that the military power of Babylon was increasingly restricted during the seventeenth century. The year names of Abi-eshuh {1711–1684} mention several defensive campaigns against the Kassite invaders from the mountains, but no major victories in the south. Ammi-ditana {1683–1646} was also apparently on the defensive, focusing on fortifications. He repaired the walls of Babylon (R4:412), and built Fort Ammi-ditana (R4:413). A fragmentary inscription by Ammi-saduqa {1646–1626} claims that Babylonian power was temporarily restored in Nippur, where a cult figure of the goddess Ishtar was installed (R4:426). Samsu-ditana {1625–1595} was the last king of Hammurabi's dynasty. Although the details were not known, he was killed during the Hittite conquest of Babylon in 1595, bringing an end to Hammurabi's dynasty (see p. 301).

The four centuries between the fall of Ur {2005} and the fall of Babylon {1595} are characterized by a remarkable political and military instability in

Mesopotamia. A number of quite successful warlords rose to power during this age – Ishbi-Irra of Isin {2017–1985}, Shamshi-Adad of Ashur {1809–1776}, and Hammurabi of Babylon {1792–1750} – but each of their empires rapidly collapsed under less talented successors. In contrast to Egypt, which emerged united and powerful under the New Kingdom in the Late Bronze Age, this long-term internal instability left Mesopotamia consistently vulnerable to outside invasions during subsequent centuries, including attacks by Elamites, Kassites, Hurrians, Amorites, and Hittites. Only in the ninth century under the great Assyrian warlords would political unity and military strength be restored to Mesopotamia.

CHAPTER SEVEN

Warfare in the age of Mari

The most detailed textual sources we have for warfare in the Middle Bronze Age is the extraordinary archive from Mari, which contains more than 20,000 cuneiform tablets, many of which are military dispatches from field and garrison commanders to the king of Mari, Zimri Lim {1776–1761}.[1] Remarkably for the ancient Near East, the military letters from Mari give us the words of actual commanders written within days or even hours of the events they are describing. Nothing is filtered through the royal propaganda machines. We are, in a sense, transported into the midst of Middle Bronze Age battles.

There are, however, a number of historiographical limitations and problems with the Mari archive. First, chronologically the tablets come largely from the reign of Zimri-Lim, king of Mari, and hence cover only a narrow period of Mesopotamian history. None the less, that period was one of the most militarily important and active, covering the rise of Hammurabi of Babylon {1792–1750} to imperial predominance in Mesopotamia. Indeed, the destruction of Mari, which ironically preserved the clay tablets, occurred two years after Hammurabi conquered Mari {1759}. The archive also presents us only with the Mari perspective; we are left with limited information concerning the views of their enemies. The archive also includes only letters *to* king Zimri-Lim; unfortunately his responses to his commanders are included only incidentally in quotations within the letters. Likewise the words of other kings, such as Hammurabi, are occasionally indirectly quoted in the Mari letters.

Our second problem in interpreting the Mari archive is that some of the texts are broken or damaged, leaving lacunae – gaps created by lost text. Tablets can be broken in a number of different ways, losing the top, bottom or one or other side of a particular missive; other lacunae are created by a gash in the middle. The net result is that many of the letters are obscure and difficult to interpret. To the problem of lacunae is added philological difficulties relating to uncertain grammar or meaning of words. The result is that the exact meaning of many texts is often uncertain. This is especially a problem in relation to technical terminology.

Finally, we have the problem of historical contextualization. Many of the letters are undated, meaning we don't know whether the events in one particular letter occurred before or after the events in another. The letters also often contain numerous references to unknown people and places. The result is that, although we know what happened, we frequently are uncertain about when it happened, where it happened, or who was doing what to whom.

Trying to reconstruct military history from the Mari archive is thus rather like trying to reconstruct the events of the Napoleonic wars from a disorganized pile of often damaged and semi-legible dispatches of Napoleon's commanders to Napoleon, but none of his responses. Remaining with the analogy, it is unclear if the battle of Waterloo occurred before or after the invasion or Russia, or if Austerlitz is in Germany, France, or Spain. It is also uncertain if Wellington is an ally or an enemy of Napoleon. Nor do we have a French dictionary – we have to make up our own as we go along. Fortunately, great strides have been made in recent years through painstaking study of the Mari letters. The recent publication of Wolfgang Heimpel's *Letters to the King of Mari* has given us both a historical framework and a translation of many of the letters.[2]

Battle divination and martial ideology[3]

Ancient Near Eastern armies operated in a world in which belief in the supernatural power of the gods was an omnipresent assumption. Battles were fought and won by the will of the gods. The prophet of one god promised Zimri-Lim "O Zimri-Lim, swear that you will not neglect me, and I shall hover over you and deliver your enemies into your power" (ARM 10.8; MK 138). Whereas Napoleon claimed that "God is on the side with the big guns", the ancient Mesopotamians would have countered "God is on the side with the big temples". To insure that a king, general, or army were operating in accordance with the will of the gods, Mesopotamian rulers employed diviners and prophets who would interpret the will of the gods. A wide range of methods were used to accomplish this. Few kings dared go to war without the explicit approval of the gods.

In the Mari texts, the most important form of martial divination was extispicy (*tērtum*), the ritual examination of the liver of a sacrificed animal for patterns and markings which were interpreted according to a complex set of rules.[4] Mari commanders invariably consulted the diviners (*bārûm*) before undertaking any major military operation; special martial diviners were assigned to accompany military units on campaign (L 225, 463; ASD 176–9). They were obviously important officers, since one is described as riding in a chariot like the generals of the army (L 225). One *bārûm* seems to have been the independent commander of a force of several hundred men:

> Ilushu-nasir, the *bārûm*-priest ... leads the forces of my lord. A Babylonian *bārûm*-priest goes with the Babylonian forces. These 600 troops are now in Shabazim. The *bārûm*-priests are now gathering omens. (ARM 2.22; WM 130)

Frequently the letters give no details about divination, mentioning only that the omens were favorable or unfavorable (L 210–11, 214–15). Other times, more precise questions were asked and specific detailed prophecies were given; examples of oracular responses to divination include:

- "The king's hand will catch territory that is not his" (L 175);
- "My lord will seize the city [he is besieging] in a hard battle" (L 221);
- "The enemy will attack and carry off livestock" (L 175);
- "The enemy will not make an incursion [into the king's land]" (L 229);
- "Those extispicies were bad. Rebellion [in the city] was repeatedly indicated. I have put the [guards] of the city gates on notice about the citizens" (L 230);
- "When [the allied Babylonian soldiers] enter Mari, they will not cause rebellion to be committed and seize the city of Mari" (L 235–6);
- "This month the enemy will not move against you with his troops and his allies, and he will not besiege you" (L 239);
- "Zimri-Lim, do not go on the road [on campaign]! Stay in Mari!" (L 268).

Sometimes, alternative plans were made depending on the forthcoming results of the extispicy. One commander ordered: "Make an extispicy, and if that [rebel] village still holds out at the end of the month, leave the fifty men behind [to blockade it], and depart! If the extispicies are bad, [capture the city] and take down [its fortifications]" (L 236). On other occasions double extispicies might be taken, asking the same question in two different ways to get confirmation, or perhaps to get the answer one wanted.

> I made extispicies as follows: I asked, "If [king] Zimri-Lim cedes [the city of] Id to the king of Babylon, will [king] Zimri-Lim be well? ..." I made [extispicies] on two more lambs as follows: "If Zimri-Lim cedes Id to the king of Babylon, will Zimri-Lim be well? ..." My extispicies were not sound [indicating a negative answer]. I did [extispicy again] as follows: "If Zimri-Lim [does not] cede Id to the king of Babylon, will Zimri-Lim be well?" My extispicies were sound [indicating a positive answer]. (L 237)

Battle could not be undertaken without favorable omens. One priest reported the results of his pre-battle extispicy. He first listed the question asked, and then the answer derived from his divination:

> Should Sumu-Dabi, with troops few or many, however many he can readily equip, draw up in battle formation against Zimri-Lim, should he do battle with him, and be safe, defeat him, be victorious? ... [The result of the extispicy was that] he must not do battle. (L 240)

When the result of the extispicy was favorable, the commander would carry out his plan: "I had extispicies done for the well-being of the troops of my lord ... and the extispicies were sound, and the troops may move from their position" (L 216, 242). Another officer reported: "We are having extispicies done now. If the god answers, we will do what the god says to us. May the god of our lord go by our side [into battle]!" (L 329). If unfavorable omens occurred, however, the plans were generally put on hold. In such a situation, the commander could wait a while, and consult the oracles again, hoping for a better result. "I made extispicies for the well-being of the messengers, and they were bad, [so I did not send them]. I will make [extispicies] for them again, and when the extispicies have come out sound, I will dispatch them" (L 210). Some oracles were given as a conditional warning; an ecstatic prophet proclaimed, "If you do not make that [new] city gate, there will be a corpse heap [of the soldiers killed in battle at the gate when the city is sacked by the enemy]" (L 263).

When the omens were bad the king or his priests sometimes had to intervene ritually, by making special offerings to re-establish good relations with the gods. Impurity or other types of sin that could antagonize the gods had to be ritually purified to insure success in battle: "There is a taboo [of sin or impurity] among you. The [exorcists and purifiers] must wash off the taboo" (L 199). The king was required to expiate for sins and impurities; according to one oracle: "If my lord stays for seven days outside the walls [of the city] when he does his ablutions [then the gods will grant] well-being" (L 261, 177). In such situations, if the king personally made sacrifice, cosmic order could be restored. One minister advised: ". . . our lord [Zimri-Lim] must come to Hanat to meet the troops, and our lord must perform an offering before [the goddess of] Hanat. And he must see the troops whom we moved and calm their hearts, which are frightened" (L 196). Bad omens could be changed to good omens by the king making an offering in expiation and taking another extispicy: "I have obtained the [sacrificial] offering that my lord [king Zimri-Lim] offered and whose extispicies he sent, and the god accepted the offering of my lord [and the omens are favorable]" (L 212).

In addition to divination by extispicy, natural phenomena were sometimes seen as ominous. An eclipse of the moon caused panic among the troops (L 209). Eclipses were often, but not universally, associated with disaster, but it was not always clear for whom. In different months an eclipse might presage that "a city loses its population", "many troops fall", or "a defeat of the other king will happen" (L 271). A prodigious birth of a deformed lamb was seen as ominous, requiring careful study by the diviners (L 510). Dreams were often thought of as prophetic: "Yasim-Dagan had a dream before his eyes. The dream is serious and is raising concern [among the soldiers]. I had an extispicy of his dream done.... [The meaning of the dream is that] my lord must give strict orders to guard the strongholds" (L 209). Another oracular dreamer wrote: "In my dream the allies of Zimri-Lim defeated Elam" (L 264).

Oracular prophecy is also described in the Mari letters in which ecstatic prophets spoke the words of the gods from trance-like states. Sometimes such prophecies were highly metaphorical and enigmatic. For example, does the prophecy "a wind rises against the land" (L 255) refer to a desert sandstorm or an enemy invasion? Others used simile prophecies: an ecstatic prophet ate a lamb alive, then pronounced, "A devouring will occur" (L 256), possibly an allusion to an invading army consuming a land.

The gods frequently requested specific offerings or behavior from the king. The prophet of the god Shamash told Zimri-Lim:

> I [the god Shamash] am the lord of the land. I requested from you [as votive offerings] a great throne as seat of my plenitude and your daughter [to serve as a priestess in Shamash's temple] – let them be rushed quickly to Sippir, city of life. Herewith I deliver into your hand the kings who stood against you [in battle]. (L 249)

Other prophets made independent prophecies not requested by the king:

> One "shock-head" (qammatum: an ecstatic spirit-possessed prophetess with disheveled hair) of [the god] Dagan of Terqa came and spoke to me as follows. She said: "The peace offers of the Eshnunakeans are deceit.... I will collect him [the king of Eshnuna] in the net that I knot. I will erase his city. And his wealth, which is from old, I will cause to be utterly defiled." (L 251)

As it turned out, Eshnuna was in the end defeated by Hammurabi.

Some oracles were very detailed, promising that the gods themselves would fight on the side of the king:

> I [asked the prophets]: "Will my lord [Zimri-Lim] come close to battle?" They [the prophets replied]: "Battle will not be done. As of the arrival [of Zimri-Lim] his [Ishme-Dagan's, son of Shamshi-Adad, king of Assyria] allies will scatter. And they will cut off the head of Ishme-Dagan, and they will place it under the foot of my lord [Zimri-Lim], saying, 'the troops of Ishme-Dagan were many. And although his troops were many, his allies scattered. My [Zimri-Lim's] allies are [the gods] Dagan, Shamash, Itur-Mer, and Belet-Ekallim and Addu, lord of determination; they [these gods] go at the side of my lord [into battle].' " (L 257)

Unlike the mortal allies of Ishme-Dagan, who will desert him, Zimri-Lim's allies are the gods, who will stay by his side and lead him to victory. Another prophet agreed, repeatedly shouting his prophecy by the palace gate: "Ishme-Dagan [son of Shamshi-Adad] will not escape the hand of [the god] Marduk" (L 325). As it happened, Ishme-Dagan died and lost his kingdom (L 145–6).

When a king wanted to go to war, he had to consult the gods, both to increase the morale of his troops, but also because a favorable oracle from the gods was considered a justification for war. Hammurabi, when he attacked his erstwhile ally Larsa, proclaimed:

> "I now requested [an oracle about going to war with Larsa from the gods] Shamash and Marduk and they answered me with yes. I would not have risen to this offensive [against Larsa] without consulting a god [first]." To his troops

he spoke as follows: "Go [to Larsa], may the god go in front of you [into battle]!" (L 333)

It is possible that Hammurabi had no desire to attack Larsa before the oracle from the gods, but more often kings were simply seeking divine permission to do what they had already determined to do.

Sometimes a commander or a king ignored the omens, though they were repeatedly advised by the diviners not to do so. One commander was adamant: "Only go out [on campaign] upon sound extispicies!" (L 458). Another oracle declared: "I am afraid the king [Zimri-Lim] will commit himself to [peace with] the Eshnunakean [king] without asking a god.... He must not commit himself without asking the god" (L 253). One priest complained that the commander was considering acting against the omens:

> The enemy are enlisting border guards from the elite troops and enlisting additional troops [in preparation for war] but my lord must [wait] and keep catering to the wishes of [the gods] Dagan, Shamash, and Addu about these things.... My lord must not hurry into battle, and my lord must not [attack] the enemy.... When Dagan, Shamash, and Addu, these gods, have answered you with yes and your extispicies are sound, then my lord must do battle! (L 243)

In general, however, the omens and prophecies were ignored at great peril. Bad omens and military misfortunes were blamed on the inscrutable will of the gods: "have I done anything that does not please [the sun-god] Shamash so that he has done this to me? ... Why has the god treated me this way?" (PH 33). Although most of us today are rather dubious that the will of God can be found in the blotches on the liver of a sheep, we should never doubt that the ancient soldiers had absolute belief in the efficacy of extispicy and prophecy. If a commander operated against the omens, the morale of his army suffered drastically. Omens changed the course of battle not because they were real, but because the Mesopotamian soldiers *believed* they were real, and behaved in rational response to that belief. Although generals might miss important military opportunities by refusing to march when the omens were bad, campaigning with bad omens could bring disaster because of the devastating psychological impact on the morale of the troops.[5] All successful ancient commanders instinctively acted upon this, whether they themselves actually believed in the gods and the omens or not.

Middle Bronze generals well understood the importance of maintaining high morale among their soldiers, as is reflected in this dispatch:

> The last of the Hana [nomad auxiliaries] have arrived here.... No one is sick. No one! There are no losses.... When I observed all [previous] expeditions there were many worries; but in this expedition I observe no sorrow or anything of that kind, only laughter and joking. [The soldiers] are as happy as if

they were living at home. The hearts of my lord's servants think [only] of the endeavor of fighting battles and defeating the enemy. Rejoice, my lord! (WM 101–2)

Bad battle omens were one sure way to destroy this type of good morale.

Modern disbelievers in ancient prophetic techniques might naturally expect a high rate of inaccuracy from ancient omens and prophecies. And, indeed, many of the oracles are manifestly false. One prophet, for example, proclaimed: "kingship, scepter, throne, reign, the upper [land of Syria] and lower land [of Mesopotamia] are given to Zimri-Lim" (L 267). In fact, it was Zimri-Lim's erstwhile ally Hammurabi of Babylon who became universal king of Mesopotamia, by sacking Mari and killing Zimri-Lim. This naturally leads us to wonder: if the omens and prophecies were frequently inaccurate, why didn't military commanders simply abandon their use altogether? To answer this question we must remember that omen interpretation was an art, not a science, and there was a great deal of "wiggle-room" possible in extispicy, allowing a range of possible interpretation by the diviner. We must also remember that the diviner-priests were among the most educated men of their day. They were well-informed high courtiers with close associations with the power elites of the kingdom. Julius Caesar, for all his greatness as a commander, also occasionally served Rome as a diviner, as *pontifex maximus* and *auger*.[6] Like Caesar, Mesopotamian diviners led troops in battle (ARM 2.22). They frequently served as spies, sending detailed reports on political and military matters back to the king (L 94–5). Whether intentionally or subconsciously, the interpretation of omens and extispicies could be manipulated by the diviners. The results of oracles and divination were thus not merely random, but were informed interpretations of omens made with knowledge of the major military and political issues facing the commander. Court and regimental diviner-priests were undoubtedly often wrong, but overall they were probably not much more inaccurate than modern political pundits and intelligence services. When a modern intelligence service fails, we blame human error. We may try to change the personnel or fix the system, but we don't abandon it. When ancient oracles failed, it was likewise seen as a mistake made by the diviner rather than evidence that the overall system itself was faulty. A particular diviner-priest may have been dismissed from court, but the practice of divination continued.

Oddly enough, battle-divination was one of the most pervasive and long-lasting military practices of ancient Mesopotamia. Long after chariots and slings were abandoned, battle divination continued. Divine sanction for Saul's reign over Israel was withdrawn when he disobeyed his diviner-priest, the prophet Samuel (1 Samuel 13). Likewise there was a dispute between Ahab of Israel and the prophet Micaiah over battle divination (1 Kings 22). A thousand years later, Greek and Roman generals were still practicing essentially the same type of battle-divination rituals.[7] The last pagan Roman battle divination was requested by Julian the Apostate in 363 CE, 2100 years after the writing of the Mari letters.[8] Medieval

Christians had their own forms of pre-battle divination, beginning with Constantine's vision at the battle of Milvian Bridge in 312 CE.[9] Indeed, in its core feature pre-battle divination has continued in use to the present, for when a military commander today prays for God's help in the planning and execution of his battle and for the protection of his troops, he is, in essence, engaging in the same practice as the ancient Mesopotamian diviners.

Military organization

There are few texts in the Mari archive which explicitly discuss military organization (L 498–500, 507–8). However, there are a number of incidental allusions to such matters which give us a fairly detailed view of how a Mesopotamian Middle Bronze army was organized and functioned (MK 141–5; MM).

Conscription and records
(MM 7–11; MK 141–5; WM 66–88)

In order to know the proper duties owed by each community, Mesopotamian rulers are known to have instituted censuses. The most detailed account we have is the census of Zimri-Lim of Mari (MK 142–3). The census was called a *tēbibtum*, which literally means purification, probably related to religious rituals associated with the census. The people were required to gather to be counted. The common people were understandably wary of a census that would be used to determine both their financial obligations to the state and the number of men they would have to provide for military and labor drafts, and the records of Zimri-Lim's census show that many tried to avoid being counted (ARM 14.64).[10] One official suggests parading the severed head of an executed prisoner as an inducement to those villagers who refused to be counted (ARM 2.48).

Troops were recruited for military service in three broad categories: professional soldiers, militias and mercenaries. Recruitment (*puhrum*) procedures were run by a sophisticated military bureaucracy led by the "secretary of the army" (DUB.SAR MAR.TU) (ASD 106–9). Each regiment had a scribe attached to it who received the pay equivalent of a lieutenant (L 500; MM 9, 12–13). These military scribes kept detailed complete lists of the names and hometowns of all of the soldiers, from which were derived lists of casualties and deserters, a frequently mentioned problem (MM 45–7; WM 72). Each village mayor (*suqāqum*) was required to oversee the recruitment in his village, and to make sure his village's quota was fulfilled. The recruits were required to "swear an oath [of loyalty] by Dagan" or some other god, after which their names were recorded on clay tablets; a copy was kept by the regimental scribe and another sent to the central archive (L 461, 482; WM 73–5). When called up, new recruits were inspected and those unfit for duty – the sick and old – were sent home (L 483). None the less, unfit soldiers could be found in the ranks; one general complained: "Reliable troops are not at hand" (L 400). Another echoed this sentiment: "Why do you release reliable men [from service] and then replace them unnecessarily with [inexperienced] little children?" (L 330).

In times of peace soldiers are frequently described as being on furlough (*patīrum*) (L 224; WM 75–6). Specific lists of furloughed soldiers were recorded and forwarded to the central government (L 194). One commander reported to king Zimri-Lim:

> My lord wrote me about dead and runaway troops. My lord said: "Write down a name-list and send it to me!" Because I watch the troops closely over here, I have sent for the soldiers on furlough twenty days ago. Let the soldiers on furlough arrive here, and I shall inspect the name-list on the tablet and see who are the troops on hand and the runaway troops, and I will send a complete report to my lord. (L 297)

A commander forwarded to the king the "name lists of the men on hand, the troops of the garrisons, the soldiers on furlough, the deserters, and the dead, place by place, on tablets" (L 348, 462). One such furlough tablet survives, listing individual soldiers by their regiment, personal name, and home town (L 464). One text mentions that sixteen out of fifty soldiers were on furlough (L 224); another unit had twenty-five on furlough and only twenty-two on duty (L 312). When war breaks out, these furloughed troops are immediately called back to service (L 243). Sometimes a commander was not able to muster the requisite number of troops; one officer was reprimanded for having only 800 men instead of the required 1000 (L 487).

As in any army, officers and soldiers grew weary of extended duty away from home. One city commander wrote to the king, complaining: "I have been staying in [the city of] Ilan-Sura [on duty] in the garrison for five years. Now, if it pleases my lord, let my lord dispatch an alternate for me!" (L. 310). Ordinary soldiers also expected to rotate after a certain term of service. "My lord instructed us as follows: 'Go and stay three months'.... Now we have fulfilled three months.... If my lord will dispatch to me a replacement for these troops, let those troops go!" (L 312). When conditions of service became bad enough, the troops became mutinous. Fifty men deserted when there was insufficient food (L 213), and others threatened to do so as well (L 314). One commander reported growing dissatisfaction in the ranks, with his soldiers complaining:

> Why did we go on campaign, and why did we not return to our lord at the end [of the campaign]? ... [The soldiers] hearts are angry, and they will rise [and desert] and depart for somewhere else.... [The king] must give them flour. He must replace these troops! (L 313–14)

Soldiers also complained of serving in winter, apparently expecting military service to be seasonal (L 185, 192–3). Punishment for disobedient or cowardly soldiers could be harsh, including being stripped naked, bound, beaten, and paraded before the troops to be mocked (L 463).

Nomad mercenaries

Mercenaries were frequently recruited from the nomads (L 222–3; WM 67), and the Kassite and Elamite highlanders (ASD 88–9). Most prominent sources of nomad mercenaries for the king of Mari were the Hana tribe of the Sim'al tribal confederation.[11] Another major tribal confederation, which seems to have been less willing to serve in the armies of Mari, was the Banu-Yamina (Yaminites, Benjaminites) to the north-east around the Khabur River (WM 95). These groups were divided into a number of clans, each ruled by a *sugagum* – a chief or shaykh. In the Mari archives they make frequent appearance both as raiders attacking the kingdom and its caravans, and as mercenaries in the service of the king. Under the right conditions, the nomadic tribes could muster sizable forces in service of a kingdom. Zimri-Lim mobilized some 7000 nomads for one of his campaigns: "Two thousand [soldiers from the] Hana [nomad tribe] were assembled in Qattunan, and they keep assembling as scheduled.... Five thousand Numha and Yamutbal troops are assembled together. They go to [military service for] my lord" (L 416). The nomads needed both monetary and verbal inducements to join the king's campaign. One commander reported: "the Hana [nomads], all of them, are assembled now and I delivered the instruction of my lord [king Zimri-Lim]. I caused them relief with words; and they arose and proclaimed favorable words and greetings to my lord" (L 200). There was a downside to using nomad mercenaries. The passage of nomad troops, often together with their families and herds, could cause problems for farmers in the campaign area. "There were masses of Numha and Yumutbal [nomads], together with their little boys and girls, slaves, maids, oxen, and donkeys. After they use up the grain, they will destroy the sedge and reed of the bank of the Euphrates" (L 204).

Organization[12]

Reports of the payment of some Mariote regiments in Babylonian service provide us with a basic outline of both military organization and pay rates (L 498–500, 507–8). Compensation for military service took a number of forms, including land grants (L 446), clothing (L 507–8), food (ASD 88), weapons (see section on logistics on p. 21), silver wages (L 498–500, 507–8), and slaves (L 225, 349). One tablet records the daily grain distribution to soldiers: high officers received two-thirds of a liter (*qa*) of barley per day, lower officers half a liter, and ordinary soldiers about a third of a liter (WM 140); there were also occasional distributions of vegetables, beer, and mutton (WM 14).

Land (*sibtu*) was given to a soldier's family in return for military service, and was governed by strict laws in Hammurabi's Law Code (LC §26–38 = ANET 166–8; ASD 96–101; L 446). Land was distributed in varying amounts to different ranks; one general was given a huge estate of 190 hectares of land (MAS 26), while common soldiers were given small, single-family plots. If the soldier failed to report for duty or sent an unauthorized substitute, he was to be executed (LC §26).

On occasion, however, soldiers were permitted to send substitutes (*takhkhu*) to fulfill family military obligations (ASD 91–3). Soldiers who were taken prisoner in war were to have their land protected, and passed to a son who was to assume his father's military responsibilities (LC §27–9); land with a military obligation attached to it could not be sold (LC §36). Officers were forbidden upon pain of death to take the goods of a soldier, to hire the soldier out for labor, or appropriate his land grant (LC §34). Soldiers were also forbidden to sell the provisions given them by the state (LC §37).

Plunder (*šallatum*) (WM 76–9) was an important element in the soldier's pay; a portion of all booty was kept by the king, but soldiers expected their share:

> Let your troops seize booty and they will bless you. These three towns are not heavily fortified. In a day we shall be able to take them. Quickly come up and let us capture these towns and let your troops seize booty. (ARM 5.16; WM 77)

The documents mention soldiers who stole booty from the king's share, and also officers who kept booty that should have been given to the soldiers. One commander complained that some of his officers . . .

> have stolen the soldier's booty! I put an oath of the king into my mouth . . . not to rob the booty of a soldier. Not ten days had passed after my decree when a tablet . . . arrived, saying "Whoever has taken away the soldiers' booty has committed a sacrilege against me." (ARM 2.13; WM 78–9)

In Table 7.1, I give very rough hypothetical equivalents to modern military ranks. The fundamental military leader was the general (GAL.MARTU, *rab Amurrim*), literally the "great man of the Amorites". Generals are mentioned as commanding regiments of sizes ranging from 500–2000 men (L 581, index; MM 12), but perhaps ideally standardized at 1000 (MK 142). At Sippar the rank was not permanent; rather it rotated among different officials every one to three years (ASD 93–6), perhaps to prevent officers from gaining a permanent independent power base.

Mention is also made of two colonels (*šāpirū ṣābim*) as assistants to the general (L 508). Under the generals were captains (*rab pirsim*, GAL.KU), who commanded a standardized company of 100.[13] Each captain was assisted by two lieutenants (*laputtūm* or NU.BANDA).[14] There is also mention of 50 "standard bearers" (*mubab-bilum*) in a regiment of 1000 men (L 597, index). This would make five "standard bearers" assigned to each 100 men. They may have been something like a sergeant, commanding twenty men each (L 508). Finally, there is the corporal (UGULA 10 LU.MEŠ, *wakil 10 awīlum*, literally, "overseer of ten men"), who commanded ten men (L 499, 581 index). A quasi-military commander was the mayor of a royal city (*sugāgum*). These served as citadel-commanders and were responsible for equipping and feeding troops, and sometimes leading troops in battle (L 587, index; MM 13).

That these were somewhat standardized ranks rather than merely vague titles is indicated by the proportional pay scale associated with each rank. The following chart (Table 7.1) shows the scale of pay.

In interpreting these figures, it must be emphasized that the shekels mentioned here are measures of weight, not coins. The Middle Bronze Mesopotamian shekel weighed about eight grams, but the actual weight of a shekel could vary from region to region and time to time. Broadly speaking, a talent was the load a man could carry – roughly 30 kilograms. This was divided into 60 *mina*: roughly 500 grams or 1.1 pound. The mina was further divided into 60 shekels, of about 8 grams each (L xiv).

To complicate matters, the Mesopotamians in this period indulged in the time honored practice of devaluing their currency. The texts speak of, for example, "silver rings of five shekels nominal value, their [real] weight four shekels" (L 500). It seems that the Babylonians were either adding 20 percent copper to their silver, or trying to pass off shekels that were in reality only 80 percent of their supposed weight. On the other hand this discrepancy might reflect a distinction between different weights of a shekel in different regions. The silver was not in the form of coins, but in the form of jewelry, cups, or plates, though these could have a standardized weight. The texts mention rings, cups, disks, and collars (L 498–500, 508).

Table 7.1 Pay scales associated with military ranks

Ancient rank	Modern parallel	Payment L 498–9	Payment L 500a	Payment L 500b	Payment L 508
rab Amurrim	general	8 G 30 S 3 garment	–	20 G 1 garment 1 shirt	–
šāpirū ṣābim	colonel	5 G 10 S 1 garment	–	10 G 1 garment 1 shirt	10 G 8 S 2 garment 2 shirts
rab pirsim	captain	7 S 1 garment	–	20 S 1 garment 1 shirt	20 S 1 shirt
laputtūm	lieutenant	5 S 1 garment 1 shirt	7 S 1 garment 1 shirt	10 S 1 garment 1 shirt	11 S 1 garment 1 shirt
mubabbilum	"standard bearer" = sergeant	–	? 1 shirt	6 S 1 shirt	6 S 1 shirt
wakil	"overseer of ten" = corporal	2 S 1 shirt	–	–	–
	10 soldiers	2 S = 0.2 S /man	2 S = 0.2 S /man	3 S = 0.3 S /man	3 S = 0.3 S /man

Abbreviations: G = gold shekel; S = silver shekel; a shekel weighed roughly 8 grams

To give a sense of the economy of scale, we can look at other prices mentioned in the Mari archive. The price of a boat ranged from 10–30 shekels depending on size and quality (L 407). A slave cost 10 shekels, while three sheep could be bought for two shekels (MM 13). Six (large?) jars of wine cost one shekel (L 407), as did twenty arrows. Men who brought back a prisoner of war were given two shekels of silver and a new shirt (L 467). A horse, on the other hand, cost five minas (300 shekels), fifteen times the wages of a captain.

One can see from this chart that payment was proportionally relatively stable, although the specific amounts varied. The variation in pay is probably because of differences in the period of time which the soldiers served; was this payment for a month, two months, or a full campaign season? The pay may have been campaign pay rather than monthly or annual pay; an army of 650 was paid two shekels per ten men, and their leader eight shekels and a shirt for a short campaign (L 467), roughly the same as indicated in Table 7.1. Some of the payments were also given to allied troops or nomad mercenaries, who may have been paid at a different scale than the king's own professional troops.

Mesopotamian armies were also divided into categories based on equipment, training and experience (MM 17–25). The precise meaning of many of the terms discussed here is unknown, and must be inferred from the context. It is also unclear if some terms designate a specific assignment or function given to soldiers on an ad hoc basis, rather than indicating separate permanently organized regiments.

The normal term for a simple soldier is *be'rum* or *erin* (MM 22–3); generically, soldiers or troops are *ṣābum* while an army is *ummanātum* (L 598–601, index). The term *ṣābum* is used with all sorts of qualifiers indicating specific assignments for troops. Mesopotamian armies clearly understood the importance of reconnoitering before battle. Scouts (*sakbum*) are mentioned frequently (L 594, index), as are skirmishers or reconnoiterers (*baddum*) (L 592; MM 16–17). Armies were sometimes divided into different columns, marching ahead or behind each other. The vanguard (*rāsum*) seems to have been composed of elite troops who could march faster than ordinary soldiers, and were sent ahead of the main body (MM 18). They were more than just scouts; one letter mentions that a commander "led the vanguard of 1000 men and reached Qaṭunnan. The rest of the troops will come after me in battle formation to Qaṭunnan. The [total] force of 3000 men ... will be gathered" (ARM 3.14). According to contemporary itineraries, armies generally made 25 kilometers (15 miles) per day, but could march 35 (21 miles) on a forced march.[15]

There were also different classes of troops serving as guards and garrisons for cities. The border guards (*bazāhātum*) (L 573, index) seem to be small outpost and patrol units which were stationed away from the main city and who watched the border and reported to the commander on the movement of troops, nomads, merchants, messengers, or any other significant groups of people. Garrison troops (*birtum*), on the other hand, were assigned to defend cities (L 581, index; WM 98; ASD 87–8). *Maṣṣartum* or guards may be a different term for a similar function; they are mainly described as guarding cities (L 582, index).

There are also classifications of troops which seem to apply to their state of readiness. The regulars (*pihrum*) seem to be permanent professional troops (L 592, index). They are mentioned as receiving tracts of land in return for their military service; whether they were to farm these lands or receive the produce or revenues is unclear. They received "five dike plots", whereas ordinary farmers had only "three dike plots" (L 446). Another category were the reservists (*diriga*), who were called up only in times of war (L 593, index). This category may be related to "replacement" troops (*ruddum*) (MM 19). Archers are rarely mentioned as a separate category of soldier in the Mari texts (MK 63), though there is some evidence for a low level of military archery. It may simply be that archers are assumed to have been included in the broader categories of troops mentioned above, but it may be that archery was not widely used in Middle Bronze Mesopotamian armies. In conditions of extreme emergency the entire population could be mobilized for military and labor in the service of the state (L 319, 386).

A strange category of troops are the "fishermen" (*bā'irum*) (ASD 101–2). They have sometimes been interpreted as being enlisted to fish for the army on campaign, or for using their nets to entangle the enemy (WM 93–4). A more likely explanation is that the "fishermen" were more generically simply boatmen, who were enlisted to run the boats servicing the army, and probably to act as marines fighting from boats. One Mari text shows that they were clearly expected to fight: "When you hear this tablet send me the *bā'irum* who are with you, all who are present. They can carry their axes and equipment" (ARM 1.31; WM 94). In the contemporary Law Code of Hammurabi the military obligations of the *bā'irum* are precisely the same as those of the ordinary soldier (*rēdūm*).[16] In the military context I would suggest that marine might be a broadly analogous modern term.

Troops were also classified by their arms (see pp. 252–6) and function. Light troops (*qallatum*) are frequently mentioned in association with ambushing enemies (L 474; MM 17–18, 43–4). Elite or heavy troops (*kibitum*) seem to be more heavily armed and better trained than ordinary soldiers, but also to move more slowly.[17] Rulers, governors, commanders, and kings were frequently served by personal retainers (*šūt rēšim*), who were presumably the most experienced and skilled warriors they could find (L 591, index). The king's personal retainers formed the Royal Bodyguards (*kisrum*; *girseqū*), who accompanied the king wherever he went (MM 18–19). The royal bodyguard of Shamshi-Adad numbered 200–400 men (ARM 2.1; WM 99). Charioteers were undoubtedly also elite warriors (see pp. 145–53).

Numbers
(MM 7–9; L 599–601 index)

A wide range of numbers are given for military forces in the Mari tablets, from a few dozen to tens of thousands. The figures provided in the sources are sometimes based on propaganda, attempting to inflate the glory of a king either by increasing the strength of his army, or that of a defeated enemy. Other faulty figures frequently derive from ignorance, and were no more than wild guesses. However, many numbers provided by the sources are derived from internal archives, which were intended for day-to-day operation of the state. These figures are probably quite reliable (MK 141–2; MM 7–8).

The largest force mentioned during this period is a claim of 120,000 men by the king of Eshununa. The king claimed "he inspected my troops at the gate of Bab-Kikurrim and now from my 600,000 troops I will send [as an allied contingent] 120,000 good troops" (PH 79). Given the demographic and logistical realities of the day, these figures are undoubtedly sheer hyperbolistic propaganda (L 599, index). Other extraordinarily large armies include one of 60,000 (MM 8; L 599), 40,000 (L 329), and 30,000 (L 418, 459, 460; ARM 2.69). Six armies of 20,000 are mentioned and another four of 10,000.[18]

However, such large armies were certainly exceptional and in some ways the numbers are problematic. One of the letters in the Mari archive contains a remarkable statement of intentional disinformation by Hammurabi: "When I dispatch 100 troops the one who hears it will quote it as 1000. And when [I dispatch] 1000 troops, he will quote it as 10,000." It seems here that Hammurabi was worried about enemy spies hearing about the number of his soldiers, or capturing the messenger and reading the dispatches from the clay tablets. Thus, in at least some of his correspondence and communication, Hammurabi used a simple code: multiply his real troop strengths by ten. Thus, if the enemy somehow intercepted the message, they would be confused by how many men Hammurabi really had, thinking he had more men than he did and hopefully causing confusion and hesitation, perhaps even forestalling an attack altogether. The problem is that, though Hammurabi wanted to confuse the enemy, he may also have succeeded in confusing later scholars. Was this a permanent policy on the part of Hammurabi, or was it used only for a limited period of time in a particular campaign? Which of the numbers for Hammurabi's army found on the clay tablets are accurate, and which should be divided by ten? Did other rulers also use similar codes for the actual numbers of troops? Or did other rulers use a different code system: should the numbers given for Zimri-Lim's Mariote armies be divided by two, or four, or ten? Or should they be read as the actual numbers? Unfortunately, we can't be sure.

Based on archaeological evidence we can obtain good information on city size, and from that, a range of population for cities based on an assumption of potential population density per hectare.[19] Unfortunately, even here we are left with estimates. How many floors did a building have? How many people slept in a room? We cannot be certain. But the overall population of the largest Mesopotamian cities was probably around 50,000 people. If there were armies of 20,000–60,000 regularly operating in Middle Bronze Mesopotamia, these forces undoubtedly included large numbers of militia conscripts, and even laborers to build siege ramps. Due to logistical limitations such huge armies would be able to stay in the field for only limited periods of time.

On the other hand, as discussed above, Mesopotamian military scribes kept detailed censuses with tablets recording the name of each individual soldier. It is clear that kings had good information on their potential and actual manpower.

Shamshi-Adad {1809–1776} wrote a letter to his son Yasmah-Adad, who had been installed as king of Mari {1796–1776} before being ousted by Zimri-Lim in 1776. This letter explains how Shamshi-Adad planned to raise an army of 20,000 men for his campaign.

> [One of my officials] has inspected the Hana [nomad mercenaries] of the encampment and I have fixed at 2000 men those who are to go on a campaign with Yasmah-Adad [king of Mari]. All of these men are now inscribed by name on a tablet.... [These men] will march with you, plus 3000 men [you will mobilize from Mari].... All those people who go with you should be inscribed, by name, on a tablet.... Collect 1000 men between the two [nomad tribes?], 1000 men among the Hana [nomads], 600 men from among the Uprapu, Yarihu, and Amnanu [clans of the Yaminite nomad confederation]. Pick up here and there two or three hundred men according to the circumstances and collect 500. With your [own personal military] attendants, 1000 men will suffice. Then you will have assembled 6000 men. As for me, I will send you 10,000 men of the land [of Assyria].... They will be a strong and well-equipped contingent. I have also written to [our allied kingdom of] Eshnunna. Six thousand men will come up from Eshnuna. These [added] upon those [troops you will raise will total] 20,000 men, a strong army. (MM 8–9; WM 66–7)

Shamshi-Adad seems to have had a little trouble with math; his numbers are confusing, but I interpret his figures as follows. The first part of the letter describes 2000 nomad mercenaries and 3000 regular troops from Mari. The next mention of 1000 men from a clan whose name is lost and the 1000 Hana nomads, I believe repeats the original number of 2000 nomads, but breaks the total down into smaller clans. To these are added 600 men from smaller nomad clans, creating a total of 2600 nomads, plus 500 men recruited from odd sources to bring the total up to over 3000. This figure is then added to the 3000 men mobilized from Mari mentioned in the first half of the letter, of whom 1000 are the personal attendants or elite troops of Yasmah-Adad. The two groups added together make up the 6000 men Shamshi-Adad expected from Mari, to which he adds the 10,000 men he will send from his forces in Assyria and 6000 Eshnuna allies, giving the grand total of 20,000 (actually 22,000) he wants for the campaign. The numbers are obviously vague estimates, but indicate that Shamshi-Adad, an experienced warrior, believed it was realistic for an alliance of three of the most powerful kingdoms of the age to raise an army of 20,000. He also states, however, that this is "a strong army", implying that most armies were smaller than 20,000.

In extreme emergency a general mobilization of the entire population could occur, as happened when the Elamites invaded Babylon:

> The conscripts of Hammurabi have positioned themselves for battle.... Hammurabi has ordered a total mobilization in his land. He called up troops

of all merchants, all males, including releasing slaves [from slavery if they serve in the army], and they are ready. And he sent high-ranking servants to Rim-Sin [king of Larsa] asking for [allied] troops. (L 319, 386)

It is thus likely that figures mentioning armies larger than 20,000 men were either disinformation, included a large number of laborers, or represent a temporary total mobilization for a state emergency. Generally, most armies mentioned in the Mari tablets ranged in the hundreds and low thousands, even in major wars.[20]

Logistics (MM 34–6)

Depending on the circumstances, the state frequently provided soldiers with weapons, clothing, and food. An official known as the *abi sabi* was a type of logistical officer (ASD 102–5). Troops going on campaign are often said to have been given provisions for a certain number of days (L 361–4, 368), ranging from ten (L 458, 507) to forty days (L 383). Delays in campaigning were often caused by difficulties in collecting enough supplies: "he is staying in Manuhatan and secures their travel provisions" (L 191–2, 487–8). Requests for supplies are frequent in the letters, including oil (L 193). Sometimes troops show up without weapons and have to be equipped by the state (L 516). Weapons were stored in government arsenals, and were issued to troops as they were mobilized: a commander ordered that his men "open the storehouse, provide a spear [for each soldier], and add travel provisions for forty days."[21] Weapons mentioned in texts from the Old Babylonian period include the standard Middle Bronze panoply.

State storehouses also contained thousands of bushels of grain (L 409), but getting these supplies to the troops in the field was frequently a problem. Commanders often complained of lack of supplies (L 213, 262); one officer, exasperated by such grumbling, responded, "Stop griping! Accept those provisions [we sent]!" (L 464). A bad harvest or a plundered crop could send a city-state into crisis. When armies were in the field, there were sometimes not enough men to collect the harvest (L 421–2); soldiers might therefore be temporarily assigned to aid with the harvest (L 457). One officer says his soldiers could not be mobilized until after the harvest is over (L 520). Armies sometimes confiscated local carts and boats for military transport, with the result that the harvest could not be collected for storage and rotted in the fields (L 413). Good boots are always in short supply in war. One commander asked his friend, "Send me good boots!", to which his friend replied, "Send me an impression of your feet and I shall have good boots made" (L 308).

As warfare continued, supplies could dwindle; people were sometimes reduced to eating the seed-crop for next year, insuring ongoing grain shortages (L 419). Ishme-Dagan's crops were destroyed in war, leaving "no grain whatsoever in his land" (L 402); he was forced to send his sons as hostages along with boats and eight talents of silver as tribute, to buy grain from his enemy (L 389, 396, 403). In the end he sold 400 "little boys and girls" into slavery to buy grain (L 390). As famine spread, the poor were forced to move in search of food, spreading the crisis: "Any strong man who has grain is staying [in the city]. Any weak commoner who has no grain departed for the [Euphrates] River [in search of food]" (L 419, 420). As in any other war, the supplies were not always in the same place as the soldiers: "The troops are hungry. They have not received provisions" (ARM 13.33, WM 141).

Natural disaster, drought, or bad harvest could exacerbate food shortages. Locust attacks wiped out one harvest (L 420–2), causing a commander to recall an army:

> My lord must dispatch troops, and they must save the grain of the palace, and [come] over here for harvesting. These commoners – they suffered last year. They now saw the hand of the locust and said, "If the locusts [eat] the grain plantations, we will not stay on [but will leave in search of food]." (L 422)

The problems of garrisoning troops are discussed in some of the letters. One letter mentions a plan to move a force of "two thousand strong spearmen.... [But] if you evacuate the troops, their [total] population is ten thousand [including the] men and [their] women [and children].... If we evacuate a population of ten thousand and also leave their grain behind, it will be a heavy burden for the palace to feed them.... Boats and pack asses, indeed carts [will be needed to move them]" (L 195). Keeping an army stationed in one region for too long could put a strain on local food resources, since the land where the troops were stationed was expected to provide half of the supplies for the army each month (ARM 1.60; WM 142). One commander complained: "The load [of feeding the army] has become great. The garrison troops, all of them, consume [our] grain rations" (L 417). In another city, the commoners rioted because too much of the city grain supply was being taken by the army (L 521).

Corruption and war-profiteering were problems four thousand years ago as well as today. One disheartened quartermaster was shocked at the disarray of the grain supplies for the soldiers in one city:

> I came down and found the earlier troops [who had been quartered in a city] have sold [the army's] grain for silver. The later troops came and wasted grain. Now there are fifty donkey-loads of grain.... Not that they gave grain rations to anybody – and five hundred measures of grain are gone from the granary for no reason whatsoever! (L 271)

When soldiers were serving on campaign with an allied king, the ally was expected to provide their supplies (L 281, 438), though he didn't always fulfill his responsibilities properly (L 215). Some allied logistic services were better organized, with precise amounts of provisions prepared for a specific number of soldiers, who were also provided with quarters by the allied commander (L 323).

Transport

Supplies, equipment, and men needed to be transported to the war zone, and many of the Mari letters deal with the problems of military transportation. Ancient commanders recognized that the type of transport used was in some ways determined by ecology and terrain. Hammurabi made the following observation: "The means [of transportation] of your land [the city of Mari in Syria] is donkeys and carts; the means [of transportation] of this land [Babylon] is boats" (L 379).

As Hammurabi noted, the transportation of supplies in ancient Mesopotamia was done by human porter (L 178), donkey (L 271), cart (L 223), or boat (*maturrum*) (WM 143–4). One caravan included 300 men and 300 donkeys; another thirty men and 60 donkeys (L 365). A commander received a shipment of flour, but complained: "sixty donkey-loads of flour . . . are not enough. They must provide us with 100 donkey-loads of flour" (L 454). Was the failure to send 100 donkey-loads because of a lack of flour, or of donkeys? Lack of transport was a frequent problem. One commander complained that "the baggage of my lord has been left behind in Saggaratum . . . because of the lack of porters" (L 178). If he was relying on human porters he obviously had no pack animals or carts. Heavy baggage was frequently left behind or taken on different routes to allow the army to move faster (ARM 1.35; WM 142–3).

Boats were frequently used to transport both men and supplies by river (L 184, 223, 324). One quartermaster sent this order: "Load onto ships 3125 bushels of barley, 313 bushels of flour and 313 bushels of *billitum*, at the rate of 156 bushels [per boat] and send it downstream.... This grain is the regular barley ration for the fortress Yabliya" (ARM 13.33, WM 141). Boats were often simply requisitioned from the local population (L 505): "he must seize ten small-boats on the right bank [of the river] and ten small-boats on the left bank upstream from Dir and collect for me as many boats as there are, be it from the palace or be it from the commoners" (L 203). Another general "gathered together as many boats and small-boats as there were available to bring up grain" (L 309). Soldiers would disrupt the river traffic of their enemies to prevent shipment of supplies (L 278). When moving upstream against the current or wind, boats would sometimes be pulled by men on the shore (L 185). Combat from boats is not mentioned in the letters, but presumably did occur.

Fairly large forces could be moved by ship; 6000 men are mentioned with ships, but it is likely that many of these walked on shore alongside the fleet in the river (L 320). Another force of 5000 men was accompanied by 600 "small-boats" (L 381, 514; ARM 6.68), about eight men per boat; clearly more or less the entire army could have been moved by river in a fleet that size. On the other hand, another army of 5000 men had only 120 "small-boats" (L 384) – about forty-two men per boat. This force seems to have marched by foot and had the boats bring their supplies and equipment (L 383). Troops are described as crossing rivers, presumably by boat (L 323). An army of Hammurabi, which was covering an enemy army besieging the city of Upi, withdrew by boat (L 324). Boats were also used to transport sick and wounded soldiers (L 281).

Boats could be expensive, and prices fluctuated wildly as war brought soaring demand for a limited number of ships. Depending on the size and circumstances, a boat could cost from 10 to 30 shekels of silver (L 407).[22] Furthermore, the price of a boat varied, depending on whether one was going up or down stream. One commander complained: "Once I buy a boat here for ten shekels of silver, will it then not be worth [only] one shekel in Mari?" (L 407). Carts were likewise sometimes in short supply, especially at harvest time when everyone needed as many carts as possible (L 413).

Trips could be slowed by lack of supplies and logistical difficulties. One commander reported on the logistics of his operation:

> On the third day of the month of Kinunum ... we started out from [the city of] Rapiqum and went to [the city of] Harbe [in one day]. We stayed five days in Harbe [fourth through ninth of Kinunum], until the troops had secured their travel provisions. We started out from Harbe and reached Yabliya in one day. The tenth [day] of the month of Kinunum was in progress when we set to fortifying Yabliya.... We brought the grain, belongings, and gear that we shipped [by boat] upstream from Rapiqum into Harbe. (L 383)

Here a journey of less than two days actually took seven days to complete because the troops had to wait for extra supplies. The army seems to have marched on foot, while the supplies and equipment were brought by boat. It is not clear if the five-day delay at Harbe was because the soldiers were collecting supplies from the countryside or were waiting for the river fleet to catch up with them.

The army on campaign

There are no detailed narrative accounts of Mesopotamian armies on campaign (*harrānum*). A coherent picture must be cobbled together from scattered bits of information in the military dispatches. There is none the less enough information to give us a broad picture of life on campaign.

Scouting and spies (MM 37–42; WM 116–18)

Scouts are frequently mentioned as both spying on the enemy and openly observing enemy movements. When enemy troops were seen operating in a hostile fashion, a king might send a letter of ultimatum: "Withdraw your troops that are with Atamrum and withdraw your encampment that is settled in my district!" (L 338). But even in the course of such ultimatums military vigilance was never relaxed: "The scouts must stay on the right bank [of the river] from Appan to Niattum-Burtum, and anyone who is headed toward ... an [enemy] encampment, [the scouts] must arrest" for interrogation (L 198–9). Armies operating in unknown areas used local people for scouts and guides (L 391, 397, 470). Spies were sent into enemy camps during sieges to discover enemy plans (L 359).

Spies and informers would frequently report on the movement and plans of enemy kings (L 291, 303, 503), but despite such efforts the fog of war is everywhere apparent in the Mari military dispatches (L 364). Agents were frequently called the king's "eyes" and "ears", while enemy informers were called "tongues" (WM 116). One report states that "[the enemy] general La-Awil-Addu went out from Shubat-Enlil together with three thousand Eshnunakena troops. Perhaps he is headed for Ashnakkum, perhaps for Shuruzum. Who would know?" (L 313). Another report claims La-Awil-Addu had 5000 men instead of 3000, but still cannot say where he is bound (L 313). Yet another report is similar: "I do not know whether those [enemy] troops are headed for laying siege to Andarig or else to Karana. I will [make] a determination of [where] they are headed [and report later]" (L 336). Mesopotamian commanders recognized the problem of uncertain intelligence, and refused to commit themselves to battle without proper information. "Within five days we will see a [more] complete report. And in view of that report that we see, we will consult and act. As long as we do not understand the details of the situation, I will not dispatch any troops!" (L 475, 477).

Enemy spies naturally tried to infiltrate an army, and could undermine the plans of a general. One report mentions the discovery of men at the court of Zimri-Lim who had been sending information to the enemy (L 295). An allied force of 2000 Mariote and 3000 Babylonian troops went on campaign against Eshnuna, but were thwarted because a spy revealed their plans to the enemy: "A secret agent went out [from the enemy], and the enemy got hold of the news about them, and the troops returned [from their campaign] empty-handed.... How can 5000 troops return empty-handed to camp?" (L 458). One captured enemy spy was kept bound in prison (L 319).

Raids

Raids are frequently mentioned in the Mari letters (L 332–3). The purpose of many raids was simply plunder. Capturing enemy livestock was common,[23] as well as taking human prisoners for slaves (L 309, 349). Grain was also plundered (L 362); however, since it was bulky and difficult to move rapidly, it might simply be burned (L 458, 511). Orchards were also cut down (L 479). Thus, in addition to plunder, raids were intended to undermine the enemy's will and capacity to resist. When enemy armies attacked, it caused a cessation of both communication and commerce between cities: "The land is stirred up [by the enemy invasion] and the routes are cut" (L 410); this would naturally disrupt economic exchange. When a marauding enemy was raiding the countryside, the people would flee to the nearest fortress city for protection (L 361).

Borders were closely guarded against raids and incursions (L 233). King Zimri-Lim instructed one of his commanders:

Do not neglect guarding the district and guarding against expeditions of the enemy. As for the Hanean [nomad chief] Yahsib-El, together with his troops – employ them forthrightly [in exchange] for grain, and let them strengthen the [boundary defenses] of the district. Let the border guards depart [the city for duty at their outposts]. They must not let the enemy pass freely through the interior of the land. (L 229)

Some raids were small affairs, capturing only thirty people (L 384) or "two Sutean women and three donkeys" (L 385). Another raid "captured thirty men and women [and] fifty head of cattle. They killed two men and one woman.... A rescue detachment of seventy troops of the city of Nusar went in pursuit. The enemy killed twenty troops from among them" (L 397).

Other raids could be much larger and more destructive (L 399). A successful raid netted "forty men and women, 100 cattle and 2000 sheep" (L 398, 511). Another large-scale raid brought widespread devastation:

[Sasiya, the king of] the Turukkean [highlanders] raided the land of Ekallatum on the other [east] side of the [Tigris] river and went [all the way] to Kurdishatum. They took the sheep of [the king] Ishme-Dagan, all of them. There was nothing left for miles. They carried off [the inhabitants] of four of his cities [as slaves] and defeated 500 soldiers [of the king]. (L 362)

He was encroaching on my land. And I wrote you for troops but you did not give me troops. Yet you gave troops to another place. (L 332)

Expeditions were sent out from cities to try to rescue captured slaves or animals (L 384, 387, 458, 467); presumably a raiding party would move slowly when herding captured sheep and could be more easily ambushed. On the other hand, many rescue expeditions failed (L 398). In such cases war-slaves could be ransomed; a family paid twenty-three shekels (184 grams) of silver to ransom their captured brother (L 360). On the other hand, there could be haggling for the ransom price. A man offered 67 shekels of silver for his son, but the captor demanded 100. The father couldn't raise the additional money, and in the end the son was tortured to death (L 366). Sometimes prisoners managed to escape, showing up at their home town naked and starving (L 487). The Law Code of Hammurabi has an interesting clause relating to the ransoming of captured soldiers:

If a merchant has ransomed either a private soldier (*rēdûm*) or a marine (*bā'irum*), who was captured in a campaign of the king, and has enabled him to reach his [home] city, if there is sufficient to [repay the merchant the] ransom in his house, he himself shall ransom himself; if there is not sufficient to ransom him in his house, he shall be ransomed from the [temple] estate of his city-god; if there is not sufficient to ransom him in the estate of his city-god, the state shall ransom him, since his own field, orchard and house may not be ceded for his ransom. (LC 87)

Thus the state had the ultimate obligation to ransom prisoners of war.

As in all other times in history the devastation caused by raids and plunder, along with the disruption of the agricultural cycle and the displacement of populations, frequently brought famine in the wake of war. Hungry people were seen wandering the countryside in search of food (L 309). There was sometimes little difference between planned, government-sponsored raids and mere marauding and brigandage by soldiers. Hungry soldiers and nomads might simply take to murdering the peasants, pillaging the countryside, and alienating the people, though such practices were usually counterproductive: "The Turukku [highlanders] could hardly have taken along food for even five days.... They sacked [a village], and this land, which had [once] been sympathetic to them, is hardened and become hostile to them. Now the Turukku are constantly hungry" (MM 11).

Battle

The importance of strategy and battle tactics was emphasized in a letter from Shamshi-Adad to his son, "You think up stratagems to beat the enemy and to maneuver for position against him. But the enemy will likewise try to think up stratagems and to maneuver for position against you, just as two wrestlers use tricks against each other" (ARM 1.5; MM 43; WM 171). Unfortunately, detailed descriptions of field battles are relatively rare in the Mari letters. Often we are simply given a terse report: "The troops of the land of Mutiabal, all of them ... drew up in battle formation. Hammurabi gave battle and defeated them" (L 321). Victory in battle was always attributed to the gods: "Today the god of my lord went in front of the army of my lord, and the spear of fiend and foe has been broken!" (L 334).

Generally speaking, when facing a stronger enemy, an army would withdraw to a fortified city or camp rather than engage in open battle (L 329). When battles are described, they are sometimes an attempt to drive off a besieging army. In this sense it may be that Middle Bronze warfare in Mesopotamia was broadly parallel to late medieval warfare in western Europe, where raids, sieges, and attempts to rescue besieged cities were more frequent than efforts to defeat an enemy field army in open battle.

One Mari commander, Yanuh-Samar, reported the following engagement, showing how armies maneuvered back and forth before battle.

> I [Yanuh-Samar, general of Mari] equipped 500 troops of Huziran and dispatched them to [fight the enemy at] Mariyatum. On the second day a rescue detachment [of the enemy] came from Kahat.... Seven hundred Kahatean troops came to the rescue.... [But later they] retreated [back] to their city. As the Kahateans [retreated] on the road to Kahat, [I sent] 100 troops of [commander] Ishhi-Addu [from Mari] and 150 troops of Huziran [a vassal of Mari], 250 troops [total] with Ishhi-Addu at their head with the order: "Go! Lay an ambush for the [retreating Kahatean] troops toward [the city of] Pardu." They took [a back route] and came out toward Pardu to meet the Kahateans and

fought, and the servants of my lord pushed the Kahateans back, and [the Kahateans] abandoned six corpses. All of them [the soldiers allied with Mari] seized one [prisoner of war] alive. And the troops are back alive. Of the 200 [of our troops in the battle] – they were not more numerous than that – not one was missing. The Kahateans were defeated good. The Servants of my lord were victorious. (L 315)

Here a battle is described in which 250 soldiers of Mari ambushed and defeated 700 enemy soldiers. There are a number of uncertainties in this narrative. Yanuh-Samar claimed his force suffered no casualties, but reports that 250 soldiers attacked and 200 returned safely; is this bad math, or a tacit admission of fifty casualties? The enemy left "six corpses" on the field; does this imply that only six men were killed, or that they managed safely to carry away the rest of their dead and wounded?[24] He also reports that "all" the soldiers of Mari took one prisoner, apparently meaning that each soldier took one prisoner, making 200–250 total prisoners. Despite these ambiguities, one gets a feel from this report for both the chaos of war, and the possibility of an officer exaggerating the extent of his victory.

As in any age, the panic of troops with low morale or who were surprised could cause a quick collapse of resistance (L 346). A defeated enemy might abandon their shields and heavy equipment on the battlefield in order to flee more quickly. "Those troops [of ours] got going [in battle] and [the enemy was] pushed aside. They [the enemy Ekallateans] left their gear behind and their shields lying on the ground. [The enemy king] Ishme-Dagan got away by a hair" (L 481).

Campaigns did not always conclude with battle. One army of 5000 marched off to battle, but returned without ever encountering the enemy, to the dismay of the king, who protested, "how can 5000 troops return empty handed to the camp?" He gave them two days rest then ordered them back to battle (L 458). Armies faced each other across a major river to prevent the enemy from crossing (L 500); this could create a stand-off where enemies camped on opposite sides of a river, neither force willing to cross and engage in battle at a disadvantage (L 474, 478). Kings might also mobilize their armies, come face-to-face with the enemy, but make peace before the fighting actually began (L 478).

Prisoners

War prisoners were invariably enslaved and often shared among troops as booty (L 225, 349), or purchased from the captors by the king (L 467). After one battle, each soldier was said to have had one prisoner (L 315). Torture, mutilation, and other atrocities were sometimes inflicted upon prisoners in order to terrorize enemies. Some prisoners had their throats cut or heads severed (ARM 2.33, 48); others were impaled on stakes (ARM 13.108). Corpses might be ritually abused, with heads or other body parts being sent to the king, paraded through towns, or hung on walls of temples in triumph (ARM 2.33, 48), like the fate that befell king Saul and his son Jonathan at Beth-Shan (1 Samuel 31.8–13). One commander ordered his men to "take along two Hanean [nomads] to the border alive and mutilate them at the border. Let them go alive to the [nomad confederation of the] sons of Yamina and tell how my lord seized the city of Mishlan by force" (L 283). Another man was tortured to death in a most gruesome manner to terrorize the enemy:

> He [a commander] pierced his [a prisoner's] nose and placed a nose-rope in it. He opened [wounds] in both thighs, skinned his rib-cage, cut off his ears. [The prisoner] passed through agonies. Thirty times they took him [the prisoner] around the city [to terrorize the people in the city, and then killed him].... His [the prisoner's] father was present. (L 366)

Important prisoners were frequently executed when captured: "Let him hand [the enemy prisoner] Ashkur-Addu over to me, and then I shall cut off his head.... Now, let a god hand two or three of my enemies over to me and I shall cut off their heads" (L 298). Heads of executed kings or nobles were sent to the victorious king as trophies (L 479). The king of the Turukkean highlanders "cut off the head [of one of Ishme-Dagan's generals] and sent it to Ishme-Dagan, saying: 'Herewith the head of one who relied on you' " (L 396).

Of course the fate of all prisoners was not so gruesome. Though commoners were generally enslaved, the elites could hope for prisoner exchange or ransom. Prisoners were occasionally released and resettled on their lands, as described by Samsu-iluna of Babylon after his conquest of Eshnunna:

> After two months had passed, having set free and given life to the people of the land of Idamaraz who he had taken captive, and the troops of Eshnunna, as many prisoners as he had taken, he rebuilt the various fortresses of the land of Warum which he had destroyed and regathered and resettled its scattered people. (R4:389–90)

Priests, priestesses, and other religious personnel were sometimes treated with special dignity so as to not offend the gods. In a letter, King Zimri-lim of Mari wrote:

> Indeed, the god Adad of Kulmish must have organized this disruption for the sake of his priestesses! On the tablet of captives that I have sent to you the priestesses of Kulmish and the priestesses of other gods are listed separately on a different tablet.... Give them clothes to wear (ARM 10.123; MK 145).

When peace was finally established between rival kingdoms, the peace treaties could include not only the large-scale strategic issues, but a number of details concerning prisoners and refugees. A treaty between Shadlash and Neribtum (PH 53–61) from the mid-nineteenth century makes special provision for refugees – "whoever fled from the war" – to be allowed to return and be restored to their lost land and property (PH 55). Likewise, an exchange of prisoners was mandated (PH 55).

Diplomacy (MK 150–4)

The Old Babylonian period was an age of complicated diplomatic intrigue in which kings needed to win diplomatic victories to prepare the way for military victory. In many ways Hammurabi was victorious in the overall power struggle not so much because he was the superior soldier, but because of his diplomatic finesse. Although details are often lacking, it is clear from surviving diplomatic archives such as that of Mari that diplomacy in the ancient Near East was highly sophisticated. Many kings kept permanent ambassadors at rival courts; as today, these men often served as spies as well, occasionally distributing judicious bribes. King Zimri-Lim of Mari kept two ambassador-spies at the court of Hammurabi, Ibalpiel and Ibalel (CAH 2/1:180–1). Such spies were used to gather intelligence, both about the general policies and goals of an enemy, and about the specifics of their military plans and dispositions (HTO 239–42). Their correspondence with their king demonstrates a detailed knowledge of and wide range of interests in all military matters.

Council meetings between allied princes or their diplomats were summoned to deal with mutual dangers (PH 27–8). Some used thinly veiled intimidation to coerce unwilling allies, along with occasional overt threats of war (PH 28–9). Weak rulers groveled to more powerful allies, begging assistance. One weak prince, Iluma, wrote to two of his allies: "Apart from you two, I have no brother [ally] . . . Save me!" (PH 29); "I have taken refuge under you in my fear" (PH 33). Yet in another letter he attempts to arrange a secret meeting with only one of the two (PH 30–1). Diplomats frequently ask each other for intelligence and gossip about other rulers, and tell each other of the plans and activities of various rivals (PH 32, 36).

As with modern diplomacy, the personalities of the rulers and their representatives were often an important factor in the success or failure of negotiations. One prince in the nineteenth century complained that he was not being treated with the honor he felt was due to him:

> Is the prince who sent you superior to me? Does he have troops superior to mine? Or does he rule a land superior to mine? As he rules in his city, I rule in my city. As he is the king of Eshnunna, I am the king of the land of Urshitum. In what way is he superior to me and why does he always send his envoys here to take tribute? (PH 79)

Of course, the very fact that such questions needed to be asked is a reflection of the relative unimportance of the king of Urshitum.

Vassal kings

Sometimes, when a city was conquered, its former king was replaced by a governor of the conqueror (L 482). On other occasions, however, a king who was defeated or forced to submit was allowed to retain his throne, but became a vassal of the conqueror. These vassals were required to take the "oath of god" that they would be loyal to their new overlord, and were expected to provide soldiers, tribute, and other services to their new master. Kings also had an obligation to provide assistance to a vassal who was under attack (WM 48); vassalage to a stronger ruler could thus be a favorable option when facing an aggressive enemy bent on overthrowing a weak king. This naturally had the potential for creating an unstable political situation, where vassals chafing at the bit of their overlords might seize any opportunity for mischief-making or rebellion. Kings might also try to undermine a rival king's vassals by supporting revolts (L 511).

A major victory in battle could cause cities to shift allegiance rapidly. One commander reported to Zimri-Lim:

> I kept pulling in city after city [into our alliance], and I was making each declare a sacred oath [of loyalty to Zimri-Lim].... Now, I caused the land to change sides to my lord. May my lord be happy! And may my lord not be late [in arriving to take control]. If my lord is late, he must dispatch me troops [in his stead], any that may be dispatched, and I shall cause the land of Idamaras [and] the upper land to reject the Elamites. (L 501)

In a Middle Bronze version of public opinion polling, the commander continued:

> I keep pulling in [information] on the opinion of the commoners of the land, and they fall down [in reverence] before my lord [Zimri-Lim].... My lord must dispatch me 1000 or 2000 troops, and we shall pacify this land. Otherwise ... they will bring up the gods and bind the land up to the [enemy king of] Zalmaqum with an oath. I am afraid the land will swear [allegiance] in its fear [of Zalmaqum], and matters will become troublesome. My lord must dispatch troops quickly. (L 501–2)

It is important to note that the volatile public opinion of the commoners, with mixed loyalties, religious oaths, alternating fear of attack from different kings, played an important part in the realistic ability of a king to subjugate new lands or maintain control over conquered lands.

Smaller cities were often treated as feudal property, to be exchanged between rulers and given to followers and vassals (L 294, 337). Frequently the citizens of a city were unhappy with new rulers, and sometimes took matters into their own hands. When the city of Kahat was conquered by king Haya-Sumu, he installed one of his soldiers, Attaya, on the throne. There was unhappiness with this move, however, requiring that "twenty troops ... attend him [to protect him from possible attacks by the citizens].... Until things calm down, those troops must attend him" (L 299–300, 440). It was always possible that rebellion was simmering beneath the surface of a vassal city. When a vassal king was ready for succession, he had to write to his overlord for permission: "He does not ascend the throne without [permission from] my lord [king Zimri-Lim]. Write to my lord! A servant of my lord must come and let him ascend [the throne]" (L 311, 317).

In times of crisis, a new king might be installed by a military coup. The city of Eshnuna was captured and looted by the Elamites, who did not feel strong enough to hold the city and thus withdrew. Thereafter, the surviving army of Eshnuna raised one of their commanders to the throne: "The Eshnunakean troops have installed a king of their own. The man who was installed to be their king, that man is a commoner.... His name is Silli-Sin. He [had previously] exercised the rank of company captain (*galku*)" (L 328, 506).

Alliances

A diplomat of the Mari period summarized the political realities of his age thus: "There is no king who is strong by himself: 10 or 15 kings follow Hammurabi of Babylon, as many follow Rim-Sin of Larsa, Ibalpiel of Eshnunna and Amutpiel of Qatna, while twenty kings follow Yarim-Lim [king] of Aleppo" (ANE 1:99; L 290). Political power in the Mari period was based on having as many vassals and allies as possible: "The spear of Zimri-Lim and [his nomad allies] the Hana is strong over all the land, all of it!" (L 290).

Military treaties were frequently established between rival kings, either to end a war or to create a new military alliance. Representatives of the kings would meet and discuss the terms, which were often spelled out in great detail. Terms might include trade agreements, rights of passage for merchants or armies, extradition clauses, mutual defense agreements for allied military operations, and distribution of booty after an allied victory. Then, as now, different rulers could use different interpretations of ambiguous language in order to attempt to manipulate treaties to their advantage. Rim-Sin of Larsa, for example, wrote a letter making excuses as to why he failed to provide the promised troops for a military operation with his ally Hammurabi (CAH 2/1:179). Treaties invariably involved an invocation of the gods to witness the oaths. A special religious ceremony was undertaken, usually involving a sacrifice, after which both parties swore the "oath of the gods". Each party to the treaty received a duplicate copy of the particulars, which were deposited in temples for safekeeping (MK 126–7, 140–1).

Allies were independent kings who were treated as equals, or "brothers" in Middle Bronze diplomatic parlance. Many of the Mari tablets center on diplomatic negotiations and requests between the allies Zimri-Lim of Mari and Hammurabi of Babylon. Though allies were not required to provide each other with troops or tribute, there was a strong expectation that they would support one another in times of crisis. Allies were expected to honor requests for troops. As Hammurabi put it: "when [an allied king] requests troops from me, I will give troops to him to let him accomplish his objective. [An ally] who does not dispatch me his troops [when I request it], I will give him no troops when he writes to me for troops" (L 334, 479). Having an alliance, however, did not preclude the need for hard-nosed negotiations (L 374, 379–81). It also often meant paying for at least part of the food and wages of allied troops. The king of Eshnunna, for example, expected to be given thirty talents of silver in return for sending troops to assist his ally (PH 78).

Alliances and treaties were always reinforced by a shared sacrifice and mutual "oath of the gods" (MK 140–1). We have the text of an alliance treaty between Hammurabi and Zimri-Lim, illustrative of the diplomatic mentality of the age:

> [By the sun god] Shamash of the sky, lord of the land, [by the storm god] Adad of the sky, lord of determination – by these gods Hammurabi, son of Sin-Muballit, king of Babylon [swore]: "From this day, as long as I live, I will be an enemy of Siwa-Palar-Huhpak [king of Elam]. I will not [assist him and] I will not write to him. Without [the agreement of] Zimri-Lim, king of Mari ... I will not make peace with Siwa-Palar-Huhpak." (L 512–13)

Military cooperation was a key element in a successful alliance. Many of the letters discuss plans for different allied units to meet at specified times and places (L 190). Sometimes, of course, units missed their rendezvous, causing problems and confusion: "I waited three days in Terqa and no [allied] troops whatsoever were assembled ... Where are the troops?" (L 191). When an enemy army approached Babylon, Hammurabi of Babylon and his then ally Rim-Sin of Larsa made a coordinated plan for mutual defense: "My troops are assembled in my land, let your troops be assembled in your land. If the enemy heads for you, my troops and small-boats will get there [to help you]. And if the enemy heads for me, your troops and your small-boats must get here" (L 322). In addition to sending troops, allies might send money and grain to support the war effort; Hammurabi sent "two talents of silver [60 kilograms] and 70 bushels [21,000 liters] of grain" to aid one of his allies (L 327).

On occasion, however, allies failed to observe the terms of the alliance. When the king of Elam invaded Mesopotamia, one of his ministers reported:

> My lord [the King of Elam] wrote me: "Right now Zimri-Lim will go against you. And he will stir up the land. Write the Turukkean [highlanders], and the Turukkean will come down to you. [Then] do battle with Zimri-Lim." And he wrote to the Turukkeans, and they did not come to him [to help fight Zimri-Lim]. (L 294)

Peace treaties

War was frequently declared and peace negotiated in the letters. As in all political systems, there often existed among ancient Mesopotamians real causes and justifications for war which were shrouded in various more or less transparent pretexts. The political order of Mesopotamia was guaranteed by taking oaths by the gods to insure proper fulfillment of treaty obligations. Violation of treaties was described in terms of violation of the oath to the gods, which was considered justification for warfare. Around 1800, "Ila-kabkabu [king of Terqa] and Yagid-Lim [king of Mari] took a grave oath by the god [Nergal] between them and Ila-kabkabu never committed a sin against Yagid-Lim [i.e. he never violated the provisions of the treaty]. It is Yagid-Lim who committed a sin against Ila-kabkabu" which led to war (PH 68). Thereafter, because of the violation of the oath to Nergal, the god "decided to punish [Yagid-Lim] and went to the side of Ila-kabkabu ... [who] destroyed [Yagid-Lim's] city and defeated his son Yahdum-Lim" in battle (PH 68). Treaty or covenant violations are thus viewed as violations of oaths and commitments to the gods, who punish the violators by granting military victory to the other party of the oath and covenant.

Peacemaking was accompanied by a shared equid sacrifice and oath-taking: "I shall kill a stallion of peace between me and [the enemy king] Mutebal" (L 197). Peace was made through diplomatic councils (L 344), exchange of cities or land (L 337), sacred oath taking (L 337, 345), a ritual equid sacrifice (L 344, 351, 363), and sharing food and drink at a feast (L 345). Oaths and divination were required to accompany all treaties and alliances; bad omens from extispicy could at least temporarily derail agreements; as one diviner advised: "the sign is not right; wait for one month" (PH 31–2). Peacemaking could include an exchange of prisoners and captured plunder: "I will release to you your losses [of prisoners, booty, and captured land] that I am keeping ... and you will release my losses" (L 351, 368).

The specific details of one peace treaty were recorded, requiring a mutual renunciation of feuding. The defenders required of the attackers: "Do not hunt us [for slaves], do not kill us, and do not deport us to another land!" In return the people of the city, under the new king installed by their conquerors, were similarly required: "Do not hunt him [the new king], do not kill him, and do not bring your former king back!" (L 350). These peace oaths were often taken very seriously. One allied commander refused to fight with the troops of the ally of an enemy because of a sacred peace oath sworn by his own king with the ally of the enemy king (L 346). Such circumstances could obviously very quickly become complicated: "Let eternal peace be established between us!" one treaty proclaimed (L 374) – a peace to end all wars. Unfortunately, like the rest of the world, such peace efforts were always temporary in Middle Bronze Mesopotamia.

CHAPTER EIGHT

Mesopotamian siegecraft

Whereas battle narratives are relatively rare, sieges (*lawītum*) were quite common in Mesopotamia and are discussed in some detail in the Mari archive, allowing us a fairly good understanding of Mesopotamian siegecraft.[1] Fortification existed in Mesopotamia from at least 6000, when Tell al-Sawwan near modern Samarra was fortified with a thick brick wall and a three-meter-wide moat (EA 4:473). Siegecraft undoubtedly began when wall building began. By the third millennium every major city in Mesopotamia had massive walls. With a large number of fortified towns and cities closely packed into the river valleys, sieges, rather than open battles, became the normal mode of warfare. If one seeks the face of battle of Middle Bronze Mesopotamia, it is not to be found in the open fields of combat, but in the long, tiresome, dangerous, desperate, hungry and dirty soldiers in sieges.

Pre-Dynastic {3500–3000}

The first artistic evidence we have of siegecraft comes from the Pre-Dynastic period in Mesopotamia {3500–3000}, from the art of the so-called Priest-king (see pp. 37–9). Two different cylinder seals show the Priest-king with a drawn bow shooting at a besieged city. In one scene the defenders are outside the wall in a sortie, punctured by arrows as they flee (Figure 5a, p. 218). The other scene shows the Priest-king with five bound captives, kneeling outside the wall of the city. One man on the wall is fighting, while another falls from the ramparts, apparently as a result of the archery of the Priest-king (AFC 24, PAE 68/1–2, 70, FI §743). A third Pre-Dynastic scene, from Elam, shows a siege with four defenders on a three-storied rampart wall throwing rocks, or perhaps sling-stones, at besieging solders on the ground below (FI §748). Archaeological evidence from destruction levels at some sites provides confirmation that sieges occurred, and that the results of defeat could be devastating. Although the seals show us that sieges occurred, they unfortunately show us little about how sieges were actually conducted. For more information we are required to wait a number of centuries until the martial inscriptions of the Akkadian warlords.

Early Dynastic and Akkadian siegecraft {2500–2200}

For the last half of the Early Bronze Age we have two cylinder seals which probably depict sieges, as well as a number of incidental references to sieges in inscriptional sources. Overall, the data is slim, but sufficient for a basic outline of early Mesopotamian siegecraft.

Later texts from the Old Babylonian period {1800–1600} describe two major types of siege engines, the battering ram (*yaššabum* or *ašubum*) (CAD 1/2:428–9) and the siege tower (*dimtum*) (CAD 3:144–7), which will be discussed in detail on pp. 229–30; they are generally mentioned together in most Old Babylonian siege descriptions. Ironically, although our earliest texts about sieges do not mention these siege engines, two cylinder seals depict sieges using what are very probably the ram and tower.

The first seal, from the late Early Dynastic period, is unfortunately badly worn (Figure 5f, p. 219).[2] In the center a tower or city wall is under siege, with two men on the ramparts, one facing right and one facing left. The building is shown with at least two stories. If the proportional heights of the men to the wall is accurate, the wall would be about 20–25 feet tall. To the right of the wall stands a large siege tower (*dimtum*). It rests on a base roughly the size of a four-wheeled war-cart. The top of the tower overtops the wall slightly. A man on the top of the tower is attacking a man on the wall. Two other men appear in the tower on two different stories, indicating the tower has a base level on the vehicle, a middle level, and a top platform. To the right of the tower five men are shown; although a ladder is not clearly visible, I interpret these men as climbing up ladders which are resting against the back of the siege tower. The tower protects the men from missiles shot from the city and allows the men rapidly to ascend the tower for an assault on the wall. To the left of the city wall we see the same type of four-wheeled vehicle, but this one is without a tower. Three men may be standing in the vehicle, while a fourth stands behind it. There are no equids pulling the vehicle and its front rests near the wall. There appears to be a knob projecting from the vehicle against the wall. I interpret this to be a ram (*yaššabum*) smashing into the side of the wall. Above this vehicle two men, seeming to float in the air, are probably ascending ladders to assault the wall. If one compares this ram with similar, more detailed renderings from the Assyrian period, it appears they are quite similar in form (AW 2:401).

Recently-published cylinder seals from Tell Beydar (Nabada) {c. 2400–2250} in north-eastern Syria show another very early depiction of the siege tower and battering ram (Figure 5g, p. 219; EEH 116 §10–11). Here we again see a four-wheeled vehicle with a three-storied tower upon it: the base, resting on the wheels, a middle level, and an upper platform on which stand two men. Behind the tower stands another four-wheeled vehicle with some type of protective cover on it and a large projecting beam. This second vehicle is again similar in general form to later Assyrian siege rams (AW 2:388, 391, 407–8, 413, 422–5).

Another seal (EEH 116 §10) shows two four-wheeled vehicles with square boxes on them. They are not in the standard shape of chariots, and have no equids pulling them. Instead each has a long rope in front, perhaps used by men to pull it. The scene is a martial one, for there are two dead bodies and men with long hafted maces. One of the vehicles is empty, but the other has three men standing it, with only their chests and heads protruding above the walls of the vehicle. These are perhaps wheeled heavy shield platforms that could be used as a portable wall. The vehicles could be pulled into position and the wooden walls of the vehicle would serve as a shield wall, behind which the soldiers could shoot missiles, undermine a fortification, or throw baskets of dirt to make a ramp. This vehicle may be the enigmatic *samukanum* (CAD 15:132), occasionally mentioned along with the ram or tower as a siege device: "even if the Amorites should make war for ten years and bring ten battering rams ([*y*]*ašubum*), ten siege towers (*dimtum*) and twenty *samukanu*, I will remain strong in my city" (OBLTA 14, 46–7). The *Epic of Gilgamesh* describes "a battering ram that destroys the walls of the enemy" (EOG 49), but we do not know how far back that element of the tale originates.

When a city faced the imminent threat of a siege, special precautions were taken. Walls are described as being strengthened and repaired in the face of enemies (LKA 329). Special guards were mounted on the wall when the city was under threat: a garrison at Eshnunna was informed that the Amorite warlord "Zikhada has taken two thousand Amorites and they are marching against you. It is urgent. Do not do any work [in the fields outside the city]. Night and day the guard should not come down from the wall" (OBLTA 44).

In such circumstances the assistance of the gods was always invoked. A garrison commander assured the king of Eshnunna that "the city is safe. The omen report concerning my lord is strong. My lord should not worry" (OBLTA 46). Religious icons and standards were placed on city walls and gates to assure divine protection.

> [The god Ningirsu's weapon] "Slaughterer-of-a-myriad" he drove in [the wall] as a huge banner at Lagash; he had it placed at [the gate] Shugalam, the dreadful site. He let terror emanate from it; from the dais of Girnun, where judgment is issued, the provider of Lagash [Ningirsu] lifted horns like a mighty bull. (R3/1:83)

We have a few incidental references to siegecraft in Akkadian and Neo-Sumerian inscriptions. The most important method described in the texts is undermining (*pilshum*), when the attackers simply dug through the mud brick wall. Shulgi's armies are described as "ripping out the brickwork of the foundations of the walls [of Der]" (R3/2:103; R2:135; LKA 123–5). The fact that most fortifications in Mesopotamia were built from sun-dried bricks meant that undermining the walls amounted essentially to digging through dry clay. Although specifically describing the building of a temple, an inscription from Ur-Bau of Lagash gives us an idea of the construction procedures: "I excavated a large building plot [x] cubits deep; its earth I shifted like gems . . . This earth I then returned from there. I piled up the foundation. Over it I built a retaining wall, 10 cubits (5 meters) high, and over the sustaining wall I built the Eninnu [temple] . . . 30 cubits (15 meters) high" (R3/1:19, cf. R2:80–2).

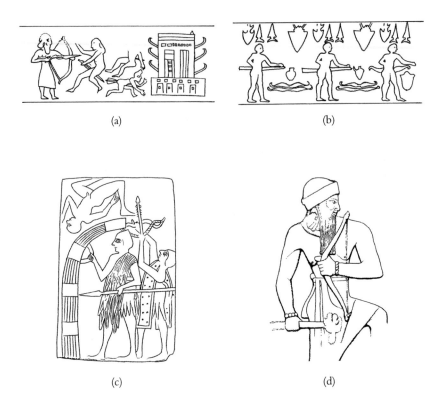

(a)

(b)

(c)

(d)

Figure 5: Archery and siege techniques (drawings by Michael Lyon)

(a) The early Mesopotamian "Priest-king" shooting his enemies with a bow during a siege of a city, {32–31C}; cylinder seal from Susa, Iran; see FI §743

(b) Craftsmen making bows and javelins {32–31C}; cylinder seal from Uruk, Iraq; see FI §742.

(c) Incised plaque depicting spearman with shield protecting an archer; Mari, Syria {26–23C} (Museum of Deir ez-Zor, Syria 11233); see AFC 158 §99.

(d) Naram-Sin, king of Akkad, striding forward in victory with bow and axe or mace; victory relief of Naram-Sin from Darband-i Gawr, Iran {23C}; see AAM §157.

(e)   (f)

(g)

(e) Akkadian archer with quiver and drawn bow; fragment of stele attributed to the period of Rimush {2278–2270} (from Telloh, Iraq; Louvre AO 2678); see AFC 201 §129a.

(f) Badly worn cylinder seal depicting a Mesopotamian siege tower (*dimtum*) and ram (*yaššabum*) assaulting a city; southern Mesopotamia {mid-third millennium} (Antiquity Department of the Royal Museums of Art and History, Brussels, O 437); see FI §749.

(g) Akkadian siege tower and ram; cylinder seal from Nabada (Tell Beydar, Syria) {24–23C}; see EEH 116 §11.

The walls were massive, and the difficulty of undermining would be increased by the enemy harassing the diggers from the walls with missiles, sling stones, and rocks, but there were no fundamentally insurmountable engineering problems. Given sufficient manpower, it was essentially a matter of time until an attacking force could undermine the walls, create a breach, and assault through the breach.

Armies would on occasion march near a city, challenging the garrison to fight in open combat, hoping to avoid a lengthy siege (R2:105–6). The defenders might come out and fight to prevent their land from being devastated by the besiegers. Gilgamesh marched outside the walls to defeat Agga who was besieging Uruk (EOG 145–8). Likewise, Naram-Sin marched out from the protection of the city walls to drive off Iphur-Kish, who was besieging his capital (R2:104–6).

For the most part we have few descriptions of actual sieges; the scribes are content merely to state that a city was taken (R2:14, 41). Akkadian inscriptions include numerous references to the destruction of the walls of conquered cities, a frequent practice for defeated cities (R2:14, 28, 41, 52–5; R4:149). It is not clear from the evidence precisely what the destruction of these walls entailed; it seems most likely that it was the destruction of key sections of walls and city gates rather than the complete leveling of the walls, which would have been a massive undertaking.

The most detailed account of a siege from this early period comes from an inscription of Naram-Sin's siege of Armanum (Aleppo).

> When the god Dagan determined the verdict [of battle in favor of] Naram-Sin, the mighty, [the god Dagan] delivered into his hands Rid-Adad, king of Armanum, and [Naram-Sin] personally captured him in the midst of his [city or palace?] gateway.... From the fortification wall [of Armanum-Aleppo] to the great wall: 130 cubits [c. 65 meters] is the height of the hill [and] 44 cubits [22 meters] is the height of the wall. From the quay wall to the fortification wall: 180 cubits [c. 90 meters] is the height of the hill [and] 30 cubits is the height of the wall. Total: 404 cubits [c. 200 meters] in height, from ground [level] to the top of the [highest part of the] wall [of the citadel]. He undermined the city [wall] Armanum [causing a breach which allowed the city to be taken]. (R2:132–5)

The figures given here for Armanum, which may be exaggerated, seem to represent the overall height of the earlier levels of the *tell*, an outer wall, and then an inner citadel wall on top of the acropolis. Naram-Sin says he took the city by undermining the wall, which presumably created a breach into which the Akkadian army attacked.

Part of the later literary legend of Sargon describes an assault through a breach:

> Sargon undermined [the walls of] the city, broadened the Gate of the Princes, [he made a breach] two *iku* [110 meters] wide. He cast it down; in the highest part of its wall he made a breach; he smote all of his wine-intoxicated men. Sargon placed his throne before the gate. Sargon opens his mouth, speaking to

his warriors, he declares, "Come on! Nur-Daggal [the enemy king] . . . Let him stir himself! Let him humble himself! Let me behold [him surrender]." (LKA 123–5)

However, siegecraft was not always successful, and sieges often turned into blockades which could last for months. A siege of Kullab by the army of Uruk is described in the Epic of Lugalbanda:

Like a snake traversing a grain pile, [the army] crossed over the foothills
But when they were but one double-mile from the city,
[The soldiers of] both Uruk and Kullab threw themselves down prone
In Aratta's field watchtowers and dikes,
For from the city darts rained like rain
And from Aratta's walls clay slingstones came clattering
As hailstones come in spring.
Days passed, the months lengthened, the year returned to its mother.
A yellowed harvest was about to grow up under heaven . . .
But no man knew how to go to the city,
Was able to push through to go to Kullab. (HTO 336–7)

With the siege in a stalemate, Lugalbanda seeks an oracle from Inanna, who tells him to fell a certain tamarisk tree and make a sacrifice of sacred fish from the canals before Inanna's battle standard A'ankara (HTO 341–4). Although the end of the epic is lost, it is clear that the divination and sacrifice is successful and the city is taken. Whatever one may think of the intercession of Inanna in the siege, Mesopotamians frequently used divination, oracles, and magic as mechanisms to revitalize flagging morale. A favorable sign from the gods could encourage men to one last effort to break a stalemate. Bad omens might be sufficient to break a siege.

Thus, although the details are generally not known, it is clear from both textual, artistic, and archaeological evidence that the Akkadians were masters at siegecraft. It was this skill, more than any other, that allowed them to create their empire. Indeed, it could be argued that the Akkadian military revolution was one of siegecraft; they discovered the right balance of technologies and methods that permitted them to take cities faster and with fewer resources than had been possible before. This created a sort of force multiplier that allowed their army to accomplish more in a given year than other armies could. The basic principles of Akkadian siegecraft – towers, rams, and undermining – would remain the standard arsenal of weapons against cities throughout the Middle Bronze Age, a period for which we have much greater source materials on siegecraft.

Siegecraft in the Old Babylonian period {1800–1600}

Thanks to the Mari archive (ARM), we are better informed about siegecraft in the Old Babylonian period than about any other time in the Early or Middle Bronze ages. Although we have no artistic representations of sieges for this period, our textual information gives us an excellent understanding of siegecraft in the age of Hammurabi.

Fortifications

The nature of siegecraft in any age is based upon the nature of fortifications. Defense of cities was a primary concern of Mesopotamian kings (WM 158–60). The basic defense pattern of cities is described in one report: "The inner city wall is surrounded by an outer wall, and the palace [citadel] by an outer wall and a moat" (ARM 6.29; WM 158). Some of the larger cities had concentric fortifications, with outer walls (*dūrum*) around the main city as well as inner fortifications (*šalhum*) for the citadel which could be defended separately, and to which the population could retreat if the outer city fell (MM 4; MK 145; Figure 6, p. 267).

When city walls were destroyed by old age, natural disaster, or enemy attacks, soldiers were used as labor crews to repair them (L 231, 497; MM 4). Royal inscriptions frequently describe the fortifications built by the king; Gudea of Lagash, for example, built fortifications (E3/1:111, 128) and restored a city gate (E3/1:147, 161). Babylonian kings also describe "levying of the army of my land" for military construction projects (R4:335, 377). In a sense, soldiers were a form of labor conscription, and, like later Roman legionaries, could be used as ordinary laborers.

On the other hand, repairs were often put off until the enemy was at the gates:

> The city where our lord is staying is not in good repair. Already before an alarm of the coming [of enemy] troops is heard, our lord must give strict orders to guards and border guards outside. They must not be negligent.... He must not neglect the guard of the wall. Here, we are very concerned about the guard of the wall and the city gates. (L 242)

Brick walls required regular repair, and numerous inscriptions describe the building or refurbishing of city walls. Shu-ilishu {1984–1975} rebuilt the walls of his capital Isin (R4:19). A century later, Enlil-bani of Isin{1860–1837} found it necessary to "build anew the wall of Isin which had become dilapidated" (R4:80). A letter requests bricks to repair a wall (L 376). In reality, the walls of major cities probably required frequent if not constant upkeep.[3] In 1733 Samsu-iluma repaired six forts which "in their old age had fallen into ruin of their own accord" (R4:381–2). Repair projects usually took several months (R4:382, 390). Nur-Adad of Larsa {1865–1850} lists the daily wages of each worker on his walls, giving a sense of the expense of such repairs.[4]

Warad-sin {1834–1823} describes his monumental rebuilding of the walls of Ur:

> [At the] fine base [of the walls of Ur] the [Sumerian] people multiply and are able to save their lives. The god Nanna entrusted me the building of [Ur's]

wall. In the course of that year five months had not passed when I baked its bricks. I finished the great wall and raised up its parapet. Like a verdant mountain I caused it to grow up in a pure place. I made its height surpassing, had it release its terrifying aura. I raised its head commensurate with its name and greatness. I caused it to shine forth splendidly to the wonder of the nation. I chose the place for my royal foundation inscription in its foundation, and raised the head of its gate there. I made its fosse strong, circled it with bricks, and dug its moat. I built for him [the god Nanna] the great wall, [the top of] which like a mountain raised high cannot be touched.... I surrounded his [Nanna's] city. The name of that wall is "The god Nanna makes the foundation of the land firm".[5]

Samsu-iluna, son of Hammurabi, also has a detailed description of the city walls of Kish: "by means of the labor of his army [Samsu-iluna] built the city of Kish. He dug its canal, surrounded it with a moat, and with a great deal of earth made its foundations firm as a mountain. He formed its bricks and built its wall. In the course of one year he made its head rise up more than it had been before" (R4:385–8).

Many walls had water-filled moats surrounding them (LKA 329; MM 4). Abisare of Larsa describes digging "the canal of the wall of Larsa" (LYN 13). Anam of Uruk in the nineteenth century provides more details: he "restored the wall of Uruk – the ancient work of divine Gilgamesh . . . in baked bricks in order that the water might roar in [the wall's] surrounding [moat]" (R4:474–5). Hammurabi "raised the head of the wall of Sippar with earth like a great mountain. I encircled it with a swamp" (R4:348), probably referring to a moat (ASD 15). Likewise, Samsu-iluna of Babylon "surrounded Nippur with a moat. He dug the Euphrates and made the wall reach the bank of the Euphrates" (R4:374, 390). The moat was frequently simply the quarry pit from which the earth was taken to build the wall. Samsu-iluna claims that "in the course of two months, on the bank of the Turul river, he built Fort Samsu-iluna. He dug its surrounding moat, piled up its earth there, formed its bricks, and built its wall. He raised its head like a mountain" (R4:390–1).

Gates (*abullum*) of the city were often massive; up to six meters high and built of imported cedar wood (ARM 3.10; MM 4), with bronze reinforcing and bolts (LKA 199, 215). An artist's depiction of a Middle Bronze gate survives in a small plaque (SDA 291c). It shows high brick walls with crenellations, and a large gateway with a brick arch and projecting towers. A similar surviving arched gate and stretch of wall can be seen at Tell Dan in Israel (ALB 208; Figure 7, p. 278). Like walls, gates needed to be regularly repaired: one city ordered the construction of a new city gate (L 263). City gates were frequently named after gods. In Sippar two gates were named after the gods Nungal and Shamash, while a third was named "Stairway Gate", presumably because it included a stair leading to the ramparts. City officials included the Gatekeeper (*sha abullim*), who was in charge of security, traffic control, and duty collection (ASD 15–16, 85; cf. HTO 175).

Preparations for a siege

When a city faced imminent threat, special precautions were taken. Walls are described as being strengthened and repaired in the face of enemies (LKA 329). Border guards (*bazāhātum*) manned outposts and patrolled the land, watching for enemy raiders and troop movements (L 573, 382, 393; MM 5, 7). Such patrols were reported to have ranged fifty kilometers from their bases (L 482). This type of duty was considered onerous: "the guarding of a city is a hard [duty]; and there are few troops available" (L 449). When there was fear of approaching enemy troops, the scouts, outposts, and city-guards were increased: "Because an alarm [caused by the enemy's approach] might be heard, we ordered a herald [to be ready] to call it out over the town.... Our lord must give strict orders to keep the guards of the wall and outposts at the ready by night and siesta" (L 239–40). During wartime, officers inside cities were required to report daily to the commander at the main city gate-fortress to receive their orders (L 462). Beacon fires were lit to alert the surrounding regions of approaching enemies (L 398; MM 10; WM 119–21), as described in a dispatch:

> I departed from Mari, and spent the night at Zuruban. All the Banu-Yamina [nomad confederacy] raised fire signals. From Samanum to Ilum-Muluk, from Ilum-Muluk to Mishlan, all the cities of the Banu-Yamina of the Terqa district raised fire signals in response, and so far I have not ascertained the meaning of those signals. Now I shall determine the meaning, and I shall write to my lord whether it is thus or not. Let the guard of the city of Mari be strengthened, and let my lord not go outside the gate! (ANET 482a)

Fire signals could thus inform a ruler of a danger and perhaps the direction the danger was coming from, but additional information had to be obtained by field officers and reported in dispatches.

As an enemy army approached, sheep and other livestock were collected into safe areas (L 394); the king would "gather before him [in his city] oxen, sheep, and his population that were loyal to him" (PH 78). Border guards also went on patrol to capture enemy agents or stragglers, and sent dispatches with reports of enemy troop movements back to the commanders (L 383). When a major enemy army approached, the border guards alerted the regiment in the city, but were unable to offer more than nominal resistance, as one report indicated: "the [advancing] enemy has pushed the border guards out of the way" (L 243).

Standing orders were given to move people and troops into the city upon the approach of the enemy: "when the enemy comes, let those seeking refuge enter the strongholds" (L 398, 247, 315, 361; MM 6). Supplies and provisions were also gathered into the city in preparation for a siege. Cattle and sheep were brought into the city for protection and kept in the peoples' houses (L 466). As an Elamite army approached Babylon, Hammurabi ordered: "[The enemy] will soon cross the border. Collect cattle and grain, straw, small boys, [small girls, all of them] and bring them into Babylon!" (L 320). Panic might spread among the population as the enemy pillaged their land and surrounded their city (L 317).

Offensive first moves

When first approaching a city an army often tried to make a surprise attack, capturing the city before it could prepare a proper defense (L 314). On occasion, a city that was surprised could fall to a conqueror in a single day. "During that same night, troops [of king Haya-Sumu] went to [the city of] Kahat and, upon their arrival, seized the city of Kahat and caught [its king] Kapiya. Attaya, who is with Haya-Sumu, ascended [the former Kapiya's] throne on that early morning" (L 299). The potential of surprise attack necessitated constant vigilance by both attackers and defenders. During time of war soldiers were constantly admonished to be on the alert: "I am afraid [that the enemy king] Ishme-Dagan may be enabled, through some negligence [of the soldiers], to do harm in the encampment" (L 359).

If a surprise attack failed, cities were frequently given a chance to surrender before the siege formally commenced. One surrendered three days after a siege began (L 350). Most cities, however, seemed to have rejected these initial overtures of surrender, preferring instead to make at least nominal resistance. For example, in one siege, "after he [the enemy king] laid siege to the city, he offered it peace but kept his troops in place. And he requested [the surrender of the besieged city's] king. They [the city] did not give [their king] to him [the enemy king]" (L 399). If a city surrendered on terms, it was spared looting; if it fought on and was taken by assault, it could be plundered and destroyed, and its population taken as slaves (MM 48). Hammurabi instructed his commanders of his policy towards Mashkan-Shapir, a major city in the kingdom of Larsa in southern Mesopotamia:

> If you succeed [in negotiating a surrender], and if the city opens [its gates] in front of you, accept its peace! Even if he [the commander] violates the oath by [the gods] Shamash and Marduk, [do not plunder] that city! If the city does not open [its gates, besiege it] and send for me [for reinforcements]! (L 333)

This policy created a psychological crisis for the defenders of the town as they saw the siege ramp daily progressing towards their walls (L 352). As it turned out in this case, the city of Mashkan-Shapir did not immediately surrender, but as the siege progressed, the besieged army began to lose heart as they saw Hammurabi's siege ramp, ladders, towers, and rams moving closer. Hammurabi's commander reported:

> They [the army of Larsa] are dreading an assault [by the Babylonians].... Sin-Muballit, the brother of Rim-Sin [king of Larsa] ... is surrounded [by the Babylonian army] in the city of Mashkan-Shapir. And the land of Larsa dreads an assault and he [Sin-Muballit] is about to change sides. [Then] the city of Mashkan-Shapir will open its gates three or four days from now. (L 334)

It is not clear if the city eventually surrendered or was taken by assault, but Hammurabi was victorious and moved on to capture the capital Larsa and annex the entire kingdom.

Sometimes an attacker would give the defender an ultimatum, allowing him a few days to surrender a city before the battle began in earnest. This was potentially dangerous, however, since it gave the defenders an opportunity to receive reinforcements. One Mariote commander, Buqaqum, reported:

> Five thousand men [of Mari] are fortifying the city of Yabliya. And [the enemy general] Shallurum is strengthening Harbe together with 15,000 men.... Shallurum spoke ... as follows: "I will wait five days for you [to withdraw from the city], then [if you do not] I will commence fighting." A rescue detachment [from Mari] must get here soon [or the city will surrender]. (L 383, 384)

If a relief army came they might camp near the camp of the attackers, hoping to force the enemy to withdraw. When facing an enemy relief force, the commander of one siege hoped he could lure the enemy out to an open battle: "when I lay siege to the city, and he [the enemy relief army] quits his camp and sets himself in motion toward me, at that time I will do battle" (L 418).

Assault

If a city refused to surrender, the next alternative was assault, which could be difficult and costly to both sides. Whenever Mesopotamian soldiers campaigned in close proximity to the enemy they built fortified encampments (*nawûm*) (L 193, 319, 320, 328), especially when besieging an enemy city (L 457). Such camps were often built by the gates of a city to prevent the besieged people from leaving, communicating, or receiving reinforcements (L 301, 346). One fortified camp is mentioned as being about three kilometers from the city under siege (L 400). If the armies remained in encampments for a long period of time they built houses and towers (L 468). When two allied armies besieged the same city, they built separate encampments for each army (L 275, 346). If enough troops were available the city would be completely surrounded (L 309).

Attackers would generally plunder the countryside for food and attempt to ambush and capture anyone coming in or out of the city (L 316). If possible they would attack at harvest time, harvesting the fields to feed the besieging army while the enemy watched hungrily from their city (L 324, 396). Besieging armies naturally had their own problems with supplies. One group complained that "they transport water to the troops day and night from five kilometers away. Who from among the two to three thousand [enemy troops in the besieged city] might attack the water carriers?" (L 497). Night operations were also sometimes undertaken (L 358).

The size of armies besieging cities could vary greatly, depending on the size of the city being attacked. Vast forces were not necessarily needed. Five hundred men captured the small town of Tilla (L 455). The siege of Shehna was undertaken by 2000 men (L 301), while the same number took Urgish (L 455). A major city, however, like Shubat-Enlil, required at least 4000 men to besiege it (L 455), and sometimes more (L 383). The size of defending armies also varied. Royal garrisons of towns were often very small: 20 (L 299), 50 (L 312), and 100 (L 314) men are mentioned, though those numbers would swell dramatically when war began, by reinforcements and conscription of the city militia into service. One city was strongly defended by a garrison of 300 (L 352). The city of Ashihum was defended by "1000 good troops", which allowed that commander to make numerous sorties (L 346).

Once a city was blockaded and defensive camps constructed, the attacker had to decide on the best approach to assault the city. One method was to attempt to undermine (pilšum) the walls causing them to collapse (ARM 1.35; WM 171). Ishme-Dagan successfully took the city of Qirhadat with this technique: "As soon as I had approached the town of Qirhadat I set up siege towers. By sapping I caused its walls to collapse. On the eighth day I seized the city of Qirhadat. Rejoice!" (ARM 1.135; WM 172).

The preferred technique for besiegers, however, was to construct siege equipment and a siege ramp (epirum) (L 321, 328, 331, 356; WM 171). The purpose of the siege ramp was to provide access to the upper wall for ladders, mobile siege towers and rams, as exemplified in a siege by Ishme-Dagan:

> The town of Nilimmar that Ishme-Dagan besieged, Ishme-Dagan has [now] taken. As long as the siege-ramps did not reach to the heights of the top of the city [wall], he could not seize the town. As soon as the siege-ramps reached the top of the city [wall], he gained mastery over this town. (ARM 1.4; WM 173)

Like Roman legionnaires, soldiers of Bronze Age Mesopotamia were frequently used in military engineering, building fortified camps and siege ramps, as well as defensive engineering activities. Although a relatively small army could besiege a town, the construction of a siege ramp was a major operation requiring a great deal of labor. While the soldiers certainly provided manual labor for siege engineering, they were frequently helped by corvee laborers (L 318–19).

Mesopotamian engineers had turned siegecraft into a science, creating mathematical exercises that allowed them to calculate the volume of earth, number of men, and time it would take to construct a siege ramp reaching a given height.[6] According to one problem, the engineers had to build a ramp to assault a wall 22 meters high. The ramp began 240 meters from the city wall, and was 36 meters wide. The ramp progressed slowly towards the wall, leaving an ever decreasing gap between the unfinished end of the ramp and the wall. This was presumably done so that as much of the work on the ramp could be done as far away from the city wall as possible. The reason that siege ramps were preferable to undermining the wall is probably that all of the operation of undermining had to occur directly under the wall, and therefore was more vulnerable to enemy attacks.

The rampart and wall of the besieged city in this mathematical problem was 22 meters high;[7] the total height of the ramp at 48 meters from the wall was said to be only 18 meters. It is unclear if the end of the ramp was intended to reach a total height of 22 meters, or if it leveled off at 18 meters high for the last part of ramp. A gap of 4 meters (13 feet) between the top of the wall and the end of the ramp could be bridged by siege towers and ladders. There would be no need to construct rams, ladders, and siege towers, which were always used on the ramps, if the end of the ramp reached the height of the wall. If this interpretation is correct, it gives us a good sense that a Mesopotamian siege tower was about five meters tall, which corresponds with our artistic evidence discussed elsewhere (see pp. 216–7). Wooden planks (*GIŠ.arammum*) were laid down to form a more solid pathway up which the towers and rams could be pushed (WM 180 n16).

According to this hypothetical mathematical problem, it would take 9500 men, each carrying two cubic meters of earth per day, only five days to build a siege ramp to the top of the wall. This number, however, was derived from a hypothetical mathematical exercise assuming ideal conditions. It does not take into account the number of men who would have to blockade the city or protect the camp. It does not consider that some of the men would be required to gather and prepare supplies for food, or that some men would be sick or injured. Most importantly, it doesn't deal with the reality of building the ramp in the face of enemy missiles and sorties, requiring men with shields to defend the workers, slowing the work and creating casualties. In reality it probably took several weeks to build such a siege ramp, even with 10,000 men. Most importantly, however, this hypothetical military engineering exercise does not match the reality of the size of actual besieging armies in the Middle Bronze, which seldom numbered 10,000 men. None the less, given the right men and circumstances, towns could fall to an assiduous attacker in a week. Ishme-Dagan, son of Shamshi-Adad, reported, "I set up a tower and a battering ram against [the town of Hurara], and in seven days I captured that town" (ARM 1.131); and on another occasion "As soon as I had approached the town of Qirdahat, I set up a tower and made its wall fall down by tunneling, and in eight days I captured the town" (ARM 1.135; cf. 1.138).

No artistic depictions of siege ramps, ladders, rams, or siege towers exist from the Middle Bronze period, but they were probably broadly similar to the Early Bronze representations discussed on pp. 216–7 (Figure 5f–g, p. 219), and to the Assyrian practices of a thousand years later as depicted in the much later Assyrian martial murals (AW 2:406–49). Siege ramps and other siege earthworks were generally taken down after a siege (L 459), meaning that they survive archaeologically only if the city was captured, destroyed, and never reinhabited. An Assyrian ramp, from the siege of Lachish in Judea, was discovered during the excavations of Lachish.[8] Indeed, most of the elements found in later Assyrian siegecraft of the early first millennium seem to have been developed by the Middle Bronze Age.

While the siege ramp was being constructed, special craftsmen were busy building the ladders, siege towers, and battering rams for use in assaulting the wall when the ramp was completed.[9] They were generally used simultaneously in an assault; frequently the attacker is said to have only a single ram and tower (ARM 1.131, 135), or sometimes only two (L 457). The construction of these devices was difficult, requiring skilled craftsmen and special materials (ARM 6.65). The precise details of these siege engines are not know, but their basic function seems clear.

Ladders (*simmiltum*) (L 205) were obviously devices that allowed the soldiers to scale the last part of a wall once the siege ramp had reached it. A large number were used in sieges, and were stored after siege for reuse and transported to the siege by boat or cart. Commanders felt an assault on a city wall could not be undertaken without sufficient ladders:

> About the [siege] ladders that Ibal-Pi-El brought into [the city of] Rapiqum – they are being kept inside Rapiqum. And there are no boats inside Rapiqum for bringing them upstream to Hurban [the city that is being besieged]. We lack ladders. If it pleases our lord, we must not have a lack of ladders. (L 393)

Battering rams (*yaššabum*) were used to break down walls or gates.[10] They were also used from the top of siege ramps. Battering rams were sometimes used to break down revetment walls supporting earthworks; it was possible that when the revetment walls collapsed, the slumping earthworks would bury the ram (L 479). Siege towers (*dimtum*) do not seem to have been extraordinarily tall – perhaps about five to six meters.[11] They were essentially strengthened and protected ladders allowing the soldiers to assault the top of the wall from the siege ramp. Another siege device which seems to have been part of the tower is the "leaner" (*humadia*) (L 205–6, 393); it is either some type of ladder, or a gangplank that was lowered by ropes from the top of the siege tower onto the top of the wall. The arrival of 500 reinforcements with a siege tower caused consternation for a besieged garrison commander, but he vowed to continue the fight: "[even] if he comes with a [siege] tower, I will not permit him to enter the city" (L 305). Towers could be disassembled, moved, and used in another siege (L 470).

On some occasions the siege equipment was constructed at a distance and transported to the site of the siege, either by boat (ARM 2.107, 2.110 14.45) or by wheeled vehicles (ARM 2.7, 2.15). Shamshi-Adad ordered the transport of siege equipment by river and land: "as soon as they have brought the siege towers and the battering ram upstream to Mari they should load them on wagons". In the latter case, it is not clear if the disassembled parts of the tower and ram were transported by cart, or if the tower and ram were built on wheels and moved on their own. The latter option is probably indicated by the siege representations of the Early Bronze period, discussed on p. 216, which show siege towers and rams on wheels. As in the Middle Ages, siege engines were given special names by the soldiers; one was called *haradan* – wild donkey (ARM 6.63; CAD 6:88), which, coincidentally, in a Latin form *onager*, was used by the Romans for a type of catapult.

On the other hand, siege equipment was often built at the site of the siege. The lack of high quality building timber throughout most of the Mesopotamian floodplain caused difficulties for sieges, requiring that either siege equipment or good timber be shipped to the site of the siege. One general asked the king to ship in special wood for building siege equipment.

> About cutting trees for *xaṭṭassi*[12] and axletrees for a battering ram and towers, of which my lord wrote — [we need] straight stems which are suitable for *xaṭṭassi*, and axletrees do not exist on the bank of the Habur [River, a tributary of the Euphrates], and cornel wood, straight stems, do not exist. (L 414)

Another commander had put his assault on hold while waiting for good building timber to build thirty ladders for a siege.

> Load on one boat those pines from the dry pines that are with you, that is, 40 pines of two reeds length for ladders, 20 pines for short ladders (*kammu*), 20 pines for "leaners" (*hu-mu-da-ia*), and provide silver for buying travel provisions for the haulers [of the equipment]; those pieces of wood must arrive tomorrow. Do not neglect this letter of mine! Further: send a blade of one pound [of bronze] for the battering ram! The assault [on the city of Mishlan has been] on hold for nine days [because of this lack of siege equipment]. (L 205–6)

Archers were also used during sieges, but again apparently in rather small numbers. A small plaque from Mari shows an archer, behind another man holding a large shield, shooting upward, apparently at enemies on a wall during a siege (Figure 5c, p. 218).[13] One letter from the commander of a besieging army requested more ammunition:

> Have made 50 bronze arrowheads of 5 shekels weight (40 grams) each, 50 arrowheads of 3 shekels weight each, 100 arrowheads of 2 shekels weight each, and 200 arrowheads of 1 shekel weight each. Make it a priority, so that it is finished quickly. It looks as if the siege of Andarik may be prolonged, and that is why I am writing to you. (ARM 18.5; MK 63)

The total number of arrows requested was only 400, enough to arm only twenty archers with twenty arrows each. The urgency of the letter seems to imply that the commander felt that these 400 arrows were important, possibly reflecting the overall small levels of archery used in Middle Bronze Mesopotamia. Thirty men with javelins are also described as harassing the city walls (L 497).

Defensive operations

One standard response of a besieged city was to make sorties to disrupt the attackers (L 400). An active defense could include many sorties. One defending commander had "1000 good troops" in his garrison, allowing him to "constantly keep coming out [of the city] to do battle" with the besieging army (L 346). A well-timed sortie could break a siege: "Two hundred troops and [commander] Saggar-Abum went out from Kurda, and he defeated 500 Eshnunakean troops. He drove them from their [fortified] camp" (L 417).

A series of contemporary dispatches to king Zimri-Lim of Mari from his city commander named Zimri-Addu give a vivid description of the course of the siege of Hiritum by the Elamites in 1764 (L 103–5). The city was defended by both Mariote and Babylonian allied soldiers (L 459). The Elamites had surrounded the city, built a fortified camp, and constructed a ramp that was nearing the walls of the city. In response Zimri-Addu undertook active defensive tactics.

> To my lord [king Zimri-Lim] speak! Your servant Zimri-Addu says: "The troops of my lord [in the city of Hiritum] are well. Some time ago I wrote my lord that [we set] fire to the tower [standing on] the lower fringe [of the Elamite siege ramp], and that the enemy [are seeking materials] for obtaining another tower. Now, that method [was successful in destroying] one tower, [but one tower] remained standing. And the work within the city against the tower of the enemy and his earthworks [continues]; a counter-ramp[14] that [we defenders] made was two ropes wide, earthworks for two ropes. And the [Babylonian] servants of [the allied king] Hammurabi were talking as follows. They said: 'We will make these earthworks higher toward our [. . .] counter-ramp, and do battle from their top [against the enemy attack from their siege ramp]. The enemy will not be able to do anything to this city!' "
> (L 457–8)

The defenders seem to have been building a counter-ramp inside the city, with revetment walls and earthworks allowing them to make the overall height of their wall higher, forcing the enemy to increase the height of their siege ramp.

Zimri-Addu continued the narrative in a subsequent dispatch written on the very eve of the battle he is describing. Some unfortunate lacunae leave part of the text unclear:

> To my lord [king Zimri-Lim] speak! Your servant Zimri-Addu says: "The troops of my lord [in the city of Hiritum] are well. The day I sent this tablet to my lord, the troops of my lord and [the allied] Babylonian troops were positioned against the enemy in front of the [enemy siege] tower and the earthworks [of the enemy]; [our soldiers] fought and drove [the enemy] from his [siege ramp] earthworks.... In the morning [the enemy] returned ... to the top of his earthworks [and] was coming out toward the [gate]. One of the 'leaners' [siege gangplank] and [. . . the siege tower?] gave way [and collapsed]. And I heard the following: 'There is no [siege] tower left to [the enemy], and he [is waiting for more materials] to obtain a [new] tower.' This I heard. The day when the battle was fought, Dagan-Mushteshir distinguished himself very much. [A] fire [was lit] and was kept burning in front of the [enemy siege] tower. And of the troops of my lord, many troops distinguished themselves." (L 459)

In the aftermath of their failure to break into Hiritum and the loss of their siege towers, the Elamite army withdrew (L 460), as Zimri-Addu describes in his next dispatch:

> The troops [of Mari] are staying in the camp of Hiritum. The Babylonian troops took down the [temporary fortifications of] the city of Hiritum [including] the counter-ramp that they had built. They are spreading the earthworks [of the siege ramp] that the enemy had heaped up.... Now the enemy has crossed to Kakkulatum. He has regrouped.... The enemy has released the work detail [which had been conscripted to build the earthworks and siege ramp] to [return] to his land. (L 459)

Another siege for which we have some detailed narratives is the siege of Razama by the Elamites (L 65–9). It began when Atamrum, king of Allahad and ally of the Elamites, with an army of 700 Elamites and 600 Eshnunakeans (L 496) made an attack on the city. Zimri-Lim of Mari was overlord of the city, but he was engaged in the north, and needed time to return to Mari, refurbish his army and relieve Razama (L 496). The city was thus required to hold out on its own for nearly a month. The king of Razama, Sharraya, a loyal vassal of Zimri-Lim, strongly resisted the siege. As Atamrum made siege ramps against the walls and prepared rams and siege towers for the final assault, Sharraya led sorties to disrupt the besiegers' efforts, specifically targeting the craftsmen making siege engines.

> The city of Razama is under siege, and [its commander] Sharraya is staying inside his city [to defend it]. He put up a fight. He went out and felled 500 troops from among the [enemy] troops. [He also killed] two leatherworkers and battering-ram makers [in the sortie]. (L 489)

The ramp had progressed well, and a siege tower and ladders were ready for their final placement when Sharraya's soldiers made another impressive sortie.

> Sharraya placed lumps of pitch opposite a tower and then lit a fire under the lumps of pitch, and the tower collapsed. And the fire consumed the "leaners" [siege tower gangplanks].... [Thereafter] Atamrum wrote to Sharraya [offering to withdraw on terms, saying]: "Give me tribute! And release to me the troops that you [captured in battle] and brought inside [the city]!" But he did not give him tribute.... And the city is strong. I am afraid Atamrum and his troops will quit [the siege] before the arrival of my lord [with reinforcements]. (L 300)

At this point the attacking commander Atamrum considered negotiating, and wrote to his Elamite overlord, explaining: "I put a chokehold on the city [of Razama]. Write to me if you want me to quit, and I shall receive the tribute of the city and quit. Otherwise [I shall take down] the fortifications of the city" (L 495–6). The townspeople seemed willing to accept an offer and pay tribute, but by this time the situation had changed; Atamrum's confidence had been restored and he broke off negotiations.

> They [the attackers] took a break for ten days, and then the elders [of the city] came out to Atamrum and told him the following. They said: "We are for making peace. The [besieging] troops must withdraw five kilometers from his camp, and I shall supply silver [as tribute]." And he [Atamrum] answered them as follows. He said: "You really have decided the following: 'We shall deceive him with words. Let him withdraw from his camp, and we shall [thereby] put a stop to the exertions [of the siege]....' If you are for making peace, why does Sharraya [the king of Razama] not come out to me [personally to negotiate]? Go, put up a fight, strengthen your city [for the coming attack]!" And the townspeople answer him as follows: "The city is Zimri-Lim's, and his regular army went behind him [to Aleppo]. Stay [and fight] until the lord of the city [Zimri-Lim] comes to [attack] you!" [Thus king Sharraya] made his decision, strengthened the city, and started coming out regularly [in sorties], and he was beating the Eshnunakean troops. And he [Atamrum] was heaping up earthworks going toward the city. (L 496)

As the siege ramp advanced toward the city wall, an urgent message was sent to Zimri-Lim requesting immediate assistance.

> Atamrum is besieging Razama. [His siege ramp] is astride the lower city [wall]. The troops of the city are doing battle all the time. If the city of Razama does not stop him, the whole land of Idamaras might change sides to him, judging by what I keep hearing from those [local citizens] around me. The eyes of Yamutbal and its entire land are fixed entirely on [what] my lord [Zimri-Lim will do to respond to this siege]. (L 454)

While waiting for the relief army from Zimri-Lim, Sharraya redoubled his efforts at resistance with a secret assault on the attackers.

> The front of the earthworks [of Atamrum's army] reached the parapet of the wall of the lower town, and the townspeople ... made two tunnels [through the wall], right and left toward the front of the [enemy's approaching] earthworks. At night they [the troops of Razama] entered [the tunnels] at the front of the [enemy] earthworks, and in the early morning the troops of the city came out [in a surprise attack] and beat half of the troops [of Atamrum]. They made them drop their bronze spears and their shields [in flight] and brought [the discarded weapons] inside the city [as booty]. The townspeople keep invoking the name of my lord [Zimri-Lim in victory]. (L 496)

At this point Atamrum was reduced to attempting a rather feeble stratagem of his own.

> He supplied bronze javelins to thirty imposters [who pretended to be soldiers from Mari], and they hassled the city, saying: "Why do you keep invoking the name of [king] Zimri-Lim? Do not his troops besiege you right now?" And the townspeople answered them as follows: "You [Atamrum] equipped impostors and let them approach [the city wall]. Yes, in five days, the troops who are with Zimri-Lim will arrive for you. You will see." (L 497)

The morale of the besiegers continued to deteriorate as that of the besieged improved with the news of the immanent approach of Zimri-Lim's relief army.

> The alarm of the coming of [the relief army] of my lord [king Zimri-Lim] has been sounded for the [besieging] troops [of Atamrum], and in the course of the night the troops in camp are being woken up twice.... Those from inside the city will come out and they will kill many [enemy] troops! And those troops in that [enemy] camp are sleepless. They keep being apprehensive about [the arrival of the army of] my lord. My lord must do what is necessary to come here and save the city. (L 497)

The end of the siege is not recorded, but it appears that Zimri-Lim's army did arrive and save the city. These examples show that an active defense – with counter-ramp, sorties and fire, and hope for a relief army – could defeat a determined besieging army.

Climax of the siege

On the other hand, when an enemy siege was nearing success the morale of the defenders played an increasingly important role. In some situations, the soldiers began to panic and even mutiny. Sleeplessness and exhaustion contributed to deteriorating morale (L 347, 400, 466). At the siege of Shehna, the city commander "said to the herald, 'Get the troops up on the wall [to defend against the coming assault]!' [One of the officers] Ushtashni-El rose and said, 'My troopers will not go up on the wall.' The herald said, 'My commander sent me.' He [Ushtashni-El] acted maliciously and shoved the herald" (L 302). On the other hand, many commanders and soldiers were willing to fight to the death for their king; one defender of a besieged garrison proclaimed: "I will not open the city to anybody. If a rescue detachment of my lord arrives, I will have lived. Otherwise I will have been killed [in the fall of the city]" (L 304).

As the situation became more desperate, cities under siege usually requested a relief army to march to their rescue (L 298, 299). "A rescue detachment must arrive like one man on the day we hear the alarm of [the enemy] coming out [to attack our city]" (L 239). Sometimes reinforcements arrived just in the nick of time to save a city: "Had the troops of my lord been one day late, the city of Karan might have long since been seized [by the enemy]" (L 352). City commanders complained when they didn't get the reinforcements they thought they needed; the king, of course, wanted them to make do with the men they had: "One time, two times, and three times I made my request before Zimri-Lim, and still he did not give anything to me" (L 262). Another commander echoed the same concern: "The city was left to itself. Now, my lord must dispatch troops, and they must take control of [the city of] Nahur. That city must not slip from the hand of my lord!" The simple reply – "There are no troops" (L 311) – has been echoed throughout history.

The exasperation of the defending city commander is reflected in his refusal to take responsibility for defeat if he is not given sufficient resources:

He [the king] disregards our word! We wrote to our lord once, twice, about troops entering Mishlan, and our lord [responded], "Whom do you fear that you keep writing me for troops?" ... If our lord does not dispatch us the troops, he cannot blame us [if we are defeated] in the future. We guard the wall and the city gates. We are afraid about [enemy devastation of] the flanks of the cultivated zone [around our city]. If there were one thousand or two thousand troops staying with us, one-half we would leave on the wall [to protect the city] and one-half we would send out on rescue missions [against the enemy pillaging the countryside]. (L 241)

As a siege progressed, starvation for the garrison and citizens became a real possibility (L 465). One commander wrote asking for assistance against a besieging army, claiming: "There is no grain in the city. My lord must do what is necessary to bring grain to the city" (L 311, 304, 309; ARM 2.50). With a deteriorating situation the loyalty of some besieged towns could be dubious as a growing portion of the population came to believe that a negotiated surrender was preferable to enslavement and the destruction of their town. The king of Mari had 100 soldiers garrisoning the city of Qatara (L 404) that was besieged by an enemy general, Kukkutanum, who managed to instigate a revolt of the citizens:

He [Kukkutanum] caused the opinion of the commoners to turn against [Mari].... And the commoners turned to the side of Kukkutanum. They started seizing Qattara. If it had not been for the troops of my lord [from Mari, who were garrisoning the town], they [the rebel citizens] would have seized Qattara. (L 354)

When a besieging army took the lower city, they faced the reality of an entirely new siege to conquer the citadel. One besieging army "took shelter in [the captured lower city of] Kiyatan. He fixed up the lower city for use as his camp.... The citadel of the city is strong. The townspeople entered it and are holding the citadel. And [the enemy] is occupying the lower city. His elite troops are in his camp"

(L 362). When the lower city fell, it was plundered: "the soldiers looted the lower part of that city, but the citadel is untouched" (L 368). Often, however, when the lower city fell the citizens decided to take the last chance to surrender the citadel on terms (L 365).

Thus the entire range of siege techniques of the ancient Near East – siege towers, battering rams, undermining, ramps, protective shelters, siege shields, and ladders – were all in place by at least the eighteenth century, and probably several centuries earlier. Although there were many subsequent important technical improvements, the basic elements of siegecraft had all been developed by the Middle Bronze Age. The only siege devices unattested in the Bronze Age Near East are the large, projectile throwing devices which developed in three phases: basic torsion devises beginning in the fourth century BCE; counterweight trebuchets in the twelfth century CE, and gunpowder in the late fourteenth century CE. Despite these significant advances, the essence of siegecraft was an invention of the Bronze Age.

CHAPTER NINE

Syria and Lebanon

The two core zones of civilization in the ancient Near East, Mesopotamia and Egypt, were surrounded by peripheral regions which had their own cultures, but which were tied in various cultural, political, and economic ways to the great agricultural river valleys. One of the most important of these, with the closest cultural and political ties to Mesopotamia, was Syria,[1] which, for the purposes of this study, will be defined as the modern countries of Syria and Lebanon. The geography and ecology of this region is quite complex, ranging from narrow coastal plains to high forested mountains, rain-fed agricultural highland valleys, the upper Euphrates river basin, steppe, desert, and oases, all interlocking in complex patterns creating a number of separate micro-environments with distinctly different agricultural or pastoral potential (M = EDS 35).

Practically speaking, this area is geographically divided into four zones:

1   the coastal plains, or Phoenician zone;
2   the inland valleys;
3   the middle Euphrates basin; and
4   the steppe and desert fringe to the south and east.

Each of these zones created different styles of human social organization. Each of the first three zones was home to city-states. The Phoenician coastal zone was additionally home to the world's first great maritime civilization, best documented in the Early and Middle Bronze ages at Byblos and Ugarit. The fourth zone, the steppe and desert, was generally inhabited by nomadic and semi-nomadic pastoralists, who often played an important military role in Syrian and Mesopotamian city-states, either as raiders or as allies of sedentary armies.

The archaeological periodization of Syria (Table 9.1)[2] is not as precisely defined as that of Egypt or Mesopotamia. In broad terms Syrian archaeological periods parallel those of Canaan, but there are important distinctions, and different scholarly interpreters arrange things differently.

The earliest written texts from Syria appear at Ebla around 2500. Before that we are dependent for our knowledge of Syrian military history solely upon archaeology or incidental references to Syria in Mesopotamian sources. The military history of Syria in the Neolithic period has been discussed in Chapter One.

Table 9.1 Simplified archaeological chronology of Syria

Period	Phase	Date	Alternate names
Epi-Paleolithic/ Mesolithic		16,000–10,000	
Neolithic	Early "Pre-Pottery" Neolithic	10,000–8700	Pre-Pottery Neolithic A
		8700–6800	Pre-Pottery Neolithic B
		6800–6500	Early Pottery Neolithic
	Late Neolithic	6500–5900	Pre-Halaf
		5900–5200	Halaf
		5200–4000	Ubaid
Chalcolithic		4400–3500	Uruk
	Protohistoric	3500–3000	
Early Bronze		3000–2000	
Middle Bronze	Middle Bronze I	2000–1800	Old Syrian Period
	Middle Bronze II	1800–1600	
Late Bronze		1600–1200	Middle Syrian Period

Chalcolithic {4400–3000}[3]

The Chalcolithic period in Syria is characterized by the rise and spread of copper working for ornamentation, statues, tools, and weapons. City fortifications also make their first appearance in Syria during the Chalcolithic. Culturally, another significant development is the closer cultural and economic integration of Syria with southern Mesopotamia, with Syria increasingly sharing forms of pottery, cylinder seals, architecture, writing, and cultural institutions; this phenomenon is sometimes called the "Uruk expansion" (AS 181–4, 190–7; HE1 14–18), which naturally included an exchange of military technologies and practices – most apparent in fortifications and weapons.

While all archaeologists agree that there are significant parallels in material culture between Syria and Mesopotamia during this "Uruk expansion", they disagree as to the extent to which this integration came about by actual migration and colonization of eastern and central Syria by people from southern Mesopotamia as opposed to the influence of merchant colonies or indirect influence.[4] The Sumerian perspective of this phenomenon has been discussed in Chapter Three. Here we will look at the issue from the perspective of the Syrians.

The Sumerians seem to have tried to create a chain of towns and markets to connect them with areas containing resources crucial to the new forms of urban social organization that were developing in Mesopotamia, such as metal, building timber, stone, and precious stones such as lapis lazuli. In Syria, the major trade route passed up the middle Euphrates, thence branching into western Syria, the Mediterranean and Anatolia. A major Sumerian colony in Syria was Habuba Kabira (Tell Qannas, Jebel Aruda) {c. 3500–3200}, which was protected by three-meter-thick mud-brick walls with numerous projecting square towers and at least two fortified gates. The city had strong cultural links with southern Mesopotamia, and is frequently described as a Sumerian colony (AS 190–7; EDS 81–6; EA 2:446–8; DANE 135–6). Many surrounding sites also exhibit, to a greater or lesser degree, close parallels in their material culture to the Sumerian city-states over several centuries (AS 195–7). Smaller Sumerian outposts, such as the fortress at Mashnaqa, have also been discovered (AS 200–1). The fact that the Sumerian colonies in Syria have some of the first major fortifications known in Syria points to two important military facts. First, the colonies were not entirely peaceful and economic in nature, but felt sufficiently threatened by surrounding non-Sumerian peoples that they needed to fortify their cities. Second, the process of Sumerian colonization necessarily included a transfer of military technology and techniques from the Sumerians to the Syrians.

The occupation of Habuba lasted less than 200 years, after which it was abandoned. The precise reason for the disappearance of Habuba and related sites is unknown. The city was not destroyed, but there could certainly have been a significant military threat contributing to the decision of the Sumerian colonists to abandon the city. Phoenican city-states were also involved in the rising militarism of the late fourth millennium; city walls have been found at Dakermann in Lebanon (MW 1:187). Weapon burials in elite graves at Byblos indicate the beginning of the rise of a military elite (MW 1:187).

The precise political and military relationship between the northern Mesopotamian "colonies" and the Sumerian city-states of the south is unclear. Given the current evidence, it is probably premature to speak of an empire, where southern cities had direct control over their colonies in the north. Rather, it is more appropriate to think of the relationship between Greek city-states and their colonies in the sixth century BC, where close cultural, economic, political, and military ties existed, but without direct control by the mother city (AS 204–5). Some sites, like Habuba Kabira, seem to have been entirely new foundations created by Sumerian colonists. Others, like Tell Brak, show a mixture of indigenous Syrian material culture with significant Sumerian influences (AS 185–90; EDS 86–9; DANE 58–9). Such sites may represent Sumerian elites ruling local peoples, or local Syrian elites allying themselves with the Sumerians and adopting Sumerian culture.

What is clear, however, is that the period of the spread of the "Uruk world system" also witnessed the spread of militarism; military threat increased during the mid-to-late fourth millennium, leading to the beginning of fortification in Syria, derived from models originating earlier in Mesopotamia. Unfortunately, lack of texts from this period prevent us from understanding any of the details of warfare during the late Uruk age, but it is presumed that competition for resources and control of trade routes was an important factor.

Whatever the nature of the military component of the "Uruk expansion", it came to a relatively abrupt halt around 3000. Some of the Uruk sites, such as Habuba Kabira, were simply abandoned with few signs of military conflict or destruction. Other Sumerian sites, however, such as Jebel Aruda and Sheikh Hassan, do have destruction layers probably caused by war (AS 208). Still other sites continued in use, but without the distinctive Uruk-style pottery and artifacts. It is assumed that the Sumerian "colonists" either were driven from these sites or withdrew on their own accord under some type of pressure. Many Sumerian colonists probably merged with the local Syrian population, losing their distinctive identity, at least in terms of material culture identifiable to archaeologists. We are uncertain as to the causes of the collapse of the "Uruk expansion"; there were probably a number of contributing factors, and a military component should not be excluded.

The Early Bronze Age in Syria {3000–2100}[5]

After the decline of the initial impulse of city building in Syria during the Uruk expansion {3400–3000}, Syria experienced a decrease in the scale and complexity of urbanization for several centuries {3000–2600}. Although small towns and villages remained widespread in Syria, there is little evidence of large-scale urbanization until the twenty-sixth century (AS 233–5, 268–7). Thereafter a number of sites give evidence of rapid expansion in size and population. The largest of these reached up to 100 hectares in size, with populations possibly approaching 30,000, probably representing the maximum potential population of an ancient Syrian city given the ecological, agricultural, technological and transportation limitations of the age. For the military historian, two developments of the Early Bronze Age are most important: increased use of copper and later bronze for weapons – tin-bronze becoming common only during the late third millennium; and the nearly universal spread of fortifications for cities, after the halting beginnings during the Uruk expansion in the late Chalcolithic (AS 250–1, 268–9). Martial themes also begin to appear in royal art. This triple combination of weapons, fortification, and martial art is a sure sign of the crossing of the warfare threshold.

As with southern Mesopotamia and Egypt, the most striking military feature of Early Bronze Age Syria is the widespread appearance of massive mud-brick city fortifications at a number of sites, probably based on earlier southern Mesopotamian models and technologies. Major fortified cities of Early Bronze Age Syria include: Ebla, Mari, Qatna (Tel Mishrife), Hama (ancient Amad), Aleppo (ancient Yamkhad), Ugarit (Ras Shamra), and Damascus.[6] Each seems to have been the center of a major independent city-state (AS 244–6). In north-eastern Syria, in a region known as the "Khabur triangle" encompassing the tributaries of the Khabur River, there were three main strongly fortified city-states by the middle of the third millennium (AS 259–62): Nagar (Tell Brak; EA 1:355–6), Urkesh (Tell Mozan; EA 4:60–3) and Shekhna (Tell Leilan; EA 3:341–7), each of which controlled surrounding towns and villages. Nagar seems to have been the dominant city-state in the region. The surviving fortifications of Shekhna (Leilan) are particularly impressive, with two concentric brick walls, the largest ten meters wide and fifteen meters high, with a circumference of 3.5 kilometers (AS 262; EDS 129). North-east Syria also contained a unique form of fortification consisting of huge circular mud-brick walls and ditches known as *kranzhügel* ("wreath-mounds") by archaeologists; the outer city walls were often supplemented by inner citadel fortifications around the temple and palace complexes on the acropolis (AS 256–9).

Ebla (Tell Mardikh) {c. 2550–2300}[7]

The two major city-states of Early Bronze Age Syria were Ebla and Mari, both of which were culturally integrated in many ways with Sumerian civilization in southern Mesopotamia. The remarkable discovery of a huge archive of 17,000 clay tablets at Ebla in 1974–76 has made it the best-documented city in Early Bronze Syria, with the earliest extensive written corpus in any Semitic language (AS 239). Unfortunately for the military historian, the vast majority of the texts at Ebla were written by its extensive and highly centralized economic and administrative bureaucracy. None the less, enough military information can be extracted to provide us with an important glimpse into military affairs in the twenty-fourth century. Before the discovery of the Ebla archive, "no inscriptions prior to the second quarter of the second millennium were found in any of the north Syrian archaeological sites" (HE1 3; AS 235); until this discovery it had been presumed that writing was unknown in Early Bronze Age Syria. This provides an important cautionary tale: our understanding of ancient Near Eastern military history is always tentative and subject to sometimes radical reorientation by new discoveries.

Ebla was first settled around 3500. In the following centuries it grew in size, becoming the predominant town in the region, supported by numerous surrounding satellite agricultural villages. Ebla's significance was in part linked to its role as an entrepot of growing international trade, probably beginning with increased demand for wool in Sumer. At its height, Ebla reached a size of 60 hectares, and a population of from 10,000 to 20,000. Archaeological and textual evidence shows Ebla as a nexus of trade eastward with Mesopotamia and south-westward with Byblos, and hence indirectly with Egypt.

Although for the most part details are not known, a tentative list of rulers (Sumerian: *en*; Akkadian *malikum*) of Ebla up until the destruction of the city-state by Sargon (?) in c. 2300[8] can be reconstructed from the texts (HE1 19–26; SHP 27; CANE 2:1222). These, include, with *very* rough chronological estimates assuming a 20-year generation:

Rumanu {c. 2740}
Namanu {c. 2720}
Da [. . .]{c. 2700}
Sagishu {c. 2680}

Dane'um {c. 2660}
Ibbini-Lim {c. 2640}
Ishrut-Damu {c. 2620}
Isidu {c. 2600}
Isrut-Halam {c. 2580}
Iksud {c. 2560}
Talda-Lim {c. 2540}
Abur-Lim {c. 2520}
Agur-Lim {c. 2500}
Ibbi-Damu {c.2480}
Baga-Damu {c.2460}
Enar-Damu {c. 2440}
Ishar-Malik {c. 2420}
Kum-Damu {c. 2400}
Adub-Damu {c. 2380}
Igrish-Halam {c. 2360}
Irkab-Damu {c. 2340}
Ish'ar-Damu {c. 2320}

This list implies that the beginning of the dynasty coincided with the building of the first royal palace (G2) on the acropolis at about 2700, with the dynasty lasting until the destruction of that palace complex around 2300; it was through this destruction that the Ebla archive was inadvertently preserved. However, most of the Ebla tablets come from the period of the last three rulers on this list – roughly the late twenty-fourth century; the earlier rulers are little more than mere names.

Based on a careful study of the political implications of economic and administrative texts, Ebla should probably be seen as a hegemonic state, the major economic and military power in inland Syria during the Early Bronze Age (HE1 51–69). At its greatest extent the kingdom occupied an area roughly half the size of the modern state of Syria. Ebla ruled over two dozen or so large cities, and many other towns and villages. About half of the kingdom of Ebla was under the direct rule of the king, administered by governors (*lugal*); the other half of the cities were vassal states which retained their own kings (*en*), who provided tribute, supplies, military equipment, troop levies, and work crews to Ebla.[9] Smaller towns and villages were ruled by overseers (*ugula*) who were appointed by the king (HE1 34). The king also sent agents (*mashkim*), collectors (*ur*) and messengers (*kas*) to oversee royal affairs and interests (HE1 51–2). Members of the extended royal family often served in major positions of power or as rulers of subsidiary cities, while daughters of the king were made high priestesses (*dam-dingir*, "wife of the god") in temples in different cities (HE1 53). Some of these client kings had their own sub-client rulers; the king of Burman, for example, was a vassal of Ebla, but was himself overlord of his own vassals in the towns of Shada and Arisum (HE1 33). Many of the smaller towns and villages were treated as property, which was traded between kings, client-kings, vassals, governors, nobles, and temple-hierarchies (HE1 34,

45–9). With variations in detail, this basic pattern of political organization would continue in Syria for the next thousand years.

The royal administration included departments for the collection and distribution of metals (*e-am*, "house of metal"), textiles (*e-siki*, "house of textiles"), and chariots and draft animals (*e-gigir*, "house of chariots") (HE1 53). Ebla could be called a tribute-state, whose power was based on wealth derived from tribute collected from vassals and allies. At the height of its power the king of Ebla received annually an average of 357 kg of silver, 10 kg of gold, and 490 kg of copper, with a royal flock totaling 670,000 sheep (CANE 2:1125–6). Vassal cities were also required to supply the army of Ebla with weapons, including spearheads, arrows, and daggers.

Supplies for soldiers were also part of the vassal tribute system, including clothing, animals, wine and food, and men for labor or combat (HE1 40–1, 45–6); the small town of Armi, for example, provided 120 soldiers, while the town of Abatum mobilized 180 (HE1 44). At full mobilization the army of Ebla was thus a composite force of each of its vassal city-states; nomadic clients of the king of Ebla were also required to send troops and supplies. The Ebla texts also describe brisk river traffic on the Euphrates, including wooden and reed boats (HE1 60–1); a number of different types of boats are described, including: boats (*ma*), large boats (*ma-gal*), and deep draft cargo boats (*ma-gur*) (HE1 60–2); these boats were presumably commandeered and used during military campaigns to provide logistical and transportation support for armies marching up and down the Euphrates.

Some city-states in the region were Eblaite allies, bound together by mutual interest and marriage. Diplomatically, Irkab-Damu {c. 2340} sealed an alliance with the vassal city of Emar, through the marriage of his daughter to the king of Emar (SHP 28–9). Although the details are lacking, it is clear that there was ongoing intrigue and tension between Ebla and rival city states, creating frequently unstable and shifting patterns of alliances. Diplomatic intrigue focused on the ongoing struggle between the two main military powers of Syria in the middle Euphrates, Mari and Ebla, for hegemony over the city-states lying between them. The ruler of a city-state called Adu was lured away by Mari, apparently under some duress, from its former alliance with Ebla: "the friendship [alliance] of Ebla is not good, better to establish good friendship with Mari" (SHP 29). Tactics in this struggle included marriage alliances and diplomatic intrigue, as well as outright war – two of the year-names in the Ebla texts mention defeat of the armies of Mari (SHP 29; HE1 43).

The most important military texts describe a struggle between Ebla and its greatest rival, Mari, which lasted off and on for nearly a century.[10] Our information comes in the form of a rather laconic and formulaic combat report from the Eblaite general Enna-Dagan to an unnamed king of Ebla, perhaps Irkab-Damu {c. 2340}, describing a sequence of campaigns over the course of three generations. Here is an example of the combat report formula: "Iblul-Il [king of Mari] defeated Shada, Addalini, and Arisum, [vassal] countries of Burman at Sugurum, and raised a [burial] mound [over a pile of enemy corpses]" (HE1 29–30).

It appears that for three generations Mari had been incrementally encroaching up the Euphrates until it had reached the Eblaite vassal city-state of Emar at the great bend, forcing Ebla to pay tribute (HE1 38–9) totaling 1000 kg of silver and 60 kg of gold over the course of perhaps forty years (CANE 2:1226). At that point Ebla dispatched an army under general Enna-Dagan, who launched a triumphant counterattack. The specifics are vague, but the overall picture is clear. Enna-Dagan was victorious, retaking the cities on the middle Euphrates that had been captured by Mari. The scale of the conflict is reflected in reports of 3600 dead at a battle at Darashum and another 3200 dead at Badanu and Masanu – though it is not clear if these numbers included civilian and military casualties (HE1 43). Enna-Dagan then proceeded south-east down the Euphrates, defeating the armies of Mari and its allies several more times, culminating in the capture of Mari itself, after which general Enna-Dagan was established as the new king (en) of Mari; it is not certain if he had been a vassal of the king of Ebla, but he seems to have become essentially independent. Thereafter the boundary between Ebla was established at Halabit, with that important fortress in Ebla's hands (HE1 49–50).

Early Bronze Age Mari (Tell Hariri) {2600–2300}[11]

The remarkable archaeological discovers at Ebla, and our consequent knowledge of that site, overshadow the achievements of Early Bronze Mari. However, most evidence points to Mari rather than Ebla as the dominant city-state on the middle Euphrates. It was nearly twice as large as Ebla (100-plus hectares versus 60 hectares), and contained from 20,000 to 30,000 people (AS 263). Its double circular mud-brick fortifications measured 1920 meters in diameter, with gates protected by large projecting towers (EA 3:414; AFC 135). As noted above, Mari also seemed to be militarily predominant over Ebla during much of the twenty-fourth century, until the great victories of the Eblaite general Enna-Dagan {c. 2340}.

We are able to reconstruct a king-list for the Early Bronze Age Mari, which unfortunately is little more than names, with very rough dates for their rule.[12]

1. Ilshu {c. 2550–2520}
2. Lamgi-Mari {c. 2520–2503}
3. Ikun-Shamash {c. 2503–2473}
4. Ikun Shamagan {c. 2473–2453}
5. Ishqi-Mari {c. 2453–2423}
6. Anubu {c. 2423–2416}
   Sa'umu {c. 2416–2400}
   Ishtup-Ishar {c. 2400}
   Iblul-Il {c. 2380}
   Nizi {c. 2360}
   Enna-Dagan (conqueror from Mari) {c. 2340}
   Ikun-Ishar {c. 2320}
   Hida'ar {c. 2300}

Mari's predominance was brought to an end by the campaigns of general Enna-Daga of Ebla, as we have seen, who defeated the armies of Mari and captured the city, installing himself as king (HE1 26–51). Little is known of Enna-Dagan's successors, and by around 2300 the city was conquered by Sargon of Akkad.

Terqa (EA 5:188–90; AS 267)

Another powerful Early Bronze Age city-state on the middle Euphrates was Terqa (Tell Ashara), with some of the most massive brick fortifications of the period – three concentric walls totaling twenty meters in thickness. The first of the three walls was built about 2900, and the next two at roughly hundred-year intervals. The walls were maintained and repaired over the course of the next thousand years, indicating an early perception of increasing military threat throughout most of the Early Bronze. It seems likely that Terqa was politically dependant on Mari in some way, and served as a major bastion for the defense of that kingdom.

Warriors of Early Bronze Syria

An analysis of archaeological and artistic evidence gives us a fair idea of the armament of the Syrian warrior of the Early Bronze Age. It is important to emphasize that the term "Early Bronze" in reference to the weapons technology of the third millennium is something of a misnomer. For example, although bronze arrowheads are known, most Early Bronze arrowheads continued to be made of flint (AS 272); in general, flint or obsidian weapons remained common. Even when metal weapons were used, throughout the first half of the Early Bronze Age most weapons were actually cast from arsenic-copper. True tin-bronze was relatively rare because of the scarcity of tin sources in the Near East. Tin, along with lapis lazuli, was imported over 3000 miles from Afghanistan; city-state bureaucracies tried carefully to control the importation and distribution of tin. Only in the later Early Bronze Age had tin supplies become large and reliable enough to allow tin-bronze to become the predominant metal for weapon making. The term "Early Bronze Age" refers to the first appearance of tin-bronze weapons, not to the period of their universal adoption. Thus, Early Bronze Age weapons industries were dependent on access to the scarce resource of tin; the ruler with the best and most reliable access to tin could arm more soldiers more heavily with bronze weapons.

Perhaps the earliest martial art from Syria was erected by an unknown Early Bronze king near Jebelet el-Beidha, showing a bearded king wearing a (sheepskin?) kilt and sash on his left shoulder, holding a mace in his right hand. One of his two followers holds an axe; the weapon of the other is lost (AS 273). This stele was erected on a prominent plateau as some sort of victory monument, pointing to the rise of royal martial ideology. Other details are uncertain.

A major source for Syrian warrior armament is armed god figurines. Throughout the Levant and Syria during Early Bronze III {2300–2000} and the

Middle Bronze Age {2000–1600}, a religious tradition developed centered on the offering of copper or bronze votive statuettes to temples. Hundreds of these statuettes have been preserved. Many of them represent armed warrior gods, and hence provide for us an invaluable record of the changing dress and armament of Bronze Age Syrian and Canaanite warriors.[13] It must be emphasized that these figures are intended to represent divinities, and hence their weapons tend to reflect the weapons of the elite warriors rather than the common soldiers, but this is generally true of all Bronze Age martial art.

Several EB III {2300–2000} figurines were found at Tell el-Judeideh (SAF 8). These depict bearded nude warriors wearing an eight-inch wide leather belt around the waist, armed with a short thrusting spear or javelin and a round-headed mace. They wear a torque around the neck, and have a conical helmet, either of copper or leather (SAF §1–2). Since other contemporary art shows warriors generally wearing kilts, the lack of clothing on several of these figures in this and subsequent periods may reflect religious concerns related to fertility, or an attempt to indicate if the votive figure is a god or goddess, rather than an actual tradition of fighting in the nude, though that cannot be discounted (SAF 133–4).

Another major collection of bronze figurines comes from the mountains of Lebanon and dates to roughly the end of the Early Bronze Age {2100–1900} (SAF 15). These depict the warrior-god wearing a knee-length kilt and an eight-inch wide leather belt at the waist; some have long braided ropes hanging from the belt or wear a torque or necklace. The figures have full beards and shoulder-length braided hair. Unfortunately the weapons for these figures were cast separately and are missing from most of the figures, but those remaining include a man-length broad-headed thrusting spear and a mace or club (SAF §3–9). The helmets worn by the earlier Early Bronze III figures from Tell el-Judeideh are not present. These two sources point to the mace and thrusting spear as the standard Early Bronze III armament in Syria.

Our understanding of the arms and armor of Syria during the Ebla age {c. 2500–2300} is greatly enhanced by fragments from military murals from the palaces of the kings of Ebla (AFC 175–7) and Mari (AFC 157–60), which complement related martial art from contemporary Mesopotamia in Early Dynastic III {2650–2300} from Girsu (AFC 190–1) and Ur (AFC 97–9), which was discussed on pp. 59–60. Fragments of a palace military mural from Ebla, sometimes known as the "Standard of Ebla", give us a good view of Syrian warriors of the twenty-fourth century (AFC 175–7). Most of the surviving fragments of the martial murals from the palace at Ebla seem to be post-combat scenes related to prisoners. The first shows a soldier from Ebla wearing a leather cape as armor, typical of the Early Dynastic period found on the Standard of Ur. This warrior also has a helmet, probably of leather, and carries a short javelin which he is thrusting into the neck of a prostrate captured enemy lying bound at his feet (AFC 176). The second shows a soldier in a leather (or sheepskin) kilt, which is cut into strips at the knee to facilitate movement; this soldier has no helmet. He has a pole on his shoulder from which hangs something which looks like fabric, and has been interpreted as a banner, a battle net, or a pouch to carry equipment or booty. The pole may in fact be an axe or a javelin – there are other scenes showing weapons carried on shoulders from which other equipment or banners are hung.[14] In his right hand he carries two severed enemy heads, perhaps hoping to obtain a bounty from the king (AFC 176). The third vignette shows a man dressed precisely like the warrior in the second, but here he is grappling with a naked enemy prisoner (AFC 177). The final scene shows a man in the same type of kilt also grappling with an enemy. The warrior has a large bronze dagger in his right hand, with a "distinctive crescent-shaped pommel and ridged blade", which he is thrusting into the eye of a fallen enemy. The enemy lies on his back, holding his attacker by the knees with his right hand, using his left hand trying to hold back the dagger (AFC 177). Other fragments from the mural show an archer and a bound prisoner being escorted by a soldier (AS 241). A contemporary statue of a king of Ebla shows him holding the typical Sumerian Early Dynastic narrow-bladed axe (AFC 171).

The martial art from Early Bronze Age Mari[15] shows very close parallels to that of Ebla and Ur, indicating there was essentially a single shared military system extending from Sumer up the middle Euphrates into eastern Syria – or alternatively that they shared the same art style and craftsmen. Weapons depicted include the narrow-headed axe (AS 264; AW 1:137–9), javelin (AFC 157), spear (AFC 158; AW 1:138), and bow (AFC 158). Most of the soldiers wear leather (or metal) helmets, fastened by a strap under the chin (AFC 158); some have beret-like caps (AS 264; AW 1:139). One of the warriors carries aloft a tall pole topped by a bull-emblem – presumably a regimental standard (AW 1:138). Most of the soldiers wear knee or ankle-length kilts with fringed hems. Most also have a long, wide sash over their right shoulders, extending down to their knees in both front and back; it is marked by two rows of evenly spaced circles (AFC 157–8; AW 1:138); this sash seems to be unique to soldiers from Mari from this period. It has been interpreted as a leopard skin – though the circles seem far too evenly spaced – or studded leather (AFC 157); it may simply be a colored fabric sash used at Mari as some type of heraldic uniform. Prisoners are shown with their arms tied to their waists and pinioned behind their backs at the elbows (AFC 157; AS 264; AW 1:138). The standard Early Bronze Sumerian-style war-cart – four solid wheels, drawn by equids, with a driver and warrior with multiple javelins – is found in the Mari murals (AFC 159–60; AW 1:139). A detailed discussion of the Sumerian war-cart is found in Chapter Five, but here it should be noted that war-cart technology had spread to the middle Euphrates by at least the twenty-fourth century.

Militarily the most interesting scene at Mari is a shell plaque depicting two warriors in typical Mari military dress and a sprawling dead enemy (Figure 5c, p. 219).[16] The first soldier holds a long thrusting spear underhand in his left hand. His right hand supports a huge reed shield, with the reeds bound in leather in four evenly spaced places. The shield appears to be about two meters tall, and is strongly arched backward in its upper portion; it seems too big and bulky to be maneuvered easily in battle. Behind this shield bearer is an archer, shooting an arrow upward over the top of the curved shield. It is difficult to resist the interpretation that this scene represents a siege, in which one warrior holds a large shield for the protection of the archer. The fact that the shield is curved backward indicates the threat of missiles from above – this could occur either from missiles shot from walls or from high trajectory arrows or sling stones shot from the ground. The archer shooting his arrow upward indicates a probable target on a wall. The bulkiness of the shield would make it unwieldy in mobile combat, but it is an ideal field fortification for static siege combat. In broad terms this shield is similar to the large body-shields of Sumerian warriors discussed in pages 55–9; the same type of siege shield remained in use in Mesopotamia until Assyrian times {930–612} (AW 2:407–9, 418–19, 424, 435).

Archaeologically, weapon finds from tombs confirm the standard Early Bronze Age panoply found in Syria, including spears, javelins, maces, axes, arrow-heads, and daggers (MW; AS 270–1). The most important sites of weapon finds include Qatna (south of modern Hama), where over 100 copper/bronze weapons were discovered in tombs (MW; EA 4:35–6; AS 245); Til-Barsib (Tell Ahmar), where nearly three dozen weapons were found in local tombs (MW; EA 5:209–10; AS 249); and the tombs at Jerablus Tahtani, near Carchemish (MW; EA 1:423–4; AS 250). These weapons are mainly of arsenic-copper, with tin-bronze appearing by the end of the Early Bronze Age. Surviving weapons include narrow-bladed axes, broad spearheads, javelin heads, arrowheads, thin daggers, and broad, leaf-shaped daggers.[17]

In summary, complementary evidence from written, artistic, and archaeological sources give us a fairly good picture of Syrian warriors of the Early Bronze period. There were two overlapping military traditions in Syria. The first could be called the indigenous Syrian system, with warriors in kilts and broad leather belts armed with a combination of spear, javelin, mace, axe, and bronze dagger, probably supplemented by the bow. The second Syrian military system, found at Mari, Ebla and probably other major cities on the middle Euphrates, could probably be considered an extension or variation on the contemporary Sumerian military system. The basic dress is a leather (or sheepskin?) kilt extending from the waist to the knees. The leather is cut into strips for about six inches above the knees to facilitate movement. This basic gear is often supplemented by heavy infantry equipment consisting of a long leather cape or cloak extending from the shoulders to below the knees, and a leather or metal helmet. The weapons shown include the standard Early Bronze bow, javelin, spear, large dagger, and axe. Other than helmets, no metal armor has been found from the Early Bronze Age; it is likely that almost all armor depicted in the martial art was leather. Metal helmets have been found in the Royal Tombs of Ur, indicating that they were used at least by the warrior elites.[18]

Akkadian Empire in Syria {c. 2300–2200}[19]

The long-lasting, bi-polar military struggle between Ebla and Mari on the middle Euphrates was overthrown by the intervention of the Akkadians around 2300. The widespread destruction layers at many Early Bronze sites in Syria are generally attributed to the Akkadian conquest (AS 277–82). The major campaigns of the two greatest Akkadian warlords Sargon {2334–2279} and Naram-Sin {2255–2218} have been discussed in Chapter Three. Among the claimed conquests of Sargon are Mari, Yarmuti, and Ebla, then westward to the Mediterranean (R 2:12, 15, 28–31). We have no precise chronology for Sargon's reign, but this campaign presumably occurred rather late in his reign after he had firmly secured Mesopotamia, perhaps around 2300. His army, presumably supported by a river fleet, marched up the Euphrates to the city-state Tuttal, which submitted. There Sargon consulted the oracle of the god Dagon, "who gave him, from that time on, the Upper Country [of Syria, including the city-states of] Mari, Yarmuti, and Ebla, as far as the Forest of Cedars [Lebanon] and the [Taurus] Mountain of Silver" (C1/2:322). With the god Dagon's approval, Sargon continued his march north-westward, sacking Mari, and reaching the Mediterranean Sea. Sargon's motive for his invasion is clear; he was seeking direct access to the "Forest of Cedars and the Mountains of Silver" – in other words, he was searching for building timber and metal, both of which were in short supply in Mesopotamia itself. Archaeology confirms that Mari was destroyed about this time, a destruction generally attributed to Sargon. Many other sites in Syria show destruction layers datable to this period (AS 278). Some were rebuilt and continued as urban centers under Akkadian rule; others were never reinhabited, initiating the urban decline in Syria which would reach crisis proportions from 2200 to 2000 (AS 281–7).

The interpretation of the archaeological evidence for direct Akkadian domination of Syria is somewhat controversial (AS 278–9). Maximalists argue for a period of direct Akkadian control of Syria in the twenty-second century, interspersed with rebellions and a period of independence between Sargon and Naram-Sin, requiring a strong campaign to reassert Akkadian authority by Naram-Sin (R 2:132–5). They point to the Akkadian palaces of Naram-Sin at Nagar (Tell Brak) and Shekhna (Tell Leilan) as exemplars of Akkadian direct rule (EA 3:343–4; AS 279–81). Minimalists see the claims of the Akkadian warlords as exaggerated and their dominion limited. Some type of hegemony must have been exercised by the Akkadians; after his conquests Naram-sin was able to install two of his daughters as priestesses at Mari, and to build a palace with bricks stamped with his name; an inscription of Rimush was also found at Mari (C1/2:331–2). In either case, Akkadian intervention in Syria created a major power shift in the old political order of Early Bronze Syrian city-states. Ebla was also destroyed by the Akkadians; although it was quickly rebuilt and remained an important economic center in subsequent centuries – as attested by references to it in trading texts – it never again regained its earlier role of regional military predominance.

Crisis at the end of the Early Bronze Age {2200–2000}[20]

The defining characteristic of the end of the Early Bronze Age is a region-wide crisis reflected in widespread ecological decay, dynastic collapse, urban disintegration, and tribal migration. Similar patterns of crisis are found in Egypt, Canaan, Syria, Cyprus, Anatolia, the Aegean, Mesopotamia, and Iran during this same period. Since similar patterns of decline have been discovered throughout the Near East, some scholars have searched for region-wide factors contributing to this crisis. One theory posits that increasing aridity initiated a crisis for both farmers and herders. An extended drought reduced both annual crop yields and the overall carrying capacity of nomadic grazing grounds. An alternative, or perhaps complementary theory posits human-caused environmental deterioration through over-grazing, soil depletion, salinization, deforestation, and other forms of ecological degradation. The impact of either or both of these developments was decreasing productivity, increasing social stress, competition for resources, and population displacement through migration and war. Given that the legitimation of most Early Bronze dynasties was intimately connected to temple ideologies of divinely sanctioned kingship and promises of fertility from the gods, drought and decreasing productivity with subsequent famine, war, and chaos would have served to undermine the legitimacy of reigning dynasts, contributing to the collapse of their power and authority. The cumulative result was a period of political disintegration, war, anarchy, social upheaval, and migration.

Although the precise cause of the urban collapse at the end of the Bronze Age is uncertain, the results are clear in both the archaeological and the historical record. The major centers of urban civilization and military power in both Mesopotamia and Egypt underwent serious decline and even collapse, resulting in the fragmentation of power and a sequence of wars. At the same time, nomadic or semi-nomadic peoples from the periphery of the urbanized regions – Amorites, Canaanites, Hurrians and Gutians – migrated from their pastoral homelands, either under ecological pressure or because military weakness of the collapsing central authority in the great urban centers created an inviting target. These peoples migrated first into the fringes of the urban areas, eventually usurping power in the major city-states throughout much of the Near East. In Egypt this infiltration of Canaanite semi-nomads occurred mainly in the eastern delta, but the internal fragmentation of Egypt in the First Intermediate Period occurred throughout the entire Nile Valley. The specific military results of this region-wide transformation will be examined in the chapters associated with each region.

The two centuries following the collapse of the Akkadian empire {2200–2000} are very poorly documented in Syria. In addition to the resurrected Ebla, the major city-states of the twenty-second and twenty-first centuries included Aleppo, Alalakh, Urshu, Tuttul, Byblos, Carchemish, and Qatna;[21] there were, of course, numerous smaller towns and unfortified farming villages which were generally dependent on the larger city-states. By the twenty-first century the city-state of Ebla ruled a mere skeleton of its former empire (HE2 101–33). If Astour's reconstruction of events and synchronisms are correct, Ebla was destroyed by Hurrian invaders around 2030 (HE2 133–71). Unfortunately, we have almost no contemporary indigenous records describing the military relations between the city-states during this period. The only other textual example we have of post-Akkadian

Mesopotamian military intervention into Syria comes from the reign of Shusin of Ur {2037–2029}, who campaigned up the Euphrates to the "land where cedars are cut" (R 3/2:191; SHP 36). On the other hand, archaeological excavations often discover "burn layers" which indicate destruction by fire, frequently assumed to have been caused by war: "an unchronicled episode in the never-ending drama of warfare between neighbours that was characteristic of Syria's early history" (C1/2:339). Such burn layers can only be roughly dated by stratigraphy; furthermore, it is impossible to know for certain who destroyed the city, or why. But their existence does point to ongoing serious wars resulting in frequent sieges, capture, and the destruction of cities.

Amorites in Syria[22]

In Syria the late Early Bronze crisis witnessed widespread urban collapse, population decline, decentralization, and devastation (HE2 164–71). Some sites, like Mari under the *shakkanakku* (descendants of the Akkadian installed "governors") {2250–1900}, survived the crisis relatively unscathed, and indeed, seem to have prospered (AS 286–7). Many sites were destroyed and never reinhabited. Others, like Ebla, were burned and "reduced to minuscule, short-lived villages" (AS 283) inhabited by impoverished squatters (AS 294). Some cities, however, like Nagar (Tell Brak) and Urkesh (Tell Mozan) managed to survive the crisis, though often with reduced population, wealth, and power. Overall twenty major cities in Syria are known to have been destroyed during this period (HE2 164–71).

Many cities which survived in one form or another experienced major dynastic shifts, with new Amorite elites rising to power. Thus, by the twentieth century Amorite warlords had come to power in most of the major city-states in Syria. They were rivaled in the Khabur triangle in north-eastern Syria by Hurrians, migrants from Anatolia who slowly became the dominant ethnic group (see pp. 303–7). The shift from the Early to the Middle Bronze in Syria is clearly marked in the material culture of ceramics, figurines, and house and town planning (AS 291).

Middle Bronze Age Syria {2000–1600}[23]

By the twentieth century the crisis which had resulted in the decline of urban civilization in the Near East had largely played itself out. Changing ecological, social, and political conditions apparently again favored urbanization; major city-states reappeared, while older surviving sites grew in size and power. The transition from Early to Middle Bronze is characterized by many new archaeological typologies, including pottery styles, other forms of material culture, weapons, fortification styles, art, and language. The Middle Bronze Age is a period of the revival of urban life; one way in which this is manifest is by increasing military competition between expanding city-states. Though still woefully fragmentary and inadequate, the range, quantity, and quality of our sources for military history improve dramatically in Middle Bronze II (SHP 39–40, 44–9), especially in relationship to the late Middle Bronze archive at Mari.

Nearly all of the known names of Syrian rulers in the Middle Bronze period are linguistically Amorite; the exceptions are those of north-eastern Syria, which are predominantly Hurrian (see Chapter Eleven). Amorite-dominated dynasties were established in most major cities by the beginning of the Middle Bronze period. Some of these dynasties, such as Byblos and Ugarit, proved quite stable and long-lasting, in contrast to the political anarchy and dynastic instability characterizing the end of the Early Bronze Age. Most of the city-states of Syria shared a related military system which can be reconstructed in broad strokes from surviving artistic and archaeological sources.

Warriors of Middle Bronze Age Syria (MM 25–31; MK 148–50)

As with most of the ancient Near East, our major source of information for arms and armor in Middle Bronze Age Syria comes from archaeology and art, supplemented by important scattered references to weapons in the Mari archive and other texts. Archaeologically, we are fortunate that the massive collections of votive objects found at the temples at Byblos included a large number of actual weapons, which allows us to make a precise one-to-one correlation between the weapons seen in art and those found in the temple-offering hordes (SAF §120–30; MW; AW 1:174–5; WM 153–6). These include dagger blades (*patrum*, MM 30), javelin and spearheads, both socketed and riveted, the "duckbill" and "eye" axes, and narrow socketed axes with chisel-like heads.[24] Bronze spears (*šinnum*) are the most commonly mentioned weapon in the Mari archive (L 195, 239, 383, 446, 516); some of them were poisoned (L 385). One force consisted of 2000 spearmen (L 195). Javelins are also mentioned at Mari (L 467, 497, 516). Some of these were ornamental weapons of pure gold designed for ceremonies rather than fighting (AW 1:170–1). Such ornamental weapons were presumably for officers, elite soldiers, or troops on parade. One text from Mari mentions "ten gold-plated bronze spears, forty silver-plated bronze spears and 250 bronze spears" (L 324).

There are several significant transitions from the Early to Middle Bronze ages, such as shields, axes, socketed weapons and sickle-swords. In the Middle Bronze Age, although the mace (*kakkum*) continued in use for ceremonial purposes, such as the example found at Ebla (EDS 236, 239–40), the mace as a practical weapon essentially disappeared, being replaced by the axe (*hassinnum*) (MM 28–9; MW; AFC 76). Increasingly weapons were made with a socket which into which the wooden haft was inserted. This permitted the head of the weapon to be much more securely fastened to the haft, thereby decreasing breakage.

The tradition of making figurines of armed warrior-gods that began in the Early Bronze Age continued throughout the Middle Bronze as well. One collection comes from northern Syria around the beginning of the Middle Bronze Age {2100–1900} (SAF 15, §10–18). Each figure in this style once held two weapons, one in each hand. Unfortunately many of the weapons of the figurines are missing;

of the forty-one figures from this period, all but ten lack weapons. The early figures in this collection are very crudely done, with the quality of the later figures
improving. Many figures are nude, but others wear the standard Syrian–Canaanite
kilt with a broad leather belt. The most frequent weapon is the javelin or short
thrusting spear. Six figures have a type of baldric around their right shoulders with
bronze daggers attached, which hang about halfway down the front of the chest;
two others have daggers on their belts. Three figures hold what seem to be early
sickle-swords, which were probably elite weapons. Two figurines from Ugarit have
torques, and are armed with maces (SAF §18).

The figures associated with the Orontes Valley from Syria are found throughout
the Middle Bronze Age {2000–1600} (SAF 15, §19–27), and contain a number of
military innovations which might be associated with the Amorites. There are,
none the less, a number of points of continuity with earlier warriors. The standard
dress continues to be a knee-length kilt with a broad leather belt. However, the
fabric of the kilt is often ornamented with lines and patterns. Headdress also
becomes ostentatious, with tall, pointed conical hats (divine crowns), and sometimes fan-like flourishes which may be feathers (SAF §24–5). Several figures also
have torques around their necks. The dagger becomes more prominent, again
generally hung in mid-chest from a shoulder baldric (SAF §19), though sometimes
placed in the belt (SAF §21). Most figures have two other weapons in addition to
their sheathed dagger. The spear, dagger, mace combination of the Early Bronze
Age is replaced by spear, dagger and one of two types of axe: the "eye" or the
"duck-bill" axe (SAF §19; AW 1:166–8).

Another innovation of this period is the shield and axe combination (SAF §94,
97, 98). Shields are mentioned in the Mari texts (L 239). From the figurines they
seem to be of typical Canaanite style, shown in several Egyptian depictions of
Canaanite warriors (see Chapter Seventeen). The Canaanite shield is rectangular
in shape with small triangles cut out of the top and bottom; they appear to be
made from animal skins with the pointed projections on the four corners being the
four shoulders. If proportional, the shields held by the Orontes figurines are quite
small – almost bucklers – perhaps 35 cm long and 20 cm wide. Egyptian depictions
of the same Canaanite shields show them much larger, capable of protecting most
of the upper torso. Seeden believes that the sculpters were forced to make unusually small shields for the figurines due to the limitations of the casting process
(SAF 144); it is likely that the actual size of the shield depicted by the Egyptians is
more accurate.

The latest and largest archaeological find of armed god figurines comes from
Byblos, where several hundred have been found, again covering the entire Middle
Bronze period. Most of these are small, poorly made, and with no surviving
weapons; they seem to have been mass produced as inexpensively and quickly as
possible. Some, however, preserve a number of military details. Some have a long,
broad-headed thrusting spear in the left hand, a long-hafted semi-circular axe in
the right, and a dagger thrust in the broad belt (SAF #195, 774, 1107). The axe is
the most prominent among surviving weapons (SAF #228, 231). Another has a

small shield, axe and dagger thrust in his belt (SAF #281). The Early Bronze baldric has disappeared; the daggers of the Byblos figurines are invariably tucked in the broad belt, either at the front or the left side (SAF #769–73). Though the weapons are usually missing, by comparing poses and the empty sockets of weaponless figurines with similar figures whose weapons remain, it is possible to extrapolate that the spear–axe or shield–axe combinations are by far the most common (SAF §34, #307, 511–16). The widespread use of the dagger–axe–spear/javelin combination is confirmed by both archaeological and Egyptian artistic sources. A few figures are armed with two spears, perhaps one a javelin for throwing and the other a thrusting spear, or, alternatively, two javelins (SAF #732–4, 1502). Many of the figures seem to have tall conical hats which are probably divine crowns; some, however, may be helmets (SAF #1129–30). Helmets (*qurpissum*) (L 205) are occasionally mentioned in the Mari texts, but body armor is rare.[25] One warrior may have a bow, though this may simply be a bent spear or even a walking stick (SAF #1406); other than this one possibility, none of the Middle Bronze figurines carries a bow, though this may be because of the technical difficulties of casting such a weapon (SAF 144).

A ritual votive basin from nineteenth-century Ebla is ornamented with a number of warriors; all of them are bearded, with no headdress, wearing shoulder-to-knee robes with patterns and fringes (AANE §448–53; AS 303; EDS 242). In one panel three soldiers flanking an enthroned king all carry broad-headed thrusting spears overhand, and sickle-swords in their left hand (AANE §448). In another panel an enthroned king is guarded by warriors with man-size spears held upright and resting on the floor (AANE §450). A hunting scene shows one man with an axe on his shoulder and another with a bow and quiver (AANE §451).

Archery is relatively rare in Middle Bronze Syrian and Mesopotamian art, archaeology and texts. There are two types of bows mentioned in the Mari archive: the *tilpānum* and the *qaštum*. The *tilpānum* was once thought to have been a "throwing-stick", but recent research has confirmed it is probably the composite bow (MK 148; MM 25); *qaštum* is a more generic term for bow. These bows are mentioned occasionally in Mari texts (ARM 2.116, 7.24, 10.19), but in relatively small numbers. Zimri-Lim ordered six *tilpānum* (ARM 18.21); another text describes thirty being sent to the palace (ARM 9.102). Arrows (*ussum*) are ordered in greater quantity, but still in relatively small numbers. Shamshi-Adad ordered 10,000 bronze arrowheads (*samrūtum*) of six shekels each (about 50 grams), but was forced to reduce his order to 5000 because of lack of tin to make the bronze. At twenty arrows per archer, 10,000 arrows could equip 500 archers; the 5000 arrows he actually got would only equip 250 archers. Another order of arrowheads included a number of different weights, presumably for different types of archery: "Have made 50 bronze arrowheads of 5 shekels weight (40 grams) each, 50 arrowheads of 3 shekels weight each, 100 arrowheads of 2 shekels weight each, and 200 arrowheads of 1 shekel weight each" (ARM 18.5; MK 63). The lighter arrowheads, with greater range but less penetrating power – and also less expensive – were more popular. Even so a total of 400 arrows ordered for a siege would only equip twenty archers with twenty arrows each.

The price was one silver shekel for twenty arrowheads; it is not clear if this is just the price of the arrowhead, or if it includes the wood, feathers, and labor cost of the arrow as well (ARM 1.38; MM 26). When we remember that ten ordinary soldiers were paid 2–3 shekels for campaign service (one month? three months?) (L 499–500; pp. 196–7), we begin to see how expensive arrowheads were. Assuming the highest pay for the lowest period of service, we get a third of a shekel per soldier per month, which would equate to the value of six or seven arrowheads.[26] The third of a shekel per soldier does not represent his entire wages; he received food, housing, equipment, and booty as well. Nonetheless, in modern terms, an arrowhead would probably cost the equivalent of one or two hundred dollars. One possible reason for the relative lack of archery is simply the expense of bronze arrowheads. At the same period an axehead required 650 grams of bronze, the equivalent in weight of seven arrowheads. But the axe could be used over and over again, while there was a good likelihood that a bronze arrowhead would be lost once shot. Bronze arrow ammunition was simply too expensive in the Middle Bronze Age. This expense may have contributed to the popularity of the sling (waspum), of which 500 are mentioned in one text (MM 26; MK 148).

The royal palace of Middle Bronze Mari was sacked by Hammurabi in 1759, preserving a unique set of color frescoes on the palace wall, some of which have military aspects. The overall theme of the murals is the ceremonial investiture of the king before the gods, who are sometimes armed. I am here assuming that the weapons of the gods reflect the actual weapons used by Mari soldiers from the period – an assumption generally confirmed by archaeology and other artistic sources. The largest mural shows the war-goddess Ishtar investing king Zimri-Lim with royal authority. Ishtar holds a proto-sickle-sword in her right hand, and has a number of other weapons (axe and mace?) in a quiver on her back (SDA 279). The weapons in the back quiver are more clearly depicted in another scene showing a god seated on a throne receiving offerings. Here again the weapons, which protrude at an angle over the left shoulder (presumably held in a quiver on the back), are the axe, mace, and proto-sickle-sword (SDA 282–3). Two common soldiers are also depicted in the murals (SDA 275, 282). Both warriors are bare-chested, wearing white knee-length kilts with elaborate fringes. Both have yellow, knee-length capes tied on their shoulders with a white sash. One is beardless, with a white turban-like hat that is wrapped under his chin; a sculpted head of a soldier also shows this same head-gear.[27] This warrior seems to have two arrows or javelins protruding from his back or side; perhaps they are lodged in his cape. Despite his wounds he is brandishing a javelin in his right hand, ready to throw. Much of this painting is destroyed, but the warrior seems to be leaning slightly backward with his left arm extended forward at waist level. My impression is that he might be holding on to a chariot frame with his left hand, and leaning backward to throw a javelin behind him with his right hand. The other warrior is bearded, without head-gear, and is carrying a bundle over his shoulder on an axe or javelin (SDA 275, 282).

A final artistic source for Syrian Middle Bronze warfare is martial scenes in glyptic art (cylinder seals). Many scenes show the king (or hero, or god) armed with a mace (FI §220, 790), or double-armed with mace and dagger (FI §545, 789) and possibly mace and axe (FI §220). One warrior is shown carrying what seems to be an axe, accompanied by another with a bow (FI §686). Another weapon which appears occasionally in glyptic art is the sickle-sword (FI §872; see pp. 66–71). The warriors are generally depicted wearing kilts and turbans, or some type of horned helmet which is generally associated with mythic depictions of the gods (FI §220, 545, 789, 790).

Two late Middle Bronze cylinder seals from Syria are some of our earliest examples of the war-chariot, depicting the light, two-wheeled, horse-drawn chariot with spoked wheels riding over defeated enemies (Figure 4e, p. 133).[28] One warrior has a quiver on his back, indicating the use of the bow from the chariot; he is also followed by four infantry "runners" or support troops for the chariot (FI §729). Another Middle Bronze scene shows people riding what seems to be a two-humped Bactrian camel (FI §738), the earliest extant depiction of camel-riding, which, in the long run, would create a military revolution in the Near East and northern Africa, ultimately facilitating the rise of the medieval Islamic world empire and West African Berber empires. In the Middle Bronze Age, however, there is no evidence for the military use of the camel, though nomads were probably beginning to use it for transport and logistics in the desert fringes of the Near East (EA 1:407–8).

Maritime power[29]

Unfortunately, due to very limited artistic, textual, and archaeological data, little can be said about maritime warfare in the Bronze Age Levant. Only in the Late Bronze does the evidence become sufficient to provide details. The two most important Early and Middle Bronze maritime cities were Ugarit and Byblos, though there were half-a-dozen other major Early Bronze maritime city-states,[30] a number that expanded to nearly two dozen during the Middle Bronze.[31] All of these sites were heavily fortified during the Middle Bronze Age. Archaeological evidence makes it clear that during the Middle Bronze Age maritime trade was occurring between Syria and Egypt, Cyprus, and the Aegean. It can be assumed that competition for trade routes would have led to some type of conflict, if only piracy, but no specifics are known.

The Great city-states of Syria in Middle Bronze II {1800–1600}

Syria during the Middle Bronze Age was divided into about a dozen major city-states, often engaged in fierce military competition. The major Middle Bronze

Syrian city-states included Alalakh, Aleppo (Yamkhad), Byblos, Carchemish, Damascus, Ebla, Hama (Amad), Khana (Terqa, Tell Ashara), Mari, Nagar (Tell Brak), Qatna (Tel Mishrife), Shekhna (Tell Leilan), Ugarit (Ras Shamra), and Urkesh (Tell Mozan).[32] In addition, the city-states of Hazor (EA 3:1–5) and Megiddo (EA 3:460–9) in northern Canaan were in many ways part of the city-state military system of Middle Bronze Syria. Generally speaking, political and military power in Syria during the Middle Bronze Age was divided among these city-states in a rather unstable system of balance of power, shifting alliances, and attempts at hegemonic domination. Overall, Aleppo was the predominant military power of Syria, with Mari a close second.

From the fragmentary textual and archaeological evidence we can establish a skeletal history of these city-states and their military interrelationships. Middle Bronze I {2000–1800} is rather poorly documented (SHP 39–40), but after 1800 the archival cuneiform sources from Alalakh, Hattusis, Shekhna (Leilan), and especially Mari become quite rich by Bronze Age standards (SHP 44–9). The three dominant city-states in Syria during Middle Bronze II were Aleppo, Mari, and Qatna. After the destruction of Mari by Hammurabi {1759} – a destruction which ironically preserved the greatest surviving archive of the age, a crucial source for military history – Aleppo remained the predominant power for a century-and-a-half until defeated and destroyed by the Hittites around 1600. The great campaigns of Mursili in Syria and Babylon {1600–1595}, discussed in Chapter Eleven, brought an end to the Middle Bronze period, inaugurating the subsequent three-way struggle for control of Syria between the Hittites, Mitanni, and Egyptians during the Late Bronze Age {1600–1200}. Our information for the military history of each of the major Middle Bronze Syrian city-states is rather limited, but a skeletal outline of military history can be obtained.

Aleppo (Yamkhad, Halpa, Halab)[33]

Although Aleppo was the most powerful Syrian kingdom during the Middle Bronze period, it has yielded only limited archaeological data and no textual archive because of modern occupation over the ancient site. Enough data survives to tell us that, like most other Middle Bronze city-states, Aleppo was defended by a double wall – an outer earthen rampart surrounding the entire city, with large fortified chambered gateways and circular towers. There was also an inner citadel, now covered by the magnificent medieval Islamic citadel (AS 303). Because of the lack of texts from Aleppo, we are left largely with incidental references to Aleppo in the records of rival states to reconstruct its military history.

During much of Middle Bronze II Aleppo was one of the greatest powers of the Near East. According to the Itur-Asdu letter {c. 1775}: "There is no king who is strong by himself: 10 or 15 kings follow Hammurabi of Babylon, as many follow Rim-Sin of Larsa, Ibalpiel of Eshnunna and Amutpiel of Qatna, while twenty kings follow Yarim-Lim [king] of Aleppo" (ANE 1:99). In other words, of the six major powers in Mesopotamia and Syria around 1775 – Mari, Babylon,

Larsa, Eshnunna, Qatna, and Aleppo – Aleppo was the most powerful. The "twenty kings" who were allies and vassals of states of Aleppo included, at various times, the rulers of the major city-states of Emar, Alalakh, Ugarit, and Carchemish. They also maintained an on–off vassal relationship with two nomadic tribes in Syria, the Rabbeans and Ubrabeans (SHP 52), who sometimes served as mercenary allies of Aleppo. In the late seventeenth century Hittite rulers referred to the king of Aleppo as a "great king", hence he was the diplomatic equal of the Hittite king.

From various historical sources we can reconstruct a king-list for imperial Aleppo, up to the time of the Hittite conquest in c. 1600, with approximate dates of the rulers (CANE 2:1202):

Sumu-Epuh {1810–1780} (SHP 51–4)
Yarim-Lim I {1780–1764} (SHP 54–8)
Hammu-rabi I {1764–1750} (SHP 58–9)
Abba'el I {1750–1720} (SHP 60–1)
Yarim-Lim II {1720–1700} (SHP 62)
Niqmepukh {c. 1700–1675} (SHP 62)
Irkabtum {c. 1675–1650} (SHP 63)
Yarim-Lim III {c. 1650–1625} (SHP 63–4)
Hammu-rabi II {c. 1625–1600} (SHP 64)

The written military history of Aleppo begins around 1805 with a campaign by Yahdun-Lim, king of Mari {1820–1798}, who marched from the Euphrates to the Mediterranean in search of cedar and other building timber; he claims to have subdued the peoples of the area, forcing them to pay tribute. As a result of this invasion Sumu-Epuh of Aleppo {1810–1790}, in alliance with a number of surrounding city-states and nomadic tribes, marched against Yahdun-Lim, who claims to have defeated the coalition (SHP 50). Shortly thereafter, however, Yahdun Lim was attacked from the east by Ilakabkabu, father of Shamshi-Adad; Mari entered a life-or-death struggle with the rising power of Shamshi-Adad (see pp. 168–71), culminating in the fall of Mari around 1796. In the last few years before the fall of Mari, its king Sumu-Yamam {1800–1796} attempted to organize an alliance with his former enemy of Aleppo against the rising Assyrians, but failed to save his city (SHP 52). On the other hand, Sumu-Epah of Aleppo seems to have welcomed the refugee dynasts of Mari – some would say legitimate kings – to Aleppo, invoking the ire of Shamshi-Adad.

The subsequent power vacuum in Syria was ultimately filled by Sumu-Epuh of Aleppo {1810–1780}, who in the two decades following the fall of Mari rose to prominence in the region, becoming a major enemy of the rising Shamshi-Adad of Assyria. During the last years of Sumu-Epuh of Aleppo, Shamshi-Adad and his son Yasmah-Adad {1796–1776}, who had been installed as client king of Mari upon its conquest by the Assyrians, allied with Qatna, the major Syrian kingdom on Aleppo's southern border, sealing the alliance with a dynastic marriage. The smaller independent city-states to the north – Carchemish and Urshu – both joined the anti-Aleppo alliance, leaving Sumu-Epuh surrounded and basically without allies (ARM 1.24; SHP 53–4). Unfortunately, no surviving text describes the outcome of this contest, but somehow Sumu-Epuh managed to forestall conquest by Shamshi-Adad, probably by allegiance with Shamshi-Adad's enemies in Mesopotamia.

This military crisis was inherited by Sumu-Epuh's son and successor Yarim-Lim I {1780–1764} (SHP 54–8), who during his reign engineered a dramatic reversal of fortune. He overcame the crisis by a deft alliance with Shamshi-Adad's other enemies Ibalpi-el of Eshnunna {1779–1765} and Hammurabi of Babylon {1792–1750}; Shamshi-Adad was thus surrounded by enemies on the east, south, and west. During this alliance Yarim-Lim is credited with having "saved the city of Babylon" (SHP 55), presumably by attacking the Assyrians in the rear while they were engaged in one of their attacks against Babylon.

Yarim-Lim also had at his court a political wild-card, Zimri-Lim, grandson of Sumu-Yamam, former king of Mari (L 42), whom many at Mari would have considered the legitimate heir to the throne of Mari instead of the usurper and Assyrian imperialist Yasmah-Adad, son of the warlord Shamshi-Adad (SHP 55). With his protégé Zimri-Lim, Yarim-Lim captured the strategic fortress-city of Tuttul on the confluence of the Balikh and the Euphrates in 1777, where Zimri-Lim was installed as king (L 41). Fortuitously, Shamshi-Adad died the next year {1776}, creating succession tensions which were exploited by Yarim-Lim and Zimri-Lim who marched on Mari, defeating and ousting Yasmah-Addu and restoring Zimri-Lim to the throne of his ancestors as an ally-vassal of Aleppo (L 41–2). Yarim-Lim cemented the alliance by the marriage of his daughter Shibtu to Zimri-Lim, insuring that his grandsons would rule Mari (SHP 56). The triumphant wedding was attended by the "kings of the whole land" (ARM 26.11). Relations with Mari remained strong until the city fell to Hammurabi in 1761. In the last years of his reign Yarim-Lim consolidated his hold on Syria, bringing a number of city-states and kings into alliance or vassalage. The important and rich trading city of Ugarit was probably a vassal of Aleppo in this period (SHP 56–7). By his death in 1764, Yarim-Lim, with his twenty vassals and allied kings (ANE 1:99), was the mightiest ruler in the Near East outside of Egypt.

The reign of Yarim-Lim's son Hammu-rabi I {1764–1750} (SHP 58–9) was generally peaceful, with Aleppo maintaining good relations with most of its neighbors. The city of Carchemish seems to have come under Aleppan domination during this period (SHP 59). An expeditionary force was sent from Aleppo to aid Babylon, including both regular Aleppan troops and Yamanite tribal contingents (SHP 59). His reign coincided with the last phase of Hammurabi of Babylon's imperialism and the sack of his brother-in-law's city of Mari, but Hammu-rabi of Aleppo seemed unwilling to be drawn into the war with Babylon.

Abba-el {1750–1720} (SHP 60–1) also ruled over a fairly peaceful period for Aleppo, maintaining good relations with Hammurabi's successors in Babylon. The major recorded military event of his reign was a rebellion of Zitraddu, governor Irridi and some other vassals in upper Mesopotamia:

Zitraddu, the governor of Irridi, revolted against Yarim-Lim [brother of Abba-el, king of Aleppo] and led robber bands and brought them to Irridi, his city. He incited the whole land to rebel against Abba-el [the king of Aleppo]. The mighty weapon [of the gods, which was decorated] with silver, gold, lapis lazuli, [and] the great weapon of the Storm God [were raised against the rebels by the king of Aleppo]. As for Abba-el, he seized Irridi and captured the enemy [robber] bands. To Aleppo he returned in peace. (CS 2:369–70)

The rebellion was thus suppressed and the rebel city was destroyed. Yarim-Lim, Abba-el's brother, who had been client-king of Irridi before its rebellion, was given the city of Alalakh as compensation, where his descendants ruled as client-allies of Aleppo for the next century (see pp. 264–5) (SHP 61).

The reigns of the subsequent kings of Aleppo are only sparsely documented in military affairs. Niqmepukh {c. 1700–1680} conquered the city of Arazik near Carchemish (AT §7; SHP 62). Irkabtum {c. 1680–1660} campaigned in the region of Nashtarbi, east of the Euphrates (AT §33), probably against the expanding power of Hurrian princes in north-eastern Syria (SHP 63). Yarim-Lim III {c. 1660–1640} fought a war against Qatna to the south (SHP 63). Unfortunately, no details are known of any of these events.

Under Hammu-rabi II {c. 1640–1620}, Aleppo faced its greatest military challenge since the war with Shamshi-Adad 150 years earlier. This threat came from a new unexpected direction, the rising Hittite kingdom to the north under Hattusilis I {1650–1620} (SHP 64). Although we have no Aleppan records of this war, it is clear that Hammu-rabi II was outmatched by the Hittites. Nonetheless, through an alliance with the Hurrians, Hammu-rabi II was able to resist ongoing Hittite aggression for over two decades, at one point apparently killing the son of Hattusilis and heir to the throne in a victorious battle (KH 102). A few texts mention an Aleppan general Zukrasi, "overseer of the army", who commanded the resistance to the Hittite invaders (KH 76; CS 2:369b). In the end, however, Mursilis I {c. 1620–1590} crushed the Aleppan army, sacking the capital and destroying the kingdom around 1600 (see Chapter Eleven).

Mari[34]

From the perspective of military history Mari is the most important city-state in ancient Syria. This is in part because of its important role as a major political and military power of the day, but more because of the huge archive of 20,000 cuneiform tablets discovered at its palace, which contain hundreds of letters describing military affairs. The military system described in the Mari letters has been discussed in detail in Chapter Seven. Here I will outline the basic political history of Mari during the early Middle Bronze Age.

Geographically Mari is located on the Euphrates river at a strategic juncture between four ecological, cultural, and political zones: Babylon and Sumer to the south-east, Asshur to the north-east, Syria to the north-west, and the nomadic steppe and desert to the south-west. Its strategic location was both a blessing and a curse; it brought wealth as a trading center, but also frequent invasion as a crossroad between Mesopotamia and Syria. In classical times the strategic and economic functions of Mari were transferred to the nearby Roman city of Dura-Europos, which served as a major Roman frontier fortress against the Persians until it was destroyed by a siege of the Sasanid king Shapur in 256 CE (EA 2:173–8).

As noted above, Mari had been conquered by the Akkadians, where they installed a military governor. As Akkadian power collapsed, the governors of Mari, known as the *shakkanakku*, siezed virtual independence and formed a dynasty. Throughout the Ur III period Mari was governed by seven rulers, although little is know about their military activities (R3/2:439–50). Under the fifth ruler, Puzur-Eshtar, a contemporary of Amarsin of Ur {2046–2038}, Mari apparently became independent, with its subsequent two rulers taking the title of king. Sometime around 2000, however, it was conquered by Amorites, who thereafter ruled the city as a new dynasty.

Little is known of the kings of Mari in the early twentieth century. For the nineteenth century, however, we are much better informed. The precise details of the rise of Yagid-Lim {c 1830–1820} to power in Mari are obscure; he may have begun as ruler of nearby Suprum. At some point he gained power over Mari and proclaimed himself independent king. His son Yahdun-Lim {c. 1820–1800} was a contemporary of the great warlord Shamshi-Adad of Assyria. He undertook a successful military career, transforming Mari into a significant military power in Mesopotamia, and a major rival of Assyria. His two martial inscriptions provide interesting details of his campaigns. After securing Mari he campaigned down the Euphrates, conquering the regions to the south-west.

> Yahdun-Lim, son of Yaggid-Lim, king of Mari, Tuttul, and the land of Khana [on the Euphrates south-east of Mari], mighty king, who controls the banks of the Euphrates – the god Dagan proclaimed my kingship and gave to me a mighty weapon that fells my royal enemies. Seven kings, leaders of Khana who had fought against me, I defeated. I annexed their lands.... I built the wall of Mari and dug its moat. I built the wall of [the conquered city of] Terqa and dug its moat. Now in a waste, a land of thirst, in which from days of old no king had built a city, I took pleasure in building a city. I dug its moat and called it Dur-Yahdun-Lim ["Fortress of Yahdun-Lim"].... I enlarged my land, established the foundations of Mari and my land, and established my fame until distant days. (E4:602–3)

These victories brought Mari into contact with both Babylon to the south-east and Assyria to the north-east, inaugurating a decades-long struggle for supremacy in Mesopotamia that would be concluded fifty years later under Hammurabi.

Yahdun-Lim next turned his attention westward, towards Syria and the Mediterranean coast.

When the god Shamash agreed to his supplications and listened to his [Yahdun-Lim's] words; the god Shamash quickly came and went at the side of Yahdun-Lim [in battle]. From distant days when the god El built Mari, no king resident in Mari reached the sea, reached the mountains of cedar and boxwood, the great mountains, and cut down their trees, [but] Yahdun-Lim, son of Yaggid-Lim, powerful king, wild bull of kings, by means of his strength and overpowering might went to the shore of the [Mediterranean] sea, and made a great offering [befitting] his kingship to the Sea. His troops bathed themselves in the Sea.... He made that land on the shore of the Sea submit, made it subject to his decree, and made it follow him [as vassals]. Having imposed a permanent tribute on them, they now bring their tribute to him. (E4:605–6)

The details of this campaign are a bit obscure – no specific city-names are mentioned – and his supremacy in Syria was certainly not unchallenged by Aleppo. It is likely that Aleppo ruled northern Syria, Mari had vassals in the middle, and Qatna dominated the south.

As with all Mesopotamian warlords, Yahdun-Lim's victories did not go unchallenged. His invasion of Syria was a cause for concern for Sumu-Epuh, king of Aleppo, who orchestrated a revolt against Mari:

In that same year [as the campaign to the Mediterranean Sea] – Laum, King of Samanum and the land of the Ubrabium, Bahlukullim, king of Tuttul and the land of the Amnanum, Aialum, king of Abattum and the land of the Rabbum – these [three] kings rebelled against [Yahdun-Lim]. The troops of Sumu-Epukh of the land of Aleppo came as auxiliary troops [to aid the rebel kings] and in the city of Samanum the tribes gathered together against [Yahdun-Lim]. But by means of [his] mighty weapon he defeated these three [rebel] kings. [...] He vanquished their troops and their [Aleppan] auxiliaries and inflicted a defeat on them. He heaped up their dead bodies. He tore down the walls [of their cities] and made them into mounds of rubble. The city of Khaman, of the [nomad] tribe of Haneans, which all the leaders of [the tribe of] Hana had built, he destroyed and made into mounds of rubble. Now, he defeated their king, Kasuri-Khala. Having taken away their population [Yahdun-Lim] controlled the banks of the Euphrates.... May the god Shamash, who lives in that temple, grant to Yahdun-Lim, the builder of his temple, the king beloved of his heart, a mighty weapon which overwhelms the enemies (and) a long reign of happiness and years of joyous abundance, forever.... [Concluding curse on enemies:] May the god Nergal, the lord of the weapon, smash his [Yahdun-Lim's enemy's] weapon in order that he not [be able to] confront [the] warriors [of Mari].... May the god Bunene, the great vizier of the god Shamash, cut the throat [of Yahdun-Lim's enemies]. (E4:607–8)

Yahdun-Lim's victories in Syria, however, were occurring under the shadow of the rising power of Shamshi-Adad in Assyria, who soon came into conflict with

Mari. Yahdun-Lim's son and successor Sumu-Yamam {1800–1796} was unable to maintain his father's military success against the power of Assyria. In 1796 Mari was conquered by Shamshi-Adad, who made the city a vassal kingdom under his son Yasmah-Adad, who ruled Mari from 1796–1776 (E4:615–22). At the death of Shamshi-Adad, Zimri-Lim, probably a grandson of the former king Sumu-Yamam, was able to retake the city with the help of the king of Aleppo. During his brief fifteen-year reign {1776–1761} he brought Mari to the height of cultural glory and political power as the staunchest ally of Hammurabi of Babylon. In the end, however, relations broke down between the two allies, leading to war and culminating in the conquest of Mari by Hammurabi in 1761 {Y33}. Two years later {1759} the city was sacked and utterly destroyed, and left essentially uninhabited (ANET 270b). The military details of these events are discussed in Chapter Six.

Thereafter, the geopolitical role of Mari as the major city of the middle Euphrates was taken by Terqa (Tell Ashara) (EDS 217–22), the capital of the kingdom of Khana. Terqa remained a vassal kingdom of the Babylonians for the next century and a half until the fall of Babylon to the Hittites in 1595. Thereafter a dynasty of Hurrian kings was installed, who were integrated into the empire of Mitanni sometime during the sixteenth century.

Qatna (Tell Mishrife near Hama)[35]

Qatna was the third most powerful state in Middle Bronze Syria, and often a major regional rival to Aleppo. The city covered about 100 hectares, with a possible population of 25,000. As with most Middle Bronze Syrian cities, it was defended by a huge earthen rampart, 15 meters high, with at least four chambered gates. Qatna served as a major emporium for trade routes from Mesopotamia through Mari to the Mediterranean, Canaan and, indirectly, Egypt.

The first known ruler of Qatna was Ishhi-Adad {c. 1795–1775}. As noted above, a serious military rivalry existed between Aleppo and the house of Shamshi-Adad of Assyria. Qatna was therefore cultivated as an ally by Shamshi-Adad; an alliance-marriage was arranged between his son Yasmah-Adad, viceroy of Mari, and Beltum, daughter of Ishhi-Adad (ARM 1.46, 77; SHP 65). This alliance was intended to create a military coalition against Aleppo, which had been raiding the villages and flocks of Qatna (ARM 5.17). Assyria and Mari sent troops to Qatna to organize a unified attack, but the results are unknown (SHP 54, 66); since Aleppo survived and expanded after the death of Shamshi-Adad, it is clear that the alliance was ultimately unsuccessful.

Amutpi'el {c. 1775–1755} succeeded his father to the throne; the Mari archives describe him as the equal of Hammurabi of Babylon and Rim-Sin of Larsa, each king having "ten or fifteen [vassal and allied] kings" who "follow" them (ANE 1:99; SHP 68). Following the death of Shamshi-Adad {1776} and the collapse of Assyrian imperialism, there was reconciliation between Aleppo and Qatna (SHP 69). Qatna was occasionally involved in sending auxiliary allied troops to aid Mari (ARM 14.69), and was known for breeding fine horses (ARM 14.88). With the end of the Mari archive {1761} our knowledge of the military history of Qatna essentially ends, other than the notice of a war between Qatna and Aleppo {c. 1640?} (AT §6; SHP 60).

Alalakh[36]

Alalakh was a second-tier military power, generally the vassal of Aleppo. The excavations of the site have discovered signs of the standard rampart, fortified gates and citadel of Middle Bronze Syrian defensive architecture (EA 1:57).

In Middle Bronze II it was ruled by a subsidiary line of the Aleppan royal family after Abba-el of Aleppo {c. 1750–1720} installed his brother Yarim-Lim as vassal king of Alalakh.

> When the allies [of the vassal city-state of Irridi] rebelled against Abba-el [king of Aleppo], their [rightful] lord, Abba-el, the king, with the help of the gods Hadad, Khepat, and the spear of Ishtar, went to [the city of] Irridi, captured Irridi, and defeated its troops. At that time Abba-el, in exchange for Irridi which his father had granted [to his brother], gave Alalakh of his own free will [to his brother Yarim-Lim]. (R4:799; AT 2; CS 2:329, 369–70)

The text describing the transfer of the city to Yarim-Lim includes a vassal oath, indicative of the obligations and ritual curses associated with vassalage.

> Abba-el [the king of Aleppo] swore the oath [to give the city of Alalakh] to Yarim-Lim, saying: "If I take back [the city] that I have given you, may I be cursed." If ever in the future Yarim-Lim sins against Abba-el, or if he gives away Abba-el's secrets to another king, or if he lets go of the hem of Abbal-el's garment [as a ritual gesture of vassalage] and grasps the hem of another king's garments [thus becoming the vassal of the other king], his towns and lands he shall forfeit. (CS 2:370)

This branch of the Aleppan royal family ruled Alalakh as vassal-allies of Aleppo for the next several generations, including Yarim-Lim {c. 1740–1720}, his son Ammi-taqumma {1720–1700}, and his grandson Irkabtum {1700–1680}. It is occasionally mentioned in the affairs of state of Aleppo. Alalakh is noted for the preservation of roughly 175 tablets from the eighteenth century (level VII) and another 300 from the fifteenth century (level IV) (AT; EA 1:59–61), which highlight a few military matters of the period (AT §2). Alalakh was destroyed during the wars of Hattusilis the Hittite around 1640, but later rebuilt.

During the reign of Irkabtum {1700–1680}, the king was said to have "made peace with [the warlord] Shemuba and his Habiru[-warriors]" (AT §58). These Habiru (Hapiru, Apiru) were "fugitive" bands of nomads, mercenaries, brigands, outlaws, or robbers; similar robber bands have intermittently infested parts of the

Near East throughout its history, most recently in the form of insurgents in Iraq. They are occasionally mentioned as serving as mercenaries in armies in the Mari age.[37] The Habiru became quite widespread in the Late Bronze Age, when they were frequently mentioned both as mercenaries and as independent raiders.[38] An example of Habiru activities is found in the fifteenth-century story of Idrimi, a Robin Hood-like dispossessed citizen of Aleppo who fled to the wilderness and became a Habiru, eventually returning to capture Alalakh and become its king (CS 1:479–80).

Ugarit (Ras Shamra)[39]

Ugarit, an important Early Bronze kingdom, was destroyed in the twenty-second century in the anarchy at the end of the Early Bronze period. It was rebuilt around 2000 by Amorite warlords, whose martial tombs contain an important collection of copper/bronze duckbill axeheads, socketed spearheads, daggers, and torques – the standard axe–spear–dagger Middle Bronze armament (AS 296; MW). Molds for casting bronze weapons were also found in the city. A stele from Ugarit of the storm/war-god Baal from the end of the Middle Bronze reflects the armament of the age. Baal, with flowing shoulder-length hair and beard, wearing a kilt and (metal?) helmet, is armed with a mace, a dagger, and a long, broad-headed thrusting spear (AANE §74; EA 5:261). The city was strongly fortified by a massive rampart wall with a remarkable surviving gate complex including a stone glacis, narrow stone gate, hidden entry ramp, large square stone tower and postern gate (EA 5:258–9).

Ugarit, along with Byblos, was one of the most important Levantine maritime powers of the age, maintaining extensive trade connections with Cyprus, the Minoans of Crete, the Aegean, and Egypt. They were especially noted for their role of transshipping tin across the Mediterranean (SHP 77). Unfortunately, unlike the Late Bronze period when Ugarit's archive is one of our most important historical sources (EA 5:262–6), the Middle Bronze period at Ugarit is poorly documented. An incomplete ancestral king-list of Ugarit mentions fourteen Middle Bronze kings with Amorite names, beginning with Yaqaru, the presumed founder of the Amorite dynasty at Ugarit around 2000.[40] The kings of Ugarit were either vassals or close allies of Aleppo during most of Middle Bronze II. No details of their military history are known.

Byblos (Gubla, Gebal, Jubayl)[41]

The Phoenician coast lacked the great agricultural resources of Mesopotamia and Egypt, but was instead blessed with access to huge forests of cedar and other hard woods, some metal resources, and, most importantly, a long coastline with several natural harbors. One of the most ancient and important coastal settlements was Byblos, which during the Bronze Age was the greatest trading and maritime city in the Levant. Byblos had been settled in the Neolithic period by at least the fifth millennium, as a small village near a perennial spring, slowly developing into a full city. The earliest cultural influences, like those of all Syrian and Lebanese cities, came from Meso-potamia, but by at least the reign of Khasekhemwy {2714–2687} of Egypt, Egyptian trade and cultural influences began steadily to grow. By the Middle Kingdom, Byblos was a large and fantastically wealthy city with strong and friendly ties to Egypt.

Byblos was destroyed by war in around 2800, after which it was rebuilt with a magnificent fortification system including massive stone walls, two known gates and a glacis. The city was again destroyed sometime around 2300–2100 by an Amorite invasion; Amorite princes ruled Byblos in the subsequent centuries, including the kings buried in the nine royal sarcophagi. In the fourth millennium the primary weapon found in burials is the pear-shaped macehead, common also in Mesopotamia and Egypt (C1/2:344). This gave way in the Early Bronze Age to the standard Bronze Age arsenal of large spearheads, daggers, and axes of several different styles (MW). Some were highly ornamented ceremonial weapons, such as a gold dagger sheath (AANE §72).

As with so much of the Near East outside of Mesopotamia and Egypt, the lack of surviving historical records does not permit the reconstruction of the military history of Byblos.[42] The names of a number of the Amorite kings of Byblos have been discovered, largely from the Middle Bronze period, allowing us to recon-struct a tentative king-list.[43] The name of the first known Middle Bronze I king of Byblos, Ibdadi {c. 2000}, is linguistically Amorite (LMB 103; SHP 40); he is often thought to be the founder of the new Amorite dynasty there.

Carchemish (Karkamish; Jerablus)[44]

Militarily Carchemish was a second-level city-state. Its importance lay in its stra-tegic location on the upper Euphrates for the trade routes to Anatolia; the strategic resource tin came from Mari to Carchemish in exchange for wine and Anatolian horses – another strategic commodity for the rising importance of chariots in warfare (SHP 72). A Mari letter from around 1765 describes some of the Anato-lian horse trade of the king of Carchemish:

> I [the merchant ambassador from Mari] spoke to him [the king of Carchem-ish] in the matter of the white horses, and he said: "No white chariot horses are available. I will give orders that they lead white horses to me where they are available. In the meantime, I will have them bring some red Harsamna horses." (EEH 121a; L 406)

The mention of specific breeds and colors of horses indicates that horse breeding was already fairly developed by this time {1765}, and the search for a matched set of white horses, presumably for the king, points to the importance of pageantry in chariotry.

Like most Middle Bronze cities, Carchemish was defended by outer walls and an inner citadel. Little is known of its Middle Bronze history except for a few references in the Mari Archive in the early eighteenth century. Three kings of

Carchemish are known from this period: Aplahanda {1786–1766} (SHP 54, 70–2), and his sons Yatar'ami {1766–1764} and Yahdul-Lim {1764–1745} (SHP 73–4). Aplahanda was a strong ally of Shamshi-Adad in his unsuccessful war against Aleppo (SHP 71), but after his death the city seems to have become a client or even a vassal to the kings of Aleppo (SHP 72). Upon the death of Aplahanda he was briefly succeeded by his son Yatar'ami {1766–1764}, who may have been a vassal of Mari. He was followed by Yahdul-Lim {1764–1745}, who seems to have returned to the fold of the Aleppan alliance after the fall of Mari to Hammurabi {1761}. Thereafter the military history of Carchemish is unknown other than its participation as an ally-vassal of Aleppo in the defense of the city of Ursha against a siege by Hattusilis in the 1620s (SHP 74–7; see pp. 298–300).

Ebla (Tel Mardikh IIIA and IIIB)[45]

During the Middle Bronze period Ebla never achieved its former greatness or regional predominance, and little is known of its military history. The best-documented ruler was Mekum, the king (ensi) of Ebla, whose name is mentioned in an inscription of one of his governors, Ibbit-Lim {c. 2030}.[46]

As with many other cities in Syria, Ebla was conquered and destroyed at the end of the Early Bronze Age {c. 2000}, but was re-established as a major military

Figure 6: Ramparts of Middle Bronze Age Ebla, Syria {c. 2000–1800}. These earthen ramparts were originally surmounted by mud-brick walls and towers which have collapsed and eroded

Source: Photograph by William Hamblin.

center by the conquerors, who were either Amorites or Hurrians (HE 2:142–64; see Chapter Eleven). The new dynasty at Ebla built a massive system of fortifications, some of the most spectacular of the period, with an earthen rampart 22 meters high and 45 meters thick, supported by a stone foundation and revetment. Small six-roomed tower-forts were built at regular intervals along the ramparts. The inner citadel and palace complex were also fortified and could be defended separately. A fine gate survives on the south-west of Ebla with angular entry multiple chambers faced with large stone slabs (orthostats) (AS 295, 298–9; EDS 214).

Few military details are known of the history of Ebla during this period. Ebla's importance in the early Middle Bronze seems to have declined. It became a vassal of Aleppo in the wake of the imperialism of Shamshi-Adad {1776}, after which it played a minor role in Near Eastern military affairs. We know of an Indilimgur ruling around 1725, and a dynastic marriage of the daughter of the ruler of Ebla with the son of Ammi-taqumma of Alalakh. The city was destroyed in the Hittite invasions of the kingdom of Aleppo by Mursilis in the late seventeenth century (see Chapter Eleven).

CHAPTER TEN

Canaan

By the term "Canaan" I will refer to the region occupied by the modern states of Israel, Palestine, and Jordan. Unfortunately, textual and artistic evidence is limited or non-existent from Canaan during most of the Early and Middle Bronze ages.[1] We are therefore largely dependent on archaeological evidence, along with occasional notices from the texts of Mesopotamia and Egypt, for our understanding of the ancient military history of Canaan. Although archaeology can provide evidence that war existed, it cannot provide us with a full military history. The following chart (Table 10.1) outlines the basic chronological periods of Canaan,[2] with rough comparisons with contemporary periods in Egypt.

Chalcolithic {4300–3300}[3]

The Neolithic background to warfare in Canaan has been discussed in Chapter One (pp. 29–30). Two major innovations relating to military history occurred during the Canaanite Chalcolithic period: the introduction of metallurgy and the rise of political units known by anthropologists as chiefdoms. The term Chalcolithic

Table 10.1 Simplified archaeological chronology of Canaan

Period	Phase	Date	Egyptian periods
Epi-Paleolithic (Mesolithic)	Natufian	10,500–8500	
Neolithic	Pre-Pottery A	8500–7500	
	Pre-Pottery B	7500–6000	
	Pottery A	6000–5000	
	Pottery B	5000–4300	
Chalcolithic	Ghassulian	4300–3300	
Early Bronze	I	3300–3050	Pre-Dynastic
	II	3050–2700	Early Dynastic
	III	2700–2300	Old Kingdom
Middle Bronze	I	2300–2000	First Intermediate
	IIA	2000–1750	Middle Kingdom
	IIB–C	1750–1550	Second Intermediate

means "copper-stone" and refers to the development of early copper metallurgy which was introduced from Syria, and originally from Anatolia (see pp. 19–23). The period is often called Ghassulian, based on the largest and best-excavated site at Teleilat Ghassul (EA 5:161–3; DANE 127–8). Although copper working was known in Canaan and Jordan during the fourth millennium, it should be emphasized that most tools and weapons continued to be made of stone. Copper should be seen more like a valuable commodity such as gold, rather than a day-to-day metal for use by ordinary people.

There are a large number of Chalcolithic settlements in Canaan, indicating rising population density from the earlier Neolithic period. Many of these settlements are rather small villages, often clustering around a larger central location; this characteristic has led some archaeologists to posit the existence of chiefdoms, where a larger central city-state dominated smaller surrounding villages. It is significant to note that most Chalcolithic sites were not fortified; this does not mean that there was no military conflict during the Chalcolithic period, but probably implies that, to the extent there was warfare, it was generally of low intensity. Two temples from this period at Ein Gedi (ALB 66–8) and Teleilat el-Ghassul (EA 5:161–3) had enclosure walls which could have served as a citadel of last resort in time of war, and as a model for fortress building. At any rate, these sites demonstrate the capacity of Chalcolithic peoples to have built fortifications had they been needed.

From the military perspective the most important characteristic of the Chalcolithic period was the development of copper weapons. As noted in Chapter One, metal-working originated in Anatolia, with the earliest-known metal weapon in the world being a copper macehead dating to c. 5000 from Can Hasan in southern Anatolia (ET 125). By the fourth millennium copper-working and mace-making technology had spread to Canaan. Signs of copper-working, including copper maceheads and axeheads, have been found in the Beer Sheba region and at Teleilat Ghassul (ALB 72–3; AW 1:120), but the largest find of copper objects is from the "Cave of Treasure" in Nahal Mishmar, between Ein Gedi and Masada, south-west of the Dead Sea.[4] The weapons were cast with a sophisticated "lost wax" technique, and the copper has trace elements that show it originated in north-eastern Turkey, pointing to long-distance trade either in ore, or perhaps in the finished weapons themselves. Among 436 copper objects there are 99 mace-like objects of various types (COT 52–89; THL 74). These maces have long hollow copper shafts, ranging in length from a few centimeters to a third of a meter, ending in a metal ball and frequently with a flared disk at the top. Many have spiral or horizontal grooves. Some have rather blunt, spike-like projections (COT 53, 57, 61, 64, 83–5; THL 83); others have numerous serrated knobs (COT 89), or a flared disk alone (COT 94–7). Some scholars view these as ritual objects; others see them as weapons – of course, they may have been both.

More certainly weapons are the 249 maceheads, which lack the long copper shaft of the other mace-like objects (COT 116–31; THL 84). These maces are all smooth and polished, averaging about 5 cm high and wide, generally either spherical or pear-shaped. The vast majority are of cast copper, though some are of hematite or stone. Similar maceheads have been found at other Canaanite sites (COT 116). A few axes and spiked mace-like heads were also found (COT 98–9, 112; AW 1:126). Additionally the cave contained a number of copper standards which were placed on wooden or reed poles and carried in procession (COT 40–51, 100–3). It is not clear if the standards were designed for religious purposes or were a type of clan totem carried in battle, such as were found among the Pre-Dynastic Egyptians as depicted on the Narmer Palette (TEM 27, 37, 40). The presence of nearly 250 maceheads along with another hundred mace-like objects implies a strong militant component in Chalcolithic culture. According to the proportion of archaeological finds, the mace remained the primary melee weapon during the Chalcolithic and Early Bronze I periods, after which it rapidly decreased in importance (MW 1:173–4), being replaced by daggers, spears, and axes.

The Ghassulian Chalcolithic Age ended rather abruptly around 3300. Many of the most important sites were abandoned and remained unoccupied. It is often speculated that the large copper hoard found at the Cave of Treasure was originally from the Ein Gedi temple, which, it is assumed, served as a religious pilgrimage site for southern Canaan (ALB 66–8; EA 2:222–3). The treasure was removed from the temple in the face of some threat, and carefully buried in the cave in Nahal Mishmar, where it remained until discovered by archaeologists five thousand years later. The assumption here is that the treasure was hidden in the hope of bringing it back to the temple; but the temple was abandoned and the treasure never returned. There is certainly a strong possibility that there was a military factor in the collapse of the Ghassulian Age, although there is little archaeological evidence for fire or other violence at the abandoned sites (ALB 88–9). Some scholars speculate about the possibility of the migration of new peoples into Canaan, again with military elements in the migration, bringing with them new cultural patterns.

Early Bronze Age {3300–2300}[5]

Archaeological evidence for large-scale endemic warfare in Canaan begins in the early Bronze Age. Bronze Age Canaan is distinguished from the earlier Chalcolithic period by a number of characteristics: new styles of pottery, use of cylinder seals, changing settlement patterns, intensification of agriculture, increasing population, shifting trade patterns, and, of course, the use of bronze. Many of these developments had military significance. Intensification of agriculture and increasing population created larger cities, capable of building bigger fortifications and fielding larger armies. Broader trade connections brought cultural and technological exchange, and hence the transfer of military technology.

For the military historian, however, two characteristics are especially important. First, we see not only the spread of the use of copper in weapon making, but the development of new weapon types, including the axe, tanged daggers, and spear and javelin points.[6] The most important archaeological find of Canaanite arsenic-copper weapons comes from Kefar Monash, dating to around 2700, which reveals the standard weapons of the Early Bronze Canaanite warrior: spear and dagger (ALB 134; AW 1:42; MW). However, not all burials uniformly contain each of these weapons. Some contain only one or the other, while others contain both; a few examples of axes begin to appear as well. The dagger alone seems to be the weapon of choice for burial (MW 1:164–5). It must be emphasized that, although such arsenic-copper weapons existed, flint knives and projectile points were still widely used, indeed, probably more widely than copper (ALB 103), with copper weapons remaining "either rare or very expensive" (ABL 134). With the development of the arsenic-copper fighting axe during this period, we also see the decline in use of the copper mace, which had been the most widespread melee weapon of the Canaanite Chalcolithic (MW 1:173–4).

The second development of the Early Bronze Age is the rapid spread and improvement of fortifications (ALB 119–25; C1/2:214–18). Jericho's earlier Neolithic stone walls and tower were almost unique in Neolithic Canaan; the vast majority of pre-Early Bronze sites in Canaan were unfortified. This would imply that whatever military threat Jericho faced was intense, but local. By the Early Bronze Age military threat had become universal and constant. Although smaller villages remained unfortified, all major cities had massive stone or brick fortifications. The building of these fortifications came in two phases. The first phase of the fortification process began in Early Bronze I {3300–3050} and II {3050–2700}, when cities built defenses of simple stone walls generally 3–4 meters thick. By Early Bronze III {2700–2300}, these walls had doubled in thickness to an average of 7–8 meters, and were reinforced by semi-circular or rectangular towers, bastions, and fortified gates. Some of the towers were huge, reaching 10 meters thick and nearly 30 meters long. Glacis are found at many of the cities, both to strengthen the foundation of the walls and to prevent ladders and other siege equipment from being placed near the walls. The largest surviving fortifications of Early Bronze Age Canaan are found at the city of Tel Yarmut, with walls made of huge uncut stones surviving to nearly eight meters high; the original walls were even higher (ALB 119–23; EA 5:369–72). The foundations of the Early Bronze walls at Arad have also been fully excavated, including numerous projecting towers (EA 1:169–74).

Although the cities of Early Bronze Age Canaan shared a single material culture, it seems that they were politically divided into about two dozen rival city-states.[7] The largest Early Bronze Age cities of Canaan ranged in size from 8 to 22 acres, with populations probably ranging from 2000 to 5000 people per city (ALB 111–13). This would give a maximum fighting force of between 500 and 1000 men per city-state. However, most cities seem to have been supported by a number of surrounding farming villages, which could double or even triple the overall population, and hence the potential military force, of any given city-state. Realistically the Canaanite city-states probably seldom fielded armies of more than 1000 men. Most armies were probably numbered in the hundreds.

While the existence of fortifications in Canaan clearly indicates the presence of conflict, it does not tell us who was involved in the conflict. A destruction layer at a site can tell us there was a war, but not who attacked. The phenomenon of the intensive fortification of Early Bronze Age city-states has been attributed to a combination of three factors: inter-city military rivalry, invasion by Egyptians, and nomadic raids. Due to the nearly complete lack of indigenous Canaanite written records or martial art during the Early Bronze Age, the military history of the Canaanite city-states cannot be fully known. A number of assumptions, however, are often made. First, it is assumed that each city-state was independent, broadly along the lines of the Greek city-state system in the fifth century BC, and in Bronze Age Syria and Mesopotamia. This would imply complex shifting patterns of alliances and confederations, with one city-state occasionally rising to temporary regional hegemony. A confederation of eight of the two dozen city-states of Canaan could possibly field armies of at most 3000–6000 men, a force large enough to threaten and conquer enemy cities.

The second source of military conflict in Canaan was military intervention from Egypt, which can be documented in a fragmentary way (ALB 105–8; ECI 24–8); these military operations will be discussed later (see Chapters Twelve, Thirteen and Sixteen for Egyptian sources discussed here). Some scholars posit a possible struggle over control of the copper resources of Sinai and southern Canaan. The earliest Egyptian kings of the First Dynasty have brief notices of campaigns against Easterners (EDE 71–4). Archaeologically, Egyptian artifacts have been found in a number of southern Canaanite towns, but these could have been introduced through trade or invasions. At Tel Erani, the largest Early Bronze site in south-western Canaan, Egyptian artifacts predominate, probably indicating permanent Egyptian occupation of the city for a century or so under Narmer and his successors {c. 3025–2915} (ALB 106–7). This city would have served as a military base for further raids and attacks, such as those carried out by king Den {2965–2915}. The Canaanite reaction to the ongoing military intervention of the First Dynasty Egyptian kings into Early Bronze I Canaan was probably a key factor in the rapid militarization and fortification of Canaan.

The military threat from Egypt decreased, but did not entirely disappear, in the subsequent centuries. The large Canaanite city of Arad was sacked and burned in around 2800,[8] possibly by Egyptian invaders. Arad's connection with the copper resources of southern Canaan and the Sinai may have made it a magnet for attack (ALB 134). The Egyptian king Peribsen {2734–2714} claims to have been the "conqueror of Canaan (*inw Stt*)" and "conqueror of foreign lands (*inw h3st*)" (ANET 228a = EDE 89–90), indicating military intervention in that region. Under Khasekhemwy {2714–2687}, Egyptian trade with Canaan seems to have begun to shift to sea-routes through Byblos, bringing declining interest and military intervention in southern Canaan.[9] None the less, massive fortification of Canaanite cities continued throughout Early Bronze III {2700–2300}; if Egyptian military intervention declined during this period, there remained other significant military threats requiring continued fortification and vigilance.

Throughout its history Canaan has been a land of mixed ecological zones with sedentary and pastoral populations. Even today, a few miles west of Jerusalem on the road to Jericho, you can find Palestinian nomads herding sheep. The Early Bronze Age was no different. While there were numerous possible shared interests – kinship, religion, economic – between nomad and farmer which might lead to cooperation, there was also stress and competition that could lead to conflict, such as competition over water or other limited resources. While it is quite certain that there were struggles between the city-dwellers and the nomads, it is likely that this rarely took the form of all the nomads uniting against all the city-dwellers. Rather, based on anthropological analogy, we can assume that nomadic clans were often related by descent, marriage, or shared interests with nearby city-dwellers; wars more probably were often fought between one city-state and its nomad kinsmen and allies, and a rival city-state and its nomad confederates. Nomadic warfare would be characterized by plundering raids; generally speaking, nomads would not besiege and assault the massive city walls of the period on their own. None the less, nomads would have been a constant and sometimes decisive element in Canaanite warfare.

Middle Bronze Age I (or Early Bronze IV) {2300–2000}[10]

Although we still have found no contemporary written records and few artistic sources from Canaan during the Middle Bronze Age, we do have increased written sources from Egypt, and, for the first time, Egyptian artistic depictions of Canaanite warriors. We are thus able to have a fuller understanding of Middle Bronze warfare.

The most striking characteristic of the shift from the Early to the Middle Bronze Age is the massive destruction and abandonment of the Early Bronze Age cities. Those large cities that were not entirely abandoned were only inhabited by scattered squatters rather than the former dense urban populations of the Early Bronze period. Most of the population of Canaan early Middle Bronze I seems to have consisted of semi-nomadic herders. There were three factors which contributed to the collapse of urban life in the early Middle Bronze Age: ecological degradation, tribal migration, and Egyptian invasion. The exact balance and interrelationship between these three factors cannot be determined, but each played a significant role. As discussed elsewhere (pp. 249–51), from an ecological point of view the twenty-third and twenty-second centuries seem to have been periods of serious crisis and drought in the Near East. This was perhaps compounded by deforestation and over-utilization of limited resources by Early Bronze cities. Cities facing decreasing productivity would be hard pressed not to attack their neighbors to resolve their crisis. Extended drought would have not only created a struggle for increasingly limited resources between cities, but would have compelled the nomads to increasing militancy as they sought for depleted water and grazing lands, culminating in tribal migration from the marginal ecologically stricken steppe country into the farmland. As nomads plundered weakly defended farming villages, the already stressed food resources of the city-states would be further depleted. Such cities might be willing to submit to a rising nomadic warlord and his confederate clans, and, in predatory fashion, join the attack on the next city-state. Some scholars see widespread nomadic migrations throughout the Near East during this period, and have associated events in Canaan with the contemporary rise to power of Amorite princes in Mesopotamia and Syria,[11] broadly paralleling much later Near Eastern migrations of nomadic Arabs, Turks, and Mongols.

The third factor in the collapse of Early Bronze urbanism was Egyptian invasion. The most striking examples of these are the five campaigns of Weni, undertaken in the late Sixth Dynasty {c. 2340}, which are discussed in detail on pp. 336–40.[12] Unfortunately, we are not told the precise chronology or the motivation for these attacks. Weni simply tells us he invaded Canaan at the head of an army of "many tens of thousands from all of Upper Egypt" along with Nubian mercenaries. This number is presumably hyperbole, but none the less Weni was probably at the head of an army which was virtually unstoppable by the Canaanite city-states. The devastation wrought by Weni is vividly described in his triumph poem:

> This army returned in safety,
> It had ravaged the Sand-dwellers' land.
> This army returned in safety,
> It had flattened the Sand-dwellers' land.
> This army returned in safety,
> It had sacked its strongholds.
> This army returned in safety,
> It had cut down its figs, its vines.
> This army returned in safety,
> It had thrown fire in all its [dwellings].
> This army returned in safety,
> It had slain its troops by many ten-thousands.
> This army returned in safety,
> [It had carried] off many [troops] as captives. (AEL 1:20)

The fundamental problem in interpreting this text is to decide if Weni is engaged in vainglorious hyperbole, or an accurate description of the actual campaign. Weni describes destroying the agricultural infrastructure, fortresses, cities, and houses, and killing or enslaving thousands. Furthermore, he engaged in five campaigns:

> His majesty sent me to lead this army five times, to attack the land of the Sand-dwellers as often as they rebelled, with these troops. I acted so that his majesty praised me [for it beyond anything]. (AEL 1:20)

If each of Weni's five campaigns conquered and sacked two Canaanite city-states, half of the land would have been left desolate. And, in fact, archaeologically, that is precisely what we see; all Early Bronze Age Canaanite cities are destroyed or abandoned within a generation or two. It is quite tempting to see Weni's campaigns – and perhaps other similar unrecorded campaigns – as a crucial factor in the collapse of Canaanite urbanism at the end of the Early Bronze Age (ECI 63–9).

The long-term result of the combination of climatic change, environmental degradation, intense competition between rival city-states, nomadic migration, and Egyptian invasions was the collapse of urban life for several centuries. On the other hand, several sites in modern Jordan – such as Iktanu (EA 3:143–4), Khirbet Iskander (EA 3:188–9), and Aroer (Ara'ir) (EA 1:177–8) – seem to have escaped this collapse. These cities show continuity in urban life between the Early Bronze and Middle Bronze Ages, with continuation of the Early Bronze tradition of massive fortification building (ALB 158). For the most part, however, fortification building disappears during the early Middle Bronze period.

This is not to say that warfare disappeared; only that it changed from city-state to nomadic clan warfare. The development of pastoralism and small village subsistence agriculture as the predominant form of social and economic organization in Canaan for several centuries was not accompanied by a loss of metallurgical skills (AW 156–7). Whether acquired by trade or indigenous manufacture, copper and bronze weapons remained important in Canaan, probably used in ongoing clan warfare between rival nomadic groups. Indeed, true tin-copper bronze alloying becomes widespread only in the Middle Bronze period. Metalworking seems to have been a specialty among some nomadic clans, one of which is depicted as migrating to Egypt to sell their metalwork (ALB 166; AW 1:166–7, 59; EWP 124). Some early Middle Bronze burial sites include copper or bronze weapons with the grave goods (MW; ALB 160, 165–6). These generally include daggers and/or spearheads, precisely the same weapons found in the panoply of Early Bronze warriors, demonstrating the continuing importance of the warrior in early Middle Bronze Canaan.

In his manual of political advice for his son Merikare, king Akhtoy of Egypt {c. 2090–2070?} gave a description of these warlike nomadic Canaanites of Middle Bronze I:

> But now, these things are said about the barbarian [nomadic] bowmen: the vile Easterner is wretched because of the place where he is – lacking in water, barren of trees, whose roads are painful because of the mountains. He has never settled in any one place, lack of food makes him wander about on foot! He has been fighting since the [mythical] Time of Horus [at the beginning of the world]. He cannot conquer; he cannot be conquered. He does not announce the day of battle, but sneaks about like a gang of thieves.... Do not worry about him! The Easterner is a crocodile on its riverbank that can snatch [his victim] from a lonely road but cannot take from the quay of a populous town. (TS 223–4 = ECI 67 = AEL 1:103–4)

Even when the cultural bias of this Egyptian view of Canaanite nomads is taken into consideration, this text none the less gives us an important insight into the nomadic warriors of Middle Bronze I: migration through barren terrain; constant raids and counter-raids, stealthy tactics in search of plunder, and the unwillingness to come to decisive battle.

In one sense, the collapse of the Early Bronze city-states strengthened the military position of the Canaanites relative to Egypt. The Early Bronze city-states of Canaan represented an ideal target for Egyptian military intervention. They were small enough that they could not single-handedly resist the overwhelming military force of an Egyptian invading army such as Weni's. On the other hand, they were large enough to provide enough potential plunder to make military action attractive to the Egyptians. The nomads of the early Middle Bronze period, on the other hand, did not have sufficient wealth to economically justify a major Egyptian attack. The costs of such a campaign to the Egyptians would outweigh any potential economic benefit from plunder. Furthermore, when faced with an invading Egyptian army, the nomads would simply practice their traditional strategy of withdrawal and dispersal, waiting for the Egyptian army to depart, after which they would return to their grazing grounds. Added to this was the problem that, during Middle Bronze I, Egypt was fragmented politically into several rival kingdoms; there were therefore no major Egyptian military expeditions during this period. Rather, as discussed on pp. 379–81, there are a number of indications that Canaanite and Sinai nomads migrated into the north-eastern delta during this period, whether as mercenaries, traders, or raiders, or simply to graze their flocks in Egyptian pastures. Rather than conquering and plundering cities in Canaan, as Weni had in the late Old Kingdom, Akhtoy III was found fighting Canaanite nomads in the delta of Egypt {c. 2025} (TS 223–4 = AEL 1:104).

Middle Bronze Age II {2000–1550}[13]

With the coming of the Middle Bronze II period we find a much richer set of sources for the military history of Canaan, with archaeology supplemented by texts and martial art, both indigenous Canaanite and Egyptian. Middle Bronze II was an era of "almost total revolution in all aspects of material culture: settlement pattern, urbanism, architecture, pottery, metallurgy, and burial customs" (ALB 175). The same is true for warfare. The most striking difference between Middle Bronze I and II is the re-emergence of a number of large cities with massive fortifications (ALB 176–81, 197–208; AW 1:65–9).[14] While most small rural farming settlements remained unprotected, nearly all large cities were strongly fortified. Most of the new fortification techniques found in Canaan seem to have been introduced from Syria, from which colonists migrated into northern Canaan and down the coast (ALB 178–9). A spreading feature of Middle Bronze II fortifications is the building of massive earthen ramparts in addition to city walls.[15] These seem to have been designed largely to prevent siege equipment from being placed against the walls, but also to raise the overall height and size of the fortifications. Other sites built large glacis to attempt to perform a similar function with less expenditure of resources (ABL 202–5). Middle Bronze Canaanite fortresses were built from stone or brick, usually with massive towers and bastions at key positions. Walls ranged from 3 to 10 meters thick and up to 10 meters high. Some sites, like Hazor, had fortified citadel and palace complexes on higher ground which could be defended independently in the event of the fall of the main city. Hazor was the largest Canaanite city-state during this period, covering an area of 80 hectares, with a potential population of 20,000. One of Hazor's kings, Ibni-Adad {c. 1770}, is known from northern Syrian texts to have been involved in international affairs there (SHP 54). City gates were strongly fortified, with long narrow hallways, chambers for guards, and huge wooden gates. A remarkable arched brick gateway survives at Dan (Figure 7; ALB 207; THL 93). By the late Middle Bronze II a standardized fortified gate begins to appear; surviving examples are found at Gezer, Hazor, Yavneh-Yam, and Shechem.[16] These new gates, sometimes called "Solomonic", were flanked by two huge towers, with guardrooms, and stairs allowing ascent to upper levels. The gatehouse was divided by pilasters into two inner chambers and had two huge wooden gates, allowing a double defense against any assault (ALB 205–8). These massive fortification programs indicate that Middle Bronze II was an age of serious and sustained military threat.

Archaeologists have discovered a number of well preserved bronze weapons from Middle Bronze II which give us a good understanding of the basic Canaanite panoply of this period (MW 1:168–70; ALB 184–5, 218–19; AW 1:166–75). In addition to the spear and dagger of earlier times, the axe becomes increasingly

Figure 7 Middle Bronze Age gate at Tel Dan, Israel {c. 2000–1800}. This gate includes stone foundations, a brick arch over the gateway, thick high walls, and projecting towers flanking the gate.

Source: Photograph by William Hamblin.

prominent, as it does in late Old Kingdom and Middle Kingdom Egypt (Figure 2j–l, p. 69). This spear–axe–dagger weapon combination in tombs is not, however, universal. Some burials have only one, while others have a combination of only two of the three (MW 1:168–70). Another striking characteristic of the archaeological record is that, although the bow appears as an important Canaanite weapon in numerous Egyptian textual and artistic sources from the Middle Kingdom, arrowheads are rarely found in Middle Bronze tombs in comparison to other weapon-types (MW 1:144–6). This should alert us to the fact that weapons associated with burial practices are more concerned with social status and religious ritual than with the actual practical military usage of the living (MW 1:149–61). Likewise, perishable weapons, such as bows, will be inherently under-represented in archaeology when compared to bronze weapons.

Another development in weapons technology in Middle Bronze II is the appearance of the curved sickle-sword, or scimitar (Egyptian ḫpš) (AW 1:60–1). The origins of this weapon in twenty-first century Mesopotamia are discussed elsewhere (see pp. 66–71; Figure 2a–f, p. 67). In Palestine a single example is known from Shechem, although three such weapons were found at the royal tombs of Byblos (MA 1:142–3, 2:514; AW 1:172). Syrian or Canaanite sickle-swords may also be mentioned as plunder taken in an Egyptian raid in Syria during the reign of Amenemhet II {1929–1895} (ECI 79 n49). They are also depicted as divine weapons in contemporary Mesopotamian art (AW 1:173). Their association with royal tombs and gods has led Graham to suggest that they may have been special or even uniquely royal weapons (MW 1:170–1). A final new weapon to appear in Middle Bronze II is the almost spike-like narrow-bladed axe (Figure 2g, p. 69; AW 1:60, 174; MW 2: figs 1–4, 8, 57). Yadin suggests it originated in Mesopotamia, where it was specially designed to pierce helmets or armor (AW 1:60; MW 1:176–7); it was later traded or copied in Canaan, even though there is no evidence of armor in either Egypt or Canaan during the Middle Bronze.

Egyptian artistic sources confirm and supplement our archaeological information about Middle Bronze Canaanite dress and weapons.[17] The most famous of these is the tomb of Khnumhotep at Beni Hasan (Tomb 3), with its splendid color murals depicting the arrival in Egypt of an armed Canaanite caravan under the chieftain Abisha (AW 1:166, OHAE 192). Canaanites in Egyptian art are generally shown dressed in multi-colored kilts and tunics, but none are shown with armor or helmets. Canaanite warriors are armed with all types of Middle Bronze weapons, including bows (AW 1:166–7; EWW 38), javelins (AW 1:166–9), fighting sticks (BH 2 §15b; AW 1:159, 166–7), slings (BH 2 §5b, §15b; AW 1:159), axes (BH 2 §5b, §15b; AW 1:59, 169), large curved axes (BH1 §16; AW 1:166–9), and bronze daggers (BH 2 §5c). Many Canaanite warriors were double-armed with either a missile and a melee weapon, or with two melee weapons. These include nearly every possible combination of weapons:

- axe and fighting stick (or sling?) (BH 2 §15b)
- bow and sling (or fighting stick?) (BH 2 §5c, 1 §47)

- bow and bronze dagger (BH 2 §5c)
- sling and bronze dagger (BH 1 §47)
- bow and axe (BH 2 §5c, 1 §47; AAK 2/1.8)
- large curved axe and javelin (AW 1:169; AAK 2/1.7)
- large curved axe and axe (AW 1:169)
- bronze dagger and large curved axe (TEM 150–1)

Although no Canaanites have armor or helmets, some are shown carrying a distinctive rectangular shield with triangular indentations on the top and bottom (BH 2 §15b; EWW 38; AAK 2/1.9); only one Canaanite is shown with an Egyptian-style shield (BH 2 §5b). All Canaanites with shields are armed with axes.

Egyptian martial art depicting Canaanite warriors can be supplemented by indigenous Canaanite art from scattered scarabs, seals, and religious artifacts, much of which is stylistically strongly influenced by Egyptian, Syrian, and Mesopotamian iconography (ALB 222–3). From the military perspective, these sources often depict gods or heroic figures armed with contemporary weapons. The weapons depicted include knives (GG §7–8), bronze daggers (GG §39c[18]), axes (GG §29), and long-handled "duckbill" axes (GG §35). Some warrior-gods are double-armed with mace and axe (GG §30) or mace and sickle-sword (GG §31a). Highly abstracted and stylized depictions of the Canaanite weather-god shows him standing in the traditional pharaonic smiting pose; the weapon held by the god, if any, is unclear, but would presumably be an axe or mace (GG §32). These few examples of Middle Bronze Canaanite martial art confirm the archaeological and Egyptian data reflecting the military importance of daggers and axes. To these can be added an eighteenth century vase painting showing two Canaanite warriors in a duel with daggers (AW 1:72). Both the overall quantity and detail of art and the prevalence of martial themes greatly increase in the Late Bronze Age (GG 49–132).

Indigenous contemporary Canaanite written sources appear for the first time in the Middle Bronze Age. Unfortunately, these amount to half a dozen texts from Hazor and Gezer written in Akkadian on clay tablets, none of which contain significant military information (ALB 224). The other major possible Middle Bronze text is the Abraham tradition in the Bible. However, the use of the Bible as an historical source for the Middle Bronze Age is fraught with controversy. Interpretations range from fundamentalist views that every detail of the biblical narrative is not only historical, but inerrant, to minimalist views that nothing in the biblical accounts can be accepted as authentic history unless confirmed by non-biblical sources.[19] In many ways such debates are more about theology than history, often thinly masking a much deeper debate about the overall spiritual authenticity and authority of the Bible. None the less, similar debates have occurred in classical studies, concerning for instance the historicity of Homer's account of the Trojan War, or late Greek traditions about much earlier Greek history. The fundamental question is: how much historical credence should be placed in a late text purportedly describing events that occurred centuries earlier? This is linked to related questions concerning the reliability and durability of oral traditions. The answer is, of course, that some parts of oral traditions preserve authentic ancient information, while other parts represent later misunderstandings, accretions, conflations, or outright fabrications. The problem becomes determining which parts of the ancient tradition are authentic and which parts are inaccurate. Thus, although the biblical Abraham tradition should be approached with caution as a source for Middle Bronze warfare, it should not be ignored.

From the perspective of military history, the most interesting Abraham tradition is Genesis 14, which describes a war between rival city states in Canaan (M = MBA §24). The story is apparently a very old one, since the author of the text feels the need to repeatedly explain things to his contemporary readers (i.e. Iron Age Israelites), such as the current names for a number of the ancient place-names he uses (Genesis 14.3, 6, 7, 15, 17). Attempts to identify the kings mentioned in the story through other contemporary records have failed. In military terms the story tells of a coalition of four kings from the north (14.1), who forced a coalition of five kings of Canaan to "serve" them as tributaries for twelve years. After this, the southern Canaanite kings rebelled (14.2–4), bringing swift reprisal by way of an invasion from the army of the northern coalition. The story describes a patchwork of ethnic groups in Canaan – Rephaim, Zuzim, Emim, Horites, Amalekites, and Amorites (14.5–7) – each of whom inhabited small independent enclaves in Canaan and Transjordan, and were defeated in turn by the northern coalition. The land of Canaan is inhabited by numerous tribal groups and city-states, each ruled by an independent king (*melek*), which form into rival coalitions competing for hegemony. Defeated enemies flee and are ruthlessly hunted down (14.10); defeated cities are plundered and their inhabitants enslaved (14.11). A wealthy and powerful nomad, Abraham, whose semi-urbanized kinsman Lot is swept up in the chaos of war (14.12), calls upon his allied tribal chiefs (14.13), while mustering men from among his own tribal warriors (*ḥanīk*: "trained" or "dedicated"?) (14.14) to rescue his captured kinsman. Abraham's tribal army of 318 men was perhaps matched by similar numbers from his three allied Amorite nomadic chiefs Mamre, Eshkol, and Aner; this would give the nomads an army of 1000–1200 men, a force which was apparently strong enough to ambush and defeat the combined field armies of the four enemy kings (14.15) and free his kinsman Lot and all the other captives (14.16). A sacrifice of thanksgiving for victory in battle, along with a tenth of all the plunder, is piously offered to Melchizedek, the priest of the god El Shaddai ("God Most High"), who then blesses Abraham (14.18–19). Thereafter some of the remaining spoil is returned to its rightful owners and punctiliously divided among the nomads (14.21–24). The story makes overall military sense when compared with all the other fragmentary contemporary Middle Bronze evidence that we have. This does not, of course, prove that the story is historical – it may simply be a fictional legend with historical verisimilitude. But this obscures the real point for our purpose here; as we have seen elsewhere, ancient military fiction often tells us more about the realities of ancient warfare than the often tendentious contemporary royal propaganda inscriptions.

Biblical traditions also provide us with possible ethnographic and geographic information on the Middle Bronze Age, in the form of traditions about ancient inhabitants of Canaan who preceded the rise of Israel. These people are known as Nephalim (Numbers 13.33), Anakim (Numbers 13; Joshua 14–15), Rephaim, Emim and Horites (Deuteronomy 2:10–12). They are described as ancient, war-like, and fearsome people of great strength and size (Numbers 13.32–3). Such descriptions are believed to represent Israelite recollections of the warlike pre-Israelite peoples from perhaps the late Middle Bronze through the Late Bronze Age who built the huge ancient ruined fortresses the Israelites saw – it must be remembered that, by the time of the Israelite kingdom, some of the ruined Bronze Age cities were already well over a thousand years old.[20]

Egyptian military intervention in Middle Bronze Canaan will be discussed in detail in Chapter Sixteen. These Egyptian sources contain several striking descriptions of the warfare of Middle Bronze II Canaanites. The historicity of the Egyptian "Story of Sinuhe", like the tale of Abraham's war with the four kings, is disputed. None the less, the tale of Sinuhe is certainly contemporary with the Middle Bronze Age, and thus provides a crucial snapshot of contemporary Canaanite warfare. The broader context of the story will be discussed later (pp. 430–3); here we will only review Sinuhe's description of Canaanite arms and warfare. Sinuhe describes the military life of Amorite pastoralists in the nineteenth century:

> When the Canaanite [rulers of the city-states] conspired to attack the [nomad] rulers of the Hill-Countries, I opposed their movements. For this ruler of Canaan [Amunenshi, the tribal chief and Sinuhe's father-in-law] made me carry out numerous missions as commander of his troops. Every hill tribe against which I marched I vanquished, so that it was driven from the pasture of its wells. I plundered its cattle, carried off its families, seized their food, and killed people by my strong arm, by my bow, by my [tactical] movements and my skillful plans. (AEL 1:227)

Sinuhe also provides us with the most detailed narrative description of the arms and combat methods of an unnamed Middle Bronze Canaanite warrior, with whom Sinuhe engages in single combat; "Easterner" is an Egyptian term for Canaanites, who lived to the north-east of Egypt.

> He [Sinuhe's Canaanite enemy] raised his battle-axe [*minb*] and shield, while his armful of javelins [*nywy*] flew toward me. When I made his [missile] weapons attack me, I let his arrows pass me by without effect, one following the other. Then, [when he was out of missiles], he charged me, and I shot him, my arrow sticking in his neck. He screamed and fell on his face; I slew him with his [own] axe. I gave my war cry, standing on his back, while every Easterner [in my tribe] bellowed [in triumph]. (AEL 228)

Complementing both the archaeological and artistic data discussed above, Sinuhe's Canaanite enemy is armed with shield, axe, and multiple javelins. The warrior first engages in an exchange of missiles, after which he charges for a melee with his axe.

Another Egyptian warrior, Sebek-khu, described an undated campaign of Senwosret III {1878–1843} against Palestine:

> [After the Nubian campaign] his majesty traveled downstream [northward] to overthrow the Bedouin of Canaan. His majesty arrived at a foreign land, Shechem [*skmm*] by name.... Then Shechem fell, together with the vile Retjenu [Canaanites], while I acted as the rearguard [for the army on its return march to Egypt]. Then the soldiers joined in to fight with the Easterners [who attacked the rear of the column]. Thereupon I [personally] captured an Easterner. Then I had his weapons seized by two soldiers. There was no turning back from the fray, but my face was [always] to the fore [of the battle]. I did not show my back to the Easterner [in retreat]. (AI 120 = ARE 1:304–5)

Here we see an army from Egypt invading Canaan and sacking one of the city-states. As in the story of Abraham's war, other Canaanites wait until the Egyptian army is marching homeward, slowed down by plunder and women and children slaves. The Canaanites then ambush the Egyptians, but, unlike Abraham, their attack is thwarted by Sebek-khu's firm defense.

Like the Early Bronze Age, Middle Bronze Canaan was organized into about two dozen major city-states, each ruled by its own independent king (*melek*), and dominating the surrounding satellite agricultural villages. These city-states formed various coalitions, with shifting patterns of dominance and submission punctuated by warfare between rivals as well as battles with Syrian, Egyptian, and nomadic enemies. The names of most of these city-states, kings, and wars are lost to history. None the less, a very broad pattern can be discerned through the Egyptian Execration Texts, ritual magic designed to curse the enemies of Egypt.[21] Scholars generally think that the early Execration Texts (the Mirgissa and Berlin collections) {c. 1950} (CS 1:50–2) describe a different political situation in Canaan than the later Execration Texts (Brussels collection) {c. 1800}. The earlier texts appear to describe regions and tribes rather than towns. The later texts focus more on specific towns and individual rulers following more organized itineraries. This has led scholars to speculate that we are seeing a military transformation in these texts from domination of the region by semi-nomadic clans and their chiefs representing the type of political situation in Middle Bronze I, to the world of Canaanite city-states and kings of Middle Bronze II. This seems to confirm the evidence of archaeology concerning the domination of Canaan by nomads during Middle Bronze I and the restoration of urban life at the beginning of Middle Bronze II. What is clear is that Canaan is a land fragmented into numerous clans and city-states, and that the Egyptians felt the need to curse the lot of them: "their strong men, their messengers, their confederates, their allies, the tribesmen in Canaan, who will rebel, who will plot, who will fight, who will say that they will fight, who will say that they will rebel in this entire land" (CS 1:52). Unfortunately, the texts amount to little more than a list of place, tribal and personal names, providing no specific information about alliances or ongoing feuds. None the less, we get a quick glimpse at the complexity of Canaanite political order, with dozens of cities, kings, and tribal chiefs.

Middle Bronze IIB Canaan {1750–1550} belongs to a new phase in ancient Near Eastern military history. This period was the most dynamic in ancient Canaanite military history, in which the introduction of the chariot, composite bow and metal armor from Anatolia and Syria (see Chapter Five) revolutionized warfare, both in Canaan and throughout the Near East. During this period Canaanites first emigrated into and later invaded the Egyptian delta, creating the most powerful Canaanite military confederation of the late Middle Bronze known to the Egyptians as the "foreign rulers" or Hyksos.[22] This will hopefully be the subject of a future study.

CHAPTER ELEVEN

Anatolia

For the purposes of this study I will use the term Anatolia to describe the region more or less coterminous with the modern country of Turkey (into which Turks first migrated in the eleventh century CE). Background on Neolithic Anatolia can be found on pp. 24–7. The following chart (Table 11.1)[1] outlines the major archaeological and historical periods of ancient Anatolia.

Chalcolithic Anatolia {5500–3000}[2]

Overall the evidence for military activity in Chalcolithic Anatolia is certainly sketchy, but does fit a basically consistent pattern. The transition from the Neolithic to the Chalcolithic period in Anatolia is not only defined by the appearance of copper casting of large objects, but also by the spread of militarism. The number and size of settlements expands, as does trade and other forms of contact between city-states. Competition develops between these small city-states, culminating in the building of increasingly sophisticated fortifications, along with an increasing frequency of arsenic-copper weapons. A number of sites show evidence of destruction in war, sometimes repeatedly. Cities that are destroyed in war are

Table 11.1 Simplified archaeological chronology of Anatolia

Period	Phase	Date	Historical
Neolithic	Early Neolithic (Pre-pottery)	11,000–6500	
	Late Neolithic	6500–5500	
Chalcolithic	Early	5500–5000	
	Middle	5000–4500	
	Late	4500–3000	
Early Bronze	Early Bronze I	3000–2700	
	Early Bronze II	2700–2300	
	Early Bronze III	2300–2000	
Middle Bronze	Middle Bronze I	2000–1800	Old Hittite
	Middle Bronze II	1800–1600	
Late Bronze		1600–1200	New Hittite

rebuilt, generally with larger fortifications, indicating a perception of increasing military threat.

A number of specific sites and finds point to spreading militarism. Fortification building expands, with the best-preserved Chalcolithic Anatolian fortress at Mersin, which was strongly fortified with a wall, gate, and glacis, dating from about 4500. Storerooms near the gate had piles of sling stones ready for use by defenders of the walls, with quarters for a garrison. The fortress was destroyed in war in about 4300.[3] Arslantepe was another major site in southern Anatolia during the late Chalcolithic (EA 1:212–15). From 3300 to 3000 it seems to have been part of the Uruk expansion from Sumer, and may have been colonized in part by the Sumerians; twenty-one copper spears and daggers were found at this site. The city was violently destroyed in 3000 by a group from eastern Anatolia who rebuilt a fortified city on the ruins. A "warrior" burial at late Chalcolithic Korucutepe {3500–3000} included a copper dagger and a mace made of iron ore (ET 137). A royal tomb from about 2900 included metal weapons, with royal retainers buried alongside as human sacrifices. Thus, although a true military history of Chalcolithic Anatolia cannot be written, the evidence hints that Anatolia may have crossed the warfare threshold by the fifth millennium, and was possibly the first region in the world to do so. If so, military history can be said to begin in Anatolia.

Early Bronze Age Anatolia {3000–2000}[4]

The Early Bronze Age was a period of significant change in Anatolia. As a major source of copper and silver for the Near East, Anatolian city-states became increasingly wealthy; the famous treasures of Troy are a striking example.[5] The lack of almost any military art or written records from the Early Bronze Age makes a detailed reconstruction of a specific military history impossible, but broad general trends are clear. All major Anatolian cities of the Early Bronze Age were strongly fortified, generally with high, thick, citadel-like stone walls. This, along with arsenic-copper and eventually bronze weapons, shows the perception of serious military threat.

By the middle of the Early Bronze Age a number of city-states had risen to positions of prominence in Anatolia, including Troy (Willuša; Hisarlik) (DANE 302–3; CANE 2:1121–34) in the north-east and Beycesultan (DANE 51–2) in the south-east. Troy {level II, 2500–2300} was well fortified by a stone wall with brick superstructure, where sixteen rich treasure troves were found in Schliemann's famous excavations. Schliemann mistakenly identified this level of the city as Homer's Troy. Troy II was destroyed in war around 2300, perhaps by the invasion of the Luwians (see p. 289). Related Early Bronze fortresses were found at Poliochni on Lemnos and Emporio on Chios (C1/2:374), fleshing out our understanding of fortifications of the period, which included narrow tower-flanked gates and arrow slits (C1/2:374). In some ways these fortresses should be conceived more as palace–fortress complexes designed for the royal residence of a

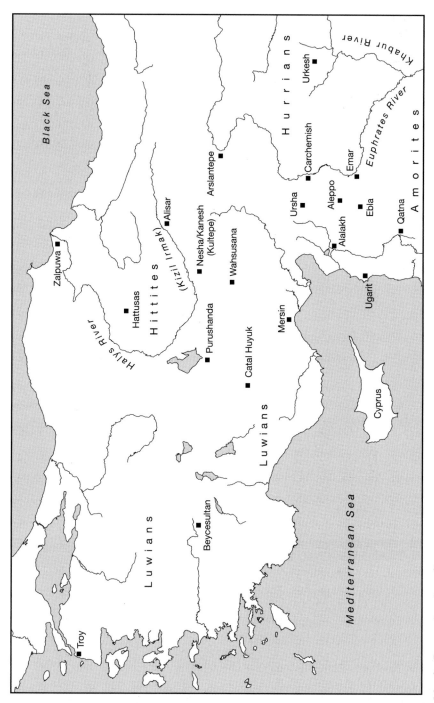

Map 3 Bronze Age Anatolia

dynasty ruling over a more rural population. The size and population of these sites tends to be limited, often measuring from 100 to 250 meters in diameter (C1/2:387). In central Anatolia Hattusas (Bogazkoy) (EA 1:333–5) – destined later to become the capital of the Hittite empire – was a major city-state in the Early Bronze period, ruled by an ethnic group known as the Hattians. Other city-states which have been excavated include Alisar (Amkuwa), Zalpa, and Kanesh (Nesha; Kultepe) (EA 3:266–8) in south central Anatolia. Demirci Hoyuk is an Early Bronze fortress city built in a circle 70 meters in diameter. The wall is of mud brick with a stone foundation, defensive ditch, fortified gates, and projecting round towers (ET 164). Overall, Anatolian Early Bronze II {2700–2300} is characterized by opulent war-like dynasties ruling strongly fortified citadels.

Weapons in Anatolia include the standard Early Bronze arsenal of dagger, spear, and axe, supplemented by stone maces (C1/2:377–8). One set of controversial artifacts, has sometimes been associated with this period. In 1959 James Mellaart claims to have been shown the so-called "Dorak Treasure", a collection of weapons that were said to have been taken from a royal grave in northern Anatolia (DANE 94–5). The weapons included the standard axes, maces, and daggers, but also included iron weapons, and short swords about 60 cm long. Mellaart produced drawings of these weapons, but the actual weapons were never photographed, nor were they ever seen again. Although Mellaart claimed they were authentic,[6] most scholars now believe the artifacts either never existed or were forgeries which the forger was planning to sell, but eventually panicked and withdrew from the market.

Early Bronze Age III {2300–2000}

The Indo-European invasions {2300–2200}[7]

The twenty-third century witnessed widespread destruction in western and southern Anatolia. Three-quarters of the Early Bronze II sites were destroyed and abandoned (C1/2:406–10). Of those sites that survived, many were greatly reduced in size, and were inhabited by peoples with new types of pottery and other material culture. Although the lack and ambiguity of evidence makes certainty impossible, many scholars associate this devastation with the migration of Indo-European peoples into Anatolia (KH 10–11). The designation "Indo-European" is a linguistic concept based on the fact that many languages spoken in India, Iran, Central Asia, and throughout most of Europe are all linguistically interrelated. It is assumed that all these languages developed from an archaic Proto-Indo-European language, and that the ancestors came from a single "homeland" generally placed north or east of the Black Sea in the fifth millennium. From there, the Indo-Europeans are thought to have migrated in all directions. In the ancient Near East Indo-European languages are found in Anatolia and Iran. There are two fundamental methodological problems relating to the study of these archaic Indo-European migrations solely from non-written archaeological evidence. First, language and ethnicity cannot be determined by material culture – that is to say, we cannot tell the language a person spoke by the type of pot or tool he used. Second, language and material culture are not coterminous – people using the same type of pot or tool may speak different languages, while people speaking the same language may use different types of pots or tools (DANE 153; EA 3:149–58).

Thus, although it is clear that there was widespread warfare and devastation in Anatolia in the twenty-third century, in the absence of written records we cannot determine with certainty the ethnicity of the peoples involved.[8] Here I will assume the theory that there was a major migration of Indo-European-speaking peoples into Anatolia in the mid-to-late third millennium. Two possible routes of a twenty-third-century Indo-European invasion are posited. One is from the Balkans into western Anatolia; this group is generally called the Luwians, assuming they are the ancestors of the Luwian ethnic group inhabiting western Anatolia in the Middle Bronze Age. Another possible route was over the Caucasus Mountains into northern Anatolia, which may have been the path of migration for the ancestors of the Hittites, who will be discussed on p. 292. From the vague evidence we have it appears that the Indo-Europeans were warlike, bronze-using, cattle-breeding peoples formed into loose tribal confederations.

From the military perspective, it is clear that there was widespread devastation in Anatolia in the late Early Bronze period, resulting in the dissolution of the old political and military order. When we begin to have the first written records in Anatolia of the Middle Bronze Age, the names of the peoples of Anatolia and the languages they speak are largely Indo-European, divided into three groups: the Luwians in the south and west, the Palaians in the north, and the Nesites in the central area around the city-state of Nesha (Kanesh), of whom the Hittites were a part (KH 10–20). In addition, the Hurrians, a non-Indo-European ethnic group, appear to have originated in eastern Anatolia. They are first mentioned in the Akkadian period {2334–2190}, when they are seen migrating southward out of Anatolia into northern Mesopotamia and Syria, quite possibly under military pressure from Indo-European migrants further to the north (see pp. 303–4).

At roughly the same time that Indo-European tribesmen were devastating much of Anatolia, the southern regions of Anatolia bordering on Syria and Mesopotamia faced invasion by the Akkadian empire. Late Mesopotamian traditions remember Sargon {2334–2279} defeating Nur-Dagan, the Anatolian king of Purushanda. Later Naram-Sin {2254–2218} fought against a rebellious coalition of seventeen kings; the list of rebel kings included Zipani, king of Kanesh and Pamba, king of Hatti, both Anatolian rulers (KH 9, 24–5). The nature of Akkadian rule in south-central Anatolia is unclear, but it appears that the Akkadians had established some type of hegemony over those regions – probably to insure access to silver and other metal resources. The overall result of the combination of Indo-European migration, Hurrian migration, and Akkadian militarism was several centuries of military anarchy in Anatolia in the late third millennium.

Though the Indo-European invaders devastated much of Anatolia, they did not completely destroy urban civilization. Though many sites were abandoned, other cities were burnt but rebuilt. The Indo-European-speaking peoples intermarried with local conquered peoples, and adopted many beliefs and practices from them, laying the foundation for the revival of large city-states and the rise of empire in the Middle Bronze period. Overall the basic pattern of scattered regional independent city-states continued.

Middle Bronze Age Anatolia {2000–1600}

By the beginning of the Middle Bronze Age a number of new city-states in central Anatolia were rising to importance, among them Nesha, Zalpa, Purushanda, Wahsusana (Nigde), Mama, and Kussara. Writing makes its first appearance in the form of an archive of Old Assyrian merchants at the city of Nesha. The key to the success of the new central Anatolian kingdoms was the two-way tin–silver trade with Mesopotamia. Anatolia was rich in silver and copper, but lacked tin, the key ingredient in bronze-making. The most reliable source of tin in that period was Afghanistan. Mesopotamian merchants, whose homeland lacked copper, silver, and tin, acted as middle-men in the tin trade, creating a "Tin Road" stretching from Afghanistan to central Anatolia. Those kings who participated in the silver–tin trade were able to receive more tin at a cheaper price. They could thereby create more bronze weapons and equip larger and better-armed armies, giving them military predominance in the region. Initially the city of Nesha controlled this trade, making it the predominant power in central Anatolia. However, the city-state destined to transform the military history of Anatolia and the Near East was Hattusas, capital of the newly rising Hittites.

Nesha (Kanesh) {2000–1750}[9]

The military history of Middle Bronze Anatolia is illuminated to some degree by the discovery of an Old Assyrian colonial archive at Nesha (Kanesh, modern Kultepe) in Anatolia. Although most of the 15,000 tablets from this archive are legal and commercial, there are a number of important military implications of this remarkable colony. In the wake of the collapse of the Ur III political order in Mesopotamia, merchants from the newly independent Assyria gained control of the rich tin trade to Anatolia, founding a merchant colony at Nesha which flourished from roughly 2000 to 1750. Twenty-one Assyrian merchant settlements are mentioned in the texts. Some, known as *karum*, were large trading colonies, while others, the *wabartum*, were apparently military garrisons assigned to secure the trade routes. These Assyrian colonies did not represent an actual military conquest by armies from Assyria, but a network of alliances and power-sharing with local Anatolian city-states, who benefited greatly by being the recipients of the Assyrian tin trade. The system was perhaps broadly analogous to the early European colonies in south Asia in the sixteenth and seventeenth centuries.

The Assyrian merchants traded tin (ultimately transshipped from Afghanistan) and Assyrian and Babylonian textiles for the gold and silver of Anatolia. The trade was undertaken by donkey caravans, taking three months for the journey from Nesha to Ashur. Over the fifty years described by the archive, 80 tons of tin was exported to Anatolia, enough to make 800 tons of bronze (KH 27); certainly not all of this was devoted to bronze weapon making, but large quantity of tin imports permitted the development of true bronze-armed armies. It is a long-standing principle of military history that, where merchants travel, armies are eventually able to follow. As we shall see, Hittite armies would eventually march along this "Tin Road" opened by Assyrian merchants and their caravans, culminating in the sack of Babylon in 1595.

The city of Nesha {level II, 1920–1850} was strongly fortified with a wall 2.5–3 kilometers long, one of "the largest in the Near East" at that time (EA 3:266). The Assyrian colonies flourished during the period covering the reign of Erishum II of Assyria through his great-grandson Puzur-Ashur II, but was destroyed around 1850 by the rival Uhna, king of the city-state of Zalpuwa (Zalpa) to the north, who may have been assisted by allies from Hattusas (CS 1:183a; KH 34). After this, the city was abandoned by the Assyrians for a number of decades.

The merchant colony was re-established {level Ib, 1810–1750} during the reign of Shamshi-Adad {1813–1781}; the control of this tin and textile trade to Anatolia may have provided an important supply of gold and silver which helped Shamshi-Adad in his remarkable conquests (see pp. 168–71). A few of the military activities of the kingdom of Nesha can be reconstructed from hints in the Assyrian merchant letters (KH 34–9). There were two kings of Nesha at this time whose names we know: Inar {c. 1810–1790} and his son Warsama {c. 1790–1775}.[10] King Inar established predominance in the region, making a number of rulers his vassals, and besieging the city of Harsamma for nine years (KH 36). Thereafter Warsama had tense relations with a rival king, Anum-hirbi of Mama, who saw himself as Warsama's equal: both are described as "kings" who ruled over "dogs" – their vassals (KH 35). These vassal kings would often raid each others' lands for cattle and other plunder. One such occasion caused Anum-hirbi to complain to Warsama of Nesha that one of Warsama's vassals had perfidiously attacked Anum-hirbi while he was engaged in warfare on another front:

> When my enemy [invaded my country and] conquered me, the Man [vassal king] of [the city of] Taisama invaded my country, and destroyed twelve of my towns, and carried away their cattle and sheep ... Did my people invade your land [as provocation for this attack], and did they kill a single [of your] ox or sheep? (KH 35–6)

The kings negotiated and agreed to "take an oath" of peace in order to "free the road" for the all-important tin and cloth trade from Asshur (KH 36). Sometime thereafter, Warsama was overthrown by an invasion by the king of Kussara, the ancestral homeland of the Hittites.

The early Hittites {2300–1600}[11]

Origin of the Hittites {2300–1900}

The basin of the Halys River (Kizil Irmak) in north-central Anatolia was known to the ancients as Hatti-land, from the name of the early non-Indo-European inhabitants, the Hattians (M = CAM 139). The Hattians, although they gave their name to the land and later empire of the Hittites, were not, in fact, the ethnic ancestors of the Hittites. Rather, sometime around 2300, Indo-European tribesmen migrated into the Halys River basin, settling among and eventually coming to dominate, intermarry with and eventually assimilate the local non-Indo-European Hattian peoples. In the process the new invaders adopted the name "the people of the land of Hatti", or Hittites (KH 16–20).

The most important kingdom of north-central Anatolia in Early Bronze III was not the eventual Hittite capital of Hattusas, but the nearby city-state of Alaca Hoyuk (DANE 9–10), which flourished in the last centuries of the third millennium {2300–2100}. The royal dynasty of the city was buried in thirteen shaft graves containing splendid treasure and numerous weapons. Finds at Alaca Hoyuk include standards with bulls, stags, and lions; these were possibly religious, but may have been military clan or regimental standards (AH 2, 17–23, §1–12). Some scholars view Alaca Hoyuk, and related sites such as Horoztepe and Mahmatlar, as Indo-European centers of power which had newly come to dominate the area (KH 12).

The conquests of Pithana and Anitta
{1775–1750} (KH 36–43)

The original homeland of the Hittite royal dynasty, however, was Kussara, a city to the south-east of their later capital at Hattusas. Our major source for this period, the Anitta inscription (CS 1:182–4; MHT 24–7), describes the rise to power of Pithana {c. 1790–1770}, king of Kussara, and his son Anitta {c. 1770–1750}, rough contemporaries of Shamshi-Adad of Assyria and Hammurabi of Babylon (KH 36–43). Kussara, the Hittite ancestral home, was a city to the south-east of Nesha on the Tin Road to Ashur. Around the year 1775, probably in an attempt to gain more control of the tin trade, Pithana . . .

> the king of Kussara came down out of the city [of Kussar] with large numbers [of soldiers] and took Nesha during the night by storm. He captured the king of Nesha [Warsama] but did no harm to any of the citizens of Nesha. He treated them [with mercy as if they were his] mothers and fathers. (CS 1:182)

By protecting the city and the Assyrian merchant class, Pithana guaranteed that the valuable tin trade would continue unabated, but with the profits in his hands.

Pithana moved his capital to Nesha, where his son Anitta built a great palace, mentioned in an inscription on a dagger (MHT 22).

When Pithana died a few years later {c. 1770} while still in the process of consolidating his new conquests, a revolt broke out in a number of his vassal cities which his son Anitta ruthlessly crushed. The major rebel cities were "devoted" to the Storm god, and were left completely desolate and depopulated, with a curse placed upon anyone who would rebuild them (CS 1:183a). Thereafter Anitta devoted himself to transforming his kingdom into an empire. His first campaign was northward against the alliance of Zalpuwa and Hattusas in the basin of the Kizil Irmak river, which had earlier sacked Nesha around 1850. It appears that Anitta was victorious, making "the sea of Zalpuwa [Black Sea] my boundary [to the north]" (CS 183a) {c. 1765?}.

It was not a decisive victory, however, for Huzziya king of Zalpuwa, and Piyushti king of Hattusas, remained on their thrones as Anitta's vassals, and quickly rebelled against him. Anitta marched north again and met the army of Piyushti of Hattusas and his vassals, forcing them to flee into Hattusas and fortify it for a siege. Zalpuwa was captured and sacked, after which Anitta blockaded Hattusas. "Subsequently, when [Hattusas] became most acutely beset with famine, the goddess Halmassuit gave it over to me, and I took it at night by storm." Anitta's revenge against this rebel vassal was again ruthless; Hattusas was sacked and sown with weeds and perpetually cursed: "Whoever after me becomes king and resettles Hattusas, let the Stormgod of the Sky strike him!" (CS 1:183b). Ironically, the city would eventually become capital of the Hittite empire.

With the north secure, Anitta turned westward against Salatiwara, whose army met Anitta in the field and was defeated and made vassal; he celebrated his triumph with a great hunt of wild boar, lions, and leopards (CS 1:183–4). With the plunder from his campaigns Anitta naturally dedicated wealth to the gods and built great temples at his capital of Nesha. He also strongly fortified the city, which became one of the great fortresses of the age (EA 3:266). Anitta's triumph was short-lived; Salatiwara revolted and marshaled his army on the Hulanna River. Anitta evaded this army, and "came around behind him [the king of Salatiwara] and [captured and] set fire to his city." Seeing their city in flames, the army of the king of Salatiwara apparently escaped with "1400 infantry and 40 teams of horses [for chariots], and [his] silver and gold" (MHT 27). This incidental reference gives us the interesting figure of 1400 men and forty chariots as the potential size of an army of a Middle Bronze Age Anatolian city-state, or about thirty-five infantrymen per chariot; it further implies that chariot warfare was a part of the Anatolian military system in the mid-eighteenth century, an issue that was discussed in Chapter Five.

Where did the king of Salatiwara go? Anitta does not say, but it is possible that he fled to his ally the king of Purushanda, a west-central Anatolian city-state near Lake Tuz, since Anitta's next campaign was an attack against that king. The king of Purushanda, however, quickly sent tokens of submission and vassalage – an "iron throne and scepter" to Anitta forestalling a major confrontation (CS 1:184b). By the end of his reign Anitta was lord over all of central Anatolia.

A period of anarchy {1750–1670} (KH 64–65)

Anitta's empire was not to last, however; around the time of his death {c. 1750?} his erstwhile vassals unanimously rose in successful rebellion. Nesha was destroyed by fire around the time of Anitta's death, and his empire collapsed, with the political order of Anatolia returning to feuding city-states. The last of the Assyrian merchant letters bemoan the toll taken on their trade by the unsettled conditions in Anatolia (KH 42), and at some point the tin trade ceased, adding economic problems to political anarchy. Hurrian peoples migrated into the south-eastern fringes of central Anatolia, while the warlike Kaska mountain tribesmen, who would later repeatedly raid and invade the Hittite empire, make their first appearance on the north-eastern frontier; the Luwians dominated the south-west. The gap of about 80 years between the death of Anitta and the rise of Labarna is essentially a blank in terms of specific military history. It seems, however, that during this period Anitta's dynasty lost control over its original city-state of Kussara, which passed into the hands of either a collateral branch of the royal family or a rival Hittite clan whose dynasty would found the Hittite empire. Kussara remained one of many petty city-states in central Anatolia until the reign of Labarna, the founder of the Hittite empire.

Labarna (Tabarna) {c. 1670–1650}[12]

When Labarna came to the throne, he was only the ruler of the city-state of Kussara, whose "land was small". During the course of his reign, Labarna claimed to have conquered seven rival city-states south of the Halys (Marrassantiya) river to the Mediterranean Sea, establishing his sons as kings in these cities (CS 1:194a). It appears that he also campaigned to the north-east of Kussara, capturing the city-state of Sanahuitta, where he also installed one of his sons as king. As he neared his death Labarna attempted to secure the succession to his throne for a son, also called Labarna, who was governor of Sanahuitta. However, a large faction at court supported a rival son, Papahdilmah, who seized the throne in a coup (CS 2:81a; KH 70–1). The details of the factional fighting or even civil war are not known, but it appears the state was split in two, with one faction ruling from Sanahuitta and the other ruling Kussara and the southern domains. This was the political situation at the succession of Hattusilis I, said to be the grandson of the first Labarna.

Hattusilis I {c. 1650–1620}[13]

Hattusilis described himself as "son of the brother of [the] Tawananna [Queen Mother]" (KH 73).[14] He also implied that he was the grandson of Labarna. The exact genealogical relationship of the Hittite royal family at this time is muddled (MHT 57). In the Wars of the Roses-style political crisis following the coup attempt by Papahdilmah, Hattusilis somehow became the prime candidate for one branch of the family, and ascended to the throne at Kussara, while a rival branch of the family under Papahdilmah (or his successor) ruled at Sanahuitta.

The military historian is fortunate to have two fairly detailed records from the court of Hattusilis – his Annals and his Testament – though, as is not unusual with ancient Near Eastern historical documents, they often create more questions than they answer. Early in his reign, perhaps in his first year, Hattusilis moved his capital from the traditional Hittite homeland in Kussara to the ancient ruined city of Hattusas (Bogazkoy), which had been destroyed and ritually cursed by Anitta a century earlier (KH 73). This city was to become the imperial capital of the Hittites for the next four centuries, and would eventually become one of the great cities of the ancient Near East, whose ruins still awe visitors today.[15] Hattusilis apparently took his throne-name at this time from the name of the city he made his new capital. The "land of the Hatti", from which is derived the dynastic name of the Hittites, occupied the region around the city of Hattusas. It is not certain why Hattusilis moved his capital. It may have been initially planned as a temporary move to be closer to the rival dynasty at Sanahuitta; on the other hand, his own hold on the throne was probably still dubious, and he may have moved to escape from the powerbase of rival political factions at the old capital of Kussara.

The first order of business upon his enthronement was to deal with the rival Hittite faction to the north.

> He [Hattusilis] marched against Sanahuitta. He did not destroy it, but its land he did destroy. I left my troops in two places as a garrison. I gave whatever sheepfolds were there to my garrison troops. (MHT 50)

Although unable to conquer his rival at Sanahuitta, Hattusilis plundered the territory, leaving the city blockaded by two garrisons and hoping to starve it into submission. His reason for not undertaking a more rigorous siege of the city was apparently a threat from the king of Zalpuwa (Zalpa) to the north, the rival of the earlier proto-Hittite king Anitta. Hattusilis destroyed and plundered Zalpuwa, taking the statues of its gods and three divine chariots captive to his royal temple at his new capital of Hattusas (MHT 50–1).

With the north secure, Hattusilis turned his attention to Syria – the first-known time a major Anatolia military power intervened outside Anatolia. At this period northern Syria was ruled by the powerful kingdom of Aleppo (Yamkhad, Halpa; see pp. 257–60). No reason is given by Hattusilis for his invasion of Syria, and perhaps none was needed. It may be, however, that Aleppo had been allied to Hattusilis' rivals for the Hittite throne, or to another of his enemies. On the other hand, he may have simply needed a new source of plunder to keep his soldiers and supporters satisfied. Whatever the motivation, the Syrian war would inaugurate a half century of Hittite military adventurism in Syria which would culminate in the sack of Aleppo {c. 1600} and Babylon {1595} by Hattusilis' grandson Mursilis. At his point, however, Hattusilis' immediate goal was more modest. He sacked one of Aleppo's vassals, Alalakh (Tell Atchana; EA 1:55–9; DANE 10–1) – leaving a precious cache of cuneiform tablets in the ruins (AT) – and plundered the surrounding countryside (MHT 51; KH 75–7).

Hattusilis' third campaign was against Arzawa, the land of the Luwians in southwestern Anatolia. There, as he was plundering the countryside, he received shocking news. The king of the Hurrians, an ally of Aleppo which Hattusilis had attacked the previous year, had invaded central Anatolia from the south-east. Hittite vassal city-states in that region, whose loyalty was nominal at best, seized the opportunity to rise in rebellion, and most of the region south of the Halys river was swiftly lost. Hattusilis retired at speed to his capital of Hattusas, where he regrouped and launched a counter-attack against the rebel cities (MHT 51).

> The Sun Goddess of Arinna put me in her lap and took me by the hand and went before me in battle. And I marched in battle against Ninassa [which had rebelled], and when the men of Ninassa saw me before them, they opened the gate of the city [and surrendered without a fight]. (MHT 51)

He subsequently attacked the cities of Ulma (Ullamma) and Sallahsuwa:

> Thereupon I marched in battle against the Land of Ulma, and the men of Ulma came twice in battle against me, and twice I overthrew them. And I destroyed the Land of Ulma and sowed weeds [as a ritual symbol of a divine curse]. I brought the [statues of the] seven gods [of Ulma as symbolic prisoners] to the temple of the Sun Goddess of Arinna.... I marched against the Land of Sallahsuwa ... and on its own it delivered itself by fire. (MHT 51–2)

The act of the city of Sallahsuwa "delivering itself by fire" apparently has reference to burning the city gates as an act of submission, thereby rendering the city indefensible (HW2 67).

By this swift response Hattusilis prevented the complete collapse of his kingdom, but his situation was still far from fully stabilized. His dynastic rival still controlled the city of Sanahuitta, which Hattusilis had blockaded four years earlier. He now undertook a full-scale six-month siege at the end of which he finally sacked the city, removing his potential rival as a possible focus for rebellion. Thereafter a number of cities submitted, and the few that still resisted were ruthlessly sacked and destroyed (MHT 52–3; KH 81–2).

With internal stability restored in Anatolia, Hattusilis undertook a second campaign against northern Syria, in which he crushed the army of the coalition of Aleppo in open battle. With the field army defeated, Hattusilis was able to conquer a number of cities in the region.

> In the following year I marched against Zaruna and destroyed Zaruna. And I marched against Hassuwa and the men of Hassuwa came against me in battle. They were assisted by [their allies, the] troops from Aleppo. They came against me in battle and I overthrew them. Within a few days I crossed the

river Puruna and I overcame [the city of] Hassuwa like a lion with its claws. And when I overthrew it I heaped dust upon it [in a ritual burial mound] and took possession of all its property and filled Hattusas with it. I entered [the city of] Zippasna, and I ascended [the walls of] Zippasna [by stratagem] in the dead of night. I entered into battle with them and heaped dust upon them.... I took possession of [the statues of] its gods and brought them to the temple of the Sun Goddess of Arinna. And I marched against Hahha and three times made battle within the gates. I destroyed Hahha and took possession of its property and carried it off to Hattusa. Two pairs of transport wagons were loaded with silver [from the plunder of the victories]. (MHT 52–4; KH 82–4)

Hattusilis' force then briefly raided crossed the Euphrates, allowing him to boast that he had surpassed the military achievements of Sargon of Akkad, who had crossed the Euphrates from the other direction, and whose martial fame was still pre-eminent 600 years after his death.

No one had crossed the Euphrates River [with an army], but I, the Great King Tabarna [i.e. Hattusilis], crossed it on foot, and my army crossed it on foot. Sargon also crossed it [600 years ago], but although he overthrew the troops of Hahha, he did nothing to Hahha itself and did not burn it down, nor did he offer the smoke [of the burning city as a sacrifice] to the Storm God of Heaven. (MHT 55; KH 84)

Hattusilis' army made no attempt at permanent occupation of Syria at this point, but, rich with plunder (MHT 54–5), withdrew back into Anatolian Hittite territory. Although he had devastated part of the kingdom of Aleppo, and defeated their army in battle, he had not decisively defeated them nor taken their strongly fortified capital. Unfortunately his detailed Annals end at this point and we are left with only vague references to later campaigns against both Arzawa and Aleppo (KH 88–9). A later document, the "Alaksandu Treaty", possibly alludes to the subjugation of Arzawa late in Hattusilis' reign (MHT 89), but stalemate seems to have ensued on the Syrian frontier. Overall, Hattusilis' victories established the Hittites as the pre-eminent power in Anatolia, and one of the leading empires in the Near East, allowing Hattusilis to claim the title of "Great King" (MHT 100, 107).

Part of the reason for Hattusilis' failure to fully capitalize on his initial victories in Syria may have been factional feuding among his potential heirs, as described in his deathbed Testament (CS 2:79–81; MHT 100–7; KH 89–99). As the old king began to age, he lost control of his kingdom:

Each of his sons went to [rule] a [conquered] country; the great cities were assigned to them. Later on, however, the servants of the princes [the sons of Hattusilis] became rebellious, they began to devour their [the princes'] houses; they took to conspiring continually against their lords, and they began to shed their [lords'] blood. (CS 1:194)

One son, Huzziya, who had been made governor of Tappassanda, unsuccessfully rebelled against Hattusilis and tried to seize the throne (CS 2:80). A daughter in the capital Hattusas plotted with some of the nobility of that city to overthrow her father and place her son on the throne. She seems to have been temporarily successful, massacring her opponents in the capital, but was eventually overthrown and banished (CS 2:81). Another son, Labarna, plotted with his mother – "that snake", as Hattusilis describes her – to murder the king and seize the throne. Considering Hattusilis' record of devastation and massacre against his enemies, it is with no apparent irony that he criticises his son: "He showed no mercy. He was cold. He was heartless." Labarna's plot was exposed and he too was banished (CS 2:79–80). Despite these plots and rebellions, Hattusilis is never said to have ordered any of his children to be executed; banishment was the usual punishment.

This type of dynastic instability, presumably occurring when the Great King was either away from the capital on campaign, or mentally or physically debilitated with age, seriously undermined the military potential of the Hittites by regularly requiring the king to abandon a campaign and rush back to the capital to secure the throne. It would be a problem that would plague the dynasty throughout its history. Hattusilis finally called an assembly of all the "army and dignitaries" of the kingdom and formally adopted his grandson Mursilis as his heir: "In the place of the lion [Hattusilis] the god will establish only another lion [Mursilis]" (CS 2:80a). At the time, Mursilis was still a young man, and was placed under the regency of Pimpira, a minister, for three years (CS 2:80a; KH 101).

Hittite siegecraft: the siege of Ursha (Warsuwa) {1620s?}[16]

Although the precise date is unclear, at some point in Hattusilis' reign he undertook a major siege of the city of Ursha in northern Syria (MHT 65–6; SHP 76–7). It may have been during his second Syrian campaign, or in one of his later unrecorded campaigns. When an enemy army invaded, some cities preferred to meet the enemy in open battle rather than having their countryside ravaged while they retreated into their main fortified city (HW2 66–7; CS 1:183b). Other cities, seeing no hope of victory, would simply submit without a fight and become vassals (CS 1:184b).

The city of Ursha decided to resist. It was apparently a vassal of a Hurrian king (KH 78; SHP 76), but was also in alliance with the king of Aleppo, both of whom provided support during the siege. When a siege began, the besieger would build a fortified and entrenched camp near the city (HW2 67). Thereafter a siege ramp was constructed, providing access to the upper walls for battering rams and siege towers (HW2 67–8). A later literary account describes some of the events surrounding the siege of Ursha, giving us insight into the nature of Middle Bronze siegecraft. The first part of the text is lost, and the account begins in the middle of the siege:

The [defenders of Ursha] broke the [Hittite] battering ram. The king [Hattusilis] was angry and his face was grim: "They constantly bring me bad news; may the Weather-god carry you away in a flood! Be not idle! Make a [new] battering-ram in the Hurrian manner and let it be brought into place. Make a 'mountain' [siege-ramp] and let it also be set in its place. Hew a great battering-ram from the [large trees in the] mountains of Hassu and let it be brought into place. Begin to heap up earth [into an assault ramp]. When you have finished let everyone take post. Only let the enemy give battle, then his plans will be confounded." (GH 148)

It is not clear why the first battering ram broke; it could have been destroyed by a sortie from Ursha, but it seems that it was poorly made out of inferior materials. Hattusilis therefore ordered a new ram constructed "in the Hurrian manner", implying that Hurrian and Mesopotamian siege technology was superior to that of the Hittites at that time. He also ordered the new battering-ram to be made from trees from the "mountains of Hassu", implying that the local trees were too small and the wood too soft to make a sturdy enough ram. There is a lacuna in the text, with some missing events, in which a Hittite ally or vassal named Iriyaya apparently failed to bring promised reinforcements. Hattusilis then complained:

Would anyone have thought that Iriyaya would have come and lied saying: "We will bring a tower and a battering-ram" – but they bring neither a tower nor a battering-ram, but he brings them to another place. Seize him and say to him: "You are deceiving us and so we deceive the king." (GH 148)

This combination of siege-ramp, tower, and battering-ram was the standard siege equipment for the Middle Bronze Age. Following another lacuna, in which the siege did not progress well, Hattusilis again berated his officers for their failures:

"Why have you not given battle? You stand on chariots of water, you are almost turned into water yourself ... You had only to kneel before him [the enemy king in Urshu] and you would have killed him or at least frightened him. But as it is you have behaved like a woman." ... Thus they [the kings officers] answered him: "Eight times we will give battle. We will confound their [defensive] schemes and destroy the city." The king answered, "Good!" (GH 148)

Despite these assurances, the siege still dragged on interminably. In the meantime, the Hittite army had not fully blockaded Ursha and the agents of allied kings – and presumably reinforcements and supplies – were continually entering the city under the eyes of the Hittite army.

But while they did nothing to the city, many of the king's servants were wounded so that many died. The king was angered and said: "Watch the roads. Observe who enters the city and who leaves the city. No one is to go out from the city to the enemy." ... They answered: "We watch. Eighty chariots and eight armies [one army for each gate?] surround the city. Let not the king's heart be troubled. I remain at my post." But a fugitive [enemy deserter] came out of the city and reported: "The subject of the king of Aleppo came in [to Ursha] five times, the subject of [the city-state of] Zuppa is dwelling in the city itself, the men of Zaruar go in and out, the subject of my lord the Son of [the Hurrian war-god] Teshub [the Hurrian king, overlord of Usha] goes to and fro." ... The king [Hattusilis] was furious. (GH 148–9)

The text ends here, but there is no evidence that Hattusilis was successful in the siege. The use of eighty chariots, ten for each of eight companies, to patrol the entrances to Ursha emphasizes that, although the Hittites seem to have inferior siegecraft at this time, they are none the less at the forefront of chariot warfare.

The weakness of Hittite siegecraft in this early period is reiterated by an examination of the overall ineffectiveness of their sieges (HW2 67–9). The siege of Harsamma by king Inar of Nesha lasted for nine years (KH 36); Sanahuitta was blockaded for four years, after which it was actively besieged for six months (MHT 52); Zalpa was besieged for two years (CS 1:182b). On the other hand, cities could fall quickly to a surprise assault, sometimes at night (CS 182–3). In comparison, sieges in the Mari documents often proceed relatively rapidly (see Chapter Eight).

Mursilis I {c. 1620–1590} (KH 101–5; SHP 80–3)

Militarily, Mursilis was one of the most successful kings of the Middle Bronze period. Unfortunately, our records for his reign are few and short. None the less, the basic outline of his campaigns can be determined. His succession to the throne seems to have been a last-minute decision by his grandfather, Hattusilis, in response to the plots and intrigues of his children (CS 2:79–81). Mursilis' father had been killed in Hattusilis' wars against Aleppo (KH 102), leaving Mursilis a minor upon his succession to the throne; he ruled for three years under the tutelage of a regent (CS 2:80a). Presumably the political instability plaguing the Hittite royal family continued in the first years of Mursilis' reign, but, if so, no records of such disturbances have been preserved. Rather, later historical recollection idealizes Mursilis' rule:

> When Mursilis was King in Hattusas, his sons, his brothers, his in-laws, his extended family members and his troops were united. They held enemy country he subdued by his might, he stripped the [enemy] lands of their power and extended his borders to the sea. (CS 1:195a)

The emphasis on "subduing" and "stripping" enemy lands "to the sea" may imply that the vassal states of Anatolia rebelled at the death of Hattusilis, requiring military campaigns to bring them back into submission, extending Hittite borders back to both the Mediterranean and Black Seas.

Upon subduing any last rivals for the throne and restoring order in Anatolia, Mursilis, by now probably in his twenties, turned his attention to the unfinished conquest of Syria, which had been begun by his grandfather and father.

> Mursilis set out against Aleppo to avenge his father's blood [who had earlier been killed in a war with Aleppo]. Hattusilis had assigned Aleppo to his son [Mursilis' father] to deal with. And to him [Mursilis] the king of Aleppo made atonement. (KH 102)

This laconic text leaves many questions unanswered, but it appears that in his old age Hattusilis had ordered his unnamed son – Mursilis' father – to continue the wars against Aleppo. While on one of these campaigns Mursilis' father was killed in battle, and, as a dutiful son, Mursilis invaded Syria on the pretext of avenging the death of his father. In the coming campaigns the king of Aleppo, whose kingdom had been devastated during Hattusilis' wars, finally agreed to become the vassal of Mursilis, thereby "making atonement" for the death of Mursilis' father. This state of vassalage did not last, however. Presumably at some point the king of Aleppo rebelled against Mursilis, requiring a new campaign to punish the rebellious vassal, probably around 1600, which is only briefly described in Hittite records: "Mursilis went to the city of Aleppo, destroyed Aleppo, and brought Aleppo's deportees [as slaves] and its goods [as plunder] to Hattusas" (CS 1:195a).

With all of Syria subdued, Mursilis faced two enemies to the west: the Hurrians in northern Mesopotamia and the Babylonians in central and southern Mesopotamia. Again the details are scanty, but in 1595 Mursilis marched to Babylon, and destroyed and sacked the city. On his return march he was apparently attacked by the Hurrians, but defeated them as well: "Now, later, he went to Babylon, he destroyed Babylon and fought the Hurrian troops. Babylon's deportees and its goods he kept in Hattusas" (CS 1:195a; MHT 143–5). Meso-potamian records confirm the fall of Babylon: "In the time of Samsuditana [king of Babylon], the Man of Hatti marched against Akkad [i.e. Babylon]" (MHT 143).

The capture of Babylon by Mursilis was the most audacious military achieve-ment of the Middle Bronze Age. Given the relative technological and logistical capacities of Middle Bronze armies, Mursilis' victory probably appeared to con-temporaries rather like Alexander's conquests 1300 years later. On the other hand, the long-term impact of Mursilis' conquest of Babylon was ephemeral, for he was murdered by his brother-in-law, Hantilis, in a palace coup shortly after returning to Hattusas in triumph.

> Now Hantilis was cupbearer [to king Mursilis] and he had Mursilis' sister Harapsilis for his wife. Zidanta had the daughter of Hantilis for a wife, and he plotted with Hantilis and they committed an evil deed: they killed Mursilis and shed his blood. (CS 1:195a; MHT 145)

Although his sister Harapsilis was able to seize his throne after this murder, the Hittite state collapsed into quasi-anarchy, with several successive coups; the Hittite records claim the gods abandoned these wicked Hittite kings, and "wherever their troops went on campaign they did not come back successfully" (CS 1:196a; KH 101–30). By the time that Hittite stability and military power were restored in the fifteenth century, the political situation in Syria had changed dramatically. The Kassite dynasty in Mesopotamia (DANE 164–5; EA 3:271–5) and the Hurrians of Mitanni in Syria (see pp. 303–7) became the real benefactors of early Hittite imperialism.

Hittite military ideology

The Middle Bronze Hittite records present a consistent pattern of military ideology. The Hittite king was chosen by the gods to rule the land of Hatti and subdue all enemies (KH 87–8; HW2 71–2). He was successful in battle when he properly served the gods, and was "beloved of the gods" (MHT 24, 51), but failed in battle when the gods turned against him for his sins (CS 1:195–6). Victories were won "with the help of the Sun God" (MHT 25). Hattusilis, the "Great King", was the "beloved of the Sun Goddess of Arinna"; "she put me [in her lap as her son] and took me [by the hand] and went before me in battle, granting victory" (MH 51). Hittite kings might also attack under direct oracular instructions from the gods, presumably pronounced by temple prophets. One oracle read: "the Sun goddess is sitting [on her throne in the temple] and sends out [her] messengers [the prophets to the king, saying]: 'Go to [attack] Aleppo!' " (CS 1:185a). Cities that resisted the Hittite king were resisting the gods; rebellion was tantamount to apostasy and resulted in complete devastation of a city, often with a ritual curse forbidding its future rebuilding (MHT 26; CS 1:183). This curse was symbolized by sowing the land with weeds (MHT 26), or covering the ruins with dust (MHT 53–4).[17]

In return for military victory, Hittite kings shared their plunder with the gods, just as they would with any other military ally: "I delivered [the plunder] up to the Storm God of Heaven" (MHT 25). The "deeds" of warfare and destruction are themselves "offerings" to the gods (MHT 52–3); the rising smoke of a sacked and burning city ascends to heaven like the smoke of a burnt offering on an altar (MHT 55). New temples were built by slave labor captured in war and from the plundered wealth: "whatever possession I brought home from the field [of battle] I thereby supplied [to the temples of the gods]" (MHT 27, 50–5). Part of the plunder dedicated to the gods included the images of the gods of conquered cities, which were taken captive and brought to serve the gods of the Hittites in their temples, symbolized by setting up the captured statues in subservient places in the Hittite temples (MHT 26, 51–2, 54).

Early Hittite military system[18]

While Late Bronze {1600–1200} artistic and textual sources for Hittite military history are quite rich, for the Middle Bronze period our materials are still rather scanty. While most Hittite soldiers were infantry (HW2 55–7), chariots none the less began to make an appearance in both art and texts. Middle Bronze Hittite infantry are depicted with the standard Near Eastern weapons: mace (AH §20), javelin, axe (AH §35c-d, §44; WV §29), and thrusting spear (FI §737). Some warriors are shown with helmets and shields (FI §737). From the few examples where numbers of soldiers are recorded, Hittite armies seemed to have numbered in the low thousands: numbers mentioned include 300, 700, 1400, and 3000 (HW2 72–3).

When details are mentioned, most Middle Bronze Hittite armies are described as consisting of both infantry and chariots (HW2 57–8; MHT 27; GH 149). Texts from this period mention capturing enemy chariots (MHT 54, 55); thirty chariots are part of the spoil at the fall of a city (HW2 59). One Anatolian army consisted of 1400 infantry and 40 chariots, a ratio of 1 to 35 (MHT 27). Another early Late Bronze text mentioned 200 chariots (HW2 73). Middle Bronze Hittite chariots should not be confused with the later Late Bronze chariots depicted on the famous thirteenth-century Kadesh battle-reliefs of Ramses II, which show three-man crews for many Hittite chariots (EAE 2:219–20). Contemporary depictions of Anatolian chariots show standard Middle Bronze two-horse, spoked-wheel vehicles with either one or two riders (see Chapter Five). One charioteer has an axe, while others use the bow from the chariot.[19] Horseriding was also known among the Hittites; a cylinder seal shows two helmeted men on horseback with reins; the context is apparently military, since they are accompanied by a man on foot with shield and spear (FI §737).

The importance of plunder in Hittite warfare is emphasized in many of the texts (HW2 69). When a country was first invaded, if the enemy king and his army withdrew to their citadel, the countryside was stripped of livestock and foodstuffs and small, poorly defended villages and towns were plundered (HW2 69–70; MHT 51). These captured supplies were used to feed the army during the forthcoming siege (MHT 50). People who were captured were enslaved; some were put to work at forced labor to support the army in such tasks as building a siege ramp. Others, however, were simply rounded up and deported back to the capital, creating large displaced slave populations (CS 2:195a). When a major city was captured it was looted of all valuable possessions, and frequently burned. The Hittites paid special attention to captured gold and silver, which is sometimes described in great detail in lists of plunder sent back to the capital (MHT 51–55). This plunder is naturally shared with the gods – the most important allies of the Hittite kings – and presumably with the soldiers as well, though this is generally not explicitly mentioned.

The Hurrians[20]

Early Hurrian conquests {2400–2190}[21]

The Hurrians first appear in historical records as mountain tribes of south-eastern Anatolia. From surviving linguistic evidence, philologists have determined that the

Hurrian language is non-Indo-European; they appear to be related to the later Urartians who also inhabited south-eastern Anatolia in the first millennium (DANE 311–12). Around the twenty-fourth century, Hurrian names began to appear in the records from the Khabur Triangle region of north-eastern Syria and northern Mesopotamia. It was likely that the Hurrian conquest of that region was a complex phenomenon including peaceful migration, infiltration by mercenary bands in the pay of local city-states, followed by the rise to power of Hurrian mercenary warlords over predominantly Semitic inhabitants, and culminating in the eventual full-scale migration of Hurrian herding tribes out of the mountains into the more fertile river valleys (HE2 160–4). The lack of Hurrian names at Ebla in the twenty-fourth century indicates that they were still restricted to the Khabur triangle at that time (AS 285).

Although the precise sequence of military conquests cannot be determined, dynasties with Hurrian personal names and worshipping Hurrian gods – particularly the storm god Teshub and goddess Shauskha – appear in a number of Northern Mesopotamian city-states, including Kharbe, Nagar, and Urkesh.[22] Tupkish, king of Urkesh, is the only Hurrian ruler known from this period (AS 284–5), during which Hurrians for the most part adopted the urban culture of the city-states they conquered. We have no evidence of a distinctive Hurrian military system.

Hurrian migration and domination of northern Mesopotamia and Syria was temporarily slowed during the period of Akkadian imperialism (HE2 161–3). Sargon {2334–2279} campaigned in northern Mesopotamia, probably in part against Hurrian city-states (R2:12, 15, 28–31; WH 7–8). His grandson Naram-Sin {2255–2218} also campaigned in the north, capturing a number of Hurrian city-states (R2: 91, 141; LKA 176–87; WH 8–9). The names Tahishatili of Azuhinnum and Puttim-atal appear to be Hurrian city-state rulers who were among the rebellious vassals of Naram-Sin (WH 8). Naram-Sin made the Hurrian city-state of Nagar his regional capital, where he built a large administrative palace (AS 278–81).

The second phase of Hurrian expansion {2190–1900}

The power vacuum left in Mesopotamia in the wake of the fall of the Akkadian empire in 2190 was filled in part by two non-Mesopotamian peoples: the Gutians in the south (see pp. 102–4) and the Hurrians in the north. Throughout this period Urkesh seems to have been the principal Hurrian city-state. We should not, however, think of a Hurrian "empire" during this period. Rather, there were a number of northern Mesopotamian city-states ruled by independent Hurrian dynasties, perhaps in some sort of loose confederation, sometimes allied together but sometimes feuding. We have only vague hints from scattered fragmentary records alluding to Hurrian-ruled city-states (WH 9–10). Talpus-atali ruled Nagar in the twenty-second century, one of the first independent Hurrian rulers after the fall of the Akkadians. The most important Hurrian ruler of this period was

Atal-Shen {21C}, who was king of the two major Hurrian cities of Urkesh and Nagar, and probably of other cities as well (WH 9).

Hurrian arms met a second setback during the Ur III period {2112–2004}. After the Gutian warlords had been overthrown and driven from Mesopotamia by king Utuhegal of Uruk {2117–2111}, the successor Third Dynasty of Ur attempted to expand Sumerian power into northern Mesopotamia as well. Shulgi of Ur {2094–2047} in particular is noted for his campaigns up the Tigris river, where he engaged and conquered several Hurrian cities (see pp. 109–11).[23] Lists of war-slaves obtained by the Sumerians during Shulgi's wars include numerous Hurrian names (WH 10). Shulgi's grandson Shusin {2037–2029} continued campaigning against the Hurrians in the north until his attention was diverted by the Amorite threat from the west (WH 10–11). Despite their success in the Tigris valley, neither of these two kings were able to capture the Hurrian heartland in the Khabur triangle, nor take the Hurrian's capital city of Urkesh.

In the last decades the Ur III dynasty, Hurrian fortunes revived under their great king Tish-atal {Y3 of Shusin = 2034}, who ruled from his capital Urkesh but included the cities of Nagar and Nineveh in his domain (WH 11–12). He seems to have successfully resisted further Ur III expansion into northern Mesopotamia, and wrote a temple dedicatory inscription, the oldest document in the Hurrian language:

> Tish-atal, *endan* [god-king] of Urkesh, has built a temple for [the god] Nerigal.... Who destroys it, him may [the god] Lubadaga destroy.... May the mistress of Nagar [the goddess Shauskha?], the sun-god, and the storm-god [Teshub] [destroy] him who destroys it. (WH 11)

An exasperating piece of evidence is a seal of unknown date and provenance which mentions "Tish-atal, king of Karahar [Harhar]" (WH 11). It is sometimes assumed that this has reference to the city of Harhar in western Iran, north-east of Babylon. A maximalist interpretation of this data is that the Hurrian king Tish-atal's domain included not only the Khabur Triangle and the upper Tigris valley, but also part of western Iran in the Zagros Mountains. The minimalist interpretation is either that the city is misidentified, or that the king is a later Tish-atal. Unfortunately, the issue cannot be resolved with our limited evidence (WH 11–12).

Another source has recently come to light giving us additional evidence of Hurrian militarism at the end of the Early Bronze Age. Based on a recently discovered Hurrian mythological text on the fall of Ebla, Astour sees a description of an historical war between Ebla and the Hurrian kingdom of Ikinkalish (HE2 145). In the course of the war the Hurrian god Teshub ordains the destruction of Ebla for attacking Ikinkalish and enslaving some of its citizens (HE2 142):

> I [Teshub] will smash the outer wall [of Ebla] like a goblet
> I will trample the inner wall like a heap of refuse.
> In the middle of the market I will crush the menfolk like a goblet

I will cast the incense burners of the upper city into the lower city
And cast the incense burners of the lower city into the river. (HE2 156–9)

In response to the oracle from the gods, a coalition of three Hurrian kings, Arib-Ibla, Paib-Ibla, and Eshe-pabu, gathered their armies and captured and sacked Ebla. Astour believes that the city was subsequently ruled by a dynasty of Hurrian descent (HE2 164). Others attribute this destruction of Ebla in around 2000 to the Amorites.

The subsequent history of the kingdom of Urkesh is obscure due to lack of textual sources. Based on later Hurrian traditions tracing their kingship back to Urkesh (WH 12), it is presumed that the kingdom or confederation lasted several generations. By the eighteenth century the rulers of most of the city-states in northern Mesopotamia and north-east Syria were still Hurrian.

Hurrian expansion into Syria {1900–1600}

In the nineteenth through the sixteenth centuries Hurrian names begin to appear in records throughout Syria, indicating ongoing migration. Much of this migration was probably through the peaceful movement of merchants, mercenaries, craftsmen, nomads, slaves, or farmers. There is also, however, a good deal of evidence for ongoing and increasing Hurrian militarism. During these centuries Hurrian names appear in the texts of Mari, Emar, Ugarit, and Alalakh – where 50 percent of the names are Hurrian – indicating the migration of either groups or individuals into these areas. In some of these areas Hurrians appear to have risen to positions of power; the king of Ursha in northern Syria seems to have a Hurrian name (WH 15). By the seventeenth century some Hurrian clans have also migrated as far as Canaan, where their descendants later appear as the Horites (or Hivites) of the Bible (Gen. 34.2, Josh. 9.7).[24]

Hurrians were also active on the south-eastern fringes of Hittite central Anatolia, and strongly resisted Hittite imperialism in Syria. A letter from the Nesha archive {18C} mentions a Hurrian king Anumhirbi, king of Mama, a city apparently near modern Maras in eastern Turkey (WH 12). When Hattusilis I {1650–1620} campaigned against Arzawa (south-west Anatolia), the army of "the enemy of the city of the Hurrians entered my land" and attacked him from the rear (MHT 51). Throughout the Hittite wars, the Hurrians seem to have been strong allies of Aleppo. The city of Ursha, which strongly resisted a Hittite siege by Hattusilis as described above (pp. 298–300), appears to have been ruled by a Hurrian dynasty (KH 78; WH 15). During the siege, Hattusilis ordered his soldiers to "Make a battering-ram in the Hurrian manner", indicating that he recognized the superiority of Hurrian siege technology (GH 148). On his campaign against Babylon in 1595, Mursilis mentions fighting Hurrians (CS 1:195a); he does not, however, claim to have conquered their land nor destroyed their cities. The later, more famous wars between the Hittites and the Hurrian kingdom of Mitanni were thus merely the continuation of an ongoing struggle which began in the seventeenth century.

By the late sixteenth century, the Hurrian city-state confederations of north-eastern Syria and northern Mesopotamia appear to have coalesced into a major kingdom, destined to become one of the most powerful states of the Late Bronze Age: the kingdom of Mitanni (Hanigalbat), whose capital was Washukanni.[25] During the fifteenth and sixteenth centuries the Hurrian king of Mitanni was considered the equal and rival of the other contemporary "Great Kings" of Egypt, Babylon, Assyria, and the Hittites.

CHAPTER TWELVE

Pre-Dynastic and Early Dynastic Egypt {3500–2687}

Geographical constraints on Ancient Egyptian warfare

The existence of Egypt as a coherent geographical and cultural concept is based on the interaction of the ecology of the Sahara and the Nile. The Sahara, the largest desert in the world, is capable of supporting only small foraging clans of hunters and herders. The Nile River, with its source in the rains of highland Ethiopia, transects the Sahara on its eastern edge, cutting a narrow and shallow canyon through the region (EAE 2:16–20; AAE). Before the building of the Aswan Dam the Nile flooded regularly, based on rain patterns in north-east Africa. The Nile floodplain provided a haven for animal and human life in the otherwise barren Sahara. Along with scattered oases, it is the only region in the Sahara where agriculture can flourish.[1] Thus, in the words of the fifth-century BC Greek historian Herodotus, Egypt "is a gift of the [Nile] river" (Her. 2.5). Egyptian civilization flourished in the Nile valley and surrounding oases, and was intimately tied to the Nile ecology in many ways (EAE 2:543–51).

The geographical and ecological foundation that created Egypt also set the stage for Egypt's military history. Surrounded by desert and ocean, the Nile valley of Egypt formed a coherent and highly defensible military region. Egypt is separated from the southern or Nubian Nile valley by a cataract, or rapid, at Aswan, which prevents river traffic, but which is easily bypassed by overland portage. The barrier of the First Cataract formed both the geographical and the cultural boundary between Egypt and Nubia (modern northern Sudan), and Kush (modern central Sudan) to the south. The Nile floodplain in Nubia and Kush is often too narrow and rocky in many regions to permit the same degree of intensive agriculture found in Egypt. Thus, Nubia and Kush were less densely populated than Egypt, and consequently generally less powerful economically and militarily than their northern neighbor. Although there were frequent tensions and raids on the Nubian frontier, the Nubians and Kushites were able to present a serious military threat to Egypt only when it had become internally weakened or broken into several rival states.

To the east and west, the desert regions were inhabited by nomadic peoples, but the limited population levels in these regions generally prevented them from raising military forces strong enough to pose a major military threat to Egypt as a

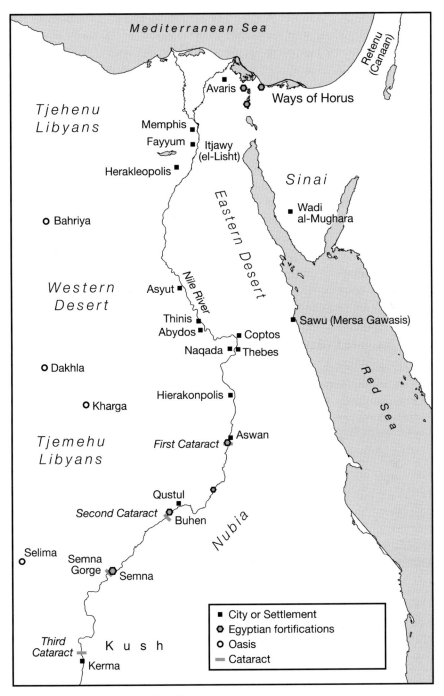

Map 4 Bronze Age Egypt and Nubia

whole. They could raid and plunder, and even do significant local damage, but could not threaten the state or conquer a united Egypt. To the north, Egypt was bordered by the Mediterranean Sea. Egypt did not face major military invasion from either the western desert or by sea until the time of the Libyans and Sea Peoples in 1190 (EAE 3:257–60), and the rise of the Libyan Twenty-second Dynasty under Sheshonq in the tenth century (EAE 3:280–1). Both of these events are outside the chronological purview of this volume.

Before the rise of the New Kingdom, therefore, Egypt faced only four potential military threats:

1   raids from the Sahara desert by Libyans;
2   the Nubian frontier beginning at Aswan, but later pushed further south;
3   the north-eastern frontier with the Sinai and Canaan;
4   internal wars when the Egyptian Nile valley was fragmented into rival states.

All of ancient Egyptian military history falls into patterns based on the shifting balance of power and fortunes of war in these four military zones of threat.

For the purposes of this study I will adopt a simplified version of the periodization schema presented in the *Oxford Encyclopedia of Ancient Egypt* (EAE 3:61–5) (see Table 12.1). Developments in early Neolithic Egypt are discussed in Chapter One.

Naqada I (Amratian), Middle Neolithic {4000–3500}[2]

Naqada (ancient Nubt), an archaeological site about 18 miles north of Luxor, was one of the most important fourth-millennium cities in Egypt, revealing a number of important early military transformations.[3] A crucial development manifest at Naqada was the rise of copper working, entailing the shift between Neolithic and

Table 12.1 Chronological periodization for Egypt

Dates	Historical period	Tool age	Material culture
To 8500		Paleolithic	
8500–5500	Prehistoric (Pre-Dynastic)	Mesolithic	
			Badarian 5500–4000
5500–3150		Neolithic	Amratian (Naqada I) 4000–3500
			Gerzean (Naqada II) 3500–3150
3150–2687	Early Dynastic	Chalcolithic "Copper Age"	
2687–2061	Old Kingdom		
2061–1569	Middle Kingdom	Bronze Age	
1589–1081	New Kingdom		
1081–332	Late Period	Iron Age	

Chalcolithic periods. Although in many respects Egypt remained a Neolithic society, with most weapons made from stone, the introduction of copper initiated a new weapons' technology that would culminate in full-fledged Bronze Age armies in the third millennium. The search for copper also contributed to an expansionistic mentality in Egyptian society. Although some copper was accessible to Egyptians in the Eastern Desert, the most important copper sources were at Wadi Maghara in the south-west Sinai, where an estimated 100,000 tons of copper was excavated throughout antiquity (EAE 1:295). Some copper was mined by local peoples and imported into Egypt in the form of flat ingots. By the Early Dynastic period, however, Egyptians began to intervene militarily in Sinai and Nubia in an attempt to access directly or even control the sources of copper mining, along with rare prestige items such as gold from Nubia and turquoise from Sinai (see pp. 317–21).[4] Thus, the increasing importance of a copper-based economy created both the demand for secure access to those resources (and hence for military intervention to control the mines), and rising military power as copper (and later bronze) became increasingly used in weapons industries (which in turn provided improved means to secure those resource centers).

The earliest method of working copper was cold hammering; eventually smelting developed and copper came to be melted and poured into stone or ceramic molds (EAE 295). Many of the earliest surviving copper artifacts are jewelry, including pins, beads, bracelets, and rings. Cold hammered copper also began to be used for tools and weapons, including surviving examples of heavy copper axes, knives and daggers, spearheads, and projectile points (EE 43, 51, 85; FP 22–3). The latter are frequently described as "harpoon tips", and may be associated with the royal ritual hippopotamus hunt (see pp. 313–4). However, such weapons could obviously also be used in war. Copper knives and axeheads are known to have been poured into molds, with their cutting edge created by hammering. As elite burials show, with the rise of proto-kingdoms (known by anthropologists as "chiefdoms") at Naqada, we find a large copper axehead in Tomb 3131 (EDE 29; FP 22).

Another development in Naqada I {4000–3500}, in part associated with the search for copper, was the rise of international trade, especially with southern Canaan and the Phoenician coast. From a military perspective, the importance of international trade is reflected in three developments. First, trade brought increasing economic specialization and contributed to the rise of social elites, and eventually of military specialists. Second, trade introduced new military resources and technologies into Egypt, such as copper for weapons and the donkey for logistics. Finally, trade brought Egypt into contact with surrounding peoples, creating zones of interaction with Nubia, Libya, and Canaan, which would culminate in international military conflict.

The gold trade with Nubia appears to have begun in the Naqada I period; the ancient name for Naqada was Nubt, meaning "Gold-[town]", with reference to its gold trade in the Eastern Desert via Wadi Hammamat. Gold – as a source of wealth and, indirectly, military power – is an important theme in Egyptian military history, and it is quite likely that part of Naqada's early wealth and military predominance was due to its access to the early gold trade.

The Naqada I period is also associated with two other social phenomena with importance for military history. Several cities in southern Egypt associated with Naqada I show an overall increase in population density – the largest towns yet discovered in Egypt during this period. Increasing agricultural surpluses and growing sedentary populations laid the manpower and resource foundations for the rise of the great protodynastic city-states which will be discussed in this chapter. Agricultural wealth could be converted into cultural predominance as well; for the first time in the Nile Valley we begin to see elements of an Egypt-wide shared material culture, as elite trade goods were transported and imitated throughout Egypt. Although Egypt still consisted politically of a number of independent proto-city-states, for the first time we can begin to speak of Egypt as a cultural entity. This process continued into the Naqada II period {3500–3150}. Finally, the egalitarian settlements of earlier periods were transformed, as control over the increasing surpluses and wealth tended to create small religious and political elites within the Egyptian proto-city-states; this process is most apparent in the building of monumental tombs adorned with rich grave goods. This is generally viewed as indicating a transition from the anthropological category of "chiefdoms" to regional city-states ruled by local independent military and hieratic elites.

Naqada II (Gerzean), Late Neolithic {3500–3150}[5]

As the small egalitarian peasant farming villages of the Nile valley grew and coalesced into larger confederations and city-states, evidence from burials demonstrates the rise of elites within Egyptian communities. These elites probably filled a number of different interrelated functions in society – religious, economic, and political. From the military perspective, however, the rise of elites coincides with the first manifestations of an ideology of militarism in Egyptian society – elites as warlords. The late Neolithic or Pre-Dynastic period in Egypt thus offers the first glimpses of military history. The lack of written sources during the Naqada II period prevents us from writing a full military history of this period. From archaeological and artistic evidence, however, it is possible to examine a number of military trends.

One clear indicator of rising militarism is the development of fortifications.[6] Expensive and difficult to construct, fortifications are generally made only when three military criteria are present. First, there must be a serious and sustained military threat. Occasional haphazard raids are generally not serious enough to merit the large-scale investment of labor and resources necessary to build fortifications. Second, there must be a non-moveable resource of sufficient value to merit the expense of fortification. In Egypt this was the development of sedentary cities that had become centers of agriculture, population, resource collection and storage, trade, manufacture of prestige products, government, and religious shrines. The aggregation of all these valuable resources in a single non-moveable center made early Egyptian cities a magnet for potential attack, necessitating vigilant defense through fortification. Finally, a society must have a sufficient labor surplus to invest the time and resources necessary to construct fortifications. Thus, the absence of fortifications does not demonstrate an absence of warfare, but the presence of fortifications is decisive evidence for serious long-term military threat; indeed, one could argue that serious and sustained military threat must pre-date the earliest construction of fortifications. The specific nature of the earliest Egyptian fortifications will be discussed in the section on Early Dynastic Egypt, at which stage the evidence becomes more abundant (pp. 325–6). However, it is clear that fortification building in Egypt began at least during the Naqada II period, as witness the mud brick defense built at the "South Town" region of Naqada (EAE 2:494).

The development of the mace is another clear indicator of the rising importance of military power.[7] Since weapons like axes and arrows have both military and non-military uses, they are not certain indicators of warfare. The mace, on the other hand, was exclusively and pre-eminently used as a weapon in archaic Egyptian warfare (BAH pl. 1). Technologically, the mace was simply a variation on the club or axe, with a heavy stone head designed for smashing rather than cutting. The earliest evidence for maces in Egypt occurs during the Naqada I period {4000–3500}. A recently discovered vase from tomb U–239 at Abydos depicts a series of warriors with pear-shaped maces herding, and perhaps dispatching, a number of prisoners (GP 79). The "Painted Tomb" (Tomb 100) from the Naqada IIc period {c. 3300} depicts a royal figure standing in a boat with a mace (GP 79). Early maces took two forms: disk-like (*mnw*) or conical, and pear-shaped (*ḥḏ*); the latter became the predominant form of the weapon.[8] By the late Naqada II period maces had become the pre-eminent symbol of kingship and military power. A large number of Pre-Dynastic maces have been discovered in tombs, and as votive gifts to the gods in temples, especially at the "Main Deposit" at the Hierakonpolis temple. Iconographically, Pre-Dynastic Egyptian kings are generally depicted carrying maces as the royal weapon, often in the famous "smiting" stance that was to be the norm in Egyptian royal martial iconography for the next three thousand years (Figure 8, p. 318; MB; PSE). Several maces are carved with scenes of the rituals of kingship that will be discussed on p. 316. Archaeologists have also discovered elegant flint knives (EE 43; AW 1:115), flint projectile points, and a copper harpoon point, presumably used for the ritual hippopotamus hunt (EE 51; EDE 216–17).

Although no detailed written records survive, the names of several legendary kings of the period are associated with the falcon war-god Horus, emphasizing their military prowess: "Horus Fights", "Horus Siezes", "Horus Decapitates" (ECI 24). The combination of archaeological and artistic evidence provides us with a broad outline of military trends during the Naqada II period. These include the spread of agriculture throughout the Nile valley, the development of increasingly large settlements, increasing contact between various regions of Egypt, and the slow adoption of a similar material culture throughout the Nile valley. During this period Egypt was divided into two major cultural regions that persist in varying degrees throughout its ancient history: Upper (southern) and Lower (northern)

Egypt. Politically and militarily, Egypt was further subdivided into a number of independent city-states, laying the foundation for the later "nomes" or provinces of Egypt.

In the late fourth millennium BC, evidence exists indicating steady expansion of the material culture (pottery and other artifacts) of the Naqada II peoples from the south into the north. It is unclear if this transition of material culture was caused by trade, peaceful migration, or conquest – or, most likely, a combination of all three. Certain sites, by fortune of geography, had superior access to trade routes and rare natural resources, which both facilitated the rise of internal elites, and provided a basis for potential military power over rival neighboring city-states. Economic competition between these city-states eventually took on military aspects, with weaker cities being exploited and eventually absorbed into larger proto-states.

Artistic sources for Late Pre-Dynastic {3500–3150} military history

Martial art provides an important source for understanding warfare in late Pre-Dynastic Egypt. The "Painted Cloth" from a tomb in Gebelein depicts the king in a martial stance harpooning a hippopotamus as part of a ritual hunt symbolizing the power of the king over the forces of chaos (EDE 33; EDE 216). The Hierakonpolis "Painted tomb" (tomb 100) shows a number of scenes of hunting, herding, and religious rituals, but includes three depictions of combat.[9] In the first (lower right) a soldier wearing an animal-skin jacket and armed with a javelin and knife fights another man with an animal-skin shield. Nearby a similarly-armed man has defeated a fallen enemy. Finally, in the lower left, the king with upraised mace in the archetypal smiting posture prepares to execute three kneeling captured prisoners.

The most detailed Pre-Dynastic artistic scene of battle is the Gebal el-Araq knife handle.[10] Here nine warriors in loincloths engage in various stages of hand-to-hand combat. Some warriors have their heads shaved, while others have long hair, apparently indicating hairstyles of the rival tribes. The scene is divided into four registers; in the upper register two soldiers armed with maces and flint knives grapple with one another. One longhaired warrior has been captured by a shaven-headed mace-wielding foe. The lower two panels show a flotilla of riverboats interspersed with corpses of slain enemies, perhaps indicating the post-combat slaughter of prisoners. This is also the first clear evidence of naval combat on rivers.

The "Hunter's Palette" is also a rich source for understanding Pre-Dynastic warfare.[11] The scene probably depicts a great hunt rather than actual combat. However, since kings can be depicted by their tribal totems in Pre-Dynastic art, it may symbolically represent combat.[12] For this discussion it will be assumed that, even if the scene depicts a pure hunting expedition, the military and hunting equipment and techniques overlapped during this period. Indeed, the palette may represent a military unit hunting while on campaign. From the military perspective we see the soldiers are all similarly dressed, wearing kilts, with some type of animal tail in the rear as adornment. Most warriors also have ostrich feathers in their hair. None carries a shield or any type of chest or leg protection. However, since the Painted Tomb demonstrates that both animal-skin jackets and shields were used in Egypt during this period, their lack of representation here may indicate that such items were not used in hunting. Most of the men in the lower column carry some type of bundle on their backs, probably a bag of supplies. The palette depicts two columns of warriors encircling antelopes, rabbits, and two lions, probably implying the use of flanking tactics. Both columns have a man with a Horus banner near the front. The upper column consists of twelve men, the lower of seven (two of whom are largely lost in a missing piece of the palette); most of the men are double-armed. Their weaponry includes: bow alone (1); bow with three arrows (1); banner with mace (1); banner and double-headed axe (1); mace and throwing stick (1); spear and fighting stick (3); spear with axe (1); bow with mace (3); spear and mace (1); lasso (2); bow with double-headed axe (1); two spears and fighting stick (1); bow and perhaps another weapon on the lost fragment (1); unknown, due to lost fragment (1). In total the nineteen men are armed with seven bows, six maces, six spears, five fighting sticks, two double-headed axes, two lassos and one axe. The presence of a man with two spears may indicate that the spears could also be thrown. Nearly all the men are thus armed with both some type of missile weapon (bow, fighting stick, and perhaps javelin), and some type of melee weapon (mace, axe, spear).

A fifth source of military information for the Naqada II period is the "Battle-field Palette".[13] This scene depicts the aftermath of the battle. In the upper register – which is fragmentary – at least three captive enemies, stripped naked with their arms bound behind their backs, are marched off the battlefield by totem standards symbolizing the victorious clans. In the lower register six enemy corpses, limbs akimbo, lie naked on the battlefield, being eaten by vultures and a lion. One of the corpses, whose eye is being eaten by a carrion bird, has his arms bound behind his back, indicating that at least some of the prisoners were executed or sacrificed after the battle.

Thus, although no precise dates, battles, or commanders can be given, the combination of several lines of convergent evidence – fortifications, elite tombs, war maces, and martial iconography – indicates that city-state-sponsored militarism had become widespread in Egypt during the Naqada II period. This process would culminate in the rise of competing regional kingdoms in southern Egypt in the Naqada III period {3150–3050}, and the military unification of Egypt around 3050.

Naqada III (Proto-Dynastic, Dynasty "0") {3150–3050}[14]

Intelligible military history of Egypt begins with wars between rival city-states of southern Egypt around 3150.[15] The sparse protohistorical evidence for this period – consisting of a few single-word inscriptions of king's names and icono-graphic representations of royal rituals and warfare – makes any interpretation of events ambiguous and dubious at best. The following reconstruction is necessarily speculative. Although the military aspects of the unification of Egypt will be the focus of attention here, it must be emphasized that this process undoubtedly included a combination of peaceful activities such as developing cultural and economic bonds, political marriages, alliances, etc.

By around 3150 southern Egypt – for which we have the most documentation in the Pre-Dynastic period – was divided into at least four independent states: Naqada (Nubt), Abydos (This), Hierakonpolis (Nekhen), and Qustul (Ta-Sety) in northern Nubia (Sudan) (M= HAAE 22–3). Each had access to trade routes for gold, stone, copper, or other important resources (EDE 36–41). The thirty-second century was one of increasing competition between these and other rival city-states. As one proto-kingdom absorbed another, its military resources concomitantly expanded, making it increasingly difficult for rivals to defeat, thus creating a type of snowball effect. This period of military competition and expansion culminated in the unification of all Egypt under Narmer, to be discussed on pp. 318–20.

The wars of unification of Egypt began with a three-way struggle between the confederations of Abydos, Naqada, and Hierakonpolis. Around 3125, king Uj[16] of Abydos was buried in the largest monumental tomb yet built in Egypt. It is often assumed that Uj had expanded his kingdom from Abydos, to the north, thereby becoming the dominant power in Middle Egypt. The extra resources obtained by this expansion permitted him to construct his monumental tomb. At the same time in the south, the kingdom of Hierakonpolis emerged victorious over the rival kings of Naqada, whose lineage disappears around 3100, probably indicating conquest by Hierakonpolis (EDE 47–8). Thus, by about 3075 two major powers had emerged in middle and southern Egypt: king Scorpion of Hierakonpolis and Uj's successor, king Ka of Abydos. These rivals soon became enmeshed in a struggle for domination of Egypt.

King Scorpion {3085?–3060?}[17]

Scorpion is known largely from the ritual scene depicted on the ceremonial "Scorpion Mace" found at a temple in his capital of Hierakonpolis.[18] The overall ceremonial context depicted on the mace-head is uncertain, but perhaps involved the ritual opening of irrigation canals, the foundation of a temple, or the *heb-sed* festival. From the military perspective the upper register is the most important. It depicts a row of captured enemy banners, from each of which hangs a dead lapwing bird. This is generally thought to depict the conquests of Scorpion, or his immediate predecessors. Included among the conquered banners is the bow symbol of Nubia, probably indicating a campaign to the south of the first cataract. One can conclude from this that there was ongoing warfare during Scorpion's reign, with substantial military success against his rivals.

Ka {3075–3050?} (EDE 57–8)

Scorpion of Hierakonpolis' great military rival was king Ka of Abydos. Seals bearing Ka's name have been discovered in the north-eastern delta. Although they could have been introduced into the area by traders, the seals may indicate some type of military intervention and perhaps the beginning of the conquest of the delta by the kings of Abydos. At some point, perhaps around 3060, Ka seems to have defeated Scorpion (or his immediate successor) and conquered his kingdom in southern Egypt. This left Ka with only one serious rival in the Nile Valley, the Nubian kings of Ta-Sety (Qustul) {3200–3000}.[19] The existence of the Pre-Dynastic Nubian kingdom of Ta-Sety in northern Sudan was virtually unknown until excavations carried out in the late 1960s and 1970s. These revealed a cemetery with about a dozen royal burials, rulers of a powerful Pre-Dynastic kingdom that was the equal and competitor of contemporary kingdoms in Egypt. Although there are a few tentative proto-hieroglyphs, written texts are lacking, making a precise reconstruction impossible. None the less, Ta-Sety shared many elements of military technology and royal military ideology with its Egyptian rivals.

As with all Pre-Dynastic Egyptian history, the details of the struggle between Ka of Abydos and the kings of Ta-Sety cannot be recovered. It appears that Ka campaigned south to the Second Cataract in Nubia, defeating the kingdom of Qustul, as memorialized by the Gebel Sheikh Suleiman monument in Nubia, which depicts a boat – presumably used for military transport – surrounded by slaughtered and captured enemies, along with proto-hieroglyphic signs of the conquered cities of Ta-Sety.[20] There is also slight evidence of a possible campaign into southern Canaan (EDE 51). By his death around 3050 Ka had conquered his major military rival at Hierakonpolis and unified all Egypt south of the delta into a single kingdom. He had probably begun the conquest of the north-eastern delta as well. The completion of his conquests of unification was to fall to his son Narmer, who founded the First Dynasty of Egypt.

Early Dynastic Egypt {3050–2687}

Sources for the military history of the Early Dynastic period are quite sparse, allowing only an uncertain reconstruction of broad patterns. None the less, there is a substantial increase of data when compared with the Pre-Dynastic period. The sources for the military history of Early Dynastic Egypt can be divided into six categories, in order of importance:

1   rock-cut victory stele;
2   annals (principally the Palermo Stone);[21]
3   military art;
4   archaeological remains of weapons and fortifications;
5   seals or other name inscriptions possibly representing the authority of the pharaoh in a particular region; and
6   later martial legends collected by Herodotus, Manetho, Diodorus, and other Classical historians.[22]

Each of these categories of evidence is fragmentary and ambiguous, creating a number of difficulties in historiographical interpretation. Although I will not endlessly use the adverb "probably", its presence should be ubiquitously assumed.

First Dynasty (Thinite) {3050–2850}[23]

Narmer/Menes {3050–3025?}[24]

Later Egyptian legend, as transmitted by the Greeks, viewed Menes as the first human ruler of Egypt who "built the city which is now called Memphis".[25] This legendary Menes is frequently identified by many scholars with Narmer, the first king of the First Dynasty.[26] The famous "Narmer Palette" shows the king – overshadowed by the falcon war-god Horus, who granted victory in battle – wearing the White and Red Crowns of both Upper and Lower Egypt (EAE 1:321–6). Narmer is depicted defeating his enemies, ritually smiting a prisoner

Figure 8   The "Narmer Palette", Hierakonpolis, Egypt {c. 3040}
Source: Cairo, Egyptian Museum CG14716; drawing by Michael Lyon.

with his mace, marching in triumph among the corpses of his enemies whose decapitated heads are placed between their legs, and capturing rival cities (symbolized by a bull smashing through city walls).[27] The symbolism of the king-as-bull is also found in the Pyramid Texts (PT 205, 409, 474, 572), in a passage which may well be describing the same mythic scenario as that depicted on the Narmer Palette. "King is the Bull ... the King has united the heavens, the King has power over the southern and northern lands ... the King has built the city of the god [Memphis?] in accordance with its proper due" (PT 319). The Narmer Palette, celebrating Narmer's military victories and prowess, is often seen as a memorial of his military unification of Egypt. At the very least, it symbolizes the ritual military prowess and activities that Egyptian kings wished to memorialize (DAE 196). Two mace heads from roughly the time of Narmer celebrate bearded captives bearing tribute to the king (EWA 5–6; FP 161).

Another memorial often associated with Narmer's campaigns is the "Cities Palette", which may depict a king's conquest of the north-west delta and Libya, with seven cities symbolically represented by walled enclosures surrounding proto-hieroglyphs for city names. Animals from tribal or city banners – representing military units – are depicted digging through the mud-brick city walls with hoes, symbolizing their assault and conquest of enemy cities. The opposite side of the palette shows rows of cattle, donkeys, and goats, probably representing the plunder from the expedition.[28]

The new unified domain of all of Egypt established by Narmer and his successors was consolidated by the creation of a new capital at Memphis, originally called *Ineb Hedj* (*inbw-ḥḏ*), or "White Fortress".[29] The construction of this fortress as the symbolic act of the primordial unification of Egypt was remembered as a fulfillment of a divine commission in later theological texts. The Shabaqa Stone explains that the king as personified by the war god Horus "stood over the land. He is the uniter of this land.... He is Horus who arose as king of Upper and Lower Egypt, who united the Two Lands in the Nome of the Wall.... There [at Memphis] was the royal fortress built at the command of [the god] Geb" (AEL 1:53). Defended by a massive mud brick wall and strategically located at the apex of the Nile delta, Memphis controlled communications and trade between southern and northern Egypt, allowing the rapid transportation of troops and supplies anywhere in the Nile valley. Memphis thus became both a symbol of the new united kingdom, as well as a practical means of militarily enforcing that unity.[30] By about 3025 Narmer's united Egypt stretched from Aswan to the Mediterranean, creating the first trans-city-state kingdom in world history. During the ensuing First Dynasty, we begin to see written language, professional administration, centralized kingship, the extension of irrigation and agriculture, mining, monumental architecture, and increasing wealth and social stratification. From the military perspective Narmer's Egypt had become the most powerful state in the world.

While the unification of Egypt solved the problem of military struggle between competing city-states in the Nile Valley that had characterized Egypt in the Pre-Dynastic period, it created new external military problems. The cultural and ethnic unity of the new state did not extend beyond the geographical boundaries of the Nile Valley, leaving three potential external enemies: Nubians to the south, Libyans to the west, and Sinai nomads and Canaanites to the east. Having completed the conquest and subjection of the independent Egyptian city-states begun by his father Ka, Narmer appears to have undertaken external campaigns against Libya and southern Palestine to secure those frontiers.[31]

Seals of king Narmer have been found at Arad, indicating that at the very least trade was occurring with Egypt. Given the fact that, for Egyptians of this period, trade, exploration, and military action were intrinsically intertwined, it is not impossible that Narmer may have campaigned in the region, establishing hegemony over Arad in southern Canaan.[32] The massive fortifications of Arad were first built in Stratum II (3000–2800), probably at least partly in response to Egyptian military threat (EA 1:169). Narmer's external campaigns may be vaguely remembered in the later legends that Menes "reigned for thirty years, and advanced with his army beyond the frontiers of his realm, winning renown by his exploits" (Man. 33).

Narmer's successors {3025–2965}

Records of the military exploits of Narmer's first four successors, if any occurred, have not been well preserved. Seals with the name of Aha {3025–3000?},[33] Narmer's son, have not been found in southern Palestine, leading some to speculate concerning a possible decline of the Egyptian presence there – though this may simply represent the vagaries of survival and discovery. Two labels, however, depict campaigns, one showing the execution of a bearded enemy (EWA 8), the other recording a campaign by Aha against the Nubians (*Ta-Sety*) (EDE 178; AE 51). Djer (Zer) {3000–2977?}[34] is noted for an expedition to Palestine,[35] – perhaps to shore up the decline of Egyptian influence there during the reign of his father – as well as a victory over the Libyans.[36] Djer's son Djet {2977–2965?} had only a brief reign, leaving his young son Den under the regency of Djer's wife Merneith – the first woman known to have ruled Egypt as regent.[37] Evidence of military activities during Djet's reign and the subsequent regency of his mother has not survived.

Den {2965–2915}[38]

Den was the second great martial king of the First Dynasty, "the preponderance of entries [in the annals of the Palermo Stone] from the reign of Den referring to military activity is particularly striking" (PS 245). Den was a long-lived ruler who during his fifty-year reign celebrated two sed festivals (DAE 256) – religious rituals of recoronation for the renewal of kingship. His military efforts were focused on the eastern desert and Canaan, commemorated by five decorative ivory panels. The most important, from a tomb in Abydos, shows the king smiting a cowering Easterner, and reads "the first time of the smiting of the east [by king Den]".[39] Others depict the destruction of fortified cities in Canaan, symbolized by a hoe breaking through a symbolic city wall surrounding the name of an enemy (EDE 156). These, or related expeditions, are also recorded in the Palermo Stone, which preserves accounts of three campaigns against Canaan over a fourteen-year period, describing the "smiting of the bowmen (*sqr 'Iwntiw*)," referring to tribes to the northeast of Egypt (PS 106, 242). The exact referent of the campaign against the "dog-[like] people" is uncertain, but probably refers to the ongoing wars with southern Palestine as well (PS 244–5). Another entry may describe the "sailing downstream [north] by boat ... and smiting of [the city] Werka" (PS 116). This brief statement highlights the importance of river transportation in Nile Valley warfare. Part of Den's royal titles included Khasty (*ḫ3sti*), with a determinative sign for "foreign desert", perhaps alluding to a campaign into the Sinai or Negev (PS 245). If so, this would anticipate the later practice of Roman emperors taking the triumphal titles of enemies or regions they had conquered. Given this emphasis of military effort, southern Canaan may have come under direct rule of Egypt during at least part of Den's reign (ECI 29–37).

Last kings of the First Dynasty {2915–2850?}

Records of military activities for the last three kings of the First Dynasty are sparse. Enedjib {2925–2900?} and Semerkhet (Semsem) {2890–2880?} made no recorded campaigns.[40] The last king, Ka'a {2880–2850?}, has an ivory rod depicting a bound nomad, which is possibly commemorative of a campaign into the Sinai or southern Canaan.[41] Thus, by the end of the First Dynasty, the basic strategic patterns associated with later Egyptian military history had already been established. Military activities focused on attacking enemies of Egypt residing in southern Canaan, Libya, and Nubia, either as punitive expeditions, plundering raids, or to defend trade and mining operations. Dealing with potential threats from these three frontiers would be a strategic constant throughout Egyptian military history.

Second Dynasty {2850–2687}[42]

Origins of the Second Dynasty {2850–2790}

Although the details of the transition between First and Second Dynasties are obscure, it seems to have been relatively peaceful. A possible attempt at usurpation by the shadowy Horus-Ba is speculated, but the first king of the Second Dynasty, Hetepsekhemwy, oversaw the burial rituals of the last king of the First Dynasty, Ka'a, indicating a regular transition of legitimacy (EDE 82–3). The history of the Second Dynasty is rather obscure, with a number of kings known only by name.

Hetepsekhemwy and Ranebi

Except for the reigns of kings Ninuter and Khasekhemwy, military events of this period are difficult to reconstruct. Hetepsekhemwy {2850–2820} is not credited with any military activities (EDE 83–4; AE 91–2), while a stele found on the desert road near Armant indicates his successor Ranebi (Nebra) {2820–2790} undertook an expedition of some sort – perhaps with a military component – to the Kharga oasis in the Western Desert (EDE 84; AE 92–3).

Ninuter

The only known military campaign of Ninuter (Ninetjer) {2790–2754} is described in the Palermo Stone for year 13 {2777}: "hacking up [the place] Shem-Ra; hacking up [the place] Ha".[43] Neither of these sites can be precisely identified. It has been speculated that Ha, meaning "North", refers to a location in the delta, and this campaign was to suppress rebellion there, which is certainly possible (EDE 85; AE 93).

It is also possible that Shem-Ra and Ha/"North" are references to southern Canaan, where archaeological evidence shows that the stone walls of the city of Arad were breached and the city sacked and burned at the end of Stratum III {c. 2800}.[44] It is possible that a rival Canaanite city-state, or even nomads, could have been responsible for the sacking of Arad around this time. But the city's massive fortifications – a 1700-meter circuit of mud-brick walls 2.5-meters thick on stone foundations, defended by several dozen projecting towers – indicate that only a determined and powerful enemy could have taken the city by assault. Given the repeated military activity of Egypt in southern Canaan, one is tempted to conclude that Arad had built its massive fortifications in defense against Egyptian incursions, but was ultimately destroyed by the Egyptians. Chronologically, the rough archaeological dating of the fall of Arad to 2800 fits into the mid-Second Dynasty in Egypt, and early in the reign of Ninuter.[45] If the Egyptians did conquer Arad, they were not able to maintain control over the region for long; the walls of Arad were rebuilt in subsequent years, which might correspond to the period of Egyptian weakness and turmoil that followed Ninuter.

Ninuter was succeeded by several obscure kings, Wadjnas (Weneg), Senedy, and possibly Nubnefer {2754–2734?}, for whom we have no recorded campaigns. It has been suggested that the succession to Ninuter was contested, and Egypt entered a period of civil strife with rival kings, which culminated in the civil war between Peribsen and Khasekhemwy (EDE 87–9).

Peribsen

The known military activities of Peribsen {2734–2714}[46] are based on several brief inscriptions in which he claims to be "conqueror of Canaan" and "conqueror of foreign lands".[47] Another small seal from the period mentions an "administrator of the foreign land", pointing to some type of officer in charge of foreign areas (EWA 24). Additionally, however, Peribsen is a unique king in Egyptian history, the only native Egyptian to have been associated with the chaos-god Seth (EAE 3:269–71; DAE 264–5). This is often interpreted to reflect a religio-political revolution of some sort during his reign, in which Egypt was split into rival factions or even separate kingdoms supporting the traditional Horus kings against the upstart radical Seth king Peribsen.[48] Details of any military activities associated with this conflict are unknown, but the struggle culminated in a civil war during the succeeding reign of Khasekhemwy.

Khasekhemwy {2714–2687}[49]

The military activities of Khasekhemwy are well documented by Early Dynastic standards. Due to the strife engendered by Peribsen's "Seth rebellion", during the early part of Khasekhemwy's reign he ruled only in southern Egypt with his capital at Hierakonpolis. The exact chronology and relative order of campaigns in his reign is unclear, but in the "year of the fighting the northern enemy" he defeated the "rebels" in the north (AE 100; EDE 91), a probable reference to the Seth king Peribsen. This delta campaigns culminated in claims of killing "47,209 northern enemies" (AE 99, MB 128, 216, TEM 45; EDE 92), a number often thought to be an exaggeration. But, exaggerated or not, it is clear that Khasekhemwy succeeded in reunifying Egypt after the troubled reign of Peribsen. Following the reunification, Khasekhemwy undertook the "humbling of foreign lands" as well (AE 100; EDE 92). Nubia was invaded, and the fragmentary remains of an inscription at a temple in Hierakonpolis list foreign countries which were apparently defeated, while another inscription mentions an office of "overseer of foreign lands", indicating that some type of direct Egyptian control may have been established outside the Nile valley (EDE 92). Maritime trade to Byblos was also renewed (EDE 92). Khasekhemwy's walls surrounding his tomb complex at Hierakonpolis provide some of the best evidence from the period for the design of fortifications. Khasekhemwy's victories, combined with a thriving economy and intense cultural and religious activity, laid the foundation for the rise of the Old Kingdom, which his son Djoser {2687–2668} was to found (see p. 329).

The Early Dynastic Egyptian military system

Organization

Only the faintest hints survive concerning Egyptian military organization in the Pre-Dynastic and Early Dynastic periods. The Early Dynastic Egyptians had a large and well-organized bureaucracy – 10,000 graves of government officials from this period have been discovered at subsidiary non-royal cemeteries near the capital Memphis (EDE 109–49). This did not necessarily translate, however, into a permanent military bureaucracy or standing army. Specific military duties and responsibilities were generally organized on an *ad hoc* basis. Officials could have concurrent economic, ceremonial, religious, administrative, and military responsibilities. This is illustrated by the most detailed funerary inscription from the Early Dyanstic period, that of of Merka {2850?} from Saqqara (EDE 148–9, AE 92).

A member of the extended royal family, Merka's offices included priest, governor of the Hare-nome, "follower of the king" – probably courtier – and "comptroller of the palace." Militarily he was "district administrator of the desert," which seems to have involved security of the frontier.

The state organized a vast system of taxation, collection, storage, manufacturing, and redistribution of food, goods and equipment, creating an unprecedented logistical foundation for military activities, one that was absent in all of Egypt's nearby military rivals during this period. Combined with its vast wealth from agricultural surplus, gold, and trade, Egypt had a significant military advantage over all her potential enemies.

Military expeditions – led by a "commander of the expedition" – were often not solely military in purpose, but rather combined exploration, trading, resource exploitation, and military functions. Titles such as "controller of the desert" or "keeper of the Canaanites" probably point to regional military frontier commanders, while the "overseer of the foreign land" was apparently the military governor of Sinai or southern Canaan (EDE 134, 143–4, 149).

Arms and armor[50]

Although we lack any detailed combat narratives from this period, we have a number of surviving weapons and combat scenes preserved in military art that provide us with a basic understanding of Egyptian military equipment. Generally speaking, Egyptian warriors are depicted as wearing a kilt, with no helmet or shield, nor any armor for chest or lower legs. The major exception to this is found in the "Painted Tomb" which shows warriors wearing animal-skin jackets and carrying a shield of animal skin (EE 36–7; AW 1:117). Melee weapons depicted in contemporary art include fighting sticks, clubs, stone-headed maces, axes, double-headed axes, spears, and daggers.

Missile weapons included bows and arrows, throwing sticks (broadly similar to boomerangs; LA 6:1299–300), and javelins. The bow during this period was relatively small, with light arrows averaging slightly under 50 cm in length; hundreds were found in leather quivers from a tomb at Saqqara. The short arrows indicated a limited draw capacity for the bows, and hence limited penetrating power. The arrows include a number of different styles with different-shaped arrow-heads made from agate, bone, and ivory; some lack fletching (AE 113–14; FP 42). The bow was also a royal weapon, as indicated by a late Second Dynasty {2700?} fragmentary temple relief from Gebelein depicting the king in martial stance carrying a bundle of four arrows in his right hand – his left hand, missing from the relief, probably held a bow (EWP 39). The mace seems to have been the preferred melee weapon, with numerous depictions of the king using it to ritually slaughter his enemies.[51]

Throughout most of the Early Dynastic period most arrow and spear-heads, axes, maces and daggers continued to be made from stone (FP 49–50; AW 1:11; TEM 29, 39). A number of copper axes and daggers survive from tomb excavations, but these were probably expensive weapons of the elite that were rarely found in the hands of the ordinary soldiers. Although the fundamental military technology of the Early Dynastic period remained Neolithic, the importance and number of copper weapons increased steadily throughout the period. Copper axes are especially prominent, with fewer daggers (EE, 85). Copper axes are found in a number of Early Dynastic burials, with an especially large hoard of copper weapons and tools from the reign of Djer {3000–2975?} (EDE 72). The search for copper also probably stimulated Egyptian military activities outside the Nile Valley. Copper sources exploited in the Early Dynastic and Old Kingdoms were found in the Eastern Desert, Sinai, and northern Nubia, each of which were zones of known Egyptian military intervention in the Early Dynastic period. The discovery of copper smelting at the Early Dynastic level at the Buhen fortification in northern Nubia demonstrates the increasing importance of copper exploitation and trade in Egyptian relations with Nubia (DAE 71). Khasekhemwy {2714–2687}, the last king of the Second Dynasty, is noted for two developments in metallurgy with military significance. He is the first Egyptian king known to have built a copper statue of himself (PS 133), which would indicate that although copper was now becoming relatively plentiful, it was still rare enough to warrant special attention in the royal annals when a statue was made of that metal. Second, the oldest surviving examples of bronze-working in Egypt – two ritual vessels found in a tomb (EAE 1:417b) – date to his reign. Thus, although Egypt could be said to have entered the Bronze Age around 2700 BC, in reality most weapons continued to be made of stone, and thus Early Dynastic Egypt was, practically speaking, a militarily Neolithic state.

Fortifications and siegecraft

Although the archaeological remains of Early Dynastic fortifications are sparse, there is sufficient evidence to show a great deal of sophisticated military engineering (EAE 2:552–9). The ongoing wars for domination within Egypt led to expanding fortification of all major cities in Egypt with increasingly massive mud-brick walls.[52] Memphis was the greatest fortress of the age, but no remains of the walls have been discovered from this period. The only surviving remains of an Early Dynastic Egyptian fortress are at Elephantine, fortifying the Nubian border. This had large, thick mud-brick walls with semi-circular projecting bastions, square towers on the corners and a fortified gate (AEA 80). In addition, it is often assumed that funerary enclosures and outer temple and palace walls paralleled the basic architecture of fortifications. The enclosure wall of Shunet el-Zebib at Abydos, and the tombs of Khasekhemwy {2714–2687} and queen Neithhotep {3000?} are well preserved.[53] The remains of some palace walls may reflect military architectural features as well (EE 58, 72–3). Hieroglyphic symbols for cities show a fortress wall with square projecting towers surrounding a glyph with the city name.[54] The importance of fortifications is emphasized by the ritual "circumambulation of the [city] wall" at Memphis, which was undertaken as part of the coronation ceremony of the kings.[55]

En Besor, in southern Palestine, was a small fortified Egyptian way station on the route to Palestine, protecting an important spring for merchants and armies crossing the Sinai (EAE 1:552–9). Art from the period depicts stylized representations of square fortresses with projecting towers. Little can be said of Early Dynastic siegecraft, but it is clear that fortresses were captured on a regular basis. Military palettes show animals – probably clan totems – assaulting the walls of cities with large triangular Egyptian hoes, presumably representing the undermining of mud-brick walls (EE 53; AW 1:122–3). As noted on p. 319, brief historical inscriptions also make mention of "assaulting" various towns, which may be a generic term for any type of siege.

The fragmentary "Cities (or Libyan) Palette", which depicts seven cities with mud-brick walls and towers being assaulted by armies represented by animals of their clan or nome totems, such as a scorpion, lion, and falcon. These animal totems wield large Egyptian agricultural hoes to undermine and destroy the brick walls of the besieged towns. As described above, it probably memorializes the Egyptian conquest of the north-western delta and parts of the Libyan desert during the Protodynastic period or the early First Dynasty {3100–3000}. Presumably, with enough time and manpower, the unbaked mud-brick walls of Early Dynastic fortifications could be undermined and breached, either forcing the city to surrender or permitting an assault to take the city by storm.

Naval warfare[56]

The importance of the Nile in the Egyptian economy and culture was associated with the very early use of river craft in Egypt. The earliest vessels seem to have been either canoes made of skins, or skiffs made of papyrus bundles; models indicate that such boats were in use by at least the Badarian period {5500–4000} (EBS 11). There are a number of artistic representations of Pre-Dynastic and Early Dynasty boats.[57] Most of these are in the context of either religious and royal processions, or the transport of gods or the soul of the king to the other world. These illustrations demonstrate that the Egyptians used multiple oars – one boat having twenty-two oars on one side (GP 154) – and a rudder; sails also appear by at least late Naqada II {c. 3200}.[58]

There are, however, two early illustrations of possible naval combat. The first is the Gebel el-Araq knife handle, which depicts boats in the background of combat by rival armies.[59] The second is from the Gebel Sheikh Suleiman monument from the Second Cataract in Nubia, which depicts a boat surrounded by corpses and bound prisoners (EDE 176–9; EBS 20). These sources, along with the Palermo Stone (PS 116), show that the transport of armies by river occurred from the very beginning of Egyptian military history; they may also illustrate the earliest actual combat aboard ships. Although a river war fleet was a crucial element in Early Dynastic Nile military power, there is no evidence of a permanent naval organization. Rather, it seems, ships were commandeered or even built as needed to serve the immediate transport and logistic requirements of the army. Naval warfare could have consisted of exchanges of missile fire as well as boat-to-boat combat; one of the figures by the boat in the Gebel Sheikh Suleiman monument has been pierced by an arrow.

Sea-going vessels are also attested to in the Early Dynastic Period, though the first recorded example of the military use of sea vessels dates to the Old Kingdom. Sea trade with Phoenician coastal cities is found as early as the Naqada II period {3500–3150}, with Byblos being especially important (EAE 1:219–21). Khase-khemwy {2714–2687} is the first king who included shipbuilding activities as a major event in his royal annals (PS 134–5 = ARE 1:64). Since artistic evidence demonstrates that Egyptians had various types of river craft for centuries, Khase-khemwy's emphasis on shipbuilding in his annals is generally associated with the sea trade to Byblos, where a stone vessel with his name was also discovered, confirming such contacts (EDE 92, 160).

By the end of the Early Dynastic period {2687} we find naval technology already being quite developed, including wooden ships with rudders propelled by multiple oars and sails. Sea-going vessels could make round-trip journeys of at least 500 miles to Byblos, and could probably go much further. In the Old Kingdom this maritime technology would be transformed into the ability to project military power hundreds of miles across the sea.

Treatment of prisoners

Iconography repeatedly shows the ritual slaughter of prisoners of war.[60] The upper register of the Battlefield Palette (EE 54, EWP 29) depicts naked prisoners of war being marched in procession. They are bound with their arms pinioned behind their backs at the elbows, a technique that appears repeatedly throughout subsequent Egyptian military art. The lower register shows the bodies of dead warriors being eaten by carrion birds and a lion. Importantly, the lower right section depicts a bound corpse being eaten by a bird, indicating that the scene shows not only the corpses of military casualties left on the battlefield, but bound prisoners who were executed after capture.

CHAPTER THIRTEEN

Old Kingdom Egypt {2687–2181}[1]

During the first millennium of its military history, Egypt continued to face its four basic military problems: potential for internal revolt, the Nubian frontier to the south, the Libyan frontier to the west, and the Canaanite frontier to the northeast. All of the military campaigns of the Old Kingdom can be related to one of these four strategic issues.

Sources

As with much of the ancient Near East, the sources for a military history of the Old Kingdom are fragmentary and unsatisfactory. Royal inscriptions give only laconic references to the king "smiting" his enemies, but can provide a rough chronology of military activity. Military art memorializing the great martial deeds of the king or his commanders is potentially a valuable source of information for the Old Kingdom. This can be organized into two types: royal temples and tombs; and the private tombs of nobles. Unfortunately, neither source is very fruitful for the Old Kingdom. For the most part, both royal and private tomb art was concerned with funerary ritual, prayers and offerings preparing the tomb's occupant for the afterlife. Kings were generally depicted as divine figures fulfilling their cosmic religious functions. From surviving architecture and fragments of murals from royal temples, however, it is clear that they once contained important reliefs of royal military campaigns broadly similar to the massive monumental military murals of the New Kingdom. Unfortunately, Old and Middle Kingdom temples were used for centuries as quarries by later builders, and only fragments of these have survived, which will be discussed in this chapter (BSMK; NEA 21–3).

The biographical inscriptions of Egyptian nobles have proven to be our most important sources for military history (EAE 1:184–9). The purpose of the auto-biographical inscriptions in ancient Egypt was threefold: first, to insure that the proper funerary rituals, offerings, and prayers were conducted; second, to describe the moral perfection of the deceased as one worthy to obtain a happy afterlife; and finally to memorialize the greatest achievements of the deceased (AEAB, 5–7). The earliest archaic prototype of the funerary autobiography is the inscription of Merka {2850?}, which amounts to little more than a list of titles including the military offices he held (EDE 148–9). More detailed autobiographies begin during the Fifth Dynasty {2513–2374} (AEAB 5–20; ARE 1:99–127). For the most part the earliest biographies contain little military information, dealing instead with ritual and courtly functions, and honors received by the deceased from the king. By the Sixth Dynasty {2374–2191}, however, some autobiographies begin to emphasize the military exploits of the deceased, providing us with the major sources of information on military campaigns and organization during the Old Kingdom.

Third Dynasty {2687–2649}[2]

Despite the cultural and architectural splendors of the beginning of the Pyramid Age, the Third Dynasty is very poorly documented in military matters. Indeed, the cultural magnificence of the Pyramid Age is based in part on the absolute military predominance Egypt had achieved during the Early Dynastic Period over any potential rival military power. The exact order and length of reigns of the kings of the Third Dynasty is only poorly understood. Whatever military activities occurred were either left largely unrecorded, or such records have perished – for example, the section of the royal annals known as the Palermo Stone dealing with Third Dynasty kings is lost. This may in part be because there were relatively few military campaigns during this era. Given the great resources and military potential of Egypt during this period, its military strength probably seemed overwhelming to its possible enemies. On the other hand, since the major royal inscriptions of this period relate to the ritual and religious functions of the kings, military matters may have been deemed unimportant for the funerary cult, and may thus be under-represented in surviving funerary evidence. It should thus be emphasized that it is likely that Third Dynasty kings undertook unrecorded military expeditions, and the picture we have of Egyptian military history is thus a minimal one.

The major source of military information is a sequence of victory reliefs and inscriptions at the Egyptian malachite, turquoise and copper-mining camp and military outpost at Wadi al-Mughara in the south-western Sinai.[3] Turquoise was a highly prized gemstone for jewelry and ornamentation (DAE 297). Copper was an increasingly important metal for tools and weapons, and was thus at least in part a military resource. The pharaohs of the Third Dynasty therefore made every effort to keep control of their mines in the Sinai, and to protect the caravan routes connecting those mines with the Nile Valley. The scarce water and food resources at Wadi al-Mughara in the Sinai meant that only a limited number of men could be maintained as a garrison in the area. It is likely that many of them served double duty as both quarry-men and soldiers.

The precise nature of the relationship between the Second and Third Dynasties is uncertain. There is some evidence that the first king of the Third Dynasty, Djoser, was the son of Khasekhemwy, the last king of the Second Dynasty from his wife Nimaathap. Whatever the exact interrelationship, there was strong continuity between the two dynasties, indicating a peaceful transition.[4]

Djoser (Netjerikhet) {2687–2668}[5] is rightly renowned for constructing the first great stepped pyramid at Saqqara. Militarily, his only major recorded expedition was to the mines at Wadi Maghara in south-west Sinai, where he claims to have defeated bedouin raiders (PSE Figure 11). His successor Sekhemkhet (Djoser-Tety) {2668–2662} recorded three expeditions to the Sinai, where stylized reliefs show the king smiting the cowering bedouins.[6] Sanakht (Nebka) {2662–2653} has two victory reliefs at Wadi al-Mughara. The first depicts the king carrying a mace, worshipping at a shrine of Horus with a banner of the wolf war-god Wep-wawet, while the second is the traditional "smiting-the-enemy" pose.[7] Huny (Qahedjet) {2653–2649}, the last king of the dynasty, probably built or expanded the fortification at Elephantine,[8] perhaps against a rising Nubian threat which would be fully faced by Sneferu, first king of the Fourth Dynasty. A statue base from an unknown king of the Third Dynasty depicts the king standing on the bearded heads of executed Canaanite war prisoners (ISP 95).

A very late Egyptian legend recorded by Manetho claims that, during the reign of a Third Dynasty king called Necherophes, "the Libyans revolted against Egypt, and when the moon waxed unseasonably, they were terrified and returned to their allegiance" (Man. 11–12). Assuming that this incident is not entirely legendary, it is not clear with which king of the Third Dynasty Necherophes should be equated. The Horus name of Djoser, Netjerikhet, is a weak possible parallel; if so, this Libyan war may refer to the final subjugation of the western delta or desert in the wake of Khasekhemwy's reunification of Egypt at the end of the Second Dynasty, described on p. 323.

Fourth Dynasty {2649–2513}[9]

Although military records for the Fourth Dynasty are still fragmentary, we begin to see, for the first time in Egyptian history, details on military affairs beyond variations of the stylized "smiting-the-enemy" motif. The transition from the Third to the Fourth Dynasty seems to have been relatively peaceful, with power passing from Huni to Sneferu, his son by a concubine Meresankh.

Sneferu {2649–2609}[10]

The founder of the Fourth Dynasty was also its greatest martial king, who was active in all aspects of Egyptian military affairs. In part this may represent the fact that we are fortunate to have Sneferu's reign relatively well preserved in the Palermo Stone and related annalistic fragments. Other kings may have been just as militarily active, but records of their campaigns, if any, are lost. None the less, Sneferu's military achievements are impressive. During his reign he campaigned against Nubia, Libya, and the Sinai, built fortifications in the north and south to strengthen the defense of Egypt, and engaged in a substantial naval building program. His military successes and expansion of trade laid the foundation for the cultural glories of his successors in the Pyramid Age.

In twelfth year of his reign {2637} Sneferu invaded northern Nubia, "smiting Nubia, bringing 7000 male and female live captives [as slaves], [and] 200,000 sheep and goats".[11] Assuming such figures are not exaggerations, this would represent a catastrophic defeat of the northern Nubians. Northern Nubia seems to have been temporarily occupied by Sneferu, for following his invasion he "built of the wall of the south" (PS 141), apparently referring to the construction or expansion of the great Egyptian fortress at Buhen.[12] At the same time Sneferu also built the "wall of the north" (PS 141), a reference to unknown fortifications on the fringes of the delta for defense against either Libyans or Canaanites. Two reliefs at the Egyptian mining outpost at Wadi al-Mughara in the Sinai show that Sneferu was also militarily active in that region, describing "Sneferu, the great god ... subjugating foreign countries".[13]

Later in his reign, in a campaign against Libya, the military pattern was the same, with Sneferu describing "what was brought [as plunder] from Libya [*Thnw*]: 1100 live captives [and] 23,000 sheep and goats".[14] Such raids against Libyans in the Western Desert were probably not uncommon during the Old Kingdom. Sneferu's brief account provides our first glimpse of the scale of such operations; the total number of Egyptian soldiers involved was probably a few thousand at most.

Sneferu also greatly strengthened the Egyptian navy, building a number of ships up to 100 cubits (c. 50 meters) long, and a fleet of "sixty 'sixteener' royal boats of cedar" – a "sixteener" probably refers to a boat propelled by sixteen oars per side.[15] A trading expedition to Byblos in Lebanon returned with forty shiploads of cedar wood for naval and building construction (PS 141; EWA 26a). Although these expeditions appear to have been solely trading voyages, there was often little distinction in the Egyptian view between military, trading, exploration, or mining expeditions; there was probably a military component to these merchant fleets, both for their protection and for "influencing" Egypt's trading partners. At the very least this incident demonstrates the development of the Egyptian navy, which by this time could man and supply a fleet of forty large ships and sail to Lebanon, foreshadowing more purely military expeditions in subsequent reigns. The full military implications of the rise of Egyptian naval power in the Mediterranean will become clearer in the reign of Pepi I in the Sixth Dynasty (pp. 336–40).

Khufu (Khnum-Khufu, Cheops) {2609–2584}[16]

As builder of the great pyramid of Giza, Khufu – better known by the Greek mispronunciation Cheops – is rightly one of the most famous kings of ancient Egypt. From the military perspective, however, he is an undistinguished successor to his martial father Sneferu. It may be that Senferu's many military victories left Egypt with a period of predominance and peace, but, whatever the reason, Khufu's reign records few military activities.

A relief at Wadi al-Maghara in Sinai describes "Khnum-Khufu, the great god smiting the nomads".[17] Another inscription records a similar expedition to the quarries at Hatnub on the west coast of the Red Sea (LHAE 249). A third expedition seems to have been undertaken to diorite quarries to the west of Abu Simbel in Nubia, perhaps indicating a continuation of the hegemony over northern Nubia that had been established by Sneferu (HAE 71; C1/2 167). We have no information during this period of the size of these mining expeditions, nor the details of their activities. In general, however, such expeditions had three major functions: protecting caravans going to and from the mines; protecting the miners and mining operations outside the Nile Valley; and undertaking punitive operations against bedouin raiders (LA 2:55–68).

Two other military artifacts from the age of Khufu merit attention: an archery scene, and the royal ship of Khufu – which will be discussed in detail on p. 366. The archery scene is a fragment of battle relief from Khufu's mortuary complex depicting archers drawing their bows (AW 1:146; EWA 29). This scene is remarkable in a number of ways. The mere existence of this fragment from the temple murals implies that Khufu undertook unrecorded military expeditions, once depicted on now-lost murals. Artistically it represents the first surviving example of the stylized representation of Egyptian warfare that would, broadly speaking, remain the normative style for Egyptian martial art for the next 2500 years. It is stylistically quite different than the martial representations of the Early Dynastic Period, yet obviously has a long period of artistic development behind it. Such a highly developed style might indicate that it is quite likely that more martial art was created during the Old Kingdom, although only fragments survive. Third, in contrast to the rough-and-tumble chaos depicted in Early Dynastic martial art, the archers in the Old Kingdom are in orderly ranks drawing their bows in unison, possibly pointing to the development of more formalized organization and tactical formations. Finally, the bows themselves are self-bows, with braided strings; several arrows are held by each archer; the bows are drawn only to the elbow.

Successors of Khufu {2584–2513}[18]

We have almost no information concerning the military affairs of Khufu's successors. Khufu's son Djedefhor {2584–2576} succeeded his father to the throne; there are no known military activities of this rule, but some scholars speculate, based on deliberate damage to tombs and inscriptions, that there may have been some type of power struggle for the throne with his half-brother Khafre (HAE 72–3). However this may be, Khafre {2576–2551} – better know by his Greek name Chephren – came to the throne and ruled for a quarter of a century, and is renowned for building the Sphinx and the second pyramid of Giza.[19] We have no information about any military campaigns save for a fragmentary relief of a bound war-captive from Khafre's pyramid causeway (NEA 22). Under Khafre, mining expeditions were sent to Toshka, in Nubia, and the Sinai (EAE 2:231). The military affairs of Khafre's son Menkaure (Mycernius) {2551–2523} – builder of the third pyramid of Giza – and grandson Shepseskaf {2523–2519} are likewise obscure.[20]

The exact genealogical relationship between the Fourth and Fifth Dynasties is somewhat uncertain, but succession seems to have passed through Khentkawes, Menkaure's daughter, whose descendants formed the Fifth Dynasty.

Fifth Dynasty {2513–2374}[21]

As with most of the Old Kingdom, we have only limited and fragmentary information about the military history of the Fifth Dynasty. It is not until the end of this dynasty that we begin to see details of military history emerging. There are a number of indications of the increasing importance of the solar cult and the power and wealth of the priesthood of the Sun-god Re at Heliopolis (ancient Iunu, biblical On). The annals from the Palermo Stone record numerous large gifts to the cult of the Sun-god (PS 152–80). Theophoric names of the pharaohs associated with Re, the rise to prominence of the sun-temple of Heliopolis, and changes in funerary ritual and practice all indicate a shift in religious ideology and power.[22] From the perspective of military history the rise of the power of priestly elites reflects a decentralization of royal authority to both priestly and secular regional powers. This trend is confirmed late in the Fifth Dynasty when we see provincial authorities gaining greater local autonomy, the ability of ministers and courtiers to make their offices hereditary, and the building of magnificent and richly endowed tombs (mastabas) for important court officials. These trends, beginning in the Fifth Dynasty, culminated in the collapse of a united Egypt at the end of the Sixth Dynasty.

The first king of the Fifth Dynasty, Userkaf {2513–2506}, is believed to have carried out expeditions into the Eastern Desert and against Nubia (EAE 598a, 588b). He recorded that 303 prisoners from an unnamed campaign were given to his pyramid, probably to serve as slave laborers for its construction (PS 217–18), as well as 70 foreign women as tribute (EWA 30). Sahure {2506–2492}[23] carried out three recorded military expeditions. The first was to the mines in the Sinai, which returned with "6000 measures of copper", and which also hailed the king as the "smiter of all countries".[24] The second two are campaigns against Libya and Canaan, which were memorialized in his funerary temple (AEA 207); they are the first surviving examples of fully developed martial murals, and remain a mainstay of Egyptian military history and ideology for the next 1500 years. The first mural, on the south wall, depicts an expedition against Libya,[25] showing the king in his stylized mace-smiting scene. There are a number of registers showing Libyan captives and spoils being brought before the gods, including the wife and children of the Libyan chieftain (AAK 2/1:5). There are no surviving scenes of actual combat. The emphasis is on how the gods granted victory to Sahure, who in return gave slaves and tribute to the gods (presumably via donations to temples). The second mural, on the east wall, depicts an expedition to Syria, which shows a fleet departing, and returning in glory, hailing the king as "God of the living".[26] This may have been an entirely peaceful trading expedition, but is important evidence of the rise of Egyptian naval power, which will be discussed on pp. 366–7.

We have no military information about Sahure's two successors, Neferirkare Kakai {2492–2482} and Shepseskare {2482–2475}. Raneferef (or Neferefre) {2475–2474} undertook military expeditions into southern Canaan and Nubia, depicted in fragmentary statues of Nubian and Canaanite prisoners from his funerary temple.[27] At his death there may have been a struggle for succession between rival branches of the royal family. The details are not known, and the struggle may have been peaceful, but it could have included some military operations in association with an attempted coup. The next two kings of the dynasty, Newoserre Any {2474–2444} and Menkauhor {2444–2436} each record expeditions to the mines at Wadi Mughara in the Sinai (ARE 1:114, 120; PSE Figure 17); Newoserre also has a statue of a bound Canaanite captive in his mortuary temple, perhaps alluding to a campaign in Canaan (EWA 34; PSE Figure 18).

Djedkare Izezi (Isesi) {2436–2404}[28] campaigned twice in the Sinai, declaring himself in memorial inscriptions to be the "Great God [who] smites the Canaanites" and the "smiter of all countries" (ARE 1:121; EWA 36; PSE Figure 19). He also continued his predecessors' maritime relations with Byblos, and with Punt, which may have included a military component (EWA 36a). Punt is a somewhat vague geographical term referring to lands on the south-west coast of the Red Sea – broadly the coasts of modern southern Sudan, Ethiopia, Eritrea, Djibouti, and Somalia – and was the source of many highly prized exotic trade goods such as aromatics and panther skins (DAE 231–2; EAE 3:85–6). The expedition to Punt was under the command of the "seal-bearer Bawerded", who brought back a "pygmy of the god's dances" to court, an event remembered at court a century later (AEL 1:26). Statues of bound Canaanite captives were found in Djedkare's funerary temple, with an inscription describing "the prostration of all the multitudes [and the] overthrowing of the foreign lands" (EWA 36–6a). A mining–military expedition was also sent to the diorite quarries to the west of Abu Simbel (HAE 79). The date of the important military mural from the tomb of Inty at Deshasheh is uncertain; some scholars think it may represent a campaign by Djedkare; others date it to the early sixth dynasty (NAE 30; EAE 2:590b). It will be discussed on pp. 358–9 in the broader discussion of Old Kingdom siegecraft.

The final king of the Fifth Dynasty, Unas (Wenis){2404–2374} (HAE 80; EAE 2:590, 600–1), is noted for his pyramid at Saqqara containing the earliest Pyramid Texts, which will be discussed on pp. 353–4, and fragmentary murals from its associated causeway (EWA 38). From the military perspective the most important mural is a battle scene depicting Egyptian soldiers armed with bows and daggers "smiting the Shasi", or eastern bedouins, while the mortuary temple contains statues of bound Canaanites (NEA 24–5; EWA 38–9; PSE Figure 22b). The causeway also depicts maritime expeditions to Byblos. Unas is said to have met for negotiations with chieftains of the Nubians at Elephantine. It is sometimes inferred from this that there was increasing unrest in Nubia as Egyptian domination began to subside – instead of issuing the standard claim that the king had crushed the Nubians, Unas was forced to negotiate (EAE 2:590a). The most famous mural from Unas's causeway depicts starving people begging for food (ISP 120); one of the figures is bearded, possibly representing a Canaanite (ANEP §102). The precise context for this scene is unknown, but is probably meant to memorialize Unas's beneficence in providing food to the hungry. From the military perspective, it reminds us that starvation has frequently been associated with war, either because natural disasters leading to hunger can be a contributing cause of war, or because war frequently brings hunger and deprivation in its wake.

Sixth Dynasty {2374–2191}[29]

The exact relationship between the fifth and sixth dynasties is obscure; some scholars assume that Teti {2374–2354}, its first king, was the son-in-law of Unas, last king of the Fifth Dynasty (EAE 3:379–81). Teti's Horus name, Seheteptawi, means "He who pacifies the two lands", and has been taken by some scholars to imply a contested succession to the throne which required some "pacification" to secure completely. A number of Teti's important ministers, including Mehu, Kagemni, and Isi, all had served in the administration of the former king Unas, however, indicating a strong continuity between the dynasties. Military activities during Teti's reign are poorly documented. His mortuary temple includes stylized statues of bound captives, indicating the defeat of Canaanites (EWA 41a–2); there is also mention of an expedition to the alabaster quarries at Hatnub. Maritime expeditions to Punt and Byblos are implied in surviving artifacts (C1/2:190). Graffiti found at Tomas in Nubia indicate caravans to Nubia were active in this period (EAE 3:380). Later legends – which cannot be confirmed by contemporary sources – claim that Teti was murdered by one of his guardsmen (Man. 19–20). Teti was briefly succeeded by an ephemeral and poorly attested ruler, Userkare, who may have been the instigator of the palace coup.

Pepy I (Phiops) {2354–2310} (EAE 3:33–4; LA 4:926)

Whatever the authenticity of the legends of assassination, Teti's legitimate and stable successor was his son Pepy I. Inscriptions record expeditions to the Sinai, the Hatnub quarries, and Wadi Hammamat (ARE 1:136–40; PSE figs 20–1). Most of these expeditions had at least a military component to them, and for the first time we begin to see the names and deeds of the actual commanders. The Sinai rock relief shows the traditional head-smiting scene, with an inscription, "The Great God [Pepy I] it is that smites and subdues the Montiu [*mntw*] of all foreign lands" (EWA 43). In reality, the Sinai expedition was under the leadership of the "commander of the army Ibdu, son of the commander of the troops Merire-onekh" (ARE 1:139). The Wadi Hammamat expedition likewise had a military escort, commanded by "God's [Pepy's] seal-bearer, overseer of the army ... overseer of foreign lands" (EWA 44). At least one maritime expedition to Byblos was also undertaken (EWA 45), as well as a gold-seeking expedition to Nubia (HAE 81).

Pepy's court, however, was not without intrigue, perhaps reflecting ongoing instability spun off by the usurpation of Userkare. Pepy's first wife was charged with conspiracy, and tried in a secret tribunal (AEL 1:19). He thereafter married two daughters of Khui, a noble of Abydos, one of whom was the mother of Merenre, Pepy's successor. The fact that Pepy was succeeded by a younger son has led some to speculate that the elder heir apparent was involved in the coup attempt associated with his mother, and thereby lost the throne, if not his life. In any event, through its marriage to the royal family, the clan of Khui would come to play a prominent role in the rest of the Sixth Dynasty (HAE 83), providing further evidence of the rising power of the regional nobility that would eventually destabilize Egypt. Pepy I is also noted for his decentralizing reforms of the Egyptian administration. A large portion of royal property devolved into the hands of private courtiers or temple priesthoods, encouraging the cults of local deities. This included exemptions from taxes and labor obligations to the king, as well as giving increasing autonomy to regional governors and priests. This culminated in the rise of semi-independent nomarchs (governors of nomes or provinces, EAE 1:16–20; LA 2:385–417), whose growing power is symbolized by their large rock-cut tombs and mastabas (brick tomb mounds, EAE 3:433–42). Pepy attempted to secure the loyalty of these rising nomarchs by intermarriage with them, including the marriage of his daughter to his vizier Mereruka. In one sense these actions certainly strengthened the immediate power of Pepy I and his dynasty by binding regional strongmen to his family. On the other hand, the rise of these semi-independent nomarchs laid the foundation for the fragmentation of the Egyptian state in the First Intermediate Period (see p. 368).

A life-size copper statue of Pepy I was found at Hierakonpolis, the earliest copper statue discovered in Egypt (TEM 89). From the military perspective it represents the expansion of the availability of copper, and hence the potential for more copper-based weapons. None the less, it is likely that the average Egyptian soldiers were still largely armed with stone weapons at this time; copper remained a metal for the elites. As is traditional in Old Kingdom mortuary temples, Pepy's temple contains statues of bound captive Canaanites and Nubians, emphasizing the military exploits of his reign (EWA 46, EAE 3:33). His copper statue also depicts Pepy trampling the "Nine Bows", a symbolic name of Egypt's traditional enemies (HAE 84). Since such statues are stylized, and perhaps even ritual in purpose, they may simply represent the ideal order of the universe rather than actual military expeditions that returned with real captives. However, that the captive statues in Pepy's mortuary temple could represent the results of real campaigns is confirmed by the most important military document of the Old Kingdom, the autobiography of Weni.

Weni's campaigns to Canaan {c. 2350–2330}[30]

With the reign of Pepy I we begin, for the first time, to see written details of Egyptian military campaigns. The most extensive and important source is the autobiography of Weni of Abydos {c. 2375–2305?},[31] one of the leading generals and courtiers of the age. It is the first eyewitness account of any detail of warfare in

Egypt. Weni's battle narrative of his campaigns to Canaan begins with a description of the mobilization of the army of Egypt:

> When his majesty took action against the Eastern Sand-dwellers, his majesty made an army of many tens of thousands from all of Upper Egypt: from Yebu [Aswan] in the south to Medenyt [Aphroditopolis] in the north; from Lower Egypt: from all of the Two-Sides-of-the-House and from Sedjer and Khensedjru; and [mercenaries] from Irtjet-Nubians, Medja-Nubians, Yam-Nubians, Wawat-Nubians, Kaau-Nubians; and from Tjemeh [southern Libyans]. (AEL 1:19)

This text first tells us that, unlike later pharaohs, king Pepy did not go on this campaign himself. It is not clear if this was the norm for the Old Kingdom, but there is little evidence from this period for kings engaging in actual combat. The enemy was the "Sand-dwellers" an Egyptian ethnonym referring to the peoples of the Sinai and southern Canaan. We are not told the background to the campaign, but apparently it was a fairly serious matter, for the army allegedly consisted of "many tens of thousands". This may be an example of the hyperbole that sometimes infects the tomb autobiographies of Egypt, but certainly the army would have numbered in the thousands. It is also unlikely that the entire force was composed of combatants. Areas of recruitment were divided into three categories: troops of Upper Egypt, of Lower Egypt, and Nubians. There is no direct evidence of a standing army in the Old Kingdom, and it is not clear from this text if the soldiers were professional or militia – or, most likely, a combination of both. Faulkner argues that there must have been some type of standing army for policing the country, royal security, responding to raiders, and maintaining control of Nubian mercenaries (EMO 33). At any rate, most nomes in the country were required to supply men for military service for the war in Canaan.

Weni's description of the Nubian mercenaries is interesting for a number of reasons. There are five specific Nubian tribes mentioned: Irtjet, Medja (or Medjay), Yam, Wawat, and Kaau. These names represent regions or clans in Nubia from between the First and the Third Cataracts.[32] The most famous of these are the Medjay, from the Eastern Desert and eastern banks of the Nubian Nile, who served as light infantry mercenaries in later periods. The final group of auxiliary troops was from "Tjemeh-land", generally thought to be Libyans from the deserts to the west of southern Egypt and northern Nubia. The exact political relationship between Egypt and northern Nubia is unclear. Egyptians probably had some sort of hegemony over these tribes, but apparently did not have direct administrative control over the region. As tributary tribes the Nubians were required not to raid southern Egypt, but instead to serve as Egyptian mercenaries, probably for both pay and plunder. Using Nubians as mercenaries had a number of advantages for the Egyptians. First, it limited Nubian raids against Egypt. Second, it provided a source of war-like manpower. The Nubians could be used as border guards to defend the southern frontier against other raids from rival Nubian tribes, as well as troops for campaigns elsewhere, as in Weni's invasion of Canaan. The Egyptians were thus employing for the first time what would become the time-tested tactic of "using barbarians to fight barbarians".[33] A strong force of Nubian mercenaries could also provide a counter-balance to the growing independent military power of the nomarchs.

Weni next provides a list of the various Egyptian officials who took part in the campaign:

> His majesty sent me at the head of this army, there being counts, royal seal-bearers, sole companions of the palace, chieftains and mayors of towns of Upper and Lower Egypt, companions, commander of foreigners, chief priests of Upper and Lower Egypt, and chief district officials at the head of the troops of Upper and Lower Egypt, from the villages and towns that they governed and from the Nubians of those foreign lands. (AEL 1:20)[34]

Weni's purpose here is to describe his own remarkable authority, listing all the mighty officials of Egypt who were under his command. But, from the military perspective, this text also tells us two other important things. Most of the leaders of the expedition had some type of normal non-military function, and were doubling as military leaders. For the offices listed by Weni, only "commander of foreigners" seems to be a military title. The regional governmental administrators and officials were in command of the military units raised in their villages and nomes. This is perhaps an indication that the provincial Egyptian army was a militia force, but it also implies that local nomarchs had command over their own regional military units; this apparent regional military autonomy would culminate in full independence of warring nomarchs during the First Intermediate Period.

Weni took his duties as commander seriously, boasting of the logistical efficiency with which the army operated.

> I was the one who commanded them – while my rank was that of overseer of [royal tenants] – because of my rectitude, so that no one attacked his fellow, so that no one seized a loaf or sandals from a traveler, so that no one took a cloth from any town, so that no one took a goat from anyone. I led them from Northern Isle and [gate] of Iyhotep [in] the district of Horus-lord-of-truth [north-eastern Delta] while being in this rank.... I determined the number of these troops [through a military census]. It had never been determined by any servant. (AEL 1:20)

Weni's emphasis on the fact that under his command the army was orderly and did not plunder Egyptian villages through which it passed on the way to Canaan could be seen as an indictment of the typical behavior of an Egyptian army in this age, which presumably engaged in precisely these types of activities – otherwise, why would Weni boast of accomplishing something that was the norm for Egyptian armies on campaign? This passage also implies that the Egyptians were well aware of logistical issues – an army needed bread, sandals, clothing, and goats, and if they were not provided by the leader, the soldiers would plunder them from the people. In this regard Weni emphasizes that he actually "determined the number of these troops", something which "had never been determined by any servant" before. In other words, his ability to prevent the army from plundering was directly related to the fact that he had numbered his army, and therefore knew something of the order of magnitude of supplies that would be required – something that had apparently seldom been done before. In a sense Weni's former functions as a court administrator prepared him for the logistical demands of his military campaign to Canaan. We see, in other words, the birth of logistics – the fact that getting an army intact to the battlefield was in many ways just as important as tactical leadership during the battle.

Weni also provides us with the world's first example of martial poetry. While not giving any tactical details of actual battles, Weni makes the overall results of the campaign very clear.

> This army returned in safety,
>   It had ravaged the Sand-dwellers' land.
> This army returned in safety,
>   It had flattened the Sand-dwellers' land.
> This army returned in safety,
>   It had sacked its strongholds.
> This army returned in safety,
>   It had cut down its figs, its vines.
> This army returned in safety,
>   It had thrown fire in all its [dwellings].
> This army returned in safety,
>   It had slain its troops by many ten-thousands.
> This army returned in safety,
>   [It had carried] off many [troops] as captives. (AEL 1:20)

In this poem, already discussed on pp. 275–6, Weni provides us with no geographical specifics of which cities were attacked, but the descriptions of capturing fortresses and destroying agriculture makes it clear that the war was with the urban city-states of southern Canaan rather than merely bedouins. An Egyptian army of as many as ten or twenty thousand would have been an overwhelming force to the Canaanite city-states of the twenty-fourth century; Weni's description of devastating the land, capturing fortified cites, destroying agriculture, burning, plundering, and enslaving is probably an authentic picture of an Egyptian army marauding through southern Canaan.

With booty and slaves, Weni and his army returned to praise and triumph in Egypt: "His majesty praised me for [this victory] beyond anything" (AEL 1:20). Unfortunately, from the Egyptian perspective, the invasion only served to further inflame anti-Egyptian sentiments – "rebellion" as the Egyptians viewed it – requiring four additional campaigns, in which Weni also claimed victory.

His majesty sent me to lead this army five times, to attack the land of the
Sand-dwellers as often as they rebelled, with these troops. I acted so that his
majesty praised me [for it beyond anything]. (AEL 1:20)

The fact that the Egyptians were compelled to make five major expeditions
into Canaan demonstrates that, even with their overwhelming military might, they
were either unable to, or uninterested in, establishing permanent stable control
over Canaan.

Weni's biography provides additional strategic details for one of his five
campaigns – though which one is uncertain.

Told there were marauders among these foreigners at the nose of Gazelle's-
head, I crossed in ships with these troops. I made a landing in the back of
the height of the mountain range, to the north of the land of the Sand-
dwellers, while half of this army was on the road [approaching from the
south]. I came and caught them all and slew every marauder among them.
(AEL 1:20)

This passage first tells us that the Egyptians had some type of intelligence available
concerning Canaan, whether from returning merchants, collaborating kings of
city-states, or, possibly, Egyptian garrisons. However the information was
obtained, the Egyptians responded quickly. Splitting his force in two, Weni sent
half by sea and half by land in a strategic double envelopment, crushing Egypt's
enemies. The location of the "Gazelle's-head" mountain is uncertain, but most
scholars associate it with Mt. Carmel near modern Haifa in Israel. If this is correct,
the Egyptians were able to mobilize a fleet capable of transporting at least hundreds, and possibly several thousand men, for several hundred miles. While it is
likely that soldiers had accompanied earlier trading expedition both for the protection of Egyptian merchants and the intimidation of trading partners, this is the
first account we have of transporting a major army by sea. Large-scale maritime
trade, which had begun at least three centuries earlier during the reign of Sneferu
{2649–2609}, who received forty shiploads of timber from Byblos (PS 141–3),
had by now developed into the capacity to successfully transport major armies
across the Mediterranean Sea, illustrating the important military principle that
where merchants go, armies can eventually follow.

Weni's remarkable autobiography thus provides us with a number of Egyptian
military "firsts". It is the first example of a detailed eyewitness military memoir,
the first evidence of the extensive use of foreign mercenaries, the first recognition
of the importance of logistics, the first martial poetry, the first example of strategic
double envelopment, amphibious operations, and combined operations by land
and sea. But although Weni's autobiography provides the first *surviving* recorded
examples, centuries of military development lay behind Weni's remarkable
achievements. There were undoubtedly earlier examples for which no evidence
has survived.

Merenre II (Antyemsaf) {2310–2300} and Nubia[35]

Merenre, son of Pepy I, had a short but eventful reign. The redoubtable Weni again appears in the reign of Merenre again as governor of Upper Egypt, where he records leading quarrying expeditions to Aswan for granite and Hatnub for alabaster (AEL 1:21). More importantly, however, he constructed "five canals" designed to allow boats to float around the First Cataract at Aswan for transporting granite. The "foreign [Nubian] chiefs of Irtjet, Wawat, Yam and Medja cut the [acacia] timber" for the boats used on the canal (AEL 1:21–2); these are precisely the same tribes who sent troops with Weni on the Canaanite expeditions described above, further emphasizing their probable tributary status to Egypt. In theory these canals could have had military applications by floating troops and supplies around the First Cataract, thereby facilitating Egyptian military operations in Nubia. The building of this canal may thus in part be connected to Merenre's overall Nubian policy; we shall see that direct Egyptian dominance of Nubia increased in the following centuries.

The expeditions of Horkhuf (Harkhuf) {2310–2300}[36]

However that may be, it is clear that, whereas Pepy had focused his attention on Canaan with the five campaigns of Weni, the reign of Merenre is closely associated with the foreign affairs of Nubia. Several inscriptions at Tomas, in the modern northern Sudan, record the passing of Egyptian expeditions through the region (HAE 85). The most important record of Egyptian intervention into Nubia was the autobiography of Horkhuf, apparently Weni's successor as governor of southern Egypt. Horkhuf's autobiography is important because it provides the clearest evidence as to how Old Kingdom trading, exploring, and mining expeditions were often indistinguishable from military operations. Horkhuf was governor of Upper Egypt, as well as a royal administrator, mayor of Nekheb, and a lector-priest (AEL 1:23–5), again reflecting the wide range of civil, economic, religious, and military offices held by Egyptian officials. From the military perspective, Horkhuf's major offices were "commander of foreigners" and "governor of all mountain lands belonging to the southern region", meaning the desert and mountain regions outside the Nile valley. In this function, Horkhuf claims to have "cast the dread of [the war-god] Horus into the foreign lands", or, in other words, to have intimidated the Nubian and Libyan tribes of the region to acquiesce to Egypt's wishes (AEL 1:25).

Horkhuf undertook three expeditions into Nubia, which provide the most detailed surviving accounts of the trade–military expeditions of the Old Kingdom. The major purpose of these expeditions was trade or tribute – the two are barely distinguishable in the Old Kingdom. As Horkhuf put it, he was to "bring the produce of all foreign lands to his lord" king Merenre (AEL 1:25).

In his first expedition, Horkhuf went with his father Iri, who may have had actual command of the expedition. In his second expedition Horkhuf was clearly in charge.

341

The majesty of Merenre, my lord, sent me together with my father, the sole companion and lector-priest, Iri, to Yam [between the Second and Third Cataracts], to open the way to that country. I did it in seven months; I brought from it all kinds of beautiful and rare gifts, and was praised for it very greatly.

His majesty sent me a second time [without my father]. I went up on the Yebu [Aswan] road and came down via Mekher, Terers, and Irtjetj (which are in) Irtjet in the space of eight months. I came down bringing gifts from that country in great quantity, the likes of which had never before been brought back to this land. I came down through the region of the house of the [Nubian] chief of Setju and Irtjet, I explored those foreign lands. I have not found it done by any companion and commander of foreigners who went to Yam previously. (AEL 1:25)

These two journeys each took seven to eight months, covering a route along the Nile of 300–350 miles each way, or 700 miles for the round trip. This gives an average travel distance of only 100 miles a month, 25 miles a week, or only four miles a day. Obviously Horkhuf's men spent a great deal of time trading, but probably also explored side wadis such as the Wadi 'Allaqi, which could have added several hundred miles to the overall journey. The tribal names mentioned in the text – Mekher, Terers, Irtjetj, and Setju – are all tribal areas between the First Cataract at Aswan and the Second Cataract near Buhen; the entire region has been flooded by Lake Nasser since the building of the Aswan Dam in the 1960s. Given that Weni had constructed a canal around the first cataract a few years earlier, it is possible that the expedition was accompanied by a river fleet on part of its journey.

The first expedition was essentially a trading operation to bring back "all kinds of beautiful and rare gifts". The second, however, although it was also concerned with trade, or "gifts", was much more focused on exploration – Harkhuf "explored those foreign lands" that had never been explored before. From the military perspective, we find an Egyptian armed caravan seemingly operating with impunity in the lands of ostensibly autonomous, and possibly hostile Nubian chiefs, implying that there was a strong military component to the second expedition, which is explicitly mentioned in Horkhuf's third expedition. This Egyptian predominance seems to have been possible because of disunity among the Nubian tribes of the region. The presence of father and son together on the first expedition is another indication that provincial authority was becoming increasingly hereditary in the late Old Kingdom.

From the military perspective, Horkhuf's third expedition is the most interesting. The date is not given, but it is generally assumed that it occurred near the end of the reign of Merenre {2300}.

Then his majesty sent me a third time to Yam. I went up from the nome of This [Abydos] upon the Oasis road [via the Kharga Oasis]. I found that the ruler of Yam [the land between the Second and Third Cataracts] had gone off to Tjemeh-land [deserts west of the Nile valley, home of the Tjemeh tribe of Libyans], to smite the Tjemeh [Libyans] to the western corner of heaven. I went up after him to Tjemeh-land and satisfied him, so that he praised all the gods for the sovereign [king of Egypt].

I sent a report with a [Nubian] man from Yam to the retinue of Horus, to let the majesty of Merenre, my lord, know [that I had gone to Tjemeh-land] after the ruler of Yam.

Now when I had satisfied this ruler of Yam, I came down through [the Nile Valley and the Second Cataract] south of Irtjet and north of Setju. I found the ruler of [the Nubian confederacy of] Irtjet, Setju, and Wawat. I came down with three hundred donkeys laden with incense, ebony, *ḥknw*-oil, *s3t*, panther skins, elephants' tusks, throw sticks, and all sorts of good products. Now when the ruler of Irtjet, Setju, and Wawat saw how strong and numerous the [allied Nubian mercenary] troop from Yam was which came down with me to the residence together with the [Egyptian] army that had been sent with me, this ruler escorted me, gave me cattle and goats [for supplies], and led me on the mountain paths of Irtjet [on the ridge to the west of the Nile valley] – because of the excellence of the vigilance I had employed beyond that of any companion and commander of the foreigners who had been sent to Yam before. (AEL 1:25–6)

Reading a bit between the lines, we can broadly outline the military relations on the Nubian frontier as follows. Around 2330 Weni was using Nubian mercenaries from the Irtjet, Medja, Yam, Wawat, and Kaau tribes for Egyptian campaigns in Canaan. It is unclear if the Nubians participated because of coercion or were voluntarily seeking adventure and a share of the plunder of Canaan; most likely a combination of both. By around 2310, however, relations on the Nubian frontier seem strained. Horkhuf is able to operate relatively freely in northern Nubia, but the passage of his expedition was probably expensive and disruptive. The Nubians therefore formed a confederacy of the disunited Nubian tribes of Irtjet, Setju, and Wawat to unite under the leadership of the "chief of Irtjet".

This forced Horkhuf's third expedition to take the Oasis Road (LA 4:541–2) through the desert, thereby bypassing northern Nubia between the First and Second Cataracts, to reach Yam, the land between the Second and Third Cataracts. There Horkhuf "satisfied" the chief of Yam, apparently allying with the chief of Yam against his Libyan Tjemeh enemies, and greatly strengthening his overall position. In return the chief of Yam agreed to send a mercenary force back to Egypt with Horkhuf. The Nubian confederacy between the First and Second Cataracts was now surrounded by Egyptians to the north, and the allied chief of Yam to the south. Facing a large Egyptian–Yam Nubian army that accompanied the expedition, the chief of the Irtjet confederacy agreed to provide supplies for Horkhuf's force and permitted Horkhuf to return to Egypt through his lands – not through the Nile valley itself, but rather on the Mountain Road along the ridges to the west where the Egyptian army would be unable to plunder or harass the Nubians. This type of fluctuating state of affairs on the Nubian frontier was probably the norm in Egyptian–Nubian relations during most of the Old Kingdom. These relations are brought into focus here only because of the fortunate survival of the tomb autobiographies of Weni and Horkhuf.

Thanks in part to the efforts of Horkhuf, the Nubian frontier seems to have stabilized, at least temporarily. Following the success of Horkhuf's second expedition, Merenre went in person in the last year of his reign {2300} to Aswan to receive the submission of the northern Nubian chiefs. An inscription from the First Cataract at Aswan shows Merenre flanked by the god Khnum receiving the submission of the Nubian chiefs. The inscription reads "the coming of the king [Merenre] himself … while the chiefs of the Medja, Irtjet and Wawat did obeisance and gave [him] great praise" (ARE 1:145–6); again we see three of the same tribes (excluding Yam and Kaau, who dwelt further south) in a formal act of submission to the Egyptian king. This Nubian peace, however, was not to last.

The logistical capabilities of the Egyptian army are also made manifest by Horkhuf's expedition. First, we see the Egyptians could keep a small army in the field in foreign lands for up to eight months, in part by plundering or requisitioning supplies from the local people. They could also march through the open desert, using the Sahara oases as supply bases, with hundreds of donkeys for carrying supplies, equipment, and trade goods. We also see Harkhuf marching west into the open desert following the Nubian chief of Yam in his pursuit of Libyan Tjemeh raiders. Thus, by 2300 the Egyptian army had developed the logistical and technological capacity to operate by land and sea in all types of terrain, to keep armies in the field for months, and to move troops up to at least 500 miles by land or sea from their nearest frontier bases in Egypt.

The Western Desert and Libyans[37]

Horkhuf's decision to take the desert road through the oases of the Western Desert highlights the role of the Libyans of the Western Desert in Egyptian military history. Unlike the Eastern Desert, with its rich natural resources, the Western Desert is a vast region of barren dunes and dry rock, essentially devoid of resources to attract Egyptian attention. Also unlike the Eastern Desert, the West has five oases that can sustain agriculture and human and animal life; today these are known as Siwa, Bahriya, Farafra, Dakhla, and Kharga. Further south opposite the Nubian Nile is a sixth oasis, Selima (M = AAE 13, 287; HAAE 27). In Islamic times (after 640 CE) the route from the Nile through Kharga to Selima was called *Darb al-Arba'in* – the "Forty-[Day] Trail". The entire desert journey from Abydos to the Nubian Nile was roughly 430 miles. Since the camel was not available in Egypt until Hellenistic times, the ancient Egyptians would have made the journey by donkey caravan, which would not only have added several days to the trip, but would have compounded the logistical problem of water supply for both men and donkeys. None the less, Horkhuf's expedition, along with other evidence, demonstrates that this route was practicable to both donkey caravans and their military escorts.

The Western Desert was inhabited by peoples the Egyptians called *Tjehenu* and *Tjemehu* (or *Tjemeh*), terms used for both the land and its peoples that are generally translated as Libyan.[38] The Tjehenu occupied the Western Desert from the Mediterranean south through the Fayyum; the Tjemehu from the Fayyum south to the Selima Oasis and the Third Cataract of the Nile. Both of these groups were pastoralists, eking a slight subsistence from the fierce Saharan desert. The Tjehenu centered on the Mediterranean coast of Libya, where the marginal rainfall was sufficient to sustain their herds. It is possible that some of the people living in the north-western delta of the Nile were also linguistically related to the Tjehenu. The Tjemehu focused on the oases of the Western Desert, and a few scattered wells and other scanty water resources.

Strategically speaking, the Libyans of the Old and Middle Kingdom periods were not a serious military threat to Egypt. The pastoral economy of the Western Desert simply could not sustain a sufficient number of people to seriously threaten the Nile Valley. Although there are no records of any major attacks by Libyans against Egypt before the New Kingdom, it is likely that they occasionally raided the Nile valley or plundered caravans passing on the Desert Road to Nubia.

On the other hand, the Libyans offered the Egyptians a potential source of plunder through livestock and slaves. From Pre-Dynastic times through the end of the Old Kingdom, we have eight accounts of wars between Egyptians and Libyans.

- The "Battlefield Palette" {c. 3200} depicts what appear to be slain and captured Libyans (EWP 29, MB 119–44).
- The "Cities" or "Libyan Palette" {c. 3100} depicts an assault on Libya (or perhaps Libyans in the north-western delta) and rows of livestock plundered during the campaign.[39]
- King Djer (Zer) {3000–2977} of the First Dynasty has a stele showing him smiting a cowering Libyan (AE 60).
- Sneferu {2649–2609} gives us the earliest written account of such a raid, describing the plunder "from Libya [*Thnw*]: 1100 live captives [and] 23,000 sheep and goats" (PS 235).
- The mortuary temple of Sahure {2506–2492} contains a relief depicting the submission of a Libyan chieftain and his family, along with plunder or tribute from the Libyans (PE 161–2; AEA 207).
- Weni's autobiography {c. 2340} mentions the Egyptians using Libyan mercenaries from the southern "Tjemeh-land" in his campaign against Canaan (AEL 1:19).
- Horkhuf's third expedition {c. 2296} allied with the Nubian chieftain of Yam in a war with the Tjemeh Libyans in the deserts west of Nubia (AEL 1:25).

- Pepy II {2300–2206} has a stylized "smiting-the-Libyans" scene in his mortuary temple, which seems to be an exact duplicate of Sahure's earlier relief, discussed above (PE 181; AEA 173).

These records indicate sporadic warfare between Egypt and Libya, essentially taking the form of plundering expeditions by Egyptians against Libyans. The absence of accounts of Libyan attacks against Egypt does not necessarily mean they did not occur. The records for this period are quite fragmentary, and the Egyptians seldom recorded accounts of defeats at the hands of their enemies; Egypt is always portrayed as victorious. Some of these Egyptian attacks on Libyans may also have been essentially retaliatory expeditions in response to Libyan raids. None the less, the picture derived from the sources is not one of Libyans threatening Egypt, but of Egyptians plundering Libyans.

This general picture is partially confirmed by archaeological evidence, which indicates that the Dakhla and Kharga oases were colonized by the Egyptians by the Sixth Dynasty. Dakhla, in particular, had a Sixth Dynasty fortress, which served both as protection for Egyptian colonists in the oases, control of the desert trade route to Nubia, and probably as a base for offensive or retaliatory operations against Libyans (AEA 26; EAE 2:290). The Pyramid Texts mention a fortress "which keeps Libya out" of Egypt (PT 665C); although its location is not identified, it may refer to the Dakhla Oasis fortress, or perhaps border forts on the western edge of the Delta.

Thus, throughout the Old Kingdom there was internecine warfare between Egyptians and Libyans, generally taking the form of raids and counter-raids. Although the Libyans lacked the manpower seriously to threaten the stability of the Egyptian kingdom itself, they were strong enough to require fortification of the oases, and their martial qualities were such that they were used as mercenaries by the Egyptians. The role of the Libyans as mercenaries for the Egyptians would expand greatly during the First Intermediate Period and the Middle Kingdom.

Pepy (Phiops) II {2300–2206}[40]

Pepy II came to the throne at the age of six, and had a reign lasting an incredible ninety-four years, making him the longest-reigning ruler in world history.[41] We first meet him at the age of ten, when he sends a letter (transcribed onto Horkhuf's tomb wall) congratulating Horkhuf for his successful third expedition. In it, young Pepy was not overly concerned with trade, war, or the affairs of state. He was most interested in . . .

> the pygmy of the god's dances from the land of the horizon-dwellers [at the end of the earth].... Hurry and bring with you this pygmy ... get worthy men to be around him on deck [of the boat], lest he fall in the water [on the trip down the Nile]! When he lies down at night, get worthy men to lie around him in his tent. Inspect him ten times at night! (AEL 1:26–7)

The arrival of a dancing pygmy, however entertaining to the boy-king, did not represent a solution to the problems of the Nubian frontier.

A few inscriptions and reliefs point to military activities during Pepy II's long reign. Murals at Pepy II's funerary complex show the king as a mythic sphinx trampling his defeated Libyan enemies, along with statues of bound captives from foreign lands. This scene seems to be a close duplicate of the funerary relief of Sahure. While it may represent an actual campaign against the Libyans – which for simplicity's sake was merely copied from Sahure's temple in a stylized form – it is also possible that it is a ritualized depiction of the royal ideal of the king as ruler of the world and victor over all enemies (PE 181; AEA 173; PSE Figure 22a). Inscriptions also record an expedition to Sinai (ARE 1:156–7), along with additional trading–military expeditions to Nubia and Punt mentioned in an inscription by Khui (ARE 1:164). In a passage from the Pyramid Texts dating to the reign of Pepy II, the god Horus "sets Upper Egypt in order for [the King], he sets Lower Egypt in order for him, he hacks up (*b3*) the fortresses of Canaan for him, he quells for him all the hostile peoples under his fingers" (PT 650, EWA 51). Although this is a mythical text, it may contain an allusion to a historical campaign. The most important historical source, however, is the autobiography of Pepinakht.

The campaigns of Pepinakht[42]

The tomb complex at Qubbet el-Hawa at Aswan contains two autobiographies of courtiers during Pepy II's reign – Pepinakht Heqaib and his son Sabni – that contain accounts of military affairs along the Nubian border. The career of Pepinakht again demonstrates the overlapping of religious, civilian, and military offices in the Old Kingdom – indeed, it is probably anachronistic to impose such modern categories on ancient Egyptian officials. Pepinakht's titles include Lector Priest, Scribe, Royal Seal-Bearer, and "Commander of the Foreigners" (AEAB 15–16), which meant both that he was responsible for border affairs, and that he commanded Nubian mercenary troops. In this capacity he "brought the produce of foreign lands to his lord [Pepy II]" and went on punitive military expeditions to "cast the terror of [the wargod] Horus into foreign lands" (AEAB 15).

The submission of the Nubian chiefs of Wawet and Irtjet to king Merenre (ARE 1:145–6), described on p. 341, was nominal at best. We do not know the exact cause, but Pepy II ordered two campaigns against some of these Nubian tribes. The first was a raid to plunder and devastate ("hack up") northern Nubia:

> The majesty of my lord [Pepy II] sent me [Pepinakht] to hack up [the Nubian principalities of] Wawat and Irjet. I acted to the satisfaction of my lord. I slew a large number of them, [including] sons of the ruler, and excellent troop leaders. I brought a large number of them to the [royal] residence as captives, while I was at the head of numerous and strong troops in boldness of heart. (AEAB 16)

The second campaign was more successful, resulting in the capture of the Nubian chiefs.

> [Pepy II] also sent me to pacify these lands [Wawat and Irjet].... I brought the two rulers of these lands to the residence [of Pepy II] with offerings of live cattle ... together with the sons of the rulers and the troop leaders who were with them. (AEAB 16)

They thus ritually renewed the submission that had earlier been given to Merenre. Some of the captured "sons of the rulers" may have been kept at court as hostages for future good behavior.

The importance of military affairs in Nubia during the reign of Pepy II is also reflected in Execration Texts found at Giza.[43] Clay figurines of Nubians were made, inscribed with ritual curses, and then shattered and buried as a means of "sending" the curse to the inscribed victim. Some of the curses were generic, against the entire people and country of Nubia. The following is typical:

> [Let a curse fall upon] every rebel of this land [Nubia], all people, all nobles, all commoners, all males, all eunuchs, all women, every chieftain, every Nubian, every strongman, every messenger, every confederate, every ally of every [foreign] land who will rebel in [the Nubian provinces of] Wawat, Zatu, Irjet, Yam, Yanakh, Masit, and Kaw, who will rebel or who will plot by saying plots or by speaking anything evil against Upper Egypt or Lower Egypt forever.
>
> [Let a curse fall upon] every Nubian who will rebel in [the Nubian provinces of] Irjet, Wawat, Zatu, Yam, Kaw, Yanakh, Masit, Medja, and Meterti, who will rebel or who will make plots, or who will plot, or who will say anything evil. (MAEM 139)[44]

Other, smaller clay figurines, representing specific named individuals – possibly enemy rulers or commanders – were also cursed. The Execration Texts will be discussed more fully on pp. 415–8, but it is important to note both that magic power was considered an important supplement to military power in foreign affairs, and that the Nubians were perceived as posing a serious enough threat to warrant these types of curses.

Pepinakht's third recorded campaign was a punitive expedition to the Sinai, which offers our first insight into the nature of combat in that region, and the first indirect indication that Egyptian combat with foreigners was not aways the victorious triumph of the king and his soldiers that funerary inscriptions and reliefs unusually claim.

> [Pepy II] also sent me to the land of the Easterners [in the Eastern Desert and Sinai], to bring him the sole companion, ship's captain, and Commander of the Foreigners An-Ankhet, who had been equipping a ship there for Punt when the Easterners belonging to the Sand-dwellers slew him together with

the company of soldiers that was with him … [text lost] I drove to flight and slew some of their men, I together with the company of soldiers that was with me.… [I] cast the terror of [the wargod] Horus into foreign lands. (AEAB 16)

Before Pepinakht's punitive expedition, an earlier mission under the command of An-Ankhet had apparently crossed from the Nile to the western shore of the Red Sea, where they were preparing a ship to sail to Punt, when they were attacked by nomad raiders who killed most of the soldiers and plundered the merchandise and other equipment and supplies. Since Egyptian texts almost never mention defeat by enemies, this allusion is instructive, and no doubt reflective of an ongoing threat from nomads that is generally obscured by the sources.

Pepinakht's account reflects a number of realities of Old Kingdom warfare. First, the Eastern nomads, while generally not a threat to Egypt itself, were a constant potential threat to any Egyptian expedition into the Eastern Desert or Sinai. Nearly all of these expeditions would thus have to have been accompanied by a strong military escort. The relative proportion of soldiers to workers is illuminated in two inscriptions from Wadi Hammamat with reference to the quarrying of stone. The first included 200 soldiers and 200 workers (ARE 1:174).[45] The second mentions 1100 men and 1200 soldiers, with 200 donkeys for carrying supplies and returning with the quarried stone (ARE 1:175). If typical, these numbers indicate that the standard proportion for these types of expeditions was 50 percent soldiers and 50 percent laborers, with about one donkey per ten men. We should, however, assume that the workers would fight when needed, and that soldiers would often form part of the labor force.

Pepinakht's mission had not only been to punish the nomads for daring to attack Egypt, but also to recover the bodies of the dead for proper burial in Egypt. Dying in a foreign land, and thereby missing a proper burial in Egypt, was of serious eternal concern to ancient Egyptians. Without a proper burial, ritual, and grave goods, the soul of the departed would suffer in eternity.[46] This would have been of great concern to soldiers and officers going on foreign military expeditions. To die and have one's corpse left rotting in a foreign battlefield was tantamount to a condemnation to hell, probably creating a type of "leave no man behind" mentality among Egyptian soldiers.

Other Egyptian texts confirm the importance of proper burial to the Egyptians. The mortuary inscription of Sabni, son of Mekhu, the governor of southern Egypt – not to be confused with Sabni, son of Pepinakht, discussed on p. 350 – describes a similar expedition to Nubia to retrieve the body of his father who had died in Wawat, apparently of natural causes. Sabni brought a group of his personal retainers, along with 100 donkey loads of incense, honey, clothing and oil as presents for the Nubians, probably to "ransom" his father's corpse. The line between gifts, trade goods, and bribes is greatly blurred in these texts; trade with Nubia often seemed a combination of extortion, tribute, the ritual exchange of gifts, along with more mundane economic business. There are naturally hints of military activity in the text, with the mention of soldiers accompanying the expedition and the "pacification" of Nubia (ARE 1:166–9). The Middle Kingdom "Tale of Sinuhe" (see pp. 430–3) also emphasizes this fear; the desire for a proper burial in Egypt was one of the prime motives for Sinuhe to return from exile (TS 40). If the corpses of the dead were not recovered and returned to Egypt, the morale of future expeditions could seriously suffer. Thus Pepinakht's expedition was more than merely punitive. It was also necessary to maintain the morale of the Egyptian army. This fear of being left behind and unburied may in part account for the expansion of the use of non-Egyptian mercenaries in foreign campaigns during the Old Kingdom, mercenaries who, with different religious traditions, might not have felt this concern to the same extent as the Egyptians.

Sabni

Sabni (Sebni), the son of Pepinakht, succeeded his father as "Commander of the Foreigners" on the Nubian frontier (AEAB 17 = ARE 1:164–9). Like his father's, Sabni's autobiography recounts his command of a military expedition to Nubia. As military commander of the Nubian frontier, or the "southern gate" to Egypt as it was often called, Sabni was ordered by the king to "build two great barges in [the] Wawat [province of Nubia], in order to convey two great obelisks to On [Helio-polis, near Cairo]". Despite the earlier claims that Nubia had been "pacified", the animosity of the Nubians continued, forcing special tactical arrangements to pro-tect the barges and their obelisks.

> I went forth to Wawat [in northern Nubia] with two troops of soldiers, while the [Nubian mercenary] scouts who I had paid were on the west and east [banks of the Nile] of Wasat, so as to bring back my troops of soldiers in peace. Never did I let a man's sandal or loaf be stolen [by the Hostile Nubians]. (AEAB 17)[47]

It appears from this description that the Egyptian army was divided in two, with half on each bank of the Nile accompanying the flotilla bringing the obelisks. In addition to the Egyptian troops in the Nile valley, however, Nubian mercenaries were enlisted. It is not clear if they were paid protection money to allow the expedition to pass, or if they were more permanently hired mercenaries to accompany the Egyptian force. At any rate, the Nubians were apparently sent to the edges of the Nile valley on the desert ridges and fringes, to protect the far flanks and scout for possible hostile movement. This account gives the distinct impression that the armed expedition was undertaken without the permission of the Wawat Nubians and in the face of a potential serious threat of attack.

The collapse of the Old Kingdom {2206–2191)[48]

There were a number of factors at work in Egypt that undermined the strength of the monarchy. One major problem was the devolution of power and the wealth of

the king to the regional nomarchs. Land, titles, authority, and wealth were naturally given to loyal and successful soldiers, ministers, and nomarchs throughout the
Old Kingdom. Since government office and land could on occasion be inherited
by a nomarch's successors, this wealth often became permanently alienated from
the crown. Furthermore, pious and for the most part perpetual endowments were
made to temples. There were also rising numbers of mortuary temples for the
ever-increasing numbers of royal ancestors; many of these were exempt from taxes
or other forms of royal service. The land and wealth necessary to maintain the cult
of the dead divine ancestors thus progressively increased. The construction of
temples and pyramids and great funerary complexes absorbed an increasing portion
of state revenue and resources. The priestly bureaucracy necessary to run the
estates designed to maintain the proper rites for the temples and pyramids likewise
grew in size while decreasing in efficiency. Thus, slowly, the resources of the
central state were diffused to regional rulers and religious institutions. At some
point the resources of the state became insufficient for the demands placed upon
them. Some speculate that the advancing age and possible incapacity of Pepy II at
the end of his reign may have left rival ministers and governors increasingly independent. At the death of Pepy II {2206} a succession crisis erupted, culminating
within fourteen years in the fragmentation of Egypt into a number of small
regional kingdoms, inaugurating what is know as the First Intermediate Period.

Economically, this period seems to have been one of extended drought and low
flooding levels of the Nile, decreasing food production and creating the potential
for famine, while increasing competition for decreasing food resources. Furthermore, drought and food shortages undercut both the real economic power of the
king and his ideological legitimacy, which was based on the claim that the king
was the divinely sanctioned sustainer of moral and natural order. The transition to
the First Intermediate Period was also characterized by the devolution of power
from the centralized royal court to provincial governors and mayors, who
increasingly claimed the credit for regional administration and building projects
and who chose to be buried in their own provinces rather than near the king.
Provincial rulers also managed to make succession to their offices hereditary,
thereby further undermining central control. To some extent these developments
are simply a matter of degree, since regional leaders were also prominent and semi-
autonomous during much of the Old Kingdom. None the less, during most of the
Old Kingdom provincial rulers at least nominally submitted to royal authority.

Pepy II's death, after a reign of 94 years, left numerous sons as possible rival
heirs to the throne. The declining power of the Sixth Dynasty is apparent in the
succession of ephemeral short-reigning rulers during its last half-century {2206–
2165}. Pepy II was succeeded by his son Antyemsaf II, who, given his father's
ninety-four-year reign, was apparently already an old man at his ascension. He ruled
for only a year, and was succeeded by his wife, Nitokerty (Nitocris) {2205–2200},
apparently the first woman to rule Egypt independently.[49] Her brief rule was followed by possibly five ephemeral rulers over the course of nine years {2200–
2191}. The details are not known, but it seems clear that provincial nomarchs

rapidly asserted independent power, fragmenting the kingdom into a number of separate regional warring nomes. The collapse of royal authority was probably accompanied by decreasing security on the frontiers; there is evidence of incursions of Easterners into the north-eastern delta shortly after the death of Pepy II (HAE 139–40). This collapse of royal authority inaugurated what historians call the First Intermediate Period {2190–2061}, which will be discussed in Chapter Fifteen.

CHAPTER FOURTEEN

Warfare during the Old Kingdom

Ideology of sacred warfare

The Pyramid Texts[1] are a collection of Old Kingdom funerary prayers and rituals designed to assist the king in obtaining eternal life in the realm of the gods after death. The surviving texts are composed of nearly a thousand "spells" or "utterances" dating to roughly two centuries spanning the reigns from Unas {2404–2374} through Pepy II {2300–2206}. Many scholars believe, however, that some of the texts may have originated centuries earlier – the first surviving copies are thus rather late versions. Although primarily ritual and religious in purpose, they contain a number of passages describing weapons and the martial virtues of the king, thus providing us with insights into the ritual and ideology of Old Kingdom warfare.

Warfare in ancient Egypt was not perceived as merely the struggle between the mortals; it was theomachy – the war of the gods. As in the *Iliad* and *Mahabharata* – or the Bible, for that matter – the gods themselves came to earth and intervened in battle to assist the king. The gods gave the king a divine mandate to conquer and rule the entire world. An inscription from the mortuary temple of king Sahure makes the divine mandate for foreign conquests clear. In this inscription, a god addresses king Sahure, proclaiming: "I grant thee all western and eastern foreign lands with all the Montiu bowmen who are in every land" (EWA 137).

The war god Horus particularly aids the king in battle: "May you be mighty in Upper Egypt as is this Horus through whom you are mighty; may you be mighty in Lower Egypt as is this Horus through whom you are mighty, that you may be mighty and protect yourself from your foe" (PT 645). The victory in battle of the king over his enemies is frequently described in mythic terms relating to the archetypal combat between Horus and his enemy, the god Seth.

[Horus] has driven back the heart of Seth for you, for you [the king] are greater than [Seth].... [Horus] has caused the gods to protect you, and Geb has put his sandal on the head of your [defeated and prostrate] foe, who flinches from you. Your son Horus has smitten him, he has wrested his Eye [the mythical talismanic Eye of Horus] from him [Seth] and has given it to you....

353

Horus has caused you to lay hold of your foes, and there is none of them who shall escape from you.... Horus has laid hold of Seth and has set him under you on your behalf ... Horus has caused you to examine [Seth] in his inmost parts, lest he escape from you; he has caused you to lay hold of him with your hand, lest he get away from you. (PT 356)[2]

And again:

O Osiris the King, mount up to Horus ... [for] he has smitten Seth for you bound ... Horus has driven him off for you, for you are greater than he.... Horus has protected you, and he will not fail to protect you. (PT 357; see also 364, 606)

In the end, its seems that even the gods must surrender to the overwhelming power of the divine king: "The gods come to me bowing, the spirits serve me because of my power; they have broken their staffs and smashed their weapons [in submission] because I am a great one" (PT 510).

Commanders faithfully serving the pharaoh would likewise be aided by the gods in battle. Sabni, the "Commander of the Foreigners", describes himself as "herald of the words of [the wargod] Horus to his following"; he is metaphorically a weapon wielded by the gods, the "throwstick of Horus in foreign lands" (AEAB 17). The king, and indirectly his duly appointed commanders, were in reality the representatives of the war god Horus. His commands reflected the will of the gods, not merely political or military decisions of human beings. The pharaoh and his commanders were the weapons of the gods to do their will on earth.

The propaganda of the king as the ideal warrior and athlete is particularly well represented in the mortuary statues of the three great builders of the pyramids of the Fourth Dynasty. Enthroned or standing, the mortuary statues of these kings depict the idealized, well-muscled physiques of powerful young warriors, symbolizing the ideal of the pharaoh as warrior-king.[3] Ritually the king was the ideal athlete – the strongest and fastest man in the kingdom (SGAE 19–59). From Pre-Dynastic times the king's physical prowess was demonstrated by a ritual run associated with the *Heb-sed* festival, the Jubilee or festival of renewal of the king's power and authority, in which the king was required to run around set markers to demonstrate his physical strength. One of these *Heb-sed* running tracks is preserved south of the pyramid of Djoser at Saqqara, in what seems to be the oldest formal racetrack in history (EDE 212–15).

Military organization in the Old Kingdom (EMO 32–6)

R. Faulkner has rightly noted that "regarding the organization of the army during the Old Kingdom there is not a great deal of evidence" (EMO 32). There is, none the less, sufficient to give us a broad understanding of the subject. Much of our knowledge on military ranks and commissions comes from tomb autobiographies, from which we learn that there probably was not a professional military officer class in the Old Kingdom. Rather, courtiers and government officials served in a wide variety of religious, administrative, legal, economic, and military capacities, according to the immediate needs of the state.

The most fully documented example of such a mixed military–civilian–religious–administrative career comes from the autobiography of Weni (AEL 1:18–22; EMO 34–5). Weni began his career as "custodian of the storehouse" under king Teti, rising to the office of inspector and "overseer of the robing-room" under Pepy I (AEL 1:18–19). Thereafter he became "senior warden" of Nekhen, serving as a judge as well. He then became "overseer of the royal tenants", and was a judge in a case involving charges against the first wife of Pepy I. He thus already had a distinguished career as administrator and judge before beginning his military duties, probably in his thirties (AEL 19). After distinguishing himself in several campaigns in Sinai and Canaan, he became governor of Upper Egypt, in which capacity he supervised or led expeditions to Nubia for granite, and to Hatnub for alabaster, along with digging canals, boat-building, and negotiations with Nubians (AEL 1:21–2). Weni's career is thus the classic Old Kingdom example of the Egyptian practice of having courtiers and officers assigned to tasks on an *ad hoc* basis – scribe, administrator, judge, governor, explorer, engineer, diplomat, miner, ship-builder, priest, and soldier, all combined into one.

Other autobiographies give hints of the same type of *ad hoc* recruitment of military officers. The autobiographical inscription of Meten, from the Third Dynasty Mastaba at Saqqara, describes his roles as administrator, judge, and governor, noting as well that he served as "commander of the fortress of *Snt*", "governor of the stronghold *Hsn*", and "governor of the Cow-stronghold" (ARE 1:77–8), indicating that civil administrators served as garrison commanders of the fortresses in their provinces. Mention is also made of commanders of individual arsenals and fortresses, as well as a "commander of the affairs of the fortresses" who seems to have had broader authority over fortifications throughout the kingdom (EMO 36). The tomb of Ka-aper contains an inscription describing the presence of "the scribe of the king's army" during expeditions (EWA §41), indicating the presence of literate military officers providing logistical and administrative support on Old Kingdom campaigns. Military and other official positions could be inherited from father to son. Ibdu and his father Merire-onekh were both military commanders (ARE 1:139), as were Heqaib and his son Sabni (AEAB 15–17).

It is unclear if the Egyptian army was organized into formal, permanent military units. Rather, it seems that each nome or province of Egypt was required to muster a certain number of troops for a military campaign, and that these troops were commanded by the government officials of those nome. Egyptian armies were thus organized on a provincial basis with soldiers serving with their kinsmen, friends and neighbors (EMO 32; AEL 1:19). This regional military organization with nomarchs in command of their own provincial troops seems to have laid the foundation of semi-autonomous nomarch military power which would contribute to the fragmentation of Egypt during the First Intermediate Period. Whether these provincial troops were purely irregular militias or included professional soldiers stationed in the provinces is unclear (EMO 33). These Egyptian troops were frequently supported by Nubian and Libyan mercenaries (EMO 33).

The only military unit mentioned during the Old Kingdom was the *teset* (*ṯst*), a battalion or regiment; this seems to be a general term for any ordered body of soldiers rather than a technical term for a formal military unit of a specific size (EMO 32). Soldiers are generically known as *meshe⁽* (*mšꜥ*), while the only regular officer mentioned is the *imy-r mšꜥ*, the "commander" or "overseer of the soldiers" – perhaps roughly "captain" or "general". This title is held by commanders of quarrying expeditions as well as more strictly military campaigns (EMO 33–4).

Weapons

Our knowledge of weapons from the Old Kingdom period, and, indeed from all of Near Eastern military history, comes from three sources: archaeology, artistic depictions of weapons, and texts. A section of the Pyramid Texts describes the ritual clothing and arming of the king in preparation for religious ceremonies and battle, and gives us a detailed description of elite Old Kingdom armament. In general the king is described as being equipped with weapons like those of the gods (PT 68, 222). Paralleling representations in royal iconography, the king wears sandals (PT 106), a kilt or loincloth and belt (PT 57L–O, S, 58, 59A, 225), and is sometimes described wearing a "tail", which probably alludes to bull tails attached to the back of the belt as depicted in the Narmer palette and other Early Dynastic art (PT 57N–O, S). He also occasionally wears a "leopard-skin" (PT 469, 485). The king receives four different types of "mantlets" associated with fighting, which may be some type of shield (PT 71F–I).

The three primary royal weapons in the arming ritual and other parts of the Pyramid Texts are mace, bow, and dagger. The most frequently mentioned weapon is the mace, which the king's "fist grips" in preparation for battle (PT 412, 512, 555, 675). There are several types: *mḫn*-mace, *ḏsr*-mace, *izr*-mace, (PT 62–4; LA 3:414–15). It is impossible to tell precisely what is meant by these different mace names. They may refer to different structural designs or military functions, but it is more likely a reference to art motifs or engravings, ritual function, or perhaps even a personal name for the weapon, like naming King Arthur's sword Excalibur.

Archery is particularly associated with the war god Horus. Horus is "Lord of the Bows" (PT 437), and "the shooter" of the bow (PT 659). In mythical stories he "draws his nine bows" against snake demons (PT 385).[4] The king, as Horus's counterpart on earth, is "he who draws the bowstring as Horus and who pulls the cord as Osiris" (PT 390). In the ritual arming ceremony the king is given several different types of bows (*iwnt* and *pḏt*), bowstrings and arrows (PT 57A–H, 71G).

Two types of dagger are mentioned in the ritual arming text: *Mtpn(t)*-dagger and *M3gsw*-dagger, (PT 57Q–R). One knife is described as "black" (PT 290), which may refer to the obsidian or dark flint of the blade. In battle, the king "bears a sharp knife which cuts throats" (PT 251). Like other weapons, the king's daggers parallel those of the gods, such as the "knife of Seth" (PT 666A, 674). The dagger is described as delivering the *coup de grace* to the king's enemies: "Sharpen your knife, O Thoth, which is keen and cutting, which removes heads and cuts out hearts! He will remove the heads and cut out the hearts of those who would oppose themselves to me" (PT 477).[5]

All the archaeological evidence indicates that the weapons in Old Kingdom Egypt were in a transitional phase between Neolithic and Bronze Age. While copper daggers and axes are known, most daggers, maces, and projectile points used by the ordinary soldiers of this period still seem to have been made of stone. In this context the frequent mention of iron in the Pyramid Texts is, at first glance, puzzling. The gods in heaven sit upon an "iron throne" which the king shares in the afterlife.[6] In heaven the king receives an "iron scepter" (PT 665C), and the god Horus wears "iron bands on [his] arms" (PT 214). In the resurrection the king's bones will be made of iron (PT 570, 684, 724), strong and everlasting. The gates to the gods' celestial castle are protected by "doors of iron" (PT 469). Although the earthly realm of the king is perceived as the mirror image of the celestial realm of the gods, these texts should not be understood as reflecting the real weapons of the king. The Egyptians understood that meteoric iron fell from heaven – it was sometimes called "copper from heaven" (EAE 2:183). Thus, heaven, the realm of the gods, was the place where iron came from; indeed, the metal is described as "god's iron" (PT 38), while the very firmament of heaven is itself made of iron (PT 509). Heavenly weapons and other items made of iron would be the celestial counterparts of earthly weapons made from stone or copper. During the early Old Kingdom the weapons of the gods were of iron, those of the king and nobles of copper, while those of most common soldiers were of stone.

Combat

Once the arming ceremony was complete the king set out for battle. Several texts seem to describe a pre-battle ceremony in which the King opens the city gates, marshals and counts his soldiers ("slayers" or "slaughterers"), and then marches to defeat the enemy.

> The bolt is opened for you in the double Ram-gate which keeps out the [enemy] peoples; may you number the slaughterers [in your army] (PT 611). The six door-bolts, which keep Libya out, are opened for you; your iron scepter is in your hand that you may number the slayers, [and] control the Nine Bows [enemy nations] (PT 665C). Your scepter is laid in your hand that you may open the bolt in the double Ram-gate which keeps out the Fenkhu ["Phoenicians" or Canaanites]. May you number the slayers, may you control the Nine Bows. (PT 716)[7]

When the army marched to confront the "Nine Bows" – a generic term to describe all the enemies of Egypt – the king was, naturally, always victorious in battle; at least this is what the Pyramid Texts would have us believe. "I have subdued those [enemies] who are to be punished, I have smitten their foreheads, and I am not opposed [by enemies] in the horizon" (PT 251) – the Egyptian way of saying to the end of the earth. In battle the king will always "smite [the enemy], destroy them, drown them on land and sea" (PT 717), an interesting possible reference to river or naval battles. In the end, "the bowmen ... are felled" (PT 231) by the king's army, and "the [enemy Nine] Bows bow to" the king in submission (PT 693), an act also depicted on some martial reliefs.

Battle scene from Inty's tomb[8]

Two scenes from tombs, probably dating to the late Old Kingdom, provide fascinating glimpses of tactics and siegecraft in this period. The first, and most illuminating, comes from the tomb of Inty (Inti) at Deshasheh in middle Egypt. Although the inscription is lost, most scholars believe the scene depicts a siege in southern Canaan. The scene is divided into two halves. The left half, in four registers, depicts a battle outside the city – presumably leading up to the siege. The right half shows the siege itself. Inty's siege mural gives us our best understanding of both the tactics of combat and methods of siegecraft in the late Old Kingdom.

The upper register is partly lost, but depicts Egyptian soldiers advancing over wounded Canaanite enemies who are pierced with arrows. The next two scenes show Egyptians fighting the Canaanites. Here the Canaanites are stumbling and fleeing in disarray from the Egyptian attack. All are pierced with multiple arrows; one has six such wounds. None of the Canaanites offers serious resistance; the orderly Egyptians are all armed with axes, marching through and dispatching the Canaanites with blows to the head, neck, and shoulders. The Canaanites seem to be armed only with bows, although one or two may have other weapons (the murals are badly damaged, leading to some uncertainty in interpretation). The fourth and lowest register, possibly reflecting events after the successful siege, depicts bound prisoners of war – men, women, and children – being led off to captivity in Egypt.

In both of these scenes the numerous arrows stuck in the Canaanites imply that some Egyptian soldiers had bows. Most of the Egyptians carry axes; none are shown with a shield, spear, mace, or dagger. They wear kilts, but no other armor or helmet. The Canaanites likewise have no armor or shield; they too wear a kilt and are distinguished from the Egyptians only by their longer hair and headbands. In terms of weapons technology, the implication of the Inty mural – confirmed by that of Kaemheset – is that the stone-headed mace, which had been the pre-eminent weapon during the Early Dynastic period and early Old Kingdom, had been largely superceded among common soldiers by copper-headed axes by the late Old Kingdom, as copper became more available and less expensive.[9] The axe-heads in the two battle scenes are of two types; examples of both have been discovered from archaeology (EWW 35; EAE 2:407; BAH pl. 2–3). The first, sometimes called the "epsilon" (E-shaped) axe, has a long and broad blade (AW 1:146, 154–5, 168–71; FP 49); the second type has a semi-circular blade sometimes described as "eye"-shaped (AW 1:12, 147; BAH 22–3). The proportional relation of the haft to the size of the Egyptian soldiers implies the haft was 50–75 cm long. It is shown wielded with either one or two hands. Both of these weapons seem to have been known to the Egyptians as *mibt* in the Old Kingdom and *minb* in the Middle Kingdom (EG 511, sign T7).[10] It is not clear if this shift in terminology merely reflects a change in pronunciation, or is related to the difference between the "epsilon" and "eye" styles of axes.

Battle tactics

Whereas the autobiography of Weni shows us the sophisticated strategy of the Old Kingdom, the Inty siege mural allows us for the first time to get a glimpse of Old Kingdom battle tactics, if only inferred from a hypothetical reading of the narrative scene. The battle began with a missile barrage from archers. Although no Egyptian archer is actually depicted on the surviving portions of the scene, the upper half of the first register is lost, and the four advancing soldiers in that panel may have been archers. However that may be, every Canaanite soldier is wounded by multiple arrows, implying massed archery by the Egyptians. The individual effectiveness of Egyptian arrows, however, seems to have been rather limited. None of the Canaanites is armored, and although there appears to be one man killed by archery – struck by six arrows in the legs, back and head – several Canaanites have three or four arrow wounds and are still alive and resisting. One is still fighting with two arrows in his leg, one in his arm and two in his head. This implies that the wounds from arrows were not very serious, and therefore that either the arrows were shot from a great distance, or they did not have great penetrating power, or both. The effectiveness of Egyptian archery was thus most likely based on the large number of arrows shot at unarmored targets.

When either the missile supply was exhausted, or the enemy was sufficiently disorganized and debilitated, the axe-armed Egyptian infantry advanced into a melee. The two middle registers show a chaotic melee in the heat of battle, but the damaged upper register shows Egyptian soldiers advancing into combat in ordered ranks. It is unclear if the Egyptian army at this time had separate regiments specializing in archery or axe combat. One man holding the siege-ladder and another supervising the mining operation both have their axes stuck in their belts behind their backs, allowing them to use both hands. The Kaemheset mural, discussed on pp. 362–3, also shows the Egyptians putting the haft of the axe in their belts leaving their hands free to climb a ladder. Since no Egyptian is shown with a shield or a bow, it is possible that the Egyptian soldiers were double-armed with bow and axe. They first exchanged missile fire with the enemy, then dropped their bows, drew their axes from their belts, and charged. On the other hand, it is also possible that the archers simply are not depicted in the melee scene, having remained in the rear when the axe-armed shock infantry advance into battle.

Fortifications[11]

Fortifications (*wmtt*, EG 496, sign O36; and *mnw*) are found in Egypt in Pre-Dynastic times, and were well developed by the Old Kingdom. Many, if not all, cities were fortified with mud brick walls; one archaic hieroglyphic symbol for a city is simply a turreted wall (HEA 1:48, 177–8). The mud brick walls (*inb*, EG 496, sign O36) were up to five meters thick, with numerous projecting bastions and towers (*tsm*); gateways (*sbḫt*, EG 494, sign O13) were heavily protected by mud-brick towers as well. Principles of concentric fortifications were understood by the Egyptians. The city walls of Buhen in Nubia included a central keep, the main wall with eighteen projecting semi-circular towers, a dry moat, and a barbican 65 meters from the main wall (AEA 40).

A number of archaeological remains of Old Kingdom fortresses have survived (Figure 9). The fortified city of Balat in the Dakhla Oasis had rectangular city walls (110 × 230 meters) with a separate citadel on the south (AEA 26). The Nubian frontier was the most highly fortified – or at least has the best surviving examples – which have been studied in great detail before they were submerged by Lake Nasser and the Aswan Dam (FB). The First Dynasty fortress on Elephantine Island at Aswan – sometimes called the "southern gate" to Egypt – continued in use during the Old Kingdom. The city itself was surrounded by a wall with semicircular towers, which followed the contours of the terrain of the island. A separate

Figure 9 Mud-brick city walls at El-Kab, Egypt {c. 1600–1000}. Although these well-preserved fortifications date to the New Kingdom, the basic size and structure are similar to earlier Middle Kingdom city-walls

Source: Photograph by William Hamblin.

53×53 meters citadel added to the defensibility of the site (AEA 81). In addition to the Elephantine fortress at the First Cataract, three Old Kingdom fortresses were constructed in northern Nubia itself: Ikkur (82×110 meters) (AEA 115), Kubban (70×125 meters) (AEA 132), and Aniba (87×138 meters) (AEA 18; HEA 1:178). Ikkur and Aniba had dry moats and semi-circular towers. The spectacular fortress of Buhen in Nubia (150×70 meters) dates to the Middle Kingdom, and will be discussed below (pp. 443–5). However, the Old Kingdom town at Buhen (120×950 meters) was also fortified, with eighteen surviving semi-circular towers and a barbican 65 meters from the main wall (AEA 40). In general, fortified mud brick walls are essentially the same as the enclosure walls of temple complexes, of which several examples have also survived.

Texts of the Old Kingdom provide some additional information about fortifications and siegecraft. Egyptian titles from Old Kingdom mortuary inscriptions include officers who were responsible for the garrisons and upkeep of fortresses, such as the Third Dynasty "commander of the stronghold of *Snt*", "commander of the stronghold *Hsn* in the Harpoon Nome", and commander of the "the Cow Stronghold". These titles indicate that there were fortified sites in various nomes of Egypt, even though the surviving archaeological evidence in the Nile valley is sparse (ARE 1:77–8). Other titles mentioning fortresses include: "Commander of the Desert Keeps and Royal Fortresses", and "Commander of the Way(s) of Horus", which was the road through the northern Sinai to Canaan (EAE 1:553).

The Pyramid Texts, which have been introduced above, also contain important – though rather mythical – allusions to fortifications and siegecraft. Specific historical fortifications are possibly mentioned in the texts. The king "is the Great Bull who smote [the city of] Kenzet" in Nubia (PT 205). An allusion to the "Fortress of the Bitter Lakes" (PT 366) – the lakes and marshes between modern Suez and Port Said (AAE 167) – indicates that the western frontier was fortified against incursions from the Sinai during the Old Kingdom. This may be related to the "double Ram-gate" which "keeps out the Fenkhu [Canaanites]" (PT 716). There is another fortress "which keeps Libya out" of Egypt as well (PT 665C). Vague details of fortress design are alluded to in the texts. The "double Ram-gate" is bolted shut (PT 611); one fortress gate has "six door-bolts" (PT 665C). Standing on the ramparts in defense of his fortress, the king is described as "a great falcon which is on the battlements" (PT 627).

The most frequent allusion to fortifications in the Pyramid Texts is the mythic "Castle of the Mace of the Great Ones [gods]" to which the king gains entrance during his ascent to heaven (PT 262, 600, 611, 665). It is also called the "castle of the Mace of *p3'r* wood" (PT 219), and is frequently associated with the god Thoth.[12] What is important from the military perspective is that the gods in the celestial world dwell in a fortress-palace (PT 322); the king on earth, who imitates the gods in all things, does as well. The king's fortress-palace at Memphis may be the earthly counterpart to the gods' heavenly "Castle of the Mace".

Siegecraft (LA 3:765–86)

The mural from the tomb of Inty, introduced on pp. 358–9, also shows a siege in progress.[13] Having lost the open battle, the surviving defeated Canaanites fled to their fortified city, depicted as walled with regularly-spaced, semi-circular projecting towers. Following their victory in the field the Egyptians assaulted the city, using two different siege techniques. First, as also described in the Pyramid Texts (discussed on pp. 353–4), they placed a tall siege ladder against the wall for an assault. In the Inty relief the assault has not yet begun. The siege scene from the tomb of Kaemheset at Saqqara, however, complements our knowledge of Inty's siege scene.[14] Here the wooden ladder is apparently on wheels – though how the axle could rotate while the ladder remained stable is unclear from the illustration. The wheeled ladder is braced by a man wedging it in place with a thick piece of wood, while five soldiers ascend the ladder. All five wear brown kilts and are unarmored and unshielded. All are also armed with axes. Rather than climbing over the wall into the city, two of the soldiers seem to be hacking at the brick wall with their axes.

The second siege technique shown in both the Inty and the Kaemheset reliefs is undermining the base of the wall. Here Egyptians with long wooden beams or crowbars are attempting to dislodge the mud bricks from the base of the wall, hoping to get the wall to collapse and form a breach. Given that all fortifications from this period were of mud brick – although some had stone foundations at the base – undermining a wall would only have been a matter of time, though such efforts could have been seriously hindered by stones and missiles thrown by defenders from the top of the wall. Thus both the Inty and the Kaemheset reliefs show the same siege techniques: a ladder assault combined with undermining the brick wall.

The reliefs also give us important information about defending fortified cities. The defenders in the Kaemheset relief are divided into four registers, but unfortunately the upper two panels are severely damaged. They possibly show soldiers throwing stones or javelins, or shooting bows at the Egyptian assaulters. The third panel depicts the herds of the Canaanites – cattle, goats, and donkeys – being brought into the city for safety, and being fed from a pile of grain. The fourth panel seems to show the women and children of the city being given a grain ration.[15] The Inty relief is even more evocative of life in a besieged city, focusing on the important role of women in logistical and medical support for the army. The first panel shows a woman extracting an arrow from a wounded Canaanite soldier, probably one who had escaped the battle that is depicted on the left side of the relief. The second panel shows a woman embracing (or throttling?) a returning soldier, and the women and children mourning before the Canaanite king on his throne.[16] In the third and fourth panels the women are again helping wounded soldiers, one who is staggering from his wounds. In the last scene some men are listening at the wall opposite to where the Egyptian soldiers are undermining from the outside. The lower left corner of the wall shows three semi-circular bastions in close proximity where the Egyptians are attempting to undermine, which may represent either additional towers used to strengthen a weak section of the wall, or a gate flanked by protecting towers.

The after-life ascent of the king into heaven is occasionally described in imagery that is probably associated with siegecraft. The king storms heaven like a fortress (PT 255, 257); he "overthrows the ramparts [of the heavenly fortress], he removes the ramparts" (PT 667C), and "demolishes the ramparts of Shu" (PT 509), probably by undermining as shown in the siege reliefs. In the process the king boasts he "will smite away the arms of [the god] Shu which support the sky and I will thrust my shoulder into that rampart on which you lean" (PT 255). One text describes how the "King takes possession of the sky, he cleaves its iron" (PT 257), probably alluding to the "doors of iron" (PT 469) of the heavenly castle. As noted above, these references to iron in the Pyramid Texts are probably mythical – since meteoric iron falls from heaven, iron is the metal of the gods. It is quite possible, however, that Old Kingdom fortress doors were reinforced at their joints and bolts with copper bands.

The gods sometimes assist the king in his victorious conquest of this mythic fortress by the use of siege ladders. In one text the four Sons of Horus aid the king in his siege by preparing both wooden and rope ladders for the king:[17]

> [They] tie the rope ladder for this King, they make firm the wooden ladder for this King, they cause the King to mount up [to heaven] . . . [The wooden ladder's] timbers have been hewn by *Ss3*; the lashings which are on it have been drawn tight with the sinews of *G3swty*, Bull of the sky, the rungs have been fastened to its sides. (PT 688)

In attacking the celestial fortress, the king "sets up the ladder" (PT 333), which the gods hold steady for him (PT 304). These textual references to the use of ladders in siegecraft are confirmed by contemporary military art from Deshasheh and Saqqara, discussed above, both of which show men assaulting city walls with ladders held firm by other soldiers at the bottom.

Treatment of prisoners (LA 3:786–8)

After the battle, "the enemies are hunted down" (PT 724), and the prisoners brought bound before the king (PT 222, 357) under the "guard of the prisoners after the great battle" (CT 493). The Coffin Texts describe a magical spell designed to prevent capture in battle, providing a description of the treatment of prisoners: "you shall not be imprisoned, you shall not be restrained, you shall not be fettered, you shall not be put under guard, you shall not be put in the place of execution in which rebels are put" (CT 23). Captured enemies might be physically abused, even tortured, and their corpses mutilated and dismembered; mercy is unthinkable. The king is promised by the gods that he "will not be hanged head downwards" (PT 694), apparently a reference to the public exposure of the corpses of enemies. The treatment of prisoners is often described in mythic terms relating to the tale of the primordial combat between Horus and Seth. Horus "bound [Seth's] legs and bound his arms and threw him down on his side" (PT 485B). He "sets [Seth, the King's] foe under your feet" (PT 368, cf. PT 371). The king's enemy "is smitten by the children of Horus, they have made bloody his beating, they have punished him" (PT 369). Captive Seth is castrated (PT 570), and dismembered: "Horus has cut off the strong arms of your foes and Horus has brought them to you cut up" (PT 372). Although these are mythic narratives, there is no reason to think the Egyptian kings did not do these types of things to their real enemies, as depicted on several of the artistic sources mentioned earlier.

The fate of the enemies of pharaoh is described in gruesome, and almost gleeful detail in the Pyramid Texts:

> I am stronger than they . . . their hearts fall to my fingers, their entrails are for the denizens of the sky [carrion birds], their blood is for the denizens of the earth [carrion animals]. Their heirs are [doomed] to poverty, their houses to conflagration . . . But I am happy, happy, for I am the Unique One, the Bull of the sky, I have crushed those who would do this against me and have annihilated their survivors. (PT 254)

In the Horus–Seth combat myth, Horus takes revenge for the death of his father Osiris, who is later resurrected by his wife Isis (EAE 2:188–91). "O Osiris the King, I bring to you him [Seth] who would killed you; do not let him escape from your hand.... A knife is made ready for him ... he having been cut three times" (PT 543, cf. 545). Torturing the defeated enemy Seth is described as retaliatory revenge for the torture Seth had previously inflicted when he temporarily defeated Osiris.

> O my father Osiris this King, I have smitten for you him [Seth] who smote you ... I have killed for you him who killed you ... I have broken for you him who broke you.... He who stretched you out is a stretched bull; he who shot you is a bull to be shot.... I have cut off its head, I have cut off its tail, I have cut off its arms, I have cut off its legs. (PT 580, cf. 670)

Such mythic texts represent a military worldview in which retaliatory raids and personal revenge on enemies were a positive moral responsibility.

The most ghastly passage in the Pyramid Texts is the so-called "Cannibal Hymn" (PT 273–4), which describes the king dismembering, cooking, and eating the bodies of his enemies to absorb their spiritual power.

> The sky is overcast,
> The stars are darkened,
> The celestial expanses quiver,
> The bones of the earth-gods tremble,

The planets are stilled,
For they have seen the King appearing in power ...
The King is the Bull of the sky,
Who conquers at will,
Who lives on the being of every god
Who eats their entrails ...
The King is a possessor of offerings who knots the cord [binding captives]
And who himself prepares his meal;
The King is the one who eats men and lives on the gods ...
It is "Grasper-of-topknots" who is Kehau,
Who lassoes them for the King
It is "the Serpent with raised head"
Who guards them [the prisoners] for him [the king]
And restrains them for him;
It is "He who is over the reddening" [blood-letting]
Who binds them for him;
It is Khons who slew the lords
Who strangles them for the King
And extracts for him what is in their bodies ...
It is Shezmu who cuts them up for the King
And who cooks for him a portion of them
On his evening hearth-stones;
It is the King who eats their magic
And gulps down their spirits;
Their big ones are for his morning meal,
Their middle-sized ones are for his evening meal,
Their little ones are for his night meal,
Their old men and their old women are for his incense-burning;
It is the Great Ones [circumpolar stars] in the northern sky
Who set the fire for him
To the cauldrons containing them
With the thighs of their oldest ones....
[The King] has traveled around the whole of the two skies [the whole earth],
He has circumambulated the Two Banks [of the Nile]
For the King is a great Power....
The King has appeared again in the sky,
He is crowned as Lord of the horizon;
He has broken the back-bones
And taken the hearts of the gods ...
The King feeds on the lungs of the Wise Ones,
And is satisfied with living on hearts and their magic ...
He enjoys himself when their magic is in his belly ...
Lo, their souls are in the King's belly,
Their spirits are in the King's possession ...

Lo, their souls are in the King's possession,
Their shades are (removed) from their owners.

Here we see martial cannibalism, with the king taking bound captives, slaughtering and dismembering them, and finally cooking and eating them to obtain their magical power. The cannibalization of defeated enemies is also mentioned in passing elsewhere: "I will eat a limb from your foe, I will carve it for [the god] Osiris" (PT 477). A variant on the "Cannibal Hymn" is found again in the Middle Kingdom Coffin Texts (CT 573).

The imagery of warfare in the Pyramid Texts describes a world filled with magical and divine power where the gods intervene in battle for their son, the king. The victorious king is merciless to his enemies, rejoicing in their downfall and suffering. For the ancient Egyptians war certainly was a physical activity in the material world; but it was also much more. For the Egyptians, war was a heady mixture of violence, religious ritual, magic, and divine sanction and intervention. War was a ritual act by which the mythic combat of Horus and Seth was re-enacted, and, through the king's ultimate victory, the cosmic balance of the universe maintained. The gods had granted pharaoh the authority to rule the world, and the king's enemies were the enemies of the gods.

Maritime developments (EBS 21–6; SP 26–69)

Egyptian ships of the Old Kingdom ranged from small three- or four-man papyrus fishing skiffs to large cedar oared and sailing ships capable of sailing throughout the eastern Mediterranean and the Red Sea. The oldest fully preserved ship ever found from this region is the royal ship buried near the pyramid of Khufu {2584}, intended to be used by the king in the afterlife.[18] This 43-meter vessel was buried in specially designed pits to the south of Khufu's pyramid. Made entirely of cedar wood imported from Phoenicia, it was designed for river travel and was propelled by oars that also survive. A complex system of nautical knots and lashing was used on the boat (FP 29). Its purpose was probably ritual rather than military, but it none the less stands as a remarkable example of Egyptian shipbuilding skill in the Old Kingdom. Sea-going vessels were larger and propelled by sails (SP 63–9), as seen from a depiction in the tomb of the Vizier Mehu {2330?} from the early Sixth Dynasty (EWP 89); the tomb of Inti also depicts a large vessel under sail (EBS 24).

It is clear that Egyptian maritime capacity developed significantly during the Fifth and Sixth Dynasties. This is reflected in three trading and exploration expeditions. A marble vessel bearing Userkaf's {2513–2506} name was found in the island of Kythera in the Aegean, the earliest indication of maritime contact between the Minoans and Egyptians – though it may have been brought to the Aegean later than Userkaf's reign (EAE 2:588b). Sahure's {2506–2492} funerary temple at Abusir depicts naval vessels returning from an expedition to Phoenicia, probably from Byblos bringing valuable cedar wood (ECI 52, EBS 23). Sahure also undertook the first recorded Egyptian naval expedition to Punt, the south-western coast of the Red Sea, which returned with "80,000 measures of myrrh, 6000 measures of electrum, 2900 measures of malachite, and 23,020 measures of [text lost]" (PS 168). Djedkare Izezi {2436–2404} likewise undertook trading expeditions to both Phoenicia and Punt. Although none of these maritime expeditions were strictly military affairs, the distinction between trading, exploring, mining, and warfare was rather vague in ancient Egypt. It is quite likely that each of these maritime expeditions had a military component, if only a company of soldiers, to protect the ships. More importantly, the ongoing maritime trade to Phoenicia and Punt provided the foundation for the capacity of the Egyptian navy to move large bodies of troops in true amphibious operations. This culminated in the Sixth Dynasty with the amphibious operations of Weni in Canaan {c. 2340}, discussed on p. 340.

We have funerary inscriptions of two naval captains, Inikaf and Khenty, from Sixth Dynasty Coptos. Among other ritual and administrative functions, both are described as "One who puts the Fear of Horus [the King] into the Foreign Lands, who brings the treasure of the King from the Southern Lands" (ICN 31, 33), reflecting the dual function of naval captains – warfare and trade. "Putting the fear of Horus [the King] into foreign lands" is often a euphemism for military action which intimidates the enemy, while "bringing the treasure" refers to either plunder or trade.

River combat undoubtedly remained the most important aspect of naval warfare during the Old Kingdom. Some indication of the nature of ship-to-ship combat can be found in some interesting jousting scenes and harpoon hunts from Old Kingdom tombs at Saqqara.[19] Fishermen often used long poles to propel their bundled papyrus skiffs in the marshes and shallows of the Nile. In the murals some of the fishermen are depicted using their poles to propel their ships, others use the long poles to jab their rivals or swing them overhead. When two skiffs collide, the fishermen are depicted as wrestling on the bow (TEM 53; SP 97). A least part of the goal is to knock the opponent into the river, from which some of the fishermen are being recovered by their friends (TEM 53). The hippopotamus-hunting scene from the tomb of Mereruka at Saqqara (EWP 93; ISP 13, 42; SP 94) shows papyrus craft approaching three hippopotami from two different direction. They have used ropes to either lasso or hook the hippos, and have long harpoons raised overhead in preparation for the kill. Although neither the jousting nor the hunting scenes are strictly military, if we add the use of archery from on board ship, these scenes provide our best window into the rough and tumble melee of Egyptian river warfare.

CHAPTER FIFTEEN

First Intermediate Period Egypt {2190–2061}

The First Intermediate Period[1] is the name given by modern Egyptologists to the time in Egyptian history from the end of the Sixth Dynasty {2191} to the reunification of Egypt by the fourth king of the Eleventh Dynasty, Montuhotep I {2061–2011}. It is characterized by political fragmentation and instability, in contrast with the political unity of Egypt in the Old and Middle Kingdoms. Royal monumental building declines and even disappears during this period, replaced by local tombs and cults in the provinces. Instead of centralizing surplus wealth to build royal tombs and temples, regional nomarchs and priests kept local resources and developed local power bases. In terms of power, wealth, and ideology, the First Intermediate Period is thus characterized by decentralization and fragmentation.

Militarily this decentralization is manifest in military conflict between rival regional Egyptian states. Egyptian military intervention outside Egypt ebbed as the grand trading and exploration expeditions of the Old Kingdom into Nubia, Punt, and Canaan largely disappear during the early First Intermediate Period (HAE 139–40). In some ways the records for this period are quite fragmentary and ambiguous, making precise reconstruction of events and dates difficult and controversial. On the other hand, military historians are provided with a number of important tomb autobiographies that contain a great deal of military information. Following late ancient Egyptian historiographic tradition, the First Intermediate Period is divided by scholars into five dynasties, the Seventh through the Eleventh. In some ways these divisions simplify a complex political and military situation.

Seventh Dynasty {c. 2190}

The numerous problems facing Egypt at the end of the Sixth Dynasty were exacerbated by a power struggle for the throne among the numerous progeny of the centegenarian Pepy II. The political chaos following the death of Nitokerty (Nitocris) {2205–2200}, Pepy II's daughter-in-law, was remembered in later Egyptian legends as the "Seventh Dynasty" of Memphis {c. 2190}, which is said to have consisted of "five kings of Memphis who reigned for seventy-five days", or alternatively, even "seventy kings of Memphis, who reigned for seventy days" (Man. 23–4). These phrases are not seen by modern scholars as specific numbers, but rather a vague recollection of a period of instability. We have no specific information about rulers or military events of this period of coups, civil war, and anarchy, as the power of the Sixth Dynasty collapsed.

Eighth Dynasty {c. 2190–2165}

Thereafter, royal power at Memphis passed into the hands of the so-called Eighth Dynasty, which is tentatively and hypothetically reconstructed with eighteen kings ruling for a mere 25 years in total {2190–2165}, averaging a reign of less than one-and-a-half years per king (CS 1:70). However, the existence of many of these rulers cannot be confirmed by any contemporary records, and the precise number, names, and lengths of reign cannot be determined with certainty. Some scholars suggest that the kings of the Eighth Dynasty may have been descendants of Pepy II of the Sixth Dynasty through a subsidiary line, and were thus the branch of Pepy's family that emerged in a dominant position following the anarchy of the Seventh Dynasty. Nominal authority of the Eighth Dynasty was recognized throughout Egypt, but the nomarchs were becoming increasingly autonomous (HAE 140–1; C1/2:198–200).

The weakening internal situation of the Eighth Dynasty left Egypt more vulnerable to outside military threat than it had ever been before. Bedouins from Sinai and Palestine are thought to have migrated into or possibly even invaded the delta toward the end of the Eighth Dynasty, contributing to the collapse of the dynasty and perhaps establishing some kind of Canaanite hegemony in the northeast delta (HAE 139–40).

The combination of social chaos, political impotence, regional autonomy, ideological instability, and economic crisis, all complicated by low flooding of the Nile and occasional famine, culminated in the complete fragmentation of the Egyptian state, with regional nomarchs transforming their former semi-autonomy into real independence. Famine is mentioned in a number of texts from the First Intermediate Period, and efforts to alleviate or avoid famine appear frequently among the merits in funerary inscriptions of contemporary nomarchs. The nomarch Henqu of the "Mountainviper", or twelfth southern nome, emphasized that he "gave bread and beer to all the hungry" and "resettled the towns that were enfeebled in this nome with persons of other nomes" (AEAB 23–4, 32–3; M = AAE 14–15, HAAE 31). In part this may simply be vague pious claims to have performed good deeds, as are often found in funerary autobiographies, but it quite possibly reflects the actual circumstances of hunger and depopulation. Contemporary autobiographies from Edfu, Thebes, and Coptos mention "painful years of distress" due to drought and famine, and efforts to transport grain to afflicted cities during this period (AEL 1:87–90, HAE 142).

Ninth Dynasty of Herakleopolis {2164–2040}[2]

The nome of Herakleopolis in central Egypt was the largest and most powerful state during this period, remembered in Egyptian tradition as the Ninth and Tenth

Dynasties, which controlled the sacred Old Kingdom capital at Memphis. Its formal establishment of full independence occurred under Akhtoy I (Khety, Achthoes) {2165–2135?}, founder of the Ninth Dynasty, who may have been a descendent of Pepy II through a subsidiary line that had traditionally served as governors of Herakleopolis. The kings of Herakleopolis seem to have retained control of Memphis and maintained at least part of its religious cult – Akhtoy I was buried there. Later Egyptian legends remember Akhtoy I as "behaving more cruelly than his predecessors" (Man. 27–8), which is sometimes thought to be a legendary recollection of attempts to suppress the independence of rival nomarchs. For a decade or two Akhtoy I seems to have exerted at least nominal influence as far south as Aswan, where his name is recorded in an inscription. But his dynasty's power in the south ultimately proved ephemeral. Under subsequent rulers southern Egypt emerged fully into independence, precipitating a civil war.

The struggle for the South {2134–2061}

The move toward the regional autonomy of nomarchs, which had begun during the late Sixth Dynasty, reached its culmination in the Ninth, with the establishment in the 2130s through 2120s of at least six separate states in Egypt. Some of these remained, formally and nominally, loyal to the kings of the Ninth Dynasty at Herakleopolis. Others became defiantly independent. As far as can be determined, the Ninth Dynasty retained control of Middle Egypt from the ninth nome to the southern part of the delta. The rebellion was most pronounced and successful in southern Egypt from the first through the eighth nomes. The following list shows the nomes, capital cities, and rulers of the major players in the southern civil war, dating to roughly 2130 (EAE 1:528–30; M = HAAE 31):

- first nome, at Aswan/Elephantine, ruled by Setika;
- second and eventually third nome, at Hierakonpolis, ruled by Ankhtifi;
- fourth nome, at Thebes, ruled by Antef I (of the Eleventh Dynasty);
- fifth nome, at Coptos, ruled by Shemai and his son Idi, who were the semi-autonomous official governors of southern Egypt for the Ninth Dynasty kings. Tjauti and Woser were also leading figures of this nome;
- sixth, seventh and eighth nomes, at Thinis, ruled by Abichu.

Middle Egypt, from the ninth nome northward, remained loyal to the Ninth Dynasty kings of Herakleopolis. Conditions in the delta are uncertain; some delta nomes may have been independent, while Easterners – Canaanites or Sinai bedouins – may have held hegemony in the north-east delta.

The precise dates and sequence of events in this civil war cannot be determined. However, the surviving records give us occasional incidental snapshots of warfare in southern Egypt. The autonomous nomarchs of southern Egypt caused concern for King Neferkahor of the Ninth Dynasty {c. 2130?}. Neferkahor sent his son-in-law Shemai to serve as "Governor of Upper Egypt", based at the fifth nome of Coptos, apparently with instructions to regain control of the situation (EAE 1:528). Shemai in turn assigned his own son Idi as governor of the turbulent nomes One through Four. Their attempts to reassert royal control in the south were plagued by recalcitrant nomarchs who refused to submit to royal authority on the part of what they viewed as the upstart kings of Herakleopolis. This defiance soon developed into military conflict.

The campaigns of Ankhtifi of Hierakonpolis {c. 2130–2125?}[3]

The most instructive source on the early southern civil war is the autobiography of Ankhtifi, nomarch of Hierakonpolis (nome three). Although functionally independent, Ankhtifi's titles include reference to royal offices, indicating a lingering nominal respect from the kings of Herakleopolis – at least he sometimes claimed to be acting in the name and interest of the king. In addition to governor, his titles include military offices such as "General", "Commander of Mercenaries", and "Commander of Foreign Lands", the last title, if not sheer boasting, presumably referred to Nubia. In an attempt to lend legitimacy to his rule, he claimed that the god "Horus brought me to [rule] the Horus-Throne [of Edfu] ... for Horus wished to re-establish it, because he brought me to [be ruler to] re-establish" the prosperity and peace of Edfu (AEAB 25); no reference is made to royal investiture. Thus, Ankhtifi claimed to be acting not for personal power or aggrandizement, but according to the will of the gods. The power base of the First Intermediate Period nomarchs was often solidified by local priests and gods. Many rulers, like Ankhtifi, were themselves priests, and were careful to care for and build temples to local deities. Ankhtifi claimed that the "temple of Khuu was inundated like a marsh, abandoned by him [the former nomarch] who belonged to it, in the grip of a rebel" (AEL 1:85). Part of Ankhtifi's justification for seizing power was the restoration of the proper ritual order for the gods. As we shall see, when the nomarchs of Thebes eventually reunite Egypt, they bring to power with them the regional Theban gods Montu and Amun.

Ankhtifi's first campaign was against Edfu (nome Two). Ankhtifi overthrew the rebel and re-established law and order (AEAB 25). This type of breakdown of authority is also reflected in another text which describes a local leader who "kept alive every man of this province ... while the great ones [former nomarchs?] were dead", and who provided food for the people, not because of "an order that is sent to a servant of the king" but on his own initiative, "out of love for [the god] Min" (EAE 1:530a).

Although no details are given, Ankhtifi also at some point campaigned southward to the first nome, Elephantine, which was under the command of the nomarch Setika. He boasted that "my speech was clever and my bravery won the day when it was necessary to join the [southern] three nomes together" into a single state by conquest (HAE 142). At his death Ankhtifi's domain included "the provinces of Hierakonpolis [the third nome] and Edfu [second nome], Elephantine [Aswan] and Ombos [in the first nome]" (HAE 142).

At the time of this consolidation of power over the southernmost three nomes of Egypt, Ankhtifi's major rival was Antef I, ruler of the fourth nome of Thebes, and founder of what was to become the Eleventh Dynasty of the Middle Kingdom. During the ongoing struggle between Thebes and Ankhtifi, an unnamed general of the Theban city of Armant – supported by allied troops from Coptos – issued a challenge to battle to Ankhtifi, which Ankhtifi accepted:

> The commander of troops of Armant had come to say: "Come [to battle], you hero, come [north] to the [war] camps of the Theban and Coptite district, which have separated." When I went north in the west channel of [the Nile at] Armant, I found the [armies of] the entire districts of Thebes and Coptus as they were making ready the [military] camp of Armant at the mount of Semekhsen. [I said:] "I myself shall approach it! May the strong armed [god] stand for [me in battle]! [I shall pin them down] as with a harpoon on the nose of a hippopotamus ready to flee, after I turned south from destroying their camp with the victorious troops of Hefat. I truly am a man like no other." (AF 29–30)

The details of the battle are lost in a lacuna in the text, but Ankhtifi was apparently victorious. Later he continued his campaign against Thebes:

> When I had sailed north [to attack Thebes] with my troop of victorious trustworthy [warriors] and had landed on the west side [of the Nile] in the Theban district: the south of my navigation [of the naval operations of my fleet on the west bank of the Nile] was at the mount *Smhsn*, the north of my navigations [in the Theban district] was at the estate of *Tmy*. While my troop of trustworthy [warriors] was seeking to fight throughout the west side of the Theban district, no one would come forth for his fear [of my army]. When I had sailed north and I had landed on the east side of the Theban district: the north of my navigation [of the naval operations of my fleet on the east bank of the Nile] was at the tomb of *Imbi*, the south of my navigations was at the ford of *Sg3*, which was probed against the walls [of Thebes] after it had closed the doorbolts [of its gates] as it was not ready [to fight] for fear of this troop of victorious trustworthy [warriors]. And so this troop of trustworthy [warriors] became challengers [to the enemy to come out and fight in open combat] through the west and east of the Theban district, while seeking battle, but no one would come forth [from their fortified cities] because of his fear. I, truly, am a man, of whom there is not another [like me]. (AF 37; OHAE 131)

This narrative gives us an excellent view of the use of river fleets in campaigns. It appears that, after his victory over the Theban–Coptos alliance at the earlier Battle of Armant, Ankhtifi took his army in his fleet and sailed up and down both banks of the Nile. His army was either on foot and accompanied and supported by the fleet, or perhaps was entirely carried by the fleet and dropped off at strategic points for land operations. They were able to sail and march unhindered throughout the entire Theban district – presumably plundering as they went. The Theban troops, being cowed by their defeat at Armant, refused to leave the safety of their city fortresses and meet Ankhtifi's army again in open battle. On the other hand, Ankhtifi did not feel strong enough to undertake a serious long-term siege of Thebes itself. His victory over Thebes was thus only temporary; Thebes remained independent and would later challenge Ankhtifi's descendants.

After establishing his predominance in the south, Ankhtifi sought further legitimization of his conquests by asking "the Overseer of Upper Egypt [for the king of the Ninth Dynasty] who is in the Thinite nome" – probably referring to either Shemai or his son Idi – to accept his authority as "the Prince, Count, Chief Priest, and Great Headman" of the south (AEAB 26). The *de facto* nature of independent rule was apparently recognized by the kings of Herakleopolis, perhaps in return for shipments of grain. The combination of low Nile flooding and political and economic collapse caused "all of Upper Egypt [to die] of hunger and people were eating their children.... The [people of the] whole country had become like locusts going upstream and downstream in search of food." Presumably in return for recognition of his authority, Ankhtifi sent food to the surrounding nomes (OHAE 129 = AEL 1:87). He may even have made an armed demonstration up the Nile as far as the eighth nome of Thinis, for he claims: "when I travel to the nome of Thinis against one who forgot himself" – presumably meaning he questioned Ankhtifi's authority – "I find it with its watchmen on the walls. When I hasten to the combat [against them], 'Woe!' says the wretch" (AEAB 26). This policy of using a combination of carrot and stick made Ankhtifi the predominant military power in southern Egypt.

Ankhtifi's autobiography also reflects the martial braggadocio of the warlords of the First Intermediate Period. He calls himself "Ankhtifi the Brave", and boasts that he is the "vanguard and rearguard" of his men, a "champion who has no peer". He threatens that, "as for any fool or wretch who sets himself against me, I shall give more than he has given" in battle – "my like [in battle] has not been, nor will be!" (AEAB 26). At his death sometime around 2120, Ankhtifi had reason to boast. He ruled the first three nomes directly, and had subjugated, but did not directly rule, the Egyptian nomarchs of the fourth through the eighth nomes. However, his conquests were to prove ephemeral, for Antef II of Thebes {2118–2068} would eventually conquer his kingdom from Ankhtifi's successor.

The Early Eleventh Dynasty at Thebes {2134–2061}

During the Old Kingdom, Thebes (ancient Waset) had been a rather small, sleepy provincial town, dedicated to its local gods Montu and Amun, and adorned with small tombs for the regional aristocracy (EAE 3:384–8). As elsewhere in Egypt, the breakdown of central authority during the early First Intermediate Period led to increasing autonomy of the local elites. According to later Eleventh Dynasty genealogies and legends, by perhaps the 2150s a local nomarch Montuhotep

(Mentuhotpe) {2155?–2134} had established semi-independent power at Thebes. He is remembered as the first "ancestor" and father of the "gods" of the Eleventh Dynasty. His position, however, was relatively weak, and judging from Ankhtifi's account of his war with Thebes, discussed on p. 372, his authority was not even secure in his own province.

Ankhtifi of Hierakonpolis' victory over Thebes made him the dominant power in southern Egypt in the 2130s and 2120s. None the less, although defeated, Thebes under Antef I {2134–2118}, son of Montohotep I, remained independent of Ankhtifi (LA 1:300–1). There is some indication that the Hierakonpolis principality in southern Egypt collapsed shortly after the death of Ankhtifi, allowing Antef I to assert authority over the three southernmost nomes of Upper Egypt, proclaiming himself "great overlord of Upper Egypt" (OHAE 133).

On the other hand, the full subjugation and conquest of the southernmost three nomes of Ankhtifi's domain seems to have occurred early in the reign of Antef I's brother and successor, Wahankh Antef (Inyotef) II {2118–2068}, during whose half-century reign Thebes conquered all of southern Egypt. The details and precise order of Antef II's conquests are not known. In his autobiography he set Thebes's "northern boundary up to the nome of Wadjet [the tenth nome].... I conquered Abydos [the eighth Thinite nome] and the whole surrounding region. I captured all the fortresses of the nome of Wadjet and I made them into the Gateway of the North", meaning the border with the northern Ninth Dynasty of Herakleopolis. His conquests were "splendid for the glory of Thebes" (HAE 145 = ARE 1:200). We also have a brief autobiographical inscription by the actual commander of the army that led this campaign, Djari, "commander of the foreigners". He "battled with the House of Akhtoy [Ninth Dynasty] in the west of Thinis", where he "raised a storm over the nome ... [and] made the [new] boundary at Wadi Hesy" in the tenth nome (AEAB 40–1). As reward for his victories, he "was promoted among the elder [commanders] because I was fierce on the day of battle" (MKT 13). Antef II appears to have made use of flanking operations via desert roads to assault his enemies in the Nile valley. A graffito was left by one of his soldiers on the 'Alamat Tal Road in the Western Desert, recording the march of "the assault troops of the Son of Re, [king] Antef [II]", which could have given him some element of strategic surprise contributing to his victory.[4] The struggle for strategic control of the desert routes allowing surprise flank attacks into the Nile valley is also reflected in an inscription of commander Tjauti's expedition. When Shamai, the pro-Herakleopolitan governor of the fifth nome of Coptos sent general Tjauti on an expedition against Thebes to the south, Tjauti recorded that he was forced to "make this [the 'Alamat Tal Road] for crossing this desert [with his army], which the ruler of another nome [Thebes?] had closed".[5] Overall the ability to move armies, as well as merchant caravans, overland through desert roads complicated the seemingly straightforward strategy of defending the borders on the Nile River alone. If an army could operate several hundred miles along desert roads, large stretches of the Nile would presumably be vulnerable to surprise attack, requiring the dispersal of garrison troops throughout the entire Nile valley rather than concentrating forces solely on the border regions.

In addition Antef II claims to have subdued the southern Libyan "chiefs who rule the Red [Western Desert] Land" (AEL 1:91), and placed his treasurer Thethi over the regular tribute required from the Libyan chiefs (ARE 1:202). By the death of Antef II {2068}, he ruled the southern eight nomes from "Yebu [Aswan, first nome] to Thinis [eighth nome] ... [receiving] tribute from this entire land, owing to the fear of him throughout this land" (AEL 1:91).

The wars of Akhtoy (Khety) III {c. 2090–2070?}[6]

The martial progress of Thebes and the decline of the Ninth Dynasty at Herakleopolis was halted, though only temporarily, by king Akhtoy III. In his famous *Instructions* for his son and successor King Merikare (see pp. 377–9), he describes how he mobilized a strong army, stopped the Theban attack at Thinis, reconquered the Delta from Eastern nomad invaders, and refortified the frontiers, leaving the Ninth Dynasty in its strongest military position in decades.

Counterattack from Asyut {c. 2080–2070?}

Some aspects of resistance to Antef II's invasion of Middle Egypt can be found in the autobiographical inscriptions from the tombs of the nomarchs of Asyut (AEA 23; EAE 1:154–6). From these sources we learn that Antef II's triumphalist rhetoric masks a more problematic reality. His campaigns into middle Egypt were strongly resisted by a family of nomarchs of Asyut allied to Akhtoy III {c. 2090–2070?} of the Ninth Dynasty at Herakleopolis. The exact chronology cannot be determined – all dates given in this section are quite speculative, and are intended only to give a rough sense of chronology. It is clear that the territory between Thinis and Asyut (Siut) (nomes 8–12) became a battleground between Antef II of Thebes and the nomarchs of Asyut, the provincial allies of the Ninth Dynasty.

In a fragmentary inscription Tefibi (Ity-yeb), nomarch of Asyut {c. 2090–2070?}, describes his successful counterattack against the invasion by Antef II. Tefibi's father, the nomarch Akhtoy {c. 2110–2090?} – not to be confused with king Akhtoy III – had laid the foundation for resistance to growing Theban power in the south. His autobiography emphasizes his efforts at canal construction and agricultural restoration after the lean years of the late twenty-second century (ARE 1:188–9). This economic revival also permitted him to restore the strength of the pro-Ninth Dynasty provincial Egyptian army in Middle Egypt.

Thus, when Antef II's invasion of Middle Egypt occurred, Tefibi was able to benefit from the military foundation laid by his father. According to Tefibi's autobiography, "my soldiers fought with the [armies of the] southern nomes [of Antef II]", describing the advance of Antef II on the "west side" of the Nile to an unnamed city north of Asyut – presumably beyond Thinis in the eighth nome, which according to his own inscription is the maximum extent of Antef's conquests.

When I [Tefibi] came to the city [that was besieged or recently conquered by Antef], I overthrew the foe, and drove him as far as the fortress of the port of the South. [Antef] gave to me the land [which he had previously attempted to conquer]. (ARE 1:182)

His offensive toward Asyut thus foiled, Antef of Thebes attempted a different strategy, sailing an armed fleet up the Nile. When word of this second attack reached Tefibi in Asyut, he mobilized his own fleet and took to the river. Tefibi's autobiography describes a naval victory on the Nile – which will be discussed on pp. 453–5 – and concludes with a discussion of restoring order in Egypt.

When a man did well, I promoted [him] to the head of my soldiers.... The land was under the fear of my soldiers; no [enemy from the] highland [desert surrounding the Nile valley] was free from the fear [of my soldiers]. (ARE 1:183)

Tefibi's great victory may also be remembered in the *Instructions* of Akhtoy III (discussed on pp. 377–9), although with a different emphasis on who was responsible for the victory. "I [claims King Akhtoy III] went to Thinis on the southern border; like a thunderstorm I seized [Thinis from the king of Thebes]; [my predecessor] King Meriibre, the justified, had not done this" (TS 222). This last phrase is presumably an allusion to the earlier sequence of victories of Antef II of Thebes before the counterattack by the nomarch Tefibi and Akhtoy III. During this campaign there was apparently the destruction or desecration of a necropolis – perhaps the famous mortuary complex of Abydos. A battle may actually have taken place there, for Akhtoy's *Instructions* mentions this battle as fulfilling a prophecy that "Egypt will fight in the necropolis, destroying tomb-chambers in a destruction of deeds" (TS 221). Akhtoy, however, refused to take personal responsibility for the sacrilege: "a vile deed happened in my time: the nome of Thinis was destroyed. It happened, but not as my action, and I knew of it only after it was done" (TS 225). He instructs his son to "destroy not the [sacred and funerary] monuments of another" (TS 222).

Following this victory, there seems to have a temporary truce between Thebes and the Ninth dynasty, bringing peace to Middle Egypt {c. 2070–2060?}, and the boundary was set at the northern border of the eighth nome. Near the end of his reign, king Akhtoy told his son Merikare "there is now no enemy on your borders.... All is now well for you with the Southern Region [of Thebes], which comes to you bearing produce, bearing tribute.... to you comes granite [from the south] unhindered." Merikare is therefore instructed "to be kind to those who yield to you" and "renew the treaties" with Thebes (TS 222). None the less, he should be prepared for war: "Arm your border against the South [kingdom of Thebes] – they are bowmen who take up the war belt!" (TS 224). This was excellent advice, for within two decades after the death of Akhtoy III, Thebes renewed the offensive {2047} under the great warlord Montuhotep I, who would destroy the Ninth Dynasty and conquer all Egypt.

According to Tefibi's son and successor Akhtoy (Khety) {c. 2070–2050?} (again not to be confused with king Akhtoy III), "there was no one fighting, nor any shooting an arrow" during his administration at Asyut (ARE 1:187). He none the less maintained a strong army in the face of possible renewal of the Theban threat: "I am one strong of bow, mighty with his army, much feared by his neighbors. I formed a troop of spearmen and a troop of bowmen, the best Thousand of Upper Egypt. I have a fine fleet" (AEAB 28–9). The nomarch Akhtoy served Merikare, son of king Akhtoy III, the last (or next to last) king of the Ninth Dynasty at Herakleopolis, who claims to have "repelled the evil-doer" Antef III and "overthrown the rebels" of Thebes in alliance with Tefibi and Akhtoy of Asyut (ARE 1:184–5). The victories of the Asyut nomarchs in Middle Egypt were secured by a grand river campaign through Middle Egypt led by king Merikare, who sailed his fleet to Shashotpe (Shutb), near Asyut, intimidating and stalemating Theban aggression for a time (ARE 1:185–6 = MKT 23).

"Akhtoy III's Instructions for his Son Merikare"[7]

One of the most intriguing and potentially useful texts of the First Intermediate Period purports to be the political and military instructions of king Akhtoy III {c. 2090–2070?} of the Herakleopolitan Ninth Dynasty to his son and successor Merikare {c. 2070–2050?}, the last (or next to last) king of the line. Unfortunately, both the authorship and the date of this text is controversial. Wendy Raver, for example, argues that "the text may be pseudepigraphical, but it was most probably composed in the court of Khety [Akhtoy] III during the tenth dynasty (EAE 2:169)."[8] R. Parkinson, on the other hand, believes the text "is not contemporaneous with the Heracleopolitan [Ninth–Tenth] Dynasty" but should "be dated to late in the Middle Kingdom" (TS 212). Given the paucity and ambiguity of the data, it is impossible to resolve this question with certainty. For this discussion I will assume the text originated in the court of the late Ninth–Tenth Dynasty, and that it reflects the historical realities of that period.

At the very least the *Instructions for Merikare* represent Egyptian views on dealing with periods of internal turmoil and military crisis such as the First Intermediate Period. As such, it is an excellent reflection of the practical military policies of ancient Egypt, even if it cannot be linked to the specific historical situation in the late First Intermediate Period. The advice given in the *Instructions* is both practical and ideological – how to raise armies and win battles, as well as how to gain the support of the gods. Akhtoy III gives a great deal of didactic military advice to his son, reflecting the standard military policies and practices of ancient Egypt. Although the work by China's great military theorist Sun Tzu *The Art of War* is frequently described as the earliest surviving military manual,[9] Akhtoy's *Instructions*, written fifteen hundred years earlier, contains sufficient military advice to consider it an archaic military manual, perhaps the first surviving military handbook in history.

In the First Intermediate Period the king was dependent on the support of the nomarchs. "Great is the great one [king] whose great ones [nomarchs] are great.

The king who is the lord of an entourage [of nomarchs] is strong" (TS 219). Nomarchs and other powerful officials must be cultivated to insure their allegiance. "If you encounter a mighty man who is the master of a town [i.e. a nomarch], and is the lord of a clan, care for him" (TS 216–17). Diplomatic skills are crucial for the king. "Be skillful with words, and you will be victorious. The strong arm of the king is his tongue. Words are stronger than any weapons" (TS 218).

The power of the nomarchs is also reflected in the fact that, for Akhtoy, a major concern is the ever-present danger of rebellion. For such there should be no mercy: "Do not be lenient to [the rebel]! You should kill those who owe him allegiance.... Punish the people who are conspiring.... Drive him away! Kill his children! Erase his name!" (TS 216–17). At the same time, the king must "beware of punishing wrongly" (TS 220).

Proper recruitment and pay of troops is emphasized, for "soldiers are good for their lord" (TS 221).

> Raise your Youth [*shwt*], so that the [royal] Residence will love you! Make your supporters plentiful among the Veterans [*s'qyw*]! Look, your town is full of new growth [of the next generation ready for military recruiting]. These twenty years, the Youth has been happy, following its heart; and the Veterans are now going forth once again; the recruits are recruited to it [the army]. ... On my accession I raised up troops from them. So make your great ones [nobles] great! Advance your fighters! Increase the Youth of your following, equipped with amounts [of wealth], established with fields, and endowed with cattle! (TS 220–1).

The precise meaning of this passage is uncertain, but the general picture is fairly clear. The "Youth" or "Young Men" seem to be a military or paramilitary group recruited from the populace. It is possible that they are the town militia, but also possible that they are professional soldiers. Throughout the ancient Near East the term "Young Men" commonly refered to men in their late teens and twenties at the prime age for military service. These Young Men are contrasted with the Veterans, an older, more experienced class of soldier. It is possible that these are simply generic terms for young and old people, but they may reflect technical categories, rather like the Greek and Roman practice of categorizing soldiers according to age groups.[10] The phrase "twenty years" may refer either to the length of military service, or the length of Akhtoy's reign during which his policies were followed. Akhtoy emphasizes not only the importance of continually recruiting soldiers into the two classes of troops, but also of ensuring their happiness and loyalty by paying them well in moveable wealth, agricultural fields, and domesticated animals. These types of payment are reflected in the autobiographies of soldiers as well. The importance of a fortified and garrisoned frontier is emphasized in the *Instructions*: "Strengthen your borders and your [frontier] patrols! ... Protect your border! Secure your fortresses!" (TS 219, 221).

Akhtoy also gives some very specific military advice for dealing with the nomadic Easterners:

But now, these things are said about the barbarian [Eastern] bowmen: the vile
Easterner is wretched because of the place where he is – lacking in water,
barren of trees, whose roads are painful because of the mountains. He has
never settled in any one place, lack of food makes him wander about on foot!
He has been fighting since the [mythical] Time of Horus [at the beginning of
the world]. He cannot conquer; he cannot be conquered. He does not
announce the day of battle, but sneaks about like a gang of thieves.... Do not
worry about him! The Easterner is a crocodile on its riverbank that can snatch
[his victim] from a lonely road but cannot take from the quay of a populous
town. (TS 223–4 = ECI 67 = AEL 1:103–4)

These ideas are remarkably similar to the broader views of sedentary peoples
about their nomadic enemies. The nomads are described as destitute raiders from
the wilderness, who make sneak attacks and plunder, before fleeing back into the
desert. Although they can raid and plunder, they are not viewed as posing a serious
military threat to security.

As is normal in Egyptian warfare, religion played a crucial role in military policy. The gods are in control, and ultimately determine military success or failure:
"God will impose his doom with blood" (TS 220). Disaster will strike anyone
"who goes against God" (TS 222). Because of this, the gods must be placated with
proper cultic piety. "Make many monuments for God.... Make the [sacrificial]
offering tables [in the temples] flourish" (TS 221). Royal patronage of the proper
religious rites will insure the gods' blessings. "Act for God – with great offerings
for a flourishing altar, and with inscriptions [in temples] – and he will act for you"
(TS 226). Opposing the king was equivalent to opposing the gods: Indeed, "to
revolt against [the king] is to attack [the gods of] heaven" (TS 225). Likewise,
"God will attack someone who rebels against the temples" (TS 224).

Magical practices, such as Execration Texts, were also "a weapon" against enemies (TS 226). Prophecy and divination could play a key role in military decision-
making. Akhtoy refers to one such prophecy: "The Youth will attack the Youth
[in civil war] just as the ancestors foretold it. Egypt will fight in the necropolis,
destroying tomb-chambers" (TS 221). It was also generally believed that divination and oracles revealed the will of the gods and could therefore influence military policies and practices. Referring to his campaign against Thinis, Akhtoy
describes the fatalistic belief in the inevitable fulfillment of prophecy: "You [my
son Merikare] know what the [temple prophets at the royal] residence foretold it.
As such things happen, these happened. Those things could not go otherwise,
even as they [the prophets] said it" (TS 22).

Akhtoy III's reconquest of the Delta {c. 2075?}

Although we have no details or archaeological confirmation (OHAE 139) it
appears that, during the decline of royal power under the Ninth Dynasty, the delta was
raided and partially occupied by both Libyan and Eastern nomads {c. 2125–2075?}.

After securing the southern frontier with Thebes, Akhtoy's "heart grieved because of the [situation in the] Delta" (TS 222), and he undertook two campaigns to restore Egyptian authority there. They first focused on the western delta: "from Hetshenu to Sembaqa, and south to Two-Fish Channel [a south-western branch of the Nile], I pacified the entire West as far as the sand-dunes of the [coastal?] lake" (AEL 1:103 = TS 222). This may have been a reference to the restoration of royal authority over recalcitrant nomarchs of the western delta, but could also include punitive expeditions against Libyan nomads who had been raiding or infiltrating the delta.

The reconquest of the Libyans in the western delta was followed by an offensive in the east against Sinai and Canaanite nomads who had penetrated that region. Thereafter, Akhtoy recaptured some of the Delta cities the nomads had occupied:

These [barbarian nomad] bowmen were [like] a walled fortress, whose fortifications I breached, [and] which I had isolated [as in a siege]! I have made the [Egyptian army of the] Delta attack them, I have enslaved their underlings and taken away their cattle, to horrify the Easterners who are enemies of Egypt. (TS 223–4 = AEL 1:104)

The eastern nomad threat, however, was not completely eliminated. Akhtoy describes his efforts to restore Egyptian power in the delta:

The [land of the delta] which [the eastern nomads] had destroyed is made into nomes; every great town is refounded; what one man ruled now belongs to ten [nomarchs loyal to the king] ... The taxes of the Delta belong to you [my son and successor]. Look, the border marker [of Egypt] which I have made in the East is driven in, from Hebenu [in Middle Egypt] to the Ways of Horus [roads leaving eastward from Egypt from Sile in the north-east delta], [Egypt is] founded with townspeople, full of people, the best of the whole land, to beat back attacks on them [from the Canaanite and nomad raiders]. (TS 223)

His defensive preparations are further emphasized. The region of the apex of the delta was said to be the "defense against foreigners. Its walls and fighters are many, whose commoners know how to take up weapons" – probably an allusion to a regional militia. The area of Memphis had "ten thousand men [in the army], commoners and freemen who are without labor duty [because of their military service].... its borders are firm, its strongholds are mighty" (TS 224). This is possibly a reference to a form of tax exemption in return for military service, but whatever the exact meaning, it is clear that Akhtoy was engaged in raising troops and fortifications for the defense of his delta conquests.

If Akhtoy III's *Instructions* are to be believed – and they may be pseudepigraphical hyperbole – Akhtoy in many ways prepared the path for the unification of Egypt by reuniting the delta with Middle Egypt. The fruit of his victory, however, would be harvested by Montuhotep of Thebes, the founder of the Middle

Kingdom, as will be discussed in Chapter Sixteen. Additional characteristics of the military system of the First Intermediate Period will be discussed along with those of the Middle Kingdom in Chapter Seventeen.

Nubia and Nubian mercenaries in the First Intermediate Period

It has been observed that "the periods of [northern] Nubia's greatest prosperity were usually those of Egypt's greatest weakness" (AAA, 47). This was certainly true for the First Intermediate Period, when Nubia witnessed increasing population and prosperity as attested by the "C-group" archaeological finds (EAE 258–9). During most of the First Intermediate Period there are no records of conflict along the Nubian frontier. Although Nubian mercenaries had served in Egyptian armies from at least the Sixth Dynasty of the Old Kingdom, during the First Intermediate Period the use of Nubian mercenaries expanded rapidly throughout southern and middle Egypt.[11] Indeed, it is likely that the ongoing civil wars in Egypt during the First Intermediate Period increased the demand for Nubian mercenaries. The Thebans may have ultimately emerged victorious from their war with northern Egypt in part because they had ready access to the Nubian mercenary market, thereby bolstering their military strength relative to the north's. Nubian mercenaries intermarried with Egyptian women during this period; a mortuary stele from Gebelein shows Nenu, a tall Nubian mercenary, holding his bow, with his Egyptian wife by his side (OHAE 129).

In his biography, Qedes, a common soldier from Gebelein, boasts of his military prowess, claiming to be "the foremost [soldier] of his whole troop", and that he "surpassed this whole town in swiftness – its Nubians and its Upper Egyptians" (AEL 1:90). This text reflects both the obvious fact that soldiers were selected for their physical prowess, and that Nubian mercenaries made up a significant portion of the armies of southern Egypt. Qedes's biography also makes it clear that a common man could become relatively wealthy through mercenary service in the Egyptian army. During his military career, Qedes "acquired oxen and goats. I acquired granaries of Upper Egyptian barley. I acquired a title to a great field. I made a boat of 30 cubits [12 meters] and a small boat."

CHAPTER SIXTEEN

Middle Kingdom Egypt
{2061–1786}

The Middle Kingdom[1] was a three-centuries-long period of essential unity in Egypt and concomitant international military power. Unfortunately, the Middle Kingdom "remains one of the most enigmatic periods in the sphere of foreign relations" which has "bequeathed us precious little evidence" on military matters (ECI 70). None the less, there are sufficient sources with enough detail to allow us to reconstruct the broad outline of military history.

The Eleventh Dynasty {2061–1998}[2]

From a military perspective, the reunification of Egypt and the beginning of the Middle Kingdom was the work of the great Theban warlord Montuhotep I {2061–2010}. In subsequent Egyptian history his great military achievements caused him to be remembered – along with Narmer/Menes and Ahmose of the New Kingdom – as one of the three unifiers of Egypt (EAE 2:437; MKT 31).

Montuhotep (Mentuhotep; Mentuhotpe) I {2061–2011}[3]

As has been discussed on pp. 373–7, the foundations for Montuhotep I's reunification of Egypt were laid by both his grandfather, Antef II of Thebes, and his grandfather's rival, Akhtoy III of Herakleopolis. The stalemate between these two kings that had developed in Middle Egypt during the 2060s seems to have continued during the first decade-and-a-half of the reign of Montuhotep I {2061–2048}, when he was essentially the regional king of southern Egypt. Although the chronology is uncertain, it appears that during these years, however, he undertook an invasion of Nubia.

Nubian campaigns of Montuhotep I {c. 2050?} (C1/2:485–8; AAA 48–9)

At an unknown date Montuhotep personally led a major expedition into Nubia, which reached Buhen at the Second Cataract; it may have occurred during the fourteen years of his reign that preceded his reunification of Egypt {2061–2048}. The two royal inscriptions, which will be further discussed below, mention "enslaving the Nubians . . . [of the] Medjay and Wawat [tribes]", indicating that warfare against Nubia was part of the royal agenda (C1/2:480–2 = MKT 24, 28). The el-Deir inscription of Montuhotep I, though fragmentary, provides a few details about this Nubian campaign:

> . . . [from] Wawat [in Nubia] and the Oasis . . . I drove out the troublemakers in them. I annexed them to Upper Egypt. There is no [Egyptian] king whom they [the Nubians] served in his time [i.e. in the First Intermediate Period before Montuhotep] . . . My wrath [against the enemies of Egypt] was slaked . . . [by the victories of] the strong troops of my recruiting. (ICN 113)

Later in the inscription he recounts: "[as for] Wawat [Nubia] and the Oasis [of Kharga?]. I annexed them to Upper Egypt. I drove out the rebellious [enemy]" (ICN 114). To maintain his control of Nubia he "placed reinforcements in Elephantine [Aswan]" (ICN 114), under the command of an official, Akhtoy, who left a number of inscriptions in the region (C1/2:480). In the year 39 {2022}, Montuhotep again visited the borders of Nubia, commemorating his reunification of Egypt and other triumphs by celebrating a great *sed*-festival (C1/2:479–80; MKT pl. 12). Two years later, in year 41 {2020}, the "triumphant" commander Akhtoy "took ships to Wawat [in Nubia]" (ARE 1:206–7); the details of this expedition are not known; it may have been largely a trading operation. At the least Akhtoy's fleet would have reinforced the nominal submission of northern Nubia. None the less, the Nubian frontier was by no means permanently subjugated; as described on pp. 397–9, later Egyptian kings were required to undertake regular Nubian campaigns.

One important outgrowth of Montuhotep's relationship with Nubia was the enlistment of Nubian warriors to strengthen his army in its wars against the rival Ninth Dynasty at Herakleopolis.[4] We have a remarkable autobiographical inscription by one of these Nubian mercenaries, Tjehemau, who served in Montuhotep's army and described his participation in these campaigns, unfortunately without giving a precise chronology. Both Tjehemau and his son enlisted in the Egyptian army at the time of Montuhotep's Nubian campaigns, subsequently serving in the reunification of Egypt and the invasion of Canaan. His autobiography, recorded in two inscriptions from Abisko, near Aswan, is the best account of the career of a Nubian mercenary.

> Inscription which Tjehemau made. Year of smiting the foreign land of the south: I began to fight [as a mercenary for the Egyptians] in the reign of Nebhepetre [Montuhotep I] in the army, when it [the Egyptian army] went south to Buhen. My son went down with me towards the king [to offer our service as mercenaries]. He [the king] traversed the entire land, for he planned to exterminate the A'amu of Djaty [in southern Wawat]. (ITM 11–20)

Here we find Montuhotep I personally commanding one of his Nubian expeditions. As the Egyptians sailed south, Tjehemau and his son – and presumably other Nubians – were recruited to serve as mercenaries to fight those Nubians who were still hostile to Egypt. As Montuhotep's campaign continued, Tjehemau described the decisive battle.

> When they [the rival Egyptian and hostile Nubian armies] approached [to give battle, the Egyptian regiments from] Thebes [were put to] flight [by the hostile Nubians]. It was the [pro-Egyptian] Nubian [mercenaries serving Montuhotep] who brought about the rally [against the hostile Nubians]. Then he [king Montuhotep] overthrew [the hostile] Djaty [Nubian tribe]. He [Montuhotep] raised sail in sailing southwards to the south [into Nubia] as a result of raising the arm against the [enemy] ruler of the [Nubian] lands . . . pleasing the king as when were surpassed those who fled among the people. (ITM 11–20)

Even if Tjehemau's ethnic pride in the Nubian mercenary regiment perhaps led him to exaggerate the role of his fellow Nubian mercenaries in the battle, none the less the martial qualities of the Nubians were highly – and, based upon this battle, rightly – regarded by the Egyptians. On the other hand, it is also important to note that Tjehemau feels no compunction about fighting in the service of the Egyptian king against other Nubian tribes. This reflects an important factor influencing the success of the Egyptian domination in Nubia. Tjehemau's loyalty, and that of most Nubians, was to his own specific tribe of Nubians, rather than an amorphous trans-tribal "Nubian people" as a whole. Most Nubians often viewed other Nubian tribes as rivals and enemies, rather than potential allies against Egypt. This tribal disunity was a major factor contributing to the eventual Egyptian subjugation of Nubia, as discussed on pp. 397–9. After contributing to Montuhotep's victory in Nubia, Tjehemau continued in Montuhotep's service in his campaigns of unification of Egypt.

Montuhotep's unification of Egypt {2047–2035?}

Montuhotep's fourteenth year {2047} was "the year when Thinis rebelled" (ITM 25), apparently with the support of the Ninth Dynasty of Herakleopolis. In response Montuhotep mobilized his army; his el-Deir inscription provides a rare glimpse of the pre- and post-battle celebrations of the Egyptian army. Before the campaign the troops were marshaled for ritualized war speeches and chants that inaugurated the campaign.

> The king's army addresses him [as they prepare to go into battle]: ". . . it is by thy hand [O King] . . . [that we triumph]"
> The King addresses his army: ". . . I come and destroy [my enemies]. We shall go downstream [north] when we have crushed the foreign lands . . . I will give you full title to it [lands captured from the northern kingdom], [and] everything which you desire [in plunder]." (ICN 112)

The king's emphasis on the material rewards of victory highlights the role of plunder as a motivating force for Egyptian armies. After the campaign, the victorious army is again marshaled for a victory triumph, with more ritualized victory speeches:

> And when [the army] had landed in health [after their victory] . . . the King's army addresses him: ". . . the chiefs of the foreign lands come to thee bowing, kissing every limb of yours. Your heart in your body reposes. Upper Egypt and the southern lands [of Nubia] . . . the [foreign] bowmen [submit] . . ."
>
> [The King speaks:] "My ancestors in the necropolis [of Thebes near where the army is marshaled in triumph], at the place where the gods are, they see this thing. (ICN 112)

Later, however, in proper Egyptian fashion, the king piously attributes his victories to the blessings of the gods:

> It was the god . . . who caused Upper Egypt to be broad for me [i.e. easy to traverse and conquer]. I did this while I was King. . . . I caused the Two Lands to come to it [in unification] . . . Wawat [in Nubia] and the [Kharga?] Oasis. I annexed them to Upper Egypt. I drove out the rebellious [enemies] . . . (ICN 114)

We have some further details of Montuhotep's campaign of reunification. Montuhotep first subdued the rebellious nome of Thinis, driving off their allies from Herakleopolis who may have instigated the rebellion. These initial victories encouraged him to continue his march further northward, where some of the nomarchs in middle Egypt apparently shifted allegiance, wisely throwing in their lots with rising Thebes. Their descendants were thus able to retain their positions as nomarchs under the Montuhotep and his successors in the Eleventh Dynasty (HAE 144). Other recalcitrant nomarchs, however, were eventually replaced with trusted ministers, strengthening Montuhotep's direct control over middle Egypt (C1/2:483).

The autobiography of the redoubtable Nubian mercenary Tjehemau, now promoted to officer status, provides an eyewitness account of Montuhotep's conquests from the perspective of an officer on the front battle lines.

> Then, [after his Nubian campaign, Montuhotep sailed northward] . . . to northern Egypt to kill [the rival king of the Ninth Dynasty] . . . Going forth . . . against the Lake of Sobek [Faiyum] . . . I overthrew the [enemy on the] sandbank . . . [and] the river, to lead the sand-dwellers [nomad mercenaries] and [the Nubian mercenaries of] Wawat . . . to put to flight the man [king] of the North. Then it [the northern kingdom of Herakleopolis] mustered its war-fleet and it traversed all its nomes of the entire [northern] land to defend itself. (ITM 11–20)

The details of the next phase of the campaign are not clear. It seems that the army of the Ninth Dynasty won some initial victories and invaded Montuhotep's domain of Thebes. In defense of Thebes, Tjehemau and his Egyptian–Nubian force was required to make an amphibious assault from their boats against an enemy who was marshaled on the banks of the river.

> Tjehemau sailed north like a lion in the following of the king [Montuhotep], together with this, his army [of Nubian mercenaries], which he had brought. He tasted of the fighting, his arm being strong due to what he did to the north. I went down to the district of Thebes. I found [the enemy] standing on the riverbank. They planned fighting. The opposition fell [before our attack], fleeing because of me ... in the district of Thebes. Then I came and was at peace together with its people, for I was strong against [their enemies] ... A herdsman of account of driving off [the enemies'] cattle [as plunder] – it is I, Tjehemau the bold! Extend the arm to me, ye who depart. The lord Tjehemau says: Live, prosper, be healthy! (ITM 11–20)

After this victory Montuhotep I's forces advanced on Herakleopolis, where the crumbling resistance of the Ninth Dynasty was shattered by the death of king Merikare in unknown circumstances – his tomb is at Memphis, indicating that his successor was still in power long enough to bury him. This successor apparently ascended the throne and ruled for only a few months, for the capital Herakleopolis was soon captured {2040} and the Ninth Dynasty ended. Funerary monuments at Herakleopolis were ritually hacked to pieces by the conquerors (OHAE 145), perhaps in revenge for the earlier desecration of the tombs of Abydos that had occurred in the days of Akhtoy III (TS 221, 225). Thereafter Montuhotep I continued the conquest of the delta, completing his subjugation of the Nile Valley. Tjehemau mentions sailing through "all the nomes of the entire land ... in the north, against the king of Lower Egypt [Merikare of Herakleopolis] and his army" (C1/2:482).

The grim reality of warfare during Montuhotep I's reconquests is illustrated by the "Tomb of the Warriors" at Deir el-Bahri in Middle Egypt, where the partially preserved bodies of sixty warriors of Montuhotep I were discovered. All had been killed in Montuhotep's wars of unification, with war wounds preserved for forensic analysis. The exact circumstance of their deaths and burials is not known, but it is generally assumed that they died during a siege in some heroic and decisive circumstances that merited special burial honors, perhaps in the final assault on Herakleopolis itself (SSN, discussed on pp. 438–40).

Foreign campaigns of Montuhotep I {c. 2035–2022?}

The conquest of the Nile Valley did not end Montuhotep's military activities. The traditional desert enemies of Egypt – the bedouins of Sinai and the Libyans of the Western Desert – remained recalcitrant. Although, again, the exact chronology cannot be determined, the conqueror undertook expeditions against the Sinai, Canaan, Libyans in the Western Desert, the western Oases, and Nubia. The evidence for these campaigns, though vague and fragmentary, points to an overall policy of subduing any possible enemy surrounding Egypt. However, permanent Egyptian occupation outside the Nile Valley remained flimsy at this time.

Two royal inscriptions speak rather generically of Montuhotep's foreign campaigns. The Dendera chapel inscription describes "clubbing the eastern lands, striking down the hill-countries, trampling the deserts, enslaving the Nubians ... [of the] Medjay and Wawat [tribes], the Libyans and the [Easterners], by [the power of the war god] Horus" (C1/2:480; PSE Figure 25). Inscriptions from a temple at Gebelein also celebrate the reunification and subsequent campaigns. The first shows the kings smiting a Libyan called "Hedj-wawesh, Prince of Libya" (FP 177; PSE Figure 23). The second relief shows Montuhotep smiting four cowering prisoners: an Egyptian – representing his conquest of northern Egypt – as well as a Nubian, a Canaanite, and a Libyan (PSE Figure 24). The king is described as "conquering the Chiefs of the Two Lands, the South and the North [of Egypt], [and] the foreigners and the two Nile banks [east and west], the Nine Bows and both Egypts" (MKT 24 = ARE 1:204–5 = C1/2:482). From these two inscriptions (NEA 36) we see royal propaganda claiming to have not only reunified Egypt, but defeated all of Egypt's traditional foreign enemies.

Montuhotep's el-Deir inscription describes the defeat of the foreigners, and their subsequent ritual acts of submission and oath of loyalty taken to the king.

His [the king's] flames fell among the foreign lands ... the foreign lands were hastening [to fight] ... the hinterlands were blocked and the Qedem lands were closed [after the Egyptian victory]; ... the Easterners came bowing head [in submission] to the banks of the sea. I went downstream to the estate of *Khss*-seat of the Rule of the Two Lands.... the people of the foreign lands came with arm bent [in submission]. They made the Oath of the God, everyone [of the defeated foreign enemies] therein upon his head, and the subjugated man therein was put to work [as forced laborers for Egypt]. (ICN 113)

Other contemporary inscriptions confirm that this is not mere royal braggadocio. The Western Desert posed two threats: Egyptian fugitives from the Ninth Dynasty and Libyan nomads. Some officials and leaders from the collapsing Ninth Dynasty at Herakleopolis fled into the Western Desert, taking last refuge in one or more of the oases there. One of Montuhotep's commanders named Kay was sent to the oases, where he defeated and captured the fugitives, bringing them back to Egypt for punishment. The oases were apparently permanently occupied, since they were later administered for Montuhotep by Henenu (C1/2:482–3). The efforts to capture the last supporters of the Ninth Dynasty may have been combined with the aforementioned punitive raid against the Libyans in which

"Hedj-wawesh, Prince of Libya" was captured (MKT 24). Montuhotep's hegemony over the Eastern and Western deserts is confirmed by a funerary inscription of an official of the Coptos nome, whose name is lost. His titles included "Overseer of All Hunters of the West and East", indicating responsibility for the nomads of those deserts (ICN 107–8).

Three pieces of evidence describe Montuhotep's campaigns through the Sinai and into Canaan (ECI 69–70). The Deir el-Ballas inscription gives vague reference to military activity in the "Eastern lands" (ECI 69). More detail is provided in the account of an expedition to the "mineral country" in the Sinai – undoubtedly meaning the mines at Wadi Maghara – by an official named Akhtoy. His goal was to re-establish Egyptian mines and quarries that apparently had become largely inactive since the end of the Old Kingdom. Akhtoy reported: "I punished the Eastern [nomads] in their land. It was the fear of the king that spread respect for me and his influence that spread terror of me, so that those countries in which I went [in the Sinai] cried out 'Hail! Hail!' to his might" (MKT 35). One suspects that at least some of the nomads' salutations were less than sincere.

At some point thereafter further expeditions were apparently taken to the urban areas of southern Palestine; the tomb of general Antef at Thebes depicts an Egyptian army assaulting what is clearly a Canaanite city (EWW 38; NEA Figure 3). No text accompanies the mural, but it seems to depict a major siege. Additional details from this scene concerning siegecraft will be discussed on pp. 447–51. The Nubian mercenary commander Tjehemau may have participated in this campaign; in the murals of Antef's tomb Nubian archers are shown along with the Egyptian infantry assaulting the Canaanite fortress.[5]

By the end of his reign in 2011, Montuthotep I had reunited Egypt, subdued the Nubians, overcome the Libyan nomads and captured the oasis, defeated the eastern nomads, and campaigned in Canaan. His military victories represent a brilliant beginning to the military predominance of Egypt during the reigns of his successors.

Montuhotep II {2011–2000}[6]

The long and successful reign of Montuhotep I meant that his son, Montuhotep II, came to the throne at an advanced age and ruled for only a decade. The military success of his father on all fronts also meant that Montuhotep II faced no serious military threat, and only few recorded military activities survive from his reign. Instead we find a reign focusing on building, art, and trade.

Montuhotep I's earlier punitive expeditions against the Easterners of Sinai and Canaan, despite their nominal submission, were apparently insufficient to entirely quell their military ardor. Montuhotep II's approach to the military problem of the Canaanite frontier focused on expanding an elaborate fortification system on borders of the eastern delta to prevent further incursions – the "Great Wall" mentality which in military history has only worked in conjunction with a strong army with a policy of regular punitive expeditions beyond the wall. The details of Middle Kingdom fortifications will be discussed on pp. 440–5.

Henenu's expedition to Punt {2004}[7]

The most notable military mission during the reign of Montuhotep II is Henenu's expedition to Punt – the south-west coast of the Red Sea – which is especially interesting for its detailed description of logistics. Building on the military victories of his father, Montuhotep II was able to reopen the Red Sea maritime trade to Punt, sending his important minister Henenu, governor of southern Egypt, as leader of the expedition. When he had successfully returned from Punt, Henenu carved an inscription describing his expedition on a rock face in Wadi Hammamat. The initial part of the inscription contains the self-adulation so typical of Egyptian autobiography, but the second half provides a detailed description of his expedition to Punt, under orders to return with myrrh, a precious incense.

> I set out from Coptos [in the fifth nome] on the way his majesty commanded me, with me being an army of Upper Egypt from the *w3bw*-garrisons of the Theban nome, from Imyotru to Shabet. All royal offices from town and country were assembled and followed me, and four companies of scouts [*s3-pnw*] cleared the way before me, smiting any [nomads] who rebelled against the king. Hunters, natives of the deserts, were employed as bodyguards ... Setting out with an army of 3000 men, I made the road into a river, the desert into a field border. For I gave a water skin and a bread bag, with two *ds*-measures of water and twenty loaves, to every one of [the 3000 men in the expedition] every day. Donkeys were laden with sandals; when a foot became unshod another sandal was ready. I also made twelve wells on the valley floor and two wells in Idahet, one measuring twenty cubits, the other thirty. I made another in Yaheteb of 10 by 10 cubits at all water levels. Then I reached the sea and then I built this fleet. I loaded it with everything when I made for it a great sacrifice of cattle and goats. When I had returned from the sea I had done what his majesty had commanded me, bringing for him all kinds of gifts that I had found on the shores of god's land [Punt].... Never had the like been done by any King's Friend since the [mythical] time of the god. (AEAB 53–4)

The extensive logistical and scouting preparations described in this account demonstrate why Egyptian armies were able to operate successfully hundreds of miles from their military bases in Egypt. Nomads were hired – or perhaps bribed – to serve as scouts and guides. Four companies of scouts – perhaps one vanguard, one rearguard and one on each flank – kept the army safe from ambush. Donkeys were organized for supply transport, including food, water, and spare sandals, and presumably other equipment. Although generally not mentioned in the sources, similar logistical planning undoubtedly lay behind all successful foreign campaigns.

Montuhotep III {2000–1998}

Major military activities are not recorded in this short and poorly documented reign. One mining expedition was dispatched to the Wadi el-Hudy amethyst mines under Shed-ptah, "commander of the foreign troops". Another was sent to Wadi Hammamat, possibly to establish some water stations on the desert routes to the quarries. It was commanded by Se'onkh, "the general responsible for the [desert] highlands" who, like Henenu, equipped his men, numbering only 60 adults, with "water skins, baskets, bread, beer and every fresh vegetable of the South" (ARE 217 = ECI 72), again emphasizing the logistical basis of Egyptian expeditions.

The most notable mission, however, occurred in 1999 and was commanded by the vizier Amenemhet, who led an expedition to the quarries in Wadi Hammamat, reaching the port of Mersa Gawasis that was destined to become the principal Red Sea port in future years.[8] His expedition, said to have numbered "10,000 men from the southern nomes of Upper Egypt, and from the garrisons of Thebes", was sent to "bring a precious block of the pure stone of this mountain" for the king's sarcophagus. The expedition included "miners, artificers, quarrymen, artists, draughtsmen, stonecutters, and gold-workers". Three thousand sailors later transported the huge block down the Nile to the delta. Amenemhet emphasized his personal administrative skill, noting that not a man nor animal perished on the expedition – a not uncommon claim in autobiographies from this period, implying divine blessing on the journey. It is important to note that Amenemhet's ability to mobilize, supply, and command 10,000 men in the Eastern Desert probably contributed to his later victory in the civil war that followed the death of Mentuhotep III.

Civil war {1998–1991} (ECI 72–4)

The Turin Canon records a gap of seven years after Montuhotep III; this possibly covers a year or two of the reign of an ephemeral Mentuhotep IV, but probably indicates a period of chaos and civil war, the details of which have not been preserved (C1/2:492–3). It is sometimes suggested that the vizier Amenemhet, who led the Wadi Hammamat expedition described in the last section, rebelled against Montuhotep III or his successor. However that may be, some fragments from contemporary biographies reflect the problems of the time. These come from the family of Nehry, nomarch of Hermopolis (the fifteenth "Hare" nome, ECI 73). After the standard flamboyant self-aggrandizement, Nehry records a battle with an unnamed king who had besieged Nehry's army in Hermopolis and was challenging Nehry to come out of his city to battle: "[The king challenged:] 'draw you up the battle line! See, I too am in battle line!' But I [Nehry] was a fortress for fighting in Shedyet-sha to which all the people rallied ... who rescued his city on the day of terror instigated by the [attack of the army of the] king's house" (ECI 73). Meanwhile, Nehry's son Kay aided in the defense of Hermopolis [I]:

recruited the city's draftees of young men in order that its levees be numer-ous.... I trained my draftees of young men and went to fight along with my city. I acted as its fortress in Shedyet-sha. When there was no one with me except my retainers; [while the king's army included mercenary Nubian] Medjay, Wawat, [Egyptian] southerners, Easterners, the Southland and the Delta being united against me. I emerged, the affair being a success, my entire city being with me without loss. (ECI 73)

Kay is apparently describing a more professional army of the "young men" in his service supported by the city militia mobilized to defend his city when under attack. But the exact background and circumstances of this battle are unclear. Since his family retained power in Hermopolis, it appears that he was in alliance with the upstart Amenemhet against the soon-to-be-toppled "king's house" of Mentuhotep IV. Here we see a local nomarch, mobilizing his provincial army, resisting a royal army behind fortress walls, but unwilling to leave the safety of those walls and face the enemy in open battle. The king's army, it will be noted, included troops from Egypt, and mercenaries from Nubia and Canaan.

Two literary sources provide a broader context for the events of the civil war and the rise to power of Amenemhet I: the "Instructions of Amenemhet" and the "Prophecy of Neferti". Although purporting to describe events associated with the reign of Amenemhet I, both works are at least semi-fictional, and their precise historical significance is debated. These texts none the less provide insights into the Egyptian view of the rise of Amenemhet, at least from the perspective of the later royal propaganda of the victor.

The "Prophecy of Neferti"[9]

This is a fascinating proto-messianic text – a prophecy of the coming of a future king who will free Egypt from its enemies and restore the divinely established order of the gods. Although the "prophecy" is set in the time of king Sneferu of the Fourth Dynasty, it is generally assumed to be a work of propaganda from the reign of Amenemhet, which justifies his ascension to the throne as the fulfillment of the gods' plan as described in an "ancient" prophecy. According to the text, all the courtiers and priests are gathered to pay their respects at court; the king is informed of a great sage named Neferti, a priest of the cat-goddess Bastet of Bubastis in the eastern delta. Neferti is brought before the king and asked to pro-phecy the future. The prophecy begins with a vision of devastation in Egypt before the reign of Amenemhet – presumably during the period of instability and civil war before his ascension {1998–1991}. The Nile is dry, storms rage, the land is infertile and depopulated. Then the Easterners invade the Delta from the east:

The land is burdened with misfortune
Because of those searching for food,
Easterners roaming the land.

Foes have arisen in the east,
Easterners have descended into Egypt.
The [frontier] fortifications are destroyed . . .
The animals of the [nomads] of the desert
will drink from the river of Egypt (CS 108)

Chaos spreads, as civil war breaks out in Egypt:

I will show you the land in turmoil
That which has never happened [before] has happened
One will seize the weapons of warfare,
The land lives in confusion
One will make arrows of copper,
One will beg for bread with blood . . .
A man sits with his back turned,
While one man kills another.
I show you a son as an enemy,
A brother as a foe
A man killing his own father.. . .
The land [ruled by the king] diminishes
But its [small independent] rulers are numerous
[The land is] bare, but its taxes are great . . .
Re [the supreme god] separates himself from mankind. (CS 108–9)

All is not lost, however, for in his vision Neferti sees the coming of a redeemer king who will drive out the enemies of Egypt and restore order. He reunites Egypt, defeats rebellious Egyptians and drives out the Libyan and Eastern invaders:

Then a king will come from the south
Imeny [Amenemhet], the justified, is his name
A son is he of a woman of the land of Nubia,
A child is he of Upper Egypt.
He will take the white crown [of south Egypt],
He will wear the red crown [of north Egypt];
He will unite the Two Mighty Ones [goddesses of Upper and Lower Egypt] . . .
Rejoice, O people of his time
The son of man [Amenemhet] will make his name forever and ever.. . .
The Easterners will fall to his slaughter,
The Libyans will fall to his flame,
The rebels [within Egypt] to his wrath,
The traitors to his might,
He will build the "Walls of the Ruler" [on the north-east Delta]
To prevent Easterners from descending to Egypt . . .
Then order will come into its place. (CS 109–10)

Amenemhet's rise to power is thus portrayed as the divine mandate of the gods to save Egypt from chaos and invasion.

Amenemhet's victory in the Civil War {1993?–1991}

The rather vague and propagandistic panegyrics of the "Prophecy of Neferti" are supplemented by several more concrete reference to Amenemhet's victories in the civil wars. The first comes from an inscription of Khnumhotep I, a nomarch of Beni Hasan in Middle Egypt:

> I went down with his majesty [Amenemhet] to Im[et] in twenty ships of cedar; then he came to Pelusium [in the north-east delta] ... When he had expelled him [the rival in the civil war] from the two banks of Horus [the Nile].... Nubians perished ... and Syrians fell. [Amenemhet] organized the land [of Egypt] ... the two banks [of the Nile]. (AIB 148–9 = ARE 1:225, 283; C1/2:496–7)

In return for his services, Khnumhotep was appointed "overseer of the eastern desert in Menat-Khufu" (AIB 152).

The Nesu-Montu inscription, written by one of Amenemhet's generals, probably recalls some of the battles of the civil war as well:

> I am one firm of foot, excellent of counsel, one whose conduct his lord [king Amenemhet] praises. The conscripts of Thebes adore me, as I never made display of cruelty [in disciplinary punishment].... I am the only one worthy to be called the hero of this land, swift of hand and quick of pace, a citizen skilled in arms. I trained the troops in ambush, and at daybreak, the landing-stage [of the city] surrendered. When I grasped the tip of the bow, I led the battle for the Two Lands. I was victorious, my arms making so much spoil that I had to leave some on the ground. I destroyed the foes, I overthrew the enemies of my lord [Amenemhet], there being none other whole will say the like. (AIB 108)

Thus, despite the uncertainties concerning the specific course of the civil war, the final result is clear: the prime minister Amenemhet emerged victorious, ascending the throne as king Amenemhet I, founder of the Twelfth Dynasty.

Twelfth Dynasty {1191–1786}[10]

Amenemhet I {1991–1971/1962}[11]

In the posthumous "Instructions of Amenemhet",[12] the dead king appears to his son Senwosret I as a ghost in a dream or vision after his assassination, giving his son a broad summary of his military career in rather generalized and poetic terms:

I [Amenemhet] strode to Elephantine [Aswan in the far south]
I traveled to the Marshes [of the delta in the north]
I stood firm on the limits of the land, having seen its midst
I attained the borders of the [frontier] strongholds
With my strong arm, and my [military] feats.…
All that I decreed was as it should be.
I tamed lions, and captured crocodiles.
I subjugated the Nubians, and captured Medjay;
I made the Syrians do the "dog-walk". (TS 207–8 = AEL 1:137)

Though this is a stylized and poetic summary, the essence of Amenemhet's campaigns is clear from the text. He conquered all Egypt during the civil war (as in the previous section), established firm frontier fortifications, and campaigned against both Nubia and Canaan.

Upon securing the throne through victory in the civil war, the new king built a new fortified capital named Amenemhet-Iti-tawy – "Amenemhet, seizer of the Two Lands", some fifty miles south of Cairo (modern el-Lisht; EAE 2:294–7; AEA 84), perhaps in part to establish a new secure base of operations outside the sphere of influence – and possible intrigue – of the priests and courtiers of the old regime he had overthrown. Amenemhet also reorganized the nome structure and appointed new officers to insure personal loyalty to himself (AIB 152–3), and continued royal sponsorship of expeditions to the diorite quarries to the southwest of Aswan (C1/2:497).

With Egypt unified, Amenemhet faced the two standard military problems of all Egyptian rulers: the Nubian frontier, and the north-eastern frontier. On both frontiers Amenemhet's policy was the same: offensive invasion aimed not so much at direct occupation, but at undermining the military capabilities of the Nubians and Canaanites, while securing the frontier with a strong fortification system.

Amenemhet's Nubian policy (AAA 49–50)

Amenemhet was said to have been "the son of a woman from *Ta-sety*" (TS 138), a term often associated with Nubia. Though he was half Nubian, he did not show any particular favor towards his mother's ancestral homeland. The broad outlines of Amenemhet's Nubian strategy can be learned from archaeology and some fragmentary inscriptions from Girgawi, which describe a campaign against northern Nubians – called the "C-group" by archaeologists (EAE 1:258–9). The expedition was under the command of the vizier Intefiqer, who left a description of the desolation caused by his invasion.

This [temporary fortified] enclosure being built, then I slaughtered Nubians and all the rest of Wawat [Nubia]. Then I went upstream [south] in victory, slaughtering the Nubian in their own land, and came back downstream stripping crops, and cutting down the rest of their trees so that I could put fire to their homes, as is done against a rebel against the king. I have not heard of another soldier doing the like.... Intefiqer [sailed] in the ship called "Great Oar". (VAE 95–6 = AIB 134)

From this account it appears that the Nubians had "rebelled" against Egypt, perhaps simply implying either a refusal to accept Amenemhet's suzerainty, or some type of raid by Nubians into Egypt. In response, the Egyptians sent a fleet around the First Cataract at Aswan, probably through the canal originally cut by Weni in the Sixth Dynasty (AEL 1:21). The army regiments either marched on the riverbank, supported by the river fleet, or were transported by the fleet. At some point they built a temporary fortified camp as a base for military operations. Thereafter, the army advanced further southwards, systematically slaughtering any Nubians they found, while destroying their crops, orchards, and cities, and leaving devastation in their wake.

The Korosko inscription allows us to date the campaign to year 29 {1962}, and mentions a number of the other commanders: Shnumu, Amenemhet (not the king), Ishteka, and "the king's son Nakhti" who "came to overthrow Wawat [northern Nubia]" (AIB 128 = ARE 1:228). Intefiqer's fleet, described as "coming and going against Wawat", was under the command of "Redis, the overseer of the ships" (AIB 129). Amenemhet's Nubian campaigns resulted in the extension of Egyptian military power to the Second Cataract, where he built the Semna fortress (HAE 161), the first in a string of fortresses designed to give Egypt direct domination over northern Nubia and control over trade between Nubian Africa and Egypt.

The northern frontiers

Whereas Amenemhet's Nubian policy was one of invasion and pushing the boundaries southward, in the north he remained essentially on the defensive. The earlier problem of Eastern bedouin incursions continued, compelling Amenemhet to strengthen the eastern delta fortifications with the "Wall of the Ruler" at Wadi Tumilat (CS 1:110; C1/2:497); archaeological remains of these fortifications have not been discovered. This fortification process was supplemented by punitive raids against the nomads beyond the Egyptian fortified border. The Nesu-Montu inscription describes one such expedition in Year 24 {1967}:

I destroyed the [nomadic] wild bow-people, the Sand-dwellers. I demolished [their] fortresses and prowled like a jackal on the desert's edge. I went up and down through their streets, there being not my match therein, because [the war god] Montu had ordered the victory. (ECI 77 = AIB 109 = ARE 1:227–8)

As on the north-eastern frontier, fortresses were also built in the western delta at Qaret el-Dahr south of Wadi Natrun to defend the Western Desert approaches to Egypt. Details about campaigns against the Libyan western frontier are not known, though the "Prophecy of Neferti" claims "the Libyans will fall to [Amenemhet's] flame" (CS 110), implying that some type of punitive expeditions were undertaken to subdue the Libyans. Indeed, when Amenemhet was assassinated in 1962, his son Senwosret was on a campaign in the Libyan desert, from which he was quickly recalled to secure the vacant throne (TS 27).

In year 20 {1971} the aging Amenemhet made his son Senwosret I co-regent {co-regent, 1971–1962; sole ruler, 1962–1928}. Thereafter Senwosret seems to have controlled foreign policy and led most major military expeditions. The military affairs of the last decade {1971–1962} of Amenemhet's reign, during his co-regency with Senwosret I, will thus be discussed in the next section, since they represent the military policy of Senwosret. Despite his great military achievements, Amenemhet's political policy caused dissatisfaction and instability at court, where he was assassinated by a harem conspiracy that was organized by a vizier but implemented by his own bodyguard. According to the "Instructions of Amenemhet", the ghost of the murdered king returned to his son and successor Senwosret and described his murder:

> After supper, when darkness had fallen ... I was lying on my bed ... I woke to fighting, and I found it was an attack of the bodyguard ... Had women [of the harem] ever before commanded troops [to attack the king]? (TS 207; Man. 34–6)

Amenemhet's murder apparently created a temporary succession crisis, but ultimately the conspirators failed, and his son Senwosret was able to succeed to the throne.

Senwosret (Sesostris) I {1971/1962–1928}[13]

Senwosret's personal reign began with a crisis {1962}. He had been sent by his father on a punitive expedition into Libya, and "was returning [to Egypt], having carried off Libyan captives and all sorts of cattle without number", when a messenger met his army on the march and informed him of the assassination of his father. Remembering his father was himself a usurper, and realizing that his throne was at stake, "he did not wait a moment; the falcon [Senwosret] flew off with his [personal] followers (*šmsw*), without informing [the rest of] army" of the death of king Amenemhet. His quick march to the palace at el-Lisht forestalled the assassins, and he was able to claim the throne (TS 27–8).

Although the first ten years of Senwosret's reign {1971–1962} had been spent in co-regency with his father, Senwosret appears to have been in charge of foreign and military affairs during most of this period. Some punitive expeditions were undertaken against the Libyans (TS 27); an officer, Ded-Iqu, who is proud of having "secured his majesty's borders", records that "as commander of young recruits" he was sent "to secure the land of the oasis-dweller", probably the Libyans around the Kharga Oasis (AEA 93–4).

None the less, for the most part Senwosret was satisfied to maintain his northwestern and north-eastern frontiers secure by strongly garrisoned fortifications that had been begun by his father (C1/2:500–1). This policy is explicitly stated by

Sinuhe, "he [Senwosret I] will conquer the southern lands [of Nubia], without yet considering the northern countries [of Syria]" (TS 31). The maintenance of the northern frontier required occasional expeditions against the Sinai bedouins, perhaps in conjunction with mining expeditions to the Sinai for turquoise and copper (LA 5:892). A nobleman named Montuhotep described one such punitive expedition in his funerary inscription: he "put his terror among the barbarians when he silenced the Sand-dwellers, pacifying the rebels because of their [rebellious] deeds" (ARE 1:256).

The Eastern Desert of Egypt was also the scene of other paramilitary mining expeditions (SI 361–400). Senwosret sent an expedition under the vizier Intefiqer to Wadi Gawasis on the Red Sea, from which ships were built (or assembled from transported parts) and dispatched to Punt (AIB 139). Several expeditions were sent to the quarries in Wadi Hamammat; an inscription from year 38 {1933} describes one with 17,000 men that transported 210 huge stones to make sphinxes (C1/2:500). Although not strictly a military expedition, the huge size of the force reflects the Egyptians' logistical capacity to mobilize and sustain large armies in the field. The military prominence of the reign of Senwosret I is also reflected in some of the tomb paintings of the period. The Beni Hasan rock-cut tombs of Khety (tomb 17, c. 2000) and Amenemhet (tomb 2, c. 1950) both contain depictions of wrestlers training, and of actual combat (EWP 120–1, 126), which will be discussed in greater detail on pp. 433–8.

The Nubian frontier

Senwosret's major military efforts, however, were centered on the Nubian frontier, focusing on securing access to the mineral resources of Nubia (SI 237–360; M = HAAE 45; AAE 41). Expedition inscriptions tell us that he exploited gneiss at Toshka, amethyst at Wadi el-Hudi, and gold and copper at Wadi Allaqi in the Nubian eastern deserts. Ameni, commander of the troops of the Oryx nome, participated in two of these gold-seeking expeditions, which he described in his autobiography:

> I sailed south [into Nubia] to fetch gold ore to the majesty of King Kheperkare [Senwosret I], living forever and ever. I sailed south with the Prince, Count, Eldest King's Son of his body, [the future] Amenemhet II, life–prosperity–health. I sailed south with 400 conscripts, the choicest of my troops, and returned in safety without loss to them. I brought the gold he had demanded, was rewarded for it in the king's house, and the king's son thanked me. (AEAB 138 = ARE 1:251–2)

The second expedition is similarly described:

> Then I sailed south to bring gold ore to the town of Coptos.... I sailed south with 600 conscripts, the bravest of the Oryx nome. I returned in peace, my

soldiers safe, and I had done all I had been ordered. (AEAB 138 = ARE 1:251–2)

Senwosret's increased military activity in Nubia was closely linked to the economic importance of gold, intended to protect the mining expeditions, control trade, and prevent possible raids by Nubians into Egypt. In the sixth year {1965}, Ibes, son of Id, participated in an expedition to Nubia, in which he "traveled downstream with the army". However, he laments: "there was no fighting", because of which he was unable to "bring a Nubian back as captive from the land of the Nubians" (VAE 95). These incidents reflect the fact that even a moderate Egyptian force of from 400 to 600 men could at this time operate with some impunity in northern Nubia, perhaps because of the devastation wrought by former campaigns such as that of Intefiqer, described on pp. 394–5. Ibes's complaint that he was not able to bring back Nubian slaves also illustrates the importance of personal plunder to Egyptian soldiers.

In his eighteenth year {1953}, Senwosret launched the major campaign of his reign, an expedition into Nubia, commanded by his general Montuhotep (C1/2:499–500). In the first phase, Montuhotep led his army to the Second Cataract, where they established a new fortified base at Buhen, intended to be the basis for permanent Egyptian occupation and annexation of Nubia. (The nature and importance of these fortifications will be discussed on pp. 443–5.) A fragmentary inscription by the "commander of the army" Montuhotep describes the devastation wrought on the local population by this campaign: "[the Nubians'] life is finished, [they are] slain ... [their] tents are burned ... their grain cast into the Nile" (ARE 1:249).

An inscription near Buhen commemorates this campaign, showing Senwosret and the war-god Montu with ten bound and cowering Nubians symbolizing ten cities, regions, or tribes defeated in the campaign (ARE 1:247). The first name on the list is "Kush", the leader of the enemy confederation. This is the first historical mention of an important new military power in the Sudan, which will be discussed on pp. 402–6. Although permanent Egyptian occupation under Senwosret I ended at the fortress of Buhen at the Second Cataract, the army campaigned further south into to the land of Kush. Ameni, "commander of the troops of the Oryx nome", described the second phase of the expedition:

> I followed my lord [Senwosret I's heir apparent Amenemhet II] when he sailed south to overthrow his enemies [in Kush] among the foreign barbarians. As Count's Son, Royal Sealbearer, and Chief Troop Commander of the Oryx nome did I sail ...
> I passed by Kush, sailing south,
> I reached the ends of the earth;
> I brought back tribute of all kinds
> And praise of me reached [even] to heaven.

Then his majesty returned in safety, having overthrown his enemies in wretched Kush. I returned in his following in alertness and no loss occurred in my troops.[14]

Like Alexander's army on the banks of the Indus, Ameni and his Egyptian soldiers felt like they had marched to the end of the earth.[15] It is possible that the Egyptians were militarily active as far south as Argo Island, near the Kushite capital of Kerma (twenty-five miles north of modern Dongola), where the name Senwosret was found inscribed on a vessel – whether it was brought by trade or military expedition is unclear (C1/2:500). The new military frontier of Kush was not completely stabilized by Senwosret I's campaign and fortress building; his great-grandson Senwosret III was required to undertake a number of additional campaigns and build more fortresses a half-century later. None the less, the military successes of Senwosret I laid the foundation for the permanent Egyptian occupation of Nubia and a century of prosperity for Egypt.

Amenemhet II {1929–1895}[16]

Until 1980, historians of ancient Egypt generally described the reign of Amenemhet II as one of peace (C1/2:503, HAE 165). The publication of a recently discovered inscription from Memphis, however, contains passages from Amenemhet's "Daybook" describing details of his military campaigns into Syria during a single year. Beginning in the Middle Kingdom the Egyptian court kept a "daybook or journal (*hrwyt*) as a means to record day-to-day accounts (income and disbursements) and events (arrivals, departures, civil and military matters, court cases, etc.)" (EAE 1:97a; LA 3:789–90). Nearly all of these records have perished, but some passages have survived and other sections were used as the basis for official military inscriptions on stone.[17] In the case of Amenemhet II, the recently discovered inscription includes a portion of the court journal for a single year – often called by Egyptologists the *annus mirabilis*, or "amazing year" – which includes accounts of tribute received and military campaigns to Syria.

Unfortunately the beginning of the inscription is lost and the year in question is not certain. None the less, the inscription describes a number of different military expeditions during this single year. First, there is the "dispatch of the army to Khenty-she [Lebanese coast]" and its return later in the same year: "the return of the army dispatched to Khenty-she in ten ships" (ECI 78–9). The size of the expedition, ten ships, indicates that the total size of the force involved was probably in the hundreds, certainly not many more than a thousand men. None the less, this force was able to return with substantial wealth – though it is not clear if this was trade, tribute, or plunder. Their goods included "1665 units of silver; 4882 units of gold, [and] 15,961 units of copper" (ECI 79). The list of wealth also included bronze weapons inlaid with gold, silver, and ivory. A second army left Egypt that year, but is not described as returning. It laconically

mentions the "dispatch of the army together with the commander of the
elite troops and the commander of the army to hack up *Iw3s* [Alse?] in Syria"
(ECI 79).

Two other armies returned to Egypt in this year, although they had apparently
been sent out the year before. The first "army" returned with wealth from the
"turquoise terraces", presumably an expedition to the Sinai mines. The second
was more clearly military, a naval plundering raid to Cyprus and another land,
perhaps on the Levantine coast:

> Arrival of the shock troops sent to destroy the towns of *Iw3y* and *I3sy*
> [Cyprus]. Tally of prisoners of war brought back from these two foreign lands:
> 1554 Easterners [as prisoners]; bronze-and-wood [weapons]: 10 battle-axes,
> 33 scimitars; 12 daggers; 11 knives; [?] javelins, as well as copper, gold, lapis
> lazuli and gems. (ECI 79)

From the military perspective one thing is particularly striking: although fifteen
hundred people were taken prisoner, only 66 weapons (and an unknown number
of javelins lost in a lacuna) are included in the plunder. This first indicates that a
large number of the prisoners would have been women and children. The weapons list may, in fact, include only bronze weapons, which were considered worthy
of special attention as plunder for the king. There is also the mention of thirty-
three "scimitars" – literally "reaping implements" (ECI 79 n49) – taken as plunder. Presumably these are the curved "sickle-swords" found in Royal Tombs I–III
at Byblos in Syria and Shechem in Canaan during the late Middle Bronze Age {c.
nineteenth century} (MW 1:142–3, 2:514; AW 1:172–3, 206–7; FP 51). The
Egyptians called this weapon the *kopesh* (*ḫpš*, EG 513, sign T16); there is limited
evidence for the use of these weapons in Egypt before the New Kingdom, when
they became more widespread.

In summary, Egypt had four separate military expeditions underway in a single year.
Two were naval expeditions, one to Lebanon and the other to Cyprus. Two others
were overland into the Sinai and Canaan. Egypt was successfully able to exert moderate levels of military force throughout Cyprus, Lebanon, southern Canaan, and
Sinai in a single year. In the same year, emissaries arrived from both Nubia and Syria
bringing "tribute" for the king – often a euphemism for merchants arriving with trade
goods – as well as "suppliants of the *Tmp3w* [Ugarit?]" with "238 ingots of lead"
(ECI 79). The inscription also records a large number of donations given to the gods
and temples, exemplifying the symbiotic relationship between the gods, who granted Egypt prosperity, wealth, and victory in battle, in return for which the pharaoh
gave a portion of this wealth back in the form of donations to the gods, through
priests of the temples, in thanks for divine blessings. While praising and thanking
the gods for their assistance, however, the army was not forgotten; the Daybook
also records distribution of rewards to the military officers in command (ECI 79).

The survival of Amenemhet II's journal for this one year points to an important
historiographical principle that needs to be repeated when trying to reconstruct

the military history of the ancient Near East: absence of evidence is not necessarily evidence of absence. Before the publication of this inscription in 1980, Amenemhet II's reign was described as essentially peaceful. In reality there were four simultaneous campaigns underway in a single year – the only year for which we have surviving evidence from the Daybooks. Records for most of Egypt's military history simply have not survived. All we can do is reconstruct a minimal account of Egyptian militarism.

That the military affairs of Nubia were not neglected by Amenemhet is indicated by an inspection tour of some of the Nubian frontier fortresses (ARE 1:278). Two mining expeditions were undertaken to the Sinai in which the local chiefs were "suppressed" (VAE 137 = ARE 1:274). In addition there is one record of military intervention on the Nubian frontier, commanded by the "assistant treasurer" Sihathor, who "reached the land of Nubia [where] the Nubians came bowing down [in submission] for fear of the Lord of the Two Lands [king Amenemhet II]" (VAE 138 = ARE 1:274). There were likewise at least two trading voyages to Punt from the major Egyptian Red Sea port of Sawu (Wadi el-Gasus). The first was in 1901, when "Captain of the Gate" Khentekhtay-wer returned safely from an expedition to Punt, "his army being with him" (ARE 1:275). The second, in 1897, was under the Treasurer Khnumhotpe (C1/2:504).

Commercial relations played an increasingly important role during this period. In addition to the Nubian trade for gold and semi-precious stones, Egyptian commercial and cultural contacts flourished with Syria, and extended into Anatolia and Crete as well. A number of Egyptian artifacts have been found at Ugarit, Megiddo, and other Canaanite cities. Byblos was especially important as an Egyptian ally; its rulers took the Egyptian title ḥ3ty-' ("count" or "mayor"), and the court at Byblos was strongly influenced by Egyptian culture (C1/2:503–4; EAE 1:219–21; DANE 62). Byblos probably served as a naval base for at least some of the maritime expeditions of Amenemhet II described in the Daybook. Although the presence of Egyptian artifacts in Syria is generally thought to represent prestige items acquired through exchange (possibly even in exchanges that occurred several generations after the artifact was made), given the previously unknown military activities of Amenemhet, it is not impossible that some may represent the extent of potential Egyptian military activity as well.

A treasure consisting of four bronze caskets filled with gold and silver tribute from Syria was discovered at the temple of Montu at Tod in Upper Egypt, indicating the rich trade, tribute, or plunder – the Egyptians didn't necessarily always distinguish between these categories – that was obtained during the reign of Amenemhet II. The growing wealth of Egypt from trade, tribute, plunder, mining expeditions, and expansions and improvements to irrigation systems (such as those undertaken by Senwosret II in the Fayyum, OHAE 164), laid the foundation for Egypt's military power. The Tomb of Khnumhotep at Beni Hasan (Tomb 3) has splendid color murals depicting the arrival of a Canaanite caravan under the chieftain Abisha in Egypt (AW 1:166–7; EWP 124; OHAE 192; BH 1 §30; AAK 2/1:6). This mural gives us a good indication of the dress and weapons of

Canaanite soldiers during this period. The men of the caravan are dressed in colorful kilts and tunics, and are armed with bows, javelins, throwing sticks, and a curved axe. The fact that the men in this caravan are armed indicates the dangers of crossing the Sinai, and adds support to the assumption that most trading expeditions mentioned in Egyptian texts were paramilitary affairs.

No major military campaigns are recorded for Amenemhet II's successor, Senwosret (Sesostris) II {1897–1877}.[18]

Senwosret (Sesostris) III {1878–1843}[19]

Militarily, the thirty-five-year reign of Senwosret III was one of the most important of the Middle Kingdom. Senwosret III's military prowess became the stuff of later legend; he was remembered over 1500 years later by the Greeks as a conqueror greater than Alexander.[20] Within Egypt, Senwosret III suppressed the semi-independence enjoyed by some of the nomarchs, contributing to a stabilization of the internal political situation for the next century, while also increasing the central resources of the king (C1/2:505–6). It is unclear if these activities involved the exercise of military power, or were purely political in nature. Outside of Egypt, Senwosret III campaigned on both the Nubian and Canaanite frontiers.

Nubian campaigns {1870–1859}[21]

In order to facilitate both trade and military access to Nubia, Senwosret III repaired and expanded earlier Old Kingdom work on the Aswan canal which allowed ships to bypass the First Cataract. In his eighth year {1870}, the king had the canal enlarged to 75 meters long, 10 meters wide and 7 meters deep (ARE 1:291–2). With his communications and logistics between Egypt and Nubia secured by the refurbished canal, Senwosret marched his army southward, past the fortification line of Buhen at the Second Cataract that had been established by his grandfather, conquering to half-way between the Second and Third Cataracts and establishing a new southern military boundary for Egypt at Semna (ARE 293–4), where in the coming years he built and garrisoned eight large mud-brick fortresses.[22] According to Senwosret's official policy declaration, the new fortified boundary was designed . . .

> to prevent any Nubian from passing it downstream, either overland or by boat, or any herds of the Nubians, apart from any Nubian who shall come to trade at [the Egyptian fortified, officially sanctioned trading center at] Iken [at the Second Cataract], or upon any good business that may be done with [the Nubians], but forever forbidding a ship of the Nubians to pass by [Fort] Heh [Semna]. (EP 135 = ARE 1:293–4)

As with most Egyptian campaigns, efficient young officers who caught the eye of the pharaoh were given rewards and promotion for their successful service. On this or one of the later campaigns, Senwosret was accompanied by one of his courtiers, Sebek-khu, who served as a commander in the army and left an account of his promotion during the campaign in his autobiography.

> I commanded sixty men when his majesty traveled upstream to overthrow the tribesmen of Nubia. Thereupon I captured a Nubian in Kenket [while fighting] alongside the regiment of my city. Then I returned downstream [north], following with six men of the [royal] residence. Then his majesty appointed me as inspector of the retainers and [command of a company of] 100 men were given to me as a reward. (AIB 120 = ARE 1:306)

Another undated text from the mortuary biography of Ibia describes his command of a campaign in Kush, probably under Senwosret III, but perhaps under another ruler:

> The king sent me to open up Kush because he deemed me efficient. I set the power of the Lord of the Two Lands [the king of Egypt] in the midst of rebellious foreign lands [of Kush], and followed the monuments of the king into remote foreign lands. (AEA 127)

This text indicates the difficulty of subduing Kush, the land beyond Nubia; the view that it was a "remote foreign land" implies that military operations in Kush stretched the logistical limits of the Egyptians to their maximum capacity. The phrase "following the monuments of the king" into foreign lands possibly has reference to images of the king carried with the army and set up in a portable shrine (e.g. BH 2 §15c). Since the king was always the official, though frequently absent, leader of the campaign, images of the king may have been carried with the army; statues and stele of kings were certainly erected along the campaign trail. Alternatively, the phrase "following the monuments of the king" may refer to the stele of Senwosret at Semna, or a similar monument.

The goals of Senwosret III's original campaign were not immediately fully achieved. The Nubian frontier was by no means stable and secure in the coming years, requiring several additional punitive expeditions. In 1866 Senwosret III again "journeyed to overthrow Kush" (ARE 1:294); four years later, in year 16 {1862}, Senwosret erected a victory and boundary stele near fort Semna, which describes his ongoing efforts at the pacification of the Nubians.

> [The King] making the southern boundary [of Egypt] at Semna:
> I have made my boundary, going further south than my forefathers.
> I have exceeded [the military conquests] that were handed down to me.
> I am a king, whose word becomes deed . . .
> One who is aggressive to capture, swift to success . . .
> Who is unmerciful to the enemy that attacks him;
> Who attacks when attacked, and is quiet when it is quiet; . . .

For he who remains quiet after [an enemy] attack,
He is making the enemy's heart strong.
Aggression is bravery; retreat is vile.
He who is driven from his boundary is a true back-turner,
Since the Nubian only has to hear [of the approach of the Egyptian army]
to fall [in submission] at a word:
Answering [the Nubian] makes him retreat.
One is aggressive to him and he shows his back;
Retreat and he becomes aggressive. (VAE 43–6 = ARE 1:294)

Perhaps protesting too much, Senwosret's grandiose claims are undoubtedly a reflection of the problems of securing his new southern border beyond the Second Cataract. When Senwosret talked of "he who remains quiet after [an enemy] attack is making the enemy's heart strong", he was probably alluding to an actual military experience of Nubian insurgency against Egyptian occupation. When strong Egyptian armies were present on the southern frontier, the Nubians and Kushites submitted. But such submission was nominal, and when the major Egyptian field army withdrew or they saw other signs of Egyptian weakness on the frontier, the Nubians and Kushites recommenced resistence and raiding. Senwosret's statement is given in the form of military advice, probably representing the conventional wisdom of Egyptian policymakers on dealing with recalcitrant enemies on their frontiers.

Senwosret faced this ongoing Nubian insurgency to his invasion with usual Egyptian brutality.

[The Nubians are] not a people to be respected....
I have seen it in person, it is not an untruth,
For I have plundered their women, and carried off their underlings,
Gone to their wells, driven off their bulls,
Torn up their corn, and put fire to it.... (VAE 43–6)

The plunder from Nubia also included gold, one of the principle reasons for the Egyptian desire to control the trade there. The holy of holies in the Osiris temple at Abydos was adorned with some of the Nubian plunder, a gift for the victory the gods had given him, "which he [the god Osiris] caused my majesty [the king Senwosret III] to bring from Upper Nubia in victory and in triumph" (ARE 1:298).

Even after the expeditions in 1866 and 1862, another campaign was necessary in year 19 {1859}, in which "the King of Upper and Lower Egypt Khekure [Senwosret III], living forever, journeyed [southward], overthrowing the wretched Kush" (ARE 1:301). Thus, the pacification of the Nubian frontier required military intervention every three to four years, frequently under the command of the king himself; it is likely that there were other campaigns whose records are lost. Obviously aware of the potential difficulties of the Nubian frontier, Senwosret concluded his victory stele at Semna with a special plea to his descendents to maintain his territory in Nubia:

> As for any son of mine who shall maintain this boundary which My Majesty has made, he is my [true] son and was born to me ... but he who shall destroy it and fail to fight for it, he is not my son and was not born to me. (EP 135)

Senwosret was obviously concerned that the ongoing military difficulties and expense of his occupation of southern Nubia might encourage his successors to abandon his hard-won conquests. In order to administer his new domains, Senwosret created a third Egyptian administrative ministry (*waret*) alongside the standard two of northern and southern Egypt. He called it the "head of the south", which incorporated Elephantine and Nubia (HAE 167).

The Confederation of Kush[23]

The people of central Sudan south of the Second Cataract who faced the Egyptian onslaught are known historically as the Kushites, and archaeologically as the Kerma Culture. The kingdom of Kush centered on their capital city of Kerma (EAE 2:227–8), a few miles north of modern Dongola, in a fertile agricultural basin on the southern Nile. By the time of Senwosret's invasion the inner city of Kerma was surrounded by imposing fortifications, probably built in response to the growing Egyptian threat. The site has been occupied since around 2500, but the region seems to have coalesced into a kingdom perhaps around 2000. The kingdom – perhaps more accurately described at this time as a confederation – encompassed the land from the Second to the Fourth Cataracts. By the Second Intermediate Period it would become a serious military rival to Egypt, intervening militarily in Egypt; a thousand years later the other Kushite kings would conquer and rule Egypt as the Twenty-fifth Dynasty {755–656}.

Due to lack of surviving indigenous written sources, we are forced to rely on Egyptian records and archaeology for historical information about Kush. From the Execration Texts (discussed on pp. 415–8), we know the names of several rulers of Kush during the nineteenth century. Unfortunately, little more is known about them than their names; the following dates can be nothing more than vague estimates. King Kaa ruled around 1900. He was succeeded first by his son Teriahi {1880?}, and then by a second son Awawa {1870?}; Awawa was in turn succeeded by his son [Uterer]ses {1850?}. The Execration Texts also contain the names of a number of other Nubian commanders and chiefs, and of queens (CS 1:50–1; SIP 253–4).

Although generally described as "wretched" and cowardly in Egyptian military propaganda, their military prowess in facing the Egyptian invasion can be inferred by reading between the lines. As described above, Senwosret III was forced to undertake four known campaigns – there were quite possibly others for which records have not survived – in a dozen years against the Kushites, building six large fortresses at the Semna rapids (midway between the Second and Third Cataracts) to control the border. Given Egypt's overwhelming superiority in wealth, resources, and manpower, the Kushites obviously defended their homeland with valor; their capital and three-fourths of their kingdom remained unconquered. The new boundary at Semna also probably in part represents the maximum Egyptian logistical capacity at this time.

The Canaanite campaigns of Senwosret III (M = HAAE 49)

The military activity of Senwosret III in Canaan is much less well documented than his Nubian campaigns. This may in part reflect less interest in Canaan, but, if the example of the inscription of Amenemhet II discussed above is typical, it more likely represents a dearth of surviving sources. It seems, however, that there was no attempt by the Egyptians to establish permanent colonial rule in Canaan as there was in Nubia. None the less, the sparse evidence demonstrates that Egyptian armies and navies did operate throughout Canaan, and on the coastal regions of Syria.

The most important military text relating to Canaan is the Inscription of Sebek-khu, an important military commander of the age who had begun his military career during Senwosret's Nubian campaigns. Sebek-khu described an undated campaign of Senwosret against Canaan:

> [After the Nubian campaign] his majesty traveled downstream [northward] to overthrow the Bedouin of the Canaan. His majesty arrived at a foreign land, Shechem [*skmm*] by name.... Then Shechem fell, together with the vile Retjenu [Canaanites], while I acted as the rearguard [for the army on its return march to Egypt]. Then the soldiers joined in to fight with the Easterners [who attacked the rear of the column]. Thereupon I [personally] captured an Easterner. Then I had his weapons seized by two soldiers. There was no turning back from the fray, but my face was [always] to the fore [of the battle]. I did not show my back to the Easterner [in retreat].... [In reward, Senwosret] gave to me a staff of electrum into my hand, a bow, and a dagger wrought with electrum, together with the weapons [I had captured from the enemy]. (AIB 120 = ARE 1:304–5)

This text is interesting for what it both does and does not say. The purpose of this mortuary inscription is to glorify the deeds of the deceased Sebek-khu, and thus it unfortunately provides neither a date nor a broader strategic context in which the campaign occurred. None the less, if the identification of *skmm* with the biblical Shechem is correct, it demonstrates that the Egyptian army at this time could operate well into northern Canaan. In any event, it is clear from the text that the Egyptians did not permanently occupy Shechem, nor decisively defeat the Canaanites, for as Sebek-khu leads the rearguard of the withdrawing Egyptian army, the Canaanites are still bold enough to attack the retreating Egyptians. There are hints of other military activity in Canaan as well; a mining inscription in Wadi Hammamat records a "smiting of the four eastern countries" (ARE 1:302), which may have reference to Canaan, but could alternatively refer to nomads in the Eastern Desert or Sinai.

The legend of Sesostris the Conqueror

Senwosret is also an important figure in later Greek legends, which seem to conflate several different kings into a single composite figure whom they called Sesostris or Sesoōsis.[24] Manetho records late Egyptian legendary recollections of Senwosret's Canaanite campaigns.

> In nine years [Senwosret] subdued the whole of [the Near East], and Europe as far as Thrace, everywhere erecting memorials of his conquest of tribes. Upon pillars he engraved for a valiant race the secret parts of a man, for an ignoble race those of a woman. Accordingly he was esteemed by the Egyptians as next in rank to [the god] Osiris. (Man. 32–6)[25]

According to Diodorus, Sesostris's conquests outstripped those of Alexander the Great, including India and the Ganges valley, and Scythian Central Asia (1.55). Whereas Alexander only dreamed of an Arabian campaign before his death, Sesostris accomplished it: "he overcame drought and failure of provisions to subdue the entire nation of the Arabians, which had never been conquered ere this time"; Sesostris is likewise said to have "reduced the greatest part of Libya to subjection" (Diod. 1.53). He also organized a fleet of 400 ships for the conquest and exploration of the Red Sea (Diod. 1.55). Diodorus claims that Sesostris's victories were stopped in Thrace – by the unconquerable ancestors of the Greeks, of course – only because of lack of supplies. However exaggerated these tales may be, they none the less demonstrate that Senwosret's military career was extraordinary enough for him still to be remembered 1500 years later as the greatest Egyptian conqueror.

Amenemhet III {1843–1797}[26]

Amenemhet III is most famous from later Greek legend as Ammenemes, the builder of the fabled Labyrinth, which was actually the pyramid and temple complex at Hawara.[27] His prominence as a cultural figure is well justified by the prosperity and achievements of most of his nearly half-century reign, including both Nubian and Syrian trade, the agricultural expansion of the Fayyum, and mineral exploitation of the Sinai and Nubia (HAE 169–70; C1/2:509–12). From a military perspective, his reign seems to have been largely a period of peace, though there are a few indications of some low-level military activities.

The north-eastern frontier

An inscription from year 2 {1842} mentions "the opening of the land of the Easterners" by the "army commander" Amenemhet son of Ibeb (ARE 1:313).

Some military activity in Canaan is confirmed, at least in an idealized sense, by a splendid pectoral of the princess Mereret, showing a scene of her brother Amenemhet III in the traditional "smiting" stance, grabbing the hair of a Canaanite bedouin and raising an axe–mace to smite him, with a generic martial inscription: "the good god [the king], the lord of the Two Lands [of Egypt], smiter of all foreign lands, Nimaatre [Amenemhet III]" (EWP 116; TEM 150–1; RA3 122). Other glyphs speak of him as "he who defeats the Eastern bedouins" (TEM 151). In general, however, the north-eastern frontier seems to have been relatively peaceful. By the end of Amenemhet III's reign a policy of more or less open borders seems to have allowed the peaceful migration of Eastern nomads into the north-east delta, laying the foundation for the rise of semi-autonomous Canaanite rulers in the delta in subsequent generations (OHAE 169; see Chapter Eighteen).

The Sinai (RA3 217–27)

Throughout the Middle Kingdom the turquoise and copper mines of the Sinai continued to be exploited by regular Egyptian expeditions. This exploitation reached its peak in the reign of Amenemhet III, perhaps achieving the point where we can speak of a quasi-permanent Egyptian garrison at the mines. The reign of Amenemhet III is particularly rich in surviving inscriptions of such expeditions; 59 graffiti or inscriptions from Amenemhet III's reign have been discovered in the region, nearly three times the number of those from all his Middle Kingdom predecessors combined (RA3 251; OHAE 168). These expeditions presumably reflect the overall pattern of Egyptian paramilitary operations in the Sinai throughout this period. Although frequently commanded by Treasury officials, and generally concerned solely with mining turquoise and copper, there seems to have been a military component to most, if not all, expeditions to the Sinai mines.

Some inscriptions mention explorers in the Sinai (RA3 22), presumably prospecting new areas for precious stones and metals. On the other hand paramilitary forces are occasionally described as "opening up the foreign lands" and "trampling" enemies (RA3 16; ECI 80–1). Since such phrases are generally descriptions of military conflict, it can be assumed that there were military activities designed to protect the miners from raids from Sinai nomads (RA3 70). On the other hand, there does not seem to have been a formal invasion, conquest, or permanent military occupation of most of the Sinai (RA3 217–19). Relations with local peoples could also be peaceful: one inscription implies peaceful interaction with the "brother of the Prince of Retjenu [Canaan], Khebded" (RA3 21–2, 45, 155–6).

An expedition in year 2 {1841} to the Sinai to mine malachite and copper numbered 734 men (RA3 221; ARE 1:315). This expedition, or a related one, went overland from the Nile to the coast of the Red Sea, crossed by sea to the Sinai, and then marched inland to the mines at Wadi Maghara, presumably thereby avoiding the arduous journey through the Sinai desert, and also possible conflicts with Sinai nomads (RA3 32, 53, 224–6; ARE 1:316). A second Sinai expedition is recorded for year 6 {1837} (VAE 97–8). Additional inscriptions about expeditions to the Sinai mines are recorded for years 41 through 45 {1802–1798}, but most contain no military information (ARE 1:316–18).[28] None the less, there was clearly a paramilitary component to these expeditions, if only for protection from possible bedouin raids. Ptahwer, the commander of the expedition of year 45 {1798}, wrote that "I was sent to bring plentiful [resources] from the land of [Sinai] … delivering the East to him who is in the palace [Amenemhet III], bringing Sinai at his heels, traversing inaccessible valleys, reaching the unknown extremities [of the world]" (ARE 1:319). Similar quarrying expeditions were also sent to Wadi Hammamat by Amenemhet (RA3 38–41), one of which included 2000 men (RA3 41).

Nubian frontier

In the south, Amenemhet's reign was again relatively peaceful. Some of the frontier fortresses at Semna were repaired and perhaps enlarged in year 33 {1810} (RA3 58–9, 212; OHAE 168), indicating that there was still tension and possible danger from the kingdom of Kush. The repair of the fortresses was undertaken by the Overseer of Treasure Intef, son of Sem-ib, who tells us that "the number of bricks which went into the rampart … when [I] was on frontier-patrol from Elephantine was 35,300" (RA3 59). The need to count every brick used in repairing the fortress is quite typical of the Egyptian bureaucratic mentality. The repairs to the city fortification at El-Kab in Egypt are also recorded (RA3 73). A royal river fleet was also maintained in Nubia (RA3 213), probably to control trade and to transport men and supplies.

There are only two recorded military expeditions against Kush in Amenemhet's nearly fifty-year reign. An inscription by the "army commander" Amenemhet son of Ibeb in year 2 {1842} alludes to the "smiting of the Nubians" (RA3 16; ARE 1:313). This may have been the final phase of the preceding Kushite wars of Senwosret III, described above, which finally forced Kush into submission. As long as access to the trade, gold, and other mineral resources of northern Nubia was secure, Amenemhet did not seem interested in further expansionist conquests; the majority of the Nubian-related texts of his reign deal with day-to-day administration (RA, 210–16).

An inscription near the Semna fort from Amenemhet's ninth year {1835} describes the suppression of a Nubian rebellion, indicating that not all was stable and peaceful in the region. A local commander, Nekhen Samontu, describes a punitive expedition:

> Together with my crews, I sailed downstream through Nubia, without a casualty among them. I did not put any [Nubian] man in jail, but I destroyed and killed those rebels of [the Nubian chief] especially for the praise of the king who desires justice. (RA3 26–8, 193)

This text implies that local leaders and their garrison troops in the Egyptian border fortifications were generally able to deal with the problem of "rebellion" in Nubia without the need for the direct involvement of the central government. It is possible that there were a number of similar local punitive expeditions undertaken on the authority of local commanders which were never recorded.

Byblos in Syria[29]

The full military implications of Egypt's relationship with Byblos are not clear. Byblos was certainly ruled by a local Canaanite dynasty, whose tombs from a Middle Bronze Age cemetery have been excavated. However, some of these rulers took the Egyptian title of "mayor" (or "count", *h3ty*), suggesting some type of Egyptian hegemony over Byblos, if only nominal. It may be that the kings of Byblos wanted to be seen as allies of the Egyptians by the kings of their rival Canaanite city-states. The kings of Byblos also wrote inscriptions in hieroglyphics, indicating either the presence of Egyptian scribes, or that Byblite scribes were familiar with the Egyptian language. Middle Kingdom statues and other inscribed objects have been found in the city.

Egypt's major interest in Byblos was trade, which focused on the all-important cedar wood for palace, temple, and shipbuilding. Other products were imported from Syria and beyond, including lapis-lazuli and tin. One can thus probably speak of Egyptian hegemony over Byblos, with strong political, cultural, religious, and economic ties of mutual interest. There were probably permanent Egyptian merchants and administrators in Byblos, with perhaps a regular military presence. The port of Byblos would certainly have been available to the Egyptian fleet for repairs and resupply, as well as serving as a potential base of embarkation for land forces.

Amenemhet IV {1798–1790} and Sobekneferu (Nofrusobk) {1790–1786}[30]

The reigns of the last two rulers of the Twelfth Dynasty are short and poorly documented, with no recorded military activities. The exact nature of the succession is also obscure. Manetho claims that Amenemhet IV was the son of Amenemhet III and brother of Sobekneferu (called "Scemiophris", Man. 34), but this is unconfirmed by any contemporary evidence. Some scholars think Sobekneferu, daughter of Amenemhet III, was the wife of Amenemhet IV, who ruled Egypt as husband of the legitimate queen; when her husband died, Sobekneferu continued reigning in her own right (OHAE 170). On the other hand, it is possible that Amenemhet III had no surviving male heir, and chose one of his court officials to succeed him as Amenemhet IV. Sobekneferu, as the daughter of Amenemhet III, might thus have been seen by some as the legitimate heir in place of the usurper Amenemhet IV. This might suggest a succession crisis and possible strife or even civil war during the 1780s, though this is quite uncertain (SIP 294–5).

Amenemhet IV was probably an older man when he succeeded to the throne, reigning only eight years before being succeeded by Queen Sobekneferu {1790–1786}, one of the few women to rule Egypt independently. Despite the lack of recorded military activities during the reigns, it is clear from a Nile inundation inscription at the Nubian fortress of Kumma that Egyptian military control over the Nubian fortresses and frontier continued until at least the third year of Sobekneferu's reign {1787}. A statue depicting the Queen trampling the "Nine Bows", the traditional enemies of Egypt (EAE 3:301), could memorialize some type of military campaign during her reign, but is also possibly a stylized depiction of royal power. At the end of the reign of Sobekneferu {1786}, Egypt entered another period of crisis and fragmentation known as the Second Intermediate Period {1786–1569}, which will be discussed in Chapter Eighteen.

CHAPTER SEVENTEEN

The military system of the Middle Kingdom

Ideology of sacred warfare

Throughout ancient Egyptian military history, victory in battle was attributed to the will and blessings of the gods.[1] The king is described, in an ideological and ritual sense, as ruling the entire earth: "may fear of you resound in the lowlands and the highlands, for you have subdued all [the lands] that the sun encircles!" (AEL 1:230), which was the Egyptian way of describing the entire world. Although there are certainly elements of boasting and perhaps megalomania in these types of claims, within the limited geographical knowledge of Egyptian society during the Old and Middle Kingdoms the Egyptian king was, in many ways, ruler of the entire world. Enemies from Canaan, Libya, or Nubia are frequently described as "rebels" against the god-given rule of the Egyptian world-king. The conceptualization of the king as divinely established ruler of the world is the central martial ideology of the Egyptians, and is reflected in a number of ways in their texts.

Montuhotep I {2061–2011}, founder of the Eleventh Dynasty, reported that his conquests were accomplished "by [the power of the god] Horus" (MKT 28). The twenty-first-century tomb of Meru reflects this same attitude in a pious inscription proclaiming "a good beginning [for the new Eleventh Dynasty] came about when [the Theban war god] Montu gave both lands [of upper and lower Egypt] to King Montuhotep" (OHAE 132). This intimate connection between the kings and the gods was most clearly reflected in texts describing the king's deification in temple inscriptions. In the thirty-ninth year of his reign {2022}, Montuhotep celebrated a great festival commemorated in the Shatt er-Rigal relief, taking upon himself the glories of godhood and using the title of Sematawy – "He who unites the Two Lands [of Egypt]" (C1/2:479–80; MKT pl. 12). He is remembered in later Egyptian legend as a god who restored unity and glory to Egypt (Man. 34).

Inscriptions by many other kings reflect the same belief that the gods have established the power of the king and granted him victory in battle. The "Loyalist Instruction" {c. 1790}, an ideological statement emphasizing the proper respect for the king, advocates that all men must venerate the king, for "he is the sun god under whose governance one lives ... It is [the gods' divine] power that fights for him [the king]. His ferocity emits dread of him [to his enemies]" (TS 238). Antef II {2118–2068} was also careful to honor the gods and to stress that his authority derived from them. In two hymns to Re and Hathor, Antef claims that he is the "deputy" of Re, and is "honored by Osiris, son of Re" (AEL 1:95). Amenemhet's coup and foundation of the Twelfth Dynasty {1991} was likewise divinely ordained. The king "appeared like [the god] Atum himself that he might restore what he had found in ruins [in Egypt]" (AIB 152). Likewise, victory in battle was given by the gods to their fellow god Senwosret I {1971–1928}: "[The war-god] Montu, lord of Thebes [says]: 'I have brought for you, beneath your feet, Good God [Senwosret I], all the countries which are in Nubia' " (ARE 1.247). On a pectoral of princess Mereret, king Senwosret III {1878–1843} is depicted as a griffin-like creature, with the hawk-head of the war god Horus, and the body of a lion, mauling cowering Canaanites (TEM 137, 139).

Special deities were entrusted with the defense of the Egyptian frontiers for each of the four cardinal directions:

> Those [enemies] who shall come against you from the South shall be driven off by Satis, Lady of Elephantine [Aswan; guardian goddess of the southern frontier], who will shoot at them with her arrows, which are painful and sharp.
>
> Those who shall come against you from the North shall be doomed to [the gods] Hekes and to Hephep.
>
> Those who shall come against you from the East shall be doomed to Sopd, Lord [and guardian of the frontier] of the East, and they shall be driven off with your knives in them.
>
> Those who shall come against you from the West shall be doomed to Ha, Lord of the West, and they shall be driven off by the striking-power of Atum in his ascendings from the horizon. (CT 313)

The Coffin Texts (EAE 1:287–8) present precisely the same ideology of the gods commanding the kings to go to war and granting victory in battle. "I have gone up and have set my [defeated] foes under my sandals, that I may have power over them, in accordance with what [the sun-god] Re commands for me" (CT 87). Horus, in particular, is invoked as war god (EAE 2:119–22). "I have assaulted and conquered the horizon by my own hand ... The kingship on the thrones of Horus is given to me, he shoots down the slaughterers for me" (CT 256). "Horus will not let you perish; Horus has set your [defeated] foes under you[r feet]" (CT 835).

The ideology of the king as the divinely predestined conqueror is most clearly enunciated in a temple building inscription of Senwosret I {1971–1928}. Royal conquests were undertaken at the explicit command of the gods.

> I [the king] will set firm decrees for [the god] Harakhty[2]
> He [Harakhty] begat me to do what should be done for him,

To accomplish what he commands to do.. . .
I am a king by nature . . .
I conquered as a youth . . .
He [Harakhty] destined me to rule the people [of Egypt] . . .
Mine is the land, its length and breadth,
I was nursed to be a conqueror.
Mine is the land, I am its lord,
My power reaches heaven's height.
I am his [Harakhty's] son and his protector,
He gave me to conquer what he conquered.
He [the god] will enrich himself [with tribute and plunder from conquests]
Because he made me conqueror.
I will supply his altars on earth [with offerings provided from plunder].
(AEL 1:116–17 = VAE 40–3 = ARE 1:241–5)

The king's role as triumphant defender of Egypt is similarly lauded in a hymn to Senwosret III {1878–1843} as divinely ordained protector:

How great is the lord of his city:
He is unique and millionfold; a thousand other men are little! . . .
Lo, he is a rampart, walled with copper of Sinai! . . .
Lo, he is a shelter, rescuing the fearful from his enemies! . . .
Lo he is [the god] Sekhment against his enemies who have trespassed his boundaries! (VAE 46–7)

On the other hand, despite claims of divine kingship, the pharaohs were sometimes subject to quite ordinary plots and coup attempts. After Amenemhet I was assassinated by his own guardsmen {1962}, his ghost appeared to his successor Senwosret, warning: "Do not approach them [your subjects] when you are alone! Trust no brother! Know no friend!" (TS 207). Even god-kings, it seems, were potentially subject to the effects of an assassin's dagger.

Evidence of divine support and blessings on military campaigns was believed by the Egyptians to be manifest through omens in nature. On his expedition to Wadi Hammamat, the vizier (and later pharaoh) Amenemhet I recorded two prodigies from the god Min. In the first, "a pregnant gazelle" wandered into the midst of the army camp and gave birth directly on the large stone block they were quarrying. The animal was promptly sacrificed to Min (ARE 1:212 = ECI 71–2). In a similar way, other animals were sacrificed before battle (AEAB 54).

A second wonder was apparently a flash flood, bringing divinely provided water to the army in the desert:[3]

The power of this god [Min] was seen and his might manifested to the plebs: the upland was turned into a lake, and water arose over the hard stone. For a well was found in the midst of the valley, ten cubits [c. five meters] square, filled with water to its brim.... It had been bypassed by the former expeditions of kings ... Only to His Majesty [Amenemhet I] alone was it revealed [by the gods]. (ECI 72 = ARE 1:216)

Although this specific omen did not occur in a military context, it represents the supernaturalistic orientation of most Egyptian warriors, where unusual natural occurrences are interpreted as signs from the gods. The importance of divination through prophecy and oracular dreams is reflected in a number of texts, such as the "Prophecy of Neferti" (TS 134–9; AEL 1:139–44) and the "Instructions of Amenemhet" (TS 206–8; AEL 1:136–8), which have been discussed on pp. 391–4. We should assume that belief in the importance of omens, dreams, and divination was an integral part of the martial mentality of the age, and could affect troop morale for good or ill.[4]

Although generally reflected in royal propaganda, the divine-king ideology of the Egyptians had an impact on the rank and file as well. As servants of the pharaohs, commanders and even common soldiers were also entitled to the blessings of the gods. A royal inscription included an invocation by king Amenemhet III to the gods for the safety of his army on an expedition to the Sinai: "O you who live on earth, who shall come to this Mine-land [Sinai]! As your king has established you, as your gods favor you, may you arrive home in safety" (ARE 1:318). An officer, Amenemhet son of Ibeb, records his personal thanks to the gods for his successful expedition: "I came to this highland [in the Eastern Desert] in safety with my army by the power of [the god] Min, lord of the highlands" (RA3 16; ARE 1:313). The Egyptian ideology of divine favors and omens could have an important impact on the ordinary soldiers as well, who believed their gods would intervene for them in battle. In military crises, belief in omens and promises of divine aide could improve or undermine the morale of troops, thus indirectly contributing to victory or defeat.

Execration Texts and war magic[5]

The belief that the gods controlled the fate of kings and nations is reflected in another body of evidence known as the "Execration Texts". The image of the smiting or trampling of bound captives was a mainstay of Egyptian ritual art for over 3000 years, with such images appearing on temple walls, tombs, doorposts, thrones, statues, footstools, canes, chariot decorations, and sandals (MAEM 112–36; PSE; MB). While many of these images had artistic or ceremonial purposes, they none the less reflect the brutal reality of the ritual execution of defeated enemies. These monuments may represent the actual execution of real war-captives, but they are also ritual acts, designed not only to commemorate previous victories, but to guarantee future victories. This ritual smiting of enemies was also practiced vicariously by priests, who used figurines for magical cursing of enemies. From the military perspective, the Execration Texts are examples of military magic, or "spiritual warfare", designed to defeat enemies through supernatural rather than merely material weapons. These texts and figurines – made of clay, stone, alabaster, wood, and wax – are broadly similar to "voodoo dolls". A curse was magically bound to an image, and transferred to the actual enemy through the destruction or burial of that image. Of these, those made of wax would have left almost no identifiable archaeological remains. Alternatively, clay pots were also inscribed with the curses and names of enemies, and then ritually destroyed.[6] There are over 1000 surviving examples of pots and figurines used for the ritual cursing of enemies, covering almost of the entire range of Egyptian history (MAEM 137).

The essential purpose of the Middle Kingdom Execration Texts was to curse the enemies of Egypt "who may rebel, who may plot, who may fight, who may think of fighting, or who may think of rebelling on this entire earth" (MAEM 140). Curses are issued against all the traditional enemies of Egypt – Nubians, Easterners, and Libyans – as well as any potential internal Egyptian rebels. Some curses are generic, against entire peoples, tribes, cities, or regions. Others are focused on specific individuals. The curses are formulaic and standardized, with a type of fill-in-the-blank format for the name of the enemy. Even the dead, who have potential supernatural power as hostile ghosts, are cursed in some of these texts (VAE 126; CS 1:52).

An important collection of Execration Texts from the Middle Kingdom was discovered at the Egyptian fortress at Iken (Mirgissa) at the Second Cataract, which includes burial pits with shattered pots and figurines (MAEM 153–80). Presumably these cursing rituals were performed by Egyptian priests assigned to the frontier garrisons. A decapitated human skull was also discovered, indicating the ritual sacrifice of a Nubian prisoner as part of the cursing ritual; significantly, many of the figurines were also headless (MAEM 162–3). Burial upside down without the severed head was a particularly abhorrent form of netherworld cursing from an Egyptian funerary perspective, and thus represented a particularly vicious form of curse meant to destroy the enemy not only in this world but in the next (MAEM 168–72). An archaic form of this practice may be seen in the Narmer Palette {c. 3050} which shows rows of bound, decapitated prisoners with their severed heads between their legs.[7]

The Execration Texts are generally quite formulaic; the following is a typical example:

> [A curse upon] every rebel who plans to rebel in the entire land: all the Medjai [Nubian nomads of the south-eastern deserts] of Webat-sepet; all the Nubians of [the tribes or provinces of] Wawat, Kush, Shaat and Beqes, their [elite warrior] heroes, their [light infantry] runners, all Egyptians who are with them, all the Nubians who are with them, all the Easterners who are with them ... all the foreigners who are with them, all the [Libyan] Tjemhu of the western hill-countries of Libya, of [the Libyan chiefs?] Hekes and Hebeqes, their heroes and their runners. (VAE 125–6)

This text includes the interesting reference to "Egyptians who are with" the Nubian enemies, perhaps indicating that there were frontier renegade Egyptians serving with Nubian armies and raiders.

A similar type of Execration Text is found in the Coffin Texts, a collection of Egyptian rituals designed to preserve the soul in the afterlife.[8]

> "May your soul be strong against [your enemy].... May you break and over-throw your foes and set them under your sandals." [These words are] to be spoken over a figure of the foe made of wax and inscribed with the name of that foe on his breast with the bone of a Synodontis fish: to be put in the ground in the abode of Osiris [in Abydos]. (CT 37)

The Coffin Texts describe a heady mix of war, magic, religion, shape-shifting shamanism, and cruel human sacrifice which was probably not uncommon in mythic idealizations of Egyptian warfare.

> It is granted that I have power over that foe of mine so that I may conquer him in the presence of the people who came to contend with me by means of the magic spells which were on their lips. I have appeared as a great falcon [the god Horus], I have grasped him [the enemy] with my talons, my lips [beak?] are on him as a gleaming knife, my talons are on him like the arrows of [the lion goddess] Sekhmet, my horns are on him as the Great Wild Bull ... [I] alight upon his spine, I cut his throat in the presence of his family, I take out his heart unknown to them, for I am a human falcon.... See, I have come and I have brought my [defeated] foe, I have crushed his family, I have thrown down his house, I have crushed his surviving children, I have crushed his cultivator who is in his field. The spirits are glad; Osiris is joyful when he sees me mount aloft as a falcon. (CT 149, cf. CT 995)

Weapons were often viewed not merely as physical objects but as things having a spiritual or magical power as well. Kings could be invested with special weapons as divine gifts from the gods.

> This strong arm of yours is in the realm of [the creator god] Atum. Receive your weapons in your hand [from the gods]; ... Smite this killer ... with the strength and might of yours, with this power of yours ... for I [the king] am [the god] Atum equipped with my [divine] weapons. (CT 586)

Magical spells were also used to ward off the power of enemy weapons, such as throwsticks (CT 418) or knives (CT 335b.2).[9] One spell from the Coffin Texts promises immunity from arrows:

> I am one mighty and aggressive.... I am one more powerful than you, so prepare a path for me. I am a vindicated one who serves Him of blood; I am a man of a million who cannot be seen by those about him who shoot arrows. (CT 1145)

It is likely that many Egyptian warriors used such magical prayers or charms which were intended to protect them from enemy weapons and magic.

From the Egyptian perspective, the ritual cursing of enemies and the invocation of magical protection was a natural part of any military campaign, simply another form of invoking the aid of the gods in battle – always the ultimate source of victory in war. In another sense, however, these texts may also represent an early form of "psychological warfare", in which the morale of the Egyptian soldier could be hardened by priests and magicians calling blessings upon the Egyptians and curses upon their enemies. At the same time, the morale of enemy troops might suffer with the knowledge that Egyptian magicians and priests were cursing them. Similar attitudes are perhaps reflected in the Bible where, during the Exodus, the Israelites, although certain of the ultimate superiority of their god Yahweh, none the less believed that Egyptian priests and magicians had real magical powers (Exodus 7.11–12, 22, 8.7, 18).

From the perspective of military history, these types of magical text not only give us an insight into war magic and psychology, but also provide a type of enemies-list, showing the regions of military concern for Middle Kingdom Egyptians (ECI 87–93). These texts confirm our other historical data, that Nubia and Canaan are the regions of central military concern, with Libya in the Western Desert a distant third.

The Execration Texts against Canaan and Syria are particularly rich in lists of cursed places and rulers, providing a brief snapshot of the political and military situation in Canaan during the eighteenth century (ANET 328–9; CS 1:51–2). It is clear that most of Canaan and Syria were divided into a number of independent or semi-autonomous city-states ruled by Semitic-speaking peoples, most of whom were considered to be at least potential enemies to Egypt. Some curse-lists give two to four entries for the same city, each listing a different ruler (CS 1:51–2). These are presumably either several different leaders of the same city – king, priest, general, or minister – or perhaps represent an updating of the lists; when one ruler dies his name is kept on the list to curse his ghost, while his living successor's name is added. The implications of these texts for understanding the political and military situation in Syria and Canaan have been discussed on pp. 283–4.

Military organization and administration
(EMO; LA 4:128–34)

The army of the Middle Kingdom was organized into province-based regiments, named after the nome (district) or city in which they were recruited or stationed (AEMK 191–2). Each nome recruited its own provincial regiment or company ($s3$), while also occasionally supplying troops to the national army of the king. Recruitment was supervised by a military scribe ($\check{s}s\ n\ m\check{s}^c$) – a type of quartermaster or logistics officer – who kept recruitment and service records, administered supplies, and accompanied armies on expeditions (EMO 39). One text describes a representative of the king passing through a province and recruiting "one man in a hundred males" into the royal army (EMO 37). Individual soldiers mentioned in administrative papyri are identified as "X son of Y", sometimes referring to the region or regiment of recruitment: "from Z". Soldiers thus generally served in companies with friends and kinsmen, under officers from their hometowns. During periods of collapsing central power and civil war, these provincial regiments were transformed into the quasi-independent private armies of the nomarchs. As discussed on p. 438, in addition to Egyptian troops, the kings recruited large numbers of mercenaries, including Nubians, Libyans, and Canaanites into foreign mercenary regiments (ECI 73), Nubians being especially prominent.

Although most of the documents have vanished, it is clear from surviving fragments that the Egyptians maintained extensive written records of military administration, kept by the military scribes. One census record from el-Lahun describes the household of "the soldier Djehuti's son Hori, of the second company of troops raised up for service in the [northern?] Sector" (VAE 112). Although not strictly military, papyri documents of the dockyard at Thinis record the specific number of men required in a work crew, along with the food to be allocated to the workers and the number of copper axes, adzes, and chisels needed by the crew (VAE 85–8). People who fled from such corvee labor assignments were listed by name, household, and village, and pursued by government officials (VAE 101). Although these records describe work crews, military records kept by the army scribes presumably contained precisely the same type of information about numbers of men, supplies, and weapons needed for the army.

Details on the payment of soldiers are vague, but the broad pattern is clear. Remuneration for military service occurred in at least five different forms: daily food allotment, clothing and equipment, land or livestock endowments, plunder, and "gold of honor" – special gifts from the king for exceptional service in combat. On campaign, soldiers were provided with food, clothing, and other equipment (AEAB 53–4). The ordinary soldier was given ten small loaves of bread a day, along with three jars of beer, two "units" of meat, and three cakes. Company commanders were given proportionally higher allotments of 100 loaves, while expedition commanders were given 200 loaves. (EAE 2:404–5). The extra food allotment of the officers was presumably used for slaves, servants, attendants, retainers, or family members.

Administrative papyri from the late Middle Kingdom provide hints of the sophisticated administrative machinery that operated behind the scenes to maintain the Egyptian army. Administrative control over this bureaucracy was an important and lucrative position run by a type of quartermaster corps of military scribes. A military scribe named Ameny described himself as the "King's favorite who controls the supply depots" (AEA 137). Surviving administrative documents include lists of provisions to be given to different groups in Egyptian society, from the royal family to government officials, priests, craftsmen, and common workers. From the military perspective, these include specific allocations of "provisions for the town militia", and for the "Medjay men" and "Medjay leader" – presumably Nubian mercenaries – "who have arrived at the palace" in Thebes (AEMK 19–22).

Soldiers and officers were often given at least partially tax-exempt tracts of land in return for service (AIB 127; TS 224; EAE 2:405). Many texts emphasize the importance of the plunder they obtained in battle, including weapons, valuable objects, and slaves (ARE 1:305). In addressing his troops before a campaign, Montuhotep I {2061–2011} promised: "I will give you full title to it [lands to be captured], [and] everything which you desire [in plunder]" (ICN 112). One soldier complained that, because of lack of fighting on a campaign, he was unable to "bring a Nubian back as captive from the [war in the] land of the Nubians" (VAE 95). Rewards were often given to successful soldiers at the end of campaigns. The "Daybooks" or court journals of the kings recorded the distribution of rewards to the military officers after an expedition (ECI 79). Sebek-khu records that, in reward for his exemplary military service, king Senwosret "gave to me a staff of electrum into my hand, a bow, and a dagger wrought with electrum, together with the weapons [I had captured from the enemy]" (AIB 120). The career of the Nubian mercenary Tjehemau, described on pp. 383–4, demonstrates that a recruit could rise through the ranks and obtain great wealth and honor through military service.

A number of technical terms were used for different types of soldiers, but the precise distinctions between these groups is not always clear. The lack of evidence makes it unclear whether these are general descriptions of broad categories, or specific technical military terms. We are dealing with centuries of history, so perhaps it is most likely that the significance of these terms changed through time. New recruits are called the "young men" (ḏ3mw), or perhaps just "recruits" (EMO 40), who need to be trained (ECI 73). When fully trained and experienced in combat they became "young warriors" (ḏ3mw n ʿḥ3wtyw) (EMO 40). Generally speaking, the term mnf3t (or mnfyt) means simply "soldier", but Faulkner believes they were distinguished from ordinary soldiers in a number of texts, and should therefore be viewed as a more professional and elite group he calls "shock-troops" (EMO 38). Another type of elite soldier is the ḳn, a "valiant man" or "hero" (EMO 40); these "heroes" formed a formal elite corps by the early New Kingdom, but the evidence for such a special unit is unclear in the Middle Kingdom, when the term may simply refer to an especially skilled and brave warrior. There is also mention in the texts of frontier and desert "patrols" (pḥrt) and fortress "garrisons" (iwʿyt) (EMO 41), but these may refer to military functions rather than special formal units.

The most elite group in the Egyptian army seems to have been the "followers" (šmsw) or royal retainers. The function of these "followers" was a mixture of personal retainer, courtier, staff officer, and bodyguard, from whose number the king often chose officers for special missions and commanders for military campaigns (EMO 38–9). Promotion through the ranks for outstanding service, culminating in enlistment as a royal retainer, was not uncommon. The military career of Sebek-khu, one of Senwostret III's "followers", shows him entering royal service as a guardsman of the pharaoh, eventually being promoted to commanding first 60 men and then 100 men (ARE 1:306; EMO 39). In Senwosret III's Syrian campaign Sebek-khu was placed in overall command of the crucial rearguard as the Egyptian army returned to Egypt. Even as an important officer, however, Sebek-khu fought in the ranks with his soldiers, where he personally captured one of the enemy (ARE 1:304). In reward for his faithful military service, he was given a staff of office and ornamental weapons made of electrum, along with booty captured from the enemy (ARE 1:305).

A number of different military ranks or functions are mentioned in Egyptian records and administrative documents. The catch-all rank of the Egyptian army was "commander" or, more generally, "overseer" (*imy*). A rather vague term, its technical meaning can only be understood in context. In its broadest sense it could be used for overseers of civilian work gangs and agricultural estates (EMO 38). From the more narrow military perspective, however, *imy* describes many different types of military officer. Supreme military command in Egypt was held by the king, but frequently exercised by the "commander of the army of Upper and Lower Egypt" (*imy-r mš šmʿw mḥw*), or "great [or supreme] commander of the army" (*imy-r mš wr*), who served as a type of minister of war (EMO 37). Generals in charge of specific expeditions were "commander of the army" (*imy-r mš*) (AIB 107; AEA 120; LA 2:524–5). The title "commander of the army" was used for officers performing many different military functions: among others, by those in charge of frontier and desert patrols, and by the garrison commanders of the Nubian frontier forts (EMO 37). Likewise, the commander of a "company" or "regiment" (*s3*) was the *imy-r s3* – perhaps "company commander" or "captain"; but in a civilian context *imy* seems to have meant simply a work crew foreman (EMO 41). Other paramilitary functions or offices included town militia, "dog keepers" with watchdogs or tracking dogs who were part of the city defense, and "baton-wielding" police (AEMK 82–4). Frontier defense duties were described by a frontier officer named Sihathor as including "defending his [the king's] boundary, watching his possessions, watchful without laxity" (ARE 1:274).

As in all ages, military life was hard, and Egyptian soldiers included the usual number of *grognards* – grumblers. An inscription by an expedition leader named Harurre describes some of the difficulties faced during operations in the Sinai and other desert regions. "When I came from Egypt, my face flinched, it was hard for me.... The highlands are hot in summer, and the mountains brand the skin ... in this evil summer-season." None the less, Harurre's "army arrived in full quota, all of it, there was none that fell among them ... [because] I led my army very kindly, and was not loud-voiced toward the workmen. I acted [well] before all the army and the recruits, and they rejoiced in me" (ARE 1:322–3). Not only did soldiers face the difficulties of campaigning and fighting in foreign lands, they also had problems on the home front with their family affairs. While away on campaign an officer named Nehesu received word of the mismanagement of his estate at home and wrote an angry letter demanding that his affairs be put in order (VAE 107–8).

The most detailed Egyptian description of the difficulties of military life comes from much later in the Twentieth Dynasty {1200–1081}, but undoubtedly reflects the realities for Egyptian soldiers of earlier periods. The text is a school essay exercise in which the students are told, in a rather satirical way, of the superiority of being a scribe over other possible professions.

> Come, let me tell you the woes of the soldier, and how many are his super-iors: the general, the troop-commander, the officer who leads, the standard-bearer, the lieutenant, the [military] scribe, the commander of fifty, and the garrison captain. They go in and out in the halls of the palace, ordering [the soldier]: "Get laborers!" He is awakened at any hour. One is after him as [if he were] a donkey. He toils until the Aten [sun] sets in his darkness of night. He is hungry, his belly hurts; he is dead while yet alive. When he receives the grain-ration, having been released from duty, it is not good for grinding [due to quartermasters giving poor-quality grain to the soldiers]. He is called up for [war in] Syria. He may not rest. There are no clothes, no sandals. The weapons of war are assembled at the fortress of Sile [on the north-east corner of the Delta]. His march is uphill through the mountains. He drinks water every third day; it is smelly and tastes of salt. His body is ravaged by illness. The enemy comes, surrounds him with missiles, and life recedes from him. He is ordered: "Quick, forward, valiant soldier! Win for yourself a good name!" He does not know what he is about. His body is weak, his legs fail him. When the victory is won, the captives are handed over to his majesty, to be taken to Egypt. The foreign woman faints on the march; she hangs herself on the soldier's neck. His knapsack drops, another steals it while he is bur-dened with the woman. His wife and children are in their village; he dies and does not reach it. If he comes out alive, he is worn out from marching. Be he at large, be he detained, the soldier suffers. If he leaps and joins the deserters, all his people [at home] are imprisoned. He dies on the edge of the desert, and there is none to perpetuate his name. He suffers in death as in life [because of lack of proper funerary ritual]. A big sack is brought for him [to be buried in]; he does not know his resting place. Be a scribe, and be spared from soldiering! (AEL 2:172)

These fragmentary glimpses show us that Egyptian soldiers on campaign had precisely the same problems and complaints as soldiers in all ages.

Arms and armor[10]

Soldiers in the Middle Kingdom period can be divided into two types according to their armament: archers (*iry-pḏt*) and close-combat warriors armed alternatively with spear (*ḥnty*) or axe (*minb*). The archers are generally depicted with one bow, but occasionally had two (BH 1 §13). Close-combat troops usually had a mottled animal-skin shield, and were armed with either spears or broad-headed axes (BH 1 §13, §30). Archers generally did not have shields, needing both hands to shoot their bows. During this period we first find both artistic and textual evidence of the Egyptian army being formally divided into tactically separate companies of spearmen and archers. We thus begin to see the tactical specialization of certain companies as either missile or melee troops. The most striking example of this is the famous model soldiers from the tomb of Mesehti at Assyut {Ninth Dynasty, c. 2156–2040}, which are organized into two companies of forty men each. The forty Egyptians are all armed with shield and spear, while the forty Nubians carry bows and bundles of around four arrows (TEM 108–11; C1/2:469). Akhtoy, the nomarch of Assyut, describes a similar organization for his army: "I formed a troop of spearmen and a troop of bowmen, the best 'Thousand' of Upper Egypt' " (AEAB 28–9). The reference to the "Thousand" may be a technical term for an Egyptian regiment, apparently composed of companies of both spearmen and archers.

Bow (LA 1:182–4)

The bow (pḏt) was the principle missile weapon during the Middle Kingdom. A fragmentary block from Lisht shows that archery was formally practiced at target ranges by the late Old Kingdom or early Middle Kingdom (SGAE 34; BAH 54). Grave goods in the Middle Kingdom tombs from Deir el-Bahri at Thebes include several bows, bowstrings of twisted animal intestines, and dozens of arrows (ꜥḥ3) with several different types of heads. Two light wooden cylindrical leather-covered quivers were also found, the oldest examples in Egypt (FP 39–46, 52). The New Kingdom tomb of Tutankhamun also has several bows that are similar in style to those of the Middle Kingdom.[11] All Middle Kingdom bows are "self" or "simple" bows, made of a single piece of wood; there is no evidence of the use of the more powerful composite bow in Egypt before the New Kingdom.[12] Different types of bows had differing draw weights, and therefore differing range and penetrating power. Like Odysseus and Rama, Senwosret I {1971/1962–1928} was said to have a bow that no one else could draw (TS 30). Bows were made in organized workshops by skilled craftsmen (AW 1:165; EWW 36). Arrows were fletched with three feathers, with arrowheads of flint, bone, or ebony, and, by the later Middle Kingdom, increasingly of bronze (FP 42–3; LA 4:1005–7). Some archery equipment was preserved in the "Tomb of the Warriors" from the time of Montuhotep I {2061–2011}. Arrow-heads discovered in the tomb were of ebony (SSN 13); bronze arrowheads are known from other archaeological sites (BAH pl. 9). Four of the soldiers had archers' wrist guards (SSN 10, pl. 4; FP 46; LA 2:948), which are also known from artistic representations of archers (FP 47). A bow tip and cord has been preserved, showing how the strings were lashed to the bows (SSN 10, pl. 5; FP 41).

A Canaanite is depicted with a bow and what appears to be a shoulder-slung quiver hanging on his back; this man also carries a curved axe, indicating that at least some archers could be armed with both the bow and a melee weapon (BH 1 §30–1; AW 1:166–7). Senwosret I and Sinuhe are both likewise described as fighting with bow and melee weapon during different phases of combat (TS 30–3). Quivers were still apparently rare among the Egyptians during this period

(LA 3:460–1); most Middle Kingdom art depicts the archers without quivers, instead carrying a bow and a packet of extra arrows, either wrapped in a piece of leather or held loose in the hand (BH 1 §47, BH 2 §5,16,17). Some of the archers are shown stacking their arrows on the ground while shooting (BH 1 §14, 2 §5).

The Coffin Texts describe bows being held in precisely this way: "my bow which I stretch with my grasp belongs to me, my arrows are in my grip" (CT 585, 1013). An illustration from Beni Hasan shows an archer with two bows, and a bundle of arrows wrapped in a proto-quiver; the fletching on the arrow is outside the leather wrap (BH 4 §24). There is evidence that quivers were introduced in the Late Middle Kingdom, probably allowing more arrows to be carried by each archer (AW 1:164–7).[13]

The tomb reliefs at Beni Hasan provide a number of illustrations of the use of the bow, some showing substantial detail. Hunting scenes generally depict archers drawing the bow to their chest or the chin rather than the shoulder or ear,[14] though the deeper draw to the ear is occasionally depicted (BAH 54). The bow-staff is sometimes depicted being held in a rather strange grip. The lower two or three fingers grasp the staff, with the upper one or two fingers extended in front of the staff serving as an arrow-guide to keep the arrow straight and stable. The thumb is extended upward and braced against the back of the staff, creating counter pressure against the lower two or three fingers. The bowstring is generally drawn oriental-style by one or two fingers and the thumb, allowing two or three arrows to be held with the other free fingers while the bow is being shot.[15] One hunter lassoes the foot of a bull while the animal is harried by a hunting dog and shot with arrows by another hunter (BH 1 §13; 2 §4); it is uncertain if the lasso was similarly used against enemy soldiers in land or naval warfare. Archers are shown stringing their bow with their knee for leverage, and stacking arrows on the ground while shooting from a fixed standing position (BH 1 §14; BH 2 §5, 15; AW 1:63).

The bow is widely depicted on funerary monuments in southern Egypt during the Middle Kingdom, showing both the social emphasis on prowess in archery, and the widespread use of this weapon during this period (ICN 58; AW 1:162–3). Nubian mercenaries are generally depicted as archers; the Nubian Nenu is shown in his funerary monument holding a bow (OHAE 129). The tomb of the nomarch Setka of Aswan likewise shows five Nubian soldiers shooting bows. They wear only leather kilts and feathers in their hair; one holds at least half a dozen arrows, and another is shown kneeling (OHAE 132).

Spear and javelin
(BAH pl. 6, 9, 14; LA 3:937, 5:1124–5)

Depictions of spears (ḥnty) from the murals at Beni Hasan show weapons apparently about 1.25–1.5 meters long (BH 1 §30–1). Some have broad, leaf-shaped heads for thrusting, while others, with narrow needle-like heads, were probably javelins (nsyw). Before the New Kingdom, most spearheads were tanged, slid into a slot in the wood, and bound to the spear shaft (AW 1:156–7, 169). The more stable socketed spearheads had been introduced by the New Kingdom (EWW 36–7; FP 39). The tale of Sinuhe describes a Canaanite warrior coming to battle with an armful of javelins (TS 33). Some spears were weighted at the back end, balancing the weapon and allowing it to be held closer to the back, giving a greater overall thrusting distance (BH 4 §23–4). The model spearmen from the tomb of Mesehi at Asyut all have copper- or bronze-tipped spears (TEM 108–11). On the other hand, the black-colored point on at least one javelin depicted at Beni Hasan may indicate a flinthead (BH 4 §24). The mortuary reliefs of Ankhtifi of Hierakonpolis shows the nomarch spearing fish with a long spear, which, if proportional to his body, would be perhaps 2.5 to 3 meters long (OHAE 128). Lances or pikes of some length were used in battle (BH 2 §5a,c, §15c).

Axe (BAH 34, pl. 10; LA 1:587)

Battleaxes (*minb*) are common in the artistic depictions of warfare in the Middle Kingdom and several examples have been recovered by archaeologists.[16] During the Middle Kingdom, axes retained essentially the same form as those of the Old Kingdom, the broad "epsilon" axe and the semi-circular "eye" blade, with the broader head becoming nearly universal in the later Middle Kingdom.[17] Axes are mentioned along with daggers and javelins as part of the plunder from an expedition to Canaan (ECI 79).

The martial scenes from the tombs of Beni Hasan depict the axe as the most common melee weapon. Tomb 15 shows Egyptian soldiers armed only with the narrow semi-circular bladed axe (BH 2 §5), while tomb 17 shows a mixture of both types, with a predominance of the semi-circular narrow blade (BH 2 §15). Both of these tombs date to either the First Intermediate Period {2165–2061} or the early Eleventh Dynasty {2134–1998} (EAE 1:175). Tombs 2 and 14, however, which date to the early Twelfth Dynasty {1991–1786}, depict Egyptian soldiers armed only with the broad-bladed "epsilon axe" (BH 1 §14, 16–17). Assuming that these differences do not merely reflect changes in artistic convention, these murals seem to indicate a shift from preference for the semi-circular blade to the broader "epsilon" blade from the early to the late Middle Kingdom. Since the broad-blade axe-head was larger and required more bronze, this shift would be consistent with the greater availability and reduced expense of bronze in the latter Middle Kingdom. While some axemen are shown with no shield, carrying their axes with both hands, most carry shield and axe (BH 1 §47).

During the late Middle Kingdom we find the first evidence of a new type of weapon, the mace-axe (*ḥ3*), a mace with a curved axe-blade attached on one side and extending somewhat down the haft (BAH 38, 69; PSE 15). This weapon is found in the smiting scene of Amenemhet III {1843–1797}, in which the blade is depicted in a different color than the mace head itself, perhaps indicating it is composed of a different material (TEM 150–1). It continued in use into the New Kingdom {post-1569}.[18]

Daggers (BAH 39, pl. 4–5, 13; LA 1:1113–16, 4:109–13)

Flint knives remained in widespread use during the Middle Kingdom in Egypt, as reflected in the numerous depictions of the use of such weapons in the martial murals of Beni Hasan (BH 3 §9–10; FP 49–50). One tomb scene depicts an organized factory producing flint knives (BH 3:34–7, §8–10). Double-edged bronze daggers, with reinforcing ribs down the center of the blade, were widely known in Canaan and Syria during the Middle Bronze Age (AW 1:61, 174–5; MW 1:102–42, 2:387–514). A Canaanite warrior is shown with a sling in one hand and a bronze dagger in the other (BH 1 §47), while each of the four cowering Canaanites in Amenemhet III's smiting scene holds a bronze dagger (TEM 150–1). Some of these bronze weapons made their way into Egypt as imports or plunder (ECI 79), where the dagger was known as *b(3)gsw* (EG 511, sign T8; EAE 2:407–8). It is uncertain when during the Middle Kingdom the Egyptians began producing their own bronze daggers imitating these Canaanite models. Bronze daggers were none the less rare enough during the Middle Kingdom that few Egyptian warriors are shown with them. One Egyptian soldier, armed with shield and broad axe, seems to have a bronze dagger in his belt (BH 1 §47). Another seems to be dispatching an enemy prisoner with a dagger thrust (BH 2 §5). Despite the occasional appearance of this new bronze dagger, it is likely that the average Egyptian soldier continued to use the much less expensive flint weapons.

Clubs or fighting sticks (EAE 2:410; SGAE 80–7)

Clubs or fighting sticks (*mks*) – also sometimes called parrying sticks – were widely used as weapons, as indicated on the murals of Beni Hasan, in which a long narrow club with a slightly curved and knotted head is used (BH 1 §16; 2 §5, 15). I will use the English terms clubs and fighting sticks interchangeably here to describe the Egyptian *mks*. Some fighting sticks have hand-guards on the haft of the weapon. One function of the club was parrying the enemy's blows, be it from club, axe or spear. Some soldiers are depicted as double-armed with either axe or short spear/javelin and fighting-stick (BH 1 §16). On the other hand, the weapons were also clearly used to strike the enemy with the end of the curved head, rather like the perpendicular projecting end of some old-fashioned walking sticks, which was often sharpened at the end of the curve to maximize damage.

Slings (FP 35; BAH 32; LA 5:656)

Slings have been known since Neolithic times. They are quite simple to make, consisting merely of a pouch attached to two long straps; in antiquity they were known to have been made of leather, papyrus, or linen. On the other hand, the sling is quite difficult to master, requiring years of practice for full proficiency. During the Old and Middle Bronze Ages slingers generally cast rocks about the size of a tennis ball. The sling made its first appearance as a significant weapon among the Egyptians in the martial murals from the tombs of Beni Hasan (AW 10; BH 1 §47; AAK 2/1.10; FP 35). It is perhaps not coincidental that the weapon is associated with Canaanite mercenaries serving the Egyptians (BH 1 §47), since the weapon was a favorite of nomads. While several Canaanite mercenaries are shown with slings, only one native Egyptian is using the weapon (BH 2 §15b); the people in a besieged city are shown throwing, not slinging, rocks (BH 1 §14; BH 2 §15). In the siege scene at Beni Hasan slingers are shown standing behind the archers, possibly indicating that their effective range was greater than that of the Egyptian bow (BH 2 §15b). These slings have rather short straps, perhaps 60 cm long.

Shields and armor (LA 2:1113–15, 4:665–6, 5:626–7)

The martial murals of the tombs of Beni Hasan depict most close-combat soldiers carrying a wood and animal-skin shield (*ikm*) (AW 1:159). This is confirmed by the model soldiers from the tomb of Mesehi (TEM 108–11). The shields are almost rectangular, square at the bottom and gently tapering to a point at the top, presumably allowing troops with locked shields still to see around the curved corners of the top. The shields were made of wood, or a wooden frame covered with animal skins, with a crossbeam handle about third of the way down. The soldiers held the shields in their left hands by the crossbeam, with their hands held upright at the elbow. Leather straps could be attached to the handles allowing shields to be slung on the shoulders when soldiers needed to use both hands (EWW 34; AE 1:14). The shields were generally about a meter tall and 60 cm wide – big enough to cover the soldier from his neck to his knees. The tomb of Nakht contains replicas of the arms of an Egyptian soldier, including half-size shields, spears, and two bows.[19]

Larger, full-body-length shields were also known; a company of about thirty Egyptian soldiers with spears and large, body-size shields is shown in the funerary reliefs of Akhtoy {c. 2000} (AAK 2/1.15). However, these seem to have fallen out of fashion, probably due to their excessive weight, and are rarely depicted during most of the Middle Kingdom (AW 1:13; FP 52; BAH 23). Soldiers are universally depicted dressed only in loincloths, and are often barefoot, though mention is made of soldiers wearing sandals (AEAB 53; CT 23; AEL 2:172). There are no surviving examples in Egyptian art or archaeology of helmets (*dbn*) or body armor (*mss*) before the New Kingdom (LA 4:665–6, 2:1113–15; FP 55–8). Some soldiers, often archers, are depicted wearing leather straps on their shoulders that cross in the middle of the chests, or are connected to a belt-like harness (BH 2 §5, 17; AW 1:159, 163); these leather bands might have provided some type of armor-like protection. The Egyptian model soldiers from Meshi's tomb wear white loincloths, while the Nubian archers have red loincloths decorated with large green diamonds. It may be that different companies wore different colored loincloths as an early type of uniform.

Training

The Egyptians recognized that new army recruits needed training before being sent to combat. The First Intermediate Period nomarch Kay described his policy: "I recruited [the city's] draftees of young men in order that its levees be numerous … I trained my draftees of young men and went to fight along with [the army of] my city" (ECI 73). Training exercises included the sport of wrestling which was depicted on the walls of several tombs from Beni Hasan.[20] Wrestlers are shown on panels which may indicate a sequence of wrestling moves, rather like a modern cartoon strip. These include body grappling, leg and arm holds, and trying to throw the opponent to the ground. These tomb murals depict dozens of different wrestling techniques, indicating that this martial sport was quite sophisticated. On the tomb of Sonebi, one wrestler taunts another: "Please be patient! And you'll see yourself on your face!" to which his opponent replies, "I'll bring you that! Look, I'll make you fall on your face!" With one wrestler down, the victor cries, "Don't boast! Look how we're here! Look at you!" (VAE 79–81). As depicted in the tombs at Beni Hasan, soldiers would train by lifting and swinging bags of sand, presumably increasing the weight of the bags as their strength increased (FP 84).

Stick fighting, both for training in using the club and for combat with axes, is known from depictions in the early New Kingdom, but undoubtedly had its origins in the Middle Kingdom, if not earlier (SGAE 78–89). Target practice for archery training is known from at least the Old Kingdom, as indicated by a fragmentary relief from Lisht (SGAE 34; BAH 54); most of the evidence for archery practice, however, comes from the later New Kingdom (SGAE 35–46; LA 5:1161–9). Combat training was also associated with funeral games, as described in the "Instructions of Amenemhet".

> Make for me mourning, such as was never heard,
> For so great a combat [at funeral games] had not yet been seen!
> If one fights in the arena, forgetful of the past,
> Success will elude him who ignores what he should know. (AEL 1:136–7)

The social importance of military skills and combat is reflected in the funerary monuments of the period. Many of the nomarchs emphasized their individual martial prowess in their funerary inscriptions (AEAB 25–6, 28, 30). Ameny, son of Montuwoser, boasts: "I am a man of the army, who attacks the [enemy] hero [in battle], but who loves life and hates death" (VAE 96). Djari, commander in the time of Antef II, emphasized that he was "calm at the moment of blows" in battle (AEAB 41). A rare glimpse into the views of the common soldier is found in the stele of Fengu from Naqada, near Thebes. He is shown carrying a bow and a sheaf of arrows, and boasts: "I am the bravest of the brave, the swiftest of the swift. The Overseer of the Priests, Weser sent me on all kinds of missions, and I returned safely" (AEAB 35). Another soldier named Ankhu likewise boasted on his funeral stele: "I am a brave one who beats one braver than himself" (AEAB 103, 104).

Overall, the evidence from the Middle Kingdom demonstrates that the Egyptian army was not a haphazard, ill-trained, and undisciplined rabble. Rather, there were formal policies of recruitment and training in a number of different weapons and combat techniques, with social standards stressing the importance of martial skill.

Combat (LA 6:1429–30)

Historical sources during the Middle Kingdom generally fail to provide details of actual combat. To understand what actually happened when Egyptian armies fought we must turn to literature and art. In the tale of his adventures, Sinuhe gives a poetic tribute to the martial skills of Senwosret I {1971/1962–1928}, in which he alludes to the major phases of Egyptian combat.

> He [Senwosret I] is a god without peer . . .
> He is lord of knowledge, wise planner, skilled leader . . .
> He was the smiter of foreign lands,
> While his father [Amenemhet I] stayed in the palace [during the co-regency],
> He [Senwosret] reported to him on commands carried out.
> He is a champion who acts with his arm,
> A fighter who has no equal,
> When seen engaged in archery,
> Or when joining the [hand-to-hand] melee.. . .
> His enemies [do not have the chance] to marshal their troops;
> Vengeful, he smashes foreheads;
> No one can stand against him [in battle].
> Wide-striding he smites the fleeing [enemy],
> There is no escape for [the enemy] who turns his back [to flee];
> Steadfast in the time of attack,
> He makes [the enemy] show his back [in retreat]
> But does not show his own back [by fleeing from the enemy]
> Stouthearted when he sees the mass [of the enemy battle line] . . .
> He is bold, descending on the Easterners
> His joy is to plunder the [barbarian] bowmen.
> Grasping his shield he tramples [the enemy] under foot,
> He needs no second blow to kill;
> None can escape his arrow,
> No [other] can draw his bow.
> The [barbarian] bowmen flee before him,
> As before the power of a great [god]
> He fights as he plans [the battle]
> Unconcerned about all else.. . .
> Enlarger of the frontiers,
> He will conquer the southern [Nubian] lands,
> Though he has not [yet] considered the northern [Canaanite] lands,

> He was begotten to smite the Canaanites
> And to trample the Sand-dwellers.[21]

Here we see all the elements of a typical Egyptian campaign: the divine imprimature given the king by the gods, preliminary orders from the king, military planning, marshaling of troops, archery exchanges followed by bloody melees, the pursuit and execution of the defeated enemy, and the collection of plunder. A victorious campaign was followed by a victory triumph as the army and fleet returned home. After one victory, the Egyptian army and fleet "returned by river and landed in Herakleopolis and the [whole] city rejoiced . . . women and men together, old men and boys. The son of the lord reached the city and entered his father's court. He brought back those [of the army] who had left home [for battle] and he buried those [who had died in battle] who had no sons [to bury them]" (MKT 23).

Provincial regiments would mobilize in their home nomes, then march or sail to the frontier fortress where the royal army was assembling. For campaigns into Canaan, this tended to be Sile (Tell Abu Sefa) or one of the other north-east frontier fortresses at the beginning of the "Way of Horus" which led across northern Sinai into Canaan. For Nubian wars, the royal assembly was generally at Aswan. Thereafter, when in enemy territory, Egyptian armies often made fortified camps as bases (AF 29; VAE 95–6). Unfortunately we have no illustrations of fortified camps from the Middle Kingdom; although Tomb 17 at Beni Hasan shows a portable shrine, offering table and supplies (or offerings?) (BH 2 §15c), there is no indication of camp fortifications. New Kingdom murals, especially the Kadesh reliefs of Ramses II, show many details of Egyptian fortified camps which may reflect earlier Middle Kingdom practices (EAE 2:219–21; AW 1:236–7).

The Coffin Texts allude occasionally to combat, complementing the order of battle described by Sinuhe. Combat begins with an exchange of missile fire, followed by an advance by melee troops. "The bowmen shot him [the enemy], [then] the spearmen felled him" (CT 1127); this text may imply that it was not necessarily expected that arrows alone would kill the enemy. Troops are described as advancing into oncoming archery: "if you [the enemy] should come against me or if an arrow should come, miss, and continue its course behind me, then Apep will thrust at you [with his spear]" (CT 1145). Daggers are drawn in the ensuing melee; a personified weapon proclaims: "I am the spear which is in the hand which is stabbed at those who are below . . . I am the knife which pierces the middle of his head" (CT 1141). Defeat is sometimes signaled by weapons breaking in the midst of combat: "my knife is broken, my shield is split" (CT 1021), mourns a defeated soldier. The victors, on the other hand, rejoice with brutal rituals of triumph: "I will cut off your heads, O you who oppose my path; I will lift up your heads on my hands" (CT 660).

Military themes in the "Tale of Sinuhe"[22]

The "Tale of Sinuhe" is perhaps the most celebrated ancient Egyptian story, and provides the most detailed description of hand-to-hand combat from ancient

Egypt. There is some controversy as to the historicity of the tale, but whether fiction, embellished history, or an authentic autobiography, it is generally agreed that the text has historical verisimilitude.

Sinuhe was a "follower" (*šmsw*) in the palace of Amenemhet I {1991–1962}, a mixture of courtier, staff officer, retainer, and bodyguard. Sinuhe was on an expedition against Libya with the heir apparent Senwosret I when the pharaoh was assassinated {1962}. Upon overhearing secret word of the coup, Sinuhe's "heart failed", fearing that he might be executed as a supporter of Senwosret I if the assassins were successful in usurping power. He therefore abandoned his master Senwosret I, making his way to the borders of Egypt and thence into Byblos and Qedem in modern Lebanon, where he spent half a year until he was enlisted in the service of an Amorite bedouin chief, Amunenshi, the "ruler of northern Retjenu [Canaan]" (TS 28–9), who wished to establish good relations with Egypt (TS 31). Sinuhe married Amunenshi's eldest daughter and became a wealthy leader and warlord of the nomadic Amorite tribe (TS 31–2).

As a champion warrior of Amunenshi's tribe, Sinuhe was eventually challenged to single combat by a rival "hero of [another tribe of the] Retjenu ... a peerless champion, who had subjugated all the land. He said he would fight with me [Sinuhe], and planned to rob me, to plunder my cattle" (TS 32), apparently in revenge for earlier nomadic raiding by Sinuhe, or perhaps to resolve a long-standing blood-feud. Sinuhe responded to the challenge: "If he has the will to fight, let him speak his wish! Does God not know what he has fated [for victory or defeat in combat]?" (TS 33). What follows is the most detailed description of personal combat we have in Egyptian literature.

> At night [before the combat] I strung my bow [*pḏt*] and tested my arrows, sharpened my [bronze] dagger [*bȝgsw*] and polished my weapons. At dawn, all Retenu [Canaan] had come, having incited its tribes and gathered its neighboring peoples, intent on this combat. He came toward me while I waited, having placed myself near him. Every heart [of the people of my tribe] burned for me; the women jabbered [in anxiety]. All hearts ached for me, thinking, "Is there another champion [as mighty as Sinuhe] who could fight him?" (AEL 1:228, TS 33)

The duel began at a distance, with an exchange of missiles. While keeping at maximum missile range to minimize the effect, Sinuhe let his opponent exhaust his supply of javelins and arrows, which Sinuhe dodged or knocked aside with his shield.

> He raised his battleaxe [*minb*] and shield, while his armful of javelins [*nywy*] flew toward me. When I made his [missile] weapons attack me, I let his arrows pass me by without effect, one following the other. (AEL 228)

The Canaanite warrior is armed with both axe and shield, which he holds in his left hand, leaving his right hand free to throw several javelins. This combination of axe and javelin is depicted several times on the Beni Hasan murals (BH 1 §14, 16).

> Then, [when he was out of missiles], he charged me, and I shot him, my arrow sticking in his neck. He screamed and fell on his face; I slew him with his [own] axe. I gave my war cry, standing on his back, while every Easterner [in my tribe] bellowed [in triumph]. (AEL 228)

As any pious Egyptian should, Sinuhe gave thanks to the gods, the true authors of his victory, after which he collected the spoils.

> I gave praise to [the Egyptian war god] Mont, while [my dead enemy's] people mourned him. The [Canaanite] ruler Amunenshi [Sinuhe's father-in-law], took me in his arms. Then I carried off [my enemy's] goods; I plundered his cattle. What he had meant to do to me I did to him. I took what was in his tent; I stripped his camp. Thus I became great, wealthy in goods, rich in herds. It was the [war] god [Mont] who acted [to grant me victory in battle]. (AEL 228)

The parallels between this story and the more famous tale of David and Goliath (1 Samuel 17) are quite remarkable. In both we see the challenge from a mighty enemy champion, whom only the hero dared face. In both, the weapons are prepared and described before battle. The enemy is wounded and felled by a missile and then dispatched with his own weapon. Victory in battle is attributed to God, and leads ultimately to wealth and power. Parallels to single-combat narratives in Homer also abound.[23] Such narratives probably reflect a widespread shared military culture, in which single combat to the glory of the gods and the plundering of a dead enemy's property were standard practices. They also reflect an oral military culture, in which such deeds were remembered and glorified in oral tales and poems, most of which are forever lost. In this sense Homer should be considered to represent the *end* of this Bronze Age Near Eastern epic tradition, rather than the beginning of Greek literature.

Despite his wealth and power in his adopted homeland, Sinuhe still longed for Egypt. From the Egyptian perspective, non-Egyptians were too culturally different to be fully integrated with Egyptians. Sinuhe, who had sojourned for many years among the Canaanite nomads, described this difference as a state of nature: "no barbarian [from Canaan] can ever ally with a Delta man [from Egypt]; what can establish the papyrus on the mountain?" (TS 33). Eventually a letter arrived from king Senwosret, assuring Sinuhe that he was forgiven and welcome at court, and encouraging him to return to Egypt, which he did (TS 35–9). He was honored by the king and welcomed by his old friends in astonishment: "look, Sinuhe has returned as an Easterner, an offspring of the nomads!" (TS 40–1). A key concern of Sinuhe was that he should receive a proper burial in Egypt (TS 36, 42–3); many Egyptian soldiers on foreign campaigns may have shared a similar anxiety that "their death might occur in a foreign country, where Easterners will lay them to rest" (TS 36) without the proper tomb and funerary rituals to insure a happy afterlife. Making offerings at the funerals of old war companions seems to have been part of a soldier's religious responsibilities. The funeral stele of Ded-Iqu records that "the soldiers serving [with me for] his majesty [king Senwosret I] presented things [at the tomb] to my *ka* [the departed spirit of the dead]" (AEA 93).

Depictions of combat in martial art (BSMK)

The tombs of the nomarchs at Beni Hasan in middle Egypt provide the best military art of the Middle Kingdom period.[24] Of particular interest for military history are four tombs:

- Khety (Tomb 17);[25]
- Baqet III (Tomb 15);[26]
- Amenemhet (Tomb 2);[27]
- Khnumhotep (Tomb 14).[28]

The precise dating of most of the tombs is uncertain, but it appears that tombs 15 and 17 date from the Eleventh Dynasty in the late First Intermediate Period {c. 2050–2000}, while tombs 2 and 15 date to the early Twelfth Dynasty {c. 2000–1950} (EAE 1:175–7). The scenes in the tombs are somewhat stylized, with similar layouts and themes, but significant differences in detail merit close attention. The tomb murals are divided into between six and nine registers, with wrestling scenes on the upper registers and combat on the lower. Tomb 2 has three registers of wrestling, two of combat and one of boats; Tomb 15 has six of wrestling and three of combat; Tomb 17 five wrestling and three combat. Tombs 2, 15 and 17 all show siege scenes on the left side of the murals, which will be discussed on pp. 447–50.

The murals depict a wide variety of Egyptian soldiers with a number of different weapons and functions. Unfortunately, most of the soldiers are shown simply marching into battle. None the less, assuming that the proportion of troop types reflects the real military situation as opposed to artistic convention, we can get a feel for the rough proportions of troop types in an early Middle Kingdom army, and the nature of Egyptian combat. The Beni Hasan tombs can be supplemented with a war scene from the tomb of Antef of Thebes {c. 2100}.

Antef {c. 2100}[29]

Antef's tomb depicts an assault on a Canaanite city, which will be discussed in the section on siegecraft on pp. 447–50. Here, the composition of the Egyptian army will be summarized. The top two panels show the assault on the Canaanite city (Figure 11, p. 447), the middle panel shows combat between Egyptians and Canaanites, while the last two panels show Egyptians carrying off prisoners after their victory. All of the soldiers are wearing the typical Egyptian white kilt; some have straps crossing their chests and some have headbands; none, however, has any body armor or helmet. The middle panel, which I interpret to depict open combat before the siege, shows the Egyptian army in victory. Three Canaanites, bound with a single long rope, are marched to the rear by an Egyptian with an axe. The center of the panel depicts the combat. Two Canaanites lie on the ground with their pointed rectangular shields and a javelin scattered around them. A wounded Canaanite is being dispatched by an Egyptian with an axe. An Egyptian shoots his bow behind two duels: in both scenes the Egyptians hold the Canaanites by their hair as they strike them with an axe and what appears to be a dagger. To the rear, five Canaanites flee. One, wounded by three arrows, is helped by a comrade. Three others, in striped kilts with short thrusting spears or javelins and the standard Canaanite shield, withdraw in good order. There are a total of twenty-three Egyptian soldiers depicted in the assault (the first two panels), of whom five are climbing the siege tower armed with axes. Of the remaining eighteen, six (33 percent) are archers while twelve are melee troops. Of the melee troops, half have shields and half do not. Two of the soldiers have spears, and two have fighting sticks; the rest (66 percent), are armed with axes, which are evenly divided between the broad-axe and the semi-circular axe blade. Two also have bronze daggers. Three of the archers seem to have a type of quiver-box for their arrows, which appears to be freestanding, and set upright on the ground allowing the archer to draw arrows to shoot. The prisoner panel shows three archers and five axemen; the middle panel three axes, one archer and one man with a melee weapon which is damaged; from the posture and thrust of the Egyptians it appears to be a dagger. Thus, the overall proportion is about one-third archers and two-thirds axemen.

Baqet III, Tomb 15
{late Eleventh Dynasty, c. 2050–2000} (BH 2 §5)

Tomb 15, from the late Eleventh Dynasty, shows the greatest number of soldiers, a total of 81, whose armament can be determined.[30] Of these, ten (12 percent) are involved with logistical support, bringing bundles of spears, bows, or arrows to the troops at the front lines; however, one of these is also armed with a bow, while two have fighting sticks, indicating that these troops were only temporarily involved with logistical support. This leaves 74 soldiers with distinguishable weapons. Of these, twenty-six are archers (35 percent), thirty-one are armed with fighting sticks (42 percent), nine are armed with spears (12 percent), six with axes (8 percent), and two with daggers (3 percent).

These broad weapon categories can be further broken down into smaller groups. Of the thirty-one men armed with fighting-sticks, eight (25 percent) have shields. Fourteen of the shieldless men are shown wielding their fighting sticks with one hand, while nine use two hands, probably reflecting different phases or techniques of stick fighting. Of the nine spearmen, two have a spear and a club, two have a spear and a shield, and five have pikes wielded with two hands. Three of the six axemen have shields, while three carry the axe alone. Neither man with a dagger has a shield or any other weapon. Only twelve of the 74 soldiers have shields (15 percent), of whom seven have clubs, two have spears, one has an axe, and two have either an axe or a fighting stick. Shields thus seem to be scattered among the troops in rough proportion to the overall number of weapons of each type.

Fifteen different melee duels are depicted in Tomb 15 (BH 2 §5). A third of the duels are between men armed only with clubs, mostly swung with two hands. In three instances a soldier has grabbed the fighting stick of his opponent by the haft. One of the combatants has a shield in only three of the fifteen melees; in no melee do both combatants have shields. This overall proportion of shielded melee duels (20 percent) is roughly the same as the total proportion of shielded men depicted on the murals (15 percent), which would seem to imply that shield-bearing warriors were not specifically organized to fight a greater share of melee combat. Indeed, the overall impression of the mural is that, while the archers are organized into special units, the melee troops seem to have a random mix of all types of melee weapons.

Three duels show a soldier holding his opponent by the hair while attempting to strike him. Another three depict combat between people with different types of weapons. The first shows a man with shield and fighting stick against an opponent with only an axe. In the second, a man with a shield and a stick faces a man with a spear wielded with two hands. Finally, a man with a shield and an axe (or a club?) faces a man armed only with a fighting stick. Two battle scenes show fighting between more than one combatant. A man with a pike has stabbed one enemy who is collapsing onto the ground, while a second enemy with a fighting stick has grasped the middle of the spear and prepares to strike the spearman. A four-way combat is also depicted: a kneeling man is grasped by the hair by an enemy who is about to strike him with a club; a man with a shield and a stick rushes to the kneeling man's rescue, but is held at bay by a man with a pike held with both hands who stands behind his companion, with the pike extending beyond him and defending him (BH 2 §5c).

Two of the duels are between an unarmed man and an opponent armed with a dagger. In the first, the attacker holds his victim by the arm or hair as he thrusts a dagger into his stomach. The second scene is somewhat ambiguous. An Egyptian appears to have a bronze dagger which he is thrusting into the face of an unarmed Canaanite, who is grabbing the Egyptian by the forearm; it is unclear if this is a fight, or if the Egyptian is attempting to help a wounded Canaanite. At any rate, the fact that both dagger combats show unarmed opponents might indicate that the daggers were generally used more for mopping-up operations than for actual fighting. In the final two melees a man with a club is beating a fallen enemy, using a double-handed blow in both cases, implying that, in the hands of a properly trained Egyptian warrior, the war-club was at the very least enough to disable an enemy or render him unconscious.

Khety, Tomb 17 {late Eleventh Dynasty, c. 2050–2000}
(BH 2 §15; AW 1:158–9)

The second late Eleventh Dynasty tomb belonged to the nomarch Khety. Here, of a total of 67 Egyptians with discernable weapons, there are eighteen archers and one slinger (28 percent), forty-one men with shields (60 percent), and eight men with spears and no shield (12 percent), six of whom have fighting sticks as well. There are finally four men in the rear carrying bundles of extra weapons to the fighters. The forty-one men with shields carry one of three melee weapons: club, axe, or javelin. Twenty-three have clubs (57 percent), and thirteen have axes (33 percent), most of which seem to be the smaller, semi-circular "eye"-style axe-head typical of the Old Kingdom, although two or three of the axe-heads may be the broad-axe more characteristic of the later Middle Kingdom. Only four have javelins (10 percent). Additionally there are eight other melee soldiers without shields, all armed with spears, six of whom have fighting sticks as well. This means that of the total of forty-nine melee soldiers – shielded and unshielded – roughly half have clubs, a quarter axes and a quarter spears.

Amenemhet, Tomb 2 {early Twelfth Dynasty, c. 2000–1950}
(BH 1 §14–16)

The early Twelfth Dynasty Tomb 2 shows a total of thirty-three armed Egyptian soldiers (BH 1 §16). Of these, eleven are archers (33 percent), seven are armed with axe and shield (21 percent), with another four (15 percent) armed with axe and javelin or short spear, and one with axe and fighting-stick. One of these axe-men has two javelins, indicating these weapons were be thrown, as was the case with Sinuhe's opponent described above (TS 33). On the other hand, two men are shown fencing with these javelins, indicating they could be used in the melee as well. This gives a total of twelve men armed with axes (35 percent); all of these axes are the larger broad-headed style. All men with shields also have axes, although one-third of the men with axes do not have a shield. The final six men are armed with one of two types of spear, but no shield. Of these, two are armed with javelins and fighting-sticks, one with a javelin alone, one with a pike wielded with two hands, and two with unclear weapons which are either javelins or longer pikes. Thus, in summary, about one-third of the army is comprised of archers, one-third axemen (of whom two-thirds have shields and one-third javelins and axes), and one-third javelins or lances without shields. Only three actual melee duels are depicted in Tomb 2. In the first a man wields a pike with two hands against an enemy with a shield and an axe. The second duel is between two men, each armed with javelin and fighting-stick. In the third a man with two fighting-sticks is beating an enemy who has fallen to the ground; the fallen man is supported by an archer in the rear shooting arrows at his attacker.

Thus, although the overall format of the battle scene in each tomb is similar and stylized, the specific armament shown is quite distinct. Assuming these differences

are due to the artists accurately reflecting changes in real armament, we can speculate that the army in Tomb 15 (BH 2 §5) represents a late First Intermediate
Period provincial army composed largely of poorly armed irregular militia. The
limited resources available to a provincial nomarch perhaps explains the prevalence
of fighting-sticks (42 percent) and the limited number of bronze weapons (23
percent). It is also likely that not all of the spearheads are, in fact, made of bronze;
some were likely made of flint, and therefore the number of men armed with
bronze weapons in Tomb 15 was probably less than 20 percent. The limited
number of bronze weapons in Tomb 15 may also reflect the ongoing transition
from Old to Middle Bronze Age armies, with bronze still relatively rare and
expensive.

Table 17.1 summarizes the differences in troop and weapon types found in the
Beni Hasan tombs over the course of 100 to 150 years {c. 2050–1950}.

A number of interesting characteristics appear from this chart. First, the percentage of archers remains relatively constant in all the murals, at about one-third
of each army. Fighting sticks outnumber axes and spears two-to-one in Tomb 15;
in Tomb 17 the proportion has become essentially even, with about a third of the
army being archers, a third having clubs and a third having axes or spears. By the
early Twelfth Dynasty Tomb 2, however, the fighting-stick has almost disappeared,
to be replaced by an even proportion of axes and spears. The proportion of axes
has nearly quadrupled from Tomb 15 to Tomb 2, and, furthermore, all the axes of
Tomb 2 are the of broad-head type, which probably required almost twice as
much bronze to make. During the same period the number of spearmen has
almost tripled. The differences between the armies depicted in the tombs probably
reflect the transition from a proto-Bronze Age army of the First Intermediate
Period to a true Bronze Age army of the Middle Kingdom. On the other hand,
the earlier tomb of Antef has more bronze weapons that the subsequent Intermediate Period tombs, a percentage that is surpassed by the period of Tomb 2. It
may thus be that the late Old Kingdom, with its control of Sinai and international
trade, had greater access to bronze weapons. The First Intermediate Period saw a
temporary decline in the availability of bronze weapons, which was restored only
by the beginning of the Middle Kingdom.

Table 17.1 Types of troops and weapons found at Beni Hasan tombs {c. 2050–1950}

Troop/weapon type	Antef	Baquet (Tomb 15)	Khety (Tomb 17)	Amenemhet (Tomb 2)
archers	33%	35%	26%	32%
fighting-sticks (clubs)	11%	43%	37%	–
axes	44%	9%	19%	34%
spears	11%	13%	18%	34%
shields	38%	15%	60%	24%
% bronze weapons	55%	22%	37%	68%

Mercenaries in the Beni Hasan murals

Though most of the soldiers depicted at Beni Hasan are Egyptians, there are a number of mercenaries involved in combat. Eleven Canaanite mercenaries are depicted in the mural of Tomb 15. Of these, three have slings, one has an axe and a shield, and two are unclear. Several three- to six-man groups of either Canaanite or Libyan mercenaries are depicted wearing bright, multi-color striped loincloths and armed with bow, axe, sling, and bronze dagger (BH 1 §16, 47; BH 2 §5b–c). The three Canaanite mercenaries in Tomb 14 are double-armed: one with both sling and bow, another with a bow and an axe, and a third with a sling and a dagger – none has a shield (BH 1 §47). Another similar company of Canaanites includes warriors with a sling and a bow, an axe and a bow, and a bronze dagger and a bow (BH 2 §5c). This implies that at least some Canaanites served as both as missile and close-combat troops, again paralleling the weapons and tactics attributed to Sinuhe's challenger (TS 33). Three of the Canaanites, again in brightly-colored kilts, are shown armed with broad, curved war-clubs or axes, along with short-spears or bronze axes (BH 1 §16 = AW 1:169). The structure of the curved weapon is unclear here, but in the Beni Hasan tomb of Khnumhotep III, a Canaanite has a similar weapon which clearly curves into a broad axe-head which is structurally different from the haft (AW 1:166–7). Some of the archers appear from their red kilts or loin-cloths – as opposed to the usual Egyptian white kilt – and their darker skin color to be Nubians (BH 2 §15a–b; AW 1:158–9). In Tomb 17 there are two squads of Canaanite mercenaries, four of them slingers and five armed with axes (BH 2 §15b). Of the five axemen, one has either a club or a sling along with his axe. The other four have rectangular shields with triangular indentations on the top and bottom and four corners projecting outwards. The shape appears to be based on an animal skin with the four projecting corners being the four shoulders of the legs, vaguely reminiscent of Tuareg *ayar* shields.[31]

There are a couple of scenes showing activities in the rear of the battle line. All the murals show columns of soldiers marching forward into battle from the rear. Logistical support of troops on the front line is reflected in several of the scenes, with soldiers in the rear carrying large animal skin packets filled with extra javelins, bows, and arrows to soldiers in the front lines (BH 1 §47, 2 §5b, 15c, 16; BAH 45, 52). Corpses are shown being dragged into piles or lines, and perhaps plundered (BH 1 §47, 2 §5c. 15b); some wounded men appear to be receiving the *coup de grace* (BH 2 §5c, 15c). A portable tabernacle with an altar table has been set up in the rear, where offerings have been presented to the gods, and a cow is being sacrificed before battle (BH 2 §15c), emphasizing the ever-present need of the aid of the gods.

Tomb of the Warriors (SNN)

The "Tomb of the Warriors" provides us with some rather gruesome detailed evidence on the nature of Middle Bronze Age warfare. The tomb contained sixty corpses, all killed in battle in the time of Montuhotep I {2061–2011}, and apparently buried simultaneously as casualties from the same battle (SSN 7). After nearly four thousand years the corpses were still sufficiently preserved to allow forensic analysis of their wounds and causes of death. The Egyptian soldiers, who, like soldiers in most ages, were probably larger and stronger than the average Egyptian, would be considered short by modern standards; the average height of the warriors in the tomb was about 1.6 meters (SSN 7). Some of the soldiers were obviously veterans, with "old, long-healed wounds" (SSN 9).

According to Winlock, ten soldiers showed signs of having been wounded by ebony-tipped reed arrows – the actual number was undoubted higher due to flesh wounds which were no longer recognizable, and the probability that many arrows and arrowheads had either been removed or had fallen from the corpses (SSN 11–13, pl. 7). One of the arrows entered the chest and transfixed the lung and heart (SSN 12, pl. 7D), indicating that Egyptian archery was powerful enough to penetrate deeply and kill. The line of trajectory of several of the arrow wounds seems to have been from above, indicating that the soldiers were probably killed while besieging or assaulting a fortress, with the arrows shot from the walls (SSN 13–14). Another eighteen wounds, many of them fatal, were interpreted by Winlock as being caused by stones thrown or slung from a fortress (SSN 14–15, pl. 8–13). Fifteen of the sixty corpses were dispatched by a *coup de grace* to the head from maces, creating traumatic shattering of the skull and facial bones (SSN 16–17, pl. 9–10). Six bodies showed evidence of having been exposed after combat, and pecked at by carrion birds, indicating there was some time between their death and the recovery of the bodies (SSN 18, pl. 12).

Winlock describes his interpretation of the battle in which these soldiers were killed:

> We have some sixty soldiers of the army of King Neb-hepet-Re' [Montuhotep I], all of whom were either killed or grievously wounded by arrows and stones hurled from the battlements of a fortress they were attacking or were dispatched by the garrison during a sortie when their companions had fled out of range. Then they were torn by vultures, during the lull before the attackers once more dared come back to the fray. A second assault saw the fall of the citadel and the defeat of its defenders, when so great was the triumph of Neb-hepet-Re' that he had all the bodies of his slain soldiers gathered up from the battlefield, including those half rotted by their exposure since the first assault.... All were borne to Thebes for burial.... None had died in hand-to-hand fights from slashes by axes, probably none were the victims of stabs by spears and daggers, nor had any of them arms broken by the blows of maces and clubs. These soldiers were killed and wounded with missiles, and such as were grievously hurt and were helpless when the garrison made its sortie had been clubbed to death. (SSN 23)

In all, the investigation of these corpses demonstrates that Egyptian warfare could be brutal, and the overall impression of combat in the martial art of the Middle Kingdom, discussed above, is confirmed by Winlock's forensic analysis.

Fortifications[32]

Archaeologically, the building of fortifications is probably the most certain sign of militarism. If so, then the Middle Kingdom in Egypt was certainly a militaristic age. A complex system of fortifications (Egyptian *mnw*) was an integral part of the overall Middle Kingdom military strategy. There were four zones of Egyptian fortification activity, corresponding to its four strategic zones: the Nile valley, the north-eastern Canaanite frontier, the oases of the Western or Libyan Desert, and the Nubian frontier.

The Nile valley

There are frequent references to fortified cities within the Nile valley, but, unfortunately, millennia of human occupation and flooding by the Nile have erased most of the archaeological evidence. It is generally assumed that most of the large cities and great temple complexes were fortified with massive walls. The best surviving remains of city fortifications comes from El Kab (Nekheb), near Edfu, whose rectangular mud-brick city walls measure nearly 500 × 600 meters, and are twelve meters thick and eleven meters high (Figure 9, p. 360).[33] The gate complex is lined with stone for additional strength. In many ways the sacred enclosure of the temple complex at Abydos (Kom el-Sultan), built by Senwosret I, is a fortification, with gates and projecting towers (AEA 3–5; EAE 1:7–12; HEA 3:42–4).

The north-eastern frontier

Despite the obvious military importance of the north-eastern frontier, and numerous textual references to fortifications there, there is little surviving archaeological evidence for Middle Kingdom fortresses from that region. None the less, textual evidence gives us a basic picture of the nature and function of that fortified zone. This strategic frontier stretched from the Mediterranean to the Gulf of Suez, roughly 120 kilometers across. However, the Egyptians made use of the impassible lakes and marshes to limit the area requiring active defense to roughly half that distance. The policy of fortifying the eastern frontier seems to have begun in the reign of Akhtoy III of the Tenth Dynasty of Herakleopolis during the late First Intermediate Period, who claims to have driven nomads from the eastern fringes of the Delta (TS 223–4). This policy, however, was rigorously maintained throughout the Middle Kingdom, and broke down only in the last years of the Middle Kingdom and the early Second Intermediate Period.

The Egyptians developed a defense in depth, composed of both frontier fortresses and fortified cities in the delta. Amenemhet I {1991–1962} is known as the builder of one of the most important frontier fortresses of the age, the "Walls of the Ruler", possibly at Wadi Tumilat near the Great Bitter Lake (LA 6:1124–6). Its precise archaeological identification is uncertain; it could have been a single fortress, a series of forts designed to control access into Egypt, or even, in part, a barrier wall. Another fortress was built at the beginning of the "Ways of Horus", the military road leading east through the Sinai to Canaan (LA 3:62–4). Again its exact location is uncertain, but it was probably associated with Sile (Tell Abu Sefa) (ECI 80; LA 5:946–7). West of the frontier, the major towns of the north-eastern delta were also fortified, providing a second line of defense against any raiders or armies who might evade the frontier fortresses.

The Western Desert

During the Middle Kingdom the Western Desert was the least militarily active and threatening, and consequently the least fortified. Most of the oases that were occupied by the Egyptians, however, probably had some type of fortification, like those surviving at the Dakhla oasis (AEA 26). At Wadi Natrun (Qaret el-Dahr), to the west of the delta, there is a 47×59-meter fortress dating to the time of Amenemhet I {1991–1962} (HEA 3:205–6). A small dry-stone fortress in Wadi el-Hudi was built to protect the amethyst miners in the Eastern Desert as well (HEA 3:207–8).

The Nubian frontier[34]

Archaeologically, the most spectacular surviving Egyptian fortifications are the four-thousand-year-old "Second Cataract Forts" in central Sudan. Indeed, they are the finest examples of Bronze Age fortifications anywhere in the world. Tragically they have been submerged and destroyed by the creation of the Aswan Dam and Lake Nasser in the late 1960s. Before their destruction, however, several fortresses received careful archaeological and photographic documentation.

Although fortification of the southern frontier of Egypt had begun in Pre-Dynastic times, the "golden age" of Egyptian fortress building in Nubia was the Twelfth Dynasty of the Middle Kingdom. The fortifications constructed on the Kushite frontier were massive, requiring the expenditure of immense resources in their creation and maintenance, and representing both the need to sustain Egyptian imperialism in Nubia through military occupation and the significant potential military threat from the southern kingdom of Kush. The Cataract Forts were not created in a haphazard manner, but represent a carefully planned defensive system with four major purposes: 1, to maintain military control over Nubia; 2, to control trade from Kush into Egyptian Nubia; 3, to prevent raids or major military invasions from Kush; and 4, to provide bases for possible military intervention south into Kush. To achieve these goals the Egyptians created four fortress zones in Nubia (see Map 4, p. 309).[35]

The first zone was at the First Cataract, the traditional boundary between Egypt and Nubia, which had been fortified since Pre-Dynastic times. There were two major surviving fortresses there:

- Elephantine (Abu), 53 × 53 m (AEA 80–1);
- Senmut (on the island of Biga).

In addition to these fortresses, Senwosret I seems to have built a wall as a barrier to further control traffic and prevent raids; it was six kilometers long, two meters thick and six meters high (AEF 71).

The second fortification zone was rather more than 100 kilometers south of Aswan, where Montuhotep I {2061–2011} and, more extensively, Amenemhet I {1991–1962} built fortresses at the mouth of Wadi Allaqi to control access to the gold and copper mining regions to the east. These included:

- Ikkur (Baki), 82 × 110 m (AEA 115);
- Kubban (also called Baki), 70 × 125 m (AEA 132);
- Aniba (Miam), 87 × 138 m (AEA 18).

The third fortification zone was at the Second Cataract, some 300 kilometers south of Aswan at the frontier established by Senwosret I {1962–1928}. Forts here included:

- Faras ("Repelling the Medjay"), 75 × 85 m (AEA 90);
- Serra East ("Embracing the Two Lands"), ? × 80 m (AEA 219);
- Buhen (Buhen), city wall 215 × 460 m; fortress 150 × 170 m (AEA 39–40);
- Khor (Buhen), 250 × 600 m (AEA 125);
- Mirgissa (Iken), 100 × 175 m (AEA 152);
- Dabenarti, 60 × 230 m (AEA 64).

A century later Senwosret's great-grandson and namesake Senwosret III {1878–1843} created the forth fortress cluster about 100 kilometers further south at Semna, about halfway between the Second and Third Cataracts. These fortresses, representing the southernmost extension of Egyptian control in Nubia during the Middle Kingdom, were:

- Askut ("Removing the Setiu"), 77 × 87 m (AEA 22);
- Shalfak ("Curbing the Countries"), 47 × 95 m (AEA 221);
- Uronarti ("Repelling the *Inw*"), triangular, 57 × 114 × 126 m (AEA 251);
- Semna ("Khakaure [Senwosret III] is powerful"), 135 × 135 m (AEA 213);
- Kumma ("Warding off the Bows"), 70 × 117 m (AEA 132).

In creating these fortification systems the Egyptians made extensive use of the defensive potential of geography. The first and third fortification zones were respectively at the First and Second Cataracts, where any Nile River traffic must necessarily stop. Thus, in a sense, the cataracts had already naturally fortified the river, to which the Egyptians simply added land fortifications. The fourth zone, at the Semna gorge, was the narrowest point in the Nile valley between the Second and Third Cataracts. The narrow Semna gorge was ideal for defensive purposes.

Although the building of the Nubian fortifications was associated with the imperialist policies of specific pharaohs, once built the forts took on a life of their own, continuing long after the original policies of the kings were abandoned or transformed by changing circumstances. Many of these forts remained in use for centuries, and were repaired or expanded a number of times by subsequent kings (e.g. ARE 1:293). Some of the forts, originally established for purely military reasons, developed into large cities and became centers of cultural and religious life in the area. Trade flourished at the forts, with a regular flow of merchandise between Egypt and Kush. The fortresses of Nubia remained in Egyptian hands into the early Thirteenth Dynasty, when the kings of Kush conquered Nubia as far north as Aswan; thereafter the fortresses remained in Kushite hands during most of the seventeenth and sixteenth centuries (see pp. 459–61). They were eventually reconquered by the Egyptians during the New Kingdom.

Characteristics of Egyptian forts: the example of Buhen (FB; BI; AEA 39–40)

Before the flooding of Lake Nasser, the best-preserved Egyptian fortress was Buhen (Figure 10, p. 444). The excavation and magisterial publication by Emery, Smith and Millard provides vital archaeological data on the characteristics of Middle Kingdom Egyptian fortifications. Built by Senwosret I {1971–1928} to consolidate his Nubian conquests, the fortress was occupied for centuries and refurbished many times. The Buhen fortress complex was built at the Second Cataract, adding man-made strength to this natural barrier in the Nile. Buhen was actually a pair – two fortresses on opposite banks of the Nile – to insure that no ship stopping at the Second Cataract could evade Egyptian notice. Modern archaeologists call these two forts Buhen and Khor, but they were both called Buhen by the ancient Egyptians, indicating that the Egyptians conceived these two fortresses as a single fortress system.

Buhen, like the vast majority of Egyptian fortifications, was constructed of mud-brick, although some other Egyptian forts have stone foundations to give the fortress greater stability. Like many other Nubian fortresses, Buhen had one wall against the Nile, allowing direct access to supplies and reinforcements from the river, again emphasizing the importance of the Nile as the logistical artery of the Egyptian army. Although Buhen was essentially rectangular in shape, many other fortresses were irregular, maximizing the defensive qualities of the terrain. The military engineers at Buhen clearly understood the principle of concentric fortification. The inner fortress measured 150 × 170 m, with walls five meters thick and up to eleven meters high, reinforced with wooden beams and reed mats to increase stability. The walls of other Egyptian fortifications measured as much as twelve meters thick. The defensibility of the walls was increased by regularly-placed square towers and huge projecting defensive bastions at the corners.

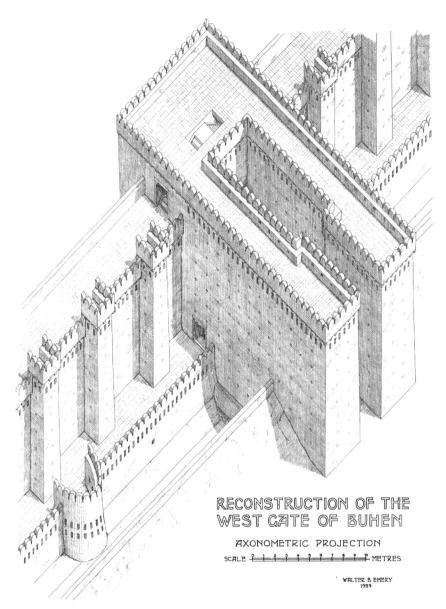

RECONSTRUCTION OF THE
WEST GATE OF BUHEN

AXONOMETRIC PROJECTION

SCALE ⊢—┴—┴—┴—┴—┴—┴—┴—┴—┴—┤ METRES

WALTER B EMERY
1959

Figure 10   Middle Kingdom Egyptian fortifications at Buhen, Sudan {20–18C}. Until its
inundation by Lake Nasser, the Egyptian fortress of Buhen was the best-preserved and most complex fortress from the Middle Bronze Age Near East. The
fortress included a dry moat, glacis, concentric walls, projecting towers, postern
gates, arrow slits, crenellation, and a massively fortified gate complex.

Source: Drawing by Walter B. Emery, from Walter B. Emery, H. S. Smith and A. Millard,
The Fortress at Buhen: The Archaeological Report (Excavations at Buhen 1) (London: The Egypt
Exploration Society, 1979). Courtesy of the Egypt Exploration Society.

Two small gates gave access the Nile, with a huge fortified monumental land-gate to the west.

This inner wall was surrounded by a second outer wall reinforced with thirty-two semi-circular towers. These towers had a double-row of loopholes for archers, angled in such a way as to allow a wide arc of fire. This entire complex was surrounded by a deep dry moat with mud-brick-lined glacis and counterscarp, creating a triple barrier against any assault. The monumental land-gate had a long narrow passageway, with tall towers projecting over the dry moat. A drawbridge on rollers within the gate could be withdrawn, blocking access to the inner gate, which was closed with heavy wooden doors. It is quite remarkable that by at least the twentieth century BC the Egyptians had already developed most of the basic concepts and principles of fortification that would remain foundational to fortification engineering until the development of gunpowder weapons nearly 3500 years later.

Garrisons and the Semna military dispatches (SD)

Within the walls of Egyptian fortifications there were a number of different types of buildings for the administration and maintenance of the fortresses. These included barracks, houses, and offices for the officers, armories, production areas, temples or shrines, granaries and supply houses, bakeries, and sometimes gardens.

The frontier fortresses were manned by permanent garrisons which sent out regular border patrols. There is also evidence of watchtowers to supplement border patrol observations. When fleeing from the turmoil of a palace coup, Sinuhe faced the problem of evading the border patrols. When he "reached the Walls of the Ruler [Amenemhet I], which were made to repel the [raids of] the Syrians and to crush the Sand-farers. I crouched in a bush for fear of being seen by the guard on duty upon the wall" (AEL 1:224). When Sinuhe returned to Egypt years later, he was stopped "at the Ways of Horus", one of the forts on Egypt's north-eastern border, probably at Sile (Tell Abu Sefa). There the garrison commander, undoubtedly astonished by a bearded man in bedouin clothing claiming to be an Egyptian who had been summoned by the king, sent a message to the royal palace asking what to do (TS 39, 42). These incidents suggest that, while individuals or small groups could evade the garrisons and border patrols, large raiding parties or armies would find it difficult to elude the strict Egyptian border garrisons and patrols.

Eight remarkable military dispatches survive from the Nubian frontier fortresses during the reign of Amenemhet III {1843–1797}, giving us a glimpse of garrison organization and administration in the Middle Kingdom. Although written by officers in the Nubian frontier garrisons to their commanders, copies were kept at Thebes, indicating "the pervasiveness of the State administration" (VAE 93). Most of the letters end with the stylized assurance, "All the affairs of the King's Domain – Life, Health and Peace [upon him] – are safe and sound." The focus of the surviving letters is on the movement of Nubians and the nomadic Medjay, and the monitoring of trading activities. Protection from Nubian raiders was obviously a high priority, and the frontier troops kept careful watch on population movements between Nubia and Egypt, with regular patrols describing sightings of people or even recent tracks in the desert. The fortresses also served as centers of trade, with the frontier garrison providing security for merchants (AEMK 191).

Nothing seems to be too trivial for recording in the dispatch archives; several letters mention the movements of only half a dozen Nubians (SD §1, 3, 5). Five Medjay bedouins, complaining that "the desert is dying of hunger", came to Elephantine begging to be allowed to "serve the Great House [of Egypt]" as mercenaries (SD §5), presumably to keep from starving. Some Nubians were turned away and not permitted to stay near the Egyptian fortresses (SD §6). Other letters discuss the arrival and departure of Nubian merchants by boat and donkey to trade at one of the forts (SD §1, 7). Medjay bedouins were hired as mercenary troops to patrol the desert against the incursions of other Nubians: "two [Egyptian] guardsmen and seventy [or seven?] Medjay-people went following a track [in the desert]". They captured three Medjay men and three women, who were brought to the fortress and questioned. "Then I [the fortress commander] questioned these Medjay-people, saying, 'Whence have you come?' Then they said, 'We have come from the Well of Yebheyet' " (SD §3).

The most complete dispatch describes such a tracking expedition which lasted three days:

> Another letter brought to him by the liegeman Ameny who is in [the fortress] Khesef-Medjaiu ["Repeller of the Medjay" = Faras], being [a message] given by fortress to fortress. It is a communication to the Lord, may he live, prosper, be healthy, to the effect that the soldier Nekhen, Senu's son, Heru's son Reniqer and the soldier from Tjebu, Rensi's son, Senwosret's son Senwosret, came to report to this humble servant in year 3 [of Amenemhet III, = 1841], 4th month of spring, day 2, at the time of breakfast, on a mission from the officer of the town regiment, Khusobek's son Montuhotep's son Khusobek . . . who is the deputy [sergeant?] to the officer of the ruler's company in the garrison of Meha [a district in Nubia] saying: "The patrol that went out to patrol the desert edge [near] the fortress of Khesef-Medjau in year 3, 3rd month of spring, last day, has returned [after three days on patrol in the desert] to report to me, saying, 'We have found the track of thirty-two men and three donkeys [. . .]' This humble servant has sent [the report from fortress] to fortress." (VAE 94–5 = SD, §4)

This remarkable document, which was preserved in a Theban archive where a copy had been forwarded from Nubia, shows that the Egyptian army maintained detailed archives with the names of each individual soldier and every patrol carefully recorded. It is likely that there were once thousands of such papyri texts in archives documenting all aspects of Egyptian military affairs, but today only the merest fragments survive.

Siegecraft[36]

The extensive program of fortification undertaken by the Egyptians in the Middle Kingdom demonstrates that they viewed such defenses as necessary and worth the expenditure of resources. The Coffin Texts describe this view of the value of fortifications, promising that "there will not go up to you those who would destroy your gate or wall" (CT 21). None the less, it is clear that, given enough time and the proper techniques, Bronze Age fortresses could be captured by assaulting armies. As depicted in the earlier Old Kingdom siege murals from the tombs of Kaemheset (AW 1:147, EWW 38; NEA 30–2) and Inty (AW 1:146, FP 141–2; NEA 30–2, Figure 2a), there were two basic methods of capturing a fortified city by assault during the Egyptian Bronze Age: breaching, and scaling. Neither ramp building nor undermining walls are attested as siege techniques in the Egyptian sources for this period.

Middle Kingdom evidence confirms the continued use of both scaling and breaching techniques, but with two major technical innovations: siege towers, and rams. Unfortunately, this Middle Kingdom evidence, though evocative, is quite limited. We have only two artistic depictions of Egyptian siegecraft in the Middle Kingdom: the siege mural of Antef (Thebes tomb 386) (Figure 11, p. 447; EWW 38; NEA 38–9, Figure 3) {c. 2100}; and the siege murals at the tombs of Beni Hasan (BH) {c. 2050–1950}.

Scaling

In a scene reminiscent of the Old Kingdom murals in the tombs of Kaemheset and Inty, the tomb of Antef has a relief depicting the siege of a Canaanite city being assaulted with what appears to be a free-standing siege tower (GJ §2; EWW 38). This device differs from earlier Old Kingdom depictions of siege ladders in two ways. First, the Old Kingdom ladders are shown leaning against the wall for support, while this siege tower is shown upright. Second, the Old Kingdom ladders have only a single set of rungs. The Antef siege tower shows three upright beams with two sets of rungs, allowing two pairs of Egyptian soldiers to ascend the tower

Figure 11 Siege and battle scene, Tomb of Antef (Thebes, Egypt) {c. 2100}
Source: Drawing by Michael Lyon.

simultaneously. There are two possible explanations for this. It may be that this is simply a double ladder with a shared middle beam. On the other hand, the artist might be trying to depict, without the benefit of artistic perspective techniques, a freestanding square tower. Another feature argues in favor of the square tower interpretation. In the depiction the tower doesn't actually touch the wall, which it would have to do if it were a ladder. Instead, it appears that a beam or plank extends from the top of the tower to the top of the wall, which the attackers would use to make the assault from the tower to the wall. A soldier on the top of the tower, armed with shield and axe, seems to be engaged in a melee with a Canaanite as the Egyptian struggles to get from the siege tower to the wall. Four soldiers with their axes thrust into their belts are ascending the tower, while a fifth man on the ground with axe and shield seems to be preparing to follow them up the tower.

This tower thus seems to be an attempt to create a more stable platform from which to assault the wall, as well as more numerous climbing rungs to allow more soldiers to ascend simultaneously. On the ground level to the left of the tower there is a partially damaged circle which may represent a wheel for the tower, similar to wheels depicted on Old Kingdom siege ladders. The city the Egyptians are assaulting has no glacis, meaning the tower can be pushed fairly close to the wall. The glacis depicted in later fortresses on the Beni Hasan murals may have been made in part to prevent siege towers from being pushed up against the fortifications. Dry moats characteristic of some Middle Kingdom Egyptian fortifications would have had a similar effect.

The Canaanite defenders of the fortress, with beards, headbands, and multicolored kilts, are fighting the Egyptians with arrows and stones. Egyptian missile counter-fire seems to be effective; two Canaanites have been wounded by arrows – one in the arm and one in the forehead – while another four have tumbled off the walls. Five Canaanites are shown with their heads barely peeking over the ramparts, while another four are standing up to shoot arrows or throw stones. One man has the pointed-rectangle style of Canaanite shield, discussed on p. 438. Beneath the siege scene we see the aftermath of the siege, with bound men being dragged off as prisoners, women and children wailing and following behind; infants are carried on their shoulders. Egyptian soldiers armed with axes (five) and bows (three) guard, and sometimes abuse, the prisoners; some prisoners are pulled by their hair.

Breaching

Breaching the fortress walls by simply digging through the mud bricks was obviously a potentially very costly operation, for the assaulting army was exposed to withering missile fire from the defenders who remained protected atop the city ramparts. The Coffin Texts describe the fear of soldiers facing such a missile barrage: "the ramparts are high, and I die in their limit" (CT 1139). The nature of the injuries suffered by the soldiers in the Tomb of the Warriors (SNN), many of whom were wounded or killed by missiles or stones throne from above, reflects the brutal fate of many of those assaulting a fortified and strongly defended city.

Thus, rather than using the Old Kingdom method of directly digging through the mud-brick walls of an enemy fortress with mattocks, axes, and crowbars, while facing deadly enemy fire from above, Middle Kingdom siege engineers developed two new technologies to protect soldiers while attempting to breach fortress walls: the battering-ram, and the penthouse or protective shed. Both of these are depicted on the martial murals from the tombs at Beni Hasan.[37]

All of the murals depict essentially the same siege scene; it is not certain if this is because the depictions reflect the standard technique of the period, or if the artists were simply repeating the same conventional scene over and over again. The castle being assaulted has either one or two gates, tall walls, and machicolation. It also has glacis – sloping earthworks at the foundation of the walls – a characteristic of fortifications which appear in both Egyptian and Canaanite fortresses from this period (ALB 202–5). The exact purpose of the Bronze Age glacis is uncertain. In one sense the glacis simply serves to stabilize the walls, allowing them to be built taller. A second possible function of the glacis would be to make breaching the walls more difficult; attackers attempting to undermine the base of the wall would have to dig through the glacis before reaching the wall itself. Finally, the sloping glacis would prevent siege towers from being placed directly against the wall, thereby limiting their effectiveness. As noted, the siege tower depicted in Antef's tomb has been placed against a wall with no glacis. It is possible, then, that glacis were made in part as a direct response to the development of siege towers. Likewise, a glacis would force attackers to place ladders further from the base of the wall and at a shallower angle; the ladders would thus need to be longer, and would be less stable. It is likely that all of these considerations were elements in the development of the glacis.

The defenders of the forts in the Beni Hasan murals appear to be Egyptians, with shields and other equipment similar to that of the Egyptian attackers; the sieges represented here were thus probably part of the wars of the late First Intermediate Period. The defenders are armed with bows, javelins, and stones (though no slings), which they hurl with great fervor at the attackers. Some of the soldiers are protected by shields from the missiles of the attackers; others hang out over the parapets to get a better aim. The attackers likewise return missile fire by both archers and slingers; arrows are shown sticking in the walls and in some of the defenders. A large part of the siege was thus a missile duel, with the defenders having the advantage of the protection of their walls and the improved view, range and penetrating power brought by shooting at an enemy from above. On the other hand the attackers might have an advantage in that they could mass more troops shooting more missiles against a single section of the wall which could support only a limited number of defenders.

The most interesting feature shared in all of the Beni Hasan siege murals is the depiction of the protected ram used by the Egyptians. The Egyptians have built a protective shelter to defend their men from enemy missiles. The exact nature of the shelter is uncertain; it clearly has a wooden frame, with crossbeams to support the structure. The roof is curved to deflect missiles. There are two uncertainties, however. First, is the structure a wooden frame covered by animal skins, or are there wooden planks on the roof and between the main structural beams? Given that the defenders' missiles are arrows, javelins, and stones, it seems likely that cured leather would provide sufficient protection for the attackers, which would also make the structure light enough that it could be easily carried into position. Second, the artist has depicted the structure in a cutaway view, allowing us to see inside, so it is not clear how much protection there really was on the sides of the shelter. Clearly there must be some type of opening to allow the Egyptians to use their ram. I suggest that the structure was completely covered on the top, had an opening at head and shoulder level which allowed the soldiers to see out and thrust their ram. The shelter was further protected by side panels on three sides, but was open to the rear allowing the soldiers to come in and out.

There are two or three soldiers in the protective structures, carrying long poles used as rams. Assuming the soldiers averaged about 1.6 meters tall (see p. 439; SSN 7), and that the artist depicted the rams in accurate proportion to the soldiers (which is not at all certain), the poles would be about 4–5 meters long. Given the height of many of the walls, however, I suspect many were actually longer than this. It is not clear from the artwork, but the poles may have had some type of metal head. It appears to me that the poles were thrust out between the gap between the roof and the protective side panel, and rested on the front crossbeam of the defensive structure, creating a point of leverage. The soldiers used their weight to hold the back of the pole down, lifting the front of the ram upward at something less than forty-five degrees. The pole was then rammed into the brick wall and used as a lever in an attempt to crush or dislodge the mud-bricks. When enough bricks had been dislodged, the upper courses of the brickwork of the fortress would collapse, creating a breach, through which an assault could be undertaken. In all of the Beni Hasan murals the ram is being used against the upper portions of the wall rather than the base. This may in part be because the glacis prevented the ram from doing much damage to the base of the wall. It is also likely that, if enough of the upper portions of the wall collapsed, the resulting slumping of the bricks would create enough of a gap and slope for an assault to be made.

Blockades

We have no accounts during the Middle Kingdom of blockades or sieges lasting for months in an effort to starve out the besieged. Why might this be? It may simply be that such sieges did indeed occur but the surviving fragmentary records do not preserve accounts of them. It is only in the early New Kingdom that we have our first account of a multi-year siege. The autobiography of a ship's captain serving in the wars of king Ahmose tells us that, during the wars of expulsion of the Hyksos from Egypt, "Sharuhen [a major Hyksos city in southern Canaan, either Tell el-Far'ah or Tell Ajjul] was besieged for three years" {c. 1550} (ANET 233b), implying that long-term sieges were feasible by this period. However, we do not know if such blockades were undertaken earlier. It may be that the mud-brick walls of most fortifications of the period could be breached with a few weeks of consistent effort, making long sieges unnecessary. On the other hand, the fortifications of Sharuhen in Canaan were also of mud-brick; if brick walls were easy to breach, thereby removing the need for lengthy sieges, why did it take three years for the Egyptians to capture Sharuhen?

It is also possible that, during the Middle Kingdom, the Egyptians lacked the logistical capacity to feed and support large armies in the field for more than a few months. If a city could not be taken within the framework of the maximum logistically feasible period, the siege would have to be abandoned; thus long sieges did not occur because the attackers starved before the defenders. But it is most likely that lengthy sieges are not mentioned in the records because, outside of civil wars in Egypt, the Egyptians generally did not face enemies with massive fortresses. The only exception to this was Canaan, where the Bronze Age city-states were highly fortified. But, as discussed on pages 406–7, the Egyptians did not, in fact, intervene extensively in Canaan during this period. The fact that they faced large, well-fortified Canaanite cities in that region may have been part of the reason. Unfortunately, the lack of data precludes a definitive answer.

Naval warfare[38]

The overall technology and pattern of naval warfare in the Middle Kingdom remained broadly similar to those of the Old Kingdom, though there were a number of technical advances. Landstrom details these in his marvelously illustrated book (SP 75–97). A number of model boats (TEM 93), artistic depictions, and archaeological remains (such as the Dashur boat, EBS 28) give us a good understanding of Egyptian nautical technology. Several different types of Middle Kingdom boats with sails, oars, and large rudders, are depicted on the tomb reliefs at Beni Hasan.[39] Some Middle Kingdom ships are depicted with shields hanging from the sides of the deckhouse (SP 78, 81, 85, 89). This may in part simply be a convenient, out-of-the-way place to store the shields, but may also be an attempt to strengthen the thin papyrus matting of the deck house against javelins or arrows in combat situations (SP 81). The Coffin Texts and other sources provide detailed nautical terminology describing many different parts of the celestial ships of the gods.[40] Although these celestial ships are close counterparts of earthly ships, they are described in mythic terms where each part of the ship represents a different god or mythic creature; the ship itself becomes a microcosm of the Egyptian universe.[41]

There were four major zones of Egyptian naval activity during the Middle Kingdom: the Egyptian Nile, the Nubian Nile (from the First to the Third Cataracts), the Red Sea and the eastern Mediterranean Sea. Fundamentally, during the two Intermediate Periods Egyptian naval combat focused on the struggle between rival Egyptian princes on the Nile river. Thereafter, although the Nile remained crucial for transporting troops and materials during the Middle Kingdom, we naturally see little river warfare on the Egyptian Nile, since Egypt was a unified state firmly controlling the Nile to the First Cataract and beyond. Instead, during the Middle Kingdom, naval warfare shifts to the Nubian Nile, the Red Sea and the Mediterranean Sea.

We have several accounts of river campaigns during the First Intermediate Period, which have been discussed in Chapter Fifteen. Henenu the steward describes part of his responsibilities as "sailing up the river at the head of his troops" (AEAB 52) indicating the importance of the river for transporting Egyptian armies. King Merikare {c. 2070–2050?} led a river campaign in Middle Egypt in person, sailing his fleet to Shashotpe (Shutb), near Asyut {c. 2055?}, where a standoff with the upstart princes of Thebes ensued (ARE 1:185–6 = MKT 23, see p. 377). Ankhtifi of Hierakonpolis' campaign against Thebes {c. 2030} included strong support from his river fleet, which sailed with impunity up and down the Nile, either carrying troops or supporting them as they marched on the banks of the river (AF 37; OHAE 131, p. 371–3). The Nubian mercenary Tjehemau mentions campaigning by river and fighting on Lake Faiyum during Montuhotep's wars of reunification {c. 2040}. He describes ...

> Going forth ... against the Lake of Sobek [Faiyum] ... I overthrew the [enemy on the] sandbank ... [and] the river, to lead the sand-dwellers [nomad mercenaries] and [the Nubian mercenaries of] Wawat ... to put to flight the man [king] of the North. Then it [the northern kingdom of Herakleopolis] mustered its war-fleet and it traversed all its nomes of the entire [northern] land to defend itself. (ITM 11–20)

Tjehemau also describes an amphibious assault against troops marshaled on the riverbank:

> I went down to the district of Thebes. I found [the enemy] standing on the riverbank. They planned fighting. The opposition fell [before our attack], fleeing because of me ... in the district of Thebes. (ITM 11–20)

These accounts emphasize the integral part river fleets played in Egyptian warfare. It would be safe to say that on the Nile river an army seldom campaigned without the assistance of a fleet for combat, transport, and logistical support.

During the campaigns against Nubia in the Middle Kingdom, Egyptian fleets played precisely the same role south of the First Cataract that they had played on the Egyptian Nile during the First Intermediate Period. Several accounts, discussed in Chapter Sixteen, describe the role of the river fleet in the Nubian wars during the Middle Kingdom. Crucial to the success of the Egyptian conquest of Nubia was the use of the canal bypassing the First Cataract at Aswan, which had been built in the days of Weni in the late Sixth Dynasty {c. 2310} (AEL 1:21–2).

This canal was dredged and widened in the eighth year of Senwosret III {1870} to facilitate his conquest of Nubia by allowing the free passage of his war fleet, troop transports, and supply ships into Nubia (ARE 1:291–2). Thereafter, a royal river fleet was apparently maintained on the Nubian Nile (RA3 213).

We have no accounts of actual sea – as opposed to river – combat during the Middle Kingdom. We do know, on the other hand, that Egyptian ocean fleets were operating widely and frequently in the eastern Mediterranean and the Red Sea during this period (EAE 2:358–67). In the Mediterranean Sea, Egyptian fleets were known to have operated as far as Crete (EAE 1:315), Cyprus (ECI 79), and Syria. The Syrian city of Byblos served as the major Egyptian naval base for resupply, fleet repair, and trade, and was crucial in the success of Egyptian maritime enterprises in the Mediterranean. (EAE 1:219–21, see p. 410). This gives a likely total range for naval operations in the Mediterranean of 700 kilometers from Egypt, and perhaps as far as 1000 kilometers, depending on how one interprets the significance of the presence of Egyptian artifacts in the Aegean Sea. The total range of naval operation in the Red Sea is even further, up to 2500 kilometers from Egypt, again depending on where, precisely, Punt was located (EAE 3:85–6). Most of these naval operations were essentially peaceful trading expeditions, but many, if not all of them, included a military component, if only a contingent of soldier for the protection of the fleet. Amenemhet II's *annus mirabilis* {c. 1910}, discussed on pp. 399–402, included the dispatch and return of a fleet of ten ships on a raid to the Lebanese coast (ECI 78–9). At the same time another fleet plundered two cities in Cyprus or on the Syrian coast and returned with 1,554 prisoners (ECI 79). The size of the fleet is not known but it must have been fairly substantial to have been able to carry enough soldiers and sailors to sack two cities and have room to return with over 1500 prisoners. The Egyptians in the Middle Kingdom clearly had the naval capacity to send several thousand men anywhere on the eastern coast of the Mediterranean.

The First Intermediate Period and Middle Kingdom preserve a number of sources which give us our first glimpses of actual naval combat on the Nile. The most impressive of these is the naval combat relief from the tomb of Antef (Intef) (Theban tomb 386), nomarch of Thebes, and early ancestor of the kings of the Eleventh Dynasty (Figure 12, p. 454; GJ §1; NEA 39; EBS 35). These murals depict three boats, all propelled by oars with large rudders at the back; no sails are visible. If the soldiers are drawn in proportion to the boat, the river boats are rather small, perhaps eight meters long; other vessels are known to have been thirty meters long with 60 rowers (EBS 36). These boats are propelled, respectively, by ten, fourteen or eighteen rowers, with half that number depicted on one side of each boat. In two of the ships they sit, rowing in unison; in the other they stand while rowing. Two of the ships have four warriors, one has at least five, and perhaps a sixth in a damaged section of the mural. Two of the ships have only archers, while the third has one archer and three men armed with shields and broad-axes. Some of the warriors stand on the prow of the ship, shooting their bows; two axemen on the prow are preparing to assault another ship, or perhaps to jump ashore.

Figure 12   Naval combat scene, Tomb of Antef (Thebes, Egypt) {c. 2100}
Source: Drawing by Michael Lyon (partly restored)

The details of the Antef naval mural thus shows that Middle Kingdom naval combat included both archery and shipboard melees, which is confirmed by textual accounts of naval combat from this period. The most detailed of these comes from the autobiography of Tefibi, nomarch of Asyut, against his rivals at Thebes {c. 2080} and is the first eye-witness narrative of a naval battle on the Nile.

> I [crossed over from the west bank] and reached the east side [of the Nile], sailing upstream [south]. There came another jackal [Antef's general] with another army from his confederacy [from Thebes]. I went out against him.... He hastened to battle to the [thirteenth] nome [of Asyut].... I ceased not to fight to the end, making use of the south wind as well as the north wind, of the east wind as well as the west wind [for maneuvering my fleet on the river].... He [the enemy general] fell in the water [after being wounded or killed]; his ships [fled and] ran aground.... Fire was set [to their ships]. I drove out the rebellion by the plan of [the jackal god] Wepwawet, [the head-god of Asyut] ... When a man did well, I promoted [him] to the head of my soldiers. (ARE 1:182–3)

This narrative depicts ships fighting a battle on the river and using the winds for maneuvering to gain tactical advantage. When the enemy general was killed in battle – by missile or melee is unclear – he fell in the river, demoralizing his troops. As the battle was won, the fleeing enemy beached their boats, abandoning them to be burned by the victors. This general pattern of naval warfare is supplemented by a passage from the Coffin Texts, describing demonic opposition to the passage of the celestial ship of the gods into the heavens in terms of naval warfare, with tactics of shattering enemy oars to prevent maneuver, and setting fire to enemy ships: "the oars of those who are hostile are broken ... I am he who opposed the destroyer who came setting fire to your bark.... They shall not attack your bark while I am in it" (CT 1099).

Thus, by the Middle Kingdom, river naval combat had become quite sophisticated, including the use of a combination of sails and oars to maneuver the ships, attempts to use the wind to gain tactical advantage over the enemy, combat with ramming to shatter oars and fire to disable enemy ships, and archery and boarding melee against enemy crews. In this, Middle Kingdom naval warfare broadly parallels the characteristics of naval combat in the New Kingdom as depicted on the famous martial reliefs on the southern wall of the temple of Ramses III at Medinat Habu.[42]

CHAPTER EIGHTEEN

Early Second Intermediate Period Egypt {1786–1667}[1]

The death of queen Sobekneferu and the end of the Twelfth Dynasty in 1786 inaugurated a period with a remarkable dearth of historical sources in Egypt. Royal and noble inscriptions with information on military affairs almost entirely disappear, in favor of formulaic ritual texts with little substantive historical content. "Sources for the period include neither royal annals nor private autobiographies with information on military events" (EAE 3:395). The names of many kings ruling Egypt during this period are unknown, due to lacunae in the Turin Canon king-list, even when supplemented by scarab seals with royal names which become popular during this period.[2] All this means that the military historian can hope to understand only the broadest trends during this period.

The paucity of sources naturally creates uncertainty and ambiguity, leading to several different ways of understanding the history of Egypt during this period. Some scholars rightly note that there are many areas of cultural continuity between the Middle Kingdom and the Second Intermediate Period. From the perspective of military history, however, the discontinuities are more significant. Among Egyptologists there are different ways of interpreting the reasons for the shift from the Middle Kingdom to the Second Intermediate Period. Some scholars include the Thirteenth and Fourteenth Dynasties {1786–1667} as part of the Middle Kingdom, with the Second Intermediate Period covering only the Fifteenth through Seventeenth Dynasties {1667–1569}. Others, whom I will follow,[3] date the Second Intermediate Period from the end of the Twelfth Dynasty in 1786 to the beginning of the Eighteenth Dynasty and the New Kingdom period in 1569. I will use the following tentative chronology of the Second Intermediate Period (see Table 18.1).[4]

In this section I will examine only the Thirteenth and Fourteenth Dynasties, culminating in the invasion of the Hyksos and the introduction of the war-chariot into Egypt around 1667.

Thirteenth Dynasty {1786–1667} (SIP 69–93, EAE 3:394–8)

Due to the paucity of sources, the military history of the Thirteenth and Fourteenth Dynasties can only be described in the broadest generalities, and this often

456

Table 18.1 Tentative chronology of the Second Intermediate Period

Dates	Dynasties
1991–1786	Twelfth Dynasty (Middle Kingdom)
1788–1667	Fourteenth (Canaanite) Dynasty at Avaris dominates the Delta
1786–1667	Thirteenth (Egyptian) Dynasty in middle and southern Egypt
1667	"Hyksos" conquest of Avaris and Memphis ends Thirteenth and Fourteenth Dynasties
1667–1602	Sixteenth (Egyptian) Dynasty at Thebes
1667–1558	Fifteenth (Canaanite) "Hyksos" Dynasty dominates the Delta
1602–1600	"Hyksos" conquest and temporary domination of Thebes
1600–1569	Seventeenth (Egyptian) Dynasty at Thebes
1569–1315	Eighteenth Dynasty at Thebes; beginning of the New Kingdom
1569	Year 1 of Ahmose of Thebes; beginning of the Eighteenth Dynasty
1558	Year 11, Ahmose conquers Avaris and ends the Fifteenth "Hyksos" Dynasty

only through inference from scanty inscriptional and archaeological remains. A basic, though fragmentary list of kings is found in the Turin King-list, which can be supplemented with scarabs and inscriptions (SIP 69–75, 94–9; CS 1:72–3). However, most of these kings remain nothing more than ephemeral names. The capital of Egypt remained at the earlier Middle Kingdom capital of Itjawy (Lisht), and there was some dynastic continuity between the Twelfth and early Thirteenth dynasties – the first two kings of the Thirteenth Dynasty were sons of Amenemhet IV of the Twelfth Dynasty (SIB 75). The major military event of the early Thirteenth Dynasty, which inaugurated the Second Intermediate Period, was the rise to independence of the rival kings of the Canaanite Fourteenth Dynasty in the eastern delta (see p. 461). This was undoubtedly accompanied by warfare, and, although we are left uninformed of the details, it is clear that the Canaanite warriors of the delta were ultimately successful in establishing their independent state. Thereafter there was at least some level of peace and accommodation between the Egyptian Thirteenth and Canaanite Fourteenth Dynasties, as indicated by trade relations and the finds of Thirteenth Dynasty seals in Fourteenth Dynasty territory.

The period as a whole was ruled by over fifty kings, generally with short reigns and few major monuments. There are no records of foreign military expeditions to the Sinai, Canaan, or Nubia, though a few inscriptions mention mining expeditions to the quarries at Wadi Hammamat in the Eastern Desert and Gebel Zeit on the Red Sea. Likewise there is inscriptional evidence mentioning a "commander" and a "lieutenant" in the western oases, indicating a Thirtheenth Dynasty military presence there (SIB 78–9). Any dynastic continuity with the rulers of the Twelfth Dynasty was ended with the rise to power of king Sobekhotpe III {1749–1747?}. He was an "elite officer", the son of the "elite officer" Montuhotep, who rose to power under unknown circumstances; Ryholt speculates that there was some type

Table 18.2 Schematized and simplified chart of the dynastic divisions of Egypt during the Second Intermediate Period, 1786–1569

Year	Thebes	Middle Egypt	Memphis	Avaris–Delta
1810	Middle Kingdom			
1800	Twelfth Dynasty, 1991–1786			
1790				
1780				
1770				
1760				
1750		Thirteenth Dynasty		Fourteenth
1740		(Egyptian)		Dynasty
1730		1786–1667		(Canaanite)
1720				1788–1667
1710				
1700				
1690				
1680				
1670				
1660				
1650	Sixteenth Dynasty			
1640	(Egyptian, Thebes) 1667–1602			
1630			Fifteenth Dynasty	
1620	1602–1600: Hyksos domination at Thebes		(Canaanite–"Hyksos")	
1610			1667–1558	
1600			(109 years)	
1590	Seventeenth Dynasty			
1580	(Egyptian, Thebes)			
1570	1600–1569			
1560				
1550				
1540				
1530	New Kingdom			
1520	Eighteenth Dynasty (Thebes) 1569–1315			
1510				
1500				

Source: Based on SIP 6, 191; all dates approximate. For map, see HAAE 52 and AAE 41.

of military coup against the weak and ineffectual kings of the early Thirteenth Dynasty (SIP 222–4, 297). However this may be, Sobekhotpe III initiated a temporary revival in Egyptian military power.

Sobekhotpe's successor, though not his son, was Neferhotpe I {1747–1736?}, under whose rule Egypt's military prestige was somewhat restored. An inscription of Neferhotpe in northern Nubia indicates that Egypt still exercised some control of that region. On the other hand, a building inscription mentions soldiers accompanying king Neferhotpe I on a pilgrimage to Abydos (ARE 1:334, SIB 226–8), which may indicate some concern for the security of the king. Seals of Thirteenth Dynasty kings and officials have also been discovered in Canaan and Syria, indicating trade and diplomatic relations with Egypt (SIB 85). Seals of Egyptian military officers have likewise been found in the Levant, implying that some type of military escort accompanied Egyptian trading and diplomatic expeditions (SIB 86). All this implies that either the Thirteenth Dynasty kings had direct access to the Mediterranean via a western branch of the Nile, or the Canaanite kings of the Fourteenth Dynasty, who controlled at least the eastern Delta, allowed southern Egyptian trade to pass through their country. The discovery of a relief from Byblos of "governor Yantinu, son of governor Yakin" with a cartouche of Neferhotpe I {1747–1736} attests that the rulers of Byblos at least nominally acknowledged Neferhotpe as their overlord (SIB 87), and may imply that the vassal relationship between Egypt and Byblos that had existed in the Middle Kingdom continued on through the early Thirteenth Dynasty; the last indications of contact between Thirteenth Dynasty Egypt and Byblos is in the reign of Sobekhotpe IV {1734–1725} and his successor Ya'ib {1721–1712} (SIB 89–90).

This resurgence of Egyptian power was brief, however. Neferhotpe was succeeded by his two brothers, but did not create a long-lasting dynasty (SIB 225–31, 298). During the last thirty-odd years of this period, from roughly 1700 to 1667, over twenty kings seem to have ruled Egypt in the Thirteenth Dynasty, indicating a period of instability and possible collapse of royal power. The military result of this instability and weakness was successful foreign invasions by both the Kushites from the south and the Canaanite Hyksos from the north, who captured the capital at Itjawy and ended the dynasty. Resistance to both Hyksos and Nubian invaders was taken up by the regional Egyptian nomarchs of Thebes, who formed a new Egyptian-controlled government known as the Sixteenth Dynasty {1667–1602}, later succeeded by the Seventeenth Dynasty {1600–1569}, likewise based at Thebes. These two dynasties retained control of much of middle and southern Egypt for nearly a century. Building on this center of military resistance, the Eighteenth Dynasty {1569–1315} would eventually arise, which would defeat both the Hyksos and the Nubians, and reunite Egypt, creating the Egyptian empire of the New Kingdom.

Nubia, Kush, and the Thirteenth Dynasty[5]

During the Middle Kingdom the Nile flood levels were recorded each year at the Semna fortress in Nubia, providing some type of advanced notice on Nile flooding, and hence expected agricultural productivity and the expected tax returns of Egypt. The custom of marking the Nile level continued through the early Thirteenth Dynasty, indicating ongoing Egyptian control and occupation of northern Nubia. An inscription mentions "the commander of the army, Renseneb", who was commander of the Semna fortress (ARE 1:331). A funerary inscription by a deputy treasurer at Abydos describes his mission to inspect the fortresses in Nubia, "in the surrounding foreign lands [of Kush] which rebel" against Egypt. Children of Nubian chiefs were kept and trained at the Egyptian court during this time as quasi-hostages (SIB 93). These texts demonstrate a continued Egyptian military interest in the Nubian fortresses, which is confirmed by Cemetery K at the Buhen fortress which has Egyptian-style burials during the Thirteenth Dynasty (OHAE 207). Diplomatic relations continued between Kush and Egypt; a papyrus details the allotment of provisions for two Nubian chiefs who were escorted to Egypt, perhaps being enlisted as mercenaries (SIB 92). At some point in the late Thirteenth Dynasty, however, Egyptian military dominance of Nubia began to erode. The exact time and circumstances in which the Egyptians withdrew from Nubia are uncertain, but strong Egyptian control seems to have continued through the reign of Sobekhotpe IV {1734–1725}. There may have been an Egyptian campaign to Sai Island south of Semna under Sobekhotpe IV, but the inscription is so damaged that the reading is quite uncertain (AN 119–20, disputed by SIP 90).

With the declining authority and competence of Egyptian kings during the unstable later Thirteenth Dynasty, however, the Egyptian commanders of the Nubian fortresses seem to have become increasingly autonomous, with power devolving into the hands of the garrison commanders who passed their offices and authority on from father to son. The fortresses became progressively more self-supporting and independent, with intermarriage between Egyptian soldiers and Nubian women, and growing reliance on Nubian mercenaries, blurring the cultural and ethnic distinction between the garrison troops and the Nubians and Kushites they were meant to defend Egypt against (BI 72–6, 83–5).

There have been a number of suggestions concerning the cause of the Egyptian loss of the Nubian fortresses.[6] The Nubian provinces may have been intentionally abandoned due to high costs and declining state revenues. Indeed two of the Nubian frontier fortresses – Semna South and Serra East – were abandoned during the last decades of the Middle Kingdom (SIP 91). Egyptian troops may have been withdrawn to face mounting danger from the Canaanite Hyksos in the Delta. On the other hand, Egyptian garrisons, finding themselves isolated and neglected by the kings of the collapsing Thirteenth Dynasty may have made a separate peace with the king of Kush to the south. However this may be, the Kushites captured some of the fortresses by siege or assault; Buhen, for example, was clearly burned and sacked. It is possible that the Kushite alliance and dynastic marriage with the Canaanite Thirteenth Dynasty in the delta (see pp. 462–3), which began by least 1720 and probably continued through 1680, might have strengthened the military position of the Kushite kings sufficiently to allow them to attack Egyptian Nubia.

The Kushite king marked his victory with an Egyptian-style stele, depicting himself with bow, mace, and the crown of Upper Egypt (BI 84).

None of these explanations are mutually exclusive: it may well be that the garrisons were neglected and weakened during the late Thirteenth Dynasty, allowing the Kushites to capture several forts by assault after which the others surrendered on terms. It is clear from tomb inscriptions of the Sobekemhab officer family at Buhen that, after the fall of Buhen, some of the surviving former Egyptian garrison troops and officers enlisted in the army of the king of Kush, and remained on garrison duty in the partially ruined Buhen fortress, from which they undertook military operations for Nejeh {1650?–1630?}, king of Kush. The fall of the Nubian fortresses probably occurred in the 1660s – at the time of the final collapse of the Thirteenth Dynasty and the rise of the Hyksos in the Delta. Thereafter, the fortresses remained in Nubian hands until the reconquest by Kamose of Thebes {1571–1569}. Nubia thus remained part of the Kushite kingdom for nearly a century (BI 80–5).

Fourteenth (Canaanite) Dynasty
{1788–1667} (SIP 94–117)

During the Twelfth Dynasty there was a slow but steady peaceful migration of Semitic peoples from Canaan into the eastern Delta. The Egyptians knew these peoples generically as ʿ3mw, perhaps pronounced roughly as *Amu*; they are probably to be related to the contemporaneous migration of the Semitic Amorites throughout Syria, Canaan, and Mesopotamia in the nineteenth century. The exact relationship between the Canaanites and the Egyptians in the Delta are vague. Some of the Canaanites undoubtedly remained semi-nomads. Others became integrated into Egyptian society. Some seem to have served the Egyptians as mercenaries or officials. It is clear, however, that many retained their separate cultural and linguistic identity, forming a significant and growing minority in the population of the Delta (SIP 293–4).

Sometime late in the reign of Amenemhet III {1843–1797}, or during the reign of Amenemhet IV {1798–1790} or Sobekneferu {1790–1786}, the Canaanites seem to have become at least semi-autonomous, as implied by the fact that there is no evidence for Egyptian expeditions to the Sinai and Byblos during the last decades of the Middle Kingdom – a fact that could be explained by an independent state in the Delta cutting Egyptian land and sea access to the Sinai and Canaan. Exactly when and how full independence was eventually achieved remains unclear. Low Nile floods late in the Twelfth Dynasty may have contributed to economic decline and political instability (OHAE 169), which may have facilitated the rise of independence among the Delta Canaanites. It may simply have been that a Delta nomarch took charge of local affairs as the central authorities proved increasingly incapable or unwilling to deal with growing problems.

However this may be, sometime around 1788 a Canaanite leader, Yakbim {1788?–1770?},[7] asserted full independent authority at Avaris (modern Tell el-Dab'a;

EAE 1:351–4; AEA 240) in the north-eastern Delta, inaugurating the Fourteenth Dynasty {1788–1667}, the first non-Egyptian dynasty to rule in Egypt. The Canaanite origin of this dynasty is confirmed by both the Semitic names of its rulers, and the Canaanite archaeological remains in the eastern Delta during this period (SIP 99–100). Although the exact nature of this transition is uncertain, there was clearly a military component in the Dynasty's rise to independence. Fifty percent of the male burials from this period at Avaris included weapons burials, with bronze daggers of the Middle Bronze IIA style from Canaan (SIP 76, 295); since many of the tombs had been plundered; the actual number of burials with weapons was undoubtedly higher, perhaps almost universal. This clearly indicates an important military component among the Canaanite population in the Delta. These weapons burials could be explained by Canaanite mercenaries in Egyptian service who eventually usurped independent power and formed their own dynasty. On the other hand, it is also possible, if not likely, that local Canaanites living in the Delta called upon their relatives from Canaan to come to Egypt and help in their efforts at independence, creating an additional influx of Canaanite warriors into the Delta at the time the Fourteenth Dynasty rose to independence. Broadly speaking, developments in the Delta may have some parallels to the rise to power of Germanic warlords and mercenaries in fourth- and fifth-century Rome:[8] a combination of peaceful migration, mercenary service, the rise to power of semi-independent mercenary warlords, militant migration, and finally the creation of a fully independent state controlled by the former mercenaries.

Within a few years the first king of the Fourteenth Dynasty, Yakbim, had conquered or otherwise come to dominate the entire eastern Delta, and possibly some of the western Delta as well. The precise boundaries of the Fourteenth Dynasty kingdom cannot be determined with certainty due to the scarcity of monuments and contemporary documents. Their control over the eastern Delta is clear from Canaanite archaeological remains. The minimalist interpretation maintains that this was the full extent of their domain. The maximalist view, however, asserts that they might also have held some type of hegemony over much of the western Delta and southern Canaan (SIP 77, 103). Yakbim's first three successors are little more than names: Ya'ammu, Qareh and 'Ammu, ruling from perhaps 1770 to 1740.

The tomb of the Deputy Treasurer of the Fourteenth Dynasty, Aamu, at the Dynasty's capital of Avaris, reflects the military culture of the age. The tomb included the sacrificial burial of five donkeys and three humans (I = OHAE 191). A bronze dagger and battle-axe were also discovered in the tomb, emphasizing the martial interests of the rulers. The burial with the ruler of donkeys rather than horses probably indicates that the horse-drawn war-chariot had not yet been introduced into Egypt in the early eighteenth century (SIP 104–5).

The discovery of dozens of scarab seals with the names of Fourteenth Dynasty rulers and officials provides insight into their foreign relations. Seal discoveries range from Nubia and Egypt to northern Canaan and Syria, and are thought to indicate the range of diplomatic and trade relationships (SIP 105–12). The connection with the kingdom of Kush in the central Sudan was important. Numerous Fourteenth Dynasty seals have been discovered at the Kushite capital of Kerma, indicating ongoing trading and diplomatic relations, perhaps by river with the permission of the Thirteenth Dynasty, or perhaps over the difficult desert trails via the western oases. It seems likely that the Canaanite kings of the Fourteenth Dynasty and the kings of Kush established a long-term alliance against the Egyptian Thirteenth Dynasty, as we find better documented in the later Hyksos period (ANET 232, 555). When – or even if – this alliance resorted to war with the Thirteenth Dynasty of Egypt is uncertain. The alliance was cemented by at least one dynastic marriage, that of king Sheshi {1730?–1710?} to the Kushite queen Tati (SIP 114–15, 252–4). Sheshi's successor, his son by this Kushite queen, was named Nehsy – "the Nubian" (SIP 115), who came to the throne around 1710. Diplomatic relations, and perhaps a military alliance, between Kush and the Canaanite Fourteenth Dynasty continued at least through the reign of Ya'qub-Har {1680s?}, whose seals have been found in Kush (SIB 300). After around 1710 the Thirteenth Dynasty was plagued by several decades of ephemeral kings with short reigns. The brief rule might indicate some type of rotating kingship, co-regency, or political instability with frequent coups. There is also evidence, however, for famine and mass burials from this period – perhaps the victims of plagues or war – which might indicate that the frequent change in kingship and brief reigns was due to an epidemic (SIP 300–1). At any rate, the dynasty was seriously weakened by 1667 when it was overthrown by rival Canaanites known as the Hyksos, who formed the Fifteenth Dynasty {1667–1558}.

The establishment of Hyksos hegemony {1667}[9]

This study comes to a close with the Hyksos invasion of the Delta and conquest of Avaris and Memphis around 1667. This date is chosen because it is generally assumed that the horse and the war-chariot were introduced into Egypt by the Hyksos, though the introduction could have occurred somewhat earlier under the Canaanite kings of the Fourteenth Dynasty (LA 6:1130–5). The introduction of the horse and the war-chariot created a military revolution in Egypt and throughout the Near East, which I hope will be the subject of a future study.

Notes

Introduction

1 Michael S. Neiberg, *Warfare in World History* (London and New York: Routledge, 2001), 9–20. Scholars now tend to replace traditional chronological markers AD and BC with CE (current era) and BCE (before the current era). Both systems still mark the transition between AD/CE and BC/BCE at the traditional year of the birth of Christ.

2 Charles Messenger (editor), *Reader's Guide to Military History* (London: Fitzroy Dearborn, 2001). See p. xxviii for a chronological listing; ancient Egypt {to 330 BCE}, pp. 151–2; ancient Near East {1000–500 BCE}, pp. 444–5. There is also one entry on China {1600 BCE – 906 CE}, pp. 96–8, and another on South Asia {to 1000 CE}, pp. 553–4.

3 Gerard Chaliand (editor), *The Art of War in World History: From Antiquity ot the Nuclear Age* (Berkeley: University of California Press, 1994), 49–60.

4 Christon I. Archer, John R. Ferris, Holger H. Herwig and Timothy Travers, *World History of Warfare* (Lincoln: University of Nebraska Press, 2002), 1–29; pages 29–61 cover ancient Persia, China and India.

5 Nine of eleven pages devoted to the ancient Near East in Chaliand's *The Art of War in World History* are on the battle of Kadesh, two are from Deuteronomy. Of the twenty-nine pages on ancient Near Eastern military history in Archer *et al.*, *World History of Warfare*, six (14–19) retell the battle of Kadesh. Likewise, Arther Ferrill, in his useful *Origins of War* (OW) devotes ten of his thirty-one pages on the pre-Assyrian Near East period to Kadesh and Megiddo.

6 For background to archaeological dating techniques and other methods, see the relevant articles in Brian Fagan, *Oxford Companion to Archaeology* (Oxford University Press, 1996), EAE 1:104–9; for radiometric dating and its use in archaeology, see EA 2:113–17. For an introduction to issues specific to ancient Near Eastern chronologies, see CANE 2:651–4; EAE 1:264–8; DANE 73; CAM 16.

7 There are several other highly technical forms of dating which are not discussed here; see EA 2:115–17.

8 EAE 1:264–8; for more technical details, see Robert Ehrich (editor), *Chronologies in Old World Archaeology*, 2 vols, 3rd edn (Chicago: University of Chicago Press, 1992). Dates for Mesopotamian rulers and dynasties are conveniently collected in chronological charts by Roux in AI 500–15, which I have followed. DANE, ANE, CAM, C1/2 and C2/1 all also follow the Middle Chronology, with some slight variations.

9 The Epipaleolithic was formerly called the Mesolithic ("Middle Stone" Age), a term still in use in some publications.

10 EAE 1:260–1, 360–3, 448–58; EA 2:130–3, 3:37–81.

11　In general, see CANE 4:2097–486: Sumerian (CANE 4:2107–16; EA 5:92–5), Akkadian (EA 1:44–9); Egyptian (CANE 4:2135–51; EAE 2:258–7); Hittite (CANE 2367–78; EA 3:81–4); Eblaite (EA 2:184–6).

12　CANE 4:2161–79; EA 2:86–9, 4:516–27, 5:352–8.

13　For an insightful discussion, contextualizing the issue in the broader range of intellectual history of the study of warfare, see John Keegan, *A History of Warfare* (New York: Alfred Knopf, 1993), 3–60, 386–92.

Chapter One

1　Some scholars suggest that war-like behavior can be found among some primates, CB 77–86; FA 20–37, and the interesting bibliography cited on FA pp. 217–8.

2　The differences between these four categories relate to both size and social organization. *Band* = egalitarian, up to several dozen people; *tribe* = egalitarian, informal leadership, up to a few thousand; *chiefdom* = formal leadership, social stratification and rank, up to tens of thousands; *state* = central government, laws, stratification, ability to enforce obedience, up to hundreds of thousands (WBC 26–7).

3　Brian Ferguson and Neil Whitehead (editors), *War in the Tribal Zone: Expanding States and Indigenous Warfare* (Santa Fe: School of American Research Press, 1992) examine warfare between "tribes" and "states".

4　For general introductions to the Neolithic period in Mesopotamia, see Hans J. Nissen, *The Early History of the Ancient Near East, 9000–2000 BC* (Chicago: University of Chicago Press, 1988); Charles Keith Maisels, *The Emergence of Civilization: From Hunting and Gathering to Agriculture, Cities, and State in the Near East* (London: Routledge, 1990).

5　For a discussion of Bronze Age nomads and their military significance, see pp. 155–7.

6　EA 4:1–15; CANE 3:1503–21, with full bibliographies to technical studies.

7　CH; EA 1:438–40; DANE 66–7; CAM 43–6; CAM 43–6; OW 30.

8　CH 171, §54, 61–4; xiii; AANE §14; for clear and detailed photographs see Astrid Nunn, *Die Wandmalerei und der Glasierte Wandschmuck im Alten Orient* (Leiden: Brill, 1988), plates 4–6, 20–29.

9　Mircea Eliade (editor), *The Encyclopedia of Religion* (New York: Macmillan, 1995), 4:199–200, 5:455–6.

10　EA 2:448–9, 1:124–5; ET 117–18; PA 151–65.

11　AS 14–98; ED 45–74. The most important Neolithic sites in Syria are Abu Hureyra (Tel Haror) (EA 2:474–6; AS 25–31, 57–9, 72–6); Bouqras (EA 1:354; AS 120–46); Jayrud (AS 27–8); Jerf al-Ahmar (AS 27–8); Mureybet (EA 4:65–6; AS 31–2, 49–52); Tell Halula (AS); Tell Sabi Abyad (AS 64–7, 112–114).

12　I. Hijjara, *The Halaf Period in Northern Mesopotamia* (London, 1997); AS 99–180; EA 2:460–2, 5:251–2; DANE 137–8, 304–5.

13　ALB 35–58; major Neolithic sites in modern Israel, Palestine, and Jordan include: Ain Ghazal (EA 1:36–8); Basta (EA 1:279–80); Jericho (EA 3:220–4); Nahal Oren (EA 4:89–90); Yiftahel (EA 5:378–9).

14　ALB 40–2; EA 3:220–4; DANE 160; M= CAM 32.

15　PAE 44–83; E. Carter, and M. Stolper, *Elam: Surveys of Political History and Archaeology* (Berkeley: University of California, 1984); W. Hinz, *The Lost World of Elam: Recreation of a Vanished Civilization* (London: Sidgwick and Jackson, 1972); EA 4:277–81.

16　Summaries and bibliographies found in PAE 45–83; EA 5:106–10.

17　PAE 69–71, 79–81; EA 3:406–9; DANE 22.

18　Barbara Adams and Krzysztof Cialowicz, *Protodynastic Egypt* (Buckinghamshire: Shire Egyptology, 1997); EBP; EE; EAE 3:61–5; LA 6:1069–76; DAE 226–8.

19   WBC 37; F. Wendort, "Site 117: A Nubian Final Palaeolithic Graveyard near Jebel Sahaba, Sudan", in F. Wendorf (ed.) *The Prehistory of* Nubia, 2 vols (Dallas: Southern Methodists University Press, 1968), 2:954–95.

20   Nissen, *The Early History of the Ancient Near East*; EA 3:476–9; CAM 18–41; M = CAM 43, 49.

Chapter Two

1   EHA 39–128; EM; AI 66–84; Charles Maisels, *The Emergence of Civilization* (London and New York: Routledge, 1990).

2   FC 10–16; EA 5:294–8; CAM 60; DANE 312–3.

3   An alternative title for many Sumerian rulers was *ensi*, perhaps "steward"; the term originally referred to the mortal ruler's role as representative and steward of the patron god of the city who was the real ruler. Its meaning was somewhat ambiguous, because an *ensi* of the god was supreme ruler on earth, but an *ensi* might also be a representative or steward for another earthly ruler (EM 260–74).

4   PAE 67–9; AFC 22–4.

5   FI; CAM 72–3; EA 4:509–12; DANE 85–6.

6   AFC 22; AM §18; AAM §14; AANE §228; SDA 75; AW 1:118. Some scholars interpret both figures as the Priest-king in two different phases of the hunt.

7   P. Hunter, *The Royal Hunter: Art of the Sasanian Empire* (New York: The Asia Society, 1978); the biblical hunter-king Nimrod is probably part of this tradition, Genesis 10.8–12.

8   Guillermo Algaze, *The Uruk World System: The Dynamics of Expansion of Early Mesopotamian Civilization* (Chicago: University of Chicago Press, 1993); ME 53–86; AS 181–201; HE1 14–18; PAE 52–71.

9   T. Jacobsen, *The Sumerian Kinglist* (Chicago: University of Chicago, 1939); a translation can be found in KS 328–31, which I will generally cite; an abridged translation of the antediluvian and proto-historic kings can be found in ANET 265–6; P. Michalowski, "History as Charter: Some Observations on the Sumerian King List", *Journal of the American Oriental Society*, 103 (1983); CANE 4:2350; C1/2:105–109. Readers of Italian can consult G. Pettinato, *I re di Sumer I: Iscrizioni reali presargoniche della Mesopotamia* (Brescia: Peideia Editrice, 2003).

10   C1/2:93–144; 238–314; for chronological charts see C1/2:998–9; AI 502–3; RH 60. Archaeological reports on the major excavated Early Dynastic Sumerian city states can be found at: Abu Salabikh (EA 1:9–10); Adab (EA 1:14–15); Eridu (EA 3:258–60); Fara (Shuruppak) (EA 3:301–3); Girsu (EA 3:406–9); Isin (EA 4:186–7); Kish (EA 4:298–300); Lagash (EA 3:406–9); Larsa (EA 4:331–3); Nippur (EA 4:148–52); Tell el-Oueili (EA 4:191–4); Sippar (EA 5:47–9); Tell el-Ubaid (EA 5:251–2); Ur (EA 5:288–91); Uruk (Warka) (EA 5:294–8).

11   AI 122–145; KS 33–72; M = CAM 83; RH 57–9.

12   HTO 341–4; C1/2:110–11; Herman Vanstiphout, *Epics of Sumerian Kings: The Matter of Aratta* (Atlanta: Society of Biblical Literature, 2003).

13   "Bilgames and Agga", EOG 143–8 = ANET 44–7 = CS 1:550–2; the Sumerian has a variant spelling, Bilgames, for Gilgamesh; I have normalized this to the standard English Gilgamesh.

14   Inscriptions, PI 97–101; C1/2:112–13; DANE 309–11; on the archaeology of Ur see EA 5:288–91 and bibliography; on the royal tombs, see RTU and AFC 93–132.

15   Trevor Watkins, "Sumerian Weapons, Warfare and Warriors", *Sumer*, 39/1–2 (1983): 100–2.

16   See cover art; Figure 5a, p. 133; AFC 98–9; AANE §46; AM 72, xi; RTU 44; AW 1:132.

17   Best viewed in AM §64; see also FI §723; cf. AAM §44.

18 A late tablet purporting to be the record of a king Lugalannimmundu of Adab, who claims hegemony over Sumer, describes an unsuccessful revolt of thirteen cities against him. Past scholars have accepted this king as authentic (KS 50–1; C1/2:115), but it is now generally thought to be a late unhistorical literary text.

19 KS 52–6; C1/2:116–20; RH; though I will cite the primary sources from PI, many of the same sources are also found in RH 44–56. Both of these translations will soon be superseded by Douglas Frayne, *Royal Inscriptions of Mesopotamia, Early Periods, Vol. 1: Pre-Sargonic Period (to 2334 B. C.)* (Toronto: University of Toronto Press, forthcoming).

20 PI 33–46; RH; KS 53–6; CH1/2: 117–19.

21 The identity of Enakale as king of Umma in Eanatum's wars is found in PI 55.

22 This stele has been photographed many times, but it is generally only the largest portion, with the chariot and phalanx, that is reproduced in military histories (FA 82; AW 1:135); the stele should be studied in its entirety to fully understand its message. The full stele, with both sides, can be seen in AFC 190–1; the entire obverse is shown in AAM §118. The most detailed photographs are found in AM §66–9, plus AAM §120 for the vultures (from which the stele gets its name) and AAM §121 for the burial mound. See also SDA 134–7. The inscription which fills the background of the stele can be read in PI 33–9. Throughout my discussion I will refer to the photograph with the most detail for the particular point under consideration. See Irene Winter, "After the Battle is Over: The *Stele of the Vultures* and the Beginning of Historical Narrative in the Art of the Ancient Near East", in H. Kessler and M Simpson (editors), *Pictorial Narrative in Antiquity and the Middle Ages* (Washington, DC, 1985), pp. 11–26.

23 PI 19, 54, 86; AM §43, 70 = AAM §35–8.

24 E3/1:150–1, 154, 166, 175, 178, 180, 189, 197, 199, 201, 206, 208, 212.

25 PI 47–54; RH 28–30; KS 56; C1/2:119.

26 The foreign mercenary are not specifically named, but in the cultural context they could have been Semitic speakers from central and northern Mesopotamia, proto-Gutians from the central Zagros Mountains, or Elamites from south-western Iran. The mention of both Mari and Elam as enemies of Eanatum (PI 42) makes either possible.

27 The Hebrew Bible is strikingly distinct in this regard.

28 Eanatum II {c. 2385–2367} (PI 68); En-entarzi {c. 2367–2350} (PI 68); Lugalanda {7 years; c. 2350–2343} (PI 69–70).

29 PI 70–85; RH 33–6, 51–2; S 58.

30 "Year names" are names given to regnal years of Mesopotamian kings and often mentioned on various administrative tablets. They are generally formulaic – "the year the king built this temple" or "the year the king conquered that city" – but are important sources for military history, since they frequently mention military events. Many of the year names have been collected on the internet at http://cdli.ucla.edu/dl/yearnames/yn_index.htm (accessed 6.7.2005).

31 PI 94–7; RH 33–6; C1/2:143–4, 331; AI 144–5; KS 58–9.

32 AW 1:60–1, 135–6; MW 1: 142–3, 170–1, 2:514. The term sickle-sword is something of a misnomer, since the cutting edge of the weapon is on the outside of the curve, rather than the inside like a sickle. However, I will retain it since it has become the standard term used to describe these weapons.

33 FA 82; AFC 190–1; AW 1:135; SDA 135; AM §66, 68; the details are most clear in SDA 135.

34 WV §13, §17, §32, §35; in AAM § 49 the upper right figure holds an object similar to Eanatum's.

35 AAM §125; the side of the stele, generally not reproduced, shows four men, all of whom seem to be carrying this same type of axe (ME 99).

467

36 There are a number of examples of the curved sickle-axe where the haft and blade cannot be differentiated: FI §540, §763; AANE §410; a bronze statue of a god also holds the same type of curved sickle-axe, Mesopotamia {19C} (SDA 285).

37 Artisitic depictions (FI §794; SDA §380; AAM §G–5, 8); archaeological find: Lagash, {c. 2000} (AW 1:172a); Shechem, Canaan, {19C} (AW 1:172d); Byblos {19C} (AW 1:172c); MW 142–3.

38 Elam: artistic, FI §763, SDA §383, EM 20, PAE 319. Syria: artistic, FI §169, AANE §448; archaeological, Byblos {19C} AW 1:172c. Canaan: artistic, FI §872, GG §31a; archaeological, Shechem {19C} AW 1:172d. Egypt: archaeological, Abydos {18C} (AW 1:172b).

39 PAE 87–100; ME 90–6; C1/2:644–7; for Neolithic Elam, see pp. 30–32. Elam is the ancient name for the modern province of Khuzistan in south-western Iran.

Chapter Three

1 R2; LKA; M. Liverani (editor), *Akkad, the First World Empire* (Winona Lake, IN: Eisenbrauns, 1993); C1/2:417–54; AI 146–60; CANE 2:831–42; EA 1:49–54; M = CAM 97.

2 R2:7–39; LKA 33–172; C1/2:417–34; DANE 251–2.

3 The chronology of Sargon's campaigns is uncertain; I here follow the suggestions of Frayne in R2.

4 Prisoners in precisely such neck stocks are found in Akkadian martial art, AM §118.

5 Campaigns in Elam: R2:22–7; PAE 100–3; ME 97–100; C1/2:432–3.

6 AM §114–5; the figure of Sargon in the Susa stele looks very similar to the famous bronze head of an Akkadian king (AM §xxii–xxiii).

7 Some scholars believe that the cultic list of cities in a hymn of En-hude-ana, high priestess and daughter of Sargon, represents the extent of Sargon's empire; see discussion and bibliography in R2:7.

8 E2:224; LKA 83, 137–9, 185, 305, 316, 321.

9 R2:40–73; C1/2:437–40.

10 The closeness of the figures for captive and expelled may indicate that the two categories are the same: those who were expelled were made slaves.

11 This insertion comes from a parallel inscription, R2:58.

12 Meluhhans are also said to have participated in an Elamite coalition against Naram-Sin, LKA 251. On Meluhha, see D. Potts, "The Road to Meluhha," *JNES* 41 (1982): 279–88; further references in LKA 251 n. 12; DANE 152–3; CANE 3:1456–9.

13 R2:74–83; C1/2:437–40; PAE 106; ME 103–5.

14 R2:84–181; LKA 173–331; C1/2:440–5; AI 156–8; DANE 206–7.

15 S. Tinney, "A New Look at Naram-Sin and the Great Rebellion," *JCS* 47 (1995): 1–14.

16 A later literary epic recounting the rebellion is found in LKA 225–61, providing interesting insights on the martial mentality; poetic lists of the city-states in the rebellion can be found on LKA 241–5, 249–53.

17 There is no firm chronology for the campaigns of Naram-Sin's reign; this outline is simply one option.

18 This is based on Frayne's reading of some obscure characters (R2:90). A later literary account of this campaign can be found in LKA 176–87.

19 For the remarkable archaeological discoveries at Ebla confirm the destruction of the city by the Akkadians, DANE 98–9; EA 2:181–3; AS 277–82; see further discussion at pp. 241–4.

20 AAM §125; AFC 192; SDA 174a; AANE §361. L. Nigro, "The Two Steles of Sargon: Iconography and Visual Propaganda at the Beginning of Royal Akkadian Relief", *Iraq*

60 (1998): 1–18; L. Nigro, "Visual Role and Ideological Meaning of the Enemies in the Royal Akkadian Relief", in J. Prosecky (editor), *Intellectual Life in the Ancient Near East* (Prague, 1998), 283–97.

21 Only two soldiers are visible from the usually reproduced front view. All five can be seen from the side view, reproduced in ME 99.

22 AM §114; AAM §138; SDA 172, 174; AW 1:151a; AANE §362.

23 AM §117; AW 1:151b; AANE §359; AAM §134–5 shows the two pieces side-by-side.

24 AM §122–3; AFC 196; AAM §155–6; SDA 176–7; AW 1:150; this should be compared with 5 in the list on p. 87.

25 AAM §153; SDA 175; AANE §360.

26 AM §118–19; AAM §136–7; the original form of the stele is reconstructed in ME 108 and AFC 204.

27 AM §xxii–xxiii; AANE §48; AAM §154; SDA 171–3; AFC 194.

28 R. Miller, E. McEwen, and C. Bergman, "Experimental Approaches to Ancient Near Eastern Archery", *World Archaeology*, 18/2 (1986): 178–95; E. McEwen, R. Miller, and C. Bergman, "Early Bow Design and Construction", *Scientific American*, 264/6 (June 1991): 76–82.

29 AW 1:6–8, 46–8, 62–4, 80–3, 150–1.

30 Y. Yadin, "The Earliest Representation of a Siege Scene and a 'Scythian Bow' from Mari", *Israel Exploration Journal*, 22/3 (1972): 89–94.

31 OW 40; FA 94, 97; EAA 180.

32 AS 133; D. Collon, "Hunting and Shooting", *Anatolian Studies*, 33 (1983): 51–56, pl. xviii.

33 AW 1:118; SDA 75; AANE §228; AFC 22; AM §18.

34 Yadin, "The Earliest Representation"; AFC §99

35 HE2:128–9; P. Michalowski, "Foreign Tribute to Sumer during the Ur III Period", *Zeitschrift für Assyriologie*, 68 (1978), 36.

36 Barry Eichler, "Of Slings and Shields, Throw-Sticks and Javelins", *Journal of the American Oriental Society*, 103 (1983): 95–102, gives an excellent review of the philological problems surrounding interpreting ancient Near Eastern technical military terms. Astour, HE2:128–132, follows Eichler's interpretation.

37 Brigitte Groneberg, "*Tilpānu* = Bogen", *Revue d'Assyriologie*, 81 (1987): 115–24.

38 In each case I will give the approximate length of the strung undrawn bow based on the proportional relation to the body of the man holding the bow, assuming the average man is 165 cm tall, a height derived from the height of the mummies of contemporary Egyptian warriors (SSN 7; see pp. 438–40).

39 AW 1:150; SDA 176–7; AAM §156; AANE §49; AM 122–3; FA 96.

40 The two can be compared side-by-side in AAM §156–7.

41 AFC §150 has the largest and clearest reproduction; see also FI §641; AM §113a.

42 AW 1:151; SDA 174; AAM §134; AM §117; AANE §359.

43 Since the data is limited, and the categories and military systems overlapping, I have combined a discussion of the Akkadian and Neo-Sumerian military systems here; much of this discussion also applies to Chapter Four.

44 MAS 27; Benno Landsberger, "Remarks on the Archive of the Soldier Ubarum", *JCS* 9/4 (1955): 121–31.

45 For the archive of Umma, see USP; specifically military records are found at USP 15–17; however, the non-military parts of the archive still illustrate the detail and complexity of the logistical system of the Sumerians and Akkadians.

46 J. S. Cooper (editor), *The Return of Ninurta to Nippur* (Rome, 1978).

47 My translation is a synthesis of R3/1:92–3 and E. J. Wilson, *The Cylinders of Gudea: Transliteration, Translation, and Index* (Neukirchen-Vluyn: Verlag Butzon, 1996), pp. 149–52.

48 R2:182–208; C1/2:454–61.

Chapter Four

1 For background on the Amorites, see pp. 155–9.

2 CAH 1/2:454–63; ME 119–21; DANE 135; RA 3:708–20; R. Henrickson, "A Regional Perspective on Godin III Cultural Development in Central Western Iran", *Iran* 24 (1986):23.

3 A letter of a farmer describes the devastation to his farm caused by Gutian raids: S. Smith, "Notes on the Gutian Period," *JRAS* (1932):295 ff.

4 The Umman-Manda appear in the Naram-Sin epics as a rather obscure but powerful enemy of Naram-sin. It is unclear if they are an ethnic group or a place-name. They are perhaps best understood more generically like the English term "horde", meaning a vast barbarian army (see LKA 265–6 for discussion and bibliography).

5 The epic "Cuthean Legend" or "Naram-Sin and the Enemy Hordes" (LKA 263–331) is set in the reign of Naram-Sin, but is generally thought to reflect memories of the fall of Akkad under his successors.

6 R3/1; DANE 134; AI 166–8.

7 There are occasional scenes of gods or kings enthroned holding weapons: AAM §201; AFC §317; AANE §404.

8 PAE 122–8; ME 122–3; C1/2:652–4; his name means the "protégé of [the Elamite god] Inshushinak", in an Akkadian and Elamite form of the name. A stele of Puzur-Inshushinak from Susa shows him with Akkadian-style regalia, AAM §158.

9 R2:280–96; Romer, W. "Zur Siegesinschrift des Konigs Utuhegal von Unug," *Orientalia* 54 (1985):274–88.

10 C1/2:595–631; AI 161–78; M = CAM 102.

11 R3/2:9–89; LC 13–22; C1/2:595–631; DANE 312.

12 R3/2:12–14, 21, 39, 41; ANET 523b.

13 On the background of the Amorites, see pp. 155–9.

14 R3/2:20; Samuel Kramer, "The Death of Ur-Nammu and His Descent to the Netherworld," *JCS* 21 (1967).

15 R3/2:91–234; DANE 270–1; C1/2:585–623; CANE 2:842–57; I follow the chronology established in R3/2:92–110, assuming that Year One of Shulgi is 2094 BC.

16 W. Hallo, "Simurrum and the Hurrian Frontier," *Revue Hittite et Asianique*, 36 (1978): 71–83; based on the year names the three Hurrian wars were in 2070–2067, 2063–2061 and 2052–2046; on the Hurrians, see pp. 303–7.

17 R3/2:235–84; C1/2:607–9.

18 P. Steinkeller, "The Administrative and Economic Organization of the Ur III State: The Core and Periphery", in M. Gibson and R. Biggs (editors), *The Organization of Power* (Chicago: Oriental Institute, 1987), 19–41; HE2:87–8; M = CAM 102.

19 On this alliance and the subsequent military campaign see R3/2:287–90 and 296–300; unattributed quotations in this section are to the latter inscription; see Piotr Michalowski, "Bride of Simanum", *Journal of the American Oriental Society*, 95 (1975): 716–19.

20 On the Hurrians, see pp. 303–7; on Tish-atal, see R3/2:457–64.

21 R3/2:191; on Ebih as Jabal Hamrin, see RGTC 2:38.

22 EA 3:186; R. Barnett, "Xenophon and the Wall of Media", *Journal of Hellenic Studies*, 83 (1963): 1–26.

23 DANE 74–5; CAH 1/2:611–17; Thorkild Jacobsen, "The Reign of Ibbi-Suen", *JCS* 7 (1953): 36–47.

24 For sources on spiraling prices and the defections of the city-states, see R3/2:366–7 and the bibliography cited there.

25 MC 243–51; Jacobsen, "Reign of Ibbi-Suen, p. 42.

26 First portion, PH 9; second portion, MC 253–68.

27 On the other hand, this could have reference to a literal flood which devastated southern Mesopotamia (LD 37), which would only have served to compound the economic, social, and military disruption of the era and further weakened Ur.

28 HTO 233–72; Ninurta is war god closely associated with Ningirsu, DANE 214; GDS 138, 142–3.

29 I have removed the refrain "before holy Inanna, before her eyes, they are parading" which recurs after each line in the poem, along with some non-military details of the procession.

30 On oracular dreams in antiquity, see A. Oppenheim, *The Interpretation of Dreams in the Ancient Near East* (Philadelphia: American Philosophical Society, 1956); similarly, Alexander's soothsayer Aristander was an expert at consistently interpreting every omen encountered as favorable to Alexander: e.g. Arrian 1.11.7.

Chapter Five

1 WV §13, 17; E3/1:73; cf. Ezekiel 1, 10, where the Israelite god rides a wheeled celestial chariot. The sun-god Shamash is described as riding his chariot through the sky (EOG 25). Ishtar's celestial chariot – presumably an exalted version of a royal chariot – is described as made "of lapis lazuli and gold, its wheels shall be gold and its horns shall be amber, driving lions in a team and mules of great size" (EG 48). M. Civil, "Išme-Dagan and Enlil's Chariot", *Journal of the American Oriental Society*, 88/1 (1968): 3–14.

2 I will use the term "war-cart" to describe the military vehicles of the Early Bronze Age, to distinguish them from the "chariot", the light, spoked, two-wheeled vehicles of the late Middle Bronze period; a full discussion of the differences between war-cart and chariot is given in this chapter. It is not clear that ancient Near Eastern peoples made this type of distinction.

3 I. Shaw, "Egyptians, Hyksos and military technology: Causes, effects or catalysts?", in A. J. Shortland (editor), *The Social Context of Technological Change, Egypt and the Near East, 1650–1550 BC* (Oxford: Oxbow Books, 2001), 59–71, discussed at 60–2; EAE 3:452.

4 Richard Bulliet, *The Camel and the Wheel* (Cambridge, MA: Harvard University Press, 1975); likewise, although the principle of the wheel was widely known in Pre-Columbian Mesoamerica, there is no evidence that wheeled vehicles were used (EWT 14–5), perhaps because of the lack of an adequate draft animal.

5 A. Schulmann, "Chariots, Chariotry and the Hyksos", *Journal of the Society for the Study of Egyptian Antiquities*, 10 (1980): 105–53; Shaw, "Egyptians, Hyksos and military technology."

6 I will use the term "equid" to refer to any of the species or hybrid species of the genus *equus* known in the Bronze Age Near East, including donkeys, onagers, onager–donkey hybrids, mules or horses. The linguistic and artistic ambiguities of our third millennium evidence often make precision and certainty in distinguishing the species difficult. Nicholas Postgate, "The Equids of Sumer, Again", in R. Meadow and Hans-Peter Uerpmann (editors), *Equids in the Ancient World*, vol. 1 (Wiesbaden: Ludwig Reichert Verlag, 1986) 1:194–206.

7 Evidence for horses equipped with bits comes from Dereivka in the Ukraine in the early fourth millennium, and from Botai in the northern steppes of Kazakhstan in the late fourth millennium, leading some scholars to argue for domestication and horse-riding in the fourth millennium steppe: David Anthony, "The Domestication of the Horse", in R. Meadow and Hans-Peter Uerpmann (editors), *Equids in the Ancient World*, vol. 2 (Wiesbaden: Ludwig Reichert Verlag, 1991) 2:250–77; D. Anthony and D. Brown, "The origins of horseback riding", *Antiquity*, 246 (1991): 22–38, and "The

opening of the Eurasian steppe at 2000 BCE", in Victor H. Mair (editor), *The Bronze Age and Early Iron Age Peoples of Eastern Central Asia*, vol. 1 (Washington D.C.: The Institute for the Study of Man, 1998). See also the webpage of the Institute for Ancient Equestrian Studies, http://users.hartwick.edu/iaes (accessed 7 July 2005). This evidence is, however, ambiguous and inconclusive, and a third millennium date appears more likely: see Marsha Levine, "The origins of horse husbandry on the Eurasian Steppe", in Marsha Levine *et al.* (editors), *Late Prehistoric Exploitation of the Eurasian Steppe* (Cambridge: McDonald Institute, 1999); Marsha Levine, "Botai and the origins of horse domestication", *Journal of Anthropological Archaeology*, 18 (1999): 29–78, and her "Domestication, Breed Diversification and Early History of the Horse" at http://www2.vet.upenn.edu/labs/equinebehavior/hvnwkshp/hv02/levine.htm (accessed 7 July 2005). Basically, the bit is not conclusive evidence of horse-riding, since a horse can be given a bit for other purposes; nor is horse-riding alone evidence for military equestrianism. To further complicate the problem it must be remembered that horses can be ridden without bridle or saddle, and hence the absence of riding accoutrements is not evidence for the absence of horse-riding. Here I will focus on the more limited question of military equestrianism in the Bronze Age Near East.

8   EEH 117–19; D. Owen, "The 'first' equestrian: an Ur III glyptic scene", *Acta Sumer-ologica*, 13 (1991):259–71; P. Moorey, "Pictorial evidence for the history of horse-riding in Iraq before the Kassites", *Iraq*, 32 (1970): 36–50; Augusto Azzaroli, *An Early History of Horsemanship* (Leiden: Brill, 1985); R. Meadows and H. Uerpmann (editors), *Equids in the Ancient World*, 2 vols (1986–1991); A. R. Schulman, "Representations of Horsemen and Riding in the New Kingdom", *JNES*, 16 (1957): 263–7; LA 4:1009–13.

9   Robert Drews, *Early Riders: The Beginnings of Mounted Warfare in Asia and Europe* (New York: Routledge, 2004); an east Asian perspective is given by Nicola Di Cosmo, *Ancient China and its Enemies: the Rise of Nomadic Power in East Asian History*, (Cambridge: Cambridge University Press, 2002). David Anthony argues, unconvincingly to me, that mounted warfare on the steppe occurred in the fourth millennium, and that chariot warfare developed after the rise of mounted warfare: "Early Horseback Riding and Warfare in the Steppes," http://users.hartwick.edu/iaes/.

10 Cavalry divisions were used in many regular armies throughout World War Two: Janusz Piekalkiewicz, *The Cavalry of World War II, 1939–1945* (Harrisburg PA: Historical Times, 1979). Horses and mules were also still used extensively for transportation in World War Two: the average German infantry division in 1939 had 4000–6000 horses; the Germans employed 625,000 horses for their invasion of Russia in 1941. The Soviet army used an incredible 21 million horses during all of World War Two, two thirds of which died: I. Dear (editor), *The Oxford Companion to World War II*, (Oxford: Oxford University Press, 1995), 37–8. Even in the late twentieth century mules and donkeys were still being used for the covert transportation of arms to Afghan rebels fighting the Soviet Union: George Crile, *Charlie Wilson's War: The Extraordinary Story of the Largest Covert Operation in History* (New York: Atlantic Monthly Press, 2003). Despite the widespread mechanization of modern armies, it is likely that the limited use of horses and mules for highly specialized military transport needs will continue into the foreseeable future.

11 Keith H. Beebe, *The Dromedary Revolution* (Claremont CA: Institute for Antiquity and Christianity, 1990); EA 1:407–8.

12 AW 1:37–40, 128–39; WV 13–36; Wolfram, Nagel, *Die mesopotamische Streitwagen und seine Entwicklung im ostmediterranen Bereich* (Berlin: Berliner Beiträge zur Vor- und Frühgeschichte 10, 1966); J. Crouwel, *Chariots and Other Means of Land Transport in Bronze Age Greece* (Amsterdam: Allard Pierson Museum, 1981); EA 1:485–7.

13 Wheels and a frame of the war-cart were discovered from Kish (AW 1:37; WV §5); a silver terret for holding the reins was found at Ur {ED IIIA, 2550–2400} (RTU 165; AFC 116; AW 1:131; WV §10; SDA 21; AM §83); while a bronze "tire" or casing for the disk wheel for protection and added traction was found at Susa (AW 1:38; WV §19).

14 WV 15–36; AW 1:37–40. In addition to the military examples presented here there are a number of recently published cylinder seals showing ceremonial four-wheeled carts from Tell Beydar {2400–2250} (EEH 116, §5–9), a terracotta model from Kish (WV §4; AW 1:132), and a shell inlay of equids pulling a cart from Nippur (WV §6); none provides any additional military information. In this chapter I will make parenthetical reference to the specific pieces evidence by citing the number assigned in the following lists; e.g. (item 1) refers to source number one.

15 WV 20–2; There is also a terracotta model from Kish {ED II?, 2650–2550} (AW 1:130).

16 WV 14–22; SDA 21; modern illustration: FA 83; Terence Wise and Angus McBride, *Ancient Armies of the Middle East* (London: Osprey, 1981), plate B.

17 AAM §121; for a detailed discussion of the overall meaning of the Stele of the Vultures, see pp. 55–9.

18 Unfortunately, this particular fragment of the stele (the third register) is generally left out of most reproductions; it shows people climbing onto a large mound of corpses with baskets of earth to cover the bodies in a burial mound (AAM §121; AFC 190).

19 Ur-namma {2112–2095} also built a ritual war-cart for the goddess Ninlil during this period, which may be fragmentarily depicted on the Ur-namma Stele (E3/2:17; cf. IYN 26; AFC 445); unfortunately, he did not leave a detailed description of this vehicle.

20 This description is repeated twice in the text (E3/1:73), once when Gudea is commanded by an oracle to build the chariot (lines vi 12–23), and again when he actually builds it (lines vii 13–23). I have merged the most important elements from both passages into one.

21 Based on E3/1:96–7 and Wilson, *Cylinders of Gudea*, 168–70; unfortunately, neither of Gudea's descriptions tell us if the chariot he made had two or four wheels. Based on the contemporary Neo-Sumerian artistic evidence discussed above, we should probably assume it was two-wheeled.

22 Debates about what is a "true" chariot seem sometimes almost to be more about the meaning of the word "true" than the word "chariot".

23 CG 74–120; WV 48–72; EWT; P. Moorey, "The emergence of the light, horse-drawn chariot in the Near East, c. 2000–1500 BC", *World Archaeology*, 18/2 (1986): 196–215; David W. Anthony and Nikolai B. Vinogradov, "Birth of the Chariot", *Archaeology*, 48/2 (1995): 36–41; M. Littauer and J. Crouwel, "The Origin of the True Chariot", *Antiquity*, 70 (Dec. 1996): 934–9; P. Raulwing, *Horses, Chariots, and Indo-Europeans*, Archaeolingua, Series Minor, vol. 13 (Budapest: Archaeolingua Foundation, 2000).

24 R. Miller, E. McEwen and C. Bergman, "Experimental Approaches to Ancient Near Eastern Archery", *World Archaeology*, 18/2 (1986): 178–95.

25 WV 50–5, §28–40; ELH.

26 Three cylinder seals from Karum Kanesh, Anatolia {2000–1850} seem to depict similar, non-military scenes of four-wheeled carts in ritual settings: 1, WV §24; ELH §2; 2, WV §25; ELH §3; 3, FI §727. It is possible that four-wheeled vehicles survived for religious and civic processions after they had disappeared from the battlefield.

27 MM 31–2; MK 159–65.

28 M. Civil, "Išme-Dagan and Enlil's Chariot", *Journal of the American Oriental Society*, 88 (1968):3–14, translation on pages 6–7.

29   Four-wheeled vehicles are *eriqqum* (Sumerian ^{GIŠ}*.mar.gid.da*); the two wheeled vehicle is a *narkabtum* (Sumerian ^{GIŠ}*.gigir*), MM 31. There is not a clear linguistic distinction in terms of the function as opposed to the structure of the vehicle.

Chapter Six

1   Non-Mesopotamian military aristocracies which ruled Mesopotamia at various times over the past four thousand years include the Amorites, Kassites, Achaemenid Persians, Seleucid Greeks, Parthians, Sasanids, Arabs, Daylamites, Selchuq Turks, Mongols, Timurids, Jalayrid Turks, Safavids, Ottoman Turks, and British.

2   AUP; M. Anbar, *Les Tribus Ammorites de Mari*, Orbis Biblicus et Orientalis 108. (Freiburg: Gottingen, 1991); M. Liverani, "The Amorites", *Peoples of the Old Testament World*, D. Wiseman (editor) (Oxford, 1973), pp. 100–33; SHP 37–8, 160–74; DANE 16–17; CANE 1231–42; EANE 1:107–11; M. Streck, *Das amurritische Onomastikon der altbabylonischen Zeit*, (Münster: Ugarit-Verlag, 2000); on the archaeological problems of dealing with archaeology of nomads and semi-nomads, see Roger Cribb, *Nomads in Archaeology*, 2nd edn (Cambridge: Cambridge University Press, 2004).

3   This description is collated from a number of texts given in AUP 92–3, 330–2.

4   DANE 215; EA 4:253–6; Victor Matthews, *Pastoral Nomadism in the Mari Kingdom, c. 1830–1760* (Cambridge MA: American Schools of Oriental Research, 1978).

5   DANE 64; EANE 1:407–8. Keith H. Beebe, *The Dromedary Revolution*, (Claremont, CA: Institute for Antiquity and Christianity, 1990). Richard W. Bulliet, *The Camel and the Wheel*, (New York: Columbia University Press, 1975).

6   Sources cited in Liverani, "Amorites", 104–5.

7   Specific details of the military encounters between the Amorites and Mesopotamians from the Akkadian to Ur III periods have been described in Chapters Three and Four.

8   DANE 156–7; AI 181–5; C1/2:631–43.

9   R4:6–14, IYN 13–21; CAH 1/2:613–17.

10   J. van Dijk, "Ishbi-Erra, Kindattu, l'homme d'Elam, et la chute de la ville d'Ur", *JCS* 30 (1978): 189–208.

11   Year names in IYN; royal inscriptions, nearly all dealing with religion in R4:15–106.

12   FSW, upon which I base my description. Four color maps based on Frayne can be found in CAM 109; the year names have been collected and collated in IYN and LYN. Many Mesopotamian year names can be found online at: http://cdli.ucla.edu/dl/yearnames/yn_index.htm (accessed 8.7.2005).

13   DANE 175; RA 6:500–6; EA 3:331–3; AI 181–5, 199–200; C1/2:631–42.

14   R4:270–316; LYN 37–60; FSW 26–8; C1/2:641–3.

15   EA 1:225–33; ANE 1:81–9.

16   A1:7–46, AR1:1–19, CS 1:463–4. OAC; H. Saggs, *The Might that was Assyria* (London: Sidgwick & Jackson, 1984), 23–34.

17   AR 1:1–8, RLA 6:101–16, CS 1:463–4; OAC 34–40.

18   The chronology of the Old Assyrian kings before Shamshi-Adad is quite uncertain. The dates given here roughly follow AI; OAC 40–3 and CAH 1/2:740–62 give slightly higher dates.

19   Military conquest theories are summarized by OAC 63–71; for Larsen's interpretation see OAC 71–80.

20   A1:47–76; PH; CAH 2/1:1–8; CANE 2:873–83; DANE 264–5; EDS 204–12.

21   OAC 42, EANE 5:188–90.

22   C1/2:636, C2/1:1; AI 190; CANE 2:873.

23   CAH 1/2:762, DANE 264; R4:560.

24 AR 1:18–28; A1:47–76; PH; C2/1:1–8; CANE 2:873–83; DANE 264–5; M = CAM 116.

25 R4:324–31; AI 181–94; C2/1:1–28; PH; M = CAM 120; D. Edzard, *Die "zweite Zwischenzeit" Babyloniens* (Wiesbaden: Harrassowitz, 1957), 122–53.

26 For a summary of our limited knowledge of Sippar during this period, see ASD 1–10.

27 Sabium {1844–1831}; Apil-Sin {1830–1813}; Sin-muballit {1812–1793}, R4:327–31.

28 Primary: R4:332–72, LC 71–142; ANET 269–71; L; Secondary: ANE 1:108–17, CAH 2/1:176–227; CANE 2:901–15; DANE 138–9, WANE 65–6; M. van de Mieroop, *King Hammurabi of Babylon*, (Oxford: Blackwell, 2005).

29 The letters of Zimri-Lim's last years, which provide great detail on military affairs in Mesopotamia, have been recently translated with numerous notes and commentary by Wolfgang Heimpel, *Letters to the King of Mari* (Winona Lake: Eisenbrauns, 2003), cited as L.

30 MK, 1–29; M.-H. Gates, "The Legacy of Mari", *Biblical Archaeologist* 47 (1984).

31 The official title of the rulers of Elam was *sukkalmah*, often translated as "vizier" or "grand regent" (PAE 160–3); for simplicity I will simply translate it as king. On Siwepalar-huppak's reign, see PAE 166–71.

32 PAE 169–71; for more details, see D. Charpin, "Les Elamites á Shubat-Enlil", In *Fragmenta Historiae Elamicae: Melanges Offerts à M. J. Steve*, edited by L. De Meyer (Paris: Editions Recherche sur les Civilisations, 1986), 129–37.

33 I generally follow the translation in LC 76–140, but occasionally prefer ANET 163–80.

34 This perhaps has reference to an inauspicious eclipse on the day of battle. Conversely, Yahweh prolongs daylight to intensify the Israelite victory on the field of Gibeon (Joshua 10.12–15).

35 In this passage the god Zababa serves as Hammurabi's bodyguard ("on my right side"), while Ishtar is Hammurabi's arms bearer; Ishtar is frequently depicted in contemporary art with a mace, axe, and sickle-sword in a quiver on her back.

36 Middle Bronze art relating to war-carts and chariots are discussed in Chapter Five.

37 FI §167, 199, 538, 772, 784; SDA 285.

38 SDA §380, 383; FI §191, 794; AAM G5.

39 R4:372–403, ANET 271; C2/1:220–2; AI 243–4.

40 AI 241–52; RA 5:464–73; EA 3:270–5; DANE 164–5; CANE 2:917–30; J. Brinkman, *Materials and Studies for Kassite History I* (Chicago: Oriental Institute, 1976).

Chapter Seven

1 For general background on Mari see DANE 189–90; CANE 2:885–99; EA 3:413–16, 419–21; MK; MM.

2 Wolfgang Heimpel, *Letters to the King of Mari: A New Translation, with Historical Introduction, Notes, and Commentary* (Winona Lake, IN: Eisenbrauns, 2003), hereafter cited as L. When possible I will cite Heimpel's translation by page number. The standard edition of the tablets, with French translation, is published in the *Archives Royales de Mari*, (Paris, 1950ff), (cited as ARM).

3 MM 36–7; WM 128–38; on Mesopotamian magic and divination in general, see CANE 3:1782–3, 1895–1909, 2013–17, 2071–4; DANE 218–19; MK 112–38.

4 CANE 3:1904–6; MK 127–33; L 656–7 gives a chart with technical terms. Letters reporting the results of extispicy are common in the Mari archive.

5 At the battle of Drepanum in the First Punic War {249}, the Roman commander Claudius Pulcher sailed into battle despite bad auguries and was soundly defeated, Cicero, *De Natura Deorum*, 2.3.

6 Mary Beard, John North and Simon Price, *Religions of Rome*, 2 vols (Cambridge: Cambridge University Press, 1998), 1:21–8, 55–8, 188; 2:205; on the importance of divination and prophecy in Roman Empire, see David Potter, *Prophets and Emperors*, (Cambridge MA: Harvard University Press, 1994).

7 On Greek martial divination, see W. Kendrick Pritchett, *The Greek State at War, Part III: Religion* (Berkeley: University of California Press, 1979).

8 Ammianus Marcellinus, *Res Gestae*, trans. Walter Hamilton, *The Later Roman Empire (A.D. 354–378)* (Penguin, 1986), 25.2.

9 Timothy D. Barnes, *Constantine and Eusebius* (Cambridge, MA: Harvard University Press, 1981), 42–3.

10 In Israel, king David's census to determine the military strength of his new kingdom was condemned as an act of impiety, bringing plague upon Israel, 2 Samuel 24.

11 Heimpel describes these groups in L 34–6, 15–18, and provides an index to all references in L 882–4; MK 142–5.

12 The administrative records of Sippar provide us some insights into military organization in the Old Babylonian state {1894–1595} (ASD 86–116).

13 L 508; MM 15; WM 91; L 578, index, where Heimpel translates this term as "division commander", which to the modern reader sounds like an officer in charge of more than 100 men; I consistently use the term "captain" where Heimpel uses "division commander".

14 L 438, 508; L 586, index; ASD 88, 93; MM 15; WM 91–2; ASD 91–3.

15 W. Hallo, "The Road to Emar", *JCS* 18 (1964): 57–88.

16 §26–38 = ANET 167–8; Meek translates *bā'irum* as "commissary", reflecting his understanding that they were to collect food for the army.

17 Heimpel translates this term as "shock troops" (L 595, index; MM 17); my sense is more of elite troops.

18 Specific passages for armies of 10,000–20,000 can be found in the index in L 599; ARM 1.42.

19 See EA 2:142–4 for discussion and bibliography. A hectare is 100 ares, an are is 100×100 meters, or 10,000 square meters, equivalent of 2.47 acres. Based on ethnoarchaeological studies, scholars have determined a population average of 250 people per hectare (or 100 per acre) in ancient Near Eastern towns. However, some sites might have had a density of as high as 500 people per hectare.

20 In the index on pages 599–601, Heimpel provides a complete list of all numbers mentioned in the texts he translates. Of these, there are fifteen references to armies ranging from 3000 to 6000 men, twenty-four references to armies from 1000 to 2000, thirty-five references to armies from 100 to 1000 men, and twenty-five references to under 100 men.

21 L 383; see also ARM 6.32, 13.54; MM 25; MK 148.

22 By comparison, six jars of wine cost one shekel (L 407); a house could be bought for five shekels (L 412). A captain of 100 men was paid 20 shekels in a campaign season.

23 L 175, 239, 306, 308, 360, 364, 393, 513.

24 Other encounters likewise point to low casualties, fifty in one case (L 342).

Chapter Eight

1 WAM 25–38; AW 1:69–71; RLA 1:471–2; MK 145–7; MM 33–4.

2 FI §749 = Brussels O. 437. It was originally published in L. Speleers, *Catalogue des intaillés et empreintes orientales des Musées Royaux du Cinquantenaire* (Bruxelles, 1917), 213. I would like to thank Professor Doctor Eric Gubel, Senior Keeper in the Antiquity Department of the Royal Museums of Art and History, Brussels, for sharing with me a recent clear digital photo of this seal, which was a great help.

3 Some examples (which could be further multiplied): Durum, R4:42; Isin, R4:79, 92, 103; Dunnum R4:98; Larsa, R4:118, 125, 191; Bad-tibara, R4:176; general R4:253.

4 R4:149, 160, 166, 240, 243.

5 R4:243, with additions from 237; cf. 237–43.

6 WM 173–5, 181 n18, with illustration; O. Neugebauer, *Mathematische Keilschrift-Texte* (Berlin, 1935), 1:149, 182–4; H. Waschow, "Wehrwissenschaft und Mathematik im alten Babylonien", *Unterrichts-blätter für Mathematik und Naturwissenschaften,* 39 (1939), 370; FA 97.

7 This figure of 22 meters for the height of the wall presumably includes the height of the *tell* (since by this time most cities were already on artificial mounds composed of the ruins of former levels of the city), the earthen ramparts built around the city, and the actual brick or stone wall which was built on top of the earthen rampart. Including all three of these elements together makes the target height of the siege ramp reasonable based on archaeological evidence.

8 David Ussishkin, *The Conquest of Lachish by Sennacherib* (Tel-Aviv: Tel Aviv University, Institute of Archaeology, 1982).

9 A device called the *kiskisum* may also have been used in siegecraft, but its precise nature is uncertain (L 364).

10 L 253, 331, 489; WM 156; CAD 1/2:428–9.

11 L 239, 253, 331; WM 156; CAD 3:144–7.

12 The meaning of *xaṭṭassi* is unknown. It is presumably a technical term for part of the siege engines, perhaps the main beam for a ram, or the large heavy corner beams for a tower.

13 AFC 158; Y. Yadin, "The Earliest Representation of a Siege Scene and a 'Scythian Bow' from Mari", *Israel Exploration Journal*, 22/2–3 (1972): 89–94.

14 The exact meaning of the word *lu'u hamannu* is unknown. Heimpel translates it as a "frontal brace", used to support steep packed earthworks (L 458). From the context I see it as some type of earthwork designed to counteract the siege ramp of the enemy, hence my term "counter-ramp". Just such a counter-ramp was discovered at Lachish in Judea, see Ussishkin, *The Conquest of Lachish* (note 8 above).

Chapter Nine

1 AS; SHP; EDS; C1/2:315–62, 532–94; C2/1:1–41, EA 5:123–31; CANE 2:1195–1218; Mark Chavalas, "Ancient Syria: A Historical Sketch", in Mark Chavalas and John Hayes (editors), *New Horizons in the Study of Ancient Syria* (Malibu, CA: Undena Publications, 1992), 1–22.

2 Based on AD; AS 102, 156, 186, 215, 236, 291–2; EDS 43; I use a simplified version here.

3 AS 181–210. Major Chalcolithic sites include: Abu Hureyra, Bouqras, Chagar Bazar (DANE 69–70), Halaf (EA 2:460–2), Mureybit, Tell Brak (EA 1:335–6; AS 185–90).

4 Guillermo Algaze, *The Uruk World System: the Dynamics of Expansion of Early Mesopotamian Civilization* (Chicago: University of Chicago Press, 1993).

5 AS 211–87; EDS 122–33; major archaeological sites of Early Bronze Age Syria include: Aleppo; Byblos; Ebla; Homs; Mari; Qatna; Tell Brak; Tell Chuera (EA 1:149–2); Tell Hamoukar; Tell Leilan (EDS 128–9; EA 3:341–7; DANE 179–80); Tell Mozan.

6 Aleppo (EA 1:63–5), Damascus (EA 2:103–6), Hama (EA 2:466–8), Mari (EA 3:413–17), Qatna (EA 4:35–6), Ugarit (EA 5:255–66); other important Early Bronze fortified sites include Tell Ashara, Tell Chuera (EA 1:491–2), Tell Khoshi, Tell Hamoukar, and Tell Mozan (EA 4:60–3).

7 HE1; HE2; AS 235–46; SHP 21–38; EA 2:180–6; CANE 2:1219–30; DANE 88–9; EDS 134–48; Paolo Matthiae, *Ebla: An Empire Rediscovered* (Garden City, NY:

Doubleday, 1981); Paolo Matthiae *et al.*, *Ebla: alle origini della civilta urbana* (Milan: Electa, 1995).

8 Michael Astour, "The Date of the Destruction of Palace G at Ebla", in Mark Chavalas and John Hayes (editors), *New Horizons in the Study of Ancient* Syria (Malibu, CA: Undena Publications, 1992), 23–40, (and in HE2 58–76) argues that the palace was actually destroyed before the Akkadian invasions.

9 HE1 25, 51–52; the client kingdoms included: Emar, Burman, Ra'aq, Abarsil, Gasur, Hazuwan, Sugurum, Ebal and Manuwat (HE1 32–6).

10 HE1 26–51, M= HE1 27; Giovanni Pettinato, "Bollettino militare della campagna di Ebla contro la citta di Mari", *Oriens Antiquus*, 19 (1980): 231–45; SHP 28 n35.

11 PI 86–9; KS 329; EA 3:413–17; AS 262–7; AFC 135–64; EDS 129–33.

12 PI 86–9; KS 328; HE1 28, 50; CANE 2:1222 the precise dates of these kings of Mari are not known. The six numbered kings are assumed to be those from the Sumerian King-list, where most names are lost but the regnal years survive (KS 328).

13 The god is presumably Ba'al (SAF 146–7), though the precise god may differ in different chronological, regional, cultural and ritual settings (SAF 145–50). Some of the armed figurines are female, probably representing the warrior goddess Ashtarte – Ishtar in Mesopotamia (SAF 145–6). Like Athena of the Greeks, Ashtarte-Ishtar was a goddess of war. For purposes of the study of arms and armor, I will simply call all the figurines gods. Excellent photographs of several of these gods (unfortunately without weapons) are found in AANE §69–73.

14 AFC 157. An eighteenth-century mural painting from Mari has a column of (mostly lost) small soldiers marching beneath the main scene; one of them has a kilt, cape, and some type of bundle hanging from a weapon on his shoulder (SDA 275, 282) – though this has been interpreted as a fisherman carrying a net. The Urnammu stele has a man with a bundle of construction equipment slung from an axe he is carrying on his back (AFC §317). It is likely that hanging bundles from weapons carried on the shoulder was a standard practice, a type of Bronze Age pack.

15 AFC 157–60; AW 1:137–9; SDA 142; AM §75.

16 AFC 158; Y. Yadin, "The Earliest Representation of a Siege Scene and a 'Scythian Bow' from Mari", *Israel Exploration Journal*, 22/2–3 (1972): 89–94.

17 For illustrations see MW 2, figs. 1–58; AW 1:12, 41–2, 60–1, 136–40, 148–9, 156–7.

18 On weapons in third millennium Syria, see MW; warrior burials at Carchemish and Tel Barsip, MW 1:188; metal helmets at Ur, AFC §56; AW 1:49; the golden helmet/ crown of Ur: AM §xvi; AANE §45.

19 See Chapter Four; AS 277–82; SHP 33–35; C1/2:321–7; HE2 78–80.

20 AS 282–7; HE2 164–71; H. Weiss *et al.*, "The Genesis and Collapse of Third Millennium North Mesopotamian Civilization", *Science*, 261 (1993): 995–1004; Nuzhet Dalfes *et al.* (editors), *Third Millennium BC Climate Change and Old World Collapse* (Berlin: Springer Verlag, 1997); more generally, N. Yoffee and J. Clark (editors), *Collapse of Ancient States and Civilizations* (Tucson, TX: University of Arizona Press, 1988).

21 SHP 36–7; HE2 101–33. Ebla (EA 2:180–6); Aleppo (EA 1:63–5); Byblos (EA 1:390–4); Carchemish (EA 1:423–4); Qatna (Tell Mishrifeh) (EA 4:35–6).

22 EDS 186–91; for the origin and background of the Amorites, see pp. 155–7.

23 AS 288–326; SHP 39–83; EDS 185–244; C2/1:1–41; CANE 2:1201–5.

24 Dagger blades (SAF §120, 124, 128; LMB 216–19); javelin and spear heads (SAF §123–5; LMB 215; AW 1:156–7); "duckbill" axe (SAF §126; LMB 211; AW 1:148; EDS 243, with a mold for casting bronze axes in EDS 183); "eye" axe (SAF §123, 128; LMB 211;); narrow-headed socketed axes (LMB 213).

25 The *qurpissum/gurpissum* has been traditionally translated as "hauberk" (CAD vol. G:139b; WM 157, 165 n26), but is now thought to be a helmet (MM 30–1). There is no artistic evidence for metal body armor until the very late Middle Bronze period;

Glock's interpretation of a royal statue with a robe with triangular markings as scale armor (WM 157, 162) is unlikely, since the king is wearing the robe on one shoulder which would have been impossible for a ten-kilogram robe of scale armor extending to the ankles. The robe would constantly fall off the shoulder. Furthermore, a woman wears the same type of dress (AFC §92), which undoubtedly represents sheep fleece.

26 Unfortunately, we are not given time of service in the pay documents from the Mari archive (L 498–500, 508). In reality, the pay could be as low as a fifth of a shekel (2 shekels per ten men) per campaign season (three months? L 312). This would make a soldier's wages for three months the same as four bronze arrowheads.

27 SDA 275; AANE §61; AM §166; SDA 270–1; AAM §206; see related paintings of elite dress at Mari in EDS 178–9.

28 FI §728–9; see Chapter Five for a full discussion of chariots.

29 Shelley Wachsmann, *Seagoing Ships and Seamanship in the Bronze Age Levant* (College Station: Texas A&M University Press, 1998); Marie-Christine De Graeve, *The Ships of the Ancient Near East, c. 2000–500 B.C.* (Louvain: Department Orientalistiek, 1981).

30 Major Early Bronze maritime sites include: Ashkelon (EA 1:220–3); Beirut (EA 1:292–5); Byblos (EA 1:390–4); Tel Gerisa (EA 2:394–6); Tel Sukas (EA 5:90–1); Tyre (EA 5:247–50); Ugarit (EA 5:255–62); most of these sites continued to be inhabited during the Middle Bronze period as well.

31 Major Middle Bronze maritime sites include: Achziv (EA 1:13–14); Akko (EA 1:54–5); Amrit (EA 1:111–13); Ashdod (EA 1:219–20); Gaza (Tell el-Ajjul) (EA 1:38–40); Jaffa (EA 1:206–7); Sidon (EA 5:38–41); Tel Michal (EA 2:20–2); Tel Mor (EA 4:49–50); Tel Nami (EA 4:96–7); Tell el-Kazel (Sumur) (EA 3:275–6); Yavneh-Yam (EA 5:374). Some of these cities, such as Sidon, have dense modern populations over the ancient sites, making detailed archaeological study difficult; some were probably inhabited in the Early Bronze period as well.

32 Alalakh (EA 1:55–61), Aleppo (EA 1:63–5), Byblos (EA 1:390–4), Carchemish (EA 1:423–4), Damascus (EA 2:103–6), Ebla (EA 2:180–3), Hama (EA 2:466–8), Khana (EA 5:188–90; AS 317–18), Mari (EA 3:413–17), Nagar (Tell Brak; EA 1:355–6), Qatna (EA 4:35–6), Shekhna (Tell Leilan; EA 3:341–7), Ugarit (EA 5:255–66), Urkesh (EA 4:60–3).

33 R4:779–97; SHP 49–64, F. Abdallah, *Les relations internationals entre le royaume d'Alep/Yamhad et les villes de Syrie du Nord, 1800 a 1594 av. J.-C.* (Paris, 1985); EA 1:63–5; CANE 2:1201–3; DANE 325–6; EDS 191–4.

34 AS 313–17; L; ARM; WM; DANE 189–90; CANE 2:885–99; EA 3:413–16, 419–21; MK; MM.

35 SHP 65–70; DANE 236–7; EA 4:34–5.

36 AT 2–4; R4:798–802; DANE 10–11; EA 1:55–9; AS 304–5.

37 WM 95–6; ARM 2.131 = ANET 483a.

38 AT 180; CS 3:237, 276–7; they are frequently mentioned in the fourteenth century Amarna Letters; see the index of William Moran (translator), *The Amarna Letters* (Baltimore: Johns Hopkins University Press, 1992), 392–3; DANE 135.

39 SHP 77–8; EA 255–62; DANE 305–6; CANE 2:1255–66.

40 CS 1:357; SHP 39, 43, 45, 77–8. Assuming a date of around 2000 for the establishment of the dynasty, the kings, with very rough estimates of their dates, are: Yaqaru {c. 1900}, Niqmaddu {c. 1880}, Ibiranu I {c. 1860}, Niqmepa I {c. 1840}, Ibiranu II {c. 1820}, Niqmepa II {c. 1800}, Ammurapi I {c. 1780}, Ibiranu III {c. 1760}, Niqmepa III {c. 1740}, Ya'duraddu {c. 1720}, Ibiranu IV {c. 1700}, Ammurapi II {c. 1680}, Niqmepa IV {c. 1660}, Ammittamuru {c. 1640–1620}. The next several names for the Middle Bronze period are lost; many other kings for the better documented Late Bronze period are also known. K. Kitchen, "The King List of Ugarit", *Ugarit-Forschungen*,

9 (1977):131–42; CANE 2:1260. Egyptian Execration Texts mention several cities and kings of southern Syria (CS 1:50–2).

41 SHP 79–80; DANE 62; EA 1:390–4; C1/2:343–51; see also the discussion om p. 410 on the relationship between Byblos and Egypt.

42 Possible exceptions are the enigmatic Byblos Syllabic Texts. George E. Mendenhall, *The Syllabic Inscriptions from Byblos* (Beirut: American University of Beirut, 1985), has provided an interpretation which has not met universal acceptance. If his interpretation is correct, the following passage represents a late Early Bronze royal inscription: "The words of Huru-Ba'il [king of Byblos]: I brought the lands into covenant to which they have bound themselves submissively because of my mighty deeds [of war]. Therefore you shall guard the ordinance of my kingship. Whoever enters honorably among us becomes one with the multitude. Thus the house has become the tribe of Huhash, and they shall be the loyal followers of [king] Huru-Ba'il" (Mendenhall, *Syllabic Inscriptions*, 33).

43 LMB 103; SHP 36, 45, 79: the kings of Byblos, with very rough estimates for dates, are: Ibdadi {c.2000}, Huru-Ba'il {19C?}, ? {1980–1820}, Abi-shemu I {c. 1820–1795}, Yapi-shemu-abi I {c. 1795–1780}, Yakin-El {c. 1780–1765}, Yantin-Ammu {c. 1765–1735}, Ilim-yapi {c. 1735–1720}, Abi-shemu II {c. 1720–1700}, Yapi-shuemu-abi II {c. 1700–1690}, ᶜEgel/ᶜEgliya (Akery) {c. 1690–1670}, RYNTY {c. 1670–1650}, Ka'in {c. 1650–1630}, Hasrurum {c. 1630–1610}.

44 SHP 70–4; EA 1:423–4; DANE 65.

45 HE2; P. Matthiae, "Ebla and Syria in the Middle Bronze Age", in E. Oren, *The Hyksos: New Historical and Archaeological Perspectives* (Philadelphia: University Museum, 1997), 379–414; E4:807–8; EDS 213–16.

46 I follow Astour's interpretation, HE2 133–64. There is a synchronism between year 7 of Amar-Suena {2040} and the reign of Mekum (HE2 133, 155); many earlier scholars have understood Ibbit-Lim, the writer of the inscription, to be the king, EER 58–9; SHP 39, 41.

Chapter Ten

1 ALB 35–231; EAE 3:335–43; C1/2:208–37.

2 Based on ALB 30. Note that the dates of each archaeological period can vary from half a century to a century among different scholars; see MW 3.

3 ALB 59–90; M = MBA §16.

4 COT; P. Moorey, "The Chalcolithic Hoard from Nahal Mishmar, Israel, in Context", *World Archaeology*, 20/2 (1988): 171–89; ALB 72–5; AW 1:126.

5 ALB 91–150; M = MBA §17, 21.

6 MW 1:164–5; AW 1:148–9; ALB 103–4; C1/2:227–9.

7 The major Early Bronze city-states larger than about 8 hectares include: Ai (el-Tell) (EA 1:32–3); Arad (EA 1:169–76); Bab el-Dhra' (EA 1:248–51); Beth-Shean (EA 1:305–9); Beth-Yerah (Khirbet Karak) (EA 1:312–14); Dan (EA 2:107–12); Ein-Besor (EA 2:219–20); Hazor (EA 3:1–5); Jericho (EA 3:220–4); Lachish (EA 3:317–24); Megiddo (EA 3:460–9); Tel Erani (EA 2:256–8); Tel Halif (Lahav) (EA 3:325–6); Tell el-Far'ah (north; Tirzah) (EA 2:304–5); Tell el-Sa'idiyeh (EA 4:452–5); M = ALB 95; MBA 17.

8 ECI 36–37; ALB 117; EA 1:170; THL 89.

9 PS 134–5 = ARE 1:64; EDE 92, 160; EAE 1:219–21; ALB 117.

10 ALB 151–173; ECI 63–9; C1/2:532–7.

11 EA 1:107–11; CANE 2:1231–42; later biblical tradition describes Amorites living in Canaan during the Israelite migration.

12 AEL 1:18–23 = ANET 227–8; EAE 3:496; M = MBA §22.

13 ALB 174–231; ECI 69–97; EAE 3:337–8; C 1/2:537–94; J. Weinstein, "Egyptian Relations with Palestine in the Middle Kingdom", *Bulletin of the American Schools of Oriental Research*, 217 (1975): 1–16; M = MBA §21.

14 Major Middle Bronze II sites with fortifications include: Acre (Akko) (EA 1:54–5); Aphek (EA 1:147–51); Ashkelon (EA 1:220–3); Beth-Shean (EA 1:305–9); Beth-Shemesh (EA 1:311–12); Dan (EA 2:107–12); Dor (EA 2:168–70); Gezer (EA 2:396–400); Hazor (EA EA 3:1–5); Jericho (EA 3:220–4); Kabri (EA 3:261); Lachish (EA 3:317–24); Megiddo (EA 3:460–9); Sharuhen (Tell el-'Ajjul) (EA 1:38–40); Shechem (EA 5:19–23); Shiloh (EA 5:28–9); Tel Gerisa (EA 2:394–6); Tel Masos (EA 3:437–9; Tel Zeror (EA 5:389–90); Tell Beit Mirsim (EA 1:295–7); Tell el-Far'ah (north) (EA 2:303–4); Tell el-Far'ah (south) (EA 2:304–5); Timnah (Tel Batash) (EA 1:281–3); Yavneh-Yam (EA 5:374–5); Yoqneam (EA 5:381–3).

15 Peter Parr, "The Origin of the Rampart Fortifications of the Middle Bronze Age Palestine and Syria", *Zeitschrift des Deutscher Palaestina-verein*, 84 (1968): 18–45.

16 Barbara Gregori, " 'Three-Entrance' City-gates of the Middle Bronze Age in Syria and Palestine", *Levant*, 18 (1986): 83–102.

17 Major Middle Kingdom art depicting Canaanites include: Tomb of Antef (Theban Tomb 386, EWW 38; NEA 38–9, Figure 3); Pectoral of Mereret (TEM 150–1); and several scenes from the Beni Hasan tombs, 2 (BH 1 §16; AW 1:169), 3 (AW 1:166–7; OHAE 192), 14 (BH 1 §47; AW 1:59), 15 (BH 2 §5), and 17 (BH 2 §15; AW 1:158–9).

18 Alternatively this figure may hold an *ankh*, an Egyptian religious symbol.

19 For an overview of the debate and a defense of the moderate historicist position, see William G. Dever, *What Did the Biblical Writers Know and When Did They Know It? What Archaeology Can Tell Us about the Reality of Ancient Israel* (Grand Rapids, MI: Eerdmans, 2001). Dever deals mainly with the royal period in Israel, after c. 1000. He is more dubious about the historical reliability of earlier biblical narratives; see his *Who Were the Early Israelites and Where Did They Come From?* (Grand Rapids, MI: Eerdmans, 2003). For a minimalist view, see Thomas L. Thompson, *The Mythic Past: Biblical Archaeology and the Myth of Israel* (London: Basic Books, 1999); Dever reviews the major minimalist literature on pp. 23–52; for a moderate inerrantist approach, see Alfred J. Hoerth, *Archaeology and the Old Testament* (Grand Rapids, MI: Baker Books, 1998).

20 E. Hostetter, *Nations Mightier and More Numerous: The Biblical View of Palestine's Pre-Israelite Peoples* (Richmond Hills, TX: BIBAL Press, 1995).

21 The Execration Texts are discussed in detail on pp. 415–8; MAEM 136–90; EAE 1:487–9. Partial translations: CS 1:50–2, ANET 328–9, VAE 125–6. M = MBA §23. On interpreting the Canaanite geography of the Execration Texts in Canaan, see ECI 87–93, and Yohanan Aharoni, *The Land of the Bible: a Historical Geography*, 2nd edn (Philadelphia: Westminster Press, 1979), 144–7; M= MBA §23.

22 An introductory bibliography on the Hyksos is given on p. 493, n. 9.

Chapter Eleven

1 Based on AFC xx.

2 C1/2:363–7.

3 John Garstang, *Prehistoric Mersin: Yumuk Tepe in Southern Turkey* (Oxford: Clarendon Press, 1953), 130–41, plates xvii–xxi; ET 128–30; EA 1:124–5, 2:8–11; PA 130–5. A photo of the fortress remains can be found in S. Lloyd, *Ancient Turkey* (Berkeley: University of California Press, 1989) 29.

4 C1/2:368–410; C2/1:228–55; EA 1:127–31; KH 7–14.

5 Irina Antonova, *The Gold of Troy* (New York: Abrams, 1996); the Aegean coast of Anatolia will not be examined in detail in this study.

6 Mellaart, C1/2:390–5; Yadin also accepts them as authentic in AW 1:142–5.

7 CG; KH 9–14; C1/2:406–10; EA 3:385–6.

8 G. Steiner, "The immigration of the first Indo-Europeans into Anatolia Reconsidered", *Journal of Indo-European Studies*, 18 (1990): 185–214.

9 M. Larsen, *The Old Assyrian City-State and its Colonies* (Copenhagen: Akadmisk Forlag, 1976); KH 21–43; ANE 1:90–5; CANE 2:859–71, DANE 163–4, EA 3:266–8; C1/2:707–28.

10 KH 35; all dates for the Anatolian kings of the eighteenth century in this section are conjectural, to give a sense of the relative chronology.

11 KH; GH; J. Macqueen, *The Hittites and their Contemporaries in Asia Minor* 2nd edn (London: Thames and Hudson, 1986). Trevor Bryce, *Life and Society in the Hittite World* (Oxford: Oxford University Press, 2002); EA 3:84–8; C2/1:228–55, 659–85.

12 KH 66–72; events in Labarna's reign are retrospectively described in the Telipinu Proclamation (CS 1:194a) and the Testament of Hattusilis (CS 2:81a). Labarna/Tabarna became a royal title among the Hittites, rather like Caesar among the Romans.

13 KH 72–89. We have three main sources (KH 66–7) for the reign of Hattusilis I: the Annals of Hattusilis (MHT 50–5 = HW2 47–55); the Testament of Hattusilis (MHT 100–7 = CS 2:79–82); these two are supplemented by a later retrospective summary in the Proclamation of Tilipinu (MHT 132–39 = CS 1:194–8).

14 Tawananna was a title of the leading female member of the Hittite royal family (KH 96–9).

15 Kurt Bittel, *Hattusha: The Capital of the Hittites* (New York, 1970); EA 1:333–5; DANE 54–5.

16 GH 148–9; KH 77–8; HW2 66–9; siegecraft in the Mari documents is discussed in Chapter Eight, exhibiting numerous parallels with the Hittite account. G. Beckman, "The Siege of Uršu Text (CHT 7)", *JCS*, 47 (1995): 23–34.

17 This practice is mentioned frequently in the Bible (where it is called *herem*, "utter destruction") and in the Mesha Stele (CS 2:137–8; ANET 320–1); P. Stern, *The Biblical Herem* (Atlanta: Scholars Press, 1989); S.-M. Kang, *Divine War in the Old Testament and in the Ancient Near East* (Berlin: de Gruyter, 1989). The practice was continued in classical warfare, such as in Alexander's destruction of Thebes {335} and Persepolis {330}, and the Romans' destruction of Carthage {146}, Corinth {146}, and Jerusalem {70 CE}.

18 WH2; For Late Bronze Age Hittite military organization, some of which probably reflects earlier practices, see Richard H. Beal, *The Organisation of the Hittite Military*, Texte der Hethiter 20 (Heidelberg: Carl Winter, 1992) and summary in CANE 1:545–554.

19 Cylinder Seal, Kultepe (Karum), Anatolia, MBI, (WV §29; ELH §4); cylinder seal, Anatolia, MBII (FI 57, §841).

20 The standard study is WH; see also DANE 150; EA 3:125–30; AS 284–7 for more recent bibliography.

21 For a summary of the theories on the origin and homeland of the Hurrians, see C. Burney, "Hurrians and Proto-Indo-Europeans: the Ethnic Context of the Early Tras-Caucasian Culture", in K. Emre *et al.* (editors), *Anatolia and the Near East* (Ankara: Türk Tarih Kurumu Basimevi, 1989), 45–51.

22 Kharbe (Tell Chuera, EA 1:491–2), Nagar/Nawar (Tell Brak, EA 1:355–6), and Urkesh (Tell Mozan, EA 4:60–3).

23 W. Hallo, "Simurrum and the Hurrian Frontier", *Revue Hittite et Asianique*, 36 (1978): 71–83.

24 N. Na'aman, "The Hurrians and the End of the Middle Bronze Age in Palestine", *Levant*, 26 (1994): 175–87.

25 The site of the Mitanni capital at Washukanni has not been identified; it is perhaps Tell Fakhariyah, EA 2:300–1. For bibliography on the Mitanni, see: DANE 200; CANE

2:1243–54; texts from fifteenth and fourteenth century Nuzi (EA 4:171–5; DANE 216; CANE 2:931–48) reflect Mitanni Hurrian culture, and include numerous items of military interest for Late Bronze warfare: T. Kendall, *Warfare and Military Matters in the Nuzi Tablets*, Ph.D dissertation (Waltham, MA: Brandeis University, 1974).

Chapter Twelve

1 For a popularized natural history of the Sahara, see Marq De Villiers and Sheila Hirtle, *Sahara: A Natural History* (New York: Walker & Co., 2002).

2 EAE 63–4; EBP; LA 4:344–8, 6:1069–76; EE 17–33.

3 EAE 2:493–4. Methodologically it should be emphasized that in the ancient Near East we are at the mercy of the happenstance of archaeological survival and discovery in attempting to reconstruct the origins of warfare. Although Naqada's importance in these developments should not be underestimated, it is quite possible that other equally or even more important sites existed, the remains of which have either not survived – potentially buried under several meters of Nile sediment – or have not yet been discovered or excavated. As a general principle, this applies to much of our historical knowledge of the military history of the ancient Near East.

4 EAE 1:200, 295; M= AAE 21 and HAAE 18, showing the major natural resources available to ancient Egypt.

5 DAE 226–8; EAE 3:61–5; LA 6:1069–76.

6 EAE 1:552–9, DAE 102–3; For the Pre-Dynastic period, see HEA 1:46–8 and A. Lawrence, "Ancient Egyptian Fortresses", *JEA*, 51 (1965): 69–70.

7 EAE 1:256–8; DAE 166–7; LA 3:414–15.

8 EG 510; AW 1:40, DAE 167, FP 33–5; EAE 2:407; disk-shaped mace heads remained in use largely for ritual purposes.

9 EDE 32, EWA 1; EWP 20–1, EE 36–7, AW 1:117, MB 44–5; PSE Figures 5–6; BAH 17.

10 DAE 109, EWP 26; AW 1:116, FP 157.

11 Hunter's Palette: EE 57; MB 93–118. Compare with figures depicted in GP 79.

12 See the "Towns" or "Libyan" Palette and the Bull Palette, discussed on pages 319 and 326. The depiction of two Horus banners among the hunters may imply some type of military function.

13 EE 54; EWP 29, MB 119–44; EWA 2; ISP 22–3.

14 Barbara Adams, *Ancient Nekhen: Garstang in the City of Hierakonpolis* (New Malden: Egyptian Studies Association, 1995); EDE 36–51; OHAE 61–7; DAE 226–8; EAE 2:98–100, 3:61–5; LA 2:1182–6; M= HAAE 22–3; AAE 30–1.

15 All dates given for this period are problematic estimates that could be higher or lower by as much as fifty years.

16 The name of this king of Abydos is actually unknown; Uj is apparently the name of the tomb that I am here using for the tomb's owner.

17 EDE 56–7; EE 56–7; AE 42–3; EBP 312–17. The name "Scorpion" derives from a hieroglyphic sign on his ceremonial mace-head; the Egyptian pronunciation is uncertain, perhaps something vaguely like Daret (*d3rt*).

18 EE 56, AW 1:121, MB 226–7, EAE 1:257; ISP 28–9.

19 EDE 39–40; AAA 28–34; Bruce Williams interprets some elements of Egyptian kingship as originating in Nubia: "Qustul: The Lost Pharaohs of Nubia", *Archaeology*, 33/5 (1980): 13–21, with a more technical presentation in *Excavations Between Abu Simbel and the Sudan Frontier. The A-Group Royal Cemetery at Qustul: Cemetary L* (Chicago: University of Chicago, 1986), 163–90; for critiques of Williams's theory, see the summary and bibliography in EDE 39–40. The Kingdom of Ta-Sety, or Qustul, is associated by archaeologists with the "A-Group" Nubian culture (EAE 1:44–6).

20 EWP 36, MB 127, AE 60; EDE, 48, 51, 177–9.

21 For translation of the Palermo Stone (hereafter PS), with detailed commentary, see Toby A. H. Wilkinson, *Royal Annals of Ancient Egypt: the Palermo Stone and its Associated Fragments* (London: Kegan Paul International, 2000). A dated translation can be found in ARE 1:57–72; DAE 218 gives references to recent studies; EWP 24.

22 Using Classical historians as evidence for Egyptian history two millennia earlier is certainly fraught with difficulties; see J. Dillery, "The First Egyptian Narrative History: Manetho and Greek historiography", *Zeitschrift für Papyrologie und Epigraphik*, 127 (1999): 93–116.

23 General surveys: OHAE 67–85; EDE 60–82, HAE, 52–4; LA 6:486–93, 1069–76.

24 EDE 67–70; EAE 2:494–5, 377–8; DAE 181,196–7; AE 43–9; LA 4:348–50.

25 Her. 2.4, 99; Man. 33; Diod. 1.45.

26 There is some controversy over whether the Menes of later Egyptian tradition should be associated with Narmer or with his son and successor Aha, or even with a conflation of several legendary kings (see discussions found in bibliography in EDE 68; EAE 2:377–8; DAE 17–18, 181, 196–7). For narrative purposes I here tentatively accept the link with Narmer.

27 TEM 40–1; AW 1.122, 124; MB 161–200; EWP 29; ISP 14–15.

28 EE 53, EWP 28, ECI 26, AW 1:51, FP 139; MB 229–32.

29 EDE 357–62; EAE 2:373–6; DAE 180, Her. 2.99; seals of Narmer's father Ka have been found in cemeteries near Memphis, indicating some type of settlement there before Narmer; Narmer probably greatly expanded the settlement and made it his capital, rather than creating an absolutely new city, EDE 58.

30 Remains of an additional Early Dynastic fortress have been found at Elephantine Island at Aswan, showing some of the characteristics of Early Dynastic fortifications, and may represent the southern frontier garrison of the new state; EWP 34.

31 Narmer's campaign – or that of a near successor – into Libya is memorialized in the "Cities (or Libyan) Palette" mentioned on p. 319 (EE 53, EWP 28, AW 1:51; TEM 38).

32 ECI 25; see also Yadin's interpretation of a symbol on the Narmer Palette as representing, in part, a campaign in Palestine, AW 1:124–5.

33 Or Hor-Aha; the name means "[the wargod] Horus fights". EDE 70–1; DAE 17–18; AE 49–56; LA 1:94–6. As noted above (note 26), some scholars equate Aha, rather than his father Narmer, with the legendary Menes.

34 EDE 71–3; DAE 86; AE 56–64; LA 1:1109–11.

35 PS 190 = ARE 1:58; EDE 71.

36 Djer Palette, AE 60; PSE Figure 7; label depicting head-smiting of a naked enemy, EWA 9; LA 6:1126–7.

37 On Djet, see EDE 73–4; DAE 86–7; AE 69–73; on Merneith, see EDE 74–5; AE 65–9.

38 EDE 75–8; EAE 1:416; DAE 18, 84; AE 73–80; EWA 10–16; LA 1:1071–2.

39 EDE 76–7; EE 87, AW 1:125, FP 164, EWP 34, EDE 156, MB 214, EWA 12. It is traditional in Egyptology to describe the peoples of the Sinai, Canaan and Syria as "Asiatics" (*ʿ3mw*), based on Classical Greek conceptualizations of "Asia" as the lands east of Europe (LA 1:462–71). In modern English, however, the term Asia(n) brings to mind India, China and Japan rather than Syria and Palestine. I therefore prefer the term "Easterner" and have changed all references in translations from "Asiatics" to "Easterners".

40 EDE 78–80; DAE 33, 257–8; AE 80–6; early interpretations of an inscription of Semerkhet in the Sinai at Wadi al-Mughara have now been shown to be from Sekhemkhet of the Third Dynasty, discussed on p. 330.

41 EDE 80–1; DAE 236; AE 86–91; EWA 17.

42 For general summaries of Second Dynasty, see EDE 82–94; Aidan Dodson, "The Mysterious Second Dynasty", *KMT*, 7/2 (1996): 19–31; OHAE 85–8; C1/2:29–35; AE 91–111; EAE 1:417–18.

43   PS 125–6 = ARE 1:62; EDE 85; EWA 18.
44   ECI, 36–7; ALB 117; EA 1:170.
45   Both the chronology of the Early Bronze Age in Canaan and that of the Egyptian kings of the early dynasties are quite uncertain. Depending on how one interprets the various possible chronologies, if Arad fell to Egyptians it could have been to any king in the Second or even the late First Dynasty.
46   EDE 89–91; AE 95–7; DAE 220. I here follow the suggestion of Wilkinson and DAE that Sekhemib-perenmaat is an alternative name for Peribsen. If not, then Sekhemib-perenmaat should be included as an additional king before Peribsen.
47   ANET 228a = EDE 89–90. In EWA 19–23, Redford interprets *inw* as "benevolence", euphemistically referring to tribute. From the Egyptian perspective, tribute and conquest were inseparably bound.
48   Some scholars believe that the myth of the war between Seth and Horus found in later Egyptian documents is in part a reflection of the cultic struggles and wars of the late Second Dynasty. H. te Velde, *Seth, God of Confusion* (Leiden: E. J. Brill, 1967); C1/2:33; LA 3:25–7, 6:84–6.
49   EDE 91–4; EBP, 348–54; EAE 2:231; LA 1:910–12; AE 98–103, who follows older views that Khasekhem is a different ruler than Khasekhemwy – it is now understood that they are the same person and the second name was taken by the king after his reunification of Egypt.
50   The major sources for the arms and army of Early Dynastic Egyptian warriors are: "Painted tomb", EE 36–7, AW 1:117; Gebal el-'Araq knife handle, AW 1:116; Battlefield Palette, EE 54; Hunter's Palette, EE 57, AW 1:118–19, FP 155; Narmer Palette, EE 52, AW 1:122–4; Libyan or Cities Palette, EE 53. Each of these has been discussed in this chapter.
51   PSE summarizes the evidence. The most prominent examples include: Narmer Palette: EE 52, AW 1.122–4, EWP 29; Den inscription, EE 87, AW 1:125, EDE 156; Cylinder seal from Hierakonpolis, AW 1:125.
52   The military art of this period includes numerous examples of icons for cities as walled enclosures; see ECI 27; EDE 119. The "City Palette" is the most famous; ECI 26; MB 230; EWA 4.
53   EWP 38, FP 128; AEA 71; HEA 1:46–8, EE 60,72–3; site plans of many tomb enclosures, presumably broadly paralleling fortification techniques, can be found in AE 38–104.
54   Bull Palette: AW 1:123; MB 144; EWA 3.
55   PS 92, 134, 136 = ARE 1:58, 64; EDE 210; LA 5:279–80.
56   SP 11–25; EBS 11–20; EAE3:281–4.
57   Conveniently collected in SP 12–25 and GP 68–74, 151–4, 192 and plates 9, 11–13, 15–16, 18–21, 23; EBS 11–20.
58   Lionel Casson, *The Ancient Mariners*, 2nd edn (Princeton: Princeton University Press, 1991), Figure 1; EBS 16.
59   DAE 109; EWP 26, AW 1:116, EBS 18.
60   PSE 4–7 discusses major examples; MB. See EWA 134–40 for a list of all Early Dynastic and Old Kingdom sources depicting the ritual execution of enemies. Other forms of early human sacrifice are discussed in EDE 265–7. Although the Narmer Palette is the most striking and famous example from the period of the iconography of the victorious pharaoh ritually slaughtering his defeated foes, it was already the culmination of several centuries of artistic and ideological development.

Chapter Thirteen

1   For general surveys and additional bibliography, see C1/2:145–207; EAE 2:585–605; EDE 94–105; EOK; HAE 63–101; OHAE 89–117; M= HAAE 27.

2   For general surveys and additional bibliography, see C1/2:145–60; EAE 2:585–6, 591–3; EDE 94–105; EOK; HAE 63–7; OHAE 90–3. Most of these accounts understandably focus on the great religious and cultural achievements, and funerary monuments such as Djoser's Step Pyramid at Saqqara.

3   Illustrations and translations of all these inscriptions from Wadi al-Mughara can be found in IS; hereafter I will provide only additional references to more accessible sources for illustrations of the Sinai martial reliefs; M= AAE 188.

4   EDE 94–5; king Djoser is more properly named Netjerikhet, but he is widely known today by the name Djoser, as preserved in later king-lists.

5   EDE 95–8; EOK 32–4; DAE 87; EWA 25a, FP 165.

6   MB 215, FP 166, PSE Figure 12; EDE 98–9; EOK 35; DAE 256–7; EWA 25b. I here follow Wilkinson's ordering of the kings.

7   EDE 101–3; EOK 36; EE 101, MB 215; PSE fig 10.

8   Inscription at Elephantine summarized in EAE 586a; a drawing of the fortress can be found in EWP 34.

9   For recent general overviews of the Fourth Dynasty with additional bibliography see: C1/2:160–79; EAE 2:586–8, 593–7; HAE 66–75; OHAE 93–109.

10 EAE 3:299–300; HAE 67–9.

11 PS 141 = ARE 1:66; the "sheep and goats" are 'wt, meaning literally "small cattle". On the dating and relative chronology of the fragments of the Palermo Stone, see PS 140, 259.

12 On Buhen, see the magnificent study by W. B. Emery et al., The Fortress of Buhen, 2 vols (London, Egypt Exploration Society, 1977–79), and discussion on pp. 443–5.

13 ANET 227b; EWP 40 and IS, figs 8 and 9, FP 167, PSE figs 13–14; EWA 27.

14 PS 235; the numbers are a bit obscure and have alternatively been read as 11,000 captives with 13,000 animals. Given the standard human-to-animal ratio of pastoral societies, Wilkinson's reading, given above, seems to be more accurate, and is also broadly proportional to the plunder figures from Nubia; see also EWA 26.

15 PS 141–3 = ANET 227a = ARE 1:65–6; for illustrations of such vessels from the Middle Kingdom, EBS 35.

16 EOK 43–5; PE 98–121; C1/2:169–72; HAE 69–71; EAE 2:234, 586; DAE 152. Greek writers (Her. 2.124–6; Man. 14–16; Diod. 1.63, calling him Chemmis) all tell tales about the Great Pyramid; none record any military legends. Unfortunately, the registers on the Palermo Stone covering the reigns of Fourth Dynasty kings after Sneferu are largely lost. Inscriptions of Khufu and subsequent rulers are largely funerary, with no military data (see ARE 1:83–95).

17 ANET 227b = ARE 1:83; IS Figure 7; FP 168; PSE, Figure 15; EWA 28.

18 On the late Fourth Dynasty, with additional bibliography, see: EAE 2:587–8, 591–3; HAE 66–75; C1/2:160–79.

19 PE 121–37; C1/2:174–6; HAE 73–4; EAE 2:229–31, 378–9, 588; DAE 149; Her. 2.127; Diod. 1.64.

20 EAE 2:378; PE 137–51; C1/2:176–8; DAE 181–2; Diod. 1.64.

21 For general overviews of the Fifth Dynasty with additional bibliography see: C1/2:180–9; EAE 2:588–90, 597–601; HAE 75–80; OHAE 109–13.

22 Stephen Quirke, The Cult of Ra: Sun Worship in Ancient Egypt (New York: Thames and Hudson, 2001); on Heliopolis, see AEA 105–6; EAE 2:88–9; LA 2:1111–13.

23 HAE 76–7; EAE 2:588–9, 598; C1/2:182–3.

24 PS 168 = ARE 1:70, 108; PSE Figure 16; EWA 31–2.

25 NEA 23; Ludwig Borchardt, Das Grabdenkmal des Königs Sahu-re (Leipzig: J. C. Hinrichs'sche Buchhandlung, 1910), plate 1. In part this scene is reconstructed by a close copy found in the Mortuary Temple of Pepi II (NEA 23).

26 NEA 24; Borchadt, Sahu-Re, plates 11 and 12; EWA 33.

27 HAE 77–8; EAE 2:589a, 599; EWA 35a. Evidence for expeditions from funerary temple: AEA 159; Miroslav Verner, *Forgotten Pharaohs, Lost Pyramids, Abusir* (Prague: Academia Skodaexport, 1974), pp. 133–54.

28 HAE 78–9; EAE 2:589–90, 600.

29 For recent general overviews of the Sixth Dynasty with additional bibliography see: EAE 3:33–4, 2:590–1, 602–4; HAE 80–9; C1/2:189–97; OHAE 113–17.

30 I will cite Lichtheim's translation, AEL 1:18–23; see alternatively: ANET 227–8; ARE 1:134–5, 140–4, 146–50; EAE 3:496; M = MBA §22. No chronological information is given in Weni's autobiography, so precise dates for his five campaigns are unknown, and are simply roughly estimated here.

31 The dates given here are a very rough estimate. Weni began service under Teti {2374–2354}; assuming he began his service late in Teti's reign {c. 2360} at around the age of 20 it would put his birth between 2380–2375. Weni apparently died during the reign of Merenre {2310–2300} (AEL 1:22) – the last king mentioned in his autobiography – which would put his death in his seventies, a venerable age for the time. His minimal dates are 2370–2310.

32 M = HAAE 27. This roughly corresponds to the modern area from Aswan in Egypt to Firka in Sudan.

33 Thomas Barfield, *The Perilous Frontier: Nomadic Empires and China, 221 BC to AD 1757* (Cambridge: Blackwell, 1989), 87.

34 Lichtheim translates *imy-r ʿw* as "chief of scouts"; I prefer "commander of foreigners", or even " commander of foreign mercenaries", on which see AAA 37, 95–6, n. 55 for extensive bibliography. The term *imy-r* is translated in different contexts as "commander", "overseer", or "chief", while *ʿw* is translated "scouts", "foreigners", or "dragomans" (interpreter) (EMO 34). I will consistently change such variants to "commander of foreigners" throughout quotations from translations without further notification.

35 EAE 2:603–4; AEN.

36 AEL 1:23–7 = ARE 1:150–4, 157–61; EAE 2:116–17; LA 2:1129; Hans Goedicke, "Harkhuf's Travels", *JNES*, 40 (1981):1–20; for map of Horkhuf's expeditions, see HAAE 27.

37 A. Spalinger, "Some notes on the Libyans of the Old Kingdom and later historical reflexes", *Society for the Study of Egyptian Antiquities Journal*, 9 (1979): 125–60; LA 3:1015–33; EAE 2:290–3, 3:497–501; maps: HAAE 27; HAE 86. For general background on this region, see Lisa Giddy, *Egyptian Oases* (Warminster: Aris & Phillips, 1987).

38 EAE 2:291; Technically, the ethnonym Libyan derives from the *Libu*, a different, though probably related ethnic group which displaced the Tjehenu by about the Eighteenth Dynasty {beginning 1569}.

39 AE 53, EWP 28, ECI 26; MB 229–32.

40 EAE 3:34–5, 2:604; DAE 220; LA 4:928.

41 These figures are from Man. 21, but are supported by some contemporary evidence; other scholars suggest a total reign of 64 years.

42 AEAB 15–16 = ARE 1:161–4; EAE 3:33; LA 4:929; M = HAAE 27.

43 MAEM 139, 149–50; related rituals may be found in the Pyramid Texts, 244, 476, as well as in numerous Coffin Texts.

44 My spelling of the names is an approximate transliteration; the original, purely consonantal spellings are given by MAEM, 139.

45 The text is somewhat obscure; a variant reading might be 200 soldiers and workers in total.

46 EAE 1:32–7. Proper treatment of war dead – or, alternatively, acts of ritual abuse and mutilation of corpses – has been a serious religious and cultural issue from ancient times to the present streets of Falluja in Iraq. For the vastly greater evidence from

classical Greece, see W. Kendrick Pritchett, *The Greek State at War: pt. 4, Religion* (Berkeley: University of California Press, 1985), 94–259; the Bible also reflects this concern in the treatment of the corpses of Saul and Jonathan, 1 Samuel 31.8–13.

47   The term "scout" appears to be a technical term for Nubian light infantry mercenaries, reflecting their frequent military function.

48   German readers should consult R. Müller-Wollermann, *Krisenfaktoren im ägyptischen Staat des ausgehenden Alten Reiches*, Dissertation (Tübingen: 1986).

49   LA 4:513–14; BDAE 93; HAE 89; for later legends see Man. 21, Her. 2.100, 134; Diod. 1.64.14.

Chapter Fourteen

1   For a translation of the Pyramid Texts, see PT; for general background with references to major studies, see Erik Hornung, *The Ancient Egyptian Books of the Afterlife*, trans. David Lorton (Ithaca NY: Cornell University Press, 1999), 1–6, and the bibliography on 159–62; EAE 3:95–7.

2   On the myth of the combat of Horus and Seth, H. W. Fairman, *The Triumph of Horus: an Ancient Egyptian Sacred Drama* (London: Batsford, 1974), J. G. Griffiths, *The Conflict of Horus and Seth from Egyptian and Classical Sources* (Liverpool: Liverpool University Press, 1960); EAE 1:294–5, 2:119–22.

3   Khafre, EWP 67, TEM 69; Menkaure, EWP 68, 77, TEM 70–1.

4   The "Nine Bows" generally is a reference to all the traditional enemies of Egypt (DAE 203–4; EAE 2:164–5; LA 1:844–5, 4:472–3).

5   One text describes the "sword which is in your hand when you ascend from the Netherworld" (PT 247), but "sword" here is an anachronistic translation.

6   PT 21, 424, 461, 483, 509, 536, 610, 667, 667A, 669, 689.

7   See also PT 666A, 667, 667A, 724.

8   AW 1:146, FP 141–2; EWA §52; NEA 30–2, Figure 2a; AAK 2/1.4.

9   A famous scene from the tomb of Niankhkhnum at Saqqara {c. 2450} depicts workmen smelting metal, confirming its increasing importance in Egyptian society by that time (EWP 88; ISP 80–1; FP 25).

10 The more narrow and elongated blade of the New Kingdom era (AW 1:180–1, 184–5; FP 47–8), designed for penetrating rather than cutting, called *3ḫḥw* (EG 511, sign T7), is not known in the Middle Kingdom.

11 AEA 91–3; EAE 1:552–3; LA 2:194–204. A. W. Lawrence, "Ancient Egyptian Fortifications", *JEA*, 51 (1965): 69–71. References in this section to AEA provide bibliography for the archaeological reports for each site.

12 PT 665, 665B, 611, 665A, 715, 720.

13 AW 1:146, FP 141–2; EWA §52; NEA 30–2, Figure 2a; AAK 2/1.4

14 AW 1:147, FP 140. EWW 38; EWA §53; NEA 30–2.

15 Gaballa (NEA 31) interprets the scene as people and animals entering a shelter. I see the objects at the right and left of the third and fourth panels as piles of grain; they bear broad resemblance to related hieroglyphs for a "heap of corn" (EG 483, sign M35), "sandy hill" (EG 489, sign N29) and "half-loaf of bread" (EG 532, sign X7). The animals are clearly thrusting their heads into the object, possibly eating from the grain pile.

16 Gaballa (NEA 31) sees the women as berating and striking the men who ran from the battle; this may be implied in a couple of instances, but in others the women seem clearly to be caring for the wounded.

17 Other passages also describe a ladder by which the king ascends into heaven: PT 271, 306, 478, 530, 572, 586A, 625.

18 P. Lipke, *The Royal Ships of Cheops* (Oxford: BAR, 1984); SP 26–34; EBS 21–2; EAE 3:281–4; OHAE 97; ISP 104–5; FP 169. Shipbuilding is mentioned in the royal annals

of Khufu (PS 223). This remarkable boat has been restored and can be seen in a museum beside the Great Pyramid.

19 SP 94–7; EWP 90–3; TEM 52–3; SGAE 101–3; ISP 41.

Chapter Fifteen

1 For general surveys see OHAE 118–47, 457–9; EAE 1:526–32; LA 6:1437–42; C1/2:464–531; HAE 137–54; Barbara Bell, "The Dark Ages in Ancient History I: The First Dark Age in Egypt", *American Journal of Archaeology*, 75/1 (1971): 1–26.

2 Modern scholars view Manetho's Ninth and Tenth dynasties (Man. 27–30) as a single dynasty, mistakenly divided in two by later Egyptian tradition (EAE 1:527–8). Here I will simply call both dynasties the Ninth, or Herakleopolitan Dynasty; there will thus be no discussion of a Tenth Dynasty. Its capital, known by its Greek name Herakleopolis (ancient: Heneneswe; modern: Ihnasiya), was the capital of the twentieth nome in middle Egypt; see EAE 2:91–3; LA 2:1124–8; DAE 124. M = HAAE 31.

3 AF 29–41 = AEAB 24–6 = AEL 1:85–6 (abridged) = HAE 142; EAE 1:94–5; LA 1:267–8.

4 John and Deborah Darnell, "New Inscriptions of the Late First Intermediate Period from the Theban Western Desert and the Beginnings of the Northern Expansion of the Eleventh Dynasty", *JNES*, 56 (1997): 241–58, quotation on 251.

5 Darnell and Darnell, "New Inscriptions", 244; EAE 1:528.

6 C2/1:466–8; HAE 143–7.

7 Background, EAE 2:169–70; translation TS 212–34 = VAE 52–4 = AEL 1:97–109 (abridged).

8 Lichtheim agrees that the text contains "valid, rather than fictitious, historical information" (AEL 1:97); Grimal also accepts its historicity (HAE 140–6).

9 Ralph D. Sawyer (trans.), *Seven Military Classics of Ancient China* (Boulder, CO: Westview, 1993), 145–186. Sun Tzu is traditionally said to have written in the early fifth century BC, but many scholars feel the text attributed to him was actually written in the third century BC (Sawyer, 149–50).

10 Adrian Goldsworth, *The Complete Roman Army* (London: Thames and Hudson, 2003), 27.

11 Henry Fischer, "Nubian Mercenaries of Gebelein during the First Intermediate Period", *Kush*, 9 (1961): 44–80.

Chapter Sixteen

1 C1/2:464–531; CANE 2:735–48; EAE 2:393–400; HAE 155–81; OHAE 148–83; MKT; Janine Bourriau, *Pharaohs and Mortals: Egyptian Art in the Middle Kingdom* (Cambridge: Cambridge University Press, 1988).

2 C1/2:472–95; HAE 155–8; OHAE 148–57.

3 EAE 2:436–8; C1/2:479–88; HAE 155–8; DAE 183; AEA 149–50; LA 6:66. His names mean "[The Theban war god] Montu is content". Some scholars reckon this Montuhotep as the second, counting his distant ancestor, a nomarch at Thebes, as Montuhotep I.

4 ITM 26–7; as noted on p. 489, n. 2, following current historical interpretation I am calling the combined Ninth and Tenth Dynasties the "Ninth" Dynasty.

5 Redford, ECI 70, believes the term "Easterners of Ḏ3ty" in Tjehemau's inscription has reference to Canaanites rather than to a Nubian tribe.

6 C1/2:488–92; HAE 157–8; OHAE 155–7; LA 6:68.

7 AEAB 52–4 = ARE 1:208–10; W. C. Hayes "The Career of the Great Steward Henenu under Nabhepetre, Mentuhotpe", *JEA*, 35 (1949): 43–9.

8 Wadi Hammamat Inscription of Amenemhet I (ARE 1:211–16 = AEL 1:113–15 and ECI 71–2 (both partial). The expedition lasted at least a month, with dates on the inscriptions ranging from day three to day twenty-eight of the "second month".

9 "Prophecy of Neferti" = TS 131–43 = AEL 1:139–45 = CS 1:106–10 = VAE 34–6; EAE 2:512–13; LA 4:380–1.

10 For general overviews with additional bibliography, see: EAE 3:453–7; C1/2:495–31; HAE 158–81; OHAE 158–83.

11 AIB; EAE 1:68–9; C1/2:492–499; HAE 158–64; OHAE 158–60; LA 1:188.

12 TS 203–11 = AEL 1:135–9 = ANET 418–19 = VAE 48–52; EAE 2:171.

13 The best study of the military affairs in the reign of Senwosret I is SI (in French); LA 5:890–9; EAE 3:266–8; C1/2:499–505; HAE 161–5; OHAE 160–2.

14 AEA 138 = ARE 1:251; See also the fragmentary inscription of the nomarch Sir-enpowet from an Aswan tomb, ARE 1:247, note b.

15 Peter Green, *Alexander of Macedon, 356–323 BC: A Historical Biography* (Berkeley: University of California Press, 1991), 402–11.

16 C1/2:502–4; HAE 165–6; LA 1:189; OHAE 163–4.

17 Donald Redford, *Pharaonic King-lists, Annals and Day-books* (Mississauga, Ontario: Benben Publications, 1986); EAE 1:95–7, 2:105–6.

18 C1/2:503; LA 5:899–903; OHAE 164–5.

19 Robert D. Delia, "A Study of the Reign of Senwosret III", Ph.D. dissertation (New York: Columbia University, 1980); C1/2:505–9; EAE 3:268–9; HAE 166–9; LA 5:903–6; OHAE 165–7.

20 Her. 2.101–7, 137; Man. 34–6; Diod. 1.53–8; Diodorus gives an extraordinarily exaggerated and anachronistic size for the Syrian campaign army – 600,000 infantry, 24,000 cavalry, and 27,000 war-chariots (1.53).

21 AAA 58–63; M = HAAE 51, CAAE 41. His achievements in Nubia led to his later deification as a patron god of Nubia. Late Greek legends on the Nubian campaign: Diod. 1.55.

22 An inundation mark from Dal near the Third Cataract, dated to year 10 {1868}, indicates ongoing Egyptian administrative activity in the area, probably associated with the building of the fortification complex.

23 On the early Kingdom of Kush, see Stuart Smith, *Askut in Nubia: The Economics and Ideology of Egyptian Imperialism in the Second Millennium B.C.* (London: Kegan Paul International, 1995); Timothy Kendall, *Kerma and the Kingdom of Kush, 2500–1500 BC* (Washington, DC: ational Museum of African Art, Smithsonian Institution, 1997); Barry J. Kemp, "Old Kingdom, Middle Kingdom and Second Intermediate Period in Egypt," in J. D. Clark (editor), *The Cambridge History of Africa, vol. 1: From the Earliest Times to c. 500 BC* (Cambridge: Cambridge University Press, 1982), 658–769; EAE 2:250–2; LA 3:888–901; M= AAE 187, HAAE 51.

24 Herodotus 2.100–110; Diodorus 1.53–58. K. Lange, *Sesostris* (Munich: 1954), reviews these classical legends.

25 It appears that the Greeks attributed a number of unknown stele and inscriptions to Senwosret (Diodorus 1.55), much in the same way that medieval Arabs would attribute many ancient monuments to the ubiquitous "Pharaoh".

26 Ronald J. Leprohon, "The Reign of Amenemhet III", PhD dissertation (Toronto: University of Toronto, 1980), hereafter RA3; C1/2:509–12; EAE 1:69–70; HAE 169–70; LA 1:190; OHAE 167–70.

27 Her. 2.148–9; Man. 34–6; Strabo 17.1.3, 37, 42; Diod. 1.61, 66, 89, 97; Pliny, *Natural History*, 36.13; EAE 14.

28 RA3, 10–184, translates all known inscriptions from Amenemhet's reign.

29 EAE 1:219–21; DANE 62; RA3 228; LA 1:889–91.

30 EAE 3:301; HAE 171; LA 1:191; OHAE 170–1.

Chapter Seventeen

1 EAE 2:238–45; D. O'Connor and David P. Silverman (editors), *Ancient Egyptian Kingship* (Leiden: Brill Academic Publishers, 1995), Oleg Berlev, "The Eleventh Dynasty and the Egyptian concept of Kingship", in Dwight Young (editor), *Studies Presented to Hans Polotsky* (East Gloucester, MA, 1981), 361–77.

2 Harakhty was a manifestation of Horus (EAE 2:146–7).

3 Divine support of Alexander the Great on his expedition to Siwa Oasis in the Western Desert was manifest by a similar unexpected rainstorm in the desert that saved the army from thirst; Peter Green, *Alexander of Macedon, 356–323 BC: A Historical Biography* (Berkeley: University of California Press, 1991), 274.

4 Descriptions by Diodorus (1.53) of oracular dreams concerning Senwosret III (Sesoōsis) derive from the Greek worldview, but may parallel earlier ancient Egyptian traditions of prophecies and oracular dreams.

5 Partial translations: CS 1:50–2, ANET 328–9, VAE 125–6. Discussions: MAEM 136–90, with detailed bibliography; EAE 1:487–9; C1/2:508–9. For general introductions to Egyptian magic see MAEM; EAE 2:321–36; Geraldine Pinch, *Magic in Ancient Egypt* (Austin: University of Texas Press, 1994); Bob Brier, *Ancient Egyptian Magic* (New York: Quill, 1981).

6 Jeremiah performs a similar ritual curse symbolized by the breaking of a pot, Jeremiah 19.1–11.

7 TEM 40–1; AW 1.122, 124; MB 161–200; EWP 29; ISP 14–15.

8 Although the Coffin Texts are mythic and magical rituals regarding the afterlife, I am here assuming that their descriptions of weapons and warfare reflect actual practices. On the background of the Coffin Texts, see EAE 1:287–8 and Erik Hornung, *The Ancient Egyptian Books of the Afterlife* (Ithaca: Cornell University Press, 1999), 7–12, 162–4.

9 Rituals of protection against enemies or cursing enemies are fairly common in the Coffin Texts; see, for example, CT 45, 49, 89, 313, 439, and 454, among many others.

10 EWW 31–9; EAE 2:406–12; BAH 20–59; FP 21–74.

11 Wallace McLeod, *Self Bows and Other Archery Tackle from the Tomb of Tut'ankhamun*, Tut'ankhamun's Tomb Series 4 (Oxford: Oxbow Books, 1982).

12 On the different designs and nomenclature of early bows, see Edward McEwen, Robert L. Miller and Christopher A. Bergman, "Early Bow design and construction", *Scientific American* (June 1991), 264/6: 50–6.

13 The tomb of the Eighteenth Dynasty {1569–1315} Nubian archer Maiherperi in the Valley of the Kings has some well preserved Egyptian archery equipment (FP 44–6), much of which would have been similar to Middle Kingdom equipment.

14 BH 1 §13, §30; BH 2 §13, §34; BAH 53; FP 40–1. Observations on the different penetrating power derived from different methods of drawing the bow were made by the sixth-century Byzantine historian Procopius, *History of the Wars*, 1.1.6–17, trans. H. Dewing, *Procopius*, 7 vols (Cambridge MA: Harvard University Press, 1914–1940), 1:4–9.

15 BH 1 §30, BH 2 §4; FP 40, 47; AW 1:9; BAH 53–4.

16 Janine Bourriau, *Pharaohs and Mortals: Egyptian Art in the Middle Kingdom* (Cambridge: Cambridge University Press, 1988), pp. 162–3, includes examples of daggers and axes from the Middle Kingdom.

17 EWW 35; AW 1:146–7, 154–5, 168–71; FP 49; BAH pl. 10.

18 FP 50–1; PSE figs 33–4, 50, 54–6, 63–6, 70–3, 85.

19 AW 1:158; FP 52; EWW 34; BAH 58.

20 SGAE 70–82, AW 1:71, EWP 120–1, 126; BH 1 §14–16; BH 2 §5, 8, 32.

21 This translation is a mixture of AEL 1:225–6 and TS 30–1, with my own interpretations added in square brackets.

22 Translations: TS 21–53; AEL 1:222–35; CS 1:77–82; ANET 18–22 (abridged). Studies: ECI 83–6; LA 5:950–5; EAE 3:292.

23 B. Fenik, *Typical Battle Scenes in the Iliad* (Wiesbaden: Steiner Verlag, 1968).

24 BH; EAE 1:175–7; EWP 120–1, 126; NEA 39–40.

25 BH 2 §15; AW 158–61; EWP 120; FA 94–5.

26 BH 2 §5; SGAE 75.

27 BH 1 §14–16; AW 169; EWP 121, 126.

28 BH 1 §47.

29 Theban Tomb 386: GJ §2; EWW 38; NEA 38–9, Figure 3.

30 There are also eleven Canaanite mercenaries in the mural of Tomb 15, which are discussed on pp. 279–80 and p. 438.

31 Christopher Spring, *African Arms and Armor* (Washington, DC: Smithsonian Institution Press, 1993), 29, pl. 4.

32 FB; BI; AEF; AW 1:16–24; EAE 1:552–9; AEA 90–3; LA 2:194–203; FP 127–38.

33 AEA 82–3; EAE 1:467–9; HEA 3:38–42; FP 128.

34 AEA 91–3; FP 130–4; HEA 3:200–29; Somers Clarke, "Ancient Egyptian Frontier Fortresses", *JEA*, 3 (1916): 155–79.

35 The major fortresses will be listed by their modern archaeological name, followed by the ancient Egyptian name where known; the Egyptian names are taken from EAE 1:555. The rough size of each fortress is given in meters, along with a reference to AEA, where full bibliographic references to the major archaeological reports and studies are provided. M = HAAE 51.

36 SW; AW 1:69–71; LA 3:765–86; FP 138–48.

37 The fullest mural is from Tomb 17: BH 2 §15, AW 1:158–9, SW 14, FA 94–5; each of the murals have slight differences in detail, making them worth consulting individually; see also Tomb 15, BH 2 §5; and Tomb 2, BH 1 §14, FP 148.

38 SP 75–97; EWW 59–63; EBS 27–36; EAE 3:281–4.

39 BH 1 §14, §16, §29; BH 2 §12.

40 Dilwyn Jones, *A Glossary of Ancient Egyptian Nautical Titles and Terms* (London: Kegan Paul, 1988).

41 CT 398, 400, 404, 405, 409.

42 AW 2:340–1; SP 111–13; EBS 45; EAE 2:356–8; AEA 143–5; Harold Nelson (editor), *Medinet Habu, vol. 1: Earlier Historical Records of Ramses III* (Chicago: University of Chicago, 1930), pl. 37–41; AAK 2, pl. 115–17.

Chapter Eighteen

1 SIP; LA 6:1442–8; EAE 3:260–5; Barry J. Kemp, "Old Kingdom, Middle Kingdom and Second Intermediate Period in Egypt", in J. D. Clark (editor), *The Cambridge History of Africa, vol. 1: From the Earliest Times to c. 500 BC* (Cambridge: Cambridge University Press, 1982), 736–60.

2 On the Turin Canon king-list for this period, see SIP 9–33, 69–74, 94–9, 118–19, 151–6, 164–5 = CS 1:71–3; for the scarab seals see SIP 34–68. The Abydos King-lists ignore this period entirely, CS 1:69–70.

3 SIP; for alternative views, see EAE 3:260–5 and the bibliography found there.

4 This chart is based on SIP 6, 186–91. However, Ryholt follows a chronological interpretation that places the end of the Twelfth Dynasty in 1803, while EAE chronology, which I follow, places it in 1786. Ryholt also dates the accession of Ahmose to 1550, whereas the EAE dates it to 1569. Thus, according to the EAE chronology the Second Intermediate Period is twenty-six years shorter than in Ryholt's chronology. To be consistent I will follow the EAE chronology, taking the surplus twenty-six years from the period of the Thirteenth and Fourteenth Dynasties.

5   Stuart Smith, *Askut in Nubia: The Economics and Ideology of Egyptian Imperialism in the Second Millennium B.C.* (London: Kegan Paul International, 1995). 81–140; EAE 2:250–2; Kemp, "Old Kingdom, Middle Kingdom and Second Intermediate Period in Egypt,": 747–60; AAA 64–72.

6   Summarized by AAA 67–70; Smith, *Askut*, 110–30.

7   Dates for all Fourteenth Dynasty kings are very rough estimates, based on SIP 114 (and elsewhere), and adjusted to match the difference between SIP chronology and that used in this book.

8   Thomas S. Burns, *Rome and the Barbarians: 100 B.C. – A.D. 400* (Baltimore: Johns Hopkins University Press, 2003).

9   On the Hyksos, or Fifteenth Dynasty, see SIP 118–50, 256–8, 301–5, EAE 2:136–43, ECI 98–122, E. Oren (editor). *The Hyksos: New Historical and Archaeological Perspectives* (Philadelphia: University of Pennsylvania, 1997); M. Bietak, *Avaris, The Capital of the Hyksos* (London: British Museum, 1996).

Bibliography

Abdallah, F., *Les relations internationals entre le royaume d'Alep/Yamhad et les villes de Syrie du Nord, 1800 a 1594 av. J.-C.* (Paris, 1985).

Adams, Barbara, *Ancient Nekhen: Garstang in the City of Hierakonpolis* (New Malden: Egyptian Studies Association, 1995).

Adams, Barbara and Krzysztof Cialowicz, *Protodynastic Egypt* (Buckinghamshire: Shire Egyptology, 1997).

Aharoni, Yohanan, *The Land of the Bible: a Historical Geography*, 2nd edn (Philadelphia: Westminster Press, 1979).

Aharoni, Yohanan and Michael Avi-Yonah, *Macmillan Bible Atlas*, 2nd edn (New York: Macmillan, 1977).

Akkermans, Peter and Glenn Schwartz, *The Archaeology of Syria: From Complex Hunter-Gatherers to Early Urban Societies, (ca. 16,000–300 BC)* (Cambridge: Cambridge University Press, 2003).

Akurgal, Ekrem, *The Art of the Hittites* (New York: Abrams, 1962).

Algaze, Guillermo, *The Uruk World System: The Dynamics of Expansion of Early Mesopotamian Civilization* (Chicago: University of Chicago Press, 1993).

Amiet, Pierre, *Art of the Ancient Near East* (New York: Harry N. Abrams, 1980).

Ammianus Marcellinus, *Res Gestae*, trans. Walter Hamilton, *The Later Roman Empire (A.D. 354–378)* (Penguin, 1986).

Anbar, M., *Les Tribus Ammorites de Mari*, Orbis Biblicus et Orientalis 108 (Freiburg: Gottingen, 1991).

Anthony, David, "The Domestication of the Horse", in R. Meadow and Hans-Peter Uerpmann (eds), *Equids in the Ancient World*, vol. 2 (Wiesbaden: Ludwig Reichert Verlag, 1991).

Anthony, D. and D. Brown, "The origins of horseback riding", *Antiquity*, 246 (1991): 22–38.

——, "The opening of the Eurasian steppe at 2000 BCE", in Victor H. Mair (ed.), *The Bronze Age and Early Iron Age Peoples of Eastern Central Asia*, vol. 1 (Washington D.C.: The Institute for the Study of Man, 1998).

Anthony, David W. and Nikolai B. Vinogradov, "Birth of the Chariot", *Archaeology*, 48/2 (1995): 36–41.

Antonova, Irina, *The Gold of Troy* (New York: Abrams, 1996).

Archer, Christon I. *et al.*, *World History of Warfare* (Lincoln: University of Nebraska Press, 2002).

Archives Royale de Mari (Paris: Imprimerie Nationale, 1950 ff.).

Arnold, Dieter, *The Encyclopedia of Ancient Egyptian Architecture* (Princeton: Princeton University Press, 2003).

Aruz, Joan (ed.), *The Art of the First Cities: The Third Millennium BC from the Mediterranean to the Indus* (New York: Metropolitan Museum of Art, 2003).

Astour, Michael, "An Outline of the History of Ebla (Part I)", in Cyrus Gordon, editor, *Eblaitica*, vol. 3 (Winona Lake, IN: Eisenbrauns, 1992): 3–82.

——, "The Date of the Destruction of Palace G at Ebla", in Mark Chavalas and John Hayes (eds), *New Horizons in the Study of Ancient* Syria (Malibu, CA: Undena Publications, 1992).

——, "A Reconstruction of the History of Ebla (Part 2)", in Cyrus Gordan, editor, *Eblaitica*, vol. 4 (Winona Lake, IN: Eisenbrauns, 2002): 57–195.

Azzaroli, Augusto, *An Early History of Horsemanship* (Leiden: Brill, 1985).

Badawy, Alexander, *A History of Egyptian Architecture*, 3 vols (Berkeley and Los Angeles, 1954–68).

Baines, John and Jaromir Malek, *Atlas of Ancient Egypt* (New York: Facts on File, 1980).

Bar-Adon, P., *The Cave of Treasure: The Finds from the Caves in Nahal Mishmar* (Jerusalem, 1980).

Barfield, Thomas, *The Perilous Frontier: Nomadic Empires and China, 221 BC to AD 1757* (Cambridge: Blackwell, 1989).

Barnes, Timothy D., *Constantine and Eusebius* (Cambridge, MA: Harvard University Press, 1981).

Barnett, R., "Xenophon and the Wall of Media", *Journal of Hellenic Studies*, 83 (1963): 1–26.

Beal, Richard H., *The Organisation of the Hittite Military*, Texte der Hethiter 20 (Heidelberg: Carl Winter, 1992).

Beard, Mary, John North and Simon Price, *Religions of Rome*, 2 vols (Cambridge: Cambridge University Press, 1998).

Beckman, G., "The Siege of Uršu Text (CHT 7)", *JCS*, 47 (1995): 23–34.

Beebe, Keith H., *The Dromedary Revolution* (Claremont CA: Institute for Antiquity and Christianity, 1990).

Bell, Barbara, "The Dark Ages in Ancient History I: The First Dark Age in Egypt", *American Journal of Archaeology*, 75/1 (1971): 1–26.

Berlev, Oleg, "The Eleventh Dynasty and the Egyptian concept of Kingship", in Dwight Young (ed.), *Studies Presented to Hans Polotsky* (East Gloucester, MA, 1981).

Berman, Lawrence Michael, "Amenemhet I", Ph.D. dissertation, Yale University, 1985.

Bienkowski, Piotr and Alan Millard, *Dictionary of the Ancient Near East* (Philadelphia: University of Pennsylvania Press, 2000).

Bietak, M., *Avaris, The Capital of the Hyksos* (London: British Museum, 1996).

Bittel, Kurt, *Hattusha: The Capital of the Hittites* (New York, 1970).

Black, Jeremy and Anthony Green, *Gods, Demons and Symbols of Ancient Mesopotamia: An Illustrated Dictionary* (London: British Museum, 1992).

Borchardt, Ludwig, *Das Grabdenkmal des Königs Sahu-re* (Leipzig: J. C. Hinrichs'sche Buchhandlung, 1910).

Bourriau, Janine, *Pharaohs and Mortals: Egyptian Art in the Middle Kingdom* (Cambridge: Cambridge University Press, 1988).

Breasted, James Henry, *Ancient Records of Egypt*, 5 vols (Chicago: University of Illinois Press, 1906; reprint, 2001).

Brier, Bob, *Ancient Egyptian Magic* (New York: Quill, 1981).

Brinkman, J., *Materials and Studies for Kassite History I* (Chicago: Oriental Institute, 1976).

Brovarski, Edward and William J. Murnane, "Inscriptions from the Time of Nebhepetre Mentuhotep II at Abisko", *Serapis* 1/1 (1969): 11–33.

Bryce, Trevor R., *The Major Historical Texts of Early Hittite History* (Brisbane: University of Queensland, 1983).

——, *The Kingdom of the Hittites* (Oxford: Clarendon Press, 1998).

——, *Life and Society in the Hittite World* (Oxford: Oxford University Press, 2002).

Buccellati, Giorgio, *The Amorites of the Ur III Period*, Publicazioni del Seminario di Semitistica, Richerche 1 (Naples: Intituto Orientale di Napoli, 1966).

Bulliet, Richard, *The Camel and the Wheel* (Cambridge, MA: Harvard University Press, 1975).

Burney, C., "Hurrians and Proto-Indo-Europeans: the Ethnic Context of the Early Tras-Caucasian Culture", in K. Emre *et al.* (eds), *Anatolia and the Near East* (Ankara: Türk Tarih Kurumu Basimevi, 1989).

Burns, Thomas S., *Rome and the Barbarians: 100 B.C. – A.D. 400* (Baltimore: Johns Hopkins University Press, 2003).

Callender, Gae, *Egypt in the Old Kingdom: An Introduction* (London: Longman, 1998).

Casson, Lionel, *The Ancient Mariners*, 2nd edn (Princeton: Princeton University Press, 1991).

Chaliand, Gerard (ed.), *The Art of War in World History: From Antiquity ot the Nuclear Age*, (Berkeley: University of California Press, 1994).

Charpin, D., "Les Elamites à Shubat-Enlil", In *Fragmenta Historiae Elamicae: Mélanges Offerts à M. J. Steve*, ed. L. De Meyer (Paris: Editions Recherche sur les Civilisations, 1986).

Chavalas, Mark, "Ancient Syria: A Historical Sketch", in Mark Chavalas and John Hayes (eds), *New Horizons in the Study of Ancient Syria* (Malibu, CA: Undena Publications, 1992).

Civil, M., "Išme-Dagan and Enlil's Chariot", *Journal of the American Oriental Society*, 88/1 (1968): 3–14.

Clarke, Somers, "Ancient Egyptian Frontier Fortresses", *JEA*, 3 (1916): 155–79.

Collon, Dominique, "Hunting and Shooting", *Anatolian Studies*, 33 (1983): 51–56.

——, *First Impressions: Cylinder Seals in the Ancient Near East* (London: British Museum, 1987).

Cooper, Jerrold S. (ed.), *The Return of Ninurta to Nippur* (Rome, 1978).

——, *Reconstructing History from Ancient Inscriptions: the Lagash-Umma Border Conflict* (Malibu, CA: Undena Publications, 1983).

——, *Presargonic Inscriptions* (New Haven: The American Oriental Society, 1986).

Cribb, Roger, *Nomads in Archaeology*, 2nd edn (Cambridge: Cambridge University Press, 2004).

Crile, George, *Charlie Wilson's War: The Extraordinary Story of the Largest Covert Operation in History* (New York: Atlantic Monthly Press, 2003).

Crouwel, J., *Chariots and Other Means of Land Transport in Bronze Age Greece* (Amsterdam: Allard Pierson Museum, 1981).

Dalfes, Nuzhet *et al.* (eds), *Third Millennium BC Climate Change and Old World Collapse* (Berlin: Springer Verlag, 1997).

Dalley, Stephanie, *The Old Babylonian Tablets from Tell Al Rimah* (London: British School of Archaeology in Iraq, 1976).

——, *Mari and Karana: Two Old Babylonian Cities* (London and New York: Longman, 1984).

——, *Myths from Mesopotamia: Creation, the Flood, Gilgamesh, and Others*, 2nd edn (Oxford: Oxford University Press, 2000).

Darnell, John and Deborah Darnell, "New Inscriptions of the Late First Intermediate Period from the Theban Western Desert and the Beginnings of the Northern Expansion of the Eleventh Dynasty", *JNES*, 56 (1997): 241–58.

Davis, Whitney, *Masking the Blow: The Scene of Representation in Late Prehistoric Egyptian Art* (Berkeley: University of California Press, 1992).

Dawson, Doyne, *The First Armies* (London: Cassell, 2001).

De Graeve, Marie-Christine, *The Ships of the Ancient Near East, c. 2000–500 B.C.* (Louvain: Department Orientalistiek, 1981).

De Villiers, Marq and Sheila Hirtle, *Sahara: A Natural History* (New York: Walker & Co., 2002).

Dear, I. (ed.), *The Oxford Companion to World War II*, (Oxford: Oxford University Press, 1995).

Decker, Wolfgang, *Sports and Games of Ancient Egypt* (New Haven: Yale University Press, 1987).

Delia, Robert D., "A Study of the Reign of Senwosret III", Ph.D. dissertation (New York: Columbia University, 1980).

Dever, William G., *What Did the Biblical Writers Know and When Did They Know It? What Archaeology Can Tell Us about the Reality of Ancient Israel* (Grand Rapids, MI: Eerdmans, 2001).

——, *Who Were the Early Israelites and Where Did They Come From?* (Grand Rapids, MI: Eerdmans, 2003).

Di Cosmo, Nicola, *Ancient China and its Enemies: the Rise of Nomadic Power in East Asian History*, (Cambridge: Cambridge University Press, 2002).

Dillery, J., "The First Egyptian Narrative History: Manetho and Greek historiography", *Zeitschrift für Papyrologie und Epigraphik*, 127 (1999): 93–116.

Diodorus, *Diodorus on Egypt: Book I of Diodorus Siculus' Historical Library*, trans. Edwin Murphy (Jefferson, NC: McFarland, 1985).

Dodson, Aidan, "The Mysterious Second Dynasty", *KMT*, 7/2 (1996): 19–31.

Drews, Robert, *The Coming of the Greeks: Indo-European Conquests in the Aegean and the Near East* (Princeton: Princeton University Press, 1988).

——, *Early Riders: The Beginnings of Mounted Warfare in Asia and Europe* (New York: Routledge, 2004).

Ebeling, Erich (ed.), *Reallexikon der Assyriologie* (Berlin: W. de Gruyter, 1932–2000).

Edwards, I. E. S., *The Pyramids of Egypt*, 5th edn (Harmondsworth: Penguin, 1993).

Edwards, I. E. S. *et al.* (eds), *Cambridge Ancient History, vol. 1, part 2: Early History of the Middle East* (Cambridge: Cambridge University Press, 1971).

—— (eds), *Cambridge Ancient History, vol. 2, part 1: History of the Middle East and the Aegean Region, c. 1800–1380* (Cambridge: Cambridge University Press, 1973).

Edzard, Dietz Otto, *Die "zweite Zwischenzeit" Babyloniens* (Wiesbaden: Harrassowitz, 1957).

——, *Royal Inscriptions of Mesopotamia, Early Periods, Vol. 3/1: Gudea and His Dynasty* (Toronto: University of Toronto Press, 1997).

Ehrich, Robert (ed.), *Chronologies in Old World Archaeology*, 2 vols, 3rd edn (Chicago: University of Chicago Press, 1992).

Eichler, Barry, "Of Slings and Shields, Throw-Sticks and Javelins", *Journal of the American Oriental Society*, 103 (1983): 95–102.

Eliade, Mircea (ed.), *The Encyclopedia of Religion* (New York: Macmillan, 1995).

Ellis, Linda (ed.), *Archaeological Method and Theory: An Encyclopedia* (New York: Garland, 2000).

Emery, Walter B., *Archaic Egypt* (Harmondsworth: Penguin, 1961).

Emery, W. B. *et al.*, *The Fortress of Buhen*, 2 vols (London: Egypt Exploration Society, 1977–79).

Fagan, Brian, *Oxford Companion to Archaeology* (Oxford: Oxford University Press, 1996).

Fairman, H. W., *The Triumph of Horus: an Ancient Egyptian Sacred Drama* (London: Batsford, 1974).

Faulkner, R., "Egyptian Military Organization", *Journal of Egyptian Archaeology*, 39 (December, 1953): 32–47.

——, *The Ancient Egyptian Pyramid Texts* (Oxford: Clarendon Press, 1969).

Fenik, B., *Typical Battle Scenes in the Iliad* (Wiesbaden: Steiner Verlag, 1968).

Ferguson, Brian and Neil Whitehead (eds), *War in the Tribal Zone: Expanding States and Indigenous Warfare* (Santa Fe: School of American Research Press, 1992).

Ferrill, Arthur, *The Origins of War: from the Stone Age to Alexander the Great* (London: Thames and Hudson, 1985).

Fischer, Henry, "Nubian Mercenaries of Gebelein during the First Intermediate Period", *Kush*, 9 (1961): 44–80.

——, *Inscriptions from the Coptite Nome, Dynasties VI–XI*, Analecta Orientalia 40 (Rome, 1964).

Foster, Benjamin R., *Umma in the Sargonic Period*, Memoirs of the Connecticut Academy of Arts and Sciences, vol. 20, April 1982 (Hamden, CN: Archon Books, 1982).

——, "Management and Administration in the Sargonic Period", in M. Liverani (ed.), *Akkad: The First World Empire: Structure, Ideology, Traditions* (Winona Lake, IN: Eisenbrauns, 1993), 25–39.

Frayne, Douglas R., "A Struggle for Water: A Case Study from the Historical Records of the Cities of Isin and Larsa (1900–1800 BC)", *Canadian Society for Mesopotamian Studies Bulletin*, 17 (May 1989): 17–28.

——, *Royal Inscriptions of Mesopotamia, Early Periods, Vol. 4: Old Babylonian Period (2003–1595 B.C.)* 2 vols, *Royal Inscriptions of Mesopotamia, Babylonian Period* (Toronto: University of Toronto Press, 1990).

——, *Royal Inscriptions of Mesopotamia, Early Periods, Vol. 2: Sargonic and Guitian Period (2334–2113 B.C.)* (Toronto: University of Toronto Press, 1993).

——, *Royal Inscriptions of Mesopotamia, Early Periods, Vol. 3/2: Ur III Period (2112–2004 B.C.)* (Toronto: University of Toronto Press, 1997).

——, *Royal Inscriptions of Mesopotamia, Early Periods, Vol. 1: Pre-Sargonic Period (to 2334 B.C.)* (Toronto: University of Toronto Press, 2004).

Gaballa, G., *Narrative in Egyptian Art* (Mainz Am Rhein: Verlag Philipp Von Zabern, 1976).

Gardiner, Alan, *Egyptian Grammar*, 3rd edn (London: Oxford University Press, 1957).

——, *Egypt of the Pharaohs* (Oxford: Oxford University Press, 1961).

Gardiner, A. H., T. E. Peet and J. Cerny, *The Inscriptions of Sinai*, 2nd edn, 2 vols (London: Egypt Exploration Society, 1952–1955).

Garstang, John, *Prehistoric Mersin: Yumuk Tepe in Southern Turkey* (Oxford: Clarendon Press, 1953).

Gates, M.-H., "The Legacy of Mari", *Biblical Archaeologist* 47 (1984).

George, Andrew, *The Epic of Gilgamesh* (London: Penguin, 1999).

Gerstenblith, Patty, *The Levant at the Beginning of the Middle Bronze Age* (Winona Lake, IN: Eisenbrauns, 1983).

Giddy, Lisa, *Egyptian Oases* (Warminster: Aris & Phillips, 1987).

Glock, Albert, *Warfare in Mari and Early Israel* (Ph.D. Dissertation, University of Michigan, 1968).

Goedicke, Hans, "Harkhuf's Travels", *JNES*, 40 (1981): 1–20.

——, "Ankhtyfy's Fight", *Chronique d'Egypte* 73 (1998): 29–41.

Goldsworth, Adrian, *The Complete Roman Army* (London: Thames and Hudson, 2003).

Grayson, Albert Kirk, *Assyrian Royal Inscriptions*, 2 vols (Wiesbaden: Harrassowitz, 1972).

——, *Assyrian Rulers of the Third and Second Millennia BC (to 1115 BC)*, The Royal Inscriptions of Mesopotamia, Assyrian periods, v. 1 (Toronto: University of Toronto Press, 1987).

——, *Royal Inscriptions of Mesopotamia, Assyrian Periods, Vol. 1: Assyrian Rulers of the Third and Second Millennia BC (to 1115 BC)* (Toronto: University of Toronto Press, 1987).

Green, Peter, *Alexander of Macedon, 356–323 BC: A Historical Biography* (Berkeley: University of California Press, 1991).

Gregori, Barbara, " 'Three-Entrance' City-gates of the Middle Bronze Age in Syria and Palestine", *Levant*, 18 (1986): 83–102.

Griffiths, J. G., *The Conflict of Horus and Seth from Egyptian and Classical Sources* (Liverpool: Liverpool University Press, 1960).

Grimal, Nicolas, *A History of Ancient Egypt* (Oxford: Blackwell, 1992).

Groneberg, Brigitte, "*Tilpānu* = Bogen", *Revue d'Assyriologie*, 81 (1987): 115–24.

Gurney, O., *The Hittites*, 4th edn (London: Penguin, 1990).

Hall, Emma Swan, *Pharaoh Smites his Enemies* (München: Deutscher Kunstverlag, 1986).

Hallo, W., "The Road to Emar", *JCS* 18 (1964): 57–88.

——, "Simurrum and the Hurrian Frontier", *Revue Hittite et Asianique*, 36 (1978): 71–83.

Hallo, William W. and K. Lawson Younger (eds), *Context of Scripture*, 3 vols (Leiden: Brill, 1997–2002).

Harris, Rivkah, *Ancient Sippar: A Demographic Study of an Old-Babylonian City (1894–1595 BC), Uitgaven Van Het Nederlands Historisch-Archaeologisch Instituut Te Istanbul, 36* (Istanbul: Nederlands Historisch-Archaeologisch Instituut, 1975).

Hayes, W. C. "The Career of the Great Steward Henenu under Nabhepetre, Mentuhotpe", *JEA*, 35 (1949): 43–9.

Heimpel, Wolfgang, *Letters to the King of Mari: A New Translation, with Historical Introduction, Notes, and Commentary* (Winona Lake, IN: Eisenbrauns, 2003).

Helck, Wolfgang and Eberhard Otto, *Lexicon der Ägyptologie*, 7 vols (Wiesbaden: Otto Harrassowitz, 1975–1992).

Henrickson, R., "A Regional Perspective on Godin III Cultural Development in Central Western Iran", *Iran* 24 (1986): 1–55.

Herodotus, *The History*, trans. David Greene (Chicago: University of Chicago Press, 1987).

Hijjara, I., *The Halaf Period in Northern Mesopotamia* (London, 1997).

Hoerth, Alfred J., *Archaeology and the Old Testament* (Grand Rapids, MI: Baker Books, 1998).

Hoffman, Michael, *Egypt before the Pharaohs*, 2nd edn (Austin, TX: University of Texas Press, 1991).

Hornung, Erik, *The Ancient Egyptian Books of the Afterlife*, trans. David Lorton (Ithaca NY: Cornell University Press, 1999).

Hostetter, E., *Nations Mightier and More Numerous: The Biblical View of Palestine's Pre-Israelite Peoples* (Richmond Hills, TX: BIBAL Press, 1995).

Houwink ten Cate, Philo H. J., "The History of Warfare According to Hittite Sources: the Annals of Hattusilis I (Part I)", *Anatolica*, 10 (1983): 91–109.

——, "The History of Warfare According to Hittite Sources: the Annals of Hattusilis I (Part II)", *Anatolica*, 11 (1984): 47–83.

Hunter, P., *The Royal Hunter: Art of the Sasanian Empire* (New York: The Asia Society, 1978).

Jacobsen, Thorkild, *The Sumerian Kinglist* (Chicago: University of Chicago, 1939).

——, "Historical Data", in H. Frankfort (ed.), *The Gimilsin Temple and the Palace of the Rulers of Tell Asmar* (Chicago, University of Chicago Press, 1940), 116–200.

——, "The Reign of Ibbi-Suen", *JCS*, 7 (1953): 36–47.

——, *Harps that Once: Sumerian Poetry in Translation* (New Haven: Yale University Press, 1987).

Jaroš-Deckert, Brigitte, *Das Grab des Jnj-jtj.f, die Wandmalereien der XI. Dynastie* (Mainz am Rhein: Verlag Philipp von Zabern, 1984).

Jones, Dilwyn, *A Glossary of Ancient Egyptian Nautical Titles and Terms* (London: Kegan Paul, 1988).

Joukowsky, Martha, *Early Turkey: Anatolian Archaeology form Prehistory through the Lydian Period* (Dubuque, Iowa: Kendall/Hunt Publishing, 1996).

Kang, S.-M., *Divine War in the Old Testament and in the Ancient Near East* (Berlin: de Gruyter, 1989).

Keegan, John, *A History of Warfare* (New York: Alfred Knopf, 1993).

Keel, Othmar and Christoph Uehlinger, *Gods, Goddess and Images of God in Ancient Israel* (Minneapolis: Fortress Press, 1998).

Keeley, Lawrence H., *War Before Civilization: The Myth of the Peaceful Savage* (Oxford: Oxford University Press, 1996).

Kemp, Barry J., "Old Kingdom, Middle Kingdom and Second Intermediate Period in Egypt", in J. D. Clark (ed.), *The Cambridge History of Africa, vol. 1: From the Earliest Times to c. 500 BC* (Cambridge: Cambridge University Press, 1982).

Kendall, Timothy, *Warfare and Military Matters in the Nuzi Tablets*, Ph.D. dissertation (Waltham, MA: Brandeis University, 1974).

——, *Kerma and the Kingdom of Kush, 2500–1500 BC* (Washington, DC: National Museum of African Art, Smithsonian Institution, 1997).

Kitchen, K., "The King List of Ugarit", *Ugarit-Forschungen*, 9 (1977): 131–42.

Klein, Jacob, *Three Shulgi Hymns: Sumerian Royal Hymns Glorifying King Shulgi of Ur* (Ramat-Gan, Israel: Bar Ilan University Press, 1981).

Klengel, Horst, *König Hammurapi und der Alltag Babylons* (Düsseldorf: Artemis, 1991).

——, *Syria, 3000–300 BC: A Handbook of Political History* (Berlin: Akademie Verlag, 1992).

Kramer, Samuel Noah, *The Sumerians: Their History, Culture, and Character* (Chicago: University of Chicago Press, 1963).

——, "The Death of Ur-Nammu and His Descent to the Netherworld," *JCS* 21 (1967): 104–22.

Kuhrt, Amelie, *The Ancient Near East c. 3000–300 BC*, 2 vols (London: Routledge, 1995).

Landsberger, Benno, "Remarks on the Archive of the Soldier Ubarum", *JCS*, 9/4 (1955): 121–31.

Landstrom, Bjorn, *Ships of the Pharaohs: 4000 Years of Egyptian Shipbuilding* (Garden City, NY: Doubleday, 1970).

Larsen, Mogens Trolle, *The Old Assyrian City-State and its Colonies* (Copenhagen: Akademisk Forlag, 1976).

Lawrence, A. W., "Ancient Egyptian Fortifications", *JEA*, 51 (1965): 69–71.

LeBlanc, Steven A., *Constant Battle: the Myth of the Peaceful, Noble Savage* (New York: St. Martin's, 2003).

Leprohon, Ronald J., "The Reign of Amenemhet III", Ph.D. dissertation (Toronto: University of Toronto, 1980).

Levine, Marsha, "Botai and the origins of horse domestication", *Journal of Anthropological Archaeology*, 18 (1999): 29–78.

Levine, Marsha et al. (eds), *Late Prehistoric Exploitation of the Eurasian Steppe* (Cambridge: McDonald Institute, 1999).

Lichtheim, Mariam, *Ancient Egyptian Literature*, 3 vols (Berkeley: University of California Press, 1975–1980).

——, *Ancient Egyptian Autobiographies Chiefly of the Middle Kingdom: A Study and an Anthology*, Orbis Biblicus et Orientalis 84 (Freiburg: Universitätsverlag, 1988).

Lipke, P., *The Royal Ships of Cheops* (Oxford: BAR, 1984).

Littauer, M. and J. Crouwel, *Wheeled Vehicles and Ridden Animals in the Ancient Near East* (Leiden: Brill, 1979).

——, "The Origin of the True Chariot", *Antiquity*, 70 (Dec. 1996): 934–9.

Liverani, M., "The Amorites," in D. Wiseman (ed.), *Peoples of the Old Testament World*, (Oxford, 1973).

Lloyd, S., *Ancient Turkey* (Berkeley: University of California Press, 1989).

Macqueen, J., *The Hittites and their Contemporaries in Asia Minor* 2nd edn (London: Thames and Hudson, 1986).

Maeda, T., "The Defense Zone during the Rule of the Ur III Dynasty", *Acta Sumerologica*, 14 (1992): 135–72.

Maisels, Charles Keith, *The Emergence of Civilization: From Hunting and Gathering to Agriculture, Cities, and State in the Near East* (London: Routledge, 1990).

Malek, Jaromir, *In the Shadow of the Pyramids: Egypt during the Old Kingdom* (Norman, OK: University of Oklahoma Press, 1986).

Manetho, *Manetho*, trans. W. G. Waddell, Loeb Classical Library 155 (Cambridge MA: Harvard University Press, 1940).

Manley, Bill, *The Penguin Historical Atlas of Ancient Egypt* (London: Penguin, 1996).

Matthews, Victor, *Pastoral Nomadism in the Mari Kingdom, c. 1830–1760* (Cambridge MA: American Schools of Oriental Research, 1978).

Matthiae, Paolo, *Ebla: An Empire Rediscovered* (Garden City, NY: Doubleday, 1981).

——, "Ebla and Syria in the Middle Bronze Age", in E. Oren, *The Hyksos: New Historical and Archaeological Perspectives* (Philadelphia: University Museum, 1997).

Matthiae, Paolo *et al.*, *Ebla: alle origini della civilta urbana* (Milan: Electa, 1995).

Mazar, Amihai, *Archaeology and the Land of the Bible: 10,000–586 BC* (New York: Doubleday, 1990).

McEwen, E., R. Miller, and C. Bergman, "Early Bow Design and Construction", *Scientific American*, 264/6 (June 1991): 76–82.

McLeod, Wallace, *Self Bows and Other Archery Tackle from the Tomb of Tut'ankhamun*, Tut'ankhamun's Tomb Series 4 (Oxford: Oxbow Books, 1982).

Mellaart, James, *Catal Huyuk: A Neolithic Town in Anatolia* (New York: McGraw-Hill, 1967).

Mendenhall, George E., *The Syllabic Inscriptions from Byblos* (Beirut: American University of Beirut, 1985).

Messenger, Charles (ed.), *Reader's Guide to Military History* (London: Fitzroy Dearborn, 2001).

Meyers, Eric (ed.) *The Oxford Encyclopedia of Archaeology in the Near East* (Oxford: Oxford University Press, 1997).

Michalowski, Piotr, "Bride of Simanum", *Journal of the American Oriental Society*, 95 (1975): 716–19.

——, "Foreign Tribute to Sumer during the Ur III Period", *Zeitschrift für Assyriologie*, 68 (1978): 34–49.

——, "The Royal Correspondence of Ur", Ph.D. Dissertation, Yale University, 1978.

——, "History as Charter: Some Observations on the Sumerian King List", *Journal of the American Oriental Society*, 103 (1983): 237–48.

——, *The Lamentation Over the Destruction of Sumer and Ur* (Winona Lake: Eisenbrauns, 1989).

Miller, R., E. McEwen, and C. Bergman, "Experimental Approaches to Ancient Near Eastern Archery", *World Archaeology*, 18/2 (1986): 178–95.

Moorey, P., "Pictorial evidence for the history of horse-riding in Iraq before the Kassites", *Iraq*, 32 (1970): 36–50.

——, "The Emergence of the Light, Horse-drawn Chariot in the Near East c. 2000–1500 B.C.", *World Archaeology*, 18/2 (1986): 196–215.

——, "The Chalcolithic Hoard from Nahal Mishmar, Israel, in Context", *World Archaeology*, 20/2 (1988): 171–89.

Moortgat, Anton, *The Art of Ancient Mesopotamia* (New York: Phaidon, 1969).

Moran, William (trans.), *The Amarna Letters* (Baltimore: Johns Hopkins University Press, 1992).

Müller-Wollermann, R., *Krisenfaktoren im ägyptischen Staat des ausgehenden Alten Reiches*, Dissertation (Tübingen: 1986).

Na'aman, N., "The Hurrians and the End of the Middle Bronze Age in Palestine", *Levant*, 26 (1994): 175–87.

Nagel, Wolfram, *Die mesopotamische Streitwagen und seine Entwicklung im ostmediterranen Bereich* (Berlin: Berliner Beiträge zur Vor- und Frühgeschichte, 1966).

Neiberg, Michael S., *Warfare in World History* (London and New York: Routledge, 2001).

Nelson, Harold (ed.), *Medinet Habu, vol. 1: Earlier Historical Records of Ramses III* (Chicago: University of Chicago, 1930).

Neugebauer, O., *Mathematische Keilschrift-Texte* (Berlin: Julius Springer, 1935).

Newberry, Percy E., *Beni Hasan*, 4 vols (London: Kegan Paul, Trench, Trubner, 1893–1900).

Nigro, L., "The Two Steles of Sargon: Iconography and Visual Propaganda at the Beginning of Royal Akkadian Relief", *Iraq* 60 (1998): 1–18.

——, "Visual Role and Ideological Meaning of the Enemies in the Royal Akkadian Relief", in J. Prosecky (ed.), *Intellectual Life in the Ancient Near East* (Prague: Academy of Sciences of the Czech Republic, Oriental Institute, 1998).

Nissen, Hans J., *The Early History of the Ancient Near East, 9000–2000 BC* (Chicago: University of Chicago Press, 1988).

Nunn, Astrid, *Die Wandmalerei und der Glasierte Wandschmuck im Alten Orient* (Leiden: Brill, 1988).

Oates, Joan, "A Note on the Early Evidence for Horse and the Riding of Equids in Western Asia", in M. Levine, C. Renfrew and K. Boyle (eds), *Prehistoric Steppe Adaptation and the Horse* (Cambridge: McDonald Institute, 2003): 115–25.

Obsomer, Claude, *Sesostris Ier: Etude chronologique et historique de règne* (Bruxelles: Connaissance de l'Egypte Ancienne, 1995).

O'Connor, D. and David P. Silverman (eds), *Ancient Egyptian Kingship* (Leiden: Brill Academic Publishers, 1995).

Oppenheim, A., *The Interpretation of Dreams in the Ancient Near East* (Philadelphia: American Philosophical Society, 1956).

Oren, E. (ed.). *The Hyksos: New Historical and Archaeological Perspectives* (Philadelphia: University of Pennsylvania, 1997).

Owen, D., "The 'first' equestrian: an Ur III glyptic scene", *Acta Sumerologica*, 13 (1991): 259–71.

Parkinson, R. B., *Voices from Ancient Egypt: an Anthology of Middle Kingdom Writings* (Norman, OK: University of Oklahoma Press, 1991).

—— (trans.), *The Tale of Sinuhe and Other Ancient Egyptian Poems, 1940–1640* (Oxford: Oxford University Press, 1997).

Parr, Peter, "The Origin of the Rampart Fortifications of the Middle Bronze Age Palestine and Syria", *Zeitschrift des Deutscher Palaestina-verein*, 84 (1968): 18–45.

Parrot, Andre, *Sumer: the Dawn of Art* (New York: Golden Press, 1961).

Partridge, Robert B., *Fighting Pharaohs: Weapons and Warfare in Ancient Egypt* (Manchester: Peartree Publishing, 2002).

Paulkner, R. O., *The Ancient Egyptian Coffin Texts*, 3 vols (Warminster: Aris & Phillips, 1973–1978; reprint 1994).

Pettinato, Giovanni, "Bollettino militare della campagna di Ebla contro la citta di Mari", *Oriens Antiquus*, 19 (1980): 231–45.

——, *I re di Sumer I: Iscrizioni reali presargoniche della Mesopotamia* (Brescia: Peideia Editrice, 2003).

Philip, Graham, *Metal Weapons of the Early and Middle Bronze Ages in Syria-Palestine*, 2 vols (Oxford: BAR International Series, 1989).

Piekalkiewicz, Janusz, *The Cavalry of World War II, 1939–1945* (Harrisburg PA: Historical Times, 1979).

Piggott, Stuart, *The Earliest Wheeled Transport: From the Atlantic Coast to the Caspian Sea* (Ithaca, NY: Cornell University Press, 1983).

Pinch, Geraldine, *Magic in Ancient Egypt* (Austin: University of Texas Press, 1994).

Postgate, J., *Early Mesopotamia: Society and Economy at the Dawn of History* (London and New York: Routledge, 1992).

Postgate, Nicholas, "The Equids of Sumer, Again", in R. Meadow and Hans-Peter Uerpmann (eds), *Equids in the Ancient World*, vol. 1 (Wiesbaden: Ludwig Reichert Verlag, 1986).

Potter, David, *Prophets and Emperors*, (Cambridge MA: Harvard University Press, 1994).

Potts, D., "The Road to Meluhha," *JNES* 41 (1982): 279–88.

——, *The Archaeology of Elam* (Cambridge: Cambridge University Press, 1999).

Potts, Timothy, *Mesopotamia and the East: An Archaeological and Historical Study of Foreign Relations, c. 3400–2000 BC* (Oxford: Oxford University Committee for Archaeology, 1994).

Pritchett, W. Kendrick, *The Greek State at War, Part III* (Berkeley: University of California Press, 1979).

Pritchett, W. Kendrick, *The Greek State at War: Part IV* (Berkeley: University of California Press, 1985).

Procopius, *History of the Wars*, trans. H. Dewing, *Procopius*, 7 vols (Cambridge MA: Harvard University Press, 1914–1940).

Ptrichard, James B. (ed.), *Ancient Near Eastern Texts, Relating to the Old Testament*, 3rd edn (Princeton: Princeton University Press, 1969).

—— (ed.), *The Ancient Near East in Pictures, Relating to the Old Testament*, 2nd edn (Princeton: Princeton University Press, 1969).

Quirke, Stephen, *The Administration of Egypt in the Late Middle Kingdom: The Hieratic Documents* (Whitstable, UK: SIA Publishing, 1990).

——, *The Cult of Ra: Sun Worship in Ancient Egypt* (New York: Thames and Hudson, 2001).

Raulwing, P., *Horses, Chariots, and Indo-Europeans*, Archaeolingua, Series Minor, vol. 13 (Budapest: Archaeolingua Foundation, 2000).

Redford, Donald B., "Egypt and Western Asia in the Old Kingdom", *Journal of the American Research Center in Egypt*, 23 (1986): 125–43.

——, *Pharaonic King-lists, Annals and Day-books* (Mississauga, Ontario: Benben Publications, 1986).

——, *Egypt, Canaan and Israel in Ancient Times* (Princeton: Princeton University Press, 1992).

—— (ed.), *Oxford Encyclopedia of Ancient Egypt*, 3 vols (Oxford: Oxford University Press, 2001).

Répertoire Géographique des Textes Cunéiformes, in *Beihefte zum Tübinger Atlas des Vorderen Orients. Reihe B, Geisteswissenschaften*, 7 (Wiesbaden: Dr. Ludwig Reichert, 1977 ff.).

Ritner, R., *The Mechanics of Ancient Egyptian Magical Practice* (Chicago: The Oriental Institute, 1993).

Roaf, Michael, *Cultural Atlas of Mesopotamia and the Ancient Near East* (New York: Facts on File, 1990).

Roccati, Alessandro, *La Littérature Historique Sous l'Ancien Empire Egyptien* (Paris: Les Editions du Cerf, 1982).

Romer, W., "Zur Siegesinschrift des Königs Utuhegal von Unug," *Orientalia* 54 (1985): 274–88.

Roth, M., *Law Collections from Mesopotamia and Asia Minor* (Atlanta: Scholars Press, 1995).

Roux, Georges, *Ancient Iraq*, 3rd edn (London: Penguin, 1992).

Ryholt, K., *The Political Situation in Egypt during the Second Intermediate Period, c. 1800–1550 BC* (Copenhagen: Carsten Niebuhr Institute of Near Eastern Studies, 1997).

Saggs, H., *The Might that was Assyria* (London: Sidgwick & Jackson, 1984).

Salonen, Erkki, *Die Waffen der Alten Mesopotamier* (Helsinki: Studia Orientalia, 1965).

Sasson, Jack, *The Military Establishments at Mari* (Rome: Pontifical Biblical Institute, 1969).

—— (ed.), *Civilizations of the Ancient Near East*, 4 vols (New York: Macmillan, 1995).

Säve-Söderbergh, Torgny, *Ägypten und Nubien* (Lund: Haken Ohlssons boktryckeri, 1941).

Sawyer, Ralph D. (trans.), *Seven Military Classics of Ancient China* (Boulder, CO: Westview, 1993).

Schulman, A. R., "Representations of Horsemen and Riding in the New Kingdom", *JNES*, 16 (1957): 263–7.

——, "Siege Warfare in Pharaonic Egypt", *Natural History: The Journal of the American Museum of Natural History*, 73/3 (March 1964): 13–21.

——, "Chariots, Chariotry and the Hyksos", *Journal of the Society for the Study of Egyptian Antiquities*, 10 (1980): 105–53.

——, "Battle Scenes from the Middle Kingdom", *Journal for the Society for the Study of Egyptian Antiquities*, 12/4 (1982): 165–83.

Schulz, Rebine and Matthias Seidel (eds), *Egypt: World of the Pharaohs* (Köln: Könemann, 1998).

Seeden, Helga, *The Standing Armed Figurines in the Levant* (München: Beck'sche Verlagsbuchhandlung, 1980).

Shaw, Ian, *Egyptian Warfare and Weapons* (Princes Risborough: Shire Publications, 1991).

——, "Battle in Ancient Egypt: The Triumph of Horus or the Cutting Edge of the Temple Economy?", in Alan B. Lloyd (ed.), *Battle in Antiquity* (Swansea: Duckworth, 1996), pp. 239–69.

—— (ed.), *The Oxford History of Ancient Egypt* (Oxford: Oxford University Press, 2000).

——, "Egyptians, Hyksos and military technology: Causes, effects or catalysts?", in A. J. Shortland (ed.), *The Social Context of Technological Change, Egypt and the Near East, 1650–1550 BC* (Oxford: Oxbow Books, 2001).

Shaw, Ian and Paul Nicholson (eds), *Dictionary of Ancient Egypt* (New York: Abrams, 1995).

Sigrist, Marcel, *Isin Year Names*, Institute of Archaeology Publications, Assyriological Series, vol. 2 (Berrien Springs, MI: Andrews University Press, 1988).

——, *Larsa Year Names*, Institute of Archaeology Publications, Assyriological Series, vol. 3 (Berrien Springs, MI: Andrews University Press, 1990).

Smith, H. S., *The Fortress of Buhen: The Inscriptions* (London: Egyptian Exploration Society, 1976).

Smith, S., "Notes on the Gutian Period," *JRAS*, (1932): 295–308.

Smith, Stuart, *Askut in Nubia: The Economics and Ideology of Egyptian Imperialism in the Second Millennium B.C.* (London: Kegan Paul International, 1995).

Smither, P., "The Semna Dispatches", *Journal of Egyptian Archaeology*, 31 (1945): 3–10.

Spalinger, A., "Some notes on the Libyans of the Old Kingdom and later historical reflexes", *Society for the Study of Egyptian Antiquities Journal*, 9 (1979): 125–60.

Speleers, L., *Catalogue des intaillés et empreintes orientales des Musées Royaux du Cinquantenaire* (Bruxelles, 1917).

Spencer, A., *Early Egypt: The Rise of Civilization in the Nile Valley* (London: British Museum, 1993).

Spring, Christopher, *African Arms and Armor* (Washington, DC: Smithsonian Institution Press, 1993).

Steiner, G., "The immigration of the first Indo-Europeans into Anatolia reconsidered", *Journal of Indo-European Studies*, 18 (1990): 185–214.

Steinkeller, P., "The Administrative and Economic Organization of the Ur III State: The Core and Periphery", in M. Gibson and R. Biggs (eds), *The Organization of Power* (Chicago: Oriental Institute, 1987).

Stern, P., *The Biblical Herem* (Atlanta: Scholars Press, 1989).

Streck, M., *Das amurritische Onomastikon der altbabylonischen Zeit*, (Münster: Ugarit-Verlag, 2000).

Strommenger, Eva, *5000 Years of the Art of Mesopotamia* (New York: Harry N. Abrams, 1964).

te Velde, H., *Seth, God of Confusion* (Leiden: E. J. Brill, 1967).

Thompson, Thomas L., *The Mythic Past: Biblical Archaeology and the Myth of Israel* (London: Basic Books, 1999).

Tinney, S., "A New Look at Naram-Sin and the Great Rebellion," *JCS*, 47 (1995): 1–14.

Tiradriti, Francesco (ed.), *The Treasures of the Egyptian Museum* (Cairo: American University in Cairo Press, 1999).

Treasures of the Holy Land: Ancient Art from the Israel Museum (New York: The Metropolitan Museum of Art, 1986).

Ussishkin, David, *The Conquest of Lachish by Sennacherib* (Tel-Aviv: Tel Aviv University, Institute of Archaeology, 1982).

van de Mieroop, Marc, *King Hammurabi of Babylon*, (Oxford: Blackwell, 2005).

van Dijk, J., "Ishbi-Erra, Kindattu, l'homme d'Elam, et la chute de la ville d'Ur", *JCS*, 30 (1978): 189–208.

Vanstiphout, Herman, *Epics of Sumerian Kings: The Matter of Aratta* (Atlanta: Society of Biblical Literature, 2003).

Verner, Miroslav, *Forgotten Pharaohs, Lost Pyramids, Abusir* (Prague: Academia Skodaexport, 1974).

Vinson, Steve, *Egyptian Boats and Ships* (Princes Risborough: Shire Publications, 1994).

Wachsmann, Shelley, *Seagoing Ships and Seamanship in the Bronze Age Levant* (College Station: Texas A&M University Press, 1998).

Waschow, H., "Wehrwissenschaft und Mathematik im alten Babylonien", *Unterrichts-blätter für Mathematik und Naturwissenschaften,* 39 (1939).

Watkins, Trevor, "Sumerian Weapons, Warfare and Warriors", *Sumer*, 39/1–2 (1983): 100–2.

Weinstein, J., "Egyptian Relations with Palestine in the Middle Kingdom", *Bulletin of the American Schools of Oriental Research*, 217 (1975): 1–16.

Weiss, Harvey (ed.), *Ebla to Damascus: Art and Archaeology of Ancient Syria* (Washington DC: Smithsonian Institute, 1985).

Weiss, H. *et al.*, "The Genesis and Collapse of Third Millennium North Mesopotamian Civilization", *Science*, 261 (1993): 995–1004.

Wendort, F., "Site 117: A Nubian Final Palaeolithic Graveyard near Jebel Sahaba, Sudan", in F. Wendorf (ed.) *The Prehistory of Nubia*, 2 vols (Dallas: Southern Methodists University Press, 1968).

Westenholz, J. Goodnick, *Legends of the Kings of Akkade* (Winona Lake, IN: Eisenbrauns, 1997).

Whiting, Robert M., Jr., *Old Babylonian Letters from Tell Asmar*, Assyriological Studies, No. 22 (Chicago: Oriental Institute of Chicago, 1987).

Wilhelm, Gernot, *The Hurrians* (Warminster: Aris & Phillips, 1989).

Wilkinson, Toby A. H., *Early Dynastic Egypt* (London: Routledge, 1999).

——, (ed. and trans.), *Royal Annals of Ancient Egypt: the Palermo Stone and its Associated Fragments* (London: Kegan Paul International, 2000).

——, *Genesis of the Pharaohs* (London: Thames and Hudson, 2003).

Williams, Bruce, "Qustul: The Lost Pharaohs of Nubia", *Archaeology*, 33/5 (1980): 14–21.

——, *Excavations Between Abu Simbel and the Sudan Frontier. The A-Group Royal Cemetery at Qustul: Cemetary L* (Chicago: University of Chicago, 1986).

Wilson, E. J., *The Cylinders of Gudea: Transliteration, Translation, and Index* (Neukirchen-Vluyn: Verlag Butzon, 1996).

Winlock, H. E., *The Slain Soldiers of Neb-hepet-Re Mentu-hotpe* (New York: Metropolitan Museum of Art Egyptian Expedition, 1945).

——, *The Rise and Fall of the Middle Kingdom in Thebes* (New York: Macmillan, 1947).

Winter, Irene, "After the Battle is Over: The *Stele of the Vultures* and the Beginning of Historical Narrative in the Art of the Ancient Near East", in H. Kessler and M Simpson (eds), *Pictorial Narrative in Antiquity and the Middle Ages* (Washington, DC: National Gallery of Art, 1985).

Wise, Terence and Angus McBride, *Ancient Armies of the Middle East* (London: Osprey, 1981).

Wiseman, D., *The Alalakh Tablets* (London: British Institute of Archaeology at Ankara, 1953).

Wolf, Walther, *Die Bewaffnung des Altägyptischen Heeres* (Leipzig: Hinrichs'sche Buchhandlung, 1926).

Wreszinski, Walter, *Atlas zur altaegyptischen Kulturgeschichte* (Leipzig: Hinrichs, 1923–1936).

Wu, Yuhong, *A Political History of Eshnunna, Mari and Assyria during the Early Old Babylonian Period (From the end of Ur III to the death of Shamshi-Adad)* (Changchun: Institute of History of Ancient Civilizations, Northeast Normal University, 1994).

Yadin, Yigael, *Art of Warfare in Biblical Lands in the Light of Archaeological Study*, 2 vols (Jerusalem: International Publishing Company, 1963).

——, "The Earliest Representation of a Siege Scene and a 'Scythian Bow' from Mari", *Israel Exploration Journal*, 22/3 (1972): 89–94.

Yakar, Jak, *Prehistoric Anatolia: The Neolithic Transformation and the Early Chalcolithic Period* (Tel Aviv: Tel Aviv University, 1991).

Yamauchi, Edwin (ed.), *Africa and Africans in Antiquity* (East Lansing: Michigan State University, 2001).

Yoffee, N. and J. Clark (eds), *Collapse of Ancient States and Civilizations* (Tucson, TX: University of Arizona Press, 1988).

Zettler, Richard L. and Lee Horne (eds), *Treasures from the Royal Tombs of Ur* (Philadelphia: University of Pennsylvania Museum, 1998).

Zibelius-Chen, Karola, *Die ägyptische Expansion nach Nubien: Eine Darlegung der Grundfaktoren* (Wiesbaden: Dr. Ludwig Reichert Verlag, 1988).

Index

Warfare in World History

Michael S. Nieburg

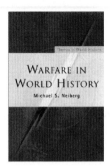

'Neiberg has produced one of the best surveys available.'

Jeremy Black, *European History Quarterly,*
vol. 33, no. 4, 2004

Despite the catastrophic effect of war, wars have also proved to be instrumental to long-term change in world history. This text is the first of its kind to survey how warfare has developed from ancient times to the present day and the role it has played in shaping the world we know. The periods discussed include:

- the pre-gunpowder era
- the development of gunpowder weapons and their rapid adoption in Western Europe
- the French Revolution and the industrialization of warfare
- the First and Second World Wars
- the Cold War and the wars of liberation fought across the Third World

With in-depth examples illustrating the dominant themes in the history of warfare, *Warfare in World History* focuses not only on the famous and heroic, but also discusses the experiences of countless millions of unknowns who have fought in wars over time

Hb: 0-415-22954-5
Pb: 0-415-22955-3

Available at all good bookshops
For ordering and further information please visit:
www.routledge.com

Routledge History

Introduction to Global Military History
1775 to the Present Day

Jeremy Black

'A lucid and succinct account of military developments around the modern world that combines a truly global coverage of events with thought-provoking analysis. By juxtaposing the familiar with the previously neglected or largely unknown, Jeremy Black forces the reader to reassess the standard grand narrative of military history that rests on assumptions of western cultural and technological superiority. . . . It should have a wide market on world history courses that are increasingly common parts of American, British and Australian university programmes.'

Professor Peter H. Wilson, *University of Sunderland*

'Jeremy Black does an admirable job in distilling a tremendous amount of information and making it comprehensible for students.'

Professor Lawrence Sondhaus, *University of Indianapolis*

'An excellent book. Too often, in military studies and histories, the land, air, and maritime aspects are dealt with in separate books. This work integrates all aspects of conflict in a reasonable manner.'

Stanley Carpenter, *Professor of Strategy and Policy,
US Naval War College, Newport, Rhode Island*

Hb: 0-415-35394-7
Pb: 0-415-35395-5

Available at all good bookshops
For ordering and further information please visit:
www.routledge.com

Routledge History

Rethinking Military History

Jeremy Black

'Jeremy Black has exercised his formidable powers of historical dissection, critical analysis, and creative cogitation to produce an exciting book ... it should spark constructive debate about how historians may better practise their craft'

Theodore F. Cook, *William Paterson University of New Jersey*

'Jeremy Black provides timely arguments against a narrowly technological perception of military history, shaped by Western experience. His survey of five centuries of global warfare shaws the shortcomings of this perspective and the necessity to uinderstand the political and cultural aspects of warfare'

Jan Glete, *Stockholm University*

'Formidable'

Paul A. Fideler, *Lesley University*

This must-read study demonstrates the limitations of current approaches, icnuding common generalisations, omissions, and over-simplifications. Engaging theoretical discussions, with reference to specific conflicts, suggest how these limitations can be remedied and adapted, whilst incorporating contributions from other disciplines. Additional chapters provide a valuable and concise survey of the main themes in the study of military history from 1500 to the present day.

Hb: 0-415-27533-4
Pb: 0-415-27534-2

Available at all good bookshops
For ordering and further information please visit:
www.routledge.com